Labored Relations

Other books by William B. Gould IV

Black Workers in White Unions: Job Discrimination in the United States.
Cornell University Press, 1977.

Japan's Reshaping of American Labor Law. MIT Press, 1984.

Strikes, Dispute Procedures, and Arbitration: Essays on Labor Law.
Greenwood Press, 1985.

Labor Relations in Professional Sports (with Robert C. Berry and Paul D.
Staudohar). Auburn House, 1986.

A Primer on American Labor Law. MIT Press. Third edition, 1993.

Agenda for Reform: The Future of Employment Relationships and the Law.
MIT Press, 1993.

Labored Relations

Law, Politics, and the NLRB—A Memoir

William B. Gould IV

The MIT Press
Cambridge, Massachusetts
London, England

First MIT Press paperback edition, 2001
©2000 Massachusetts Institute of Technology

This book was set in Sabon in QuarkXPress by Asco Typesetters, Hong Kong.
Printed and bound in the United States of America.

Library of Congress Cataloging-in-Publication Data

Gould, William B.
Labored relations : law, politics, and the NLRB—a memoir / William B. Gould IV.
   p.   cm.
Includes bibliographical references and index.
ISBN 0-262-07205-X (hc : alk. paper), 0-262-57155-2 (pb)
  1. Gould, William B. 2. United States. National Labor Relations Board—Biography.
3. Judges—United States—Biography. 4. Unfair labor practices—United States—History.
5. Industrial relations—United States—History. I. Title.

KF3372.G68   2000
354.97'092—dc21
[B]   00-041135

This book is dedicated to the career civil servants of the NLRB.

To make labor free by prohibiting that control by which the personal service of one man is disposed of or coerced for another's benefit.

Bailey v. *Alabama*, U.S. Supreme Court (1911)

Contents

Preface

In June 1993 President Bill Clinton nominated me to be the chairman and a member of the National Labor Relations Board. Article II, Section 2 of the United States Constitution states, in part, that the president "shall nominate, and by and with the Advice and the Consent of the Senate, shall appoint all other officers of the United States, whose appointments are not herein otherwise provided for, and which shall be established by Law."

When it became apparent in 1993 that the process of confirming my appointment would be tortuous and protracted, I began to keep a diary. I continued to make entries in it after I went to Washington in early 1994 and until the summer of 1998. I have not, of course, included all the entries in this book, nor even complete portions of every passage used. Editorial judgments were required.

Excerpts from the diary are clearly identified, almost always with an accompanying date. In chapter 2 and elsewhere they are mixed in with independent recollections and other source materials to present a coherent narrative. It goes without saying that the diary was extremely helpful to me in recollecting events and organizing this book. There were so many meetings and conversations and telephone calls that without this record it would have been virtually impossible to sort through and be true to the events recounted.

The organization of this book was also facilitated through a series of invited lectures I presented in late 1998 and early 1999. I gave the first talk to the San Francisco Bar Labor and Employment Law Section and the San Francisco Industrial Relations Research Association. It was appropriately entitled "Back from the Front." The second was presented at a faculty seminar my friend Professor Herman Levy asked me give near my Stanford backyard, at the Santa Clara Law School. I gave other, similar lectures to classes in the Stanford University Political Science Department and at San Jose State University.

My friend Professor Lamont Stallworth kindly invited me to be the Gallagher Lecturer at Loyola University in Chicago on October 2, 1998. On March 5, 1999, I gave the University of Washington Law School Condon-Faulkner Distinguished Lecture in Seattle. Next, after participating in a conference organized by Professor Margaret Levi of the University of Washington, I proceeded on to the Midwest, where I gave the Ralph Fuchs Lecture at the Indiana University School of Law in Bloomington on March 9. Finally, on June 14, I gave a dinner address about my work at the NLRB to the Labor Relations and Employment Section of the Nebraska State Bar Association in Omaha.

In addition to its presidential appointees, the National Labor Relations Board is composed of almost two thousand career civil servants working in Washington, D.C., and in more than thirty regional offices throughout the United States. It is to them that this book is dedicated. The Board's high standards of excellence are attributable in large part to these men and women.

The best and the brightest of them all, in my experience, were my friend, and chief counsel from 1994 through 1997, William R. Stewart, the recipient of the President's Distinguished Civilian Service Award; and my confidential assistant, Mary Ann Sawyer. I owe her intelligent and reliable help throughout my tenure to the good judgment and recommendation of Bill Stewart.

Bill is the first recipient of the President's Award in the entire history of the NLRB. I first met him when we worked together as legal assistants to Board Chairman Frank McCulloch during the Kennedy and Johnson administrations. He subsequently worked in the appellate branch of the Board, where he was involved in enforcing its decisions in the circuit courts of appeals throughout the country— the rung of the federal judiciary just below the U.S. Supreme Court.

Thus, no one knew more about the agency in the 1990s than Bill Stewart, and his background and experience stood me in good stead during my chairmanship. Bill not only helped me with the flow of cases and the interpretation of the law but also through his knowledge of where the bodies and the dollars were buried at the Board's Washington headquarters.

Like Bill, Mary Ann Sawyer was tireless, devoted, and unqualifiedly loyal in the difficult and challenging four and a half years of my stay in Washington. I could not have done my job without these two distinguished individuals.

My excellent personal staff also included Eileen Steffanick. She was and is a wonderful person and a great back-up to whom I can always turn. Also of inestimable help were Hester Taylor, Benita Riggleman, Sharon Hodge, Howard Johnson, Ralph Deeds, and Miguel Gonzalez.

I had the good fortune to work with so many very bright and capable career people at the NLRB. Alfred Wolff, who succeeded Bill Stewart as my chief counsel in 1997, and Kate Dowling, who stepped into the deputy chief counsel's position as the youngest woman ever to assume such a senior position at the Board, are excellent examples. The quality of Al Wolff's work was first-rate and, like Mr. Stewart, he provided the kind of dedication and loyalty I badly needed. Kate Dowling's superlative writing and organizational abilities were key to the upsurge in concurring and dissenting opinions I was able to produce in 1997 and 1998.

The "Four Horsemen" of my personal staff—David Schwartz, Ella Chatterjee, Steve Rappaport, and Ed Hughes—were critical to our ability to process cases promptly and meet the highest standards of professionalism. They were vital in grinding out the hard yardage: especially the drafts of opinions and the detailed research needed for the most difficult issues we confronted.

In Washington, it was also a special pleasure to be able to work with many distinguished and able career people at the Board who were not on my staff. They included, among so many others, Linda Sher, associate general counsel; David Parker, director of information services; Tanna Adde of the same section; Harding Darden, director of the Budget Division; Enid Weber of the executive secretary's office; my two appointees as inspector general, Robert Allen and Aileen Armstrong; George Constantinople, on the staff of Board member J. Robert Brame III; Harold Datz, chief counsel to Board member Peter Hurtgen; and Bill Wachter, assistant general counsel for the Contempt Section of the Litigation Branch.

As an "outsider" who had lived most of his life outside of the capital, I was particularly aware of the valuable work done in the Board's regional offices. Especially worthy of laud and honor is the fine work of the regional directors: Louis D'Amico, Baltimore; Jim Scott, Oakland; Paul Eggert, formerly regional attorney in Oakland and now Seattle regional director; Bob Miller, San Francisco; Dan Silverman, New York; Rosemary Pye, Boston; Peter Hirsch, formerly Philadelphia; Dorothy Moore-Duncan, Philadelphia; Rochelle Kentove, Tampa; Bill Schwab, Detroit; Victoria Aguayo and James McDermott, Los Angeles; Glenn Zipp, Peoria; and Roberto G. Chavarry, Indianapolis. These dedicated men and women, along with regional attorneys Al Palewicz, Baltimore; Terry Jensen, formerly in Seattle; Ron Hooks of Memphis; and Joe Norelli, San Francisco, provided exemplary leadership during periods of crisis.

Notwithstanding the conflict with the Republican Congress that extended from 1995 to 1998, my very best friend and the agency's staunchest ally in Congress for most of this period was a Republican: Senator Mark Hatfield of Oregon, who retired from the Senate in January of 1997. As chairman of the Senate Appropriations Committee, Senator Hatfield, a principled and thoughtful legislator, was particularly solicitous of the Board and its interests. He played the primary role in guiding us through that most difficult period. As a student of the War of the Rebellion and the work of President Lincoln, I saw his qualities as Lincolnesque. The Board is forever in his debt.

Besides Senator Hatfield, the agency's closest friends in the Senate were my California senators, Democrats Dianne Feinstein and Barbara Boxer; Democratic senators Paul Wellstone of Minnesota, Tom Harkin of Iowa, Edward Kennedy of Massachusetts, Jack Reed of Rhode Island; Paul Simon of Illinois; and the Republican senator from Rhode Island, the late John Chafee. In the House of Representatives, Nancy Pelosi, Anna Eshoo, Tom Lantos, Tom Campbell, Xavier Becerra, George Miller, Zoe Lofgren, and Maxine Waters—all of California—were supportive on numerous occasions, as were William Clay of Missouri, Nita Lowey and Nydia Velázquez of New York, Frank Pallone and Donald Payne of New Jersey, Tom Sawyer, Dennis Kucinich, and Louis Stokes of Ohio, John Conyers Jr. of Michigan, and Bobby Scott of Virginia. In an eleventh-hour impasse recounted in chapter 13, representatives David Bonior of Michigan and Bernard Sanders of Vermont played an absolutely vital role in moving forward the work of the Board.

I received valuable assistance and counsel from the White House through Abner Mikva, counsel to the president, Bob Nash, presidential director of personnel, and Richard Socarides, White House liaison to the Department of Labor. I am particularly grateful for their support.

Helpful support for the Board during my term of office was also generously provided by union officials, business leaders, and lawyers like Bill Coleman of Washington, D.C.—who led me to valuable contacts in the business world. The knowledge and experience of the union and management lawyers on our advisory panels was greatly appreciated. Foremost among them were Elliott Bredhoff, Lee Jackson, Betty Southard Murphy, Allison Beck, Barbara Sapin, Judy Scott, Marshall Babson, and George Murphy of Washington, D.C.; Arnold Perl of Memphis; Duane Beeson, Bob Cassel, and Morton Orenstein of San Francisco; David Ellis of Boston; Saul Kramer, Max Zimny, Gwynne Wilcox, David Prouty and Gene Eisner of New York; David Cathcart, William Emmanuel, Lloyd Loomis and George Preonas of Los

Angeles; Roderick Gillum, Theodore Sachs, and Jordan Rossen of Detroit; Andrew Kramer of Cleveland; Bob Giolito of Atlanta; Herbert Segal of Louisville; James Watson of Galveston; and Peter Anderson of Seattle.

Earlier drafts of this manuscript were read by Catherine Fisk, Donald Lamm, Robert Berry, James Gross, Leonard Koppett, Oscar Paskal, William Stewart, Paul Spiegelman, Matthew Holden Jr., and Bill Simon. I benefited from their criticisms and comments. I am also most grateful to Roberta Clark for her most thorough and meticulous review of this book. Her critique has made this a better work. Of course, I take full responsibility for the book and any of its deficiencies.

At Stanford Law School I am grateful to Judy Lawrence, Janet Jones, Carol Crane, and Bernadette Saint John, who typed the bulk of this manuscript and provided me with some valuable editorial commentary. I also express gratitude to Kathy Robinson, who assisted in typing the manuscript. Susan Quinn, research assistant and member of the Stanford Law School Class of 2000, helped with the research for this book, and Paul Edenfield, Stanford Law School '02, provided important assistance in tracking down documentation.

Dean of the Law School Paul Brest provided me with a leave of absence in the fall of 1998 as well as for my full term as chairman and the months while I awaited conclusion of the confirmation process. I am most grateful for his generosity in this regard.

Finally, I am grateful to my wife, Hilda, and to my three sons, William, Timothy, and Edward, for their patience and understanding during that challenging and sometimes stressful period of life in Washington and California.

Introduction

At the Navy Yard [Charlestown, Massachusetts] at five o'clock I received my Discharge, being three years and nine days in the service of Uncle Samuel and glad I am to receive it. . . . So ends my service in the Navy of the United States of America.

So wrote the first William B. Gould as he ended his service to the U.S. government on September 29, 1865. It is now late spring of 1999. Yet I can still recall how those words, written at the conclusion of a far more perilous period, were on my mind when my term as chairman of the National Labor Relations Board expired in August of 1998. The work in Washington was done, the race there run as best as I could run it, and the decks were clear for new assignments.

But even then I could not break daily contact with my office. For a number of days, and indeed weeks, I telephoned the office regularly to make sure that the cases the Board members signed off on before I left were actually issued as decisions and received by the parties affected.

Only a few months earlier I had endured the most tumultuous and wrenching congressional hearings of my tenure in office. After the Republicans took control of Congress in January of 1995, none of the hearings about appropriations or oversight had been friendly. Each year and each hearing the aggressiveness of House members' questioning had intensified in a rising crescendo. But the hearing in May of 1998 was a raw summation of nearly four years of outright hostility by congressional Republicans who, for the most part, remain unreconciled to the sixty-five-year old statute I was charged to administer. Ernest Istook, a conservative Republican of Oklahoma, accused me of not telling "the truth to this Committee" about the opposition to California Proposition 226 I had expressed in a statement to that state's legislature. (This unsuccessful ballot initiative would have required unions to get explicit authorization from all represented workers prior to spending dues money for political purposes.) "I don't think [you] ... should be in your position" Istook declared angrily. All the old enemies of the Board swarmed around me—Jay Dickey, Republican of Arkansas, and Henry Bonilla, Republican of Texas, in the forefront.

Much to my surprise, Proposition 226 had touched a raw nerve for the Democrats as well. The Republicans wanted to see it enacted on both the federal and state levels to eliminate a major source of funding for the Democratic party and, simultaneously, exclude the labor movement from the political process. The Democrats, however, were uneasy about my statement because it spotlighted their funding relationship with the unions. One House Democrat, David Obey of Wisconsin, lectured me about how the National Labor Relations Board cannot "afford" such statements "under any circumstances."[1] A few other Democrats, who saw my statement as a kind of revelation about the emperor's new clothes, were embarrassed and abandoned me.

For much of my Washington sojourn, the pride of service expressed by the first William B. Gould in the nineteenth century sustained me. Never, even at the 1998 hearing, did I regret accepting President Bill Clinton's nomination. I was and am proud of the mission I accomplished. But, as I think back on it, it seems more and more like a mission impossible.

On the sunshine-filled August day I stepped down from my responsibilities I felt a tremendous sense of release. I was a private citizen again as I drove from Candlestick Park toward San Francisco with the top down in the American-made Camaro convertible I had purchased while in Washington.

As I write this it is May of 1999—another of those exquisitely lovely days that seem to blend one into another at this time of year. (This month the Supreme Court called California "one of the ... most beautiful States in the Nation.") I walk the two and a half blocks from my home to my book-laden office at Stanford Law School. The memories of the nightmarish impeachment proceedings and the similar House Republican attacks on the rule of law I endured as chairman—the same rule of law that was the House Managers' mantra-like incantation—have begun to fade. The hummingbirds, palms, California live oak, and pungent eucalyptus remind me of the life I have resumed. From Stanford's baseball Sunken Diamond wafts the echoing siren song of the public address system, riding softly on a late-afternoon breeze and into the Law School's Crown Quadrangle. I promise myself to go in that direction more frequently in 2000, when the day-to-day pressures and deadlines will be less exacting.

It has all come and gone so quickly. This is what my great-grandfather must have felt in 1865 and in the years that followed. That other life, that much more public life spawned by the 1992 elections and President Clinton's appointment, is like a blur, its events sweeping by on fast-forward. Yet that other life is still only nine months past.

The almost-daily tumult and emotional exhaustion ... the sense of accomplishment laced with, and sometimes overwhelmed by, unceasing exasperation. The loneliness of decision making. The frequent visits to One Step Down, the jazz club next door to my condominium on Pennsylvania Avenue (its presence there had influenced my purchase) ... the alternately dulcet and blaring tenor saxophone sounds soothing and drowning an ever-present anxiety over the refusal of presidential appointees to do their assignments and the threats of congressional Republican to quash the National Labor Relations Board.

The sleepless nights tuning into jazz radio and reading P. D. James mysteries.... The inspirational weekend visits to Gettysburg, Antietam, Fredericksburg, The Wilderness, and Appomattox. So often, as I tried to remain faithful to the principles of the first William Benjamin Gould (adapted to contemporary realities), I felt like an arm-weary pugilist hoping that he had given as good as he got.... I was still standing last summer in the fifteenth round under a barrage of blows that said, "Don't you dare speak about the law unless you are spoken to."

Then, with little more than a week to go in my term, I picked myself up off the pavement of Connecticut Avenue and K Street after being hurled violently through the air. Now truly bloodied, and with a broken arm as well, I had been run down by one of Washington's madcap cyclists.

Frequently between 1994 and 1998 I had reflected on my good fortune, which did not oblige me to brave the bullets of that earlier Confederacy. Yet, as I struggled to put out of my mind the budget slashing and the ever-escalating attacks on the Board, I fretted about the reaction of my family to the nasty things the House Republicans were saying about me and the impact of the latest vilification on my mother's blood pressure.

The trail to that time and place had began in November 1992 with President Clinton's election. But in a sense its real origins were in 1862 and the three years following that my great-grandfather chronicled in his diary. It culminated that 1865 day that he stepped off the *U.S.S. Niagara* on the docks of the Charlestown Navy Yard.

The Civil War—or War of the Rebellion, as I prefer to call it—produced the great constitutional amendments that committed the United States to a policy of free labor. In 1911 the Supreme Court declared unconstitutional Alabama's debt-peonage law and, in so doing, held that the Thirteenth Amendment's prohibition of slavery was designed to "to make labor free by prohibiting that control by which the personal service of one man is disposed of or coerced for another's benefit."[2] In my view, this new policy was a precursor to the National Labor Relations Act, the modern labor legislation that created the NLRB. Making labor free was the goal that I tried to keep alive during my term of service.

The National Labor Relations Act of 1935 declares the practice and procedure of collective bargaining to be the public policy of the United States. The act, amended twice in major respects, is predicated upon the view that inequality of bargaining power between employers and employees who do not possess full freedom of association or actual liberty of contract depresses wage rates and wage earners' purchasing power through destabilization of competition in wage rates and working conditions. The act seeks to implement this policy through a quasi-judicial administrative agency, the National Labor Relations Board, whose role it is to rule on the "unfair labor practices" prohibited by the act. The Taft-Hartley amendments enacted by the Republican Eightieth Congress in 1947 apply the same concept to the actions of unions. A second important function of the Board is conducting secret ballot box elections to determine whether workers wish to be represented by unions.

Notwithstanding the slight diminution of its role compared to the 1950s and 1960s—because of the expansion of wrongful-discharge litigation, federal and state fair employment practice statutes, and state labor relations laws involving the public sector—the NLRB is a great agency with a proud and distinguished tradition and culture.[3] It has served the labor-management community well for most of this past century and will continue to do so throughout this one.

As stated in more detail in chapter 2, the Board is split administratively into two halves. The general counsel, who serves a four-year term, is a presidential appointee. This official is an independent prosecutor who brings cases to the Board for resolution and, paradoxically, acts as the NLRB's lawyer in the courts. The second half is the judicial side, the Board itself, which is composed of five members, all of whom serve five-year terms. The president nominates these five members and names one of them the chairman.

Board members and the general counsel tend to be Washington insiders, often people who have worked as counsels to a congressional committee or in a Washington law firm. Practical, or "hands on," experience with industrial relations or the employment relationship in the field is unusual—as is previously acquired expertise in labor law. Appointments from the western and southern parts of the country are also unusual. Because they have no home other than Washington to return to at the expiration of their terms, such insider appointees often devote a considerable portion of their effort and energy to promoting their reappointment prospects or looking for other government or government-related jobs. This preoccupation is one of the factors making the nation's capital a very insular, cliquish, and rough neighborhood. The environment there frequently called to my mind President Harry Truman's maxim: "If you want a friend in Washington, get a dog!"

The only two chairmen of the Board who shared my background as a neutral arbitrator and academic were the first two, who were appointed by President Franklin D. Roosevelt. J. Warren Madden was a University of Pittsburgh law professor, and Harry A. Millis a University of Chicago labor economist, author, and arbitrator. It is an interesting coincidence that Chairman Madden was appointed as the result of his contacts with Lloyd Garrison, a friend of President Roosevelt, when both were visiting professors at Stanford Law School in the summer of 1933. Millis, too, taught briefly at Stanford while he was a professor at the University of Chicago

Also rare are appointments of career NLRB officials whose background derived from field experience is so obviously relevant to the work of the Board. The only four examples I am aware of are regional directors: Gerald Brown, appointed by President Kennedy in 1961; Ralph Kennedy, appointed by President Nixon in 1970; John "Doc" Penello, appointed by President Nixon in 1972; and Wilford Johansen, appointed by President Reagan in 1985. I believe strongly that the absence of people with this kind of experience contributes to the excessively rarefied atmosphere of the Board in Washington.

In his history of the National Labor Relations Board, James Gross highlights the hostility of congressional conservatives to the Board and the NLRA, particularly in the periods 1947–1949 and 1953–1955, when Republicans controlled both houses of Congress. In describing the external and internal aftermath of the Supreme Court's 1937 *Jones & Laughlin* decision,[4] in which the Court upheld the constitutionality of the act by a 5 to 4 vote, he notes:

Despite the fact that the Supreme Court's decision had confirmed the Wagner Act as the law of the land and the NLRB as a permanent governmental authority and despite the appeals for labor peace and the submission of disputes to the NLRB, the opponents of the board and the act simply sought other ways to destroy the Wagner Act and the NLRB. Their attacks were shifted from the act to the board itself and indeed included a powerful new dimension— "the clamor of legislators against the board."

Not all of the NLRB's difficulties were caused by hostile forces outside the Board, however. Now that the constitutional battle had been won, the board's internal problems became more pressing and more important. As J. Warren Madden put it "prior to our Supreme Court decisions ... we were all so busy fighting the common enemy that we didn't have many disagreements. . . ." Yet, internal divisions and conflicts surfaced almost immediately after the Supreme Court decisions.[5]

It was thus inevitable from January 1995 onward, when Republicans took control of both houses, that there would be conflict between the Board and Congress. Much of the internal divisiveness that afflicted our work can also be traced, in part or in whole, to this political environment and its destabilizing impact. That environment first manifested itself vividly during debate about my confirmation as chairman; it continued to intensify until my very last day in office, August 27, 1998.

This book, therefore, is about the relationship between law, a quasi-judicial administrative agency, and politics in the volatile arena of labor policy. It is also about the balance of power between labor and management and the way the losing side's refusal to accept the results of presidential electoral polls affected the workings of labor law in the 1990s. Finally, it is about the rule of law and the role of labor in a modern economy.

Chapter 1, "The Philosophical Underpinnings," is an attempt to set forth the political and labor-management environment I stepped into when President Clinton nominated me to be chairman of the National Labor Relations Board. It also provides some insight into my own ideas insofar as they are relevant to my work with the Board and the National Labor Relations Act. Chapter 2, "A Harbinger of Hard Times," briefly describes the recent history of the NLRB and Senate confirmation battles. It also contains an account of my introduction to congressional politics and my preparation for the confirmation hearing on my nomination. Chapter 3, "The Confirmation Process," describes that hearing and the subsequent difficulties encountered by the White House and Senate Democrats in bringing the nomination to a vote in the full Senate.

Chapters 4 and 5, "First-Year Policies and Initiatives" and "First Attempts to Implement Reforms," set the stage for all that follows and attempt to describe the innovations I introduced within the parameters of the act as written and some of our early successes in paring down the backlog of pending cases. They also emphasize the internal reactions and resistance I encountered from other appointees to the Board. Chapter 6, "Balls and Strikes," after a brief summary of the history of player-owner relations in baseball, describes the Board's successful involvement in the strike negotiations of 1994–1995, the most widely publicized case we addressed during my tenure. It also turned out to be the last case in which we could operate under the law without interference by the hard-charging Republican Congress elected in November of 1994 under the banner of the Contract with America.

The remaining chapters focus on that portion of the story and the inevitable tensions that emerged between law and politics. Chapter 7, "The Idea of Independence" provides background on the peculiar independent nature of the "fourth branch of government": the quasi-judicial administrative agencies of which the National Labor Relations Board is but one. Chapter 8, "The Coming Storm," first discusses some of my predecessors' problems in dealings with the executive branch—problems I did not encounter. It then sets the stage for what lay ahead: a whole host of confrontations with the hundred and fourth and the hundred and fifth congresses. These were played out in the context of appropriations and oversight and congressional scrutiny of the Board by, mostly, conservative House members with little sympathy for the purposes of the statute we were sworn to administer. Chapter 9, "Congress Instructs the NLRB," continues this theme, providing chapter and verse on the House's interference with the idea of independent adjudication and the conflicts that emerged.

The last four chapters, while still concerned with congressional relations, also take the reader into the internal world of Board operations. Chapter 10, "The Clamor of Legislators," focuses on the Board's struggle to obtain adequate personnel and funding, while Chapter 11, "The Lights Will Not Go Out" details my frustration with the unwillingness or inability of Board members to do what they were brought to Washington to do—adjudicate disputes between labor and management and produce decisions. The environment of surveillance and repression with which the Board was surrounded had changed everything and undermined the earlier strides made toward expediting administrative processes and eliminating the backlog.

Chapter 12, "The House Republicans' 'Number One Enemy'" refers to Congressman Obey's characterization of me in 1997, even prior to the fracas and turmoil that broke out over my opposition to Proposition 226 in 1998. In this chapter the struggle with Congress and the Washington-insider Board members comes to a head. It culminates in partial success as a number of long-pending Board cases are issued just prior to my departure—which, but for the intervention of two key members of Congress (one a Democrat and the other an Independent), would never have happened.

Of course, chapter 13, "The Dilatory Virus," attempts to pull together some of the themes of the book and to suggest several policy reforms.

The appendixes at the back of the book reproduce a series of speeches I gave as NLRB chairman, several statements and letters dealing with labor law issues that faced the Clinton Board, and some of my ideas for labor policy reform. A glossary of cases provides readers with background material on relevant decisions handed down by the Supreme Court just prior to and during the Clinton administration and on cases adjudicated before the Board in my term.

1

The Philosophical Underpinnings

Two major developments in American politics and labor history emerged in the last decades of the twentieth century. First, President Lyndon Johnson's prediction that the Democratic Party w ould lose the "solid South" to the Republicans because of the Kennedy-Johnson administration's promotion of landmark civil rights legislation in the 1960s was realized. By the 1980s new-found Republican congressional strength had mirrored presidential electoral results and triggered a more rightward tilt to the Republican party nationally, although this trend was most pronounced in the South. It resulted from the "southern strategy" first adopted by Barry Goldwater in his 1964 landslide defeat and, more successfully, by Richard Nixon and Ronald Reagan.[1] Republican adoption of conservative social and economic policies—as well as conservative appointments to the Supreme Court and subordinate federal courts by presidents Reagan and Bush—were followed in the early 1990s by election of a new group of congressional Republicans and, in 1994, of Republican majorities in both houses. The fierce partisanship of these new members culminated in the 1998 impeachment trial of President Bill Clinton. Together, these developments constituted an explicit realization of Johnson's prophecy.

The second major development of the last decades of the century was the decline of unions in American society. A kind of free-fall descent began earlier but accelerated in the 1980s and was most pronounced in the private sector, in labor's traditional strongholds of manufacturing and transportation. In the 1990s the old leaders of organized labor at Washington's AFL-CIO headquarters, already hunkered down into a posture of impotent defense, experienced a palace revolt—albeit one democratically implemented—and were routed by the opposition for their failure to recruit new members. The new leaders' emphasis on organizing and electoral politics threatened business interests and the Republican elements that had had it all their own way during the Reagan and Bush administrations. The result was an even more polarized labor-management relationship than had characterized the 1980s and early 1990s. This divisiveness was particularly obvious in Washington, where policy disputes are fought out. Its implications for the struggle between the adversarial and cooperative models of labor-management relations in America are not yet fully discernible.[2]

It was inevitable that these two developments would have repercussions for the administration and interpretation of the National Labor Relations Act, the principal statute governing labor-management relationships in the United States. In particular, they would affect the work of the administrative agency created by that statute, the National Labor Relations Board (NLRB), as well as my own nomination, confirmation, and four-and-a-half-year tenure (1994 to 1998) as chairman of the NLRB.

Added into this mix of factors was the perspective on labor issues I brought to my new position from my life experience and training. I was born in Boston, Massachusetts, in 1936, the great-grandson of a former slave, William B. Gould, who escaped from Wilmington, North Carolina, served in the U.S. Navy during the Civil War, and afterward became a citizen of Dedham, Massachusetts, immediately south of Boston. As the firstborn child of university-educated black Americans—the first to attend college in their families—I was brought up with values and ideas that made me think, in retrospect, that I had been born into both the Democratic party and the Episcopal Church. Indeed, my great-grandfather was one of the founding members of the Episcopal Church of the Good Shepherd in Dedham, where I was baptized. All members of our family were staunch Republicans—because of that party's progressive position on slavery and race during the Civil War and Reconstruction—until my father broke with that tradition in 1932. It is not, therefore, surprising that I have rarely strayed from the Democratic party and its support of economic and social justice and of policies that demonstrate concern for ordinary, average Americans and those who have been ostracized and excluded.

I believe this focus has never been more vital than it is today, given the increased income disparities in our country—a gap between the rich and poor greater than in any of the industrialized free-market nations of Europe, Canada, or Japan. It is clear to me that the government must intervene in the market to help those who cannot help themselves. Such intervention and the provision of essential social services are the prerequisites for civilization—a point expressed by Justice Oliver Wendell Holmes in his 1927 maxim, "Taxes are what we pay for civilization."[3]

Inextricably tied to this idea is my own—and many others peoples'—conviction that what best unites us across racial and class lines is a government that performs well. Integral to this system of belief is a firm dedication to the rule of law, not as noisily proclaimed by the Republican House managers during the Clinton impeachment proceedings in 1998, but, rather, as a philosophy mirroring genuine commitment to independent adjudication. In such an environment, third-party adjudicators such as members of the NLRB would not be pressured in the name of partisan passions or pilloried for unpopular decisions predicated upon antimajoritarian considerations.

This adherence to judicial and administrative agency independence seems to me one of the surest means by which individuals' rights to freedom of speech, conscience, association, and religion have been protected for more than two hundred years. This is the first reason why the Bill of Rights that contains these safeguards has so well stood the test of time. The protection of such individual liberties is part of the democratic, liberal faith to which I subscribe.

A final basis for my loyalty to the Democratic party is that in the twentieth century it was an internationalist party more supportive than the Republicans of such organizations as the United Nations and the International Labor Organization. The latter association attempts both to establish a code for workers and employers around the world and to provide a means of effectively ordering international labor-management relations. Yet another part of my internationalist belief system, perhaps rooted in the military service of my forebears in the nineteenth and early twentieth centuries, is the importance of maintaining a strong military under civilian rule.[4]

As a small child and youth in Massachusetts and, later, New Jersey, I was deeply affected by the practices of racial discrimination that pervaded all aspects of American life. During and after World War II, segregation was still proudly proclaimed as the official policy of some corporations and unions. On numerous occasions my father was denied job opportunities because of racial discrimination and, in some instances, was fired from a job after it was discovered that he was black—his light complexion sometimes not immediately revealing this fact to the employer. His story, and the chronicles of so many others I knew and read about—people well qualified for the positions they aspired to but denied the chance to advance—were defining memories for me.

The second, and almost equally significant, contribution to my political outlook was the legacy of the Great Depression and the poverty into which it drew so many black and white Americans. My mother's stories of this difficult period emphasized the terrible importance of every nickel and penny and how often she and my father had to worry about where the next coin would come from. Tales of the long-lasting unemployment and misery of the thirties nurtured in me an acute awareness of, and a sensitivity to, economic inequality. In fact, this focus on economic justice led directly to my interest in and, ultimately, professional commitment to ameliorating conditions in the workplace.

These values antedated my formal education and were even more deeply entrenched. But they were complicated by a wariness of the labor movement engendered by the exclusionary policies of, in particular, the construction unions and the American Federation of Labor. This distrust was common to many black Americans at that time. The violent conduct of my future employer, the United Auto Workers (UAW) during the Kohler dispute in the 1950s caught my father's attention and elicited his unreserved condemnation. His attitude undoubtedly influenced my own view that whatever the worth of unions in protecting the wage standards and working conditions of employees, there were avenues of protest that should be discouraged as inconsistent with sound public policy. The effects of racial discrimination and arbitrary treatment generally, as well as the inequities many Americans experienced in the 1930s, encouraged in my family the conviction that the best objective for life was working for the public good, particularly for the masses of our people rather than for those already privileged by financial security and connections to the seats of power. This sense of public obligation derives, I think, from our family's political and religious values and from my great-grandfather's naval service during the Civil War—and that of his six sons in the Spanish-American War and World War I. Often during my tenure in Washington, as I came to the end of another emotionally and physically exhausting day, I found new strength in the commitment of my great-grandfather, as reflected in a diary he kept between 1862 and 1865. His firm sense of purpose was directly linked to my own professional aspirations and, ultimately, to my work at the NLRB.

I was first attracted to the rule of law and decided to become a lawyer as a senior in high school by the Supreme Court's landmark 1954 ruling in *Brown* v. *Board of Education*.[5] In it, the Court held unanimously that segregation in public education was unconstitutional. This opinion—along with a previously developed interest in government and politics—led me to the law. When I arrived at Cornell Law School in 1958, I soon realized that there were few constitutional lawyers in the United States, and fewer still who focused on civil rights matters such as those pursued by Thurgood Marshall and Charles Houston in *Brown* and its precursors. My own specialty became labor law—in part because I believed workplace democracy to be an important and relatively undeveloped value that lagged far behind the progress made elsewhere in the political arena.

The "comfortable words " of the Episcopal *Book of Common Prayer* and the New Testament (Matthew 11:28)—"Come unto me all ye that travail and are heavy laden"—were special to my father and, thus, to myself. This concern for the heavy-laden is inextricably linked to the need for society and the state to help those in need of protection from unbridled market forces. The policies of certain unions, particularly those associated with the Congress of Industrial Organizations (CIO), were deeply concerned with the kind of democratic public policies I supported. My interest in labor law was also furthered by the intellectual challenge and intricacies of the National Labor Relations Act and related legislation and case law.

This interest, facilitated and encouraged by my Cornell law professor, the late Kurt Hanslowe, took me from Ithaca to Detroit in the summer of 1960; there I began my career on the legal staff of the United Automobile Workers. In the 1960s the UAW and Detroit were excellent places in which to strengthen and fortify my interests in the unions and the Democratic party. At the same time, working there gave me a wonderful opportunity to meet many pioneers of the struggle for workers' democratic rights, men like Walter Reuther, with whom I conversed from time to time. In the Skilled Trades Department I came to know and work with Reuther's almost-immediate successor, Douglas Fraser; later, in the 1970s, I had a good deal of contact with Fraser during his presidency of the UAW.

In the late 1960s, working both within the UAW and, subsequently, in a New York City law firm representing employers, I gained considerable firsthand, practical knowledge of modern labor law. From this experience I developed the view that the laws of a democratic country must not only guarantee the right of free trade unions to exist, to bargain collectively, and to expand their membership but must also be properly rooted in a reciprocal system of rights and obligations for both labor and management. While representing employers, I particularly disliked the cases in which management arrayed itself against union representation altogether and sought, through NLRB decertification challenges, to limit labor's attempts to ballot workers or to recruit members through other means. Of course, my view has always been that, while workers have a democratic right *not* to participate in collective bargaining, collective bargaining is the system most compatible with the idea of democracy in the workplace.

Nonetheless, early in my career I accepted the view—to borrow the words of Archibald Cox in a 1960 law review article—that there are "union rights and union wrongs."[6] This approach led me to concur with Governor Adlai Stevenson of Illinois, the Democratic party's 1952 standard bearer, who supported legal regulation of unions as well as employers, thereby rejecting the party's platform plank advocating repeal of the 1947 Taft-Hartley amendments to the NLRA.

The idea that both labor and management need to be regulated was also part of my thinking about the racial discrimination practiced by some unions. The need to eliminate racial inequality in all venues prompted inclusion of Title VII in the Civil Rights Act of 1964 and its application to labor unions as well as employers.

In the early 1970s, during my first academic assignment, at Wayne State University, I represented black workers in a case involving discriminatory hiring and promotions. They were fighting both an employer, the Detroit Edison Company, and two unions with which the company customarily bargained. Thus, litigation experience and my research and writing interests—as well as my early life influences—coalesced into the conviction that both unions and employers are capable of misdeeds and good deeds.[7] Moreover, my time working for the United Auto Workers and representing employers in labor disputes convinced me that the rights of both sides must be respected. Unions should have the right to air grievances and bargain collectively, whereas management—particularly once a contract is secured —should be able to insist on receiving the benefits of uninterrupted production realizable from labor's compliance with no-strike a pledge in the collective agreement. During my student days at the London School of Economics in the early 1960s and in subsequent visits to the United Kingdom, I witnessed the plague of guerrilla warfare waged through "wildcats" or unofficial work stoppages. They reinforced my view that both unions and employers should adhere strictly to the rule of law.

In essence, I have come to subscribe to what is characterized in both the Clinton administration and the Blair administration the U.K. as a "third way" in labor-management relations.[8] I advocate government intervention to promote union recognition and collective bargaining—as do the NLRA and Britain's 1999 Employment Rights Bill. At the same time, autonomy for both sides should be enhanced, not only in the collective-bargaining process but also by using dispute-resolution procedures to decide a wide variety of issues that would otherwise burden society through litigation. A demystified law should speak, I believe, simply and clearly, so that the average layperson will be unafraid to rely on his or her own devices in seeking its protection.

By the 1980s, I was also fervently convinced that employee participation in management—particularly in industries (whether union or nonunion) besieged by foreign competition—would be advantageous to both sides. Employees would benefit from promoting their own involvement in the firm and from access to information formerly an exclusive managerial province. Employers, on the other hand, would profit from workers' help in fending off competition that would otherwise cost jobs and lower workers' wages and benefits.

In the decade or so prior to 1994, the decline in trade unions and collective bargaining begun in the mid-1950s had accelerated to a gallop. In 1955, unions represented 35 percent of American workers; by the time the 1990s drew to a close, the figure had dropped to 14 percent, only 10 percent of them in the private sector![9] The absence of unions in many areas of business during this period was one factor in the increasing income differences among workers and between workers and employers—a problem that is continuing into the new century. That inequality means, most importantly, that a democratic nation has no democracy in its workplaces.

A whole host of factors were responsible for the union decline and its consequences. Debate continues about whether income inequality has been principally fostered by foreign competition or by technology—although both elements undoubtedly played a role in weakening the unions. Well before the 1990s' debates about free trade and labor protection under NAFTA and GATT, the global economy was inducing employers to relocate factories to countries where labor was less expensive and even less well protected than in the United States, or that were closer to the ultimate consumer. At home, meanwhile, the nature of employment relationships was changing. Temporary employees (what Europeans call "atypical workers") and independent contractors were being widely substituted for permanent workers whose rights were secured by union contracts. Companies' ongoing relationships with these new groups of employees undermined collective bargaining and made organizational activity arduous or all but impossible. The advent of foreign-born workers (some of them undocumented workers) had much the same effect; such workers are afraid to protest low wages and benefits and poor working conditions, even though American labor law entitles them to the same rights as other employees.[10]

The American economy also led the western countries in substituting low-paid service for jobs in manufacturing. Employers in the burgeoning service sector resisted union organizing drives all the more tenaciously because increased costs could not be absorbed through productivity enhancement and labor-saving devices;

to them, union-negotiated wages meant either higher (and less-competitive) prices or reduced profits.

Moreover, the new information technologies developed in the last few decades of the century had spawned new high-tech industries, such as those concentrated in the Silicon Valley of California. The unions knew little about these growing industries or the firms that made them up, and they devoted insufficient resources to recruitment. The unorganized employees of such technology companies, often more mobile and less job-oriented than workers in manufacturing, were difficult to organize. In addition to the prevalence of contingent workers—part-time and temporary employees, independent contractors, and undocumented workers—the shift to white-collar jobs meant trying to recruit people for whom unions are frequently synonymous with low social status. Decades of well-publicized corruption scandals in key unions had promoted a negative image of organized labor that recruiters found nearly impossible to shake.

The Reagan and Bush administrations, meanwhile, cultivated downright hostility toward unions. This attitude was first manifested in President Reagan's discharge of illegally striking air traffic controllers in 1981; some observers have seen this stance as a signal to the many employers who subsequently began utilizing the right to replace even lawful strikers permanently, a right they had possessed since a 1938 Supreme Court ruling but had infrequently exercised.[11] Members of the NLRB appointed by Reagan and Bush reversed precedents that had protected employees' rights; they thus emasculated what was once thought of as the workers' Bill of Rights. In the 1980s, these developments buttressed Supreme Court precedents—which are not always favorable to the basic purposes of the NLRA—and encouraged some employers, from the 1970s on, to exploit newly apparent administrative loopholes and delay dispute settlement interminably.

This was the situation in the early 1990s during the Senate debate about my confirmation as chairman of the NLRB. In the private sector, the precipitous decline of trade unions to almost single-digit status during the 1990s not only meant less security for unions and individual workers but also threatened the very existence of the labor movement. More-polarized labor-management relations gave birth to new employer organizations even more aggressively committed to a nonunion workplace than such old-line groups as the National Association of Manufacturers (NAM). In an era when cooperation between employees and employers was being given much lip service—especially in debates on legislation designed to enhance workplace teamwork arrangements in, for example, the automobile industry—the effect of such hostile groups was to intensify conflict in the making of national labor policy.

There was also more overt partisan conflict. As the Reagan and Bush administrations sought to steer the Supreme Court to the right, bitter ideological and personal confrontations resulted from Supreme Court nominations—particularly those of Robert Bork in 1987, Douglas Ginsburg shortly thereafter, and Clarence Thomas in 1991. These battles were presaged by much-earlier disputes over President Nixon's nominations of Clement Haynesworth and George Harold Carswell in 1969 and 1970; both were rejected by the Democratically controlled Senate, as was Bork. The Senate majority's attack on "one of the club," Senator John Tower (R-Texas), whom President Bush nominated as secretary of defense, provoked further acrimonious and long-lasting partisan resentment.

These fights masked two profound changes occurring in the body politic: a shift of the two parties away from broad coalitions of interests and regions and the Democrats' loss of the South to the Republican party:

As long as the South was solidly Democratic, the two political parties remained broad coalitions. The Democrats were a mixture of conservative Southerners and urban Northerners. (both groups supported Franklin Roosevelt's populist economic activism, but they agreed on little else); the Republicans represented Wall Street and Main Street, the Eastern elite and the Western middle class (who agreed on a preference for limited government, and little else). In the fifties, and the first half of the sixties, the southern Democrats, who by seniority controlled many of the significant congressional committees—joined with Republicans to prevent much of anything from happening except appropriations for highways and defense.

But the "solid South" was shattered over civil rights. When Northern Democrats decided to support desegregation—a new generation of Southerners emerged within two decades and became Republicans. [They became the House Managers who impeached and sought to remove President Clinton from office.] At the same time, many of the liberal children of the eastern Republican elite joined the Democrats, as did southern blacks when they gained the right to vote. As the parties grew more ideologically "responsible," debate became more abrasive and partisan.... The musty, ornate rituals of collegiality, the respectful parliamentary language, the staff and privileges granted to the minority were gradually abandoned or severely modified to the Republicans' "disadvantage."[12]

Nothing more vividly demonstrates the role reversal of the political parties than debates on the civil rights bills of 1990 and 1991. In both years, the Democratic members of Congress sought to revise several decisions rendered by an increasingly conservative Supreme Court, decisions they viewed as at odds with the intentions of the framers of 1960s civil rights laws. On August 3, 1990, the House passed a civil rights bill by a vote of 274 to 154. Among southern Democrats, 65 members voted in favor and 10 voted against passage; all 13 Democratic representatives of border states voted for it, and 35 of 39 southern Republicans voted against it.[13] In the Senate, the bill passed as well, only to be vetoed by President Bush; his veto was upheld by the narrowest of margins, 65 to 34, with all 16 Democratic southerners voting for the bill and all 8 southern Republicans voting against it. These votes marked the completion of a remarkable political transformation.

In 1991 congressional Democrats made another attempt to pass a civil rights bill. The House voted 381 to 38 to enact the new legislation, with 77 of the 78 southern Democrats voting yea while southern Republicans split 25 to 15 against it. Again, all 14 Democratic representatives of the border states supported the legislation.

This result contrasts starkly with the votes of a quarter of a century earlier, when the southern Republicans of the 1990s were still Democrats. Of the 96 Democrats in the House who voted against the Civil Rights Act of 1964, 88 were from southern states. When the Senate ultimately passed the legislation 73 to 27, 20 of the 21 Democratic votes against passage were cast by southerners and the remaining nay vote came from by a senator from West Virginia. In the final passage by the House on July 2, 1964, 85 of the 91 Democrats voting against it were from southern states and the remaining 6 came from border states.

As historian Andrew Hacker has commented about the contemporary political situation:

One of the two major parties—the Republicans—has all but explicitly stated that it is willing to have itself regarded as a white party, prepared to represent white Americans and defend their interests. Of course, Republican administrations make sure that they appoint a few black officials, either vocal conservatives or taciturn moderates willing to remain in the background. (And they were especially adroit at finding apt candidates for the Supreme Court and Chairman of the Joint Chiefs of Staff.) An unwritten plank in the party's strategy is that it can win the offices it wants without black votes. More than that, by sending a message that it neither wants nor needs ballots cast by blacks, it feels that it can attract even more votes from a much larger pool of white Americans who want a party willing to represent their racial identity.... [A] politics purposely permeated by race has consolidated enough white Americans as a self-conscious racial majority.[14]

When I was introduced to one of these "new" Republicans, Senator Strom Thurmond of South Carolina, during the confirmation process in 1994, I said: "Senator, my great-grandmother came from Charleston, South Carolina." He had not the slightest interest, and I had no opportunity (or, indeed, inclination) to tell him about her purchase out of slavery in 1858. Thurmond, the presidential candidate of the Dixiecrats in 1948 and now a leading member of the Republican party, evidently saw before him only a black Californian who was supportive of the

NLRA and spoke in the urban accents of the Northeast. He did not attend the hearings but, like Senator Orrin Hatch (R-Utah), inserted in the record a statement against my nomination. Needless to say, he voted to deny me confirmation.

In a sense, my nomination as NLRB chairman and my tenure in that position fused together the ever-deepening antipathy of the Republican Right, particularly members of the House of Representatives, toward labor and race issues. Yet the increasingly malicious environment in Congress did not relate exclusively to civil rights or even union matters. Earlier it had become one in which newspapers began to report more intimate details of the personal lives of nominees and notable figures (e.g., Senator Gary Hart's [D-Colo.] ill-fated 1988 presidential campaign and the fights over the Supreme Court nominations of Robert Bork and Clarence Thomas).

As my nomination to the NLRB chairmanship languished in committee, the president's appointments of me and other administration officials were sometimes described as being "Borked."[15] Yet the vast difference between myself and Judge Bork was that he had opposed the civil rights initiatives of the 1960s—including public accommodations and fair employment practices legislation—that had since become part of the bedrock American consensus relating to race relations. He had thus defied the mainstream. On the other hand, my views, reflecting fidelity to the statutory goals enshrined in the provisions of the National Labor Relations Act of 1935, were, if anything, moderate and mainstream and were recognized as such by other academics. It was obvious that the Republicans' objective was to pay back the Democrats for the slights they had suffered while in the minority. Theirs was a payback rooted in vengeance, not in logic or reason.

Into this fertile ground of conflict came the new Republican leadership and Newt Gingrich, who became Speaker of the House after the "Republican Revolution" and "Contract with America" that captured both houses in the 1994 congressional elections. On the Senate side stood Majority Leader Senator Trent Lott of Mississippi, who was identified with white supremacist organizations in his state.[16] He stated in a speech that "a lot of the fundamental principles that Jefferson Davis believed in are very important to people across the country, and they apply to the Republican party. From tax policy, to foreign policy, from individual rights to neighborhood security are things that Jefferson Davis and his people believed in."[17]

This was the new ideological and regional fault line within which politics was being debated. The origins of the confrontation were admittedly racial in tone and substance, but they also had broad implications for labor policy—where the fight was about a balance of power as ideologically explosive as race. It was into this arena that I stepped a few months after President Clinton nominated me in late June of 1993. The battle that followed reflected the changing landscape of Washington and of American labor-management relations.

A prominent manifestation of this contentious atmosphere were the fights over administrative nominations; even prior to the advent of the Hundred and Fourth Congress, President Clinton had more than his share of them. The new element in the Senate was the use of the filibuster to block confirmation of nominees. Two recent students of the filibuster note that "about two-thirds of the legislative deaths by filibuster occurred between 1962 and 1994, a period of just 33 years out of the 205 year history of the Senate before 1995.... [But] the rate of death by filibuster ... has been increasing since that time.[18]

The increased use of this maneuver has transformed the constitutional requirement that a majority of the Senate give its "advice and consent" to presidential appointments to the need to obtain sixty votes to end a filibuster. It has also made the Senate a forum for a return match over issues on which the public had already expressed itself in the presidential election. The substantial increase in the number of filibusters in recent years provides, according to one nonpartisan report, "abundant opportunities for partisan mischief in the appointment process."[19] And mischief in 1993–1994 there was aplenty, as we learn in chapter 2.

2

A Harbinger of Hard Times

In November 1992, Bill Clinton was elected to his first term as president of the United States, ending the twelve years of Republican presidential dominance that began in 1980 with Ronald Reagan's election. During his first year in office Reagan had dramatically fired the nation's unlawfully striking federal air traffic controllers. President George Bush, although his January 1989 inaugural speech proclaimed the advent of "kinder, gentler" policies, seemed to reflect and reiterate the Reagan-era's inhospitability to collective bargaining.[1]

As a lifelong Democrat loyal to FDR and the New Deal, I delighted in Bill Clinton's election and hastened to San Francisco's Fairmont Hotel that November evening to celebrate the good news and admire his inspirational victory broadcast from Little Rock.

Though I had always stayed at the periphery of political activism, I had been a delegate to the 1974 Kansas City mid-term mini-convention and had drafted labor-policy memoranda for Senator Robert F. Kennedy in his 1968 presidential campaign. I did not, however, know Bill Clinton, nor, indeed, any members of his inner circle. I had sent him a small contribution during the New Hampshire primary, given a couple of speeches on his behalf during the fall campaign, and attended a large September 1992 rally in San Jose where the candidate spoke.

Shortly after the election, however, an old friend, Jack Sheinkman, president of the Amalgamated Clothing Workers, wrote saying he wanted to put my name forward for a job in the new Clinton administration.[2] I told him I was interested, and we met for lunch in mid-December 1992 at San Francisco's St. Francis Hotel.

When Jack asked me what position appealed to me, my initial inclination was to suggest something in the policy-making echelons of the Department of Labor. But Jack thought the chairmanship of the National Labor Relations Board was the place for me, pointing out that I had worked for Frank McCulloch (President

Kennedy's NLRB chairman) and that most of my professional practice, writing, and teaching involved the National Labor Relations Act. "That would seem to be a natural," he said enthusiastically.

While Jack was right—and indeed it could be said that I had fallen in love with the structure and symmetry of the National Labor Relations Act from my earliest exposure to it as a student at Cornell Law School—I had never aspired to be on the Board. Yet, from the point of view of experience and intellectual investment, Jack's recommendation was a sound one, and I agreed. When we parted that day, he told me he would recommend me directly to President-elect Clinton and I promised to follow the strategy he outlined for me.

With considerable prescience, he advised me to review my arbitration experience—I had acted as an impartial neutral between labor and management since 1965—and to contact both management and union lawyers involved in decisions I had rendered. He was concerned that my views and writings would be characterized as pro-labor—I was, after all, in favor of collective bargaining—and that some senators would be a reluctant to confirm me on that basis. Jack thought it would be useful to have management attorneys who had both won and lost arbitration cases before me attest to my fairness. After excavating a number of my files from the bowels of the Stanford Law School, I got in touch with a dozen employer and union representatives and lawyers and asked them to send letters on my behalf to the White House.

The National Labor Relations Board is one of several New Deal alphabet agencies (e.g., the Federal Communications Commission [FCC] and the Securities and Exchange Commission [SEC])—created during the 1930s.[3] The Board administers and interprets the National Labor Relations Act of 1935 (NLRA), which has been amended in key respects on at least two occasions.

The act protects employees' rights to protest working conditions they deem unfair and to organize into unions and select representatives. It obliges management to bargain in good faith with the union that represents a majority of workers in an appropriate group or unit and requires unions to bargain in good faith as well. Under the act employees also have the right to refrain from union activities, to vote against the union in a secret-ballot election, and *not* to sign authorization cards distributed to obtain their allegiance to the union. Regulations prohibiting various unfair practices by unions ensure these rights.

The National Labor Relations Board, a small, quasi-judicial administrative agency, has jurisdiction over such issues; with certain significant exceptions, its jurisdiction is exclusive. The Board consists of a general counsel—a presidential appointee with personnel responsibilities for the thirty-six regional offices located throughout the country—and five presidentially appointed members. The latter have authority to adjudicate in cases the general counsel brings before them as a prosecutor and in union representation proceedings that culminate in a secret-ballot election. The Board's orders are not, however, self-enforcing; if either side resists them, the matter is taken to the federal courts for enforcement.

Traditionally, the Board consists of three members of the president's own party and two members of the opposition. In contrast to the situation in other regulatory agencies—most of which are also quasi-judicial—this political allocation is a matter of custom, not of law.

The principal functions of the NLRA and the Labor Board (as the NLRB is often called) are: (1) to oversee elections determining whether employees wish to be represented by a particular union that has petitioned the Board for a representation election; and (2) to resolve controversies about whether employers or unions have committed unfair, and illegal, labor practices. Cases—triggered by charges or petitions filed by unions, employers, or individual employees—are heard by regional NLRB officials, whose decisions may be appealed to the five-member Board in Washington. Disputes involving elections and unfair labor practices usually arise when unions are attempting to recruit new members or to organize a nonunion workplace, but they can also occur within established union-management relationships.

The National Labor Relations Act has endured, albeit with major modifications, for sixty-five years, longer than the comparable legal or regulatory frameworks governing labor practices in Great Britain, Germany, France, Italy, and Japan. During that time it has had a major impact on employees, employers, and labor-management relations, notwithstanding its very small staff of approximately nineteen hundred employees. In the past decade, due to the decline in trade unions, the Board's caseload has diminished. In the early 1980s it reached its zenith of nearly forty thousand cases per year, since steadying at more than thirty thousand.

As collective bargaining has waned during the past twenty-five years, new issues involving the employer-employee relationship have been addressed by the courts and by other state and federal agencies. These include wrongful-discharge actions involving the propriety of employer dismissals of, mostly, nonunion workers, health and safety conditions, pension benefits, and fair employment practices law. Nonetheless, the NLRB remains the country's most important administrative entity related to employment. Its decisions are frequently cited in and relied upon in such areas as fair employment practices and wrongful discharge and under state statutes that provide public sector workers or agricultural employees (as in California) the opportunity to engage in collective bargaining.

For some time after my luncheon conversation with Sheinkman very little happened. He informed me that he had spoken to the president-elect prior to the inauguration at the annual New Year's Hilton Head social event Clinton initiated while governor of Arkansas. Then, during January of 1993, people began telling me they had heard my name mentioned as a possible head of the Labor Board. During my visit to Johannesburg that month, a leader of South Africa's Mineworkers told me American friends had advised him I would be named to the post. And in early February 1993, when I conducted my second annual round of baseball salary arbitration in Los Angeles, attorneys for San Diego Padre pitcher Andy Benes bumped into me at breakfast and said they had heard I would be appointed. A couple of months later well-known *San Francisco Chronicle* columnist Herb Caen wrote: "You may bet the farm on this: Stanford law professor William Gould as next chairman of the Nat'l Labor Relations Board."[4] But nary a word did I receive from anyone in Washington.

In the meantime, Secretary of Labor–designate Robert Reich invited me to join the Commission on the Future of Worker-Management Relations, which had as its mission the proposal of labor law reforms. When I met with Reich and the other members of the commission in Washington in March, he reminded me that he had reviewed one of my books for the *Harvard Law Review*.[5] At the time he said nothing about the NLRB and neither did I.

Finally, in mid-May 1993, I had a call from Cynthia Metzler of the White House staff inviting me to talk about the chairmanship with administration officials next time I was in town on commission business. This was the first word of an appointment I had received directly from the White House. She informed me matter-of-factly that she intended to follow through on the subject for some time. As the next commission meeting was on May 25, we scheduled the appointment to discuss the NLRB for that day.

Just before 10:00 A.M. on the twenty-fifth I walked from my room at the Mayflower Hotel down Connecticut Avenue and across Lafayette Park to the Old Executive Office Building next to the White House. Here, I met with Metzler in the first in a series of meetings she had scheduled for me. All of them were convivial and seemed to go well. After my session with Metzler I met with Reich and with

Lane Kirkland, who was then still head of the AFL-CIO. In a Democratic administration elected with labor support, it was generally assumed that the AFL-CIO had to place its imprimatur (or at least its *nihil obstat*) on any nominee in the labor field—particularly for the sensitive NLRB position, which could affect the power balance between labor and management.

Both Reich and Kirkland seemed to proceed on the assumption that I would be appointed. When we met in his office, Reich assured me, "You know that Lane Kirkland supports you for this position." In fact, I hadn't known. Because so many of my writings in the 1960s and 1970s had been critical of the AFL-CIO I had worried about possible opposition, or at best damnation through faint praise. But Jack Sheinkman was at the top of his political game in the federation as well in the Clinton administration; he had done his work well at the AFL-CIO's 16th Street offices (only a couple of blocks from the White House).

Reich formally offered me the job that day and, assuaging an anxiety I had had going into the meeting, also asked me to stay on as a member of the Commission on the Future of Worker-Management Relations. (Later he had to revoke the request because of Republican opposition to my playing both roles.) The Republicans maintained that there was a conflict of interest between proposing law reforms as a member of the commission and interpreting the NLRA as head of the Board—a theme that was to emerge time and time again during my term of office in Washington. That day, as we talked in Reich's office overlooking the capitol, I reminded him of Attorney General Robert Kennedy's threat to jump from the Capitol Building if Jimmy Hoffa, the Teamsters' president, was not convicted in the trial then pending. (Hoffa was acquitted, and RFK was offered a parachute by his critics.) Reich, who is ten years younger than I am, responded blankly and seemed unfamiliar with the story.

When I left Reich's office, I was elated at the prospect of serving as chairman while continuing on the commission. As I walked into the Department of Labor cafeteria for lunch, two cowboy dancers were twirling to the song "I Feel Lucky"— my exact feelings. Yet, though I had readily accepted Reich's invitation to be head of the Labor Board, I had tacked on one qualification: I would take the short term—member terms are staggered so that one expires each year—which began in 1993 and expired in 1996. That would be a long enough stay in Washington for me, I told him. Reich seemed to agree, although he said nothing in response to my statement. From that day onward, however, everything took much longer than I expected it to. And there were many occasions over the next five years when I felt most unlucky indeed.

Later I found that my commitment to leave Washington at a date certain set me apart from other NLRB appointees and gave me a sense of independence consistent, I believe, with the Board's role. Yet it was always a source of tension with other members of the Board and their paramount objective (i.e., to retain their government position or its substantive equivalent or better). Their overriding goal was to hang on in Washington as long as possible. In this regard, the words of Professor G. Calvin Mackenzie are right on target:

What is most distressing ultimately is the transcendent loss of purpose in the appointment process. The American model did not always work perfectly, but it was informed by a grand notion. The business of the people would be managed by leaders drawn from the people. Cincinnatus, in-and-outers, noncareer managers—with every election would come a new sweep of the country for high energy and new ideas and fresh visions. The president's team would assume its place and impose the people's wishes on the great agencies of government. Not infrequently, it actually worked that way.

But these days, the model fails on nearly all counts. Most appointees do not come from the countryside, brimming with new energy and ideas. Much more often they come from congressional staffs or think tanks or interest groups—not from across the country but from across the street: interchangeable public elites, engaged in an insider's game.[6]

At the May meetings, Reich and Metzler said that an "intent to nominate" me would be issued by the White House within a couple of weeks. But no announcement came until June 28. By late May and early June, however, newspapers like the *Wall Street Journal* were proclaiming my nomination. I have always suspected that these articles were a deliberate trial balloon put up by someone in the administration who was skeptical about my appointment and doubtful that the Senate would confirm me. When the *Wall Street Journal* piece ran on June 17, my telephone in Stanford rang off the hook.[7]

Then the real challenge began—a drumbeat of criticism and a distribution to newspaper columnists of background papers and books aimed at stirring up resistance to my confirmation. The principal opposition was led by two organizations: the National Right to Work Committee, which gained prominence a decade ago when the National Labor Relations Act was interpreted by the U.S. Supreme Court as protecting the rights of antiunion workers; and the Labor Policy Association, an extreme right-wing business group I had never heard of until I joined the worker-management commission earlier that year. Several management lawyers who had written the White House supporting my nomination that spring were threatened: their business clients, said the letter writers, would be advised of their support of me. These groups had late-May and most of June, while rumors of my appointment flew around Washington, to gear up their campaign. During the Reagan and Bush administrations they had had it all their own way—exercising, at a minimum, a virtual veto over any nominee to the Board—and they seemed to expect to continue playing the role of power broker. Their attacks on me began a stressful period that was to stretch over the next nine months.

My situation was not all that uncommon. Confirmation struggles involving NLRB appointments had occurred regularly from the 1970s onward. At that time, employer resistance to trade unions was stiffening and dissatisfaction with the NLRB's creaky administrative procedures was emerging. The first serious push for labor law reform in almost twenty years—aimed at providing more effective remedies for unfair labor practices and expediting elections and complaint handling—took place in 1977 and 1978.[8] In October 1977 the House of Representatives passed the Labor Reform Bill, which would have allowed the government to cancel and withhold contracts from employers that repeatedly engaged in labor law misconduct. Because of the inadequacy of existing remedies, the bill imposed new sanctions in the form of double damages for unfair labor practices. Inasmuch as most of the cases involved appeals that were essentially factual, it also mandated prompt review by the NLRB in Washington of the rulings of the regional administrative law judges (who acted as trial judges in these cases). But in 1978 virtually the same package of reforms, though favored by a majority in the Senate, could not be voted on because there were not sufficient votes to break the Republican filibuster.

Meanwhile, the fight over labor law reform spilled over into the confirmation process for NLRB members and heated up as labor and management squared off in the halls of Congress. The first incident involved William Lubbers, President Jimmy Carter's nominee as general counsel of the Board. The second, in 1979, concerned Washington insider–career bureaucrat John Truesdale, formerly the Board's executive secretary. In both instances the attack was led by Senator Orrin Hatch (R-Utah). These initiatives changed the way future Board nominations were treated by the Senate. Prior to that time, as political scientist Terry Moe explains,

The primary rule is deference to the president: he has a right to build his own administration as he sees fit and thus to have his appointees confirmed as long as they are not clearly unqualified. What, then, counts as "unqualified" and therefore is a legitimate reason for voting against confirmation? Here, the basic rule is that there must be a "smoking gun" of some sort—a serious character flaw, criminal conduct, demonstrable bias, or obvious inability to carry on the duties of the job. A candidate's ideology is not a legitimate basis for voting no.

For these reasons—and because senators, like presidents, must save their efforts for the bigger fish that they have to fry—senators of all ideological stripes are strongly disposed to vote affirmatively on virtually every presidential nominee.[9]

While disavowing the threat of filibuster, Lubbers's congressional opponents claimed that his close ties to NLRB Chairman John Fanning—he had served as chief counsel to Fanning—should disqualify him. They argued that the earlier connection would prevent the arm's length relationship between these two officials that is presumed necessary in some circumstances—for example, when the general counsel, acting as the prosecutor, brings unfair labor practice cases to the Board for adjudication. Hatch also focused attention on meetings related to the 1978 Labor Reform Bill that Lubbers had allegedly attended with union officials. Lubbers maintained that he had not participated in lobbying on behalf of the bill.

Ultimately, Lubbers was confirmed—over the objections of the U.S. Chamber Commerce, the National Association of Manufacturers, and other business groups —but not before a cloture petition was filed in April 1980 to break a Republican filibuster. This was the beginning of a series of difficult confirmations, most of which had formerly taken place on a voice vote without a hearing.

The basis of Senator Hatch's attack on Truesdale was more obviously ideological. He claimed that as a member of the NLRB Truesdale had never decided cases "in favor of any position which was considered contrary to those officially representing union interests." During his renomination hearing in 1980, Hatch also criticized the declining rate of appellate courts' affirmance of Board decisions and suggested that Truesdale's votes had something to do with it.

On August 18, 1980, the *New York Times* reported that Truesdale's renomination "may be filibustered in the Senate as a result of business opposition to him."[10] Though President Carter gave Truesdale a recess appointment in October, just prior to Carter's electoral defeat, after the election the renomination continued to languish in committee.

After the inauguration, the Democrats in Congress sought an opportunity to pay back the Republicans. President Reagan's first nominee to the NLRB, John Van de Water, ran into immediate trouble. Van de Water, who had been a management consultant, was opposed by organized labor. In response to questions by Senator Edward Kennedy, he admitted that companies had hired him during union organizing campaigns to keep unions out. In 1981 the Senate Labor Committee rejected his nomination, and, though serving on a recess basis, he could not get a favorable recommendation from the Senate.

Ironically, when the Van de Water nomination failed to move forward, President Reagan nominated as chairman of the Board Donald L. Dotson, who was confirmed by voice vote on February 17, 1983. His relatively easy route to confirmation—the only senators at the hearing were Don Nickles (R-Okla.) and Gordon Humphrey (R-N.H.)—resulted in part from exhaustion from the struggle over Van de Water. Though labor and the Democrats had won the battle over Van de Water, they lost the war. Under Dotson, the Board quickly shifted ground in a wide variety of policy areas, laying itself open to charges of antiunion bias. Ultimately he produced a boycott of the Board by certain union leaders frustrated by its procedures and decisions. As Moe points out,

Reagan imposed on the NLRB a brand of radical anti-unionism that business leaders did not demand and, in fact, had long resisted ... but, especially in an environment of economic adversity and union decline, some business leaders began to realize over time that the reality of an anti-union NLRB was not to be feared at all—that it proved quite consistent with their own, more confrontational approaches to unions. They were, in effect, dragged kicking and screaming into the brave new world of political anti-unionism by presidential leadership and some saw that what was clearly impossible in earlier decades was now quite possible indeed.[11]

Thus, Dotson's tenure—added to the generally hostile labor-management and political climates and to controversies over nominees to other offices—made it clear that from that time forward any nominee to the NLRB, especially as chairman, would be scrutinized carefully.

During debate over my confirmation in 1993, matters were immensely complicated by the antiunion groups' distribution of excerpts from my *Agenda for Reform*, which MIT Press was to publish later that year. In it I argued that the National Labor Relations Act was not working effectively and proposed a number of reforms to the statute and to national labor policy, in particular a wide variety of procedural and substantive reforms designed to implement the aims outlined in the preamble to the act. Among other reforms, I recommended obligatory recognition of unions on the basis of employees' signed authorization cards and payment of union dues; more rigorous guidelines encouraging the Board to seek prompt injunctive relief against labor law violations; double or triple back-pay awards for certain violations of the statute; first-contract arbitration when parties cannot reach agreement subsequent to NLRB certification or recognition; requiring employers to bargain with unions about plant closings and to open the firm's books when financial questions are relevant to negotiation issues; use of court injunctions against no-strike violations by unions in all circumstances; amendments to the act to promote and enhance employee-participation programs; elimination of employers' right to permanently replace economic strikers; and a requirement that unions hold a vote before initiating a strike.

Despite numerous amendments to the NLRA in 1947 (Taft-Hartley) and 1959 (Landrum-Griffin), the original preamble has been unamended since the statute's origin in 1935. The preamble, states that

[it is hereby declared to be the policy of the United States to . . . encourage] . . . the practice and procedure of collective bargaining and [to protect] . . . the exercise by workers of full freedom of association, self-organization, and designation of representatives of their own choosing. . . ."

It was and is my view that the creakiness of the act's administrative procedures was responsible for the new-found loopholes that allowed employers to delay realization of these rights. The lack of effective remedies and substantive decisions, which diminished the effectiveness of concerted activity generally and the right to strike in particular, undermined the statute's preamble.

I had expressed some of these ideas in earlier law review articles, and a number of other scholars had recommended similar changes both prior to publication of *Agenda for Reform* and subsequent to it. All in all, the ideas were moderate, the kind of middle-of-the-road positions I had expounded during most of my professional career in labor management. Nonetheless, as the summer of 1993 wore on, the National Right to Work Committee turned up the decibel level of its critical barrage and labeled the book a liberal or union *Mein Kampf*.

Although the Democrats controlled both Houses of Congress, strange things had begun to happen at the beginning of the Clinton administration in 1993. The nominations of first Zoe Baird and then Kimba Wood for attorney general were withdrawn after sparking considerable controversy. And only a few weeks before I was offered the chairman's job by Secretary of Labor Reich, President Clinton had withdrawn the nomination of Lani Guinier, his nominee for assistant attorney general for civil rights, when some Republicans tagged her a "quota queen" because her writings advocated several new forms of political representation. The nomination of yet another black appointee, Jocelyn Elders, to be surgeon general was then encountering stormy weather. At this point, as articles critical of me and my writings began to circulate, President Clinton's counselor Bruce Lindsay (I later learned) was expressing misgivings about my nomination.

Just before the excerpts from my book began to appear, my chief-counsel-to-be Bill Stewart (who was then working for the general counsel of the NLRB) asked me if there was anything in my book that could cause controversy. I thought long and hard and said: "There is only one thing I can think of. I advocate expanded remedies for undocumented workers, who have already been declared by the Supreme

Court to be protected as employees under the act. Aside from that, I really can't think of anything." In fact, believing that its timely appearance would help my nomination, I had asked the publisher to accelerate the book's publication. I didn't anticipate for a moment that it would cause problems for my confirmation. But Lindsay had become uneasy—particularly about my proposal to grant union recognition on a "members only" basis when there was substantial worker support short of a majority. "Was that his view of the act as currently written?" Lindsay asked Cynthia Metzler. "Of course not," I responded when she relayed the question to me.

Lindsay's confusion was genuine—but it was a result of a deliberate disinformation campaign designed to confuse my views about how the statute should be rewritten so as to more effectively implement its goals with my understanding of what the act said in its current form. This ploy was a harbinger of things to come and introduced a theme my opponents would return to frequently. They argued that I wouldn't be able to distinguish between my two roles: case adjudication by Chairman Gould, on the one hand, and ideas about law reform by Professor Gould, on the other.

Nonetheless, on June 28, President Clinton announced his intention to nominate me:

William Gould has a tremendous amount of both practical and scholarly experience in labor law and stands for the principles that I want the NLRB to uphold—the rights of all workers to participate in labor organizations, and the need for labor and management to work together to increase our nation's competitiveness in a global marketplace. I think that he will be an excellent addition to the Labor Relations Board.

On June 28 the very first person who called me from Washington to offer congratulations was the Reverend Jesse Jackson. Speaking from a car phone as he left town at the end of the day, he said he looked forward to meeting with me on my next visit. Throughout my tenure Jackson took a considerable and constructive interest in labor-management relations and the work of the Board. Most of the other the congratulatory calls that day came from close friends in California and on the East Coast. At that point none of us had an inkling of the struggle that was about to ensue.

The formal papers on my nomination were not forwarded to Capitol Hill until the first week of August. In the meantime, Senator Nancy Kassebaum (R-Kansas), the ranking Republican member of the Senate Labor and Human Resources Committee, pointed out to a news reporter that "they were very late getting the Gould [papers] back up here.... We can't do anything until the papers get here."[12]

Nonetheless, the president's announcement began the planning process. My contacts in the White House advised me to start my leave of absence from Stanford Law School in the fall of 1993 as they expected me to be sworn in as chairman by then. The plan was to nominate me formally once the FBI check was completed, though the intent to nominate was announced prior to its conclusion. Hearings of the Labor Committee would presumably be held early in the summer, and a Senate vote on my confirmation would take place by early fall. However, the nomination papers were not completed and signed by President Clinton until August 6, and the Senate recessed for its summer break on August 8. At one point, Charlie Buffon—a veteran Washington lawyer the White House and Department of Labor brought in to head my "confirmation team"—thought the hearings might be held in the middle of Washington's sweltering summer heat, but that was not to be. The committee was in no hurry. No hearing was held in August or in September. Finally, in September, the hearing date was set for October 1.

My nomination was not the only one in the Clinton administration to be affected by delay. In 1993 confirmation took an average of 8.53 months per nominee, compared to 8.13 months in the Bush administration. By these standards, the nearly nine months I waited for the Senate to confirm me (seven months from receipt of the nomination papers) was not excessive. But comparisons with the first year of the Reagan administration (5.30 months) and the Kennedy administration's record (2.38 months) is far more dramatic.[12a] For instance, President Kennedy's nominee for NLRB chairman, Frank McCulloch, was in office within two months—as was the other Board nominee, Gerald Brown, a San Francisco Democrat who had been an NLRB regional director. In those days both nomination and confirmation proceeded expeditiously.

There was yet another factor. President Clinton's election had brought the Democratic party back to the promised land; but in this first Democratic administration in twelve years inexperience reigned. On the day of my nomination, a Stanford public relations officer who had been trying to pry information about my appointment from the White House for some time said to me, "I wish I could find an adult there." And, although I appeared to be the only person ever seriously considered for the chairmanship, my appointment was affected by the party's long period in the wilderness. In the first weeks and months of 1993 the White House was besieged by the long-pent-up desires of aspiring officeholders. All of this contributed mightily to the holdup.

As the delay became more pronounced, the business groups intensified their attack on my nomination, and then some of my supporters jumped into the fray.

First, several leaders of the National Academy of Arbitrators, the blue ribbon club of arbitrators I had belonged to since 1970, made statements or sent letters supporting my nomination. Second, my friend and colleague, Professor Herman Levy of Santa Clara Law School, rallied nearly a hundred law professors to sign a letter to the Senate Labor and Human Resources Committee characterizing me as "uniquely qualified" to be chairman. Unions like the United Auto Workers, the United Food and Commercial Workers Union, and the American Federation of State, County, and Municipal Employees all began to take an interest and to support my nomination. So did a quartet of influential California labor leaders I had come to know over the past two decades: Jack Henning, Walter Johnson, Chuck Mack (a Teamster leader), and the late Jimmy Herman, president of the International Longshoremen and Warehousemen's Union (ILWU). Similarly, Bill Coday, president of the Pacific Maritime Association (which bargains with the ILWU and other maritime unions), joined in, a fact referred to by Senator Dianne Feinstein (D-Calif.) during the confirmation debate the next year.

The first of many flaps emerged during one of my visits to Washington in connection with the Commission on the Future of Worker-Management Relations. The Republicans on the Senate Labor Committee, probably encouraged by Senator Hatch, the ranking member on that side, asserted that my nomination for the chairmanship was inconsistent with membership on the commission. Of course, I, armed with Bob Reich's statement, felt confident that it was entirely appropriate for me to serve in both capacities. When the Republicans objected, however, the view —expressed to me initially by Senate Labor Committee staffers and later by Department of Labor people below Reich—was that I should not participate in commission business until my appointment was confirmed. I was advised that I should then offer to resign from the commission.

I resisted this position fervently. I believed that someone experienced and charged with the responsibility for interpreting the statute would be in a strong position to recommend useful labor law reforms. But the prevailing administration view was that the Republicans should have their way in this matter. After a long and friendly telephone call with Reich in steamy Boca Raton, Florida (where I was attending the annual meeting of the black National Bar Association), he said: "I can't tell you what to do. It's really up to you." That comment, so different from his earlier affirmative support, convinced me that it was more important for me to move ahead and get confirmed as chairman.

In the wake of the August 6 nomination, two individuals began to assume primary responsibility for preparing me for the confirmation hearing. The first,

Buffon, prepared a voluminous briefing book that analyzed all my writings going back to the 1950s. The British Labour party intellectual Harold Laski had written so extensively that wags liked to say that he contradicted himself. I was not to be allowed to do this—at least not consciously. The idea was to prepare me for all of the many possible lines of attack. The second person working with me was an extraordinarily bright guy in his early twenties who had worked in the Clinton "War Room" during the 1992 campaign. Nestor Davidson, in addition to his brainpower, had a lot of good sense. He later graduated from Columbia University Law School and became Justice David Souter's law clerk. Davidson's only drawback at the time of my confirmation battle was his relatively low status in the White House pecking order.

Just as the three of us began our preparations for the hearing, the first in an extraordinary series of bombshells dropped on me. One morning early in September as I stepped out of the shower I received a call from Mark Childress, one of Senator Edward Kennedy's aides and a counsel to the Labor Committee for the Democratic side.

"Are you sitting down?" Childress asked me.

"What is it?" I asked.

"I have to ask you. Do you gamble?" Someone on the Republican side, he said, was spreading a story that I had disastrously high gambling debts and was accepting bribes in my arbitration cases to pay them off. People who knew something about me and my interest in sports, particularly baseball—as well as my involvement in the baseball salary arbitrations in 1992 and 1993—could easily have seen this as an opportunity to find fire where they claimed to smell smoke. But no one who knew me personally would believe I would gamble—beyond making a few (mistaken!) five-dollar bets on the Super Bowl with friends.

Had I ever been to Nevada? Atlantic City? Childress asked me that morning. "Did you have arbitrations in those places?"

I answered affirmatively with regard to Nevada, but I had not been to Atlantic City since gambling casinos were set up there in the 1980s. (In the 1960s and 1970s, though, I had attended Democratic party, United Automobile Workers, and United Steel Workers conventions in Atlantic City.) Childress didn't seem completely satisfied, and when I asked him "Who is circulating this?" I got no response.

Instead he asked: "Have you been to South Africa and Cuba?"

I told him I had been to South Africa eight times. (In fact, I had just returned from giving a series of lectures there in August.) I had been going to that country since the 1970s, had given numerous lectures there under the auspices of the U. S. government, and had worked with the developing black trade unions. Another story going around, according to Childress, charged that I was connected with the South African Communist party and was visiting both South Africa and Cuba for this reason.

"But I have never been to Cuba," I protested. I told him that although I had met Joe Slovo, the head of the Communist party in South Africa—and undoubtedly others whose party affiliation I was unaware of—I had certainly never attended a Communist party meeting there.

When I repeated my question, "Who is circulating this?" Childress seemed to laugh off the stories and said he couldn't say (or, I supposed, wasn't allowed to say) and that I would be visited by an FBI agent, though I had already received my FBI clearance.

When the FBI agent arrived, she posed the same questions Childress had, and I gave the same answers. When she asked why anyone would say these things about me, I could only speculate: "Perhaps the sources of this are the enemies who are opposed to my appointment to the chairmanship."

The strategy behind the rumors soon began to emerge. As a news reporter who called my Boston College colleague and friend Bob Berry commented. "He's [Gould] known to love sports. He's black. Therefore, he must be a gambler." Though the formal debate in Congress was framed in terms of the ideas set forth in my books and articles, it became clear that my opponents were now playing the race card—sometimes subtly and sometimes not. This ploy, along with President Clinton's already acrimonious relations with Congress and my fidelity to the objectives of the National Labor Relations Act, fueled their campaign. Later in the fall, following my confirmation hearing, the dirty tricks were to continue (see chapter 3). Meanwhile, the gambling–South Africa–Cuba affair seemed to recede into the background. (It received little public attention until the following spring, after my confirmation.)

In mid-September it was time to address the hearing process, and I flew to Washington for a series of "courtesy calls." The first sessions took place on September 14 and 15, and they went well. I began with Senator Dave Durenberger (R-Minn.). We talked a good deal about sports generally and baseball in particular—the epic 1967 Red Sox–Twins struggle as well as the Twins' more recent victories. In our conversation he was effusive about me and my qualifications, stating that the government was "fortunate to have someone as qualified" as me in the chairmanship. Durenberger's praise of me seemed almost too good to be true—and, indeed, it turned out to be too good to be true. When the committee voted in October, he (along with Senator James Jeffords of Vermont) abstained. And, unlike Jeffords, Durenberger did not cast a vote when the nomination came to the full Senate in 1994.

The next visit was with Senator Paul Wellstone (D-Minn.)—a short, wiry, energetic, and bubbly fellow, as enthusiastic a man as I've ever met. He asked me about the erosion of the collective-bargaining process through unlawful means and how it could be revived. Questioning me about remedies to problems in first-contract negotiations and arbitration, he displayed a knowledge of issues most politicians— even those conversant with labor-management affairs—know little or nothing about. Wellstone was both knowledgeable and intellectually alive. I found his enthusiastic interest in the NLRB and my nomination warming. We were to form a close working relationship during my tenure in Washington.

Next came a very brief meeting with another Democratic senator, Paul Simon of Illinois. Like Wellstone, he was quite sympathetic, and he wanted me to return to discuss labor law reform bills he had introduced or planned to introduce in the near future. I gently resisted this idea, because it would conjure up memories of my commission work and invite the Republicans to attack me on the grounds that I was acting as a policy maker and not a judge. I would be glad to work with him, I said, but the timing wasn't good.

Two weeks later, on September 28, I returned to Washington for another round of courtesy calls. These meetings were more challenging than the earlier ones and were complicated by the need to prepare simultaneously for the October 1 hearing.

I began the morning of September 29 by meeting with a man who would become a good friend, the late William Curtin. Curtin was a partner in Morgan, Lewis and Bockius, a firm that represented employers in labor cases. When I met with him in his M Street office he was full of encouragement and confidence about my confirmation prospects.

The second meeting that day was with the congressional Black Caucus on Capitol Hill, and here too I met with a warm and supportive response. Bill Clay (D-Mo.), before whom I had testified in 1984 at the House Labor Committee hearings on the inadequacy of labor law, paved the way. He, along with a number of other old friends, was to be at my side throughout the October 1 hearing. Like Senator Wellstone, the Black Caucus was a group I could always turn to for support in the most difficult of circumstances.

Next I met with Senator Ted Kennedy, chair of the Labor Committee, its most important Democratic member, and (undoubtedly) one of the most important senators since the founding of the Republic. He, along with Wellstone, Simon, and Tom Harkin of Iowa, as well as my own California senators, Dianne Feinstein and Barbara Boxer, were to be my principal Senate supporters. Kennedy shepherded the nomination through and remained a friend during the Republican-controlled hundred and fourth and hundred and fifth congresses.

The critical meeting that day was with Senator Hatch, the second-ranking Republican on the Labor and Human Resources Committee and a spokesman for the right wing of his party. Hatch began by asking me why I would ever leave Stanford for a Washington job like chairman of the Labor Board. Curiously enough, a similar theme was articulated a few weeks later in a *Los Angeles Times* article linking me to a controversial appointment to the U.S. Court of Appeals. Wrote journalist Paul Roberts: "The best bet is that Gould will use his powers to stretch the law at his directions. Why else leave the palm trees in pleasant Palo Alto, if not for the pleasure of wielding power?"[13]

I responded to Hatch by saying that my stay in Washington would end a few years early, and then I would move back to Stanford and write about it—a comment that left Hatch smiling.

He then treated me to a long monologue about the changes that new Board appointees brought. "When the Democrats are in," said Hatch, "they rule for the unions. When we are in, we do what is right." Sitting in on the meeting was my friend Betty Southard Murphy—a Washington management lawyer, former head of the NLRB in the Ford administration, and a friend of Hatch's. At this point she offered her opinion that Board members shouldn't comment on legislation, but Hatch said, "That hasn't been my experience." I said nothing in response to this little colloquy; whatever I said would be harmful. If I supported Murphy's position, I would be sailing under false colors; if I supported Hatch's version of the ways things usually operated, I would give my opponents additional grounds for voting against me. I already felt badly enough about leaving the Reich Commission. (It later came to be called the Dunlop Commission after its chair, Professor John Dunlop of Harvard University.) I certainly I did not want to lose my ability to speak out from time to time on issues relating to labor law reform.

I then mentioned to Hatch the 1979 hearings for the confirmation of Bill Lubbers as general counsel during the Carter administration—a particularly contentious set of proceedings. I emphasized that, in contrast to Lubbers, I would not meet with representatives of labor and management in ad hoc strategy sessions on pending labor legislation—as Lubbers appears to have done. Said Hatch: "I am grateful for that." (In fact, during debates on the Taft-Hartley amendments in 1947, NLRB Chairman Paul Herzog and General Counsel Gerhard Van Arkel both worked with leading senators—Chairman Herzog to help draft the legislation and Van Arkel to write speeches and the Democratic minority report. In the 1960s, too, Chairman McCulloch's special counsel had drafted the Democratic House's report on labor law reform.)[14]

Toward the end of our meeting, Hatch said, "I'm aware that you don't like my views on Anita Hill." Here he appeared to be referring to a letter I had written to the *New York Times* in 1991 attacking the Republican treatment of her during the confirmation hearings of Supreme Court Justice Clarence Thomas. I smiled and said, "You are aware of that?" Hatch exclaimed, "Do you think I'm stupid?"—and we both laughed. He then plugged in a supportive comment about Thomas and how much he thought of him. I remained silent so as to avoid entanglement in something that really had nothing to do with my nomination.

It seemed to me that the meeting had concluded on a fairly positive note, but that was not to be the case with my next one. My encounter with Senator Nancy Kassebaum of Kansas—daughter of Alf Landon, the GOP standard bearer for president in 1936—presented a more formidable and surprising obstacle. She was accompanied by a young right-wing lawyer named Steve Sola who was, I was told, her Svengali. My White House consultant, Nestor Davidson, was also there. Kassebaum was very pleasant and quite intelligent in her discussion of the points raised. She sought out my views, in particular, about the right to strike and employers' right to make permanent replacements. I was hitting on all cylinders that day and happily provided her with a seminar-type exposition of the act and its provisions that I thought both clear and unassailable. It was later apparent, however, that this meeting—and the detailed articulation of my views I had given Kassebaum—was a turning point on my learning curve for the confirmation process.

She didn't like what I had to say in the least—although she listened quite politely. When I asked for her support as I left her office, she said, "At the hearing you will carry the burden of proof." I was absolutely stunned. This was such a marked contrast with the recent hearings on Supreme Court nominations in which Senator Joe Biden (D-Md.) had told nominees, "Judge, the presumption is with you." Senator Kassebaum was telling me that the presumption was against me—at least as far as she was concerned.

When Davidson and I left her office, we sat down on a park bench near the Senate office building. We were both depressed about the meeting. "This confirmation could get away from us," Davidson asserted disconsolately, reprimanding me for mishandling Kassebaum. He stressed the havoc she could cause for us among so-called Republican moderates.

Hatch and Kassebaum were at the heart of the forces threatening my confirmation. Kassebaum was the ranking Republican on the Labor and Resources Committee, and Hatch, though he had shifted his major focus to the Judiciary Committee, over the years retained his interest in the Labor Board. From my conversation with Hatch, it was clear that he had either not forgotten the Lubbers and Truesdale hearings or had been well briefed on them.

There was one more Republican moderate to see before the hearings. On September 30 I met with Senator James Jeffords of Vermont. He was careful, soft-spoken, and very much a listener. I responded somewhat affirmatively to his view that the Board should give priority to strike-replacement cases. He seemed to believe that doing so would help create a middle ground on this issue between the Republicans and liberal Democrats: the Labor Board should expedite the cases but not change the substance of the law that denied economic strikers the right to return to their jobs. His idea was to resolve quickly the question of whether strikers were protesting against unfair labor practices (and so entitled to reinstatement) or economic strikers who could be legitimately ousted from their jobs. Workers and employers could then get on with their work under existing rules without any change in the law governing the right of economic strikers to return to their jobs. Jeffords seemed, in the main, sympathetic to my nomination, and I came away thinking that this meeting, in contrast to the one with Kassebaum, had gone well.

After the Jeffords meeting I went to a luncheon at the union federation building with Elmer Chadek, director of the AFL-CIO Industrial Union Department, and his aide, Joe Uehlein. The most vivid impression I brought home from that meeting was not the discussion we had—after all, the federation, like the congressional Black Caucus and the Democratic senators, were the choir that didn't need preaching to. It was, rather, the extent to which the building on 16th Street, just a block from the White House, was festooned with anti-NAFTA banners. The North American Free Trade Association Treaty was at that time being debated in the Senate, and President Clinton—who campaigned in 1992 on providing protection for labor in any such agreement with Mexico and Canada—wanted it adopted. The AFL-CIO had become one of the major sources of opposition to the president's policy, splitting the Democratic party coalition and placing Clinton in alliance with most of the Republicans in the Hundred and Third Congress.

Though I uttered not a public word on the subject, my own view was that Clinton was right and that NAFTA's promotion of a free trade environment would boost the economy—though I too thought the labor provisions ineffectual and unenforceable. I believed, however, that subsequent revisions and future similar treaties could build in better protections. At that point nothing tougher than NAFTA had ever been negotiated.

But my views, which I kept to myself—they would have surely irritated the AFL-CIO on a matter irrelevant to my nomination—hardly mattered. What was important was that the AFL-CIO was devoting an extraordinary and unprecedented amount of legislative effort and attention to this issue. It dwarfed both the federation's support for my nomination and any attempts to pursue with a sympathetic administration and members of Congress a vast number of worthwhile legislative initiatives on behalf of labor. In October and November of 1993, NAFTA was a major distraction for some of my supporters.

On September 30, on the eve of my appearance before the Labor Resources Committee, I met with a group of people who put me through my paces with regard to the questions I would be asked the next day. I had found earlier meetings of this kind frustrating, filled with young congressional hotshots all too ready with answers to questions they thought would be posed. At one point, when I had tried to break in with my ideas about an answer, someone said: "Oh, why not let Bill give his idea?"

But the September 30 meeting was particularly helpful. It introduced me to "Washingtonese"—the art of answering questions in an evasive manner rather than displaying one's substantive knowledge. This was the mistake I had made in my dealings with Senator Kassebaum, in which I had provided very direct answers to her questions. I should have been far more circumspect. The basic advice—and I followed it fairly successfully on October 1—was to say as little as possible and not to answer questions directly but rather to give bland, general responses that were, in essence, nonresponsive. It was not really my style or instinct as an educator, but I became very good at this practice and employed it later when responding to questions about Labor Board decisions. It must have helped me on October 1, for the hearing went far better than that ill-fated meeting with Senator Kassebaum, in which I had provided very direct answers to her questions.

3

The Confirmation Process

On October 1 as Bill Stewart and I entered the Dirksen Building on Capitol Hill, a voice called out behind us: "Bill, Hello Bill, Bill...." It was Ted Kennedy, greeting us in his warm, gregarious fashion and giving me the lift I needed. I had tossed and turned throughout a sleepless night, unable to close my eyes as I thought about the issues discussed in my "prep" meeting. But by the time we arrived at the hearing I was fully alert and going on adrenaline.

I had a lot going for me that day. Kennedy, chair of the committee, was on my side, and I was accompanied by senators Feinstein and Boxer of California, Congressman Bill Clay of Missouri, and the House member from my own district, Representative Anna Eshoo. Though ready for a full-blown attack on me and my writings, my confidence was sustained by the influential and friendly Democrats flanking me at the hearing table.

Kennedy chaired the hearing. Kassebaum was not present because of illness. Hatch, who was to be my principal inquisitor, was there and in good form and as nattily attired as he had been at our meeting two days before. The initial discussion consisted of good-natured bantering, mostly between myself and senators Jeffords and Durenberger.

Then Hatch commenced a systematic cross-examination. He began with an inquiry into my views on *Pattern Makers* v. *NLRB*.[1] In this decision the Supreme Court, by a 5-to-4 vote, had deferred to the Board's expertise and held that a member could resign from the union at any time, under any circumstances. My own view was that the right to engage in collective activity should be balanced against the right to refrain from it—in this instance by resigning—but that when a union is in the midst of economic conflict, it can turn down a resignation request in the interests of solidarity. Hatch wasn't pleased.

Senator Hatch: Your criticism of this case indicates that you might well tip the scale against voluntary unionism in favor of union solidarity. If that is the case, it is a matter of great concern to me. You say that a statute protects the right to refrain from union activity, but only at the appropriate time and appropriate circumstances.

I responded by relying on Chief Justice Warren Burger's concurring opinion in an earlier decision, in which he had argued that the union's need for solidarity was most pressing at a time of economic conflict.[2] After a lengthy and thorough cross-examination, Hatch concluded:

Senator Hatch: And I presume that you will uphold the law as a member of the Board.

Mr. Gould: Under the current authority of the case law that has evolved, I would uphold that law.

Senator Hatch: That's all I need to know.

At this point, there followed a very tense moment. I had long believed—and expressed this view after I was confirmed—that the Supreme Court's statement that the Board could change its mind applied even to cases in which the Court had affirmed the Board's view—that is, when the Court had relied on the Board's own expertise in so ruling. In *Pattern Makers*, although Justice Lewis Powell's reasoning for the majority also considered substantive law—in this case the NLRA's hostility to the closed shop (which requires union membership as a condition of employment)—the Court was deferring to the Board's expertise. The justices were simply affirming a judgment previously made by the Board. Indeed, Justice Byron White's separate concurring opinion, which tipped the balance in favor of the majority view, was based exclusively on the Board's expertise.

My view was, and is, that the Board is free to exercise its expertise differently and formulate an approach in which competing interests are balanced more appropriately. I therefore said:

Mr. Gould: Senator, if I may interject a second, though.

Senator Hatch: Sure, sure.

Mr. Gould: Perhaps my last answer was not as complete as it should have been.

Senator Hatch: Okay.

Mr. Gould: The *Pattern Makers* decision was based upon—particularly in Justice White's view, Senator, he cast the deciding vote—the Board's exercise of its expertise. The Court was deferring to the Board's expertise there.

There was a moment in which I could feel all my friends holding their breath. I dared not complete my thought and say that I would exercise my expertise differently. But I wanted to get the reasoning of the Court, as I understood it, before the committee, so that I would be free to vote to reevaluate the *Pattern Makers* doctrine in a future case.[3] I feared Hatch would now ask the obvious follow-up question: Would I exercise my expertise differently? But he simply went on to his next subject (the compulsory recognition of unions), leaving unexplored an area in which my views might well have provoked even more intense Republican opposition.

Hatch's questions again skirted an area I wanted to avoid when discussing the employer's right to permanently replace strikers:

Senator Hatch: Would you press for a change in Board law?

Mr. Gould: Would I press for a change in the Board law?

Senator Hatch: Press that we change the law.

Mr. Gould: What I think you're referring to is a book in which I advocated change. But that is your job.

Again, I did not want to go on record as saying I would not speak for change. Obviously, however, it is Congress's job to amend the law, and in saying so I avoided a direct answer and the kind of commitment Hatch sought to extract from me. I had learned from my encounter with Kassebaum that the art of congressional testimony is to avoid a direct answer. On October 1, 1993, I was able to dance evasively along the lines advocated by my White House tutors.

Aside from Senators Kennedy, Hatch, Durenberger, and Jeffords, only Senator Wellstone played an active role in the hearing. His remarks focused on the deference generally shown to a presidential nomination—a deference that was eroded seriously during Clinton's term of office.

Senator Wellstone: I guess my last point, Mr. Chairman, is that once again I follow the questioning of Senator Hatch, it does strike me that the fact that someone has really been out there with a lot of important intellectual work and a lot of important articles is I think very much in the positive.

I once talked to Senator Hatch when I first came here—and this is true; you were my teacher—and I won't use the name, but there was a particular nominee and we had this discussion and I didn't agree with some of the particular issues. And you said to me: "Listen, this President decided to nominate this person and you may not agree, but if you think that that person has integrity and if you think that person is really qualified, that ultimately is what should matter." I feel that is exactly what applies to Bill Gould.

Back and forth we went for the balance of that October morning. Finally, after some bantering with Senator Kennedy, Senator Hatch said to me:

I've enjoyed chatting with you, I've enjoyed reading your book and reading other matters that you have written and spoken. You are clearly a very, very, brilliant person, and I think you have been a great teacher. I just want you to know that I'm very impressed with you personally and look forward to further dialogue here. Welcome to the Board.

Senator Kennedy interposed that he was "just waiting to hear that last sentence, that you can support the nomination." But Hatch asserted ominously that he had "deliberately withheld" that comment.

Yet when the hearing concluded, Senator Hatch rushed down to where I was standing and asked me to autograph a copy of the book (*Agenda for Reform*) he had questioned me about. Soon thereafter he was to announce his opposition to my nomination. But on that day, Ted Kennedy, standing in the background, said to a number of my supporters, "He [Hatch] never laid a glove on him."

The Hearing Aftermath

As we left the Dirksen Building on that sunshiny October day, I and my friends thought that we had handled the challenge and triumphed mightily. We were told that Ken McGuinness, the lobbyist in charge of the right-wing Labor Policy Association (which had worked so vigorously against my nomination during the summer months), had been exasperated and angry about the way the hearing had gone. Three days later, in a speech to the AFL-CIO in San Francisco, President Clinton mentioned my nomination just after a reference to Secretary of Labor Bob Reich: "We have nominated a chair of the National Labor Relations Board in Bill Gould ... who believe[s] in collective bargaining."

But, there were a number of developments that emerged from what seemed to be a great victory on October 1, all of which diminished or limited it. First of all, the dirty tricks evident in the gambling and South Africa–Cuba rumors continued. On October 31 and November 3, two remarkably similar articles commenting on racially inflammatory issues appeared in the *Los Angeles Times* and the London *Evening Standard*. Both sought to link me with the reputed views of Judge Rosemarie Barkett, justice of the Florida Supreme Court who was later confirmed to the U.S. Court of Appeals for the Eleventh Circuit. The piece by Jeremy Campbell in the *Evening Standard* alleged that

In Barkett's view, American juries are full of people with ambivalent opinions on race, but at such a deep level they are not aware of it. These distortions in the unconscious mind surface as a refusal to acknowledge that a person who commits a crime can be simply redressed in the injustices of the class-ridden society.

The idea that certain people are not responsible for their actions, but are driven by occult forces beyond their control is a recurring theme among Clinton appointees. It shows up too, in the opinions of William Gould, a law professor chosen by Clinton to head the National Labor Relations Board.

In his writings, Professor Gould suggests that a person who chooses not to belong to a trade union is really a misguided victim of years of conservative brainwashing.[4]

Paul Roberts, a Treasury Department official in the Reagan administration, sounded a very similar note in the *Los Angeles Times*:

As one of her colleagues remarked [about Judge Barkett] when she voted to vacate one death sentence, she believed the defendant "is a good man, except that he sometimes kills people."

Gould, a Stanford Law Professor, has a similar explanation about why employees reject unions. It is all due to the Reagan "whirlwind" that creates a "hostile environment" that causes workers to foolishly reject labor unions....

... Lining up with the judge who finds socially redeeming virtues in racial murders and with an NLRB Chairman who wants to cram unions down the throats of workers and managements without a majority vote, Clinton seems destined to be smitten by his own appointees.[5]

Both articles appeared designed to draw me into the emotion-laden morass of crime and race. The source of these very similar stories, and the earlier false rumors, never emerged. Mike Weiss, author of an article on my confirmation published in both the *San Jose Mercury News Magazine (West)* and *Mother Jones*, later attempted to pin them down and concluded that they came from Mark Dissler of Senator Hatch's staff.[6] Dissler had distributed packets of material about Judge Barkett and urged journalists to stir up a campaign against her. At the time, Hatch, a member of the Judiciary Committee, was busy proclaiming his indecision about her nomination; he later asserted that he had been unaware of Dissler's actions. Despite his proven involvement in the anti-Barkett campaign, Dissler denied being the source of the smears against me.[7]

In Washington, the cheerful aftermath of the October 1 hearing was soon dimmed as well. First, Senator Kassebaum immediately came out against my nomination in a statement issued that afternoon, notwithstanding her absence from the hearing. She posed to me a wide variety of written questions, some of them quite nasty. For instance, she asked: "If you believe that (authorization) cards should only be used in connection with the requirement that prospective members indicate support for the union through payment of union dues, why did you fail to mention this additional requirement in your recent book?" I replied that I did mention this point in my book and provided page citations.

In the last week of October 1993, the White House asked me to return to Washington, D.C., to speak to more senators and to woo business groups who had expressed hostility to my nomination. The first meetings were more in the nature of touching base with friendly faces. After I met with Senator Carol Mosley-Braun (D-Ill.) for a few minutes I wrote in my diary for November 28:

She carries herself like an actress, wonderful carriage, and was friendly to me. Jeff Gibbs [of California, the son of a colleague at Stanford] and Nestor sat in.
　Also met with Heflin [D-Ala.] the same day. But he really had no time to meet. "You'll be alright," he said a number of times [and he waved to me, leaving the room as he said it.] [But] the need [for him] to say that made me uneasy.

That same day my interview with Senator John Chafee (R-R.I.), with whom I arranged my own meeting without White House help, was quite contentious. When I said I wanted to extend union voting by postal ballots, he expressed concern. Earlier, he had worried that my proposed reliance on signed authorization cards wouldn't give employers sufficient opportunity to campaign against a new union. This issue, and not the secret ballot box, was his main concern about mail ballots as well. (In subsequent litigation it also proved to be the primary objection to their use.)

Next, I enjoyed meeting with Senator Tom Harkin (D-Okla.), who seemed to promise me an increase in NLRB appropriations. ("You'll be back to me about appropriations.") His parting shot was 'You'll be here by Thanksgiving." At that time, I thought that Thanksgiving would be much too late. (What Harkin lacked in clairvoyance, he more than made up for with support and commitment to the act once I got to Washington.)

I was not enthusiastic about breaking bread with people who were trying to do me in, but I bowed to the advice of those who knew better. I had a number of interesting sessions with Republican groups—in particular one luncheon where most people treated me pleasantly enough but obviously didn't change their opinions. In a later diary entry, on November 28, I recalled this luncheon with

the NAM, Chamber of Commerce, Labor Policy Association . . . and others—this was set up by Joe Velasquez [of the White House] as a particularly distasteful situation to meet with those who are trying to kill my nomination. For the most part, they were obsequious. . . . Eddes of the Chamber [was civil] and a woman who had been in the Reagan Labor Department was relatively obnoxious. I played the role, stating that I wanted their ideas—mainly because I wanted to say as little as possible.

The opposition announced by Nancy Kassebaum in the wake of the hearings had begun to take root. On October 20, she, along with senators Hatch, Strom

Thurmond of South Carolina, Judd Gregg of New Hampshire, and Dan Coats of Indiana, sent a "Dear Colleague" letter. In a broadside attack on my views, particularly those set forth in *Agenda for Reform*, the letter claimed that I espoused radical labor law reforms that had no place in the shaping of Board interpretations, enforcement of national labor law, or decision making. Ignoring the views I expressed in my dialogue with Senator Hatch on October 1, the letter declared the writers' opposition to my views on permanent strike replacements, recognition procedures, union disciplinary authority, and the obligation of employers to disclose confidential information.

Then, on October 29, Kassebaum put on another hat and sent yet another letter, this one co-signed by Jeffords and Durenberger (both of whom had abstained from the vote reporting me out of committee on October 20). This letter asserted that several Republicans would withhold their support for me until President Clinton sent a "complete package of nominees for the remaining open positions on the Board, including the General Counsel position, and consulted with the Committee Republicans and the business community regarding those nominees." Kassebaum was thus identifying herself with Republicans purportedly interested in having a balanced Board that would, they argued, redress grievances in a "fair, consistent, and even-handed manner."

This letter was a watershed development. It allowed Kassebaum to claim that she was not attempting to kill my nomination but only to condition it on Republican approval of other NLRB nominations. The truth was that she would have liked to prevent my appointment altogether. But, given the other vacancies—there were two on the Board as well as the important general counsel position—she found an alternative strategy, one that gave her the opportunity to influence the selection of these nominees. In August President Clinton had nominated another Democrat, a union lawyer from Philadelphia named Margaret Browning, for one of the Board seats. By tradition, the remaining vacant seat belonged to a Republican. It was this seat that Kassebaum and the moderates were determined to control.

The practice of "batching" appointments was not new to the National Labor Relations Board. In the early 1990s the Bush administration was being buffeted on the right by an important constituent, the National Right to Work Committee—which was preoccupied with the *Beck* issue (the expenditure of union dues for political activities)[8]—and from the left by Senate Democrats. In an attempt to mollify both sides, it had put together informal "packages" of nominees. Prior to that time, as Mathew Bodah has noted, "the only example of candidates of opposite parties being confirmed at the same time was fifty-one years ago when Democrat Abe Murdock and Republican J. Copeland Gray were sworn in on August 1, 1947. That situation, however, was extraordinary: the board had been expanded from three to five seats by the Taft-Hartley Act."[9]

But something very new was involved in the Kassebaum proposal. Throughout the Clinton administration it was to haunt the appointment process for regulatory agencies in general and for the Board in particular, especially the 1997 group of appointments. Reagan and Bush—indeed all the Democratic and Republican presidents before them—had selected the nominees of the opposition party on their own. Now the Republicans wanted direct involvement in a Democratic president's choice of a Republican nominee. G. Calvin Mackenzie has described the change in the process as follows:

The tendency to select appointees to an agency as teams and to divide up control over the choices has become the norm in Washington. The Senate, in fact, often delays confirmation until several nominations to the same agency accumulate, thus allowing it to require that the President include some nominees who are effectively designated by powerful Senators.

This kind of batching of nominations rarely happened before the present date. Even on the regulatory commissions, whose original statutes require that an only a bare majority of appointees can be from any one party, a vacancy in an opposition party chair was usually filled by the President with an enrollee in the opposition party who supported the President. These appointments, common for most of this century, came to be known as "friendly Indians" and were routinely confirmed by the Senate even when it was controlled by the opposition party. But they allowed the incumbent President to control the appointment process and to shape the majorities on most regulatory commissions.

That is nearly impossible these days. The membership of the regulatory commissions has become little more than the sum of the set of disjointed political calculations. Concerns about fealty to leadership, effective teamwork, and intellectual fealty to leadership and intellectual or ideological coherence play almost no part in the selection of regulatory commissioners. The juggling of political interests dominates. That we as a nation often get inconsistent and incoherent regulatory policies should be no surprise to those that follow the shuffling and dealing that produces regulatory commissioners.

An additional complicating factor in "batching" is that the Republicans do not have the same incentive to make a deal regarding a group of nominees for a particular agency. This is especially so of an agency like the National Labor Relations Board which operates under statutory principles in which a large number of Republicans do not believe. Accordingly … all of the incentives are weighted toward crippling the agency.[10]

As we shall see, this state of affairs later became a justification for advising the Board not to take action of any kind, because it would be illegitimate to do so when it is not at full strength. Thus, the Kassebaum–Jeffords–Durenberger approach, supposedly reflecting a compromise between complete opposition to my nomination and acquiescence to it, represented the beginnings of real trouble for the functioning of the Board and the appointment process.

In reference to my nomination President Clinton had early made it clear that he would not (as the press termed it) "do a Lani Guinier"—whose nomination for assistant attorney general he had withdrawn under Republican pressure. He appeared ready to resist the Kassebaum initiative. On November 12 he responded directly to Senator Kassebaum, stating that he shared her desire for an able and fair-minded Board and intended to consult with the Republicans about the remaining open positions.

It is my hope that, once Professor Gould is confirmed, I will be able to turn my full attention to the remaining positions at the NLRB, to move ahead expeditiously and to work with you in filling the positions in which you are interested.

It is critical at this juncture that the Board remain functioning, and, therefore, it is important for the Senate to confirm Professor Gould. I know that you share my goal of an NLRB that has the confidence of both employers and employees, and the confirmation of Professor Gould is the first step towards achieving that goal.

But, much to my surprise, and perhaps that of the White House, Kassebaum's response was to throw down the gauntlet and announce her intention to lead a filibuster until the full package was brought forward. Supported by business groups who would lobby both Democrats and Republicans against voting, she would delay confirmation as long as it took. The antilabor groups rallied their supporters to oppose me until the full package was revealed.

As Thanksgiving Day drew near, Congress stood poised to recess, and there was a growing possibility that no action would be taken on my nomination. My diary entries for late November reflect this uncertainty:

November 20, 1993   The last 72 hours have been a complete roller-coaster. A new dominant figure enters the scene after the House passed NAFTA on November 17 ... Howard Pastor, the president's congressional liaison. I find him pleasant, intelligent, quick and hard-working, but his tactics on the Republican seat seem questionable.
...
For some strange reason, it took two precious weeks for the White House to respond (to the October 29 letter).... It [the Clinton November 12 letter] was a good letter, supportive of my nomination—(at the time I first read it this past week, I wasn't even aware of the Kassebaum letter)....

The day after NAFTA, November 18, Pastor called Kassebaum and offered her a veto over the Republican seat. (Kassebaum's office was to dispute the accuracy of this.) She turned it down, insisting upon the name of a nominee. Earlier that day, my hopes had soared because of the pending discussion—but in late morning (they) plummeted. Now it appeared that there was no candidate. [Eric] Schmertz [a New York arbitrator] and [Don] Zimmerman [a former Board Member appointed by Carter] were rejected by the Republicans; Dole's candidate—Mary Harrington of Kodak—and Hatch aide Sharon Proust were rejected by the AFL-CIO.

I called Tom Donahue of the AFL-CIO [former secretary-treasurer, who held that position throughout the confirmation dispute] that evening [to discuss Republican candidates for the Board]. Soon thereafter, Reich, Kirkland, Donahue, and Glynn [Tom Glynn, undersecretary of labor] met for lunch. Pastor had said to me earlier: "The choice is theirs—do they want Gould as chairman?—If so, they must back down on the Republican seat." But this dance was complicated by organized labor's "unhappiness with Clinton on NAFTA."

With Kassebaum holding firm against compromise, AFL-CIO and Republicans defending their own candidates, the Senate about to adjourn, my fate yesterday and today was and is perilous.

Two developments brightened the prospects. The first was the active intervention of Paul Wellstone. Subsequent to my call to him, Pastor has acknowledged his interest. He has called two or three times over the past couple of days, reporting on White House activity, hopeful prospects [in Republican ranks]. He has been a good friend.

... After [my first meeting with Wellstone prior to the hearing] ... we met again the last week in October when I returned to Washington for courtesy calls with both politicians and business types. We flew from San Francisco to Washington on the redeye [sitting next to one another]. Wellstone said that conservative politicians feared me as they do liberation theology. We talked about our work and our families. He offered his help—and I have taken him up on the offer yesterday and today.

The second [development] was a Friday night call from Cynthia Metzler while we were about to sit down for dinner with Gordon and Evelyn Myatt. (Gordon [a retired administrative law judge of the Board] is teaching my Labor Law I course this semester.) Cynthia said that the AFL-CIO had approved of Kenneth Hipp of Honolulu—a management labor lawyer and Republican. Kassebaum was evaluating him and "softening." But Cynthia said that the she sensed the Republicans were seeking "revenge" for the Democrats' treatment of Van der Water, Reagan's first and failed nominee in 1981—[and] Oviatt [a Bush nominee and Board member], who was kept waiting for his seat in 1989 for a year. At this point, discussions were moving forward—but still no agreement from Kassebaum and, perhaps equally important, Dole.

November 22, 1993   Late Saturday, after the above entry, I telephoned Wade Henderson of the NAACP [he, along with the organization, had appeared with me at the hearing on October 1] in Washington at about 5:30 P.M. (P.S.T.). He responded enthusiastically and said that he would make calls. Within a few minutes, he called back with bad news—as of Friday at midnight, a nomination could be brought on with unanimous consent only. On Saturday morning, Kassebaum had told my Republican friend Rod Hills [a Washington lawyer and Stanford graduate], whom I had reached in Mexico with a request to call Kassebaum, that the issue was now "bigger than her." What she meant was that she had now succeeded in stirring up the Republicans and business and that they would object to placing my nomination in debate, even if she agreed that Hipp and I could go forward.

Shortly after Henderson's call, Pastor called to say that it was now virtually impossible and that he was focusing on the future. Curiously, he said that Henderson's call had put a "different light or dimension" to my name. It was interesting, he said, that Republicans were only attacking African American nominees and that he was not "above" playing this card at some point in the future. I was rather surprised that it had taken him so long to see the racial issue. On Sunday and today, a series of phone calls with Pastor and Cynthia. Pastor believes that a recess appointment makes sense for both me and Hipp in the interests of "parity"—though the issue of Peg Browning, the other Democratic seat, and Fred Feinstein, who was nominated for general counsel on Saturday, was not addressed. My concern is that: (1) opposition to them could grow under such circumstances—opposition which has thus far been aimed at me exclusively, and (2) I must have a date or time period certain for a confirmation vote. Otherwise, there will be an incentive to delay the vote, and the Republicans will take a referendum on my opinions.

This is the thirtieth anniversary of JFK's assassination—and I can well remember being told about it in the NLRB's offices in Pennsylvania Avenue and gathering in front of the White House as helicopters went in and out, and the crowds grew increasingly uneasy.

November 25, 1993   Thanksgiving Day: No sooner did Pastor get into all of this than he resigned two days ago. He has told me that he will continue with the nomination matter through his departure in December. Now, yet another leader is involved, John Podesta, who is number 2 to [Mack] McClarty [Clinton's chief of staff]. He [Podesta] called me yesterday and seemed sensible and promising. But, yesterday a piece appeared in the N.Y.T. [*New York Times*] stating that Podesta is in line for another position with the Veep. [Ultimately, in the fall of 1998, he would become chief of staff to President Clinton.] We'll learn more.

Spoke with Dusty Baker [San Francisco Giants manager] on Monday, and he volunteered to enlist Walter Shorenstein—which he did at the forty-niners game Monday night at Candlestick. Shorenstein swung into action on Tuesday. If only I had reached him earlier. He is one of the biggest ... Democratic party donors in the country.

Jim Stephens, incumbent chairman, called late yesterday. His attitude has changed. When he thought that I would easily be confirmed, he called frequently and was very chatty. Now his calls are infrequent and many say that he works regularly with my enemies, like McGuiness at the Labor Policy Association. Stephens's call yesterday was just to poke around and see what I knew about the administration's plans for filling the Raudabaugh vacancy [John Neil Raudabaugh, who was appointed by President Bush]. (R, [according to Stephens] a recess appointment, left [the Board] yesterday with a great flourish.) I played [it] close to the vest. He [Stephens] wants to hold [onto] the chairmanship desperately. The more that he wants it, the more that I think a recess appointment may be the way to go.

November 28, 1993   Paul Richard, an assistant to John Podesta of the White House, telephoned on Friday after Thanksgiving. ... He really had nothing to report, said that the White House was operating at half-staff and were going to "check in."

But during the past week I was dismayed as a result of a telephone conversation with [one of the country's top union leaders. He] said, "If you quote me, I'll deny it, but I'm disappointed in the leadership of the Senate leader," George Mitchell. But he, like other trade unionists, doesn't seem to have done much lobbying with the moderate Republicans and southern Democrats who are important to me. [Most of the union leaders' attention was focused on NAFTA.]

And so 1993 came to a close without a resolution of the confirmation issue. As I had been assured that I would be in Washington in the late summer or early fall of 1993, I had not planned to teach in the fall term. The confused state of affairs left me dispirited as the year ended.

1994: The New Year

My diary for 1994 began on a more promising note.

January 3, 1994 The past week or so has produced numerous phone calls with nothing definitive. A week or so ago—before Christmas—John Podesta said that a deal would be cut with Kassebaum right after the New Year. The assumption was that this would be in the first week of January.

Last night Jack Sheinkman called from New York to say that he had spoken one-on-one with President Clinton at the annual New Year's gathering [in Hilton Head] (he was the only labor leader invited there!), and that he had told Clinton that [legislative reversal of the Supreme Court decision allowing employers to permanently replace economic strikers] ... would be difficult to provide as a kind of compensation for NAFTA, [and] that therefore [Clinton] should place primary focus on the NLRB. Sheinkman spoke of all four appointments. But he mentioned me by name, told the president of our long friendship. Sheinkman said that the president was attentive and took notes. I can't imagine a more significant communication.

Today Jim Stephens [called essentially] ... to promote Chuck Cohen as a Board member. Cohen, along with [Mary] Harrington was interviewed by Reich and Glynn today. Stephens's pitch was that a deal with Kassebaum would be easy if the White House would support Cohen. Cohen is a management labor lawyer in Washington.

Stephens had not known that John Truesdale has been interviewed for a recess Board appointment. The deal would be not to make Truesdale chairman. Stephens didn't ask this, but it surely must have been on his mind.

Raudabaugh called from Chicago shortly after the Stephens call. Earlier he had called to support Harrington—as had Jean McKelvey [of Cornell] and Katherine Hagen of AT&T ([so] Stewart Schwaub of Cornell wrote me)—but now he was expressing reservations, because he had learned that Harrington was close to McGuinnis at the Labor Policy Association and there are none worse than him, except for the National Right to Work Committee....

January 8, 1994 On Tuesday afternoon January 4, Ralph Deeds of General Motors phoned to say that the GM Government Affairs people believed that a deal had been cut between the White House and Kassebaum on Monday night. Their view was that Mary Harrington had become the leading candidate for the Republican seat. This view was confirmed by both Cynthia Metzler and Nestor Davidson the following day. (Davidson said that Podesta had advised him of this on Tuesday.)

I called Podesta three times without a return call—but he did call on Wed. He denied a deal but said that they were close to one. He said that "we have accepted her [Kassebaum's] list of two." These people are Harrington and Chuck Cohen of Washington.... the AFL-CIO has apparently relented on Harrington, though Podesta emphasized (as he has in the past) the sensitivity of this matter, urging me not to speak to anyone about it. Podesta said that he wanted to have this matter finalized by today when President Clinton (who has just returned from his mother's funeral in Arkansas) leaves for Russia. (Podesta is going with him.)

Yesterday, a *Daily Labor Report* article heralded an impending deal.... The problem is that, even if a final choice is made today (optimistic view, given all the other matters before Clinton, including a Republican and *New York Times* attempt to make a scandal of the Whitewater S&L matter when he was Gov. of Ark.), an attempt could not be made until the Senate returns on Jan. 25. Given the FBI check that would still take place, the nomination couldn't be made until late Feb. This could put everything back until April or May....

January 28, 1994, Clearwater Beach, Florida   This is my time to bungle. Yesterday I gave a speech here to a Stetson Law School conference. My speech (based on notes) was divided into two parts: (1) ... a description of my odyssey since the Spring of 1993, sprinkled with a list of errors made by the Labor Policy Association on my writings, a reference to "scurrilous lies both professional and personal"; (2) a description of my goals as chairman. I had hoped that the latter would be the main feature—but it was the former that caught the attention of the *Daily Labor* reporter. This was a stupid move on my part because, of course, it gave McGuinnis free publicity, a new opportunity to create an issue and a delay —and he set about doing just that, issuing a press release which stated that he didn't get his info from William Safire (a reference to Admiral Inman's useful, but yet bizarre attack on the press) but rather from my book, again confusing my views on law reform (this time with reference to the Supreme Court's 1958 *Borg-Warner* ruling) with those relating to my responsibility as chairman.[11]

When I saw the form of the story, I telephoned both Paul Richard (Podesta was out of town) and Nestor to say that a problem had arisen; I had made a mistake. Nestor had actually telephoned on Jan. 24 to say that he had a phone message from Kassebaum's right-wing counsel Sola. Today, his [Sola's] cut on this is revealed by two questions he put to Nestor: (1) How was I identified? Answer: chairman-designate; (2) Had I received an honorarium? Answer: None. He will contend that I tried to profiteer from the publicity in this matter.

Meanwhile, [I] learned [that] (Harold) Coxson at NAM [had stated] that McG [McGuinnis] would try to get a new round of hearings on my views....

I should have left these guys alone—and I will do so from now on, if possible.

Meanwhile, the *Wall Street Journal* reported yesterday that Cohen would be nominated and that that would cut loose Peg Browning and myself....

... Yet another development—On Tues. just before the Senate reconvened, Truesdale was given a recess appointment. On the one hand, it seemed necessary to deal with [representation] elections and the backlog—on the other hand, it takes the heat off the Senate to confirm us. As Kassebaum said much earlier: "Surely you can find someone to warm Professor Gould's seat." Actually, Truesdale takes Browning's seat....

On January 31 in a piece on the confirmation process, *New York Times* columnist Anthony Lewis railed against the abuse that Clinton nominees such as Lani Guinier and Morton Halperin were subjected to.

Attacks are made on nominees, for reasons of ideology and politics, with a zealotry that knows no bounds of truth. The attackers are in both the press and the Senate. Nominees are ordered not to reply, and those who should defend them are too often inept or craven.

Lewis concluded by saying this about my protracted ordeal:

A victim of slow confirmation torture is William B. Gould 4th ... a Stanford law professor who was nominated by President Clinton last June to be chairman of the National Labor Relations Board. More than seven months later, he is still caught in a snarl caused by Republican partisanship and White House ineptitude.

The surprising attacker in this case is Senator Nancy Kassebaum—surprising because she is not usually so partisan or unfair. She has called Professor Gould "radical," though in fact he is a moderate labor-law expert respected by both sides.

Senator Kassebaum's real interest apparently is to dictate the choice for a Republican N.L.R.B. seat. The White House could probably have worked things out quickly, but it fiddled. A deal may finally be near now.

Of course politics has always played a part in confirmation. But the process is nastier now. Republicans and the right-wing press are out to harass President Clinton as if to deny the legitimacy of his election. The President, for his part, has been slow on appointments and weak in defending his choices....

If we want good people in government, decent politicians and editors are going to have to restrain their partisan zealotry. That has done more harm than the much-criticized press invasions of privacy.[12]

In early February, however, the long-hoped-for confirmation seemed to be drawing nearer.

February 5, 1994   The deal seemed to have taken more shape this past week. At long last, the White House expressed an intent to nominate Chuck Cohen this Thursday to the Republican seat. Both Paul Richards and Richard Socarides [the White House guy on labor matters] believe that a vote can be taken on the entire package on February 24–25. That seems doubtful—not only because they are always unduly optimistic, but also because the estimate is predicated on the view that hearings would be waived for the other three nominees. Interviews with committee staff will be conducted the coming week. At that point, matters will become more clear.

On Wednesday after returning from Iowa the previous evening, I spoke to a management labor law group at the Ritz Carlton in SF—the Council on Labor Law Equality. It went well: Q.: "We're concerned that, as an academic, you won't understand business." A.: "I have represented management, Proctor and Gamble, Diners' Club, negotiated, arbitrated." Q.: "You are for CB [collective bargaining]—but isn't the recovery taking place because we are free of constrictive collective agreements?" A.: "I'm against constrictive agreements. Read my book."

Later in the week I spoke with both Paul Wellstone and Tom Harkin. Wellstone was frustrated by the delay, promised to make inquiries. Harkin and I discussed our mutual uncertainty and apprehension about Cohen. He promised to do some intelligence on this. [Indeed Cohen's nomination, like that of his Republican successors after 1996, made Professor Mackenzie's remarks about the "batching" of nominations and the corrosive effect on "intellectual or ideological coherence" seem prescient indeed. We eventually came to call Cohen "Doctor No"!]

I reminded Harkin of his prediction that I would be in Washington by Thanksgiving—and how depressingly distant that seemed. When he learned of the February 24 estimate, he said; "You'll be here by St. Patrick's Day." That may be the proper estimate. [Indeed, it was, given the fact that I was confirmed a little more than two weeks before that date and was functioning in Washington by then.]

Betty Murphy and I played telephone tag much of the week. Her real purpose in calling seemed to be her desire to build bridges with McGuinnis. He had called her, she said, because he knew that we were "close" ... and he was concerned about my Fla. remarks. She said she would have him call me when I said that I would talk to him. (I really don't want to—and won't, once I am confirmed.) But I haven't heard from him.

Harold Coxson of NAM (he was at the SF lunch) told Dave Parker on Fri. that Kassebaum's people were still fishing around, trying to get a copy of a tape of my Fla. remarks—now their focus is on whether I mentioned Kassebaum.

Today I telephoned Bill Coleman.... Coleman's warm response: "Hello, friend" [cheered me immensely]. I brought him up to date. When I told him I hadn't received an honorarium for the Florida speech, he asked how many nights I had stayed there at Stetson's expense. "I've tried a few cases, Bill," he said. He promised to make some inquiries on Mon.

[Wade Henderson of the NAACP].wasn't as optimistic as the White House on February 24–25. He said that McG had called him twice—earlier in the week he had called because McG had approached him about the Florida. speech. Again, the report was that McG was uneasy—and concerned that race could emerge as a factor in this dispute.

Said I: "I think that we will know much more about timing by the end of the coming week."

February 19, 1994   The week began with Bill Coleman's report back (last Tues.) of a conversation that day with Kassebaum.... She advised Coleman that I would be confirmed. But she didn't seem to be completely on the same page on other matters. The White House—Podesta, Richard, Socarides at the Department of Labor—had been saying consistently that they expect a vote on February 24 or 25. But this is dependent upon a waiver of hearings for Feinstein, Browning, and Cohen. But Kassebaum advised Coleman that she assumed that there would be hearings and, if so, that would take us well into March or late April. Moreover, Kassebaum indicated that Mitchell needed to be (and had not been) advised of any schedule for a vote. Socarides called Coleman back and [said he] did not think that there was a basic discrepancy.

Mike Weiss of the *Mercury* [San Jose] was at our house late Tuesday P.M. and said that, as soon as the Senate vote is taken, he and two crack investigators from SF would fly to Washington to track down the origins of the stories on gambling, South Africa, and the articles about the similarities between my views and those of Judge Barkett from Florida.

Betty Murphy called to set up a Wednesday conference call with McGuinnis—but I had second thoughts, particularly when I realized that a conference call was involved. I called Podesta and Socarides and told [them] that it would be helpful if I could say that the White House "requested" that I not talk to McG. They agreed and I left a message with Murphy to that effect....

A good, lengthy midweek call from Fred Feinstein. We began to talk about jobs at the Board and pledged cooperation. (He and Browning will be interviewed by Rep[ublican] staffers this week.) We both emphasized the need for ALJ [administrative law judge] reforms, though he was [not] interested in conciliation ideas but rather the need for speed and efficiency. I have a good feeling about Fred and believe that we can work well together. We both agreed on the need for regular meetings with Peg—and indeed scheduled one for Mar. 8, based on the assumption that I will be confirmed this month and in Washington on 3/7.

Meanwhile, Washington, like the East Coast (earlier the Widwest) suffers through horrendous ice and snow and cold. It is balmy and sunny here today. In an hour, I go to a dinner at Walter Shorenstein's Portola Valley home for Ted Kennedy and his re-election campaign. [The evening was a fundraiser for the Ted Kennedy 1994 campaign and Kennedy offered words of encouragement to both my wife and myself. We sat next to James Hormel, the Hormel heir who is a gay activist from San Francisco. He also was in line for an appointment in the Clinton administration but, with fierce opposition from the Republicans over a five-year period, his wait was to prove longer than mine.]

Meanwhile, February 24–25 came and went, and I left for a speaking engagement in Chicago that weekend. On the twenty-eighth when I returned a call from Ted Kennedy in the lobby of the Chicago Hilton, he assured me that the vote would be taken on March 2. In response to my question about whether the votes were there, he responded in the affirmative. As I flew back to San Francisco from Chicago the next day, anticipating that I would be confirmed on that date, I composed a statement for the press.

The debate on my appointment took place, as Kennedy had predicted, the day after my return to the Bay Area. My wife Hilda, I, and Mike Weiss of the *San Jose Mercury News* gathered around a television set in our home to watch it.

Senator Howard Metzenbaum (D-Ohio) began the debate with "strong support" for the nomination, stating that I stood out as "perhaps the most qualified nominee in the history of the NLRB." Senator Kassebaum, the first to speak in opposition, contended that I had "lent support over the years for radical change in the labor law" and that I subscribed to "an agenda that will undermine the very legal structure his agency will oversee." As she set forth her views, her aide, Sola, held up my book, *Agenda for Reform*, in front of the television cameras, giving myself and the MIT Press a remarkable plug.

Senator Kennedy spoke next, chronicling my background and broad support and emphasizing the endorsement of the National Academy of Arbitrators. He pointed out that my views were in "the mainstream." But blistering attacks by senators Alan Simpson (R-Wyo.) and Don Nickles (R-Okla.) followed. Nickles pointed to my statement that either the Supreme Court or the Congress should reverse the law on permanent replacement of strikers: "So he's more than willing to use the Board to change the fifty-year-old statute," he concluded, even though my comment specifically referred the matter to the Court or Congress. In the written version that appears in the *Congressional Record*, he mentions the Court and the Congress but not the Board—though I could hardly use the Court or the Congress to change the statute, since I was being nominated for the Board!

The rejoinder came from Senator Wellstone, who stated his belief that future historians would see me as an even-handed chairman. Then came the most dramatic portion of the debate, an eloquent and compelling statement from my state's senator, Dianne Feinstein of California. She quoted management people who supported the nomination and argued that it offered a great opportunity to create a centrist Board. Then others, like senators Boxer and Mosley-Braun, joined in with their own articulate testimonials.

Then came the vote. Of the first thirteen votes cast by senators who were on the floor, seven were "No." Watching from the comfort of my own home at Stanford, I began to shift uneasily in my chair. In the Senate gallery, Bill Stewart, (to whom I had already offered the job of chief counsel) leaned across the aisle and said to Fred Feinstein: "I can't believe this. I can't believe that this is happening." Feinstein replied: "You know what it is?" Stewart shook his head. "It's racial. This is what their motivation is."

The vote was 58 to 38 in favor of my nomination—the most "No" votes received by any nominee up to that time. Every single Democrat in the Senate voted for me, but only five Republicans did so. As the senators and their aides departed from the floor, Senator Kennedy joked to a number of people within earshot: "Let's hope Nancy's right!"—meaning of course, let's hope Bill Gould is as radical as she claims. In a note he sent me the next day he commented with relief, "It's a good thing the Republicans decided not to filibuster!" Exhausted and yet exultant, my feelings and the mood at Stanford were celebratory. The sense of near-regret I had had as I departed Chicago, knowing that I would miss tenor saxophonist Stanley Turrentine, who was due to arrive at the Blackstone the following night, now almost evaporated. I issued the statement I had composed on the plane the night before. In it I described the vote as a "victory over a determined campaign of cynical character assassination … by right-wing ideologues" and characterized the Republican tactics as "antidemocratic." I vowed to "return the Board to the center, to promote balance" between labor, management, and employees and to "let workers, union officials and business people know that they will be treated with respect, civility and fairness."

On March 7, thirty-three years to the day after President Kennedy's Chairman, Frank McCulloch, was sworn in, I took the oath in a private ceremony at Stanford Law School attended by my colleague and friend, Miguel Mendez. A day later, a formal public ceremony in San Francisco was presided over by another old friend, Chief Judge Thelton Henderson. Before President Carter appointed him to the federal bench, he and I had been co-counsels (with others) in a class action job-bias case. Both Judge Henderson and Paul Brest, dean of the Stanford Law School, spoke. It was a grand occasion, full of the good camaraderie of many old friends and the staffs of the regional NLRB offices in San Francisco and Oakland. Standing proudly with my wife and two of my three sons, I felt cheerful and optimistic, thinking I had taken all the hits it was possible to take. Little did I know that all this was a mere prelude to the conflicts that would soon arise, both within the Board and as the result of congressional pressures.

When I returned to Washington on March 14, Bill Stewart awaited me at Dulles airport, as he had on so many occasions during the confirmation process. On that first day we drove directly to the Board's offices on 14th Street and worked for a couple of hours. It was the beginning of what would be a grueling, sometimes exasperating, and challenging four and a half years.

4

First-Year Policies and Initiatives

With confirmation behind me and surrounded by the warm glow of friends and family, I was eager to take on the challenges of the chairmanship. Before proceeding to Washington, however, I fulfilled a speaking engagement made on the assumption that I would be confirmed and able to speak out at that time. This speech to the Los Angeles Industrial Relations Research Association was attended by many friends and the regional Board employees.

In it, I announced my intention to create an advisory panel composed exclusively of labor and management lawyers. In the 1970s, during the chairmanship of Betty Southard Murphy, a similar task force had been formed; but it was designed only to provide the Board formal, written recommendations. My idea was to solicit viewpoints from all sides, so obtaining ongoing, informal inputs that might either lead to action on our part or respond to an NLRB action or proposed action. I believed that such a system would benefit not only Board members but also the lawyers who dealt with us in a much more formal manner, giving them a better understanding of the problems and perils we faced in making decisions and policy judgments.

When I announced creation of the advisory panel that day, I proposed as its very first member Bill Emmanuel, an outstanding Los Angeles management labor lawyer I had known for a number of years. Soon after my arrival in Washington, however, I discovered that my enthusiasm for this concept was shared by neither the general counsel nor other members of the Board, Democratic or Republican. In part, their resistance was simply a fondness for the status quo. But they were also concerned that some Board insiders who had hovered around the agency for years—particularly members of a special American Bar Association (ABA) Labor and Employment Law Practice and Procedure Committee—would be put out by seeing new people and fresh ideas come in the door. Of course, my public announcement in Los

Angeles made it impossible for the Board or the general counsel to prevent the panel's formation, a sequence of events that was to occur fairly frequently. When, soon afterward, the administration praised us for the use of advisory panels, it was forgotten—or at least not openly articulated—that I had been the lone wolf supporting the idea.

The advisory panel was the first of a number of my ideas that were well received by the labor relations community generally and regarded as a great success. Yet it created a problem I was never able to overcome with members of the ABA Labor and Employment Law Section. In ways both trivial and substantive, tensions and conflicts with the section were everpresent. One day Gordy Kirshner, a management labor lawyer from Los Angeles who was particularly active in the section, asked me: "Let's see, Bill, what is the role of the advisory panel?" When I told him, his brow furrowed in mock puzzlement as he said he assumed *that* was the ABA subcommittee's role. (I later learned that this committee, part of a management-dominated section, frequently treated Board members and some senior career Board employees to midwinter meetings at posh warm-weather resorts. Though House Republicans wanted to pillory me for travel reimbursements I received from the AFL-CIO, they displayed no interest whatever in the financial perks provided by ABA lawyers—many of whom concurrently had cases before the Board!)

This conflict over the advisory panel was a harbinger of future problems. The powers of the chairmanship are only nebulously defined. During most of my term, Congress (whether Democratic or Republican), the bar, the academic community, and the press were far more likely than my fellow Board members and the general counsel to accord me stature and to defer to my leadership. At a conference held in 1995 to celebrate the sixtieth anniversary of the NLRA, former Board member Howard Jenkins Jr., who had served for twenty years under half a dozen chairmen, declared that "Board members should defer to the chairman in administrative matters but should be independent in deciding cases." But the practice he outlined was not the one followed during my term. Indeed, one Board member even derided the idea in a private aside to my chief counsel, Bill Stewart.

In the final analysis, the chairmanship—given the authority of the general counsel to appoint regional staff and recommend regional directors to the entire Board (not just to the chairman)—is more like a bully pulpit than a position of authority. This was particularly true during my term because of the Board's sharply divided political composition, my troubled relations with the general counsel, the hostility of Congress, and the frequently thorny issues we had to confront (e.g., postal ballots and a variety of measures to expedite our procedures).

When I arrived in Washington on the heels of my Los Angeles speech, Bill Stewart was awaiting me at Dulles Airport, as he had been on so many other occasions throughout the long confirmation struggle. "Mr. Chairman!" he called out as I almost passed him, head down, on my way to the baggage area. We drove to NLRB headquarters—the comfortable and tastefully decorated suite of offices the Republicans would later refer to as the Taj Mahal because of its spaciousness, kitchen facilities, and modest studies for Board members. We went to work immediately, for there was no time to waste. On March 16, only two days later, we had to appear at the first of a number of hearings of the House Appropriations Subcommittee on Labor, Health, Human Services and Education. It was the only appropriations subcommittee hearing I participated in during a Democratically controlled Congress.

During that first week in Washington and my introduction to the hurly-burly of congressional hearings, I became aware of other Board members' simmering resentment over my advisory panel proposal. Yet it was another, seemingly trivial, matter that provided an indication of future troubles. Bill Stewart discovered—I believe the former chairman, Jim Stephens, brought it to his attention—that a photograph of Reagan's chairman, Don Dotson, was attached to the toilet seat in the chairman's bathroom, placed there by Stephens or one of his subordinates. They thought it was a great joke, and so did I. However, soon after Bill showed it to friends who were management labor lawyers with close connections to the Labor Policy Association we received word that the *Wall Street Journal* was about to run a small item indicating that I had placed Dotson's photo on the toilet seat. (Later the respected *Washington Post* insisted on publishing pieces of gossip about me that were almost as trivial.)

Of course, we immediately removed it to avoid controversy. We had not placed it there in the first place and had nothing to do with it. But it was a portent. Time and time again, I would be urged to make changes to respond to a perception that was completely false. The Dotson-Stephens toilet incident was only a particularly bizarre illustration of this phenomenon.

Another issue of perceptions arose out of a rather ordinary commercial transaction, the purchase of an automobile, a necessity for suburban excursions, trips to my mother's home in New Jersey, and visits to Civil War sites I wanted to see while in Washington. I had set my heart on a stylish Mazda Miata—but the staff, led by the ever-watchful Bill Stewart, recommended against it—notwithstanding the UAW's collective-bargaining agreement with Mazda. Buying it, they reasoned, would simply set me up for a questions about where my car was manufactured and for an unnecessary assault by my friends in the labor movement. So I bought a red Camaro convertible produced by General Motors' Chevrolet division and zoomed along eastern highways, gray hair flying in the wind!

The Presidential Appointees

At NLRB headquarters I soon discovered that the regular meetings Chairman Frank McCulloch (my old boss) had held in the 1960s to discuss the most important cases had fallen into almost complete disuse. I revived the practice, which, I recalled, had boosted the Board's productivity—and sometimes even its collegiality.

The latter was of particular concern to me as internal tensions on the Board were present early on. As noted in chapter 3, the Board is divided—by tradition not by statute—three to two between members of the president's own party and those of the opposition. These five, plus the general counsel, are the key players in the decisions and policies carried out by the Board.

Though the general counsel is not involved in case adjudication, given his prosecutorial role, President Clinton's appointee, Fred Feinstein, was a significant player —both in case law, through his willingness (or unwillingness) to issue complaints based on particular theories, and in internal administrative matters. Formerly a career staffer with the House Labor Education Committee under several Democratic chairs, Feinstein's major area of expertise presumably lay in relations with Congress —but only, it turned out, with a Democratic Congress, which would be history in a matter of months.

Feinstein was particularly obsequious to the House Republicans and, generally speaking, to anyone in a position of authority. (He did, however, fight the GOP on regional reorganization of the Board, the one place he should have been accommodating.) Mild mannered and, on occasion, disarmingly friendly, he tended to be secretive and was unwilling to face up to problems of internal reorganization. Both ideology and turf—and turf is no respecter of ideology—divided us more often than I would have liked. At times the Republicans appeared to hate him even more than they did me.

Senator Kassebaum's insistence on batching appointments had brought onto the Board Republicans Charles Cohen of Maryland, a management labor lawyer, and James Stephens. Stephens, my immediate predecessor as chairman, had been on the Board since 1985 and had served as its head between 1987 and 1994. His term expired in 1995. Career staffers had been impressed with the way Stephens had worked hard to learn about the NLRA. He was tight with conservative groups, particularly the right-wing Labor Policy Association, but unable to find common ground with the National Right to Work Committee (NRWC). Like Feinstein, a congressional staffer prior to his work with the Board, Stephens had served as counsel to Senator Hatch on the Senate Labor and Resources Committee. To paraphrase Professor Mackenzie, Feinstein and Stephens had simply walked across the street to new jobs, and they did not plan to leave Washington anytime soon.

The second Republican was Charles Cohen. Internally—particularly at Board meetings—he displayed the personality of a bull in a china shop, staking out consistently conservative positions and dissenting as often as possible. His extremely smart chief counsel, Harold Datz, was a great help on case production. (Datz always wanted to have the last word in our warring opinions; we usually let him have it in order to get the cases out.) Cohen knew a lot of people and was very much the Washington insider, particularly among the district's law firms. He and I shared a passion for baseball but little else. The staff called him "Doctor No" because he dissented from the simplest and most self-evident propositions and opinions. Like Stephens, Dennis Devaney, and John Higgins (the ideological comrade in arms who took his place in 1996), Cohen wanted reappointment very much but did not obtain it.

Joining me on the Democratic side was Margaret Browning, a union lawyer from Philadelphia. Disciplined in her work habits and extremely intelligent, she had refined tastes in food, wine, and clothing. Her capacity for hard work made her a major contributor to our record productivity during 1994–1995. (I thought of her as the Iron Lady.) She voted with me as often as any member of the Board, but our personalities clashed over substance and style. She almost always sided with Feinstein in the many disputes about administration, and my staff thought she aspired to be chairman. Browning, the smartest of the Board members I served with, was extremely skillful at maneuvering other members around to her position. (She was to die of breast cancer in 1997 before expiration of her term.)

Devaney, a Reagan Democrat, was a holdover from the Bush administration. He was, in retrospect, probably my best ally on the Board that first year; he sometimes deferred to me on both administrative and legal questions. He left the Board—much to his disappointment—in December 1994.

Another Washington insider, Democrat John Truesdale, received a recess appointment to replace Devaney; he had already served as a member on a recess basis immediately prior to my confirmation and was to replace me as chairman in

December of 1998. A consummate senior bureaucrat, he had a genuine dedication to case production and had survived on the Board for many years by carefully keeping a finger in the wind. He allied himself closely with Browning and Feinstein. As much as anyone, he was responsible for the nostrum that Board chairmen and members should not speak out on law reform. No basis for this conventional wisdom was ever articulated, and the idea that it evoked retaliation was never established. But that did not stop Truesdale from saying it—again and again. When he replaced me in 1998, the House Republicans grew to love him because, in their view, he had "depoliticized" the agency. Translated into ordinary English, this meant that virtually none of the pending policy decisions that were at the Board in 1998 were issued during the first two years of his chairmanship. Moreover, the number of Section 10(j) injunctions (see below) sought declined dramatically.

The first overt conflict within the Board arose over what seemed a fairly superficial matter—the official public swearing-in ceremony in early April 1994. Whereas I had fought a tough fight during the nomination process, the other new Board members had received no attention at all and had been confirmed by unanimous voice vote in the wake of my confirmation. Because my nomination was the only one put forward initially in 1993 (Browning's nomination was made later that summer), it did not occur to me that there would be a joint swearing-in. I had therefore invited one of my oldest and best friends, Chief Judge Julian Cook of Detroit, to administer the oath to me. Now, although the "batching" process had changed the situation, I continued to prefer a separate swearing in. After all, I had been the object of considerable controversy and had done all the heavy lifting in the confirmation process.

The others (quite naturally I suppose) resisted this idea. I can still see them sitting in phalanxlike formation on the couch in my office—Browning, Feinstein, and Cohen all exhibiting disapproval through their facial expressions and body language. Browning, in particular, was irritated with my choice. As she did on many later occasions, she took it upon herself to advise me about how such matters should be handled: "Your swearing-in in your own city—in your case by Judge Henderson—was the appropriate way to involve someone who has been a personal friend of yours." I disagreed. Then, and on so many larger issues, we simply agreed to disagree.

When it became clear that we would all be sworn in on the same day, I nonetheless insisted on having Judge Cook swear me in. The oath for the others was administered by Secretary of Labor Reich. The ceremony, which took place on April 11, was a pleasurable event and was attended by much of official Washington—even some of our erstwhile enemies during the confirmation process. (Most would remain opponents.) People were friendly and seemed to enjoy themselves. Bill Stewart organized a little gathering afterward at an Italian restaurant near the Board offices. It was a nice party and was attended by some of my friends and family, including my mother, my wife, and our three sons. From time to time, though, my mind drifted back to a comment made at a party we had attended a night or two earlier. Zoe, wife of the president's counsel, Ab Mikva, had introduced me as "Bill Gould ... the last chairman of the National Labor Relations Board"! This remark kept me in mind of the serious challenges that awaited me.

In April I also gave my first speech as chairman to the Detroit AFL-CIO. It was like a homecoming for me, with all my friends from the UAW and my days at Wayne State University in attendance. It was also memorable in two other respects. First, we were advised that someone had called the regional NLRB office and seemed to be threatening me. I well recall the tense look on the face of Michigan AFL-CIO General Counsel Ted Sachs as he escorted me into the convention hall accompanied by a few security people. Second, in my speech I made a remark that angered the enemies of my confirmation. Referring to the 58 to 38 vote for my confirmation and the fact that I had received the greatest number of "no" votes of any Clinton nominee, I declared: "This is my badge of honor." The crowd cheered lustily, and I received a standing ovation. Though my critics regarded the comment as impolitic—and perhaps it was—it was exactly what Senator Harkin said to me four and a half years later at a private luncheon he held to commend me for a job well done.

Shortly after the Detroit speech, I flew to Minneapolis for a luncheon address to the National Academy of Arbitrators. There, I emphasized the theme I intended to make the hallmark of my chairmanship: the establishment of policies to diminish the prolonged and expensive litigation that was so vexatious to both sides. I spoke of my earlier experience with the California State Bar, where we had recommended the substitution of arbitration for litigation in wrongful-discharge complaints. And referring to President Nelson Mandela's inauguration in Pretoria, South Africa—which I had been privileged to attend on behalf of the U. S. government—I pointed to the emphasis Mandela had given to dialogue, understanding, and reconciliation between old adversaries.

Procedural Initiatives

Back in Washington I rolled up my sleeves and got to work on a series of procedural initiatives to promote and expedite settlements. The congressional environment, notwithstanding my difficult confirmation, seemed to be somewhat positive to the Board. In July of 1994, the Senate Subcommittee on Appropriations for Labor voted to give us a two-million-dollar increase over what the Office of Management and Budget had requested. Ultimately, the Hundred and Third Congress granted us a budget in excess of President Clinton's request.

At the March 16 House subcommittee hearing, Representative Nancy Pelosi [D] of San Francisco had reflected this era of good feeling when she remarked to me and to the chair, Jose Serrano of New York:

What you should know, Mr. Chairman, is that Chairman Gould comes to this position with a widespread broad-based support in our community.... I know I speak for my colleagues from the Bay Area in expressing the pride that we all have in your appointment and your confirmation, and what it means to working people in America to have the balance that this new board will have in terms of labor relations.

In this environment, my ideas did not run afoul of Congress. But they did create a good deal of controversy inside the Board.

Administrative Law Judge Reforms

The conflict was immediately evident in the response to what I saw as a relatively moderate proposal to make the Board's administrative law judges more effective and, in the process, speed up procedures and diminish wasteful litigation. I had first propounded this theme in my October 1993 confirmation hearing and restated it in my March 1994 appearance before the House Appropriations Subcommittee.

My view was that the administrative law judges (ALJ)—career civil service officers we called *trial examiners* back when I first started practicing labor law in the early 1960s—received too little support from the Board. After the general counsel—as prosecutor—issues a complaint alleging an unfair labor practice, the matter comes before an ALJ, who hears the case, determines the facts and the law, judges the credibility of witnesses, and issues a decision. The National Labor Relations Board in Washington hears appeals from the ALJs' decisions (the majority of which are appealed as a matter of course). Though appointed by the five-member Board in Washington, the judges make their judgments independently of the Board.

My first proposal was to give ALJs the authority to issue bench decisions: that is, oral decisions issued at the conclusion of the hearing. In many of these cases, the central issues are fairly straightforward and the law is not the least bit complex; most involve issues of fact and credibility rather than of law.

Over a number of years I had advocated the use of bench decisions in lieu of the then-existing procedure, in which briefs were filed by counsels representing labor, management, or employees. This process consumed approximately four months and delayed the date at which the case could reach the Board in Washington. In many cases, briefs added little or no factual information to assist the ALJs' assessment of credibility. My own experience as an arbitrator had led me to believe that in cases based on the facts presented by witnesses, it is most useful to make a determination while the demeanor of those witnesses is fresh in one's mind. (Of course, in private arbitration cases I was not able to control the filing of briefs, whereas a public agency like the NLRB could establish rules to do so.)

Under the bench decision rule we instituted, judges have discretion to decide at the end of the trial that they will "hear oral argument in lieu of briefs" and read their decisions into the record right then and there—or within seventy-two hours of the hearing's termination. Before this rule was implemented, all administrative law judge decisions—including those involving relatively simple factual cases—had to be issued in writing after a full briefing by both parties.

In the 1970s, notwithstanding my own frustrations with brief filings in arbitration cases, other arbitrators had frequently resorted to bench decisions, most often when given explicit authority to do so by the collective-bargaining agreement. On the West Coast, because of the particular need for prompt adjudication in the shipping industry, the International Longshoremen and Warehousemen's Association (ILWU) and the Pacific Maritime Association (PMA) had provided for immediate rulings. In certain cases the arbitrator, summoned by a "beeper" (long before the advent of cellular telephones), went directly to the dock in question, heard the case, and issued a decision right then and there!

Based on the industrial jurisprudence in this area that had begun to emerge, and on my own three decades' experience as an arbitrator, I urged the Board to utilize a similar procedure in unfair labor practice cases when, in the ALJ's opinion, briefs are not necessary because: (1) issues are predominantly or exclusively questions of credibility and fact-finding; or (2) the law is clear but one side (generally the employer) chooses to litigate. As an example of the latter, I pointed to cases in which one party refuses to provide information on matters relevant to collective bargaining. Remarkably, this relatively straightforward proposal proved to be extremely controversial.

Early in 1994 I advanced another idea intended to promote earlier resolution of complaints: a rule creating *settlement administrative law judges*. Provided all parties agree, these judges could be assigned to conduct settlement negotiations for cases prior to their hearing before the ALJ acting as trial judge. Whenever feasible, settlement conferences would be held in person, allowing the settlement judge to delve more deeply into all aspects of a case than the judge who will ultimately hear and decide it if a settlement is not reached.

Before this rule change, many judges were reluctant to inject themselves into settlement discussions for fear of compromising their ability to decide cases fairly if settlement efforts proved unsuccessful. Moreover, I had to be very careful about not referring to the settlement judges as *mediators*—even though, as a practical matter, mediation or conciliation would be their role. The 1947 Taft-Hartley amendments to the NLRA prohibited the Board from engaging in mediation, because the Republicans who controlled the Eightieth Congress were hostile to outside specialist technocrats, whom they considered "radicals." (Economic studies of the effect of the amendments, or of any aspect of the law, were also prohibited, on the grounds that all economists were leftists!) In addition, as we learned in a seminar with the administrative law judges held in January of 1995, some of them simply didn't like to mediate. They believed their role as judge was inconsistent with the functions of a mediator.

My idea for settlement judges emerged in the 1970s and early 1980s from research and writing comparing the Japanese and American systems of adjudicating cases of unfair labor practices. In my *Japan's Reshaping of American Labor Law* (1984), I noted that the Japanese were good at resolving such claims informally, even after cases were brought before the Japanese NLRB. (Of course, the dark side of this state of affairs was that the Japanese were even more tardy than their American counterparts in resolving these complaints, an aspect of their work we obviously did not want to emulate.) Although the American system had always yielded a high rate of settlement—generally on the order of 80–95 percent—this was true only of cases mediated prior to either the involvement of the general counsel as prosecutor or to their hearing before an administrative law judge.

My effort drew on the Japanese experience in devising effective mediation once the battle lines had been drawn and a hearing was about to commence or had commenced. I noted too that the Japanese continue to seek a settlement even after the hearing is concluded. Not only does their NLRB encourage negotiations through its mediatory intervention, but it also promotes them through the verbal recommendations it provides the parties. I had observed that in America the tough cases about to go to (or actually in) litigation were infrequently resolved. At the stage when the Japanese are devoting a good deal of mediatory energy to litigation and finding substitutes for it, our settlement rate falls off precipitously when litigation commences —or is about to do so.

Accordingly, I proposed both that ALJs step up their conciliation efforts in the normal course of adjudication and that special settlement judges chosen by the chief administrative law judge be drawn from the ALJ corps and assigned to mediate conflicts involving unfair labor practice.[1] The basic assumption behind this concept was that the parties would be more likely to resolve their differences with the assistance of a third party who would not act as the trial judge if they failed to reach a settlement. Participants would probably be more willing to make concessions and initiate compromises if they knew that their negotiating stance would not be used against them in subsequent adjudication. The proposal therefore included a guarantee that if settlement efforts failed, a new administrative law judge—one with no knowledge of or access to the confidential records of settlement efforts—would adjudicate the case. This concept has long been used in the private resolution of labor disputes, particularly those arising in the public-employee sector; for some reason its use had apparently never been considered for NLRB unfair labor practice cases.

Internal Resistance to Reform

I made another, somewhat less-controversial proposal at this time to provide goals and timetables for the Board's own handling of administrative law judge decisions. Yet members clearly felt some uneasiness about this issue, too; in retrospect, I suspect that they did not want to impose goals and timetables on themselves.[2] During the Bush administration, the General Accounting Office (GAO) had noted that the Board, which established deadlines for regional directors and other subordinate personnel, had carefully avoided establishing any such requirements for itself. The GAO's criticism of our predecessors also applies to my tenure and the next chairman's: "The Board has no standards for the total length of time it considers acceptable for a contested case to be at the Board or the length of time a case can remain in each decision stage before corrective action is required."[3]

In yet another attempt to ensure that the business of the Board would be carried out expeditiously in Washington, I advocated revival of Rule 76-1, which had been promulgated by the Board in the 1970s but was no longer in force. It stated that if no dissent or concurrence on a draft opinion had circulated within two weeks of its approval by a majority of three Board members, the decision would be issued within the next two weeks unless a dissent circulated within that time. The majority then had two weeks to respond to the dissenting opinion, and the dissenters one week to respond to the majority. This rule was a genuine first step toward setting deadlines for the work of the agency. If revived, it would send the message that the same timely action expected of administrative law judges and regional directors would apply to presidential appointees as well. The problem was that this rule had been discontinued sometime prior to 1994.

On September 30, 1994, John Truesdale—then serving as executive secretary of the Board—recommended that it reestablish Rule 76-1 at the earliest possible date. But the Board, over my lone dissent, voted to defer implementation because of other reforms we were then instituting—in particular, "speed teaming," which placed decisions that simply ruled on the facts of a case on the fast track. Most of them were representation cases (decided by hearing officers at the regional office and affirmed or reversed by the Board); most of these decisions were issued within a month or so of their arrival in Washington.

Although the 1991 GAO report had advocated procedures akin to reforms we had already set in place, in my view Rule 76-1 and speed teams were not mutually exclusive. It was important to institute both reforms. But I could not convince other members of the Board.

I suffered several other early setbacks. The quality and clarity of Board decisions, I believed, would be enhanced if Board members were identified with particular decisions. Lack of identification, it seemed to me, meant lack of responsibility and contributed to the inferior quality and lack of precision I saw in many Board decisions—which sometimes made it difficult to rely on them as adjudicative precedents. In my view, some of the Board's difficulties in enforcing certain of its orders in the courts are attributable to this problem.

Although I did not know it at the time, some forty years before Harvard Law School Dean James Landis had suggested the same idea and attempted to persuade the Federal Trade Commission and the Securities and Exchange Commission to adopt similar procedures. "I do not like the present practice of an anonymous opinion—writing division attached to a commission for whose utterances there is only a collective responsibility and that of a rather remote nature," he wrote. In my view, the same reasoning applies to the decisions of the NLRB; although the initial draft of a decision may be prepared by an individual Board member's assistant, the final draft is hammered out in collaboration with other members' staffs, and no one member is ever identified with the opinion itself.

My frustration with this process was one reason why I wrote more concurring opinions than any other Board member (as well as numerous dissents). One of my primary incentives for joining the academic ranks had been my love of writing and the written word, and I was determined to compose my own opinions while in Washington. I think that Landis's critique of the situation in 1950s Washington is still right on target.

Imagine, for example, how the Supreme Court of the United States would have fared in our history if it had followed the practice of rendering nothing but anonymous per curiam [by the court as a whole] opinions.

Another defect of the present procedure is that it works somewhat against intellectual competition among the commissioners themselves. Very few commission opinions provide interesting reading. Substantially none of them, except dissenting opinions, reflect the internal travail that must again and again accompany the difficult process of decisions. Since no single individual takes the responsibility for or has a pride in a particular utterance, they tend to reflect a lowest common denominator rather than a piece of work whose goodness or badness can be ascribed to an individual.[4]

All the other Board members opposed my proposal. Jim Stephens argued that it would lead to more delays. My view, however, was that if my other reforms were accepted—especially the revival of Rule 76-1 or some other firm time deadline—the potential for tardiness would be diminished. In Stephens's opinion, because Betty Murphy had advanced this idea during the Ford administration and the Board had rejected it, it should be rejected now. And it was.

In truth, although I was ultimately more successful with the administrative law judge reforms, it was not entirely clear in 1994–1995 that even these reforms could be instituted. The management lawyers and some labor union lawyers on our advisory panel were skeptical about bench decisions, and union lawyers distrusted settlement judges, fearing that they would delay adjudication. At the New Orleans convention of the American Bar Association in the summer of 1994, we found lawyers of the Labor and Employment Law Section invariably hostile to both ideas. In his address, Gordy Kirshner argued sardonically that

A number of us have experienced a decline in our labor law caseload over the past few years, a decline in litigation. But then God sent us Bill Gould! He has all kinds of ideas about administrative reforms, particularly in the area of administrative law judges, which will generate more litigation! We have him to thank for this.

The reforms, of course, had their origin in the idea that the opposite was true: that is, that there would be less litigation as a result of the settlement and bench decision rules. But the evidence was not in at the time of the ABA convention because the new rules had not yet been implemented.

Ballot Issues

Meanwhile, I pushed ahead with other reforms, some of them relating to the secret ballot elections conducted by the NLRB. I believed that a greater number of elections should be conducted by mail rather than by manual voting or balloting on plant premises. I wanted the Board to act more flexibly in this regard, a point I had made in *Agenda for Reform*. But my conversation during the confirmation process with Senator Chafee, who expressed hostility to the idea, made me aware that this issue could prove controversial.

One month after I joined the Board, a case that illustrated dramatically some of the problems and deficiencies of Board procedures came up for our review. In this case, the Seattle regional director refused to fashion a mail ballot for striking workers, some of whom were working at jobs in other states. Arguing that they were scattered not because of job assignment but because they had "chosen" to be on strike, he pointed out that the Board's manual (devised for some irrational reason by the general counsel and not the Board) allowed postal voting by mail only when workers were dispersed due to job assignment. I immediately walked the halls and urged my colleagues to reverse the regional director's decision—the procedure is to grant a review to consider whether it should be reversed or not—and, *mirabile dictu*, Stephens and Cohen decided to vote with me.[5] The union and employer, without Board intervention, then provided the mail ballots for the strikers. But the issue raised was an important one, and it was to reappear several times. In the summer of 1994 we voted 2 to 1 to reverse another regional director and provide mail ballots for casual or part-time workers who were on call and would thus not necessarily be at the facility when the vote was taken.[6] In the meantime, this issue, like so many others we worked on that first long hot summer, was becoming politicized.

Another ballot issue involved challenged ballots, disputes over whether workers who have voted are properly within the unit; for example, whether they are supervisors (and thus not covered by the NLRA) or somehow else do not share a "community of interest" with other employees. Under the usual procedure, such workers had been allowed to vote but their challenged ballots were kept separate, leaving the ultimate determination of their eligibility to subsequent NLRB adjudication. But during my tenure, resolution of the dispute about workers' inclusion or exclusion was often postponed while the vote was conducted—as long as the number was not substantial. Traditionally, the Board had allowed balloting if the eligibility of no more than 20 percent of the employees was in dispute. (The reasoning is that beyond this number employees would not be able to make a genuine choice, not knowing who was in the unit, and that employers would not be able to determine who were supervisors and could therefore give orders.) I pushed for a higher percentage, on the grounds that this would expedite our procedures and thus more effectively redeem the statute's promise to provide workers with prompt representation.

In the spring of 1994 the Board proceeded with a union election in which 33 percent of the voters in one unit and 22 percent of those in another were in dispute. This case was *North County Humane Society.* In both units, the theory was that it might not be necessary to resolve such disputes if the number of challenged ballots did not affect the outcome—and this proved to be true in this case.[7] Similarly, in a second case, *Columbia Hospital for Women Medical Center, Inc.,* the ratio of challenged ballots was 37.5 percent.[8] There, too, the matter was resolved without the need for further litigation, and the union was recognized.

In yet another case—*Baltimore Gas & Electric*—which was closely watched because of the large number of employees involved and the firm's high visibility, the Board held an election to resolve a recognition dispute in which 21 percent of the ballots were questioned.[9] Since the challenged number of ballots in this case was approximately seven hundred, the election would ordinarily have been delayed for some time. Indeed, it is probable that it would not have taken place during my term if we had had to hold hearings on each individual challenged. But the approach we used was again successful, because the number of disputed ballots was not determinative. In this case, the union was defeated by a substantial margin.

Section 10(j)

Beginning in 1994 we instituted the most important reform of all—which directly implicated the general counsel and, especially, the people in the regions who had to do extremely labor-intensive work to carry it out. It was our frequent use of Section 10(j) of the NLRA, which authorizes the Board to obtain injunctions in federal district court against unfair labor practices by employers (e.g., discriminatory dismissals, discipline, or refusals to bargain), even though a case has not been brought before an ALJ or has not yet been administratively concluded. (Such actions may also be sought against unfair labor practices by unions—although most of these cases are handled under different statutory provisions that *require* the Board to seek injunctions in federal district court.)

In the late 1970s the National Association of Manufacturers (NAM) had campaigned vigorously (and successfully) against a labor law reform bill. It was designed to provide for both more effective remedies in such cases through double or treble damages—rather than, for example, back pay minus interim earnings—and to expedite administrative procedures. The NAM argued that a principal reason why such a reform was unnecessary was the existence of Section 10(j). Under this provision, the Board, generally at the application of the general counsel, can seek injunctive relief against a wide variety of alleged misconduct by either unions or employers. But, as I had noted in *Agenda for Reform*, the number of requests for injunctive relief had been declining since the early 1980s. Indeed 1990 and 1991 (the last two years for which I had figures) recorded the smallest number of Board authorizations, general counsel requests, and cases submitted to Washington of the period beginning in 1982. (The declining number of cases submitted to Washington during these years is hardly surprising, given Republican control of the presidency and the fact that regional directors take their signal about what is acceptable from the general counsel's office.)

An anomaly in the law, as reflected in the Taft-Hartley amendments, which created Section 10(j) and the parallel provisions relating to unfair labor practices by unions, is that Board action against certain unfair union practices is mandated. Thus, when a union engages in, for instance, an unlawful secondary boycott or pickets against a competing union during representation elections, regions are required to seek an injunction—even without an authorization or a determination by the NLRB in Washington. Under Section 10(j), however, when an employer is accused of an unfair practice, only the Washington Board can decide whether to ask for an injunction. It had been an infrequently used discretionary power.

When the new Board came to Washington in the spring of 1994, much of this changed. We provided the regions with new guidelines and encouraged them to identify and prepare for litigation Section 10(j) cases in which a failure to act promptly would make remedies ineffective. During the four and a half years of my term, the Board sought injunctive relief more frequently than in any comparable period of its entire sixty-three-year history. We began this policy in the spring of 1994 and fleshed it out during the hot and humid Washington summer that followed.

The Board report on the 10(j) injunctions issued between March 1994 and April 1 1998, notes that the general counsel sought Board authorization for the issuance of 10(j) injunctions in 313 cases and that the Board authorized such action in 292 cases, or 92 percent of them. Of the 270 cases pursued to conclusion, the parties reached a settlement in 133 cases (49 percent); and a favorable court order was obtained in 105 of the 137 cases(77 percent) resolved by court decision.

By the end of my term (again since March 1994), the Board had authorized 303 Section 10(j) injunctions and denied authorization in 17 (5.3 percent) of cases. I voted against authorization in those 17 cases, and in 2 other cases I dissented when the Board granted authorization.[10] As in the bulk of substantive law cases in which there were dissenting opinions, I was the man in the middle. Some members, like Browning and Truesdale, seemed to believe that whatever the general counsel requested should be authorized. Later Democratic appointees like Sarah Fox and Wilma Liebman seemed to take a similar (but perhaps not identical) view. I voted with the Democrats more frequently than with the Republicans. But, because of political and ideological divisions and Board members who automatically ratified any proposal by the general counsel, I thought it particularly important to discharge my responsibilities on a case-by-case basis, as the statute provides. The Board Republicans, of course, dissented on numerous occasions, and some House Republicans howled about our use of Section 10(j)—clearly because it was so effective.

It is the Board that authorizes injunctive relief, not the general counsel, who, in the overwhelming number of instances, requests it. I therefore resisted entreaties by Feinstein to delegate the decision to the regional offices. Before becoming chairman, I had taken the view, theoretically, that the regions should exercise the final issuing authority, to ensure that it would be done expeditiously without a convoluted and time-consuming reference to Washington. But I soon realized that, because the general counsel appointed regional personnel, delegating that authority to the regions would be a de facto transfer of power from the Board to the general counsel. And, as my votes indicated, I did not always view the general counsel's recommendations with unbounded confidence. The following diary entry is illustrative.

March 9, 1995   Today I voted, for the first time, to deny Section 10(j) proceeding authority to the general counsel in Have-A-Vend Co., Inc., 4-CA-23189 and 4-CA-23269. The vote was 3–2 and I joined with Cohen and Stephens. I did so because the regional director, Peter Hirsch, whom I knew from the early 1960s, recommended that 10(j) relief not be sought because of inconsistencies in the affidavits of key witnesses and the fact that the witnesses would only cooperate as a result of investigative subpoenas. The regional director also relied upon the fact that the discriminatees were not willing to accept reinstatement—but that was not so important to me, given my view that reinstatement is not always and should not always be regarded by the Board as a critical remedy that is integral to our enforcement efforts. Sometimes monetary relief is all that is appropriate. However, the case seemed very weak; quite frankly, given that it is Teamsters Local 115 in Philadelphia, which Feinstein is involved with in connection with protracted contempt proceedings, I wondered whether the motivation for bringing this under Section 10(j) was more political than legal. This would not be the first time—the *Mine Workers* contempt situation [discussed in chapter 5] is the most prominent example—where Feinstein was guilty of such conduct.

In this case the regional director concluded that there was "no direct admissible evidence" that the discharged employees were union supporters and that the credibility of union witnesses "must be considered against a backdrop of Union hostility to this Employer for cooperation in the Region's contempt proceedings against [Local] 115." This case, for which the general counsel sought to invoke Section 10(j), was so weak that it neither went to trial before an administrative law judge nor produced a settlement of any consequence. The employer simply agreed to post a notice in traditional form stating that it would not violate the NLRA—without admitting that it had done so and without reinstating anyone. It paid one former employee $352, a paltry sum equivalent to nuisance money to make the charge go away. The Board would have embarrassed itself by using Section 10(j) in a case of this kind. By carefully examining each case before us, I think that I was able to steer the Board during my chairmanship to a selective and appropriate use of Section 10(j).

Other Efforts to Enhance Efficiency

Several decisions made at about this time, although they did not institute new procedures or activate existing tools like Section 10(j), related directly to my endeavor to handle cases more expeditiously. In a case I thought particularly important, the Board asserted its jurisdiction over employers who operated pursuant to contracts with government entities but declined to examine whether any particular subject was a proper subject for collective bargaining.[11] This practice had been followed by earlier Boards as a basis for either asserting or not asserting jurisdiction. By ruling in this way, we established a theme that was to echo through so many of my opinions: the avoidance of unnecessary litigation over issues that should not be litigated.

Almost by reflex, both Cohen and Stephens dissented from the Board's position on this question! But even the conservative and anti-NLRB courts of appeal for the eighth and the fourth circuits, as well as the sixth and tenth, upheld our decisions as consistent with the NLRA.[12]

In this case the issue was whether or not the subject matter was capable, in the government's view, of resolution through collective bargaining. The Board held that it was a question for workers to determine for themselves in a secret-ballot election. Although the decision also drew dissent from some quarters, the proposition seems an unremarkable one; it not only kept Washington out of the business of determining what subject matter parties could bargain about but also promoted employees' free choice and reduced unnecessary and wasteful litigation.

In another case that I thought demonstrated the balanced approach of the Clinton Board, we unanimously held that a hearing in some form is required prior to an election.[13] As explained above, my approach to the challenged-ballot issue was aimed at expediting representation questions so that workers do not lose faith in the prompt delivery of the protections promised by the NLRA. However, because the act itself speaks of a hearing, it was also my view that a hearing is always required—notwithstanding the delay involved. Of course, as the Board did not establish the definition of a *hearing*, our regional directors had considerable discretion in deciding how to conduct one—and some of them used it.

The Board was especially successful in expediting the critical procedures for representation elections. During my last year in office, 62.5 percent of these elections were held within 42 days of receipt of employees' petitions; 75 percent took place within 49 days; and 87.5 percent occurred within 51 days. This forward movement was undoubtedly attributable to the more efficient handling of hearings as well as to the reforms undertaken in the challenged-ballot area.

Rule Making

For years commentators as well as the judiciary had urged the Board to consider rule making as an alternative to ad hoc adjudication in the approximately one thousand cases that come to the Board in Washington each year.[14] I advocated rule making, too, for a number of reasons. In the first place, I believed that the public would have a better understanding of the Board's position on any number of issues if we set forth the rules clearly rather than speaking enigmatically after lengthy delays in numerous adjudications. All too frequently, the Board's decision simply affirms the rather lengthy opinion of an administrative law judge and does not provide the parties or the public with guidance on how they should conduct themselves in comparable circumstances so as to avoid litigation. (Admittedly, the Board's ability to explain its decisions in clear language would have been enhanced if Board members had been required to write and sign their own decisions. But, as noted above, that idea had been rejected by the majority.)

Second, I thought that rule making provided a better avenue than litigation for parties to influence Board decisions. In litigation, parties to the dispute are frequently the only ones who receive notice of a hearing, so that interested parties such as the AFL-CIO and the NAM have no input. Rule making would allow more people to participate and submit their views of the issue in question.

Third, I thought the process of rule making would help the Board become better informed about the industrial relationships we were affecting through our actions. True, we now had advisory panels designed to provide part of the background we needed. Moreover, I, General Counsel Feinstein, and other Board members often spoke at ABA and state bar associations meetings, engaging in dialogue and receiving useful feedback. Yet it seemed to me that these occasions were no real substitute for the input obtained through public commentary. However, when I attempted to establish seminars to inform the Board and its staff about current developments and issues, I was rebuffed.

In 1995 I arranged for George Kourpias, president of the International Association of Machinists, and Duane Fitzgerald, president and CEO of Bath Iron Works in Maine, to speak to us about their highly successful union-management cooperation program. In a memorandum on October 30, 1995, John Truesdale, a recess member of the Board, objected strongly:

If I had been consulted in this matter, I would have said that I do not think it is an appropriate function of the National Labor Relations Board. . . . the NLRB is a quasi-judicial body, an administrative labor court so to speak, and I do not think that the courts do or should sponsor meetings on subjects of the day, no matter how worthy. . . . this meetings . . . will inevitably be perceived as a function of the National Labor Relations Board, and [will] presumably inject the Board into the ongoing debate over the TEAM Act (Teamwork for Employees And Managers Act). It may also have foreseeable implications in the current budget situation. I also note that the Machinists are the charging party in the Boeing case now pending in the Seattle region, and the respondent in California Saw & Knife, now pending before the Board. In addition, the Board has had cases involving Bath Iron Works. . . . For all these reasons, I will not be present at the November 9, 1995 meeting.

Members Cohen and Browning quickly concurred in this view, and though the meeting was cancelled for other reasons, their united opposition would have diminished the audience. All of this opposition was, of course, quite silly. Yet, the important point was that it existed—and interfered with the Board's ability to examine the real world in which it operated. (Board Members seemed unaware that events of this kind occur quite frequently at the judicial level. In 1999, for instance, judges of the Court of Appeals for the District of Columbia invited the president of a professional sports league that had had litigation before the court to meet with them in an "off the record" seminar.[14a]) The Board members' attitudes, which were displayed fairly frequently after I began my rule-making initiative, highlighted the difficulties involved in operating in a walled-in and rarefied environment shot full of conventional wisdom and nostrums devised by a few senior bureaucrats who had occupied Washington offices for decades!

For all these reasons, I was determined to make rule making one of my priority reform initiatives. About a month after I arrived in Washington, I sent a memo to that effect to other Board members and the senior staff. After discussing the matter with Burt Subrin, head of the representation unit, I decided that the best arena in which to begin rule making was disputes over the appropriateness of single versus multiple locations as bargaining units.

Problems over this issue typically arise when unions are petitioning for representation. An employer like Holiday Inn might maintain, for instance, that as it had four inns in a given geographical area, the election should be held at all four locations. Ever since I was a young Board lawyer in the early 1960s, however, the single location was presumed to be the most appropriate.[15] This was so, reasoned the Board in a long line of cases, because the first priority was to find an appropriate unit; and, even though a multilocation unit might also be appropriate, if the election were not held at a single facility there might be no election at all—because the union may not be able to obtain the requisite 30 percent showing of interest in all locations combined necessary to trigger a Board-conducted election at all facilities. However, because the Board is precluded from establishing units exclusively on the basis of the unions' extent of organization, it has always, properly, allowed employers the opportunity to rebut the single-unit presumption. Generally—although a large number of criteria can be invoked to rebut the presumption—the critical factors the Board considers are the geographical distance between facilities, the extent of employee exchange (particularly temporary exchanges) between locations, and whether all locations are supervised by the same individual or individuals. In the overwhelming number of cases, only this kind of thoroughgoing economic or administrative integration can rebut the presumption in favor of one facility.

The difficulty was that the Board had never spelled out precisely the circumstances under which the employer rebuttal would be upheld, thus leaving it to ad hoc litigation. A statement of the exact set of parameters necessary to rebut the presumption—for example, the required distances between facilities, the number of employees transferred from one location to another—would let the parties resolve the matter without even coming to the Board. The absence of such a rule a rule invited the sort of wasteful litigation Congress had sought to diminish or eliminate in the 1960s through the rule-making recommendations issued by the Ervin Separation of Powers Subcommittee.

Since then, the Board, after much urging by Congress and the academy, had moved into its first rule-making venture. In the 1980s confusion about the appropriate unit in the acute health care industry had invited wholesale litigation. The Board's rule making, which was approved by the Supreme Court in *American Hospital Association* v. *NLRB,* had substantially diminished litigation in this industry.[16] My hope was to extend rule making to other business sectors with similar results.

Rule making was peculiarly suited to another problem that had affected the Board since the Eisenhower administration. With each new president—be it Eisenhower, Kennedy, Johnson, Nixon, Ford, Carter, Reagan, or Bush—the Board's philosophy on major policy issues swung in a new direction reflecting the philosophy of the new administration. I thought that rule making would diminish these rapid shifts—inevitable even in the Supreme Court with the advent of new appointees—along with their polarizing political effects. It would thus strengthen the doctrine of *stare decisis*—a judicial principle to which I had expressed fidelity in responding to a question Senator Hatch asked me in my confirmation hearing.

Rule making, because it would put the public on notice, would overcome the problem of lack of input I was simultaneously attempting to solve through my other initiatives. And, because a detailed justification for each rule would be provided, future Boards might be inhibited from wholesale reversals, which would be fashioned much less frequently and with greater care. Those who wanted to reduce the role of politics in the administration of the NLRA would presumably welcome rule making. That was the theory, in any event, although it did not always play out as I had intended.

Only a month after I arrived in Washington, I sent a memo to members of the Board and the senior staff suggesting that we give priority to rule making on the single-location issue. For rule making, the journey was to be far more perilous and moved far more slowly than my proposals on administrative law judges and postal ballots. An Advanced Notice of Proposed Rulemaking was published on June 2, 1994, and the comment period—during which unions, employers and other interested parties could submit proposed views—ended on July 29, 1994. It took some time for staff to absorb and prepare these comments for the purpose of circulation. Meanwhile, political developments were to overtake this particular reform and have a major effect on the entire work of the Board.

Our efforts were not wholly successful because rule making, like oral arguments (and we held a record number of oral arguments), necessarily attracted a good deal of attention early in the process. This meant that pressure against a rule members of Congress did not like could be brought to bear before the Board made its final decision. This is what happened in connection with our rule-making proposal on single-facility units when we brought it forward near the beginning of the Hundred and Fourth Congress in 1995. Several Board members were genuinely sympathetic to rule making and to the objectives of this proposal; but they also wanted to be reappointed and so were not immune to political pressure. And there was political pressure aplenty. The new Republican Congress wanted us, in Congressman James Talent's (R-Mo.) words, to "flip" as well as "flop" on the single-location cases. The Republicans clearly feared that this rule would expedite NLRB elections, facilitate union organizing, and promote recruitment of new union members (a prospect their patrons abhorred)—and that it would be difficult to reverse.

The most politically volatile rule-making issue confronting me at the beginning of my chairmanship related to the Supreme Court's ruling in *Communications Workers* v. *Beck*, which established the right of dissident nonmembers to refrain from paying their union dues if those dues were earmarked for political and other purposes unrelated to collective bargaining.[17] The reality behind the *Beck* case, which was decided in 1988, was that unions, which are virtually always supportive of Democratic party nominees, put most or all of their political contributions in that party's coffers. Unions thereby gained a stake and involvement in the political process while Democrats acquired an important donor—one the Republicans strongly objected to their having!

The Bush Board, however, had done nothing whatsoever to implement the Court's ruling; it had not issued a single decision on pending cases; nor (as we shall see in chapter 7) had it issued a rule to deal with them—even though *Beck* had been on the books for six years by the time we arrived in Washington. Later I was to see *Beck* as the third rail for Republicans. They had not been able to decide these cases in a matter compatible with the law as long as there was a Republican president, because of the extraordinary and inordinate influence of the right-wing National Right to Work Committee, which had a veto over Board nominations and confirmations. The only option for Chairman Stephens and his Board was to remain silent and take no action; to do otherwise would require members to vote for the balanced approach to the interests of unions and dissidents contemplated by the Court in *Beck*—and that would be a vote against their own reappointment!

The problem was additionally complicated by the fact that Stephens was then being conciliatory to the AFL-CIO on a number of issues in order to smooth over the enmity created by Chairman Dotson's term. Stephens had worked hard at promoting good relations between himself and Larry Gold, then the AFL-CIO general counsel, and had also done his utmost to learn the ins and outs of the NLRA. To come down against the AFL-CIO over such a critical issue as whether the union or dissident workers bore the burden of challenging the status quo would undercut this burgeoning modus vivendi.

However, as long as the NRWC remained a political force in the Bush White House, siding with the unions also meant trouble for Stephens, and perhaps even for other Board Republicans. In the past the committee had denied reappointment to some members and stopped new nominations in their tracks. Thus the answer for Stephens was to delay rule making indefinitely. Any decision he initiated would be harmful to the Republicans on the Bush Board.

In the very first weeks of my tenure, with both houses still controlled by the Democrats and President Clinton in the White House, I promised the public that I would give priority to the *Beck* cases and see that they were processed. They had been with the Board for an inordinately long time, and I did not then understand why not one single decision had been issued. I said as much to the press. The unrelenting political pressure and interference of the Hundred and Fourth Republican Congress would soon give me a better sense of Washington politics and why the Bush Board had been so inactive in the *Beck* arena.

5

First Attempts to Implement Reforms

The sultry Washington summer of 1994 proved that there would be no letup from political pressure on a variety of fronts, notwithstanding the minority status of the Republican party. The constant threat of such pressure is evident in my diary entries for this period.

August 2, 1994   Yesterday had a longish, rather exhausting meeting with Fred Feinstein and Peg Browning, hammering out the language on postal ballots. Late last week the matter was politicized by the Labor Policy Association, which said that I wanted to eliminate manual ballots. Even by their standards, this was a rather big lie.

Today I spent a good deal of time talking with colleagues. Cohen was concerned that a brand new memo on absentee voting and neutral sites for elections had only been circulated yesterday.

But Stephens's view went beyond procedure—which upset him. Stephens said the publicity about our work (last week we received considerable attention because of our administrative law judge reforms) would politicize matters, make opponents go to Capitol Hill, and stymie all nominations—his and Devaney's. He said that this was the way (it had been done in the 1980s) that reversal of precedent could be stopped.

August 4, 1994   Postal ballots. Yesterday I met with all the Board members except Devaney to discuss competing drafts, compromise possibilities and approaches. Stephens was irritated about the procedure—particularly about Board member Margaret Browning's last-minute draft on absentee ballots and off-site or alternative-site votes. Both are good ideas—but the drafts were circulated only this week. Stephens also suspected a cabal of myself, Peggy, and Feinstein.

But Cohen has emerged as the main thorn in my side. I spent considerable time with him last night talking about a compromise. "That will help" he kept saying—but he kept asking for more. I accepted the idea that manual ballots would be the norm and probably went too far in cutting out language that gives us flexibility to have mail ballots even where the facility is not a substantial distance away and where employees are not scattered.

This morning Cohen—and also Stephens to a lesser extent—made it clear that they would use our open meeting (mandated by the Sunshine Act) [which requires certain government meetings to be open to the public] to posture for the gallery. Cohen was particularly pugnacious and adversarial and interrupted me as he did last week during our open meeting on ALJs. He used all the rhetoric, saying "If it ain't broke, don't fix it." I didn't rise to any of the bait because I didn't think it would be suitable. At one point I said to Cohen: "I think we've had some good discussions together." No response or nod whatsoever from Cohen. That was the tip-off.

On August 4 we moved ahead on the *Beck* issue as well, a problem that was sure to bedevil us politically, as it had our predecessors. We voted 5 to 0 to provide the unions a relaxed standard under the 1988 ruling giving members the right to object to the way their dues are spent. Cohen and Stephens joined us—demonstrating that they saw the National Right to Work Committee as a fringe group. I was sure there would be an uproar on this decision when it became public

Although very few published, formally bound NLRB decisions and orders were issued in 1994 (most of them being put off until 1995–1996), we had before us a whole raft of cases with wide policy import.[1] During that fall and the early months of 1995, we probably had more meetings to discuss them than any Board had held since the 1970s. One important case concerned unions' right to obtain the names and addresses of all the employees in a unit within seven days of the regional directors' order of election. An earlier Board had rendered this decision, but our Board held, in October 1994, that full names, not merely initials, must be provided.[2] The decision appeared trivial, but it had great practical significance.

In another early case, the Board erred, in my view, in holding that work-release prisoners did not share a community of interest with the regular so-called free-world employees and were therefore ineligible to vote in a Board-conducted election.[3] My dissent stated that the test of whether they share a community of interest with their fellow employees is their status in the employment relationship, not the control to which they may be subjected at other times. The Court of Appeals for the District of Columbia Circuit agreed with my dissenting view and found that the work-release employees were "completely integrated" into the workforce.[4] This decision did not bear directly on the public policy debate about prison labor and its use in the private sector. It did, however, uphold the proposition, which I promoted, that when the state decides to utilize inmates in work-release programs, they should be integrated into the bargaining process if they are integrated into the workplace, notwithstanding their status as prisoners.

In established relationships between labor and management—as in multi-employer association bargaining in the construction industry—I sometimes voted with Stephens and Cohen to require an affirmative showing binding individual employers to a successor multiemployer contract, even though I disagreed with them about the precise nature of the test to be applied.[5] Similarly, I joined them in the view that, if past practice supported the procedure, an employer could withdraw from a multiemployer association if it had taken no prior actions committing itself to be bound by the results of the upcoming negotiations. As I wrote in my separate opinion in a 1995 multiemployer case, "the fact that it may not be the most efficient or best in the view of this agency or other third parties is irrelevant. It is the process devised by the parties, which they have bargained for, that supports our decision today and not our own view about what is best for them."[6]

I wrote another separate opinion in a successorship case, joined this time by the Democrats on the Board, Browning and Truesdale (who filled Devaney's seat on a recess appointment), to form a majority.[7] Supreme Court precedent mandated that a successor company that purchased or in some other way become the new owner of an enterprise and retained a majority of the predecessor's employees—or made it "perfectly clear" that it would do so—was obligated to bargain with the union.[8] The issue before us in 1995 was whether a successor employer that planned to change wage rates and conditions of employment was also obligated to bargain with the union. The majority held that the successor employer in this case had acted unlawfully in imposing the new wage rates without first consulting with the union. I argued that under federal labor law the only prerequisite to imposing a successorship obligation to bargain with a union was that the employer planned to retain all the employees in the unit. The mere fact that the new management intended to change the conditions of employment (as well as the wage rates) did not erode its duty to bargain, since this was the only circumstance under which there was an opportunity to bargain and since employers so frequently do change conditions of employment in successor situations. I particularly enjoyed writing this and other concurring opinions. I composed it partly in my office and partly in a hotel room in Atlanta where I was giving a speech.

In a multitude of other cases, I was the man in the middle, casting my vote with either Democrats or Republicans when I thought the statute warranted it. And, almost as frequently, I stood alone in a series of concurring and dissenting opinions when, in my view, the same considerations required it.

While working on our reform proposals, we also held oral arguments on a number of cases. These oral arguments were as popular with labor and management lawyers as our advisory panels, inasmuch as they gave the bar a sense of real participation in our procedures. Sometimes the direct exposure to the litigants was helpful for the Board as well. For the parties and the public they provided an opportunity to see the Board at work and gain some understanding of the basis on which decisions were made. Foremost among these cases was a series involving unions' attempts to organize nurses.

October 28, 1994   Today we had oral argument on a very difficult matter involving the supervisory status of charge nurses. In May, the Supreme Court rejected our predecessors' attempts to say that such nurses are not "acting in the interest of the employer" within the meaning of the act and therefore could not be declared employees on this basis [and so are ineligible to vote in union elections]. Now the open question is whether they (employees) "responsibly direct or assign employees." How one defines "responsible direction" is difficult—although I find the union case more persuasive.

[Ironically, around this time] I met with American Hospital Management Association people in Houston, [to discuss] the changing nature of the industry and the attempt to decentralize and empower ... [in] a three-hour closed session marathon—at the end, Saul Kramer and Bill Emmanuel (who had invited me) said that no chairman had delivered such a fine talk.

Eventually, the Board held in two lead cases that the disputed charge nurses were not statutory supervisors within the meaning of the act because their responsibilities were of a routine nature and did not require independent judgment.[9] This was an important decision for the public policy that promotes collective bargaining and for union organizers attempting to recruit workers in hospitals frequently affected by cost-cutting. (It is extremely likely that only a short time later the Board would not have been able to hold oral arguments and reach this decision without evoking a great deal of pressure from the newly elected Republican majority.) The appellate courts are now split on this issue, which seems sure to return to the Supreme Court.[10]

ALJ Reforms

Meanwhile, discussions on my procedural reforms went forward.

September 2, 1994   These past few weeks have been tumultuous. Cohen has grown more strident over ALJ reforms, postal ballots, and now dissents in *Earl Industries,* a case involving Jesse Jackson in Arkansas, where a black union adherent was fired—unlawfully in my view—and for the third time.

Fortunately, the ALJ reforms did not really get on the Republican party's radar screen in 1994 or thereafter. But from the beginning there was both internal and external resistance to them that went beyond that of the Republican Board members. Employers were opposed to bench decisions on the grounds that they had a right to file briefs and that our proposals would create more litigation—a theme Stephens and Cohen articulated in their dissent. And General Counsel Feinstein was none too friendly to the settlement judge idea. While the unions were mildly opposed to it—arguing that these judges might become yet another factor exacerbating delays—Feinstein's objections, to judge by the comments of the regional directors we brought into the discussions, ran deeper. Regional Director Gerry Kobell of Pittsburgh said that if administrative law judges became involved in the conciliation process the regional directors would lose some of their autonomy. He thought it important for regional directors to be able, in some instances, to allow back pay to mount in order to use this "pretty piece of change" as a lever in the negotiations—a power he thought would be undercut by the involvement of administrative law judges.

The reform was also not, of course, acceptable to the two Republicans on the Board, Stephens and Cohen. Although both stated that they were not opposed to settlement judges, they voiced some concern that respondents might delay settlement talks with the regional offices and "thereby upset the highly successful efforts of those offices." This was similar to the objections voiced by some regional directors; that is, that these efforts contravened the NLRA and its provision for a hearing. The more ambitious part of Stephens's and Cohen's argument, however, related to policy considerations: they saw the reform as diminishing the role of the regional offices.

On bench decisions, their dissent was more hard-hitting. The two contended that the new rule sacrificed "fundamental fairness, procedural due process, and high-quality decision making." Without a brief, they argued, the ablest counsel could not pull together an argument just subsequent to the close of a hearing; respondents would be in a particularly unfavorable position since the NLRB could simply plot its oral presentation in light of its precomplaint investigation. Moreover, they claimed, the judge would not have an opportunity to engage in the necessary assimilation of the facts, research, organization, and reflection that make a good decision—which could "compound" the Board's difficulties in the federal courts. In any event, the dissenters contended, there would be no net savings of time because there would be new opportunities to litigate procedural issues, both before the Board and in the courts. Citing the arguments the business lobbyists had submitted to us, the dissenters predicted that our proposals would undermine the goals of fairness and be counterproductive in terms of time and costs.

So, bureaucratic infighting, as well as political resistance, imperiled our proposals.

September 2, 1994   When I was in the West—in Seattle at the Holiday Inn [in August]— I had it out telephonically with both Peg Browning and Chuck Cohen. Peg, particularly during my absence, was wheeling and dealing with Devaney and Cohen to delay my ALJ rule. Their objective was to tone down Cohen's angry dissent, [though they]promised to do so [issue the rule] on 8/18—it finally went down today and will be published next week.

We agreed, 3 to 2, to promulgate for public comment the rule containing both ALJ reforms; we adopted it on an experimental basis in February of 1995 and finalized it a year later.

The rule provision on settlement judges allows the procedure to go into effect only when all parties approve of it. I would have preferred—given the public interest in savings to taxpayers and private parties—to grant the chief administrative law judge authority to appoint settlement judges even when all sides do not consent. I held this view even though, as I always conceded, conciliation efforts were not as likely to be successful when one party objected to them.

Nor were settlement judges permitted to issue written or verbal recommendations, in contrast to the practice followed in Japan. Again, I would have liked to provide our judges with this authority to deal with questions that emerge once a hearing has commenced. But I was outvoted on this matter as well. Still, all in all, I thought that the rule adopted embodied the basic policies set forth in my proposal and that the Board acted sensibly in adopting it.

In January of 1995 we held a successful training seminar on settlements for administrative law judges. Several of them stated openly that they did not consider themselves conciliators or mediators but judges. Our chief administrative law judge, however, made certain that these judges were not given settlement assignments.

The effects of the reforms, contrary to the dire prognostication of the dissenters, were even better than we had anticipated. Following implementation of the settlement judge rule, the Board secured agreement in about 60 percent of its settlement efforts. Through July 1998 we had assigned settlement judges in 319 cases and achieved settlements in 195 of them.

Moreover, the increased focus on settlements and the training seminar led the judges, in spite of budgetary problems, to emphasize settlement and hold more face-to-face meetings in normal adjudicative situations—that is, when not acting as settlement judges. In the first two full years of the rule, judges increased their settlement rate by about 25 percent over the preceding two years—from an annual average of 572 settlements to an average of 718. Considering that many of these hearings were scheduled to take weeks to complete, the savings to the Board and the taxpayer were in the millions—no small economy in a budget of our size. We estimated that each fully litigated case costs the NLRB around $35,000, including personnel, travel, and court-reporting expenses. Private parties spend at least that much and probably more. Thus the new administrative process yielded taxpayer savings in excess of approximately $2.3 million, with an additional savings of $300,000 attributable to bench decisions. Private litigants, too, reaped significant savings.[10a]

The results for bench decisions, the major focus of the attack on the ALJ reforms, were also favorable. Between February 1995 and July 1998, NLRB administrative law judges issued 102 bench decisions. In the first six months of fiscal 1998, bench decisions accounted for about 7 percent of the total decisions issued by judges. As of August 1, 1998, 21 of those bench decisions were pending before the Board. But, of the 85 in which the time period for filing exceptions had elapsed, only 48 (or 57 percent) were appealed; the rest were adopted by the Board with no exceptions. This is lower than the roughly 70 percent rate at which written decisions by the ALJ's are appealed. The increased numbers of appeals, new issues, and litigation the dissenters had predicted simply did not materialize.

Of the 24 cases appealed to the Board and decided by it, only 2 involved reversals or partial remands. Moreover, out of the 63 bench decisions that had been decided by the Board or adopted unchanged, only 7, or 11 percent, had been taken to the courts of appeals. By 1998 two of these cases are pending, two were affirmed, and one was remanded in full. It is thus clear that the judges, as a rule, chose wisely the cases that warranted bench decisions.

In 1999, in the first legal test of the bench decision regulations, the Court of Appeals for the First Circuit in Boston upheld the Board's new rule.[11] The employer in this case contended that the regulation could not stand because it violated Section 10(c) of the NLRA, which states that parties "may" file briefs at the discretion of the administrative law judge. The court noted that the statute did not "entitle" the parties an opportunity to file written briefs instead of oral argument, as the rule provides in illustrative instances, because it is "testimony," not a brief, that must be "reduced to writing and filed with the Board." The court stated that there was nothing to preclude, either implicitly or explicitly, the Agency from adopting the procedure permitted in the challenged rule: requiring the ALJ to "certify the accuracy of the page of the transcript containing the decision" and to cause a copy of those pages to be served on the parties and filed with the Board.... In light of the deference due the Board's interpretation of the Act, we see no reason to disturb the Board's conclusion that "these provisions provide for a written decision, in the form of a certified copy of the record pages containing the judge's full decision, which is served on the parties, in full compliance with the provisions of Section 10(c) of the Act."[12]

In this case, the employer also contended that the Board did not have any reason to justify the regulation and overrule precedent—which the rule did overrule—and that it must allow briefs to be submitted. The court noted that the Board had concluded that bench decisions played a role in the expeditious resolution of unfair labor practice proceedings. Said the court:

We therefore have no difficulty upholding this procedural regulation: it is within the Board's authority and permissible under the Act. The Board considered relevant precedent, discussed the objections raised through comments submitted, and clearly articulated its reasoning in revising the regulations. Therefore the Board did not act arbitrarily or capriciously in revising the challenged regulation.

The court found that under the circumstances of this case the administrative law judge and the Board had complied with its own regulation. The regulation considers that oral arguments in lieu of briefs would be appropriate in a case that "turns on a very straightforward credibility issues; cases involving one-day hearings; cases involving a well-settled legal issue where there is no dispute as to the facts; short record single-issue cases or cases in which a part[y] defaults by not appearing at the hearing." The court rejected the employer's contention that, because the hearing in this case took two days (instead of one), it was a complex case in which oral procedures were not appropriate. Said the court:

This two day hearing is more akin to a "one-day hearing ..." than it is to a "case with [a] lengthy record...." Most of the legal issues here are "well settled" and it became clear as the hearing progressed that the factual disputes evaporated one by one, either non-existent in the first place or not genuinely contested. While at the outset the case appeared as if it might be "complex," the reality as the evidence came in was that the case presented a few rather straightforward applications of settled principles of labor law. Thus, while initially the ALJ properly left open the possibility that the case might be complex enough to require written briefs, he acted within his discretion in determining, as the evidence developed, that the case was in fact an appropriate candidate for oral argument in lieu of briefs.

Finally, the court noted that counsel, though it was only given notice on the afternoon of the second day of the hearing, had the entire following morning to prepare its closing argument. Said Judge Bownes, speaking for a unanimous court:

Such time is considered more than sufficient for attorneys to prepare closing arguments in trials and evidentiary hearings in courts and agencies throughout the country, including hearings lasting substantially more than the two days that was the case here.[13]

Again, contrary to the views of critics that bench decisions would lead to more litigation, the rule has not only saved time on Board reviews but has also resulted in the issuance of decisions, on average, some three or four months earlier than those based on briefs.

In addition, the ALJ time targets we phased in in September of 1994, have produced dramatic time savings. The median number of days from close of hearing to issuance of a judge's decision dropped from 138 in fiscal 1993 to 112 in fiscal 1997. In the same period, the median days from receipt of briefs (or submissions) to judges' decisions fell from 83 to 60. This accomplishment is all the more remarkable in that cases that do go to trial and require judges' decisions are longer and more complex than they were in the past. For example, the average transcript length of judges' decisions issued in the first six months of fiscal 1998 was 684 pages, an all-time high. As recently as fiscal 1992, shortly before the Clinton Board came to Washington, that figure was 439.

Meanwhile, the increase in productivity was accomplished with a dwindling number of administrative law judges, whose ranks were reduced to an historic low by retirements and other attrition. In November 1993, just prior to my chairmanship, the Board employed 78 judges, as compared to 58 on May 22, 1998, shortly before my departure. That is half the number (117) employed in 1981!

Obviously, this diminution required the existing corps of judges to become more productive. The overall productivity of NLRB judges has, in fact, increased very significantly. Between 1995 and 1999, judges have increased their average disposition of cases (that is, the total of decisions and settlements per judge) by 38.6 percent. In fiscal 1993, the average was 15.2 cases; in fiscal 1997, it increased to 21.07. When I left office in August 1998, only 134 cases were pending before administrative law judges. So far as I am aware, this is the smallest number in the history of the agency. Frequently during my tenure, I praised the NLRB judges as the unsung heroes of the NLRB. Their improvements in case handling and reforms were a substantial part of our achievements in attacking the backlog of cases in the early days of 1994 and 1995.

Of course, other innovations were involved. In Washington we adopted both speed teams and super panels—in which Board members made an immediate decision on a group of related cases and signed it then and there. But the administrative judge reforms were the key element in decreasing the backlog to the lowest level since statistics were kept.

Though this record was historic—at one point the backlog of cases to be decided by the Board in Washington was down to 330—other troubling trends later eliminated some of our gains and led to an upswing. By August of 1998 the backlog was almost 700 cases—double the mark of three years earlier. And the backlog gains, as well as speedier case handling evidenced by other relevant criteria (discussed in chapter 13), were eroded even more severely in 1999 and 2000 subsequent to my departure.

Postal Ballots

Our postal ballot reforms had a similar, major impact. In the summer of 1998, the Board voted 3 to 2 to approve the use of postal ballots in a wide variety of situations at San Diego Gas & Electric.[14] The majority noted that mail balloting is appropriate when a strike, lockout, or picketing is in progress and where eligible voters are "scattered" over a wide geographic area by (1) job duties or (2) their work schedule. In a concurring, separate opinion I also found postal ballots appropriate in all situations where it is necessary to conserve Board resources—a particularly important consideration given the budget constraints imposed by the Hundred and Fourth and Hundred and Fifth congresses—and/or to enfranchise employees. (At the same time, of course, I had no illusions about the reaction of congressional opponents—they cared not one whit about cutting costs when it did not suit their ideological agenda!)

The story of the Board's experience with the conduct of mail ballot elections provides some sense of what the fight was all about from 1994 onward. We doubled the use of mail ballots during the four-plus years of my term—employing them even prior to the Board's decision in *San Diego Gas & Electric*. In the Seattle office, 21.8 percent of all elections were conducted by mail, and in San Francisco 12.9 percent were postal elections. The regions that covered vast distances had a particular need for postal balloting, given the substantial travel expenses they would otherwise incur.

But the real heart of the matter was revealed by the dissent to the rule initially formulated by recess appointee John Higgins in 1997 and his Republican successors Peter Hurtgen and J. Robert Brame III in 1998. They decried the inability of employers to speak directly to workers just before elections. It must be said that the effects of captive-audience speeches (in which workers are called together to hear the company's view on company time and property twenty-four hours prior to the mailing of the ballots) may well be dissipated by mail balloting. Thus a postal election may take place over a period of weeks subsequent to management's speech, whereas a manual-ballot election conducted at the plant generally occurs twenty-four hours after the speech. The effect of this difference is dramatized by the fact that of the 3,476 elections held in fiscal 1997, a majority of votes cast were in favor of a bargaining representative in 48.2 percent of the elections. On the other hand, the number of elections won by the unions when they were conducted by mail rose to 66 percent! Thus it appears that the dispute is really about employers' loss of opportunity to influence workers' votes.

This debate came out in the open in discussions over *San Diego Gas & Electric*, where I noted that antiunion tactics like captive-audience speeches were more likely to be used in manual elections than with mail ballots. Unfortunately, the price of issuing this decision was to bowdlerize the language of my concurring opinion, which originally suggested that the genuine rationale for employers' rejection of mail ballots was the desire to engage in antiunion tactics. To assure dissenting Republicans that I was not accusing them of being "union busters," I was compelled to forsake the more direct language of earlier drafts so that the decision would issue.

One of the arguments against the mail ballot is that the participation rate is lower. It is. But the participation rate in such elections would be lower than average in any case, because mail ballots are designed for situations in which employees are difficult to reach and would otherwise be disenfranchised. The true comparison would be between voter participation rates with mail ballots in situations traditionally deemed suitable for them and manual balloting in the same situation.

Rule Making

Very soon after arriving in Washington (as noted in chapter 4), I sent a memo to members of the Board and the senior staff suggesting that we give priority to rule making on the single-location issue. The journey for my proposal on this critical issue, however, would be more perilous and progress would be far slower than it was for the ALJ and postal ballot reforms. An Advanced Notice of Proposed Rulemaking was published on June 2, 1994, and the comment period—during which unions, employers, and other interested parties could submit proposed views—ended on July 29, 1994. It took some time for staffers to absorb and prepare the comments for circulation to Board members.

Meanwhile, political developments overtook this reform and had a drastic effect on all the Board's work. President Clinton's proposals for health care had foundered in the Congress in the teeth of a withering counteroffensive by the insurance industry. The Republicans gained renewed confidence from this victory and seemed sure to strengthen their position in Congress in the off-year elections, as opposition parties in the United States have traditionally done.

But no one I spoke to in Washington thought that the Republicans would actually control Congress in 1995. This had not happened since President Eisenhower was elected in 1952; and, although the Senate had been held by the Republicans in the 1980s, at no time had the Republicans controlled both houses since Senate Majority Leader Robert Taft and Speaker of the House James Martin led the Congress in 1953–1955. But in November 1994 the political ground was shifting dramatically, producing seismic changes in both houses. The result was the emergence of the extraordinarily self-confident Newt Gingrich as House speaker and the soon-to-be presidential aspirant Robert Dole as his Senate counterpart. My diary records the sense of apprehension many of us felt after the election.

November 14, 1994   The Republican landslide of a week ago has left me and most others in a state of shock. The control of the committees is vital and we are bracing ourselves for oversight hearings and hostility to any good budget request that might come out of OMB.

Today we (Ralph Deeds [my special assistant], Fred Feinstein, Harding Darden [the extremely valuable budget analyst]) met with Isabel Sawhill and other OMB types at the Old Executive Office Building. Sawhill probed us on our contacts with the Republicans—perhaps through the Advisory Panels. Sawhill said that most of government can expect to be "flattened" at "the best." However, she said that there are "exceptions." She seemed impressed with the fact that we are streamlining—I emphasized our initiatives on rule making, ALJ's, and the like. She said that she takes this "seriously."

The political developments were soon reflected in sharp relief in the Board's internal deliberations.

November 16, 1994   A tumultuous day with Cohen and Stephens, perhaps feisty because of last Tuesday's results, attacking Korbell's [the Pittsburgh regional director] mail ballot, predicated upon unlawful conduct. Cohen threw a tantrum and said that he would attack mail ballots in the press—would stir up opposition to all reforms. This evening Peggy [Browning] and Fred [Feinstein] came in to convince me to change my vote—I finally said that if Cohen would show us the statement that he would issue in support of postal ballots and it was satisfactory, I would shift my vote to at least require the regional director to examine off-site alternatives [for voting as Feinstein and Browning were proposing] as an intermediate solution.

Meanwhile, Devaney, a Reagan Democrat, was coming to the end of his term, which would expire on December 16, 1994. He assiduously, but unsuccessfully, sought reappointment from President Clinton. (Disappointed in this quest, he supported the Dole-Kemp ticket in 1996.) His departure affected a number of issues, foremost among them rule making.

The problem erupted in an agenda meeting I called on December 8. I knew that if my rule-making initiatives on representation in single-versus-multilocation disputes did not go through by December 16, they would be considerably delayed by the new appointments and the inevitable problems of confirming them. I therefore reminded the Board that the issue had been an important priority for us as early as April 6. (The proposed rule, which I had prepared after discussion with my staff, went beyond the three industries identified in the advance notice and covered all but a few industries within our jurisdiction.)

I anticipated that both Stephens and Cohen would object to taking any action only a week before Devaney's departure. I therefore had Acting Solicitor Jeff Weddekind (one of the most talented of the Board's career civil servants) look into the question of whether we could issue the rule immediately, with dissenting opinions to follow. Truesdale informed us that when Abe Murdock's Board term expired in 1957 (after he had been the Democratic senator from Utah), he had a dissent prepared; but as the majority was not ready to issue a decision; "he just issued it, and I guess the majority . . . came later." In fact, other administrative agencies (e.g., the Federal Trade Commission) allow opinions to be issued after the deadline established in their rules.

I pointed out to the Board that we were riding two different horses on this question. On the one hand, because of uncertainty about what would happen after December 16, we needed to deal with the matter quickly; on the other, I wanted to "promote an environment where all Board Members have an opportunity to express views on issues important to them. I believe that the majority believes that the rules published on December 16 would be final for them and there would be no need to respond to a dissent filed after December 16." Browning, however, demurred and would not commit herself to signing with a majority until the final version of the proposed rule—which had not yet been circulated—was put forward.

Stephens launched into a harsh attack on the proposed process and on me, though claiming to be "as dispassionate as possible." Notwithstanding Weddekind's findings, he said he really didn't care what had happened in other agencies. He argued that the "stage is being set here for a radical departure from Board practice" and that "customary practices are going to be short-circuited." He accused me of trying to revive my failed attempt to oblige Board members to adhere to specific time limitations. He also pointed out that I had declined Cohen's proposal to hold a May 26 meeting on the subject. But, as I had told him at the time, I was concerned then that the open meeting requirements of the Sunshine Act were encouraging Board members to posture before their perceived constituencies. Said Stephens ominously (as recorded in my diary):

"If the public becomes aware of how deliberation was shortcut, how this rule was railroaded through, we are setting ourselves up for a hit from Congress, and rightly so." And later he said: "The Chairman raised the point yesterday that this is just a notice and proposed rule setting up a comment period, not a final rule. My concern is what about the next stage? If we're railroaded this time, will we be railroaded the next time? It is an outrage. An absolute outrage."

I responded that I wasn't going to be "intimidated by threats of political pressure" and stated twice that I "resent it" (the word *railroad*). But Browning would not support my position and stated that she was "on the fence." Ironically, she, having put forth her alternate-site proposal as something she thought could establish a bridge to the Republicans, found herself under attack for introducing what Cohen characterized as major changes.

And so it went. The vote was delayed beyond December 16—with significant consequences. Devaney's term expired, and he could not participate on rule making. He would not be the last member to complain about this situation.

December 31, 1994   Just a few hours left in this momentous year.... This afternoon, both Bill Stewart and I were at the office—I managed to finish work on all cases on my desk— then Bill brought in a few more (as always) and I had new tasks.
    The landscape has been changed by Republican control of Congress. I am sure that this will plague us in 1995—both on the budget and oversight hearings.... My inability to present my own views in opinion form—I seem to always be reviewing other people's work—has frustrated me. Notwithstanding the Republicans, I am hopeful that I can do more of this in 1995.
    Already both Stephens and Cohen have been emboldened—S. accused me of trying to "railroad" rule changes and threatened a "'hit" from Congress. He complained of lack of time to respond to my reforms—yet the ideas have been before the Board for a half-year now.

General Counsel Troubles

Meanwhile, it was also becoming more and more clear that I would have difficulties with General Counsel Feinstein. That fall we needed to put together a committee to address new technology problems. Although I (not the counsel general) was head of the NLRB, I suggested that the committee be composed half of the chairman's representatives and half of people from the general counsel's staff. Feinstein immediately objected to this arrangement; he stated that because of that official's administrative responsibilities, such committees in the past were dominated by general counsel representatives, and he saw no basis for departing from that precedent. He intimated—as he was to do from time to time—that others in his praetorian guard were insisting that he control the composition and that there would be morale problems if his people did not dominate the committee. We sat in my office late one afternoon and into the early evening, discussing the question, lapsing into long periods of silence, and staring at one another.

While I had not thought or written about the matter prior to my Washington stint, I came away with the view that the Taft-Hartley amendments' creation of an independent general counsel with control over so many employees had produced a two-headed monster that posed serious administrative problems. Before I was chairman, I had sometimes thought, as in the Tennessee Saturn dispute over UAW recognition, that the general counsel had usurped responsibilities for statutory interpretation that properly belonged to the Board.[15] On both policy and administrative matters, Feinstein and I were frequently at odds, and he had the advantage of not sharing his authority with anyone else. Quite frequently, he undercut my efforts by going to Browning, and later Fox and Liebman, to gain support against positions I had taken.

To compound my problems, both prior and subsequent to my arrival in Washington, I was completely unsuccessful in advancing genuinely qualified candidates for Board vacancies. I worked hard for the appointment of a hardworking and intelligent Hispanic labor law professor from the Southwest with pro-labor views, but I could not interest the AFL-CIO. I could never get the White House, the Labor Department, or the AFL-CIO to consider good people from beyond the beltway (and a couple within) who would be good allies. In this respect, Chairman Dotson of the Reagan era had an advantage. He generally had one vote upon which he could count. I had none.

Union Headaches

A second development that fall had a more direct bearing on the external world of politics. Jack Sheinkman, my old friend and "rabbi" in the confirmation process, retired as president of the Amalgamated Clothing Workers to facilitate a merger with the International Ladies' Garment Workers Union (ILGWU). In November I was one of the speakers at his retirement party in New York City. Governor Mario Cuomo, who was just about to lose a bitterly fought reelection campaign, sent a message praising Jack and saying, with obvious reference to Jack's participation in demonstrations against the Bush NLRB, "Now that Bill Gould is Chairman of the NLRB, what can Jack Sheinkman possibly protest against in the future?"

It was a convivial and memorable evening. Leaders of the New York labor movement and the Democratic party were present en masse—and many had come from Washington and elsewhere to honor Jack. But his retirement was a real loss for me, for he had continued to be a key player and my close confidante even after my confirmation.

United Mine Workers

As 1994 came to an end, a particularly thorny problem presented itself. I had already incurred the wrath of a number of business groups for promoting reforms to expedite our procedures and produce a better balance between labor and management in the cases we adjudicated. Yet I had also been quite clear about my conviction that the rule of law applied to all parties who came before the Board—unions as well as employers. In an article I wrote in the early 1970s, I had supported many of the Taft-Hartley amendments to American labor law as good policy and appropriate responses to union abuses.[16] This position was not always greeted with enthusiasm by elements within the labor movement to whom Taft-Hartley was anathema. Some union leaders who welcomed the Clinton Board's commitment to collective bargaining and the goals of the NLRA nonetheless believed that union lawlessness should not be treated as severely as employer misconduct—because the bargaining table and the cards were stacked against workers in American society. I had a different view.

The controversy over this issue first emerged in connection with a major dispute involving the United Mine Workers (UMWA) and its leader Rich Trumka, who in 1995 would become secretary-treasurer of the AFL-CIO. One day before my confirmation on March 4, 1994, the Board's solicitor, John Higgins, recommended that civil contempt proceedings be instituted against the union and some of its districts, locals, and officials pursuant to the February 24, 1994, request of Acting General Counsel Dan Silverman. "When we obtained the 1987 contempt adjudication," Higgins wrote, "it was hoped that the Decree would be the beginning of a new day in Agency proceedings involving the Mine Workers. Clearly ... we were wrong.

Not only has the Union engaged in massive and serious acts of violence, but they have failed to comply with the various steps of the Agreement that were developed to try to keep control of strike activity."

In World War II and its aftermath, the bituminous coal industry was a troublesome area of labor-management relations.; Unlawful union conduct triggered a showdown between President Truman and John L. Lewis and led to a Supreme Court contempt ruling against the UMW.[17] Again in the early 1970s, an upsurge in wildcat (unauthorized) work stoppages created havoc in the mines, sometimes accompanied by the violent conduct of union members and their officials and/or individuals in ski masks who set up picket lines and induced workers to "down tools." In my view, the Supreme Court's inexplicable failure to extend the enforceability of no-strike clauses to injunctions in disputes caused by sympathy stoppages was a direct response to the specter of unenforceability that surrounded this issue—as reflected in the frequent illegal strikes staged by the UMWA in the 1970s.[18]

In the 1990s, as strike activity waned, union-management relations had become more peaceful in all senses of the word. But there were major exceptions, and the Pittston strike of 1993 was one of them. The Silverman memo details (1) the widespread violence that occurred in connection with the UMW's 1993 strike against certain members of the Bituminous Coal Operator's Association (BCOA), in violation of a 1987 contempt citation affirmed by the Court of Appeals for the Fourth Circuit; and (2) the International's failure and refusal to comply with certain affirmative requirements for preventing strike misconduct that were set forth in the 1987 decision. The 1987 adjudication, which had emerged out of numerous violent coal strikes over many years, called for the UMWA to monitor and control authorized strikes by designating responsible picket captains, making sure that these officials were present at all locations at all times during picketing, and requiring them to take all reasonable action necessary to ensure that picketing was conducted in accordance with the adjudication order. The UMWA was also required to investigate any allegations of misconduct; remove union members who engaged in unlawful or unauthorized strike activity from the picket line; and, depending upon the severity of the misconduct, discontinue strike benefits and bring internal union disciplinary proceedings against such members. The adjudication imposed a stiff set of prospective fines: $10,000 per violation against the union, with a doubling of fines when the misconduct resulted in serious bodily injury; $1,000 per violation against individual officers and union employees; and $750 against pickets and all other persons who violate the order.

The Silverman memo catalogued many instances of mass picketing, blocking ingress and egress from mines, and threats of bodily injury that occurred in 1993. At one mine, a convoy of vehicles were attacked by masked individuals with rocks and guns and a truck driver was killed instantly by a gunshot fired by the local's mine safety chairman. Masked individuals were armed with rocks, jackrocks, jack plates, and Molotov cocktails. Other instances of violence were committed at a number of mines, and the violations continued, even after the Board obtained injunctive relief through Section 10(j). Silverman, noting that the 1987 adjudication placed responsibility on the International to ensure lawful conduct, pointed out that

Widespread misconduct occurred in the presence, and with the acquiescence, of responsible officials designated by the International, and on numerous occasions was perpetrated by the responsible officials themselves. Virtually no efforts were made to remove offending pickets from the picket line. The International has been unable to point to a single instance in which strike benefits were suspended or a member disciplined for engaging in misconduct. Nor, apparently, were any investigations undertaken by the International, even after massive allegations of misconduct were brought to its attention during the complaint and 10(j) proceedings in the various Regions.

The memo, which awaited us when we took office in early March 1994, recommended contempt proceedings and an assessment of $1.3 million in fines against the UMW. But soon after our arrival, General Counsel Feinstein received a letter from former Secretary of Labor William Usery. The latter revealed that Elizabeth Dole, secretary of labor in the Bush administration, had appointed him to mediate the 1993 strike and that the parties had recognized the need to change the nature of their relationship. Usery also noted that they had agreed to dismiss their lawsuits against one another, not to file future cases arising out of the 1993 strike, and, specifically, to request that the NLRB withdraw the charges.

A week later Feinstein advised the Board that he was in touch with UMWA lawyers and was discussing settlement. He asked the Board to defer action for thirty days so as to promote settlement. Feinstein indicated that he agreed with the thrust of the Usery letter and wanted to back away from contempt litigation.

On April 8, 1994, however, I put forward my position in a memo to Board members and Feinstein.

As I stated at our last meeting, I take a very serious view of the conduct engaged in by the UMWA in the previously discussed contempt matter. We cannot deal with employer lawlessness if we do not address union lawlessness. The above referenced matter is the second instance of contempt. This is "contempt on contempt."

A majority of the Board has already voted to authorize contempt proceedings. If there is no settlement in hand by next Friday, at 5 P.M., I propose that we authorize contempt proceedings at that time and instruct the General Counsel to proceed forthwith.

In a separate memo to Feinstein that same day, I expressed concern about delaying Board discussion and about the timetable established for evaluating the UMWA's response. At an April 15 meeting, over Feinstein's protest, the Board voted 3 to 1 (myself, Stephens and Cohen, Devaney dissenting) to authorize contempt proceedings. I noted that this action did not preclude future settlement discussions with the UMWA. On May 5, when Dave Parker, the Board's information officer, was ready to send out the usual press release on the matter, Feinstein told him not to do so because he wanted the Board to keep a "low profile." Bill Stewart commented, "I wonder if Fred really understands that contempt cases are Board cases" not a matter for the general counsel.

That same day in a speech to a labor law conference for management lawyers, I stated that the Board would not tolerate lawlessness and repeated misconduct. I pledged "an evenhanded approach against all those who break the law.... We must stand against lawlessness no matter what the source." As Dave Parker's release about the contempt action explained clearly, the Board was attempting to avoid recurrence of the violation of individual rights.

The UMWA was incensed and called the decision to initiate contempt proceedings "a reactionary ploy to satisfy board critics."[19] Pointing out that mine owners were willing to drop the charges of unfair labor practices, the union alleged that "this is being driven solely by the National Labor Relations Board." Harry Bernstein, writing in the *Los Angeles Times,* stated that

Gould ... will have to try harder to overcome the NLRB's pro-management stance of recent years.... One ominous sign was Gould's deciding NLRB vote to seek as much as $1.3 million in contempt fines from the United Mine Workers for alleged picket line misconduct during last year's seven month strike against 12 coal companies ... With his vote in the Miners' case, Gould went too far to make his point [of neutrality and impartiality].[20]

A couple of weeks later I got a taste of what was involved in this kind of dispute. Steve Tallent, a management labor lawyer, and Elliot Bredhoff, an old friend and union lawyer, cohosted a party at Tallent's house to welcome me to Washington. The angry UMWA threatened to picket the party and to dissuade union lawyers from attending it. Fortunately, through the good offices of Bredhoff, cooler heads prevailed, and Trumka was dissuaded from taking this position. No pickets appeared.

The next stage in this scenario arrived with the Supreme Court's June 30 ruling in *International Union, United Mine Workers of America* v. *Bagwell,* a case that had hovered in the background of our discussions on the contempt issue.[21] In *Bagwell,* several companies had sued in Virginia state courts to enjoin the union from conducting unlawful, strike-related activities, many of which were similar to those cited in the *BCOA* case. All in all, contempt findings were made in almost five hundred instances, many of them violent. The trial court held that contumacious acts must be proven beyond a reasonable doubt but did not afford the union the right to a jury trial and hit it with $64 million in fines. The question posed to the Court was whether the fines were civil or criminal in nature. If criminal, the Constitution requires a trial by jury. Said Justice Harry Blackmun, speaking for the Court:

For a discrete category of indirect contempts ... civil procedural protections may be insufficient. Contempts involving out-of-court disobedience to complex injunctions often require elaborate and reliable fact-finding.... Such contempts do not obstruct the court's ability to adjudicate the proceedings before it, and the risk of erroneous deprivation from the lack of a neutral fact finder may be substantial.... Under these circumstances, criminal procedural protections such as the right to counsel and proof beyond a reasonable doubt are both necessary and appropriate to protect the due process rights of parties and prevent the arbitrary exercise of judicial power.[22]

The Court pointed out that the trial court did not attempt to calibrate the fines to damages caused by the union's contumacious activities or indicate that the fines were "to compensate the complainant for losses sustained" [and] ... the "non-party governments ... never requested any compensation." The Court concluded that the fines in question were criminal because: (1) the union's sanctionable conduct did not occur "in the court's presence or otherwise implicate the court's ability to maintain order or adjudicate the proceedings before it"; (2) union contumacy did not involve simple, affirmative acts but rather "widespread, ongoing, out-of-court violations of a complex injunction"; and (3) the fines were serious, totaling over $64 million for offenses in many areas.

The Court's decision produced further pressure from Feinstein, who argued that any attempt to bring contempt proceedings against the UMWA would be, given its similarity to Bagwell, an "uphill" fight. The logic of *Bagwell* did have some applicability to our own UMWA case and its suitability for contempt; it seemed to indicate that, in part, the most violent offenses were criminal matters requiring trial by jury. On the other hand, Nort Come of our Supreme Court unit thought we had a "fair chance" to distinguish our case from *Bagwell,* given the fact that we were specifically seeking affirmative acts by unions and that the nonneutral fact-finding that had concerned the justices in *Bagwell* was not at issue here—given the Board's attempt to enforce prospective fines before a master (a person appointed by the court to provide impartial fact-finding).

In a 1999 case, *NLRB v. Ironworkers Local 433*, the Court of Appeals for the Ninth Circuit concluded that the enforcement of prospective noncompliance fines did not trigger the criminal-procedure safeguards required by *Bagwell*; it therefore upheld the Board's application for contempt adjudication.[23] The court noted that *Bagwell* was "unusual" and did not involve the NLRB. Its decision focused on the fact that while *Bagwell* concerned an injunction issued by a single trial court judge, in NLRB cases the issue of noncompliance fines arises from consent decrees the Board uses to enforce its prior orders. The court stressed that the Board's civil contempt powers are "particularly adapted to curb recidivist offenders of the NLRA" and that the fines are intended to ensure future compliance with a court order remaining in place.

Nonetheless, in 1994 *Bagwell* produced a period of uncertainty for the parties in the UMWA case, who were still feeling one another out about the prospects of settlement or litigation. Two weeks before that decision, I had lunched with Larry Gold, then the AFL-CIO general counsel. He urged me to reconsider the contempt issue and said pointedly: "You won't get any points with the opposition for doing this." I reminded him, and everyone with whom I came in contact on this and similar issues, that my view was that I could never get enough "points" with anyone to satisfy them about anything. I was strictly concerned, I told him, with the applicability of the National Labor Relations Act to labor and management. Nothing else.

Finally, as winter set in, we put this matter to rest. We began anew to attempt to settle the contempt issue before the trial, which was scheduled for early 1995. I instructed the general counsel to send a December 23 letter to the UMWA offering $250,000 compensatory damages, a $350,000 bond, and a sunset period that would expire after the next significant strike date subsequent to expiration the 1998 contract. The Mine Workers turned down our proposal.

On January 24, 1995, we were visited by Nicky Barone of Judge Knapp's office in West Virginia. (Knapp was the federal district judge who had jurisdiction over the case.) Barone emphasized that the companies wanted a settlement and that "No one could understand why the Board was now suddenly coming in and digging up this old case." She said that we should consider the fact that the Mine Workers had changed their ways, but I pointed out to her that so far there had been no opportunity to assess how well the union would carry out their intentions, "notwith-standing my faith in Rich Trumka."

I stressed to her that the Board needed to protect the public interest, which included the individuals who have been victimized by the strike—specifically, the individual who had been murdered, those who have been threatened with a similar fate, and the victims of other forms of union violence. She stated that the murder was very unfortunate. Of course, she and the courts were concerned about this—although she expressed some doubt about whether the conviction of the murderer (which took place in July 1994) would be upheld.

At the conclusion of the conversation, I told Nicky Barone that, because Fred Feinstein had prematurely revealed our bottom-line position in discussions held the day before, we had nothing left to offer her. She was quite disappointed with this statement and said that I was a "hard" man. On the contrary, I assured her, I was really conciliatory and congenial.

The day before we had had a heated discussion of the subject at our Board meeting. Stephens focused on some of the same doubts I had voiced—especially the Mine Workers' violent behavior and their continued award of strike pay to those who engaged in the violence. Both Stephens (who wrote an angry letter to the Board claiming that the settlement was "ramrodded through") and I thought that there was no room for concessions on money. But we were outvoted by the other three members. Though the settlement imposed sanctions, they were not as sweeping as I would have liked.

Teamsters Local 115

NLRB v. Teamsters Local 115 presented many legal and political issues similar to those involved in the UMWA–BCOA case.[24] The conduct in question arose during a series of labor disputes between Teamsters Local 115, a very active and politically influential union in Philadelphia, and five separate employers. The Board sought a contempt citation, because of the 1986 judgment the Board had obtained from the Third Circuit Court of Appeals. During several strikes in 1985, company officials had been punched, kicked, spat upon, and pelted with rocks. Threats of serious violence were made. The contempt proceedings were triggered by a special master's finding that a new round of violence had occurred at at least four locations. It alleged racial and sexual threats, a picket's assault of a security guard, and a male picket who threatened a female employee with a long knife, flashing it and screaming at her and her elderly mother. The master also found that union agents had engaged in reckless and dangerous driving aimed at individuals involved in the dispute.

Again, although the Board asked the court to establish prospective fines for future misconduct, the employers withdrew the charge of unfair labor practices. But, as in the UMWA–BCOA dispute, our view was that the employers' withdrawal was not dispositive and that it was in the Board's interest to prevent recurrence of unlawful behavior to protect individual employees, even though the employers— not the employees—had filed the charge.

The Teamsters, who were both friendly and helpful to the Board in the many disputes with Congress that arose during my term, were anxious to settle, as I noted in my diary.

October 28, 1994 Judy Scott [general counsel] of the Teamsters was here yesterday. She spoke about many matters—how she could help us with OMB (of course, if the Republicans take Congress two weeks from now that will be my real problem) and ideas about a suitable regional director for Cincy. But what she was really here for [was] to attempt to speak [about] a contempt matter against Teamsters Local 115 in Philadelphia. [My confidential assistant Mary Ann Sawyer, anticipating that this would be the subject of the meeting had gently tried to block it—but I agreed to meet with her nonetheless.] Like the *Mine Workers* [case]—which produced threatened pickets against me—this will be politically sensitive. I will use our contempt authority expansively and test the limits of the Supreme Court's *Bagwell* decision. The unions believe that they have won a great victory there—but if our contempt authority is crippled, it will aid recidivist employers [as well]. We must be able to use it against both.

In the summer of 1995, the Third Circuit entered a purgation order against Local 115, requiring compliance with a broad prohibition against violence—assault, blocking entrances, and so on—and a deposit of $15,000 with the district court, which would be remitted upon performance of specified affirmative acts (e.g., making individuals whole through compensation for property damage). The court also established a prospective fine schedule of $10,000 per violation and $1,000 per day against Local 115 and $1,000 per violation and $500 per day against responsible individuals, such fines to be collected "subject to the requirements of due process of law." The Teamsters, relying on *Bagwell*, petitioned the Supreme Court to vacate the order, but the Court denied their petition.

At this point the Teamsters demonstrated great interest in holding settlement talks, while the Board's contempt section, which kept my office apprised of their discussions, refused to budge. Apparently the proposals the union put forward related to sensitivity training and the like. But, as we had achieved everything we wanted in the Third Circuit's order, we had no incentive to enter into such discussions—though we gained the impression that Feinstein was willing to do so.

The *Lechmere* Cases

Another instance in which I took a position that troubled the labor movement involved nonemployee union agents' access to private property for the purpose of informing their public about the union's position. In 1992 the Supreme Court, by divided vote, held that in almost no circumstances could union agents obtain access to private employer property to recruit new members or organize a facility. I thought the decision wrong—because of the central significance of the workplace in communications about union organization by both unions and employers—and had already said so in *Agenda for Reform*.

Now, in the *Lechmere* cases, I was called upon to apply the decision. However erroneous I thought it, it was the law of the land.[25] Because I believed the Court's broad reasoning applied to these cases as well, I voted with the two Republican members to deny unions access to private property.[26] The AFL-CIO was very displeased with my stand and—as Larry Gold had predicted earlier—I got no points from the opposition. But what was important to me was that under the extant precedent I had no choice. Later, on August 27, 1998, my last day in office, I again joined the two Republican members to support this position in a case involving organizers' access to a restaurant/snack bar.[27]

Frequently, however, an important part of the Board's work was not simply to issue decisions and formulate Board policies but to engage in policy making through our posture in the courts. After the unions lost with me on the merits of the access issue, they tried to renew their argument in a slightly different form when the cases reached the appellate courts.

May 2, 1996   Yesterday, Jonathan Hiatt [AFL/CIO general counsel] came to see me, and we talked about the advisory panels. But the most important part of the conversation was related to a proposal that he made. He said that in the cases in which the unions have lost on the *Lechmere* issue before the Court of Appeals for the District of Columbia and us (I wrote a special concurring opinion expressing my profound disagreement with *Lechmere*, but stating that I was obliged to follow it in the circumstances and the issues raised) that this was their last chance to get the matter before the Supreme Court because the general counsel would not be issuing complaints in the future. He wanted us to meet to support ... [a] brief that would not oppose review by the Supreme Court (perhaps even encourage it). He felt that it would be consistent with my position (which is at odds with theirs) to take such a view. I told him that I was unaware of any practice by an administrative agency to this effect, but a subsequent discussion with Bill Stewart and Hiatt himself today led me to believe such a document can be filed. I pointed out to him that the distinction between my position, which is against theirs on union access and support of a petition for review—while a valid distinction in fact—would not easily be understood. I pointed out to him that I had come here to try to do everything in accord with principle, and yet I found myself so frequently taking into account the political environment. . . . I said that I was sure that the Labor Policy Association would immediately issue a statement attacking me if I acted in accordance with his position, stating that my finding for the employers in January 1995 in support of our acquiescence in the petition for certiorari was, as I put it, "rank duplicity." Hiatt expressed concern about exposing me to damage through the political process but, nonetheless, persisted in his view that . . . the Board should support the unions. I subsequently discussed this with Bill Stewart last night, and it may be that we will take the position that he, Hiatt, wants us to take. That is something that I will have to sort out. I still have not read his brief to the Supreme Court in its entirety.

In the final analysis, I didn't support the AFL-CIO. I was not worried about picking a fight with the Labor Policy Association—or other extremist management groups. I had a number of them going already. But promoting a view that could so easily be misunderstood and seen as logically inconsistent with the position I had taken on the particular cases seemed to me an unwise move.

This sort of issue was to reappear a couple of years later. As it turned out, 1994 and the early weeks of early 1995 were the calm before the storm. That storm was the Hundred and Fourth Congress and its Contract with America (we used to say "Contract *on* America"). But before that tempest hit, the Board was remarkably successful in displaying to the public what labor law could do in a major dispute if truly allowed to work. That opportunity arose out of the baseball strike of 1994 and 1995. We were to be very much at the center of this storm too.

6

Balls and Strikes

Early in my tenure we heard a case that raised public awareness of the work of the NLRB, especially the all-important Section 10(j) procedure. It involved America's grand old pastime—baseball.

In 1995 the Board handled a well-publicized union decertification election in the National Basketball Association. Under our decision, the league was permitted to pay the transportation expenses of all those handsomely paid players who wanted to cast their votes in cities where the polls were open on a schedule they found most convenient. Yet nothing caught the public's attention more than our involvement in baseball.[1]

During the thirty-one years that they had engaged in collective bargaining, the baseball players and the club owners had had eight strikes or lockouts. They occurred at one stage or another virtually every time the parties had to renegotiate a contract. Prior to 1994 the most extended conflict, lasting almost two months, had resulted in a considerably shortened 1981 season and in two different sets of standings for the two parts of the year. The winners of each "miniseason" played each other to determine the division champions.

On December 31, 1993, the collective-bargaining agreement between the Major League Players' Association and the Players' Relations Committee of the club owners' association expired. When negotiations commenced early in 1994, they promised to be difficult, inasmuch as the owners were persisting in their efforts to recapture portions of the players' free-agency rights lost in a 1975 arbitration ruling.[2] In 1994 the owners' mantra was reduction of the inequality among clubs in large- and small-market cities; they claimed that the disparities imperiled the economic viability of many teams and, thus, the sport's competitive balance. A salary cap, the owners insisted, would contribute substantially to resolving the imbalance.

The players' union responded by arguing that if the problem was one of economic disparity among teams, it should be reduced by revenue sharing among the clubs not economic sacrifice by players. But the owners pressed on. With more than thirty players earning $3 million a year and the average salary in excess of $1 million, it wasn't hard to convince the public that players' greediness and unwillingness to accept salary caps—as football and basketball players had—was the heart of the problem.

The players set a strike deadline of August 2, 1994, only five months after my term as chairman began. They proceeded on the assumption that the greatest pressure could be exerted in the fall before the playoffs and the World Series—the time when owners made most of their money. During the winter, by contrast, the owners would be able to impose their last offer unilaterally after bargaining to impasse—leaving the union with the weak remedy of a strike when it would hurt the owners least. Or, alternatively, owners might risk a lockout in the spring, depriving players of paychecks, again at a time when owners would not feel the pinch.

On August 2, 1994, while at the White House for a social function involving California Democrats, I chatted with President Clinton in the receiving line. I remarked that Secretary of Labor Bob Reich and I had been discussing the baseball negotiations. The president expressed dismay at the prospect of a strike that year. "This is the best year in a long time," he said, referring to the home run records that might be set by Ken Griffey, Mark McGwire, Matt Williams, and others. He remarked that it was hard to have sympathy for either side, given their wealth and "greed." As we parted he said to me, "If you guys could resolve this, they'd elect me president for life!"

I too had a deep personal and professional interest in this issue. I had written a book on sports law, as well as many newspaper pieces on baseball, and had taught a course in sports law at Stanford for a number of years. I had also arbitrated in salary disputes in 1992 and 1993. In fact, when I left the law school for Washington in the spring of 1994, I told sports journalist Leonard Koppett, my friend and co-teacher, that my deepest regret was giving up my baseball salary arbitration. Leonard replied, "You'll be more involved now than you ever were in the past. A big conflict is coming between the parties, and the National Labor Relations Board will be right in the middle of it. You'll see." Truer words were never spoken.

To understand the 1994-1995 dispute, it is necessary to look at the history of baseball and how the law pertaining to it developed. It all began long ago, in 1922, when the renowned Supreme Court Justice Oliver Wendell Holmes Jr. had what all baseball players have—a bad day. That bad day was to influence baseball for years to come.

The case before the Court, *Federal Baseball Club of Baltimore* v. *National League of Professional Baseball Clubs,* emerged out of the demise of the Federal Baseball League.[3] Several of the teams in the league thought they had been undermined by organized baseball. The frustrated owner of a Maryland ball club brought suit against each of the sixteen teams in the National and American leagues; the two league presidents; Kenesaw Mountain Landis, head of what was then called the National Commission; and three former owners or persons having power in the Federal League. The complaint alleged a conspiracy among the defendants in violation of the Sherman Anti-Trust Act of 1890—which prohibits conspiracies in restraint of trade and is anti-monopolistic. The plaintiff alleged that his attempt to launch a baseball club had been severely damaged, and he was able to prevail at the trial level. He was awarded $80,000, which would be tripled under the provisions of the Sherman Act. On appeal, however, the court held that the activities of the defendants did not fall within the terms of the Sherman Act, and the U. S. Supreme Court agreed to review the matter.

Speaking for a unanimous Court, Justice Holmes concluded that the antitrust laws were not applicable to baseball because it was not in trade or commerce, although the exhibition was done for money. Baseball was, said the Court, a mere "incident" of commerce unrelated to production. The Court's opinion did not refer to the fact that clubs telegraphed the play-by-play and news about games across state lines ; it thus did not consider whether this aspect of the game was more than incidental and constituted commerce within the meaning of the 1890 statute.

The view of commerce expressed by Justice Holmes in *Federal Baseball* was the product of a bygone era that influenced the Court up to the time of the depression but has since been discarded. Its abandonment enabled Congress to enact a series of wide-ranging social and economic reforms that began with the Court's constitutional approval of the National Labor Relations Act.[4] Nonetheless, in subsequent rulings, down to the present day, the Court has never departed from *Federal Baseball,* and so has left the sport immune from antitrust law—in contrast to the law that developed with regard to such professional sports as football, basketball, and hockey. Thus, through the vehicle of the "reserve clause" written into major league baseball's rules, players were bound to one club for life unless they were sold or barred from play for behavior unacceptable to the clubs.

Shortly after World War II, a number of major league players defected to the short-lived Mexican League and, as a consequence, were blacklisted. One of those players, light-hitting New York Giants' outfielder Danny Gardella, sued under the Sherman Anti-Trust Act. The Court of Appeals of the Second Circuit, examining the changed nature of the game of professional baseball, ruled 2 to 1 that the sport could be covered by the act by virtue of its extensive radio and television coverage broadcast across state lines—a phenomena not present at the time of *Federal Baseball*. But the case was settled before reaching the Supreme Court, allowing Gardella and three other major leaguers to return to baseball in the summer of 1949.[5] The settlement, and the fact that other cases had been decided contrary to the Second Circuit's ruling, left the issue unresolved. The fundamental question in the Mexican League litigation, and in later cases in which players resorted to antitrust law, was whether the teams could conspire to refuse to deal with certain players. In other contexts, it was whether clubs could conspire to refuse to deal with a player held by another club through the reserve clause.

In 1953 the Court again confronted the issue. Ignoring the logic of the Second Circuit opinion in *Gardella*, in *Toolson* v. *New York Yankees* the Court held once again that baseball was not within the scope of federal antitrust laws.[6] It denied free agency to a player complaining of a minor league assignment—the very circumstance in which, in 1931, Baseball Commissioner Landis had set some players free![7] The Court noted that Congress had been aware of *Federal Baseball* for the past thirty years and had not taken any legislative initiative to reverse this interpretation of the Sherman Anti-Trust Act.

The reserve clause issue was confronted directly in 1972 in *Flood* v. *Kuhn*, when St. Louis Cardinals center fielder Curt Flood protested his trade to the Philadelphia Phillies. The Court, in a memorable opinion written by Justice Blackmun, adhered to its previous position, although it candidly admitted that other sports had come under the antitrust laws in the years since *Federal Baseball*. The Court said that baseball "[with] its reserve system enjoying exemption from federal anti-trust law ... is, in a very distinct sense, an exception and an anomaly."[8]

In referring to other cases in which professional sports leagues and clubs were held to be subject to the antitrust laws, the Court could only state that baseball

is an aberration that has been with us now for half a century, one heretofore deemed fully entitled to the benefit of stare decisis, and one that has survived the Court's expanding terms of interstate commerce. It rests on a recognition and an acceptance of baseball's unique characteristics and needs.[9]

The Court held that any inconsistency or illogic between the legal treatment of baseball and that accorded other professional sports must be remedied by Congress not by the Court. A quarter of a century later, after the 1994-1995 baseball strike, Congress finally did just that in the Curt Flood Act of 1998. To that portion of the story we return later.

Meanwhile, two major developments unfolded. In the first place, as noted above, antitrust laws were used successfully to challenge reserve clauses in other sports and, therefore, to permit players to move from team to team through the provisions of negotiated collective bargaining agreements.[10] Players and teams therefore needed to negotiate some kind of compromise between complete restraint and complete free agency—which, ironically, would place everyone on the market simultaneously and, perhaps, diminish the salaries owners would be willing to pay individual stars. As a result of these cases, owners of other sports teams had an incentive to enter into collective bargaining to provide for free agency; because, by doing so, they would gain the "labor exemption" to antitrust laws, which made them as immune as baseball was from treble-damage awards if they were found acting in restraint of trade.

Second, baseball players, notwithstanding the narrow definition of commerce used in *Federal Baseball*, were found eligible to use the procedures of the National Labor Relations Act—the existence of which was predicated upon the commerce clause of the Constitution. In 1969 when baseball umpires pressed for recognition, the NLRB ruled that professional baseball was an industry affecting commerce and, thus, was within its jurisdiction; the ruling allowed the Board to hold a representation election when disputes about recognition arose. Just the year before, the players had obtained their own first collective-bargaining agreement (although they had had a union since 1954). This momentous event occurred, in turn, one year after Marvin Miller became director of the Major League Player's Association.

Thus the collective-bargaining process took the baseball players down a very different road than that pursued in other sports. In the 1973 negotiations, in the wake of *Flood* v. *Kuhn*, the players won a new and significant arbitration procedure through negotiations. In the 1960s they had obtained a grievance-arbitration procedure, which allowed for the resolution of disputes involving interpretation of the collective-bargaining agreement. Now, in 1973, they achieved salary arbitration, which provided for the resolution of salary disputes by the same kind of third-party neutral.

Salary arbitration had its genesis in the *Flood* litigation and the idea that the owners had to do something to disassociate themselves from the public perception of a master-servant relationship created by the reserve clause. When it was negotiated in 1973, salary arbitration was of the *final offer* variety—that is, it required the arbitrator to select the position or final offer of one side or the other—and it has remained so ever since. The theory behind final-offer arbitration is that if the arbitrator can choose between the positions of the two sides, both parties will be motivated to make more reasonable offers and, in the process, to voluntarily resolve most of their disputes.

The advent of salary arbitration did not, however, accurately anticipate developments in baseball's grievance-arbitration procedure. The first step toward creating the baseball free agent through grievance arbitration was initiated in 1974 by "Catfish" Hunter, then of the Oakland A's. Hunter's grievance charged the A's owner with failing to fulfill an obligation to make deferred payments so that the player could avoid tax liability. Hunter maintained that this was a breach of contract; the arbitrator agreed and held that, because the club had failed to fulfill the contract, Hunter could terminate it. He therefore became a free agent and able to entertain offers from any other major league club.

On December 31, 1974, the Catfish accepted an offer from the New York Yankees for an unprecedented salary package: a $1 million signing bonus, a $150,000 annual salary for five years, life insurance benefits worth $1 million, and a substantial amount of deferred compensation. (Only later was it learned that Hunter had received an even higher offer, having rejected a $3.8 million package from the Kansas City Royals.)

This award and its results caught the interest of a large number of players. The next step was an attack on the reserve system itself through the grievance-arbitration machinery Hunter had utilized. The next grievance was filed by Bobby Tolan—the erstwhile Cincinnati "ballhawk," who patrolled the outfield for San Diego—but he withdrew it when he signed his contract with the Padres. Andy Messersmith of the Los Angeles Dodgers and Dave McNally of the Montreal Expos were the ultimate beneficiaries. In their cases the same arbitrator, Peter Seitz, held that players could not be bound to a club beyond the renewal or option year if no contract was signed by the end of that year.

These rulings produced a new spate of collective bargaining, which led in 1976 to the first in a series of agreements addressing the free-agency issue. From the beginning, the Major League Players Association skillfully limited the number of free agents available under the negotiated procedures. They had learned the lesson of Catfish Hunter and, earlier, of Ken Harrelson, who had signed with the Boston Red Sox in the heat of the 1967 pennant race after being peremptorily dismissed by Charlie Finley of the Kansas City A's. The lesson was: When there are few, or only one, free agent on the market, the price for their services goes up. Thus creation of a relatively free market through the new free-agent agreement carefully held back the number of players who would be on the market at a given time. This, in tandem with salary arbitration, ratcheted up baseball salaries and caused great concern on the part of the owners.

The next time around, after postponing resolution of the basic issues through a 1980 agreement, the union struck on June 12, 1981, and remained out for fifty days. The NLRB attempted to intervene in the stoppage on the grounds that the owners had not engaged in good faith bargaining because they had not disclosed the financial information they had characterized as the basis for their bargaining position. But the federal district court rejected the Board's position, stating that the owners had not made a financial claim invoking economic considerations during negotiations.[11]

During the 1985 season there was another, shorter strike, which introduced into the agreement more stringent eligibility requirements for salary arbitration (i.e., three-year rather than two-year eligibility. These new requirements infuriated the 1986 Cy Young award winner, Red Sox fireballer Roger Clemens, who was not eligible and had to accept whatever the Red Sox offered that year. This requirement, in turn, helped spark a lockout during spring training in 1990, when a compromise was reached on the salary-arbitration and free-agency issues. Again the owners gave ground.

As late as June of 1994 there was little talk of a strike, although Murray Chass of the *New York Times* reported that a strike threat for August was materializing Yet, he noted, "in ownership circles, there is talk of gloom and doom but not because of the threat of a strike. The atmosphere is bleak because owners of a sizeable number of teams believe they face financial doom if they don't get the salary cap they covet."[12] He went on to say that while some owners wanted to avoid a stoppage in 1994, others thought that there was "immense cost in deferring it." As in 1981, 1985, and the lockout of 1990, the owners expressed a firm intention to change the status quo by limiting the mechanisms that had allowed players to obtain substantial increases in their salaries. It was clear that the owners' proposal of the salary cap would be the major issue in any negotiations. Some owners, however, believed that players would not strike and so relinquish their very large salaries. But, as Chass quipped, "eight labor negotiations, eight stoppages. Is that batting 1.000 or .000?"

As my diary records, we were keeping a close eye on the situation, even though we could play no adjudicative role until one party or the other brought the matter before us.

July 18, 1994   Steve Rosenthal of the Department of Labor called today to set a Friday meeting to discuss the baseball negotiations. It looks as though the parties are heading toward a strike—perhaps a rather lengthy strike. Rosenthal wants me to suggest a mediator—a job which I would love if only I wasn't supposed to adjudicate.

July 26, 1994   Discussions last Friday with Steve Rosenthal, and Bob Reich yesterday about baseball negotiations and possible (probable) strike. I told both of them that my view was that the objective (Reich asked whether we should be giving this attention) should be to have more deliberate negotiations—and to buy time for this by getting the Players' Association to agree that there is a problem that they can remedy. Differences can exist about the scope of the problem—Seattle, Pittsburgh—and the remedy—scaling back or eliminating salary arbitration or salary cap. The important concession would be for the players to agree that they as well as the owners can do something. The quid pro quo would be for the owners to give up their right to unilaterally institute their own proposal until well into the 1995 season.

Reich asked numerous questions about the industry and relations. He wanted to know whether other teams shared in postseason money, who would be hurt more by a postseason strike. These were easy factual questions.

Reich divided interests—big owners, small owners, star players, marginal players. "What did the players think would happen to the small clubs?" he asked. I told him that I thought that their answer was market-relocation or sale. I told him about the Haas family in Oakland [who], like Charlie Finley before them, had given up on free agents in the small-market Bay Area.

Reich wants to do something, fears looking bad if the strike comes along and the administration is not acting.

Between the Rosenthal and Reich conversations, I talked with Chuck Cohen, who wants the two of us to mediate. I mentioned this to Reich—and told him of the complexities of recusal [in subsequent proceedings before the NLRB]–and our conversation was inconclusive, skeptical, both of us expressing some skepticism [about this idea of Cohen's].

Meanwhile, the countdown continued while the parties met only infrequently. Negotiations languished right up to the eve of the Players' Association deadline. The dynamics between the parties made the players fear that if they did not strike well in advance of the season's end, the owners would unilaterally institute their own position on free agency during the winter months and open the camps without them—relying, if necessary, on temporary replacements. The players thought that threatening the postseason play that brought owners most of their revenues would give them the maximum amount of leverage. For this reason, they viewed as misguided the proposal Secretary Reich made at Fenway Park in Boston during a game; he wanted the parties to continue talking without resorting to warfare.[13] On August 12, while I was en route to speaking engagements in Vancouver, B.C., Seattle, and Spokane, the players struck.

In fact, their strategy misfired. The owners did not back off their positions in time to save the 1994 season and the World Series. The Federal Mediation and Conciliation Service regarded it as a victory when, in early September, they were able to induce the parties to return to the bargaining table, the talks having been in recess since late August.[14] On September 10 the players' union proposed an alternative to the salary caps: a 1.6 percent tax on revenues and a 1.6 percent tax on salaries from the sixteen top teams in each area, the sums collected to be transferred to the ten teams having the lowest revenues. The players also proposed a 75/25 percent split in gate receipts between home and visiting teams. While the American League split was then 80/20, the proposal would have provided much more for visitors in the National League, who frequently received less than 5 percent of the gate. The owners, however, wanted a more substantial package that assessed players more directly than a tax imposed only on high-revenue teams.

Then the unthinkable transpired—the World Series was canceled, the first time that had happened since 1904! After the season's collapse, negotiations continued but with little impetus until December, when the owners sought to change the negotiating environment: on December 22 they unilaterally implemented their salary-cap proposal and eliminated salary arbitration for certain players.

The month before, the owners had agreed to set aside the salary-cap proposal to explore the tax alternatives the union had been putting forward in general terms for the past couple of months. The clubs had then made their own tax proposal, and the union had responded on December 10: its economic proposal included revenue sharing funded by a flat 5.25 percent tax on club payrolls. The owners offered a counterproposal that included several refinements to the union offer: a flat tax of 4.64 percent on a broader definition of taxable revenue, a different basis for determining amounts of contributions paid to recipient clubs, a payroll-tax exemption for recipient clubs, a broader definition of taxable payroll, and an adjustment mechanism to provide additional taxes if needed.

On December 12 the owners offered further modifications, and the union suggested exchanging salary arbitration for free agency. The owners welcomed this idea, and over the next few days there were modifications by both sides and, on December 14, a new union proposal accepting the owners' definition of revenue and a number of other owner proposals. On December 19, the union put forward a more detailed explanation of its December 14 proposal. While there appeared to be no immediate prospect of an agreement, the parties were deeply involved with a sequence of serious proposals and counterproposals.

The next day, at an evening meeting between Don Fehr of the Players' Association and Colorado Rockies' owner Jerry McMorris, the latter stated that the owners still needed a "significant drag" on players' salaries—more than the union was offering. He told the mediator that he did not see any way to reach agreement. Fehr responded that he did not agree with McMorris's assessment.

The next meeting occurred on the fateful day, December 22, the day the owners planned to implement their last offer. For the first time, the union presented a revised proposal that included a marginal tax plan. The negotiations resumed. Five hours later, however, the owners rejected the players' proposal, noting that while it represented a major philosophical shift, a more stringent tax was needed to alter salary patterns. When the players asked for a counterproposal, the owners replied that they saw no reason to believe that a counterproposal within the same framework would significantly lower the brackets or that increasing the tax rates would help. They announced that the negotiations had reached an impasse.

An exchange between Fehr and McMorris reported in the *New York Times* that morning provides some support for the owners' view. Speaking to reporters, Fehr said: "This meeting, although friendly on a personal level and candid, leads to a candid description of our differences which remain. That is what we talked about."

In other words, Fehr let McMorris know the players would not accept a tax that would artificially affect their salaries, and McMorris let Fehr know that the clubs would not agree to any settlement that did not include a tax affecting players' salaries.[15]

The key legal question thus was whether there was a prospect of further negotiations, given the players' apparent interest in them. On the theory that the answer to this question was in the affirmative, the players filed a charge of unfair labor practice with the New York City regional offices of the Board. For if there was a chance for negotiation when the owners proclaimed a deadlock, their unilateral implementation of the salary cap was an unlawful refusal to bargain in good faith. Subsequently, the owners stated that they were changing the method of free-agent negotiations so that it would proceed on a centralized basis, rather than club by club. Again, the issue was whether the system of free-agent compensation could be altered under the circumstances. This point—whether proper procedures had been followed—was the question the Board would consider. We never considered the rights or wrongs of the players' and owners' positions. That was not the issue before us—and under federal labor policy, it is never the issue before the Board. Rather, the question was whether the parties had followed proper procedures.

At this point, two fronts of negotiation began to open. One was the litigation before the Board; the case was investigated by Dan Silverman, the New York City regional director acting as prosecutor on behalf of General Counsel Fred Feinstein. The other front was before Congress and in the president's attempts to resolve the matter, either by revising the antitrust exemption—thus allowing players to sue the owners in federal district court for any restrictions imposed on free agency—or through provision of compulsory arbitration.

In January the White House intervened and, late in the month, set a deadline for settlement or progress, appointing as special mediator W. J. Usery, the former secretary of labor in the Ford administration (who was also involved in the Mine Workers' contempt case). His job was to recommend terms for an agreement. Peter Angelos, the outspoken owner of the Baltimore Orioles—who had earlier warned that he would not participate in the 1995 season if temporary replacements were on the field—voiced optimism that a negotiated settlement and real baseball could ensue.[16] (Angelos objected to replacement players, in part because of the possibility that the Orioles' Cal Ripken would pass Lou Gehrig's consecutive-games record that season, and in part because he thought using them would harm the game's quality and thus the game itself.)

Bob Reich then announced that the administration was "turning up the heat" and setting a February 6 deadline before the government intervened. Stating that, "I want this thing settled," President Clinton summoned Usery to the White House a few days later. According to Chass,

although the two sides did not move closer together on the core economic issue on the second day of their resumed talks, interested Government observers said they hoped the Presidential pressure and fear of the unknown—what Clinton or Congress might do in the absence of a settlement—would hasten a deal by the Monday deadline that the President set last week.[17]

The owners now assured General Counsel Feinstein's office that it was withdrawing its salary cap, and it appeared that mediator Usery might provide recommendations that would take the form of legislation. The next day, however, the newly arrived Republican majority in Congress pulled the rug out from under the White House and refused to support such legislation. As Reich noted in his diary, the unwillingness of the owners to accept arbitration, coupled with Republican reticence, sent the White House into retreat.[18]

The potential for Board intervention thus began to appear more prominently on the horizon. The following day, after a speech in San Francisco, I spoke with Feinstein on the telephone; I emphasized that, given the imminence of spring training, the issues should be presented to the Board expeditiously. On the same day the *New York Times'* Chass wrote that the "Labor Board" had warned of "peril" to the owners.[19] Of course, the Board, which controls labor cases sent to the courts and must specifically authorize any request for injunctive relief, had taken no such action, inasmuch as the matter was still being investigated by Feinstein and had not yet been referred to the Board.

In the wake of the failed negotiations, prospects for settlement became far less promising.[20] Meanwhile, the Players Association began to display dissatisfaction with mediator Usery. This feeling had apparently grown out of the players' suspicion that Usery had expressed displeasure with their position while at the White House. As spring training was about to commence with replacement players, Congress was signaling that it would not only refuse to intervene through arbitration but would also not tamper legislatively with the antitrust exemption provided in *Federal Baseball.*[21]

At this point, therefore, all attention focused on the Board. The players indicated that if the Board sought an injunction reinstating the pre-December 22 conditions while bargaining continued, they would return to the field.

Meanwhile, inside the Board, strange things were happening:

March 9, 1995   Earlier this week, Feinstein did a very curious thing in connection with the baseball unfair labor practice litigation. The charges were filed with him around Christmas Day and were amended in February. Although the case has much visibility—when I was at the Smithsonian last night, someone looked at my tag and said, "Oh, you are from the NLRB—baseball"—Feinstein seems to be deliberately dragging his heels in completing the investigation. There may be considerable justification for this: (1) the case may be a difficult one on both the law and the facts; (2) it may be important not to move too quickly with the charges because of the impact that it might have on negotiations. All of this is understandable. However, during the earlier part of this week, Feinstein proposed to me that we disguise the fact that his role is separate from ours and create the impression in the public that we were speaking with one voice and one decision. There could be two reasons for this: (1) Feinstein recognizes what may be the rather tenuous nature of the case and is looking to us for comfort so as to be less vulnerable himself; (2) he wants to create the impression in the public—something that he seems to have been doing assiduously with the newspapers—that he *is* the Board and speaks for the Board. [The Chass piece supported this view.] My own sense is that (2) is the more likely of the two explanations, given his behavior on a whole host of matters in the past.

I told Feinstein that it was very important for us to keep our functions separate and that the public should be advised of this. When he persisted [in his proposal], I asked him whether he thought that he could fool anyone and, if so, who were we fooling? Feinstein then said—and this is a tactic that he has employed many times—that he wanted to meet with all the Board members to explain his point of view, and I said that I would set this up and consult with them. But when Bill Stewart contacted Stephens and Truesdale, at least Stephens (and perhaps Truesdale as well) indicated that they thought a meeting was inappropriate given the delicate subject matter and the sharp demarcation line between our respective functions. I advised Feinstein of this late on Tuesday, March 7, and he was extremely angry and upset. I told him that he should feel free to lobby the Board members, which he did and was able to arrange through that effort the meeting that he desired.

But the reception given this proposal on the morning of March 8, the Board agenda [meeting], was quite cool, except for the views expressed by Peggy Browning. Later yesterday afternoon, Bill Stewart told me that Feinstein would be coming in to see me, to advise me that he would do it my way, that is, do his job, issue the complaint or not issue the complaint, and be done with it—handing the responsibility over to us. Sure enough, Feinstein came in late in the afternoon and gave me just that position. He said the meeting had been "valuable" for him and that he was not going to attempt to fudge the differences between our respective roles.

March 11, 1995   Another flap with Feinstein yesterday about the respective roles of the general counsel and the Board on the baseball case. He claimed that one of the representatives of the union (it was probably Fehr) … telephoned him and advised him that I had spoken to reporters emphasizing the separate roles of the general counsel and the Board. I denied this although, in retrospect, in seemed to me that what I should have simply said was that he should not be so concerned about disguising our respective roles [as I had done before].

This incident reminds me of the fact that all the principal players [inside the Board] here are *not* friends in any sense of the word. Feinstein has been calculating … from the very beginning. This is to be contrasted with the relationship between McCulloch and Ordman [general counsel under President Kennedy] that existed when I was on the legal staff here in the sixties. They had a good relationship and consulted with one another. Feinstein rarely consulted with me, if at all, and only does so when he has already talked to many others and has a plan to promote his office. Regrettably, Browning is aligned to him and so is Truesdale.

Stephens and Cohen, of course, are completely tied into the Republicans on Capitol Hill and thus cannot be trusted at all. I continue to hear rumors from a number of sources that Kassebaum and Hatch are planning an investigation of me and are looking at my travel records.

I had a number of speaking engagements in the West and was in Los Angeles on March 17 when Feinstein presented his recommendation and requested the Board to issue an injunction against the owners. In response to press inquiries, I stated that the general counsel had submitted the case to us. My speaking to the press about the matter angered members of the Board, especially Browning. I, in turn, was irritated with their response, which played right into Feinstein's attempt to disguise what was actually going on inside the Board.

My next stop was Tempe, where I was giving a series of talks at the Arizona State University Law School. When I accepted the invitation I had hoped to catch a few games of spring training; given the dispute over the use of temporary replacements, I decided that was inadvisable. While I was there the Board held a telephone conference call to discuss the general counsel's application for an injunction. By the time I returned from the West, there were two votes for an injunction (Browning and Truesdale) and two votes against (Stephens and Cohen).

March 23, 1995   A tumultuous day—the previous evening, just as I arrived back from Arizona, Bill Stewart left a message that Bill Usery, the mediator in the baseball dispute, had left a message stating that he would like the Board to delay its decision in the baseball case and that he would like me to call him. I did so between 8 and 8:30 P.M. last night. Usery stated that he had two constructive days with the parties on a "confidential" and "fairly quiet" basis. He said that he was trying to establish a meeting with [Acting Commissioner Bud] Selig and Fehr for Saturday and Sunday and that it might possibly run into Monday. He said that if the parties made an agreement it would be this coming weekend and expressed concern that if we issued an authorization for an injunction that we would run the risk of impeding negotiations and inflaming the relationship between the parties. I asked Usery what the prospects were for a settlement, and he said he could not speak in terms of "odds"—but he stated that this opportunity was better than any other which had existed before. Usery stated that he had talked to fourteen owners that day and said: "We have a group—they have a group" which will meet with the union. He also said that Orza [Gene Orza, the general counsel of the Players' Association] had asked him not to interfere with any of the unfair labor practice aspects of this case.

I then called up Ab Mikva [the president's counsel] to send him an update about Usery's status, given the criticism that the Players' Union had sent his way. Mikva said that he would check and call me back, and he did and said that while Usery is "technically still our mediator"—he also said "nobody thinks he can reach the players. He has lost his influence." I told Truesdale, Browning, and, ultimately, Feinstein of my contact with Mikva. But at the Board meeting this morning, [Stephens and Cohen were there as well], I only related the Usery conversation and said that on balance I would recommend that we follow Usery's view even though I was concerned how much impact it might have in the future. The Board decided to do this without very much debate, and Feinstein echoed my views.

. . .

I had a couple of telephone conversations with Usery in the afternoon because of a leak to the press about his call to me. He was extremely concerned for, as might be anticipated, the Players' Union was most critical of him. He apparently turned around and told Fehr and Orza that I called him and that he had not called me. When I called him back to ask him about this, he said that of course he had called me, but did not deny directly my characterization of his conversation with Orza and Fehr.

I had scheduled a meeting of the Board at 9:00 A.M. on Tuesday. My belief is that now we have to come to a decision at this time—particularly inasmuch as Usery told me this afternoon that O'Connor [Chuck O'Connor, the lawyer for the owners] had been forced out by the militant hardliner Robert Ballow from Nashville, Tennessee, who is very close to Jerry Reinsdorf, the owner of the White Sox and the Bulls. Some of the public will be critical—particularly those who are sympathetic to the association—because it will be said that Usery called me on behalf of the owners. And perhaps he did. But I thought that the owners would simply jump in and say that I disrupted negotiations by conducting a vote today. If they do not reach an agreement over the weekend there would be no choice but to proceed.

Meanwhile, *New York Times* sports columnist Chass reported that no negotiations had been scheduled for the weekend and that the future of the talks did not "appear promising."[22]

Shortly before the weekend when it seemed likely we would be vote on the general counsel's recommendation, a television crew asked us if they could bring television cameras into our agenda room, and do some filming, preferably while Board members were present. Unsure of how this matter should be handled, I did not vote, and a majority eventually rejected the request. Before the vote, however, Cohen told Stewart he could not make up his mind on the camera question until he knew whether, if they didn't have access to the agenda room, they would come to the chairman's office. He said: "I can't vote on this issue until I know what the answer is."

Stewart replied that he had no idea what the television people intended and I didn't either. He gained the very distinct impression that Cohen's overriding concern was ensuring that no attention be given the chairman's role in the dispute. If anyone was to receive such attention, he appeared to reason, it should be the Board as a whole. This almost-puerile obsession and resentment of the press's focus on me as the chairman manifested itself again and again!

March 28, 1995   On Friday afternoon, [the 24th] I went ... to Feinstein and then to the other Board members, recommending that we meet on Sunday or Monday morning and that we try to resolve the matter at this time.... On Saturday, the *New York Times* ran a piece by Murray Chass stating that our meeting would be on Monday, and on Saturday at 11:00 P.M. I received a phone call from the Associated Press asking me whether we were having a meeting Sunday afternoon. I responded in the affirmative and was then bombarded by a series of inquiries from most of the major networks.

At the Sunday afternoon meeting on March 26 we spent half the time talking about publicity and procedure. Truesdale excoriated me for talking to the press, and the Board voted 4 to1 to have no contacts with journalists about the baseball case. I dissented and stated that I would not be bound by the vote; the Board could not tell me what to say, whom to say it to, and when to say it. Browning and Truesdale even objected to revealing the outcome of the vote. Indeed Truesdale began the meeting by saying that the "worst thing that could happen" would be for the vote to be revealed. I took strong exception to this view; I saw no basis for keeping secret any vote on Section 10(j), let alone a vote on the baseball issue. Truesdale ultimately acceded to the desire of Cohen and Stephens to publicize their positions—Cohen was particularly vehement on this matter. Next, they coalesced around another attempt to muzzle me, and again I told them that I would not be bound by any such decision.

March 28 (continued)   On the merits of the case, there was very little discussion. All of us announced our votes. [I voted with Browning and Truesdale to authorize an injunction, although I had hesitated for some period of time because I needed to examine the impasse issue carefully. And I was unsure whether salary arbitration—on which there had clearly not been bargaining to impasse—was a mandatory subject of bargaining.] Only Stephens discussed the merits in a long rather boring and pedestrian, as well as meandering, discussion of the cases. It was meandering in the sense that it would wander off into policy and his interests—whether it was feigned or not I do not know—in some of my writings in the area of professional sports and labor law. But much of what he quoted me for related to policy recommendations and proposed changes in labor and antitrust law. Stephens said that he was willing to be convinced to vote for authorization, but I sensed that he really wasn't and didn't engage him in any discussion. . . . [The vote was 3 to 2; the three Democrats in favor of an injunction and the two Republicans against it.]

[On March 27 I was quoted by Chass in the *New York Times* to this effect: "I, along with the other two members, believe that the case is a strong one under the applicable legal standards . . . that is why we voted to authorize."] Yesterday morning Truesdale walked into the office and loudly attacked me for issuing my statement to the *New York Times* and called me a "piece of work." [He acted as though I had not dissented from the Board's position on communicating with the press and had not explicitly stated that I would do so.] As I said to the *Daily Labor Report* today, I have not been the victim of such verbal abuse in my entire thirty-four years of professional experience. We had a shouting match as he walked out of the office, which upset both Mary Ann and Eileen. It was a traumatic and wrenching day.

. . .

Had lunch today with Ab Mikva . . . in the White House mess and had a very interesting discussion with him about the recent flak here over the baseball case and Section 10(j) in particular. I told him that when I issued the statement [a week ago Friday], stating that the general counsel had submitted the case to us, this became a matter of criticism by the Board members. I told him of Feinstein's reluctance to even publicize the fact that he was recommending an injunction and his attempt to confuse the public about who was doing what inside the Board. He [Feinstein had] kept stating that he wanted the "agency" to be the party that was identified in the public mind and did not want it known that the Board was discharging its responsibility under Section 10(j) subsequent to his recommendations to us.

Mikva was absolutely amazed by this, noting his recollection that Section 10(j) explicitly gives authorization to the Board and not the general counsel to proceed in federal district court. I pointed out to him that a majority of the Board seemed to be playing into this and deferring to the general counsel in this regard. This was the major reason why other Board members had been critical of me on March 17 when I was in Los Angeles and responding to the press inquiries about the submission of the matter to us.

One interesting point arose when I said that an outgrowth of my commentary in the *New York Times* on March 27 (the commentary that triggered Truesdale's attack on me— I simply had said that the baseball request for an injunction was a "strong case") was Cohen's separate opinion setting forth his reasons.

Mikva stated that he thought it would be a good idea if in high-visibility or important cases, like the baseball case, the Board members did provide their reasoning as part of their official duties. I said that I agreed with this, though in the bulk of cases it is simply impossible to do so as a practical matter. He reiterated the view that he was only speaking about the high-visibility or important cases and that the judges would find the Board's reasoning useful. I pointed out to him that a basic problem that I had throughout this process was that Truesdale and Browning were of the view that we simply defer to, or rubber stamp, the general counsel's view—and that it was essentially the general counsel's responsibility. I told him that I have had such difficulty with the Board members on all other aspects of this case that the idea of circulating opinions, as valuable as it was in theory, was simply an impossible burden with this Board and their views about the general counsel's functions.

I had called Mikva yesterday to advise him that Truesdale was about to publish critical comments about me—I thought at that time that other Board members were joining him [they did not]—and had asked for him to see if Truesdale could be taken to the "woodshed." But he told me today—as did Steve Rosenthal and Richard Socarides of the Department of Labor—that they thought this was inadvisable because of the potential for being charged with political meddling in the Board processes. This probably was the sound decision, although, in the midst of all this yesterday with a day-long advisory panel meeting going on, I did not think so at the time.

April 3, 1995 Last Wednesday I had lunch with Benedict Wolf in the midst our advisory panel meetings.... The week was an emotional roller-coaster due to the tension involved in the baseball dispute and the unprecedented attack made upon me by Truesdale. But Wolf, the former executive secretary of the National Labor Board and the National Labor Relations Board, our predecessor under an executive order [promulgated by President Roosevelt] as well as the Board itself until 1937, said that he had lost interest in the statute subsequent to the Taft-Hartley amendments—until I was appointed chairman. That gave me a real lift.[23]

After the Board authorized the injunction, Dan Silverman and the lawyer for the Players' Association, George Cohen, went before Judge Sonya Sotomayor of the federal district court in New York City to request the injunction. Her opinion exceeded our expectations. On the theory that impasse had not been reached in the bargaining process, she required that the parties come back to court prior to implementing any new set of working conditions.

April 3 (continued)   On Friday, March 31, Judge Sonia Sotomayor issued a decree upholding our position in the baseball case, and the union subsequently offered to return to work. On Sunday the owners decided not to lock out, and the baseball season is now scheduled to begin on April 26. And the Board's role was constructive and positive, and I believe that we enhanced both the collective-bargaining process and, even more important, the resumption of the baseball season itself. Even if the owners win in an appeal to the Court of Appeals for the Second Circuit, they are still looking down the barrel of unfair labor practice liability as the case comes back to us later this year or next for consideration of the refusal-to-bargain charges.

The opinion Judge Sotomayor issued prior to Opening Day 1995 was as notable for its understanding of the game as for its grasp of the law:

Issuing the injunction before opening day is important to insure that the symbolic value of that day is not tainted by an unfair labor practice and the NLRB's inability to take effective steps against its perpetuation....

The often leisurely game of baseball is filled with many small moments which can catch a fan's breath. There is, for example, that wonderful second when you see an outfielder back pedaling and jumping up to the wall and time stops for an instant as he jumps up and you finally figure out whether it is a home run, a double, or a single off the wall, or an out.

As I noted in my diary, Judge Sotomayor's order induced the players to return to the field; and the owners, notwithstanding their earlier murmurings about a lockout, accepted them because of the potential liability for large sums in back pay. The owners had planned to use temporary replacements, as they had throughout spring training, calculating that seeing the new season open with replacements would break the players' resolve and dissipate their solidarity. Their forecasts about players' resolve had proved erroneous in every single dispute from 1972 on. Yet, I was later told, they were bitter about the Board's intervention because they thought it had deprived them of their chance to defeat the players! (At the party at Shea Stadium to commemorate the fiftieth anniversary of Jackie Robinson's arrival in the big leagues, Players' Association General Counsel Gene Orza suggested that I be invited to the owners' party. He was met with a resounding "No!")

In September 1995, while Sparky Anderson's Detroit Tigers were in Baltimore to play the Orioles, the Court of Appeals for the Second Circuit—after an embarrassingly one-sided oral argument in which the owners' position was ridiculed by the court—affirmed Judge Sotomayor in an opinion written by conservative jurist Judge Ralph Winter:

We are unpersuaded that an injunction compelling the PRC and the Clubs to observe the anti-collusion and free agency provisions of the Basic Agreement infringes on their right as a multi-employer group to bargain through an exclusive representative. Free agency and the ban on collusion are one part of a complex method—agreed upon by collective bargaining—by which each major league player's salary is determined under the Basic Agreement. They are analogous to the use of seniority, hours of work, merit increases, or piece work to determine salaries in an industrial context.

... Given the short careers of professional athletes and the deterioration of physical abilities through aging, the irreparable harm requirement has been met. The unilateral elimination of free agency and salary arbitration followed by just three days a promise to restore the status quo. The PRC [was] ... embarking on a course of action based on a fallacious view of the duty to bargain. We see no reason to relieve it of the consequences of that course.

We therefore affirm.[24]

Meanwhile, in the wake of the injunction, the 1995 season ran its course. Finally, late in 1996, after completion of the next season, the parties negotiated a comprehensive collective bargaining agreement that resolved many of their outstanding differences. The Board's injunction had created the environment necessary to negotiation of a contract—exactly what an order curing a refusal to bargain is supposed to do! This was one of those instances in which the Board was able to do good, to achieve the important goal of restoring the nation's pastime, and, simultaneously, to act in accordance with the parameters of the National Labor Relations Act in a way the public could clearly understand. The case was truly a primer in American labor law.

The daily reality of my work, however, consisted of lots of hard slogging. In baseball, as the commentators noted, it took a rare Sunday afternoon meeting to bring about a resolution. My difficult dealings with the general counsel, other Board members, the parties to the dispute, and the mediator took place behind the scenes. But, like the rest of my four-and-a-half-year tenure, they helped me accomplish a job worth doing.

In April, not long after opening day, our work was applauded at a Hofstra Law School conference commemorating Babe Ruth's hundredth birthday. New York City labor arbitrator Dean Eric Schmertz introduced me as the head of the agency that had brought about the resumption of baseball. Earlier in the evening I had met Phil Rizzuto, the Yankees' shortstop when I was growing up in New Jersey. When he heard Schmertz's introduction he exclaimed to me excitedly, "You didn't tell me that! You didn't tell me that!"

Later that spring, Baltimore Orioles' owner Peter Angelos invited me to throw out the ceremonial first pitch at Camden Yards when the Boston Red Sox came to town to play the Orioles. The *Baltimore Sun* commented that the owners "despised" me more than they did Angelos, who had opposed them on temporary replacements. But the *Boston Globe* also had this to say:

A cloud of smoke from Boog Powell's tasty barbecue stand hovered over right field in front of the brick warehouse. Last Aug. 11, the last time these two teams played here, the smoke was black and ominous, signaling the end of baseball because of a work stoppage.

Last night it was like a breath of fresh air ... baseball was alive and well, at least here, where these teams ended their seasons prematurely last year....

There was a touch of irony to Bill Gould, chairman of the National Labor Relations Board, whose decisions against the owners got the game back on the field, throwing out the first ball.

[Pitcher Roger] Clemens did the most effective throwing after that.[25]

That fall I again sat in Angelos's box—this time with President Clinton—to watch Cal Ripken break Lou Gehrig's streak for consecutive games played. The Orioles owner, who had opposed the owners' position in part because it would have ended Ripken's string of games short of the record, began the conversation by saying to the president, "This is the guy that we have to thank for the 1995 season!" That was one of the moments that made me think the three-thousand-mile trek across the continent had been very worthwhile.

At other times, however, I felt melancholy that the divisiveness and distrust inside the Board—the logical corollary of the infighting that had taken place the previous year—had spilled over into the baseball case. Whether the issue was rule making, postal ballots, administrative law judge reforms, or my attempts to streamline the Board to produce cases more efficiently and effectively, I sensed that the Republican members of the Board responded, initially, to the polarization so evident in my difficult confirmation hearing. Further emboldened by the results of the midterm elections, they had even carried this attitude over into the baseball case.

Curiously enough, the congressional Republicans who had openly voiced opposition to President Clinton's desire to intervene in the dispute through some form of arbitration remained silent about the Board's handling of it. (The House minority leader, Richard Gephardt, had also opposed compulsory arbitration.) They were not so quiescent about the wide variety of issues with more direct policy implications that arose from 1995 onward. In fact, I have always assumed that some concerted effort was made to get the Republicans to pressure us—but that it was uncharacteristically unsuccessful!

7

The Idea of Independence: The Headless Fourth Branch

When my sons arrived in San Francisco for the reception following my swearing in on March 8, 1994, they asked me a very direct and fundamental question. Who, they wanted to know, was my boss? It was a tough question. I was the chairman of an "independent" regulatory agency. Yet no one in this world, I told them, is independent in the absolute sense of the word, and no one anywhere—least of all in a modern democracy—can claim to have no boss.

My response to my sons, and in public speeches thereafter, was "The law is my boss." That answer points to the quasi-judicial nature of the administrative agencies and the fact that, like federal judges with life tenure, the charge of a NLRB member is to interpret the law. (The chairman of the agency has the additional charge to act as its administrative head.)

The framework for NLRB independence is well established, thanks to the failure of FDR's secretary of labor, Frances Perkins, who sought unsuccessfully to bring the Board into the Department of Labor. The project of placing the NLRB under the Labor Department umbrella was also vigorously promoted by William Green, president of the American Federation of Labor in the 1930s. Green and other labor leaders urged President Roosevelt to take this position because the department was a friend of labor. According to Robert Cushman, Green believed that having "a labor relations board outside the Department of Labor would detract from the prestige and usefulness of the department itself."[1]

In her congressional testimony Secretary Perkins made the case for putting the Board under the Department of Labor. Such a framework would, she argued, (1) avoid creating yet another new independent government agency; (2) give the Board greater prestige; (3) provide for a more effective integration of labor activities; (4) avoid wasteful duplication of services; (5) prevent the Board from interfering in the department's conciliation work, which it might do if left on its own; (6) give the secretary of labor the power to make Board staff appointments, thus bringing its work into harmony with that of the executive branch; (7) free the Board from having to argue its case before congressional committees (because the department would speak for it in Congress); (8) avoid possible public confusion about overlapping jurisdictions; (9) give the Board a direct line to the president through the secretary of labor; and (10) replicate an arrangement that had worked well in New York with its state board.

Fortunately, the arguments of the minority report filed by New York Congressman Vito Marcantonio won the day. He contended, first, that only complete independence and the public prestige that accompanies independence would ensure the Board's complete impartiality. Being inside the Department of Labor—and subject to the department's control of budgets and personnel—would necessarily undermine its independence and quasi-judicial status. Moreover, independent status would make it easier to obtain the services of the most able and impartial people. Second, the NLRB must not only be impartial, it must also have the appearance of impartiality. Inside the department it would inevitably be regarded as a "friend of labor." Third, most of the previously established quasi-judicial agencies were independent of any executive department. The NLRB too needed to control all stages of its cases. It also needed to keep its quasi-judicial work "sharply separate," especially from the tasks of conciliation and mediation carried out by the Department of Labor. Finally, the minority report noted, the Board was being created as an agent of Congress, not of the president.

Independence won the day. The National Labor Relations Act's Senate sponsor, Robert Wagner (D-N.Y.)was able to convince the Senate Labor Committee to support the idea of a board outside the Department of Labor, and Representative Marcantonio persuaded his House colleagues to back that position. Even so, the Board's perfect independence, though frequently extolled, has always been an elusive reality.

There are a number of practical reasons for this ambiguity. The president has the constitutional authority to appoint Board members. Nonetheless, the Supreme Court, in *Humphrey* v. *Executor,* held that if Congress established an administrative agency (in that case the Federal Trade Commission) with the intention of making it independent, impartial, and free from the political process, the president could not remove its officials prior to the expiration of their terms.[2] This 1935 decision had prompted the writers of the Senate Labor Committee's report on the NLRB legislation to remove the language in the statute referring to the Board as an "independent agency in the Executive Department." The framers of the report apparently perceived an inconsistency between independence as contemplated by *Humphrey* and making the Board a part of the executive branch.

In the wake of the *Humphrey* decision, the National Labor Relations bill was therefore revised to provide that a member of the Board could not be removed by the president except for neglect of duty or malfeasance of office—and then only after notice and public hearings. The rationale for this independence is the desirability of the rule of law and due process and the view that the expertise the Board is presumed to possess is best exercised outside the immediate political passions of the day—whether they emanate from the executive or the legislative branches. Even the judiciary is supposed to defer to the Board's expertise and fact-finding, although some circuit courts—the District of Columbia, the Fourth and Eighth circuits come to mind most immediately—seem to do so very infrequently.

The justifications for independence cited by legal scholars are numerous. Back in the 1930s, James Landis recognized that regulatory policies are more permanent, consistent, and professional when they are not "too closely identified with particular presidential administrations."[3] William Cary, however, points out that although a basic purpose of independence

is to free commissions from the insidious influences of politics.... there are effects which are extremely serious. Cut loose from presidential leadership and protection, the agencies must formulate policy in a political vacuum. Into this vacuum may move the regulated interests themselves, and by infiltration overcome the weak regulatory defenses to become the strongest influences upon the regulators.[4]

Who, then, *is* the boss of the chairman of the National Labor Relations Board? In fact, in addition to his exclusive authority to appoint Board members, the president chooses—without the advice and consent of the Senate—the chairman from the Board's member complement. We cannot therefore equate the absence of traditional executive branch status with control by Congress. The fact is that the president, without any cause or notice of public hearing, may demote the chairman to ordinary Board member. Clearly, then, we have to assume with Peter Strauss that the chairman will administer the agency and conduct himself (or herself) in a manner compatible with the general policies of the administration: "Presidential influence over the independent agencies is heightened by the special ties existing between the president and the chairmen of almost all the independent regulatory commissions. Although all commissioners, including the chairmen, are appointed to fixed terms as commissioners, the chairman generally holds that special post at the President's pleasure."[5]

Cary, President Kennedy's chairman of the Securities and Exchange Commission records that he had virtually no contact with the president. Nor did I ever see President Clinton officially. My only visits to the White House were for social functions and ceremonies. Of course, the NLRB is a very small agency, indeed infinitesimal by the standards of the U. S. government. Yet, like Cary, I like to think that, in part, "the failure to see the President can be treated not as criticism but as almost as a compliment. As one of his assistants said: 'You would have heard from us if there was anything wrong.' The President had no time for, and indeed in the normal course should devote no time to, our problems unless there was 'trouble.'"[6]

Never once did I hear directly or indirectly from the White House about any matter or policy relating to adjudication or rule making. My impression is that this policy has been the rule and not the exception over the years. During the Eisenhower administration, Chairman Guy Farmer stated, "there was no presidential attempt to devise plans, discuss policy, exchange views, or play on team loyalties. He was strictly on his own."[7] After all, it was during the Eisenhower presidency that Special Assistant Sherman Adams (frequently thought of as the de facto president) had to resign because of his interference with an independent regulatory agency on behalf of Bernard Goldfine. Yet the similar Clinton administration policy promoting agency independence and noninterference astounded the Republicans in Congress who possessed oversight or appropriations responsibility. Perhaps, as suggested below, that was because the Bush administration had acted in an entirely different manner!

The independence the Board enjoys in its adjudicatory capacities is furthered by the National Labor Relations Act itself, that is, the statute's open-ended ambiguity. The act, for example, prohibits the "interference, restraint or coercion" of employees' rights to organize and engage in concerted activity. What does this language mean for union attempts to solicit and recruit workers on company property? What forms of union free speech on company property are immunized by virtue of this language? Decades of litigation have emerged to consider these and numerous other issues.[8]

By virtue of this broad and ambiguous language, Congress gave the Board wide scope, almost a tabula rasa, to make a whole host of policy decisions. Subsequently, a series of Supreme Court decisions explicitly acknowledged the Board's policy-making role.[9] Even the Taft-Hartley amendments and their prohibitions of secondary boycott have proven elusive in general; if applied literally they would eliminate virtually all forms of primary strikes, let alone secondary activity. Again, the way the amendments were written opened up opportunities for wide-sweeping policy judgments.

The opaque words *good faith,* relating to the duty to bargain fairly, are another instance of the wide berth provided for policy judgments. These words also mean, of course, that the attention of Congress and others with a political interest will inevitably be focused on the Board. At the same time, these words strengthen the independence of the agency because they necessarily invite members to exercise the kind of expertise that only an administrative agency concentrating all its energy on a relatively narrow field of specialty can possess.

I was comfortable accepting President Clinton's nomination because I saw my views as an impartial arbitrator as compatible, in a general sense, with those of the president. As an arbitrator acceptable to both sides, I was and am a centrist in the labor-management world, committed to a "third way" approach that precludes identification with either side of the bargaining table. Because I am also committed to the basic principles embodied in the National Labor Relations Act itself, my philosophy identifies me as a liberal Democrat. Not surprisingly, this brought me into considerable conflict with the Republicans during my stay in Washington.

Besides the scope of the chairman's responsibilities and the process by which he or she is appointed, there are other factors that give politics a role in the operation of an administrative agency, particularly the National Labor Relations Board. The most obvious manifestation of this influence is the short duration of NLRB appointments: five years. As a result, the Board is exposed—not only to the politics governing the initial appointment and confirmation process, which inevitably generate policy discussions—but also to political pressures from Congress and the president each time a member comes up for reappointment.

The nexus between law and politics becomes especially vivid when Board members have to decide cases involving competing, and sometimes explosive, tensions among unions, management, and employees or—as sometimes happens—when they refuse to hear cases that might prove too controversial (and would draw on the Board the fire of political friends or enemies). I became all too familiar with that problem during my chairmanship. Early in my term, I was told that one member of the Board up for reappointment was openly advertising to parties whose cases were before the agency how he would vote on such cases. His conduct represented one extreme on the politicization continuum. Fortunately, he was not reappointed.

This sort of behavior—and more subtle reappointment campaigns members waged while I was in Washington and before I arrived there—led me to advocate a reform that would diminish both politics and the appearance of politics in Board decision making. First, Board members should be limited to one term. Second, so that the public can gain from the incumbent's experience, that one term should be longer—perhaps seven or eight years, as on the Federal Reserve Board. All in all, I think the best approach for the NLRB would be that set forth by Cary:

Perhaps this problem of personal independence can best be summarized in the response to a question addressed to Newton Minow [President Kennedy's chair of the Federal Communications Commission] in 1961: "Just what makes you think you are qualified to be Chairman of the FCC?"

[Minow replied] "Two things, first, I am not looking for a job in the communications business, and, second, I don't want to be reappointed."[10]

For the "communications business" we can substitute "a labor law and labor relations practice." Even though President Clinton's new ethical rules forbid formers member from appearing before their former agency for five years (under Bush it was one year), it is all to easy to circumvent the rule by providing counsel behind the scenes and subtly letting the agency or one of its regional directors know who in the law firm is really calling the shots. And, indeed, many former Board members are very much in the labor law "business." Those who cannot obtain reappointment—and most desperately want to be reappointed—carry on in Washington, D.C. They cannot go home again because they have no home other than Washington!

Of course, the temporary nature of appointments makes it potentially possible for the president to influence Board policy through them. As soon as I was confirmed in 1994, the president had a Democratic majority at the Board; in 1961 President Kennedy, only two months after his inauguration, achieved the same result. A number of other considerations also link law to politics. First, the president controls budget requests, and I, like my predecessors, was prohibited from making representations to Congress that were at variance with White House proposals. We made our case before the Office of Management and Budget (OMB) and never before Congress.

Fortunately, during my tenure the OMB was always sympathetic to our innovations and thought highly of our accomplishments. Moreover, because the Republican Congress sometimes attempted to devise policy through so-called appropriations riders, I frequently had to discuss with OMB people policy matters that the Republicans themselves had raised.[11] I was continually asked, for example, How important was rule making to the Board? Could this be used as a chip to be bargained away for other parts of our appropriations request to Congress? My response was invariably "yes"—and it *was* used as a chip. From my perspective, money or appropriations were the sine qua non of effectiveness.

Second, we discussed with the OMB several politically sensitive issues relating to the organization of the Board itself. I had urged the Board and the general counsel (who has direct responsibility for regional office personnel) to inform Congress that—in order to promote a more efficient operation and stave off budget cuts—we were willing to consolidate and merge some regional and subregional offices. I thought this would show good faith on our part and would safeguard our interests, particularly if we stressed that the measure would result in no loss of personnel. For reasons that were never completely clear to me, General Counsel Feinstein resisted this idea vigorously, and it was not until 1998 that I was able to get a majority of the Board to support my view. Then, just as the general counsel partially relented, the White House intervened and became involved in the drafting of the language to be sent to Congress. Again, this discussion occurred as part of the appropriations process. (Ironically, in November of 1999 the new Board did reorganize and credited Feinstein for his last-minute conversion to this cause!)

Third, though the president does not control directly agency personnel, I was responsive to White House interest in placing some qualified people with us. (At the same time, I selected my own personal staff without consulting the White House). The White House was particularly important to the allocation of super grades, both in determining the number of these people we would get and in addressing internal disputes about what positions in the agency they should occupy.[12]

Another personnel issue that brought me into contact with the White House was the problem of keeping the Board at full complement. I had frequent discussions about this with Bob Nash (director of personnel and confidante of the president from Arkansas days) and, in 1997, on a more limited basis, with John Podesta. In 1996 Nash was again trying desperately to convince first Senator Kassebaum and, later, Senator Trent Lott to propose acceptable Republicans for a new "batch" of Board nominees. Kassebaum left the Senate without responding; Lott, who succeeded Senator Dole as Majority Leader and effectively supplanted Jeffords as chair of the Labor and Resources Committee, cut a deal with Senator Kennedy at the eleventh hour in the fall of 1997.

Involvement by the White House in these areas is inevitable and blurs the line between the executive and the so-called headless fourth branch (i.e., the regulatory agencies). But, it seems to me, our predecessors in the Bush administration went too far in that direction. While, so far as I am aware, they did not interject themselves directly into case adjudication, they did attempt to influence rule making. C. Boyden Gray, counsel to the Presidential Task Force on Regulatory Relief in the Reagan administration and later counsel to President Bush, described how the task force dealt with complaints about regulatory agencies in 1981:

We told the lawyers representing the individual companies and the trade associations involved to come back to us if they had a problem. They said they did, and we made a couple of phone calls and straightened it out, alerted the top people at the agency that there was a little hanky-panky going on down at the bottom of the agency, and it was cleared up rapidly. So, the system does work if you use it as sort of an appeal. You can act as a double check on the agency that you might encounter problems with.[13]

An illustration of this philosophy at work at the National Labor Relations Board occurred in 1991–1992 over the issue of *Communications Workers v. Beck*.[14] In this decision the Court held in 1988 that union dues from so called "limited members" or nonunion employees could not be used for political purposes not germane to collective bargaining if such workers objected. For more than a decade since that decision, this has been a high-visibility, politically sensitive problem, particularly for Republicans responsive to the National Right to Work Committee and its desire to eliminate the unions as a national political force. During the Bush years the *Beck* issue developed into a source of political intrigue inside the Board. This enmeshing of politics and law produced a result precisely the opposite of what I (at least prior to my Washington experience) and other commentators would have expected. Whereas during my term friction over *Beck* rule making arose between the Board and the House Republicans, for Chairman James Stephens it was tension between the Board and the executive branch that contributed to turmoil and inaction inside the Board.

In October 1991 Stephens heard that White House Counsel Gray was airing his opinion that there were problems at the Board and that it was not enforcing the *Beck* decision.[15] At the time, in fact, the Board was purportedly considering rule making on the issue and even had a proposed rule in the works.[16] Stephens, who believed General Counsel Jerry Hunter was not "biting the bullet" on the issue, telephoned Gray and asked for a meeting on *Beck*. Stephens was concerned that some White House people evidently assumed that the chairman could direct the general counsel to prosecute a complaint, even though, of course, the general counsel is completely independent of the Board in this respect.

In the October 25 meeting Stephens provided the White House staff with an update on the *Beck* cases that were pending and advised them of his interest in rule making. A draft memo of the *Beck* rule was circulated in February 1992, and

Stephens took the proposed notice on the rule making to Gray and others in the White House. Gray advised Stephens that they wanted to see the actual draft proposal of the rule and to provide input to it. It is unclear whether Stephens complied with this request.

On May 21, 1992, Stephens told Gray that public comments on the proposed rule had been made. Sometime during the same month, the Bush director of personnel told Stephens that "the president expects you to support him and to be a team player." Gray then asked to see the proposed rule. Stephens, (who had been appointed to the Board by President Reagan and made chairman by President Bush) replied that "that would be fine if the White House wanted a 'heads up.'" At this point he was convinced that there was a move afoot by Bush-appointed Board member John Raudabaugh to replace him as chairman. (As noted previously, the president could remove him as chairman, even though he could not remove him from the Board). Raudabaugh, for his part, stated that he had not sought the chairmanship, although in June 1992 the White House had asked him to consider taking it after the elections.

The matter was complicated by the fact that the Board had cases on *Beck* issues pending while it was considering rule making. Stephens was concerned that his discussions with the White House about substantive *Beck* issues might not be perceived as appropriate under these circumstances. A memo from Solicitor General John Higgins assured him that they were.

When a subsequent meeting was held, Stephens said, he was "scared to death" that Gray would say "you can kiss the chairmanship good-bye." The White House subsequently communicated with Stephens through Greg Walden, who worked for Gray and was, in Stephens's view, a "mouthpiece" for the National Right to Work Committee.

On September 3, 1992, a memo was sent to Board Executive Secretary John Truesdale indicating that the White House was preparing comments on the proposed rule for the Board and did not want to make those comments public. The White House also wanted to see any revisions the Board made after the White House proposals were received. It was clear that the White House was hopeful of integrating their executive order (which provided for posting notices on *Beck* rights in every plant in the country) with anything done by the Board—and that, indeed, it was intent on controlling the Board's actions.

On September 4, Truesdale and Higgins sent Board members a memo about Gray's comments on the proposed *Beck* rule:

The covering memo is concerned ... [about] three major issues, ... unit by unit, expenses for organizing and for litigation outside the bargaining unit and applicability of the rule to pending cases. The Board does not attempt to resolve each issue with a proposal but instead requests the public to respond to specific questions. Mr. Gray's memo does not itself advocate any specific position on any of these issues. Indeed, it suggests that the Board could present alternative proposals on these points. Mr. Gray's concerns about the failure to address these issues is expressed in the second paragraph of his memo.

"We are concerned that by failing to put forth a specific proposal or alternative proposals on these issues, the Board may be foreclosed ... from proceeding expeditiously to a final rule on such issues in response to public comments. As a result, resolution of these issues will be postponed indefinitely[,] frustrating the President's public commitment announced in the Rose Garden in April that henceforth the Executive Branch would implement the *Beck* decision promptly and vigorously."

Apparently, Higgins and Truesdale did not send Board members the full text of Gray's comments. They did, however, quote Gray's final paragraph:

Our more specific comments are provided in the attachment. We strongly urge the Board to consider our comments as expeditiously as possible. We also request that the Board allow us the opportunity to review the revised proposed rule and preamble before the document is sent to the Federal Register.

Ultimately, the majority of the Board, with Devaney dissenting, voted not to review or consider the Gray memo. Stephens said that he already knew that the Bush White House "did not believe in the independence of independent agencies."

The approach of the Clinton White House was quite different. At the time, for example, when I was pushing for contempt sanctions against unions (described in chapter 3) that were important to the Democratic party coalition and the White House, I received no communication or pressure of any kind. Indeed, when I, while discussing other matters with White House official Joe Velasquez, mentioned that the contempt sanction against the United Mine Workers had caused a stir both at the Board and in labor union circles, Velasquez responded: "We have strict instructions not to discuss anything about unions affected by your actions or the Board's." The same hands-off policy was followed in reference to Board actions against business interests. It was also reflected in Ab Mikva's refusal to take Truesdale "to the woodshed" as I requested during the 1995 baseball case. Though such a White House action would not in that case have related directly to the substance of a case before the Board, even the appearance of White House intervention in the dispute would have been unseemly and would have suggested inappropriate executive interference. In retrospect, buffeted though I was by the winds of high visibility in this important case, I erred in making the request and Mikva was correct in rejecting it.

In my view, intervention of either the executive or the legislature into the substance of particular cases is exactly where politics is inappropriate and where the idea of the rule of law is eroded. I thought that Stephens should not have taken the initiative to communicate with the White House, particularly when he thought his job was on the line in those discussions! The confluence of law, the executive branch, and Stephens's desire to remain chairman were at odds with proper independence for the Board.

The Hundred and Fourth and Hundred and Fifth congresses controlled by the Republicans, however, had no such compunctions. The involvement of certain senators and House members in case processing and decision making during this period constituted an interference with decision making comparable to the earlier interference of the Bush White House. I often thought that the many problems we had with the Republican Congress were attributable not simply to their opposition to the National Labor Relations Act itself but to a general view of administrative agencies that, like that of the Bush administration, simply did not include independence.

A February 24, 1998, letter to me from the House Appropriations Subcommittee Republicans is a classic illustration of inappropriate congressional interference with the rule of law and the substitution of politics for law. Among other things, the Republicans requested that I communicate in writing to the regional directors about the proper criteria for determining the appropriate representation units when unions were seeking single-facility units and employers were seeking multiple facilities—the very same issue on which I had attempted to initiate rule making at the beginning of my term. The letter made it clear that the Republicans were not satisfied with having stopped rule making in its tracks through appropriations riders (see note 11) and the fact that a majority of the Board, over my dissent, had voted to withdraw the rule altogether. Now, without any amendment to the NLRA, the House Republicans were presuming to instruct me to tell regional directors how to resolve the single facility unit cases.[17]

The question, of course, is always how and under what circumstances the political process can be allowed to affect an independent agency. On the issue of interference, what I said in my March 18, 1998, response to the House Republicans' letter about their inappropriate political interference with adjudication applies to both the executive and legislative branches. I wrote that their letter requesting that

I communicate with the regional directors about appropriate criteria for representation cases caused me "grave concern":

Never before has the Board been instructed or requested to advise Regional Directors how to proceed in a substantive area of Board law. Never before has Congress attempted to intrude upon the adjudicatory responsibilities of the Board with respect to classes or pending cases, and I fear that the tendency reflected in your letter, if left unchecked, will erode the system of independent adjudication and democracy in the workplace, which has been a valuable and important aspect of national labor policy.

I then quoted Chief Justice Rehnquist and the concerns he had expressed in a recent American University speech on impeachment and intimidation of the judiciary. With regard to the Board, I said that

attempts by Congress to interfere with the Board's resolution of pending cases, or cases that are likely to come before the Agency for resolution, compromise the Board's independence. This independence is a prerequisite for the confidence which the Board must enjoy if the statute is to be interpreted impartially and in a manner compatible with the purposes of the Act by those entrusted with such responsibilities by the President and the Senate.

Yet, in the case of interventions that fall short of the kind of interference engaged in by the House Republicans of the Hundred and Fifth Congress, or of interference in particular cases, lines become more difficult to draw. For example, with regard to the executive branch, former SEC Chair Cary asks whether

the expression of an attitude on the part of the President giving the heads of regulatory agencies a direction by which to sail [should] be regarded as improper or subject to Congressional criticism? My own view is that it is not improper, although by rationalizing I convinced myself that every action we were proposing to take would not "rock the boat," as [Kennedy] might construe it. I do believe that regulatory agencies are very much a part of the Federal government and affect our economy and American business so importantly that they should be subject to a general framework of national policy, which the President should feel free to express without Congressional opposition. If I had been told directly to "slow down," I might have resigned in protest, yet I believe the President should set the general tone which we follow during his administration.[18]

The complexity of the relationship is made clear by a number of other considerations. For instance, during my tenure an article in the *Wall Street Journal* asserted that the NLRB worked in concert with the White House or with Secretary of Labor Alexis Herman in regard to *Beck*: "The Labor Secretary's office traditionally advises the NLRB."[19] Like so much that this paper wrote about the Clinton Board editorially, this was a complete fiction.

In a letter to the editor, I pointed out that the Board was created as an independent federal agency and that the idea of a relationship with the Department of

Labor advocated by FDR's Secretary of Labor Frances Perkins had long ago been rejected. "The Secretary of Labor has no legal authority," I said, "to 'advise' the board on how to carry out its responsibilities, and during my term of office no such advice has ever been provided by anyone in the Executive branch let alone the Department of Labor."[20]

At the time, I did have some contacts with Secretary of Labor Herman that involved *Beck*. But they consisted simply of notifying her of our decisions. As I recorded in my diary,

September 27, 1997 ... [Secretary of Labor] Herman asked me whether the *Beck* decisions might be forthcoming soon, and I said that I did not know; but I asked her if there was some problem in connection with timing. She said, following the line of noninterference which I think has been such a hallmark of the Clinton administration, that there was no problem in timing but that she simply wanted to be on notice when the cases came out. I assured her ... that I would give them notice. This is what I did during the remainder of my term and this was the extent of the contact.

When Robert Reich was secretary of labor during Clinton's first term, he held periodic meetings of the heads of all labor relations or labor law agencies. During those meetings, he would ask us to report on our work, and we would talk about budget matters. I usually described the Board's recent decisions and the issues that were then pending. The same practice was followed by other heads of agencies. But we never discussed policy or the reasoning supporting our policies. We did, however, discuss the timing of the release of decisions during the first budget crisis of 1995–1996 and the government shutdown that ensued. (This is undoubtedly what later prompted me to query Secretary Herman about timing.)

January 17, 1996 Yesterday the Board met and we discussed, amongst other things, the question of what we should do with the cases that have accumulated since the shutdown commenced....

Browning, in accordance with the view previously expressed by the AFL-CIO General Counsel Jonathan Hiatt, was of the view yesterday that we should hold up the issuance of *California Saw & Knife* and *Weyerhaeuser*, the two lead *Beck* cases, the theory being that this would only inflame some of the more right-wing House Republicans.[21] I expressed the view—and it was concurred in by Chuck Cohen—that we should move ahead and get to the matter as quickly as possible and stated that any attempt to delay would simply give the National Right to Work Committee an ability to harp on their propaganda theme, that is, that we are holding up the issuance of these decisions in order to allow the unions to place their dues in President Clinton's reelection coffers. I stated that I thought an attempt to delay simply plays into that basic propaganda theme, which has been without any truth or merit whatsoever. Cohen and I prevailed on Browning to support the view that these *Beck* cases, along with another very controversial one involving remedies for illegal aliens as employees under the meaning of the Act [conditional reinstatement and back pay], the *A.P.R.A.* case, should get out as quickly as possible.[22]

This morning I had breakfast with Secretary of Labor Bob Reich, along with other heads of labor relations agencies. I mentioned these cases and Reich said to me: "If you were to allow an ex parte comment, I hope that you don't issue these decisions before the Congress makes a budget decision." I reiterated some of my concerns expressed previously to Browning and Cohen, and he said that he understood. However, he said that perhaps, by virtue of the sequence of issuance, that is, if the more controversial ones are put to the bottom of the pile, at least we could make a decision about issuance with more knowledge about what kind of decision the Congress is going to make and when it is going to make it. I told Reich that I was concerned about the possibility of leaks to the extent that I feared any kind of interference with the sequence of issuance might create a new round of criticism from the House. He said that he understood my position and we parted ways, as he was about to go off for some other briefing or program.

I then reflected anew on this entire matter and spoke with Chuck Cohen. From this meeting, Cohen and I agreed—sometimes at my initiative and sometimes at his—that we would do the following: (1) issue the hospital cases involving the supervisory status of registered nurses immediately, giving them absolute priority; (2) place *A.P.R.A.* at the bottom of the pile [because of its extraordinary political sensitivity, involving undocumented workers] ... ; (3) have editorial and the executive secretary advise us when the opinion is ready to go and attempt to put it out on a Friday [so as to make news only on Saturday when very few people are reading the newspapers or watching news programs on television], and at any event, evaluate the situation vis-à-vis the stage of congressional deliberation on the budget at the time that the decision comes up for editorial. My view is that it was not problematic to delay the illegal-alien issue because there is no organized constituency which has yet focused upon this matter [that was yet to come]—in contrast to the union dues issue and therefore whatever leaks occur would not create a political problem for us. All I want to do is simply place *A.P.R.A.* at the bottom of the seventy-five cases that are now pending so that Congress does not focus upon them at the wrong time. But on the union dues *Beck* issue, it seems important for us to evaluate the situation precisely at the time that editorial tells us that they have signed off and the cases are in the executive secretary's office. Moreover, it seems to me to be a good idea to issue it on a Friday if at all possible.

In essence, although Reich had put no pressure on me to do anything whatsoever, it seemed to me and the Board that the advice he provided was good. The period of the government shutdown was a particularly desirable time—in spite of our short-handedness—to issue decisions, because there was so much news about the shutdown itself. (Only Board members and sometimes chief counsel and some editorial people worked.) Getting decisions out on Friday also kept attention away from us, further diminishing the potential for budgetary retaliation.

Republican members of Congress scrutinized the Board's contacts with the executive branch and often questioned me about them. Representatives like Roger Wicker of Mississippi, perhaps aware of Bush White House policies toward administrative agencies, reacted with disbelief when I testified that I did not discuss decisions such as the *Beck* cases with the White House. The following exchange took place during the appropriations hearings on March 19, 1997:

Mr. Wicker: Chairman Gould, on February 18, Vice President Gore announced a series of new proposals at the AFL-CIO convention. One of these proposals deals with Federal contractors and their having a satisfactory record in adhering to labor laws. Because the NLRB would have an active role in ensuring that companies [that] receive Federal contracts adhere to these proposed regulations, I was wondering if you could expand on the details of the Administration's plans?

Mr. Gould: I cannot expand on the details of the Administration's plans, Congressman, because I have not been supplied any information from the Vice President's office with regard to what the actual content of his proposals will be and how they will be implemented. . . .

Mr. Wicker: Okay. I'm very glad to hear that, as a matter of fact. And I just wondered if you agree with me that it would be inappropriate entirely for any employee of your agency to work with the Vice President or with the Administration in promulgating these types of regulations, since you will be called upon to be more or less a neutral mediator should they be placed into effect.

Mr. Gould: Well, I'm called upon to be a neutral adjudicator involving the questions that arise under the statute and the interpretation of the statute and the policies of the statute. I would not want to give you an undertaking that I would not communicate with the Executive Branch about a proposed Executive Order any more than I would give you an undertaking that I would not communicate with the Congress about proposed legislation or proposed Executive Order.

The one thing that I will not communicate about with other parties, be they the Executive, Legislative, or Judicial Branch, or private parties, is cases and facts and evidence and arguments relating to law that comes before this agency or that might come before this agency, issues that involve adjudication. In this respect, again, there never has been one bit of communication between the Executive Branch and my agency, my office, about any matter which has come before us, is before us, or is likely to come before us, and there never will be. But beyond that, I would not want to give you any understanding, Congressman.

Mr. Wicker: All right. So if the Administration were to ask you for assistance in these new proposals that the Vice President announced, what would be your position about working with the Administration and assisting them in finalizing such proposals?

Mr. Gould: I frankly don't know at this point, Congressman. No one from the Administration has extended such an invitation to me. I think it's premature on my part to speculate about what my response would be. I think it might well depend upon a variety of factors. I would want to make a judgment if and when that situation arose.

Mr. Wicker: But you're certainly not ruling it out at this time?

Mr. Gould: I'm not ruling it out at this time. I said I would not give you an undertaking that I would not engage in such a communication.[23]

Indeed, the inevitable contact with the White House people on appropriations, representations to Congress, and the NLRB appointment process meant that— except for pending cases and the formulation of Board policy—the line between appropriate and inappropriate contact or discussion was inherently vague. Reich's advice about the timing of case issuance highlights the problem and shows that suggestions about matters unrelated to the actual substantive merits of particular cases were sometimes offered by members of the executive branch. Another such suggestion came up that day in March of 1995 that I had lunch with the president's counsel, Abner Mikva, and talked about the baseball injunction. I also mentioned to him the problems of separate opinions. Some Board members (as discussed in chapter 4) were reluctant to be publicly identified with their opinions. As I recorded in my diary (March 28, 1995), Mikva

thought that it would be a good idea if in high-visibility or important cases, like the baseball case, the Board members did provide their reasoning as part of their official duties. I said that I agreed with this, though in the bulk of cases it is simply impossible to do so as a practical matter. He reiterated the view that he was only speaking about the high-visibility or important cases and that judges would find the Board's reasoning useful. I noted my impression that Browning and John Truesdale, then serving on a recess appointment, were of the view that they should simply defer to, or rubber stamp, the general counsel's view [involving Section 10(j) cases relating to injunctions].

Again, the advice was good, and I was later able to use it in issuing a separate opinion in the Section 10(j) context in the *Detroit Newspapers* decision.[24]

As noted above, there were numerous contacts with the White House about budgetary matters and appointments. The former would generally involve me in discussions with OMB and, after Mikva's departure, with Harold Ickes and Leon Panetta. On appointments I worked principally with Bob Nash, director of personnel, whom I came to regard as my best friend in the executive branch during the last couple of years of my tenure.

My general relationship with the AFL-CIO is more thoroughly treated in another chapter. But, because the federation was part of the Democratic party coalition and threw itself extensively into the 1996 presidential and congressional campaigns, I was sometimes concerned about the pressure that they might bring to bear on the White House, and thus on me. But no threats were ever made, and if the White House was responding to such pressure, I never learned of it.

The closest the AFL-CIO ever came to applying pressure took place in early 1998, and in fact the incident might have had some relationship to the White House's position on Feinstein's renomination efforts that year.

March 5, 1998   A number of things happened over the past few days that highlight the political headlights in which we find ourselves. On Friday, February 27, we received a call from Senator Specter's office saying that he wanted a political meeting between myself, Richard Trumka, secretary-treasurer of the AFL-CIO [from Pennsylvania and particularly close to Specter], and George Becker of the United Steelworkers. I still don't know what this was about, and I have the sense that I will never know because I believe the meeting will not be held.

On Tuesday, March 3, I received a telephone call from John Sweeney, which may well have been in response to this proposed meeting. Sweeney's call was to urge me to be supportive of Fred Feinstein's [re]nomination to be General Counsel. Sweeney advised me that organized labor was supportive of Feinstein and that he would like me to be as well. I told Sweeney that I viewed this as the president's prerogative and, therefore, had not spoken on the matter and did not plan to do so. Moreover, I said, if I did speak out it would harm him [Feinstein]. Sweeney said that he understood all this, but he felt that I might be "called upon" to offer an opinion and he wanted me to be supportive. [I did not offer a response to this.] In retrospect it may be that he saw the meeting coming with Specter, given that Trumka was a part of it, and wanted me to come to Feinstein's defense in that meeting, sensing that Specter would want Feinstein's nomination to be withdrawn.

In any event, this afternoon Feinstein ... told me that he was withdrawing his name for nomination because he was advised that he didn't have the votes.

Curiously enough, one area of substantive contact and debate with the Clinton administration arose twice: in 1996, with a case then before the Supreme Court, and in 1998, in connection with a *Beck* case also being heard by the Court. Both times the result deprived the Court of the Board's expert view on vital areas of the law that might have led to different decisions. In the *Beck* case—*Marquez* v. *Screen Actors Guild*,[25] which the Court decided unanimously against the interests of *Beck* dissidents—a majority of the Board had taken a position supporting expanding *Beck* rights for individual dissidents. In that case, however, we were frustrated by Solicitor General of the United States Seth Waxman—whom G. Calvin Mackenzie has characterized as "an administration insider in a job traditionally reserved for a prominent law professor."[26] The heart of our problem was a 1994 decision, *Federal Election Commission* v. *National Rifle Association Political Victory Fund,* in which Chief Justice Rehnquist, writing for the majority, held that the FEC lacked authority independent of the solicitor general to present a petition for certiorari, even in actions brought under the very statute the FEC was created to administer.[27] (The Court grants review of a case to be considered on its merits by granting such a petition.)

Waxman, speaking of the FEC decision to the Supreme Court Historical Society, remarked that "given the modern inclination to create Executive Branch agencies that are 'independent' of the president, it is wise to remember the very substantial benefits in retaining approval authority centralized in the Solicitor General—so that when the United States speaks, it is with a voice that has considered, and reflects, the interests of the whole United States."[28]

In fairness, it must be said that the first difficulties over this subject between the NLRB and the Solicitor General's Office arose prior to Waxman's time in office. In both cases, however, though the contact and discussions undertaken were necessary and institutionally appropriate, the Board's independence was compromised— because the Court was deprived of the Board's expertise.

The first case, *Brown* v. *Pro Football*, was argued before the Court in March of 1996 and involved the conflict between antitrust law and labor law.[29] A union brought an antitrust action against the football owners, complaining that individual members of a team's taxi or development squad were not free to negotiate their own salaries. (These players are retained by the club as substitutes for regular players missing through injury or other causes.) The owners had unilaterally imposed salaries on all such team members employed in the National Football League.

In my view the lower court opinion—which contended that labor law completely trumps antitrust law in professional football once the parties have bargained to an impasse—was erroneous, It failed to take into account the unique characteristics of professional sports, in which player mobility has traditionally been constrained through the reserve clause draft systems and other mechanisms. Moreover, I was convinced that a blanket denial of antitrust protection in such cases would diminish owners' incentive to bargain and, thus, erode the basic purposes of the National Labor Relations Act itself. In all sports except baseball, unions have been able to bring owners to the negotiating table through antitrust litigation complaining of league restrictions on a player's ability to move from club to club. Another concern I had—and it had already been manifested in football on a couple of occasions— was that if the only way players could obtain the benefits of antitrust protection through lawsuits filed against the owners was to eliminate collective bargaining altogether (rather than by bargaining to impasse or beyond), they would simply go through the motions of a sham decertification and remove the union from the scene so as to sue the owners for antitrust in restraint of trade. Again, this poor solution had in fact already been resorted to in football on two occasions.[30]

There was a great deal of pulling back and forth inside the Board on this issue, in part because the case presented a complete reversal of the classic roles of labor and management and so was alien to the thinking of most labor lawyers. The traditional argument was that the labor exemption from antitrust law should be interpreted broadly; otherwise antitrust laws could be used to break up unions and eliminate collective bargaining, which actions are inherently anticompetitive. But in none of the classic antitrust labor cases had the argument been made that the presence of antitrust liability would promote rather than impede better working conditions by encouraging collective bargaining. And, indeed, the cases heard before this time had not presented a situation in which labor mobility was restricted.

The Board had been told by Feinstein's office that the solicitor general wanted to know whether it could represent to the Supreme Court at the March 27 oral argument that the Board subscribed to the position taken by the government in the case. On March 25, I sent a letter to Lawrence G. Wallace, the deputy solicitor general who would argue the *Brown* case.

> Please be advised that a majority of the Board subscribes to [the view set forth in the Government brief] ... that the court of appeals' expansive formulation of the labor exemption is wrong as a matter of law, and may do serious harm to the nation's antitrust and labor policies if not reversed. The Board majority would also note, however, that this dispute arises in the context of a labor market which traditionally has imposed constraints upon employee mobility and where unions are attempting to enhance not eliminate or diminish, competition. In the Board majority's view, therefore, the issues presented here should be viewed as peculiar to labor management relationships in the sports and entertainment industries and any holding in this case should be limited in its applicability to labor management relationships possessing the special characteristics described.

I received no response to this letter. As events unfolded, it became clear that the Solicitor General's Office did not like the views it expressed.

April 6, 1996 Easter Eve: On March 25, the Board became concerned about the fact that our view was not properly presented by the Justice Department to the Supreme Court, and I wrote a letter to Larry Wallace of the Solicitor General's Office. I had dinner with Paul Weiler [of Harvard Law School and on the legal team of the NFL Players' Association] on Monday night and told him of the letter. Weiler and I were both concerned about the fact that the Justice Department had written an antitrust brief that did not take labor law into account. Weiler asked me to attend a briefing session for the oral argument to be held on March 27 at the Kirkland, Ellis law firm on March 26 [they were representing the Players Association, Kenneth Starr of Whitewater fame [having been assigned the responsibility to argue the case before the Supreme Court]. After many attempts to get there, I was not able to attend—but Weiler told me that evening that Wallace had not indicated that he had received the letter. As I left my condominium here on the morning of March 27 at about 7:55 A.M., I received a call from Weiler and he asked me to give him a copy of the letter. I told him that I had one copy and that I would meet him at his hotel, the Hay Adams, and eventually we bumped into each other one block north of the Hay Adams and I gave him a copy. During the oral argument—Bill Stewart and I sat in Justice Ginsburg's special box— no reference was made to our letter, although about four of the justices constantly asked all the parties why the NLRB had not presented a view of what the NLRB's view was.

In an article that appeared shortly thereafter in the *Legal Times of Washington* I was quoted about the oral argument:[31]

"I was worried about the antitrust cast of the brief, and the solicitor general's willingness to apply antitrust law to labor-management situations beyond sports and maybe entertainment," says Gould.

The limited input from the board in the government's brief clearly caught the attention of the Court, which would normally want to know the NLRB's views on labor law issues such as the definition of an impasse and issues relating to revival of negotiations and the union decertification process.

"Why is the NLRB not included?" asked Justice Sandra Day O'Connor as soon as Wallace got up to argue. Wallace said that the NLRB does not usually speak on antitrust matters and besides, the Board was undergoing "a transition in membership" at the time the brief was being drafted. Wallace also said discussions had taken place at the staff level with the board in preparing the brief.

But the justices, who clearly viewed this as a labor case as well as an antitrust dispute, didn't buy Wallace's explanation. Justice Antonin Scalia wryly observed that it would be "rather surprising" if the AFL-CIO didn't file a brief simply because it had a vacancy on its board.

Justice Ruth Ginsburg also lamented the lack of NLRB input. "I thought we'd be enlightened by the board on when an impasse occurs and when it is over," she said. Later, after Wallace sat down, Justice Stephen Breyer said, "I want to know what the labor board thinks."

Gould sat in the audience stewing about what he viewed as the board's imposed silence in the case, but not surprised. He said he had been alerted in the hours previous to argument that Wallace had no plans to tell the Court about the board's views.

The day before the argument, Gould had sent Wallace a letter elaborating on the board's views, and the morning of the argument, he had handed a copy of the note to a lawyer on Starr's team. After the argument, Gould held a press conference in front of the Court—also a step that was severely frowned upon by the solicitor general's office, which never talks about pending cases—in which he lamented that "our views were not made sufficiently clear to the Court."

Gould also said in a later interview that it was "absolutely false" for Wallace to tell the Court that the board's transition was even partly responsible for the board's absence from the brief. In fact, for a time in January, before the recess appointment of Sarah Fox, the board's membership was down to three, instead of the five it is mandated to have. But Gould insists, "her designation did not figure in any way on the discussions in the case."

Wallace declines comment.

Gould also says Starr "confronted" Wallace after the argument about his failure to tell the Court more about the board's views.

According to the *Legal Times,* Starr sought to have Lawrence submit our letter to the Court but was unsuccessful. As the result, on March 28, Starr sent a letter to the Court in which he submitted my letter, in light of the Court's "strong interest in the views of the Board." Although Starr also suggested that the Court invite the solicitor general to file a submission setting forth the views of the Board, the Court took no action. The Board's views were not considered, and on June 20 the Court's 8 to 1 opinion in *Brown* held that federal labor law shielded the football owners from antitrust action.

Only Justice Stevens's dissenting opinion took account of the fundamental difference between collective bargaining in professional sports and other industries. Justice Breyer, writing for the majority, noted that the Court's holding was not intended to "insulate from antitrust review every joint position of terms by employers, subsequent to impasse or deadlock in the parties' negotiations." Antitrust law might still apply where it would not, said Breyer, "significantly interfere" with the bargaining process. He noted that

We need not decide in this case, whether, or where, within these extreme outer boundaries to draw that line. Nor would it be appropriate for us to do so without the detailed view of the Board, to whose "specialized judgment" Congress "intended to leave" many of the "inevitable questions concerning multi-employer bargaining bound to arise in the future."[32]

Thus, the fiasco—the solicitor general's refusal to make our views known to the Court and the inability of Starr to get the Court to consider our letter or to let the Board file a brief—left the Board, the expert independent agency, without a way to communicate its views to the Court. Rather than attempt to file the letter after oral argument—a practice frowned upon by all courts—Starr should have emphasized the Board's views during his presentation to the Court and was truly negligent in his failure to do so.

The issue emerged again near the end of my tenure on a matter far more directly related to politics and the law: the obligations of unions under *Beck* to notify dissident employees of their rights. My own approach to the *Beck* issues was complicated by the fact that I had always accepted the view of Justice Felix Frankfurter that the line demarcating unions' political and economic activities was highly arbitrary.[33] But that view, part of my policy perspective, had long since lost the day at the Court. Therefore, the position I took in relation to *Beck* as chairman fell within the parameters of Supreme Court precedent applicable to the National Labor Relations Act. *Marquez* v. *Screen Actors Guild*, the case that brought us into contact with the Solicitor General's Office once more, arose in November 1997, just after the Board had attained full strength with the confirmation of four new members.[34] It was decided by the Court of Appeals for the Ninth Circuit in San Francisco and involved the terms of a union security agreement requiring membership as a condition of employment. The question was whether the agreement must spell out (1) the Supreme Court's definition of *membership*—the payment of periodic dues and initiation fees after being on the job for thirty days—which was not a definition of *full membership*; and (2) the fact that dissidents can invoke *Beck* rights only if they do not assume the obligations of full membership. The differences in membership obligation is crucial, not only because the *Beck* protection of dissidents is not available to full union members, but also because the Supreme Court held more than thirty years ago that workers who are full members and assume membership obligations beyond the payment of dues subject themselves to union discipline.

In other words, under *Beck*, union security agreements that require membership as a condition of employment may be enforceable only to a limited extent: employees are free to pay a prorated portion of union dues for support of collective bargaining only and not pay the portion used for political and organizing expenses, which must be refunded. Moreover, employees are free under the *Pattern Makers* decision (the subject of my colloquy with Senator Hatch during my confirmation hearing) to resign from the union, removing themselves from union discipline and, at the same time, gaining the opportunity to object to political spending they could not reject if they were full members. In *California Saw & Knife* we had held that the union must advise both members and nonmembers of these terms. What was at issue in *Marquez* was whether this obligation to notify must be articulated in the union-security provisions of the collective-bargaining agreement or whether the agreement could convey a different message that fails to define membership.

Over the years I had frequently expressed my own view to labor law students at Stanford Law School. It is that, as nonlawyers and workers (and even some lawyers) do not understand the legal differences between full membership and limited membership (which requires only paying dues and initiation fees) and their implications, unions should be required to inform workers of the law. I believe that the duty to provide fair representation itself imposes such an obligation, and I voted this way in our internal Board deliberations and articulated this position in two opinions.[35] (I have also consistently upheld the view that unions are similarly obligated to inform members about other prohibited labor practices not directly implicated in the unions' duty to provide fair representation.[36])

Sarah Fox, who was Ted Kennedy's aide before coming to the Board in January 1996, was so concerned about my position on this issue that she telephoned me at home to discuss it. My opinions also upset a number of union lawyers, particularly

John Hiatt, general counsel of the AFL-CIO. At a function held at federation head-quarters to welcome new Board members shortly after my first written opinion on this subject appeared in 1997, he challenged me. The opinion, he believed, would tie up negotiations and burden them with excessively detailed language on *Beck*. I told him that my interest was simply in spelling out the meaning of membership so that employees would know about their obligations under federal labor law and understand what consequences flowed from the difficult choices they had to make. Hiatt argued that the effect on labor would be bad—and he made a motion with his finger across his throat, indicating that labor's throat was being slit!

In early 1998, after the new Republicans, J. Robert Brame III and Peter Hurtgen, were confirmed as part of the deal negotiated among the White House, Senator Kennedy, and Senator Lott, Brame said he was willing to agree with me in find-ing for the dissidents but not with my rationale. He stated that any collective-bargaining agreement that mentioned membership was invalid because, in his view, no form of "membership" could ever cause a worker to assume obligations as a condition of employment. For some reason, Hurtgen refused to express himself on the issue until August 27, the last day of my term.[37] Throughout 1998 it became clear to me that, whatever Hurtgens' view, it was impossible to bridge the divide between myself and Brame as it related to our respective rationales. It seemed to me that Brame was driven on this and other subjects by a kind of ideological fervor that, in this instance, precluded any mention of membership in the union security clause—even though the NLRA itself specifically mentions that membership, as defined, can be compelled as a condition of employment. I thought that his view badly diluted the legitimate power of unions, which is inappropriate under a fed-eral labor policy intended to foster collective bargaining. I expended some energy, unsuccessfully, in attempting to align Hurtgen with my position or find some inter-mediate common ground. In the meantime, in a pattern that was to recur again and again in 1997 and in 1998, it became clear that issuance of a Board position on *Marquez* was unlikely or, in all probability, impossible.

This made the dialogue with the solicitor general critical—and—as in *Brown* v. *Pro Football*—the stage was set for maneuvering.

April 15, 1998   Yesterday, we had a very active discussion involving *Marquez* v. *Screen Actors Guild*, 119 S. Ct. 292 (1998). In my absence on Monday—I was still returning from Boston to Washington by train—Fox and, [Wilma] Liebman [a Democrat, the other November 1997 appointee] had convened a meeting with the general counsel and his Supreme Court people. As I sensed when I learned of this meeting ... the purpose ... was carefully choreographed so as to attempt to divide myself from Brame in formulating a majority position in this arena and thus to avoid having the Board file a brief. Board silence on this union security issue, that is, the lawfulness of a clause that does not define "membership" or "membership in good standing," would be what the AFL-CIO wanted—and it is quite clear that Feinstein, Fox, and Liebman all wanted it as well.

Earlier, Fox and Liebman had tried the ploy of having accelerated briefing in another case ... but in this meeting—after I had left—they admitted that there was no way that the Board could render a decision prior to the time of oral argument by the Supreme Court or certainly during my term prior to my departure this summer. Thus, they revealed what they were really after, that is, Board silence.

Feinstein began by saying that he thought that the Board had never filed a brief ... [where] it had not issued a decision on the issue presented. [This was an error—the Board had filed a brief in *Beck* itself!] Therefore, he indicated that he was against the filing of a brief. [No majority at this point had formulated a position in a written decision holding that the terms "membership" or "membership in good standing" were unlawful under the Act]. Both he and Nort Come [deputy associate general counsel for Supreme Court litigation] were particularly anxious to draw me out into a big discussion of a number of issues about what kind of curative language would be appropriate [to put in the place of the offending language]. Of course, I think that membership must simply be defined in terms of periodic dues and initiation fees, as the Supreme Court has already done in *NLRB* v. *General Motors*, 373 U.S. 734 (1963), *Allis-Chalmers*, and *Beck* itself.[38] [But I knew that there would be] disagreement with Brame on this, and I said that it was not necessary to address the issue. Come jumped in and said, "How can you avoid discussing the issues which are presented in *Buzenius* v. *NLRB*, 124 F.3d 788 (6th Cir. 1997) [another union security case in which the Court of Appeals for the Sixth Circuit in Cincinnati had held that it was dissatisfied with our failure to condemn the term "membership" as unlawful]." I said, "Very simple. We simply address the question of whether 'membership' or 'membership in good standing' alone is unlawful [when articulated in a union security provision of a collective-bargaining agreement]. That is all we are required to do."

They were obviously frustrated with this and kept trying to paw the ground and to find new ways of exploiting differences [among the majority, which appeared to consist of myself and the two Republicans].

Hurtgen, largely through the active involvement of Harold Datz, seemed to buy into the notion of going further than simply the rationale I had set forth at one point. After the meeting, Fox and Liebman immediately indicated that they would join him in going further, even though they did not want to express a view at all and even though their view [on the substantive language in the collective-bargaining agreement itself] was completely antithetical to mine, Hurtgen's, and Brame's. [The idea was that the more ambitious the remedy, the more likely it was that Brame and I could be divided and that it could be said that there was no majority view. If Fox and Liebman could draw us into this approach, then they could draw us apart and succeed in doing nothing.] Hurtgen saw through the deceit and manipulation involved in this technique and said that he would stand with Brame and myself.

As I was discussing the matter with Datz [after the Board meeting, in Hurtgen's office down the hallway] ... Fox appeared at the door to inquire what position Hurtgen had taken. Datz advised her, and she said, "Oh, that's probably for the better. It's not good for us to have shifting majorities" [on the need for curative language beyond what I advocated and the substantive language itself] and then walked away. Datz and I looked at each other smiling and [a senior career official present at the time] … said, "She will do anything to achieve her political objective." And that is what it is, that is, an attempt to obtain a political objective. The last gasp of the Fox–Liebman initiative was the most startling and, in some respects, desperate of all.

May 4, 1998   Today we met with Seth Waxman, the solicitor general, to discuss the *Marquez* decision. As all of us anticipated, the fix was in. Lawrence Wallace [had] recommended that the solicitor general not file a brief representing the Board's position because (1) the Board had not rendered an adjudicated decision in which the majority supported the view that the Ninth Circuit was wrong and the membership must be defined in terms of dues and initiation fees; and (2) most arrogantly, their view that the Board precedent directly contrary to Supreme Court law for the past thirty-five years was correctly decided! [For some strange reason, the Board in the 1950s had held that the phrase "membership in good standing" was lawful]. Hurtgen participated, as did Feinstein, Linda Sher [deputy general counsel], and Nort Come. But Hurtgen, who was supposed to be on my side, provided very little help and seemed to be reconsidering his position out loud in light of Waxman's intellectually vigorous position.

Waxman was of the view that *Marquez* was somehow a different issue than the issues we had been confronted with in cases like *Buzenius*—that is to say, his view was that *Marquez* was a duty-of-fair-representation case and that our cases were not. I pointed out to him, both in our meeting and in a subsequent telephone conversation, that this was not the case. All of these cases were duty-of-fair-representation cases, although ironically, I am of the view that they should not be duty-of-fair-representation cases [or at least not be decided under that legal standard], a position that I expressed in footnotes in *California Saw & Knife* and in *Buzenius* (or *Weyerhaeuser* as it was styled at the Board level.[39]) I pointed out to both Waxman and Wallace that the Board had presented a brief in *Beck*, although it had not adjudicated the issue in *Beck*.

The most frustrating aspect of this was not simply the fact that we could not get our point across to the Court—they [the Court] will undoubtedly complain, just as they did in *Brown v. Pro Football*, 518 U.S. 231 (1996)—and that the majority of us recognized that our position is the only one that is essentially compatible with *General Motors* and its progeny, but also that the realpolitik of the situation is that this is the only time that the majority will support the view that unions have an affirmative obligation to define membership more broadly during the Clinton administration. No one will be appointed to take my place at the Board who does not subscribe to the AFL-CIO position on this issue. They will make sure of this because, of course, they have a complete veto over any Democratic party nominee to the Board. At one point, when we were alluding to the change in composition of the Board, I said that a frustrating element was that I would no longer be on the Board in a couple of months. Waxman and Wallace made light of this; and they, undoubtedly, have predicated their position, as legally defensible as it may be, upon that view. When there is an adjudicated case, it will comport with the age-old Board decisions that have held that "membership" or "membership in good standing" [in the collective agreement] is compatible with federal labor law, notwithstanding *General Motors*. This was a frustrating morning. Indeed, I became silent after thirty or forty minutes—I should have become so much earlier, and Waxman, indicating an interest in going on with the meeting said, "You probably want to leave right now." This was one of the few accurate comments that he made during the session.

Waxman also seemed to think that my view was the view expressed by Harry Edwards [a liberal judge appointed by President Carter to the Court of Appeals for the District of Columbia] in the [earlier] *Paramax*[40] decision, and [because Edwards is also black] I should have made ... the comment that "you have me confused with other colored folks who are rendering decisions," but I bit my tongue and did not do so even though Bill Stewart, when he heard about it this evening, said that would really have broken the ice in our favor. In any event, I didn't say it and so it is too late.

May 12, 1998   Today we were advised, that notwithstanding the fact that the Board has rejected the solicitor general's position in the *Marquez* case pending before the Supreme Court, the solicitor general is giving consideration to filing its brief setting forth its views anyway—even though the Board itself rejects them! They apparently believe that they are sufficiently expert that they can ignore the agency that Congress has chosen to act as the expert in this field! The arrogance of these people is absolutely overwhelming. First, they reject our views. Second, they propose their views, which we in turn reject. Then, third, they turn around and propose that their views go forward even without our consent. The only way that I can counter this is through a speech next week in Hartford, where I plan to review some of the major Board decisions in 1998. We will talk about *Group Health* and *Monson Trucking*, where I said clearly that union security agreements must spell out membership in terms of the obligation to pay dues and initiation fees and no more!

Ultimately the proposal I anticipated was in fact made to us, that is, that we support the filing of a brief taking a position antithetical to the one I advocated. The solicitor general suggested that he send the Court a brief putting forward his view that an undefined "membership" clause in the union security agreement was not a violation of the NLRA and that we consent to this. It was almost as though we had had no discussion with him!

On June 18, I wrote to Waxman, stating that while the duty-of-fair-representation issue involved in *Marquez*—that is, Was the negotiation of a clause merely requiring membership consistent with the union's obligation to represent employees fairly?—might be distinct from time to time from the question of the legality of the underlying clause, Supreme Court authority for the past thirty-five years had dictated the position that a majority of the Board had taken on the duty of fair representation. Moreover, I said, "your most recent draft says that the union did not violate its duty of fair representation by negotiating a union security clause requiring 'membership.' A majority of the Board disputes that your view is the correct legal position under the circumstances of this case. I urge you to reconsider your decision in light of our position, which follows."

I pointed out to Waxman that this was similar to a situation in which a union prohibited from writing a racially or sexually discriminatory clause into the collective-bargaining agreement attempts to defend its position on the grounds that it did not violate its duty of fair representation because the latter standard gives the union more latitude. I concluded by urging him again to reconsider his filing of the proposed brief.

On June 30 Waxman responded in a letter to Feinstein and copied to me. He stated that he continued to believe that his position was the correct one but had decided not to file a brief because of a "disagreement" within the government on proper resolution of the case. Meanwhile, Hurtgen and Brame had written to him, not only agreeing with my position but also stating that their disagreement "should not become a matter of public debate." To this, Waxman replied that his office had "long maintained both the practice and the position that government officials should not comment publicly on pending Supreme Court cases."

In my June 30 reply to Waxman I said that although I had no further plans to speak out on the subject, I had already mentioned the issue in a speech in Hartford the previous month and thought that it was entirely proper to do so.

I am of the view that I, as Chairman of the National Labor Relations Board—and a Chairman who has commented and written extensively on labor law issues for most of my professional career—properly should comment on matters pending before the Supreme Court. I would have thought that it is desirable for the Court to have the benefit of both the Board's view as well as those of its Chairman on a matter of such critical importance to the development of national labor law and policy. And I would think that the expression of such views is in the interest of the United States government.

I received no reply from Waxman. Quite obviously he thought the Supreme Court ought not to hear the views of the Board's expert agency. And it did not.

In the fall, the Court held unanimously—with Justices Kennedy and Thomas concurring separately but expressing some mild misgivings—that failure to negotiate a clause spelling out the meaning of membership as defined by the Supreme Court was not a violation of the duty of fair representation. The Court did not know what the Board's view was and did not know it because, just as it had in *Brown*, the path to the Court lay through the Solicitor General's Office.

Clearly, it would have been infinitely preferable to have issued a Board decision on *Marquez* in time for the Court to consider it. But aside from the difficulty of forging a majority view with Brame, the problem I confronted throughout 1997 and 1998 was getting the decision issued at all. Fox and Liebman made it clear that their accelerated-briefing idea would not provide a chance to issue a decision by the time of the Court's oral argument and certainly would not allow us to issue one prior to my departure in the summer of 1998. Brame, in fact, had detailed views he still had not articulated in written form more than a year after my departure!

Perhaps the result would have been the same even if the Board had expressed its views. We will never know. Yet it seems a pity, and inconsistent with the rule of law and the idea that the Board possesses special expertise on this subject, to deprive the Court of the Board's views.

This case was the high-water mark of executive interference—and, it must be said, it was relatively mild interference by the standards of the Bush administration. In *Marquez*, politics and the law were in tension because the case fell under the rubric of the Court's *Beck* decision. Critics of the administration, had they been fully informed about the controversy at the time, would have been perplexed (or, more likely, uninterested, inasmuch as it did not fit their preconceptions) to know that the issue transcended the ideological differences between myself and the Republicans on the Board who supported my position.

Because I agree with Cary that the president must articulate the "general tone" of his administration, I would have felt compelled to resign if I had found myself seriously at variance with it. Though I assumed that my view on the *Marquez* issue conflicted with that of the White House, I did not know. No one in the executive branch except the solicitor general communicated with me about the subject. I believed that my votes on adjudicated cases, policy initiatives, and speeches were in accord with the general philosophy of the Clinton administration. (Specifically, I thought that my statements on the permanent replacement of strikers, employee participation, and other, earlier questions related to *Beck* (described in chapter 9) fit in with the White House's general policy or "tone.")

Congress, on the other hand, expresses its policy views principally through legislation—ideally reform legislation adopted after hearings in which interested witnesses provide informed perspectives—but also in the form of appropriations riders, action (or inaction) on appointments, and comments made during oversight hearings. The issue of NLRB "independence" as it arose in the Hundred and Fourth and the Hundred and Fifth congresses is closely related to the policies the Board adopted, especially those described in chapters 4 and 5. During my term in office the Republican majority expressed continuous hostility to both the National Labor Relations Act and our initiatives. The issues I address in the next chapter can only be thoroughly understood in that highly politicized context.

8

The Coming Storm

It was a lovely spring day in 1995. As I came bounding out of my seat in the Capitol subway I ran straight into Senator Richard Shelby of Alabama. He was a Democrat when the vote on my confirmation came forward, and, like all other Democrats, he had voted to confirm me. In the wake of the 1994 Gingrich revolt, however, he had become a Republican. I couldn't help wondering whether his vote would have been the same with his new party affiliation.

"Be fair," Shelby instructed me after we had exchanged a few pleasantries. "Don't you try to unionize America! Don't let the NLRB do that," he said with emphasis.

Carefully avoiding any reference to the public policy provisions of the National Labor Relations Act contained in the preamble (which would surely have antagonized him), I assured the senator that the Board's job was to hold elections that guaranteed employees free choice about unionization. I doubt if I assuaged his concerns, or those of the many other Republicans and well-organized business groups I spoke to over the next few years.

One result of the 1994 elections was a vastly increased assertiveness and aggressiveness on the part of the congressional Republican leadership. This was particularly true in the House where Newt Gingrich presided as the speaker and leader of what he proudly characterized as a "new revolution." The assault on New Deal legislation began immediately, and the National Labor Relations Board was high on the Republican list of targets.

This was not the first time the Board had attracted hostile congressional attention. In 1938–1939, only a few years after its 1935 enactment, the Wagner Act and the Board it created were assailed in the House during a series of highly publicized hearings. The House special committee to investigate the National Labor Relations Board was chaired by an anti–New Deal Democrat, Howard Smith of Virginia.

The Senate Labor Committee held hearings in April of 1939 on bills to amend the act, and similar amendments came from the Smith Committee in the House. At that time, it was not only employer organizations that were arrayed against the Board. An unhappy American Federation of Labor thought it had been ill treated by the Board in the determination of appropriate units arising out of disputes between the industrial unions in the CIO and the craft unions of the AFL; the federation thought that the Board favored the CIO unions.[1]

A whole host of "reforms" reflected mistrust of the new agency. Although no amendments were passed, the Smith Committee hearings pushed the Board into retreat and led it to change its policy on issues such as union certification based on signed authorization cards rather than on elections. As historian James Gross has noted, "enactment of the Taft-Hartley Act [in 1947] ... was a legacy of the Smith Committee.[2]

In the wake of World War II, the Republican Eightieth Congress, finding much with which to disagree in the Wagner Act and the Board's interpretation of it, amended it to define new unfair labor practices by unions and make it more difficult for them to recruit members and obtain employer recognition. Because of allegations that the combined prosecutorial and adjudicatory functions of the Board spawned an unfair bias in favor of labor, the Taft-Hartley amendments separated the general counsel's office from the Board and made that official a presidential appointee.

The internal disagreements about the baseball strike described in chapter 6 highlight some of the tensions between the general counsel and the Board that can result from this change. Notwithstanding the fact that the general counsel's prosecutorial functions are separate from the Board's judicial role, I found during my tenure that the numerous, vague boundary lines can, and often do, produce tensions.

One illustration of how this tension is expressed involved the great interest congressional Republicans displayed in 1996 in the alleged forgery of union authorization cards by the United Food and Commercial Workers Union at Purdue Farms (a chicken processing firm owned by a politically influential citizen of North Carolina). The regional people in the field who had direct investigative responsibilities in this representation case were employees of the general counsel's office. Yet I, as head of the agency, was called upon by both the Senate and the House to respond to numerous inquiries about the case. The buck stopped with me in this and in many other cases in which I was obliged to protect the integrity of the Board's processes.

At Senate oversight hearings in September 1996, I took it upon myself to respond to the inquiries of North Carolina Republican Senator Lauch Faircloth and his thinly veiled insinuations of NLRB impropriety and partisanship. I took on that responsibility. Yet the general counsel's authority over the field offices, which gives the agency an unwieldy administrative structure, is a direct legacy of the Republican Eightieth Congress's exaggerated and unwarranted distrust of the Board.

Another bequest of Taft-Hartley with which we became familiar in the 1990s was the oversight or "watchdog hearing." Indeed, during my term, many such hearings about Board activities were held without notice to either the Board or the general counsel. They frequently involved the parading of witnesses who had a grievance against the Board in general or in particular cases. Another kind of attack on the Board during the Hundred and Fourth and Hundred and Fifth congresses was held under the rubric of appropriations hearings, a forum that does not seem to have figured prominently in congressional oversight either prior to or immediately after World War II.

Of course, it is obvious why labor law, which inevitably involves volatile and controversial competing social, economic, and political interests, attracts the attention of Congress. Sometimes senators and representatives are acting in response to aggrieved constituents, be they unions or employers. This congressional involvement, like the sometimes-uneasy relationship between the Board and the White House, can undercut the independence of the NLRB. How, then, does the agency simultaneously maintain adherence to the rule of law and the notion that it will not be influenced by parties, private or public, in the resolution of labor issues *and* maintain a proper responsiveness to the political branches of government?

At the very beginning of the Taft-Hartley era, the confirmation hearings of General Counsel Robert Denham provided an extreme illustration of deference to congressional intervention—albeit within the context of prosecutorial as opposed to quasi-judicial conduct. Here is the colloquy between General Counsel Denham and Senator Joseph Ball of Minnesota (one of the labor law reform activists of the Eightieth Congress):

Senator Ball: I wonder if you would feel, if you are confirmed, that it would be in keeping with your responsibilities to consult with the joint committee that was established by the act, as to their interpretation of those various questions before you yourself took a final position on them?

Mr. Denham: I should feel it would be a privilege to do it, sir.

Senator Ball: I take it you would feel that way generally about any questions that arose in your own mind as to the proper interpretation of any provision, to consult with this committee, which includes, I believe, every member of the [1947] conference committee of both Houses on the act, as to what they think would be the proper interpretation?

Mr. Denham: Very definitely. After all, this act has to be administered in accordance with the intent, and I definitely would not want to undertake to resolve any questions that might not be clear in the act without making sure that I know what the intent was, and this is a source of information on that subject.[3]

In his questioning, Senator Claude Pepper of Florida highlighted some of the problems with Denham's approach.

Senator Pepper: So you would be seeking the counsel of the joint committee in making an analysis of the law?

Mr. Denham: Correct.

Senator Pepper: Do you think that the Supreme Court, when they are called upon to construe this law, is going to send for anybody in the Congress to help them.

Mr. Denham: I am afraid not.

Senator Pepper: You would be rather shocked if they did, wouldn't you as a lawyer?

Mr. Denham: Yes sir.[4]

It could be argued that the difference between the roles of the general counsel and the Board allows the counsel to be closer than the Board or its chairman to the parties and the political process, both inside and outside Congress. Yet, in my view, even discounting these differences in function, Denham's testimony was remarkable, and unbelievably wrong. Since his tenure, no Board or general counsel, to my knowledge, has taken such a position—and most certainly did not do so between 1994 and 1998. It would have been highly inappropriate to do so, not only because it would diminish the Board's independence but also because, as the Supreme Court has pointed out, the question of congressional intent can only be answered by the Congress that actually enacted the legislation.[5] (Perhaps this argument can also be made against consulting with the same Congress subsequent to the time it enacted the legislation—if it is still sitting—given the possibility of changing views as well as after-the-fact explanations not originally intended.)

I would readily concede that ascertaining the appropriate line of demarcation beyond which Congress should not cross is complex. All we can say with certainty is that Congress should not intervene to attempt to influence the adjudication of cases or to require some kind of approval in advance—which seems to have been the informal understanding arrived at in the conversation between General Counsel Denham and Senator Ball. (Ultimately, President Truman asked for, and received, Denham's resignation!)

As a young lawyer working with NLRB Chairman McCulloch, I witnessed cases in which members of Congress inquired, as they do today, about the status of particular cases. This is always appropriate, since members have a direct interest in the problems of their constituents and the effective management of the agency. Indeed, as described in chapter 12, inquiries about cases by several members of Congress proved vital to our ability to discharge and issue them in 1998, shortly before my term expired. Senator Harkin, for instance (as noted in my diary), expressed interest in getting the Bridgestone/Firestone dispute resolved.

March 10, 1995   Senator Tom Harkin called late yesterday afternoon about the Bridgestone/Firestone strike, which is taking place in Iowa, Indiana, Arkansas, and Ohio. ... Senator Harkin said that he was concerned about the fact the Board had not acted on this matter, that is, the unfair labor practice charges against Bridgestone/Firestone filed by the United Rubber Workers. He said that the company had not met one single time with the union. I said that I would check into this and did not note that this is part of the general counsel's responsibility, since it is not generally understood that the general counsel is separate from us.

I then discovered that Bob Allen (of Advice) ... has responsibility for this matter. Bob told me that the charges were lodged in Indiana on August 28 and were sent to Washington on January 27. [In] ... my ... telephone conversation with Senator Harkin I apologized for this delay.

Apparently the union is filing unfair labor practice charges—arising out of forty bargaining sessions, not zero as Senator Harkin seemed to think—based on the theory that the company was engaged in unlawful refusal to bargain by taking a take-it-or-leave-it position. Of course, unfair labor practice liability is a prerequisite to reinstatement for the strikers (as unfair labor practice strikers). The company, for its part, has filed charges against the union, alleging that the union was rigid in its position and its insistence that pattern bargaining be adhered to and thus engaged in unlawful refusals to bargain. Apparently the picket line has been a rather difficult one—we issued a Section 10(j) against the picket-line misconduct, which has been recently settled a few months ago— with anti-Japanese statements and sentiment (Bridgestone/Firestone is owned by the Japanese company Bridgestone).

I called Senator Harkin today and said that he could tell the Bridgestone/Firestone workers—he is speaking to them tomorrow (Saturday)—that the ball is in the general counsel's court and a decision on whether a complaint will issue or not issue should be made by late next week....

Senator Harkin referred to [the] *Des Moines Register*, which contains comments on the Dunlop/Pirelli strike, where we recently issued a complaint, and the fact that the company was recalling the striking workers there rather than litigate further. Senator Harkin is particularly hopeful that the same thing could happen at Bridgestone/Firestone. (Incidentally, our phone lines have been flooded with calls by the scab or replacement workers who are being ousted at Dunlop/Pirelli [and] who have been told that we are the source of their problems.) I told Senator Harkin that if a complaint was issued then I could try to intervene with the chief administrative law judge to see if the case could be given some measure of priority.... Again, my impression was that Tom Harkin did not understand the different rules that the general counsel and the Board apply, but that he was more aware of this at the end of our conversation.

I hope that something favorable happens, although, as I told Senator Harkin, the case appears to be a "close one." In this connection, he was rather surprised to find out that there had been forty bargaining sessions (based upon what he had been told by the union).

Throughout my term the Hundred and Fourth and Hundred and Fifth congresses continuously complained about lack of action on the *Beck* cases involving political dissidents' objections to paying dues—cases that had been before the Board for six years prior to my arrival. This inquiry was, of course, tinged with political argumentation; that is, the Republicans wanted us to decide the cases against the unions so that life would be more difficult for the Democratic party, which was the recipient of most union funds. Yet their inquiries—like that of Senator Harkin—were nonetheless appropriate. In the summer of 1995, Congressman Cass Ballenger of North Carolina questioned me at length about the inability of the Board to decide cases in the *Beck* area, and I advised him that I was doing my best to get Board members to act on them. (As we saw in chapter 7, the Bush Board held up these cases for six years!) In the first round of House oversight hearings that year this query was raised time and time again—and I was always concerned, and in some instances embarrassed, about our tardiness in deciding these and other cases.

But the inquiries were to become even more aggressive in later hearings. During a 1996 Senate oversight hearings, for instance, Senator John Ashcroft (R-Mo.) questioned me about the Board's *Manganaro* decision.[6] This case dealt with whether certain contract language designed to limit so-called double-breasting (i.e., the establishment of subsidiary nonunion companies) was "secondary" in that it coerced or implicated so-called innocent third parties and therefore fell under the secondary-boycott prohibitions of the NLRA. The Board held in this case that the clauses at issue did not violate the act.

The phenomenon of double-breasting, a strategy of Associated General Contractors (a group of nonunionized contractors), had recently gained currency in the construction industry. It allowed employers to set up nonunion companies so as to escape both the union and the contractual regulations contained in the collective-bargaining agreement negotiated with it.

Senator Ashcroft: It seemed to me that the Longshoreman case [*NLRB* v. *ILA*, 473 U.S. 61 (1985).] had been the test established by the U.S. Supreme Court and that businesses had relied on it and had relied on it successfully for a long time, and they feel like they can no longer rely on it, and it is their perception that the rules have changed....

Mr. Gould: Well, with all respect, Senator Ashcroft, the Longshoreman case involved a dispute about containerization and whether the control language in that context was secondary or primary. This case involved a double-breasting situation which is in my view distinguishable from ILA and not the precise issue presented there....

Senator Ashcroft: So it is your view that Longshoreman is still good law and that businesses that pattern themselves upon the Longshoreman facts should be able to sustain their double-breasting arrangements consistent with the way they were sustained in the Longshoreman?

Mr. Gould: Well, of course, the Longshoreman case is the law; it is what the U.S. Supreme Court has said about the distinction between primary and secondary cases.

   With regard to the double-breasting and other language different from *Manganaro*, I would in terms of my own vote await those cases and cast my vote once I see what all the facts and circumstances are.

Senator Ashcroft: I think that is good judgment.[7]

Senator Edward Kennedy then stated that while he did not mean any "disrespect to my colleague," the committee should at least notify Board witnesses about its intent to question them about particular cases. Ashcroft, of course, was rearguing the points presented to the Board, the points an employer seeking reversal would ultimately present to a court of appeals. But Ashcroft's question about *Manganaro* and the inherent vagueness of much adjudication allowed me to slip and slide away from responding directly to the issue. I could never have responded this way to a question about rule making—whether a proposed or a final rule—because rule making is so clear and straightforward. Rule making establishes a clear and concise rule to address issues in a way that frequently ambiguous and sometimes confusing adjudicated decisions do not. In my reply I was also able to use the technique that had served me so well in confirmation hearings—falling back on the intention to decide a future case on the basis of all the specific facts and circumstances of that case. Though Ashcroft was obviously not a friend of mine or the Board, he was constrained to characterize my response as "good judgment."

   The more fundamental issue raised half a century ago in a colloquy between Senator Wayne Morse of Oregon and one of my predecessors, Chairman Paul Herzog, was never squarely joined in any of my appearances before the committees.

Senator Morse: ... Mr. Herzog, what do you think the relationship should be between the so-called watchdog committee and the National Labor Relations Board?

Mr. Herzog: I think that the relationship should obviously be a friendly one, that the relationship should be most certainly not of a sort which might create even in the conscious or subconscious of the administrators any feeling of pressure to reach certain types of results. I think it should be an approach which looks toward self-analysis and not toward self-justification....

Senator Morse: Mr. Herzog, if such a watchdog committee takes it upon itself to interview the National Labor Relations Board in respect to its policies, in respect to its reasons,
theories as to why it has reached certain decisions already announced, is there not the ever-
present danger that not only members of the Board and members of the Staff but parties
before the Board may assume that the Board is acting under pressure?

Mr. Herzog::   Yes; there is that danger.

Senator Morse: Do you think that the Board should at any time be questioned by a so-
called watchdog committee as to a decision it has already rendered?

My question goes to whether or not you think it is a good policy to have a quasi-judicial
board brought before a congressional committee and examined in regard to the reasons
that may have led the Board to render a certain decision or to take a certain administrative
course of action.

Mr. Herzog: I have no particular personal objection to anything of that kind. I see no
reason why any congressional committee can't talk to any administrator about any
problem, whether it is a joint committee, watchdog committee, or whatever it is called.

The difficulty arises when the powers of a committee are created so as to make it
possible for that committee to feel that it can question the Board about a decision. Yet it
seems to me that once a decision is issued it is out, and the public and the press can
question us. A very offensive thing, of course, would be for the Board to be questioned or
compelled in any one direction about a case before it is decided.

Senator Morse: That would be bad, too, but I certainly disagree with your conclusion if
you think that questioning the Board about its decisions after they are rendered will not
endanger as courts are and weren't questioned. . . .

Mr. Herzog: Well, I didn't say I was in favor of it, Senator. I simply said that I thought if
a regular committee of Congress could do it—I suppose it has been done for years with the
National Labor Relations Board—I don't think it makes much difference whether it is a
joint committee, or a regular committee of the Senate or the House. If all of it is to stop, I
suppose it would be better if all administrators were put in the same position as courts are
and weren't questioned. One always gets that, Senator, sometimes from labor committees
of the individual Houses, sometimes from Appropriations Committees.

I have always been treated with great courtesy in those situations and that makes me not
object too much. I think it would be safer of course, if that sort of matter were not raised.
The courts are there to review us.

Senator Morse: I happen to think that this trend in the Congress of the United States, to
place this type of restriction on quasi-judicial tribunals, is threatening the separation of
powers doctrine in this country and is always going to be a threat to the exercise of the
truly judicial functions in respect to those issues which are given over to the jurisdiction of
a quasi-judicial tribunal. I want to say that as far as I am concerned I shall always be heard
to protest calling of the National Labor Relations Board before any congressional committee, watchdog or not, for the purpose of discussing with that Board the reasons that may
have caused it in its judicial capacity to reach a decision. I think it threatens to undermine
this whole notion of decisions by an administrative law board being reached judicially and
it adds up, in my judgment, to be a threat of political pressure being placed upon administrative tribunals.[8]

From 1995 onward, and particularly in the early part of 1996, I felt as though I was spending almost as much time on Capitol Hill talking to members of Congress and testifying before committees as I was in my office at 14th Street deciding cases. Indeed, my staff and I thought that it was part of the strategy of the Republican majority to distract us from adjudication. A series of particularly time-consuming series of hearings, mostly in the House, commenced with the Appropriations Subcommittee on Labor in February 1995. This subcommittee contained members who were to be our most persistent critics and opponents during the next three and a half years, although many others got into the act. Like members of the labor oversight committees of both the House and the Senate, the Republicans on the appropriations committees tended to be from the fringe of the right wing and disproportionately from the South. The NLRB was in their sights: they targeted labor issues—just as they had previously gone after policies involving race and civil rights. As Jesse Jackson said to me in early 1995 during one of our meetings, "You really have the white folks all stirred up these days!"

The first round of hearings began in February 1995 with the House Appropriations Subcommittee on Labor, Health, Human Services and Education and related agencies. The hearings were chaired by John Porter, a distinguished-looking Republican from Illinois, who appeared to be more moderate than his Republican colleagues and sometimes even spoke more moderately. Compared to such extreme right-wing Republicans as Ernest J. Istook (Okla.), who frequently led the charge against us, Jay Dickey (Ark.), our most persistent opponent, Henry Bonilla (Texas), and Dan Miller (Fla.), Porter seemed eminently reasonable.

These southern Republicans were the ideological mirror images of those southern Democrats who had left the Democratic party over civil rights; they now represented the far right wing of the party that was so dominant in the House. The public would become much more familiar with this brand of Republican when the House Judiciary committee set off after President Clinton in the 1998–1999 impeachment imbroglio.

Their new dominance in the House, it was said, forced so-called moderates like Porter to scramble rightward to hold their positions. In the fall of 1997, during one of the appropriations debates on the floor of the House, he asserted that I had "politicized" the agency. "I am no fan of this administration's NLRB," Porter said. "I think in many instances Chairman Gould has politicized the institution beyond anybody's imagination, and I feel that that is a serious problem for our country."[9]

I was so concerned about this comment that I sought a meeting with Porter, who had been accessible to me in the past but now seemed unapproachable. A meeting was finally arranged through a note from Tom Campbell, a Stanford Law School colleague elected as a Republican in the district adjacent to mine in California. When I met with Porter, he said he had not intended to charge me with politicizing the agency and that, in fact, he had "confused me" with General Counsel Feinstein. He formally apologized to me "for having made this charge," although he did not do so on the House floor where he had made it. In 1998 he referred to the incident again during a dispute with the subcommittee about a statement I had made to the California legislature. (I attacked California Proposition 226, which sought to diminish union-dues expenditures for politics). "You took great offense at that," he reminded me, but he didn't mention that he had apologized.

On the wintry February day of our first Republican subcommittee hearing in 1995, Porter began by inquiring about the status of employee-participation cases. (They were often referred to as the *Electromation* cases after a Bush Board ruling in 1992.) These cases were of special interest to Republicans and led to their 1995 and 1996 sponsorship of the so-called TEAM Act. Porter then proceeded to a restrained inquiry about the so-called salting cases, which involved employer discriminatory retaliation against paid union organizers either employed by companies or seeking employment. This issue, too, later proved to be a volatile issue—because this tactic was becoming common in the construction industry and because of the political involvement of Associated General Contractors in the Republican party. On this occasion, General Counsel Feinstein advised Porter that the Board had sought review of the issue before the Supreme Court.

The next interrogator was Congressman Istook of Oklahoma. By the standards of what was to come—in both 1997 and 1998 Istook called me a liar during hearings—my 1995 dealings with him were mild. Because so much of his time was consumed with his antiabortion and school prayer campaigns, the Board was not quite at the top of Istook's list, but it was up there.

All my confrontations with Istook—and there really is no other word for it— were unequal duels in which I attempted to keep my temper as he poured abuse on me and the agency. Two years later, I could feel my heart pounding furiously at the end of this exchange about my answer to a question about the number of cars the Board possessed:

Mr. Istook: See, the problem we have is we can't even get simple basic information answered straightforwardly, and Mr. Bonilla asked these questions and you gave a long rambling answer that wasn't an answer. It's difficult to even get that much less technical stuff. You see the difficulty in having any level of trust or credibility in what you have to say.

Mr. Gould: No, I don't whatsoever, Congressman. I think that I'm always forthcoming. I try to answer, and I will answer, every question that's put to me, including yourself, and your characterization of me is completely incorrect and erroneous.

Mr. Istook: I think you're wrong sir, because you can read back in the record how you answered Mr. Bonilla's question by dodging it.

Mr. Gould: Congressman, I don't dodge any question. I'm not dodging any question today.

Mr. Istook: You've already dodged it and you can't go back and make up for it, sir.

Mr. Gould: Well, you know, we're getting to you said, I said....

If I may, Mr. Chairman, on the very same page where Congressman Istook asked me about the car, I see he said, "So, I'm wrong. I've been mistaken. There's only one car?" "That's correct." "Okay." "Mr. Feinstein [said] I might also add, in the field we do utilize some GSA cars in different regions for necessary case travel." Very next line in response to what Congressman Istook had said, so there can be no mistake about whether the information that we provided you at the hearing last year, Congressman—

Mr. Istook: Mr. Gould, I was talking about the information that you stated—

Mr. Gould: Well, Mr. Feinstein immediately brought this to your attention as soon as I spoke, and you know it.

Mr. Porter: Thank you, Mr. Chairman. Thank you, Mr. Istook.[10]

I had been told that Istook, a pugnacious and compactly built man, had actually tried fisticuffs with someone from the State Department who was testifying before a committee. Consequently, I was ready for anything!

But on this day in 1995, Istook merely bore in on the issue that most excited the Republicans, that is, the Board's use of a Section 10(j) injunction. As they were to make clear time and time again, the Republicans did not like our use of this provision. On this occasion, Istook purported to be interested in whether our policy was a "reflection" of a Clinton administration policy decision. It was not.

As related in chapter 7, this was a theme picked up two years later by Congressman Roger Wicker of Mississippi, who was concerned that I might cooperate with Vice President Gore's proposed executive order about government contracts and parties that violated the National Labor Relations Act or did not adhere to other standards. Both Istook and Wicker seemed to proceed on the assumption that we, like the Bush Board, would take our policy cues directly from the White House or the Department of Labor.

Subsequent to this hearing, Istook used written interrogatories to explore another issue of great interest to the Republicans (and probably the Democrats as well): the status of the *Federal Express* case then pending before the Board. The key question was whether we should automatically refer a petition filed on behalf of Federal Express's ground employees to our sister agency, the National Mediation Board (NMB), which possesses jurisdiction over railway and airline workers. Clearly, the pilots and those directly associated with the in-air aspects of the Federal Express business are within the jurisdiction of the NMB. But the basic question in *Federal Express* was which agency would make the preliminary determination on the issues, particularly those involving the status of trucking employees, who were traditionally under the jurisdiction of the National Labor Relations Board, even when they worked for air or rail carriers.

Historically, it was the National Mediation Board that made the preliminary determination, although, as I saw it and was to make clear in a dissent I filed later that year, there was no basis in law for it to do so.[11] In my reply to Istook I pointed out that the Board had ordered oral argument on December 7, 1994, and that the briefing had only ended on February 3, 1995. As noted below, others subsequently took a great interest in the plight of the Federal Express Company and expressed their interest directly to the Congress. As I noted in my diary, we soon recognized the importance of this case.

July 2, 1995   Last week at a meeting of the Board agenda, we discussed the cases that have been before the agenda since we came here in March 1994 and now. A few of the cases involved the application of the majority's view in *Federal Express*. This case is not yet issued, but now some cases have to be resolved in light of the majority's opinion, which is to hand over determinations about jurisdiction to the National Mediation Board. The majority maintains that it is not doing this, but as I point out in my dissent, there is no instance of the Board ever disagreeing with the National Mediation Board on a jurisdiction issue. During the meeting, Cohen, when confronted with one of these cases in which the NMB has already made a determination said, "What is there to be done further?" indicating that he would automatically accept what the NMB had done. Bill Stewart and I laughed aloud about this, and I said that I wish that I had the tape recorder at the meeting, because this is exactly what we had been maintaining that they are doing, that is, automatically deferring to the NMB. Stephens looked at me with a complete blank expression, not comprehending what we were saying at all—and Cohen didn't seem to pick up on it as well.

Federal Express, I was soon to learn, was an extremely important political player in Washington. Undoubtedly I was way behind everyone else in the Washington political arena and at the Board in understanding this. Yet here, as elsewhere, I do not regret adhering to the rule of law in fashioning my dissent in the case, notwithstanding some of the political problems I encountered thereafter.

Before we issued that decision, however, the next round of hearings began. This time they were of the oversight variety and were chaired by Representative Peter Hoekstra (R-Mich.).

July 2, 1995: Next week we will have oversight hearings with Congressman Hoekstra. Clearly he is going to be aggressive, and we will have to be well prepared. I spent Thursday and Friday meeting with a number of the Democratic congressmen on the committee. Last Thursday afternoon, I met with Congressman Payne, who is the head of the Congressional Black Caucus, and he was very helpful, steering me toward a number of influential Democrats on the committee. As a result of my meeting with him, I saw Friday morning Congressman Jack Reed of Rhode Island, Matthew Martinez of southern California, Tom Sawyer of Ohio, who is the ranking Democrat with particular interest in the TEAM Act, as well as Bobby Scott of Virginia. I also met with Bill Clay of Missouri, who was as congenial and friendly as ever.

I asked all of the [Democratic] congressmen if they would be there at the hearing, and they indicated that they would. Congressman Sawyer said, "I will be there with bells on!" Sawyer emphasized the fact that [through] Hoekstra ... I could expect anything to be raised in the hearing. He, Martinez, and Scott all suggested that I establish some sort of liaison with them....

Subsequently, I also met with George Miller of California, who was quite friendly and helpful. He advised me: "Never back down with these guys [the right-wing House Republicans]. To back down and to give any ground is a sign of weakness, of which they will take immediate advantage." I took that bit of advice to heart as much as any I received while in Washington.

During my tenure I met continuously with Democrats—and with Republicans I thought were sympathetic—as well as some I was pretty sure were unsympathetic! In my view, these contacts were perfectly appropriate. I was attempting to rally interest and support among individuals I perceived as supportive of the Board in a period when it was often under attack. I saw these meetings as a necessary part of preserving the Board as an effective agency. They were not, I felt confident, inconsistent with the pledge I had given Senator Hatch not to participate in partisan meetings about labor law reform.

And, although the overwhelming percentage of my support came from Democrats, I also met frequently with a number of sympathetic Republicans. I established good relationships with such Senate Republicans as John Chafee of Rhode Island, John McCain of Arizona, Susan Collins of Maine, James Jeffords of Vermont, John Warner of Virginia, and Arlen Specter of Pennsylvania. I was not able to develop the same rapport with a comparable number of House Republicans, although Stanford Law School colleague Tom Campbell met with me frequently and was helpful. I was also forever disappointed with the positions taken by so-called moderates like Senator Kassebaum and Congressman Christopher Shays of Connecticut.

Outside of Congress I met with virtually all groups and spoke before hostile audiences as well as friendly ones, Republicans as well as Democrats, management as well as labor and other interested groups. I made only one exception to this rule: I refused invitations to appear before the right-wing Labor Policy Association. Feinstein, however, readily accepted their invitations, and I believe Browning and Fox did as well. My view was that one had to draw the line somewhere in the interest of standards. Given their vitriolic attacks on me, both before and after I took office, I had to assume that any comments I might have made to them would have fallen on deaf ears. At the same time, I readily concede that the decibel level of their attacks was undoubtedly affected by the fact that I, unlike other Board members, had spurned their invitations!

In any event, I did not give ground or provide explanations, rationalizations, or apologies. Even in the early summer of 1995, well before the shutdown that came that winter, it was clear to me that we were up against people seeking to break the social contract that was fashioned by the New Deal, the Fair Deal, and the New Frontier. In this environment, conciliatory expressions were scorned. The Board and the act we administered were the enemies—I had to get used to that fact and adjust to it.

As a result of my meetings, when the July oversight hearing began there were more Democrats than Republicans in attendance; and, as I had anticipated, their presence was of considerable psychological importance. As in the appropriations hearing in February, the focus of much Republican questioning was Section 10(j), particularly an injunction we sought (and were ultimately denied) against the Caterpillar Company of Illinois. *Beck* as well as the employee participation–*Electromation* cases continued to be part of the discussion. One of my sharpest questioners was Representative Randy "Duke" Cunningham, a Republican from Southern California, who, like Istook, had the reputation of being a brawler.

Mr. Cunningham: So when we change that law [the National Labor Relations Act] after forty years of liberal rule, you are going to adhere to it?

Chairman Gould: Excuse me, Sir?

Mr. Cunningham: After forty years of liberal democratic rule and the laws that go along with it, when we change that, you are going to stand up for that same law when we change it?

Chairman Gould: Well, let me say that the Congress makes the laws under our system, and we have to interpret them, and obviously that is my role in this job, and it matters not which Congress fashions the law. Our obligation is to enforce it, and that is what I have always done in this job.

Mr. Cunningham: We are going to change that law.

Chairman Gould: Excuse me, sir?

Mr. Cunningham: I am glad to hear that because the law will be changed.

Though the Republicans were to make a pass at it in 1998, no changes in labor laws were passed. In the meantime, the fight went on—on the appropriations front and, as 1996 and 1997 unfolded, in the oversight arena as well. After we appeared before the Hoekstra subcommittee in July of 1995, the latter proposed a 30-percent cut in our budget. The full committee chaired by Congressman Robert Livingston of Louisiana (who departed from the House in 1998 under dramatic circumstances) fashioned a 15-percent cut. This was the first of a series of budget assaults the House made on the Board. Yet, as *Business Week* noted, we did not "scurry" around trying to "placate" the Republicans and their allies; instead, "Gould has continued his agency's aggressive pursuit of employers who violate federal labor laws. Gould has made plenty of enemies among companies accustomed to the less vigorous enforcement that prevailed under Reagan-Bush rule."[12]

In the midst of all this, I developed what came to be an important and cherished friendship, with Senator Mark Hatfield, a Republican of Oregon and chair of the Appropriations Committee. As it turned out, Hatfield, a former academic himself, had received an advanced degree from Stanford University. Shortly after reading a speech I had given on Abraham Lincoln's birthday, he invited me to lunch in the Senate dining room. This association was a stroke of good fortune for me, personally and professionally, for his Senate Appropriations Committee was critical to the survival of the Board. Senator Hatfield, ever a principled and thoughtful gentleman, was a student of President Lincoln and was himself genuinely Lincolnesque in demeanor, thought, and conduct. He was to be a good and valuable friend in the appropriations process during both 1995 and 1996.

July 27, 1995   Yesterday I met with both Senator Hatfield and [Senator] Specter as well as an early morning meeting with Congresswoman Nancy Pelosi, and [in] an early afternoon meeting with Congressman John Porter of Illinois. [Pelosi] ... offered to help us in any way possible to restore the loss which was incurred the evening of July 11 as a result of Congressman Jay Dickey's amendment [providing for a 30-percent cut]. She suggested that the battle in the House was basically lost, given the fact that the committee has now ratified what the subcommittee did and that it would be difficult to do anything when the

House votes next week. Congressman Porter, with whom I met with both Fred Feinstein and Harding [Darden], said that he thought he was helping us by proposing a 15-percent [cut]. He felt that that was so extreme that it would fend off any further cuts. He expressed substantial disagreement with both the labor law reform items that were adopted in connection with Section 10(j) through the appropriations process and the interference with the "rule of law," as he put it, that was involved. He noted that the Senate had more monies to work with. He stated that amendments would be allowed on the floor but that he was not sure that it would be wise for us to get someone to introduce an amendment because it might serve simply to "inflame" our opponents and work toward an even greater cut than that which we had received already. Porter said that he would support an amendment to restore the funds to the 15-percent cut that he had proposed, but that he would want to be consulted about it in advance so that he would, among other things, know where the money that we would get would come from. He stated that he would have to approve of this before he went ahead with support for us.

In the afternoon, I met at 3:30 P.M. with Senator Hatfield in his very grand offices in the chairman's office of the Appropriations Committee. He was cultivated and gentlemanly, and thoughtful, as he had been in my earlier meeting with him. We spent four or five minutes talking about the way in which his office is furnished and the shutters. He showed me the very fine craftsmanship involved with the shutters and commented about the desks, one of which had been finished in 1855. (In his office is a painting of President Lincoln—and another individual, possibly a president, whose identity I did not know).

Before I could even begin, Hatfield summarized the precise amount that we had been cut and the consequences that this would pose for us in terms of delays, closing of offices, etc. He had obviously been briefed—apparently through some of our documents—even in advance of this meeting. Hatfield expressed strong disagreement with the appropriations riders approach and I quickly pointed out to him that I would prefer to live with the consequences of much of those riders if we could get our money restored.

Senator Hatfield asked me to describe the Section 10(j) process to him, and I did so. I indicated that we had used it more frequently than our predecessors; and I pointed out to him that the opponents of labor law reform had often referred to the existence of Section 10(j) as a basis for addressing the delay-in-effective-remedy problem without any [need to amend] . . . the statute. I suggested that we were simply following the approach that had been suggested by the opponents of reform. I mentioned the baseball case and pointed out the importance of it in connection with the 1995 season. I said that our administrative process would have allowed us to move forward only when there was a 1996 or 1997 season. Hatfield nodded and seemed to understand all of this.

He suggested that we meet with Senator Specter, and I said that we had such a meeting planned for the afternoon. He said that Specter was a real "liberal"—he said "Sometimes I hesitate to use that word, but I think it is important to use it." He said, "I don't like the new word, 'moderate'—it is such a pusillanimous term."

Toward the end of our discussion, he went back to his desk and looked at the names of the committee members, suggesting that I contact Cochran of Mississippi, Bond of Missouri, and Gorton of Washington. He said that Gorton would have a real understanding of our law-enforcement problem. I [had] stressed to him that we were a law-enforcement agency at the beginning of our conversation and that he would be able to relate to this.

The meeting with Senator Specter did not begin until about 6:15 or 6:30 P.M. or so, and this was attended by Darden, Feinstein, and Peggy Browning [who hails from] ... Pennsylvania. Specter was feisty and aggressive and showed his cross-examination skills. I tried to give him a bit of chapter and verse on the Local 115 [Teamsters discussed in chapter 5] case. (Earlier, in the Hatfield meeting, I had mentioned to Hatfield that I expected some concerns [to be] expressed by Specter about Local 115 and that any modification of the court decree would undercut our credibility with both the court and the public. Hatfield said, "I'll talk to Senator Specter.") Feinstein had said that there was no violence in the Local 115 case, and I quickly corrected him by citing some of it that was in the Master's record. We are going to send Specter more material on this in the next day or so.

Specter also questioned us a great deal about the *Overnite Transportation* case [in which we sought nationwide Section 10(j) relief]. He had a letter from [its] President, Drew Lewis [Bush's secretary of commerce], castigating us and suggesting that the general counsel had not processed the charges that they had filed. On this, Feinstein was a little weak. He did not recall precisely the charges that Specter queried him about.

Specter wanted to know a great deal about the riders [and] expressed disagreement with this approach. He was quite personal, asking Feinstein and Browning and Darden a good deal about themselves, and then turned to me and asked me where I had been raised—he seemed to recognize Long Branch, New Jersey [my hometown] immediately. To Browning, he said, "Why is it that we don't know one another?" And Browning said that they did "indirectly." The conversation seemed to end on a positive note.

Our next visit was to Representative Jay Dickey of Arkansas, who was to be our major tormentor on the subcommittee, and indeed, in Congress. His constant pitch—articulated that day and during the February hearing itself as well as throughout the next four years—was that we had too much staff. "What are you doing about fraud, waste, and mismanagement?" Dickey asked me when I met him in a House corridor outside the subcommittee room later that summer. Again and again, I pointed out to him that there was no evidence of any such malfeasance. But Dickey's rhetoric resonated well with the House Republicans and those they thought had brought them to their new position of power in 1995. In their eyes, the Board had to play a role in reducing the deficit, even though the small sums allotted to us could have no significant impact on the budget or the national debt.

The balance in both the February and July 1995 appropriations hearings was struck by the Democratic members. In the February subcommittee hearing, Representative Nita Lowey of New York weighed in with serious questions about a number of our internal reforms, in particular, the administrative law judge rules. Both Lowey and Representative Nancy Pelosi of San Francisco were particularly valuable to the Board during my tenure, both through their attendance at hearings and their intelligent interest in our work. The involvement of Lowey and Pelosi and my contacts with Tom Sawyer and the other Democrats on the oversight committee taught me a lesson about how to approach future committees. When the bell rang during one of those tropical, excruciatingly humid days for which Washington is famous, I had made sure that the Democrats were on notice about what was happening and had been encouraged to attend and participate in the hearing.

For me, the aggressiveness demonstrated by the Republicans in those 1995 hearings provided a kind of introductory insight into what was to come. The questions asked, as well as the numerous interrogatories sent to us at various times, were highly confrontational and at times insulting in their pursuit of trivia and substance. It became obvious to me that these were the price of independence for a small administrative agency like the National Labor Relations Board.

Moreover, there was an obvious connection between the respective attitudes toward the Board taken by the executive and legislative branches of the government. Members of the executive branch at all levels of the Clinton administration (even the solicitor general during our contretemps with him) honored the independence of the agency. The White House and the Department of Labor scrupulously avoided interference. Ironically enough, this meant that the Board was more exposed to outright abuse and retaliation from Congress for positions we took in both adjudication and rule making. Our separation from the administration, while inherently valuable to our mission, made us an orphan more vulnerable to the harassment of congressional leaders who viewed the idea of the rule of law with suspicion, even when exercised by the independent judiciary. Its unique role meant that the Board was very much alone, and, though the Clinton administration was always supportive, the Hundred and Fourth and Hundred and Fifth Republican congresses sensed the weakness that flowed from institutional isolation.

Thus the administration, appropriately, did not identify itself publicly with our policies. Notwithstanding the profound disappointment of Istook, Wicker, and other Republican leaders at their failure to uncover a policy relationship between the Board and the administration, when the Republicans pushed against us they were pushing into a veritable political and power vacuum. And, as we see in the following chapters, there were virtually no limits to their intrusiveness.

In retrospect, I realize that the 1995 hearings were just the preliminary skirmishes. When I saw Congressman Tom Sawyer that September he joked to me, referring to the July sessions, "That wasn't so bad, was it?" But the 1995 hearings were far from the last of my problems. A whole host of confrontations with the hundred and fourth Congress lay ahead. 1995 was just the beginning.

9

Congress Instructs the NLRB

The 1949 colloquy between Senator Wayne Morse and NLRB Chairman Paul Herzog about the limits of congressional oversight reveals, at the very least, a difference in emphasis on the chairman's obligation to answer questions about cases. From time to time during both the Hundred and Fourth and Hundred and Fifth congresses, I was asked about Board decisions and attempted to respond in broad terms. Senator Ashcroft's question about the *Manganaro* decision (mentioned in chapter 8) is a good illustration.[1] Yet, while a chairman should always be unyielding and uncompromising with Congress about interpretation of the law itself, the reality is that being as polite and accommodating as possible with members is essential; they hold the power of the purse and can make life difficult through investigations, written interrogatories, hearings, and their role in confirming future Board members.

Clearly, the kind of questions Senator Ashcroft posed to me had been raised before, for example, during the Republican Eighty-third Congress when majority was concerned about whether the Board was adhering strictly to the new Taft-Hartley amendments. Neither Chairman Herzog then, nor I in 1995 had any practical alternative to responding. To do otherwise risked retaliation to the agency. In this context, independence is a somewhat mythical and abstract idea.

During the tenure of Chairman Frank McCulloch in the 1960s, most inquiries from Congress involved the status of cases. In the 1990s, too, Democrats and Republicans who appreciated the appropriate lines of separation frequently made this kind of inquiry. For example, Republican Senator John Chafee of Rhode Island had a considerable interest in the long-lasting *Brown & Sharpe*[2] dispute in his state; but, like Senator Harkin asking about the *Bridgestone/Firestone* case, he was always careful to avoid any suggestion that he wanted a particular result.

Regrettably, their approach was not always followed by others. In fact, many members of Congress sought to influence or halt decision making altogether—firing shots across the bow designed to intimidate the adjudicators before a decision could be made. This sort of interference was and is entirely inconsistent with the rule of law. For if the latter means anything at all, it means that those adjudicating questions of law involving the interpretation of statutes should function independently, without fear of retaliation and without being questioned while cases are under consideration.

But no such concept of independent adjudication prevented Representative Tom Delay of Texas and others of his ideological persuasion from calling for the impeachment of federal judges whose decisions he disapproved of. Even judges with life tenure were not immune from the kind of congressional pressure that was applied to the Board.

Industries and corporations that thought they had been (or might be) harmed by the Board's decisions immediately ran to the Republicans in Congress. And they had considerable success in obtaining the GOP's support for their attempts to induce the Board to retreat. The very first company to adopt this gambit was the Overnite Transportation Company, against which Section 10(j) proceedings were instituted in early 1995. The Caterpillar Company, too, complained bitterly about the Section 10(j) injunction filed relating to the hundreds of unfair labor practice charges filed by the United Auto Workers as a result of a strike that commenced in the early 1990s. Caterpillar, too, sought refuge among the Republican legislators.

Rule-Making Troubles

The Board's proposed rule making on single versus multilocation bargaining locations also brought complaints from the Republicans' supporters. In the restaurant industry, franchise fast food outlets were alarmed by the rule designed to take the ambiguity out of the employer's rebuttal of the single-unit presumption (see chapter 4). Congressional Republicans saw the proposed rule as likely to expedite union elections, which, the National Restaurant Association convinced them, would probably result in more workers voting for unionization. Certainly the Republicans were correct in assuming that one of the by-products of rule making would be the streamlining and acceleration of the process; whether it would also induce workers to vote for unions in greater numbers has never been tested empirically.

Of course, the issue was not always put forward in quite such a bald-faced manner. My comments about the benefits of diminishing the complicated standards of law in such disputes—and, therefore, replacing the involvement of lawyers with clear specifications about distances between units—were derided by some manage-ment lawyers as well as by the Republicans. They declared that the rule, adopted as a proposed rule only in the fall of 1995, would "balkanize" American business and force it away from centralized personnel practices. Overlooked completely was the fact that for three and a half decades the Board had favored the presumption of a single unit for organizing employees not previously represented by a union. This well-established precedent had the same balkanizing effect—to use the opposition's language—as the proposed rule. But it worked far more slowly and gave attorneys the ability to drag out proceedings considering the inherently vague circumstances under which employers could rebut the single-location presumption. Since these cir-cumstances had never been defined with precision, the older practice was an invi-tation to litigate. The restaurant industry, which provided substantial contributions to a number of the Republican committee members, obtained the support of the House Appropriations Subcommittee—which immediately became interested in attaching riders to NLRB appropriations bills.

About this time Congressman James Talent of St. Louis, chairman of the House Subcommittee on Regulation and Paperwork, began to poke around as well. (One of the ironies here is that our rule was intended to reduce regulation and the paper-work that flows from litigation!) When I learned that he was planning to hold hear-ings, I scheduled a meeting with him on December 7, 1995. I made this entry in my diary for that day:

I had a very interesting hour-long meeting with Congressman Talent about his proposed hearings into our rule-making process on single location. He proved to be an extremely able and intellectually keen legislator. We had a good deal of friendly bantering back and forth at the beginning of the meeting, which included our recollections of baseball in both Boston and St. Louis and his devotion to Curt Flood. I made three basic points to him: (1) that his hear-ing, in effect, replicates what we are trying to do [through the deliberative process]; (2) the formal hearing process [by the Board itself] here would be both arduous and expensive in these times of budget austerity; (3) our rule is proposed only and not final—although I emphasized in great detail to him my philosophy behind rule making. This led to a wide-ranging discussion of the desirability of alternative dispute resolution procedures for litiga-tion. I mentioned my chairmanship of the California State Bar Committee and my views about the need to subject wrongful discharge cases to legislation. [The committee had devised alternative dispute resolution procedures for the wrongful-discharge cases in California that were flooding the courts.] Talent stated that hearings are desirable from his perspective because they remove Congress from the "hot seat" or being "on the spot." He said that "this would give his constituency an opportunity to vent this feeling without requir-ing him to take a position."

But, like so much that was said on Capitol Hill, Talent's representations proved to be false and misleading advertising. He was holding hearings not to take himself off the spot—he would have been on the spot had he not done so—but because of his supporters' and constituents' views. He needed to show them that he was out in front and taking a position compatible with their views. When the hearings were finally held on March 7, 1996, Talent's motives became clear.

As the *Daily Labor Report* pointed out the following day, I told the subcommittee that the proposed rule would mean that cases could be processed more quickly, more predictably, and at lower cost to both the government and private parties. Employers would no longer need to rely on lawyers' interpretations of the convoluted circumstances under which the three-and-a-half-decade-old presumption in favor of a single facility could be rebutted. The rule would spell it out. The proposed rule stated that there would be no rebuttal of the presumption unless: (1) the employer's second facility is located within a mile of the petitioned-for facility, (2) 10 percent of workers are temporarily transferred from one facility to the other, and (3) there is common supervision of more than one facility. Only then could the presumption be rebutted. Given the specificity of the rules, there would be little to litigate about, compared to the inherently vague and shifting standards of applying the very same criteria in the context of litigation.

I stressed that the current system invited wasteful litigation and was a form of "crap shoot" because of the many imprecise standards. Rule making would not only create more clarity but would also eliminate the potential for the kind of "flip flops" employers and union lawyers had often complained of in Board adjudications. I emphasized that this would also diminish the role of politics in particular cases or groups of cases, avoiding a situation in which every new president could appoint a Board to change the law through adjudication, sometimes on the basis of the skimpiest of records.

But Talent deliberately misunderstood my point and applied my comment to the specific controversy in question (i.e., single or multilocation units). To the delight of those in the hearing room he said: "You're saying ... there have been flip-flops in the past. In the name of stability, under your rule from now on, it's only going to be flop.... There won't be any more flips."[3]

In this hearing and in future communications, the GOP and those who pushed them to march up the hill on this issue presented another argument against the proposed rule: that is, that it was not needed because there was already a paucity, indeed a decline, in litigation over the single-versus-multiple-location issue. I advised the committee and others with whom I discussed this subject that reported Board decisions represented only the tip of the iceberg and that most such decisions made at the Board level were unreported and, even more important, that many were resolved at the regional level and were similarly unreported. Moreover, although I did not press this point, unions filing petitions in a single-versus-multiple-facility dispute may well accede to the employers' position just to get an election in the near future without a protracted hearing.

But, like so much of the debate on this and other issues, the facts I supplied were not well received—indeed they were not received at all. The entire hearing, and those that followed, highlighted a different aspect of rule making, one with substantial implications for the relationship between politics and law. The barrage began in earnest with a March 29, 1996, letter from thirty-eight Republican senators, including the two Kansas senators, Senate Majority Leader Bob Dole and Nancy Kassebaum; Kit Bond (R-Mo.), who later publicized his position in op-ed pieces in the *Washington Times*; Don Nickles (Okla.), who had spoken so forcefully against my confirmation; and Orrin Hatch (Utah). Even the moderate senator Jim Jeffords of Vermont joined in. (A year later notwithstanding his seniority, Jeffords—who had voted for my confirmation—was almost denied the chairmanship of the Senate Labor and Human Resources Committee. He had also been attacked by the *Wall Street Journal* for supporting me and opposing Clarence Thomas.[4] Perhaps at this point he was anxious to placate the Republican leadership.)

The March 29 letter began with the usual misstatement—that is, that the Board was rejecting a test it had used for decades. The letter also sounded the theme Talent had developed in the House hearing: that litigation regarding single-facility units had dropped appreciably between 1965 and 1994 and, therefore, that there was no need to act.

On another point that was to become a recurring theme, the Republican senators said:

We doubt the wisdom of promulgating a rule that will fundamentally change such an important area of labor law at a time when less than the full complement of Members are available to consider the propriety of the rule. The Board has only three Members who have been confirmed by the United States Senate and one Member serving as a Recess Appointee.

I provide a more detailed treatment of the appointment problem in chapter 11. But suffice it to say that in 1996 it was the Republicans themselves who were blocking the president's appointments and were, therefore, the source of the problem they cited. Yet they sounded this alarm again and again. The argument always reminded me and others of the child who kills his parents and then throws himself on the mercy of the court as an orphan. The Republicans knew that, at their own insistence, only a "batching" package could go through! Stephens had departed in August 1995, leaving the Republican seat, which only they could fill, vacant. And, seven months later, Kassebaum still had not provided the White House with the names of acceptable Republicans! In the interim, Sarah Fox, Kennedy's legislative aide, had been nominated for the recess seat that had been filled by Devaney (and subsequently by career bureaucrat Truesdale). Kassebaum, notwithstanding her good relationship with Kennedy, had sworn opposition to the Fox nomination, apparently on the grounds that she was too liberal or prounion.

In the spring of 1996, one week after the senators' letter, their counterparts in the House of Representatives, sixty-seven strong, followed suit. Their similar letter stated that the proposed rule would "unfairly skew the rules heavily in favor of the union attempting to organize an employer's workforce." This, they claimed, would be "disruptive" to small business and would undermine productivity and the growth of enterprise.

In responding to both letters, I pointed out that only a very small number of the cases involving elections and appropriate units are in fact reported. Almost 80 percent of all cases coming to Washington since 1990 had raised this issue. However, these statistics did not take into account (1) cases in which neither party appealed the regional director's decision, or (2) those in which the parties had entered into a stipulation at the regional level in order to avoid the necessity of a hearing and the consequent delay in holding an election. Focusing on the argument that we were considering a reversal of precedent, I noted that in 86.5 percent of the adjudicated cases coming forward in fiscal year 1995 a single facility was found to be appropriate. I also noted that considerable flexibility was allowed for by the fact that in "extraordinary circumstances" the Board could depart from a newly promulgated rule that contained the same presumption as the majority of adjudicated cases.

There was no serious discussion of or rejoinder to the points I made. The drumbeat of criticism continued and was eventually embodied in a rider to our 1996 appropriations bill. It precluded the expenditure of any funds on the proposed rule and ensured that the issue would be nothing more than a debating point during my term of office.

The proposed rule on appropriate bargaining units appeared to dwarf, or at least diminish, congressional anger over our handling of "salting" cases (which involved employer retaliation against paid union organizers who were also employees) and use of Section 10(j) injunction actions. (The House Republicans had enacted a rider requiring a four-vote Board majority to authorize injunctions but it was not in the final bill.) In fact, the focus on rule making gave us somewhat greater discretion in the Section 10(j) arena. After all, there were only so many issues Congress could use to control us through the appropriations process—given the hostility of some senators (e.g., Specter) to legislation by appropriations rider.[5] In the 1996 budget, rule making was the one "chit" House Republicans managed to cash in.

The episode provided us with a lesson on the law of unintended consequences in dealing with Congress. The purpose of the rule-making initiative was not only to reduce waste and to streamline our procedures—as Congress had been urging the Board to do for years—but also to minimize the potential for oscillating policies from one administration to the next. Both Democratic and Republican Boards had been guilty of policy turnabouts. The Eisenhower Board of the 1950s and, more recently, the Reagan and Bush Boards, had treated similar cases far differently than their predecessors had. Rule making, because it was predicated upon substantial evidence derived from direct, practical experience with the problem, would be more lasting and would provide greater stability and less direct political influence than when each new Board appointed by each new president decides to repudiate stare decisis. In essence, rule making could provide a balance between law and politics without, it must be conceded, completely eradicating political influences on Board policy making.

What we had not foreseen, however, was the fact that rule making, by its very nature, generates publicity. That is the essence of it, for to work well it has to call publicly for the comments of the best experts from all sides. Variations on this theme, such as holding oral arguments on an issue, also attract attention—most crucially, the attention of financially well-placed Republican donors and, ultimately, the Republican politicians themselves. By using rule making and oral argument on critical issues—for example, reconsideration of the rules about whether temporary workers can vote in NLRB-conducted elections—we advertised what we were thinking of doing before we did it, thus inviting political interference from those unconcerned with the rule of law. And, unlike the interrogatories posed by Senator Ashcroft, to which we could give ambiguous but politically satisfactory responses, this kind of interference could stop the Board in the starting-block!

Adjudication, on the other hand, was a different matter. After my discussions with Secretary Reich (discussed in chapter 8) about the relationship between the

Board's decisions on back pay for undocumented workers and congressional action on our budget, we carefully released such controversial decisions without any fanfare. In that case, it was a long time before anyone even noticed. Of course, when they did, there were hostile reactions, but by then the Board had already taken action and Congress had passed our budget. So the publicity came after the horse was out of the barn. In rule making, and in oral argument, the opposite was true.

The following scenario illustrates an alternative outcome on our rule-making initiative. Suppose that we had decided that the rules relating to employer rebuttal of the single-facility presumption were too vague and had tried to change them through adjudication. If the Board had rendered such a decision at a time when the press was not watching, or during the government shutdown of late 1995–early 1996 when most people assumed we were not issuing decisions, it might have taken weeks, or even months, for the public and industry to find out what we were doing. The Republicans would have been protesting about an adjudicated rule that was already on the books and could only be changed by a statutory amendment. Whatever might have happened in the House under these circumstances, such a bill would have had to survive both a potential filibuster by Senate Democrats and the veto sure to come from President Clinton. Compare this to the relative ease with which the Republicans thwarted the prospective rule making with an appropriations rider.

In effect, our proposed rule making and, to a lesser extent, holding oral arguments on important policy matters invited congressional scrutiny. The Board held more oral arguments during my chairmanship than it had ever done in the history of the Agency. Although all Board members supported the policy of more oral argument, I must take responsibility for what, in retrospect, seems to have been an error—not simply because of the appropriations riders but also because of the havoc it created in our internal decision making. All of this, both the Republican involvement in our decisions and the internal paralyses and difficulty that it caused the Board, had unfortunate implications for the rule of law.

For instance, two years later, in 1998, a newly constituted Board evidently thought that it was politically smart—at least I assume the other two Democrats thought so, given their commitment to expediting union elections—to withdraw the proposed rule on single-location units. I dissented. And time proved the decision incorrect in two respects. The first was that withdrawing the rule invited even more congressional interference with case adjudication (as discussed in chapter 11). The action simply whetted the Republicans' appetite to intervene. As Congressman

George Miller of California had warned me two years earlier, they smelled blood and took the withdrawal as a sign of weakness! Second, it deprived the administration of a bargaining chip it could have used in its budget battles with Congress. This was particularly unfortunate in 1998, when the Monica Lewinsky matter made the Republican Congress eager to leave Washington for the hustings to exploit the scandal in the midterm elections. So anxious were the Republicans to swoop in on what they perceived as a major political advantage that they were forced onto the defensive on the budget and capitulated on virtually all policy issues, including the Board's appropriation! It is quite possible that in the peculiar political environment of 1998 the Republicans might have relinquished their hold on rule making in order to get out of town. But renunciation of the rule by the Board majority gave the rider a free ride.

Had I fully anticipated the behavior of the Republican Congress, it would have been better—notwithstanding the obvious benefits of rule making—to have proceeded quietly, through adjudication, once I could not get the rule on single-location facilities through the Board in 1994. (It must be admitted, however, that it would have been equally difficult in adjudication to obtain the votes of the Board insiders who thought they could appease the Republicans in Congress. Indeed, as in so many instances, there might have been no resolution of submitted cases at all!)

Oral Arguments

The same point can be made of my policy on oral arguments. Believing that the Board had not held enough oral arguments in the past, I thought they would bring us some of the advantages of rule making (i.e., participation by outsiders as amicus [friends of the court]). The Board would benefit through the oral argument itself, as well as through the filing of briefs, and the industrial relations community would gain a greater sense of inclusion. This proved to be an overly optimistic perception and, in the political environment of 1995 and beyond, utterly naïve.

A good illustration of the way oral arguments attract congressional attention were the cases involving so-called contingent employees, or as the Europeans call them, atypical workers in nonstandard employment relationships. Two categories of such cases came before the Board during my tenure. The first involved workers supplied by companies like Manpower to employers in need of temporary help. These workers do not have the same status as regular or permanent employees in terms of benefits and conditions, even though they often assume the same duties and are sometimes employed for substantial periods of time. This phenomenon of contingent, or temporary, workers has been one of the hurdles confronting unions attempting to organize a workplace.

Sometimes the user employee to whom the second category of contingent workers were referred had simply gone out of business as an employer of employees and contracted out with a temporary agency, with the agency placing such employees on its own payroll, providing for workers comp, etc. and then obtaining a reimbursement from the user. Either the manpower agency or the user can direct the workers, and sometimes they both do.[6]

Generally, the only genuine opportunity to reach these workers is at the workplace to which they are sent by the referring agency. But in my view, past Boards, though operating under a statute designed to promote collective bargaining as a matter of public policy, had been complicit in the de facto exclusion of such workers from the coverage of the statute.

Temporary employees, unless working under a contract of specific duration, have been viewed as employees within the meaning of the act. The critical question in the new contingent worker cases was whether such employees could be deemed to have a bargaining relationship with either or both the referring or using employer and whether, where regular employees were also present in the workplace, the temporaries could be said to share a "community of interest" with them.

Since 1973 the Board had held that when an employing agency (e.g., Manpower) sends temporary workers to a second employer (e.g., General Motors) and a union, such as the United Auto Workers, petitions to represent both the regular employees and the temporary workers at the workplace, both employers must consent to the election.[7] The underlying theory behind this approach was that this situation was similar to multiemployer bargaining, for which the consent of all parties is needed under the National Labor Relations Act. Multiemployer bargaining, however, is generally conducted among employers that are in competition with each another, which is generally not the case in the temporary-worker scenario. Nonetheless, in a series of decisions in the 1990s, the Bush Board had affirmatively expanded the 1973 precedent. The stage was thus set for us to determine whether these old doctrines should be reviewed, and possibly reversed, in the light of 1990s employment practices.

Accordingly, the Board held oral argument on this question in December of 1996 A second set of oral arguments held during the same week considered the standards for determining whether an individual is an independent contractor, and as such explicitly excluded from coverage by the National Labor Relations Act, or an employee, and thus within its protection. In a wide variety of industries—for example, the trucking industry—employees have been reclassified as independent contractors. Two such cases came before us in December of 1996: *Roadway Package System, Inc. and Dial-A-Mattress Operating Corporation*.[8] The Board sought the parties' comments on (1) whether the Board had the authority to change or modify the common law right-of-control test that determines whether an individual is an employee within the meaning of the act; (2) the relative importance of factors indicative of employee or independent-contractor status; and (3) the applicability of particular cases decided by the Board in the 1980s that raised similar independent-contractor issues. Once again the usual suspects from the House weighed in—familiar members of the relevant labor committees like Jay Dickey (Ark.), Cass Ballenger (N.C.), Henry Bonilla (Texas), Roger Wicker (Miss.), Peter Hoekstra (Mich.), chairman of the House Education and Employment Opportunities Committee, Ernest Istook (Okla.), Harold Fawell (Ill.), and Dan Miller (Fla.) In all, a dozen members of the House signed a letter in which they stressed their "concern" about our "recent actions" on the coverage of temporary workers and independent contractors under the act. They went on:

We find it particularly troubling that you would consider changes in such sensitive areas of the law when the Board is now operating with only four members, only two of whom have been confirmed by the Senate. Clearly, the law is well-settled and based upon provisions that have been the statute for almost 50 years. Throughout the country, businesses, their employees, and the unions representing those employees have entered into relationships which assume the stability of these long standing interpretations. Any sudden changes in these interpretations could have a seriously destabilizing effect on the U.S. economy.

Two weeks later I responded by noting that as the matters before us were *sub judice* it would be inappropriate for me to comment on them. However, I stated that we would decide these cases, as we did all others, on the basis of the evidence presented and relevant law. With regard to the familiar theme of the Board's lack of full membership, I said:

With regard to your comment about the Board's "current membership," please be advised that for a significant percentage of its sixty-one-year history, the Board has operated with less than a full complement of five members. For example, in the fifty years since 1947, the Board operated with less than a full complement of members approximately 27 percent of the time; for the past twenty years (1977–1996), the Board was below its full complement 47 percent of the time; and for the past ten years the NLRB operated with less than a full Board 56 percent of the time.

As to your concern that two current Members are recess appointees, I would point out that since 1980, eleven recess appointments have been made to the Board for varying periods, ranging from one to fourteen months. During one six-month period in President Bush's administration, the Board was down to three Members, one of whom was a recess appointee. On the other occasions during the Bush administration, the Board functioned with two recess appointees, once for 9.5 months and once for 7 months.

Clearly, it would be difficult, if not impossible, for the Board to perform its functions if it did not take actions on issues of consequence whenever it was below its full complement of five members or when its members included recess appointees.

But the fact is that the letter from the House had its effect. The Board never issued its decisions on temporary or contingent employees during my tenure. The cases had languished with the agency for at least four years!—and would do so for at least another two years subsequent to my departure. And, although the Board did issue the decisions involving independent contractors in the trucking industry— and did send a separate case back to the regional director for a hearing on whether physicians working with an HMO were employees or independent contractors—the letter seems to have had its effect there as well.[9] Except for my dissent in *Dial-A-Mattress,* there was no willingness to refashion the traditional standards.

My own conclusion was that the control exercised by employers by virtue of governmental regulations, whether they involve truckers or physicians, was indicative of employee status. But the majority of the Board, both Democrats and Republicans, stood pat and in *Dial-A-Mattress* reversed our own regional director, who had found that the truckers were employees not independent contractors. Thus, congressional intervention may well have achieved its purpose and contributed to our failure to issue decisions in this extremely important line of cases involving temporary workers and adoption of the rather conservative and traditional guidelines utilized in the independent-contractor cases. Congress arrested in midstream the reshaping of the employment relationship the Board could have undertaken under the existing statutory framework. The inability to produce a decision, definitive or not, in this key area is one of my major regrets.

Section 10(j)

Another area of policy initiative that produced congressional scrutiny was our increased use of Section 10(j), which authorizes the Board to seek injunctions against employers and unions in federal district court. The very first company to seek refuge among the Republican legislators was the Overnite Transportation Company, against which Section 10(j) proceedings were instituted in early 1995.

The Overnite's principal officer, Drew Lewis (President Bush's secretary of transportation), complained bitterly to several congressional committees.

Correspondence on this subject was not long in coming. All the Republican members from Virginia (Overnite is headquartered in Richmond), including Senator John Warner, wrote to me. So did Republican members of the House Appropriations Subcommittee on Health and Human Services—including Dickey, Bonilla, and Miller—as well as Representative Bill Goodling, chair of the House Committee on Economic and Education Opportunities, with whom I would later correspond on other, related matters.

A typical tactic intended to interfere with our adjudicatory process was employed by Representative Bonilla of Texas. Again, in 1995, he not so subtly reminded me that the subject of Section 10(j) had arisen in the appropriations subcommittee hearings.

> It appears to some of us that the Board's activities toward Overnite are unjust. As you recall when you came before the House Appropriations Subcommittee, of which I am a member, to justify your budget, several members expressed concern about the Section 10(j) process. The NLRB could be seriously questioned about prejudging this case. I would hope that the Board is confident that this matter is being examined in a careful and fair manner.

How the Board could be prejudging this issue was unclear to me, unless using Section 10(j)—which proceeds on the assumption that there is reasonable cause to believe that a violation exists on the merits (which are to be adjudicated later)—is always a prejudgment. Undoubtedly, this was the way a number of the Republicans viewed the statute, inasmuch as Section 10(j) was the most effective remedial tool the Board possessed. If invocation of Section 10(j) was declared a prejudgment, it would be eliminated; it would then be impossible to litigate any case before an administrative law judge, the Board, and, ultimately, the courts subsequent to obtaining a temporary injunction.

But Congress, by enacting Section 10(j) as part of the Taft-Hartley amendments in 1947, had made quite a different judgment from that of Representative Bonilla. Undoubtedly the Hundred and Fourth Congress would have liked to repeal Section 10(j) altogether, but legislation to either repeal it or require a four-vote majority to authorize it would have run up against the same obstacles as a bill eliminating the single-unit presumption: a Democratic filibuster in the Senate and a veto by the president. By voting for an appropriations rider requiring four votes in favor the House subcommittee sought to give the Republicans on the Board a virtual veto over all future 10(j) actions. In this instance, fortunately, the rider was dropped before passage of the budget.

An even more pugnacious tone was taken in a letter to General Counsel Feinstein from Republican Conference Chair John Boehner. He stated that the Board's position vis-à-vis *Overnite* would "greatly handcuff them [Overnite] in continuing to effectively communicate with their employees."

Frankly, I'm at a loss as to why you, and presumably the five member Board insist upon pursuing a highly litigious process with Overnite. Could this possibly be the best use of the Board's resources? I'm certain that many would conclude that these actions appear to fly in the face of the cost benefit analysis, paperwork reduction, and legal reform tenets in the Contract with America.

In much the same vein, House Majority Leader Delay of Texas wrote me that he failed to see the "logic" of the way the Board had handled the *Overnite* case. He also noted ominously that he wanted answers promptly "within the context" of not only the handling of the *Overnite* case but also the fact that the Board was increasing its use of Section 10(j).

In his letter Representative Miller of Florida sounded yet another theme we heard from time to time:

With the federal debt reaching over $4.7 trillion this year, all parts of the federal government are being reviewed for ways to cuts spending by streamlining procedures and eliminating unnecessary waste. Accordingly, I find it disturbing that a good faith effort by a company to save the federal government years of litigation, as well as millions of dollars, is not permitted proper review.

I would hope that the NLRB shares our concerns of balancing the budget and promoting fiscal responsibility.

Yet, as Tom Harkin pointed out in the February 6, 1996, Senate Appropriations Subcommittee hearing chaired by Senator Specter, the Board's $170 million-plus budget had little to do with the deficit or the debt.

Senator Harkin: ... of the total federal budget I would bet it [the NLRB budget] is less than 1/10 of a percent.

Mr. Gould: Yes. I would think it is something along that line.

Senator Harkin: So 1/10 of a percent, you cut 30 percent off that and you end up balancing the budget.
    Pure and simple, what this is is an attempt to do in the NLRB. That is all it is. Now, why joke around? Why beat around the bush? Why try to wallpaper it with some kind of thing about oh, we are trying to make all these little efficiencies and stuff....
    ... I think you are doing a good job. I think that the NLRB is finally doing a good job, and that is why people are after it ... the whole thing just boils down to an attack on the rights of working people to have their complaints fairly adjudicated in an expeditious manner ... if they cut this by 30 percent Mr. Chairman, you might as well forget it. You might as well pack your bags and go home. It would be a sham.

It was apparent to me as well that the Republicans' interest in saving money was disingenuous. When we proposed ways to save the taxpayers money, such as rule making, Congressman Miller and other Republicans opposed it because they perceived that unions would be able to win more elections and employees would be organized as a result of the rule. The same was true of postal ballots. When they believed that unions would be more successful and that employers would have more difficulty campaigning against them in this context, the fact that the ballots would save taxpayer money had no weight. The Republicans opposed them.

The argument that the Board should not authorize any Section 10(j) petitions for injunctions unless it was at full strength—echoing the point made by the Republicans in connection with rule making—spilled over into the Detroit newspapers strike, one of the most celebrated and contentious labor disputes in the country during my term.

In April 1995 the collective-bargaining agreement between four unions and two newspapers expired. A couple of months later the unions struck. Throughout the strike the employers continued to publish, using permanent replacements. The regional office of the Board issued a complaint that the employer had bargained in bad faith and that the strike had resulted from an unfair labor practice. In early 1997 the unions made an unconditional offer to return to work, which was rejected. Ultimately, the regional director's position was upheld by an administrative law judge, and on August 27, 1998 (my last day in office) the Board unanimously held that the strike was an unfair labor practice strike, thus entitling the strikers to return to work and to displace the permanent replacements if necessary. However, because the Board's orders are not self-enforcing and judicial review takes some time, the strikers still could not obtain reinstatement.

On March 11, 1997, senators Dan Coates (Ind.), Mike DeWine (Ohio), Bill Frist (Tenn.), and Judd Gregg (N.H.)—all Republican members of the Labor Committee—wrote to me. They expressed concern with: "reported statements of the Detroit regional director that the NLRB is contemplating an injunction in Federal Court on the issue of retention of replacement strikers and whether such a legal move by the Detroit region would be appropriate in light of the ongoing legal proceedings before the full Board."

On March 14 I responded that the question of authorizing an injunction under such circumstances was a Board decision and that neither the regional director nor the general counsel could act without the Board's authorization. I also pointed out that the Board can seek injunctive relief under Section 10(j) in federal district court only when "ongoing legal proceedings [are] before the full Board."

I myself would have voted to hear oral argument, as the Republican members of Congress had urged me to do, in either *Overnite Transportation* or *Detroit Newspapers*. There would have been no risk of publicity because the companies in both cases had already put the matter squarely on the Republicans' radar screen. In *Overnite Transportation* I was outvoted 4 to 1 at the urging of the general counsel. The theory was that oral argument would indefinitely delay proceedings that should be expeditious and that the parties were not at that juncture in a genuinely adversarial posture. I agreed with the general counsel that most Section 10(j) proceedings should not provide for oral argument but argued that it was appropriate in *Overnite Transportation* because we were seeking the first-ever nationwide injunctive remedy through Section 10(j). Since Board members had the right in Section 10(j) matters to see the papers of all the parties (employer, union, and general counsel), I saw no reason why it would be inappropriate to hear from them orally. (This was a procedure I instituted near the beginning of my chairmanship in early 1994.) But again I was outvoted.

Though I did not yield to the Republican Congress in any of these battles, in one instance I adopted a course of action remarkably similar to the way Secretary Reich had advised me to handle the undocumented-workers decisions. The "salting" cases involving employer retaliation against paid union organizers who were also employees continually enraged the House Republicans. In hearings and in letters they made this clear to me time and time again. In the fall of 1995, because the issue was pending before the Supreme Court, Senator Specter asked me to hold up such cases until the Court had resolved the issue, and I immediately agreed. The Court would rule on the issue within a matter of weeks or months, and its decision would, of course, govern the outcome of our cases. This strategic retreat was unique, but it involved what seemed to me to be an appropriate procedural concession to realpolitik. In November the Court unanimously held that such paid organizers are employees within the meaning of the act and are therefore entitled to protection against unlawful discrimination. The House Republicans, I am sure, were startled by the fact that Chief Justice Rehnquist, Justice Scalia, and Justice Thomas all joined in the majority opinion written by Justice Breyer.[10]

Nonideological Aspects of Congressional Pressure

How did all this congressional pressure on the Board come to pass? Of course, I knew from early in 1995 that we were in the sights of the Republicans—the House Republicans in particular. What I did not fully appreciate was the relationship between campaign finance and the events of those years. For instance, I was well aware that the National Restaurant Association was leading the charge against our rule making. Its members assumed that John Sweeney's Service Employees Union and others would attempt to recruit their low-wage or minimum-wage workers and would be assisted in their efforts by quicker election proceedings. What I did not realize was that the National Restaurant Association PAC had donated $820,983 to federal candidates in 1997 and 1998 and that Republicans received 81 percent of these contributions.

Representative Talent, who scheduled hearings on our rule-making initiative in early 1996, received $9,054. Other important Republican senators and representatives with labor committee responsibilities—Lauch Faircloth and Ballenger (N.C.), Gregg (N.H.), Fawell (Ill.), and Randy "Duke" Cunningham (Calif.)—received sums ranging all the way from Talent's $9,054 to Cunningham's $500. The contributions of the PAC to key Republican members of the House Appropriations Committee were even more impressive. Representative Ann Northrop (Ky.), who frequently expressed her irritation with our position on rule making, received $8,500; Bonilla (Texas) received $4,500; John Porter (Ill.), the committee's chair, received $2,500; Wicker (Miss.) got $2,000; and Istook (Okla.) received $1,000.

Thus the sustained attack of the National Restaurant Association was basically responsible for putting us out of the rule-making business during my tenure in Washington. The contributions made by its PAC (it was number 42 of the top 100 contributors to Republican candidates in 1996) made it a real player in Republican party politics and well able to call in its chits. The fact that Talent had earlier introduced a bill to extend the restaurant tax credit to tips earned on deliveries—it was blocked by the Democratic-controlled Congress—is not without significance.

The National Restaurant Association was not, of course, the only major Republican contributor focused on our actions. The nonunion Associated Builders and Contractors PAC contributed $1,004,617 to federal candidates in the 1997–1998 election cycle, and Republicans received 97 percent of these donations. Again, the same cast of characters appeared on the list: Senator Faircloth, $10,000 (he was defeated anyway); Representative Talent, $7,000; Senator Gregg, $3,000; and Representative Ballenger, $500. The list of the recipients of the builders' largesse on the House Appropriations Subcommittee are also familiar: Northrop, $10,000; Wicker, $5,000; Bonilla, $2,500; Istook, $2,500; Miller, $500; and Porter, $500.

The National Right to Work Committee PAC, though not as big a player as either the National Restaurant Association or the Associated Builders and Contractors, contributed $11,835 to Senate Republicans in 1997–1998 and nothing to the

Democrats. The Republicans always took an interest in the *Beck* cases, which were the exclusive focus of the National Right to Work Committee. But the Republicans, who saw union money being overwhelmingly bestowed upon the Democrats, did not need the Right to Work committee to remind them that it was in their own self-interest to pressure the Board about *Beck*. It was their vehicle, as they saw it, to break the financial connection between the unions and the Democratic party, thus weakening both groups.

A classic and vivid illustration of the relationship between money and politics was the involvement of Federal Express when the UAW sought desperately to keep its ground employees outside the jurisdiction of the Railway Labor Act. The reason was very simple. Whereas the Board had traditionally found single facilities to be appropriate bargaining units, the National Mediation Board (NMB), which administers the Railway Labor Act, defines units on a nationwide basis. This was good for unions with mature collective bargaining relationships with employers but difficult for those seeking to establish some kind of presence through organizing efforts. I was the only member of the Board who voted to examine the issue of our potential jurisdiction on its merits, but in 1996 Federal Express made certain that the Board would not have the opportunity to obtain jurisdiction. As the *New York Times* reported:

Federal Express wanted the language [of the Railway Labor Act] changed because it might exempt it from the National Labor Relations Act and, as a result, help it resist efforts by unions to organize its workers. Despite passionate speeches by opponents on behalf of organized labor, the company was able to engineer a remarkable legislative victory, prevailing upon the Senate to remain in session two extra days solely to defeat a filibuster by its opponents.

"I was stunned by the breadth and depth of their clout up here," said Russell D. Feingold, a first term Democrat from Wisconsin who had opposed the change. In the end, Mr. Feingold was one of thirty-one Senators who voted against Federal Express.

The article went on to note that Federal Express's success was based on its "generous political action committee, the presence of popular former Congressional leaders from both parties on its board, lavish spending on lobbying, and a fleet of corporate jets that ferry dozens of officeholders to political events around the country." Senator Ernest Hollings, the South Carolina Democrat, proposed an amendment to the Railway Labor Act providing for NMB jurisdiction over Federal Express. During congressional debate on the provision, he excoriated me for being responsible for throwing the question of jurisdiction into doubt.

We had, in fact, held oral argument on the issue, and I had expressed the view that the Board ought to consider the issue on the merits rather than blindly defer-

ring to the rulings of the NMB. On October 9 I wrote to Senator Hollings, noting
that although the case had been with the Labor Board for two and a half years prior
to my confirmation, it was an "unusually complex one involving two separate federal agencies, and it has been the subject of numerous motions and appeals by the
respective parties in the process of pursuing their legal rights in the matter." I
received no reply to my letter, which emphasized that I had always been interested
in expediting the case. Hollings explained to the *Times* reporter that he had helped
Federal Express "because he was grateful to the company for its willingness to use
its plane to fly hay to his state during droughts."[11]

Notwithstanding the opposition of Ted Kennedy, the AFL-CIO, and the UAW's
statement that "it is especially outrageous for the Senate to provide this special
interest provision for just one company," the Republicans obtained cloture, shut off
debate, and enacted the provision. In a subsequent opinion I wrote I bowed to the
amendment because, no matter how tawdry the political process, Congress is legislatively supreme.[12] This was indeed special-interest legislation—and yet it seemed
a cut above the blandishments and threats we received about Section 10(j) injunctions, the "salting cases" in which the Associated Building Contractors had such an
interest, and the contingent-worker cases. In this case, at least, there was properly
enacted legislation to which the Board was obliged to adhere.

For its part, Federal Express went from success to success. It subsequently
induced the union leadership representing its only organized employees (the pilots)
to accede to its position after breaking off negotiations.[13]

Statements About Law Reform

During my term of office, I set forth my views on reform of a number of key areas
of the National Labor Relations Act. I knew that certain people in Washington,
both inside and outside the Board, had decreed that a chairman or member of the
Board should not publicly discuss the legislation we were charged with administer-
ing and interpreting. Their thinking was that somehow such expressions of opinion
represented a conflict of interest and would prejudice the cases of parties that
appeared before the Board. Perhaps most importantly, they felt—especially after the
Hundred and Fourth Congress came to town—that speaking out would antagonize
Congress. Nonetheless, I thought it was important for me to make known my views
of certain carefully selected and important provisions of the statute. Indeed, as I was
soon to discover, if I did not do so, others, quoting from my earlier writings, would

try to characterize them for me. Therefore, from the beginning I discarded some of the recent tradition on this subject, which, in any case, contradicted earlier practice. Chairman Harry Millis, for instance, informally advised President Roosevelt in the 1940s; and Chairman Paul Herzog, who also made numerous public pronouncements about labor law reform, performed the same service for President Truman.[14] This custom was followed by all chairman of quasi-judicial administrative agencies, who frequently gave their views on legislation, both in speeches and before Congress. I could see no valid reason why the current chairman of the National Labor Relations Board should not do so as well.

I agreed fully with the statement of Chairman Robert Pitofsky of the Federal Trade Commission when he said: "It is not enough for regulatory agencies to simply enforce the laws entrusted to them.... It is equally important to decide whether the laws we are enforcing are up-to-date at a time when vast changes in global trade and the pace of technology rivalry have changed the very nature of competition."[13a]

In February 1995, speaking at the annual Yosemite Conference of the San Francisco Labor and Employment Law Committee, I expressed support for President Clinton's recent executive order seeking to restrain government contractors from permanently replacing strikers. In the 1980s I had advocated congressional reversal of the Supreme Court's *Mackay* decision, which allowed employers to permanently replace economic strikers.[15] I pointed out that this tactic actually denied workers the right to strike; in effect, it made them relinquish their job in exchange for the exercise of a statutorily protected right. In *Agenda for Reform* (1993) I had set forth this view, which had attracted the attention of the Republicans (particularly senators Hatch and Kassebaum) during debate on my confirmation.

The problem of striker replacements appeared to have grown considerably during the 1980s and early 1990s. (President Reagan's dismissal of twelve thousand striking air traffic controllers in the summer of 1981 arose out of an unlawful strike against the federal government and so was not, as it is frequently characterized, a case involving permanent replacements under *Mackay*.) Several factors appeared to exacerbate the problem: growing foreign competition in manufacturing; deregulation in such heavily unionized transportation industries as airlines, trucking, and rail; and the growing proportion of the workforce who were part-timers and temporary employees (often part of two- or more income families), who might be more prone than regular employees to cross a picket line. Major employers with what had been regarded as mature relationships with organized labor (e.g., Caterpillar Tractor, Greyhound, Phelps Dodge, International Paper, United Airlines, Trans-World Airlines, Eastern Airlines, and the *New York Daily News*) had threatened to use or had used permanent replacements.

In *Erie Resistor* v. *NLRB*, the Court's logic in condemning super seniority for nonstrikers appeared to undercut the apparent reasoning of *Mackay*.[16] Moreover, the inconsistency of the rules of the American system, which prohibited discharges for strike activity but allowed permanent replacements, left most observers puzzled and were badly out of step with developments in Canada and Europe.

President Clinton had campaigned against *Mackay* in 1992, and prior to issuing his executive order he had supported legislation designed to overrule that decision. My Yosemite speech, therefore, though prepared without any contact with the White House or the Department of Labor, was consistent with the general philosophy of the executive branch and focused on deficiencies in the legislation I administered.

On April 7, 1995, representatives Goodling, Fawell, and Hoekstra wrote to inform me that my role as chairman should be that of an "adjudicator" who "interpreted" the National Labor Relations Act. They charged that I had "repeatedly" exceeded the appropriate and traditional role of the chairman and thus undermined the "public trust" in my ability to carry out my obligations. They stated that I should recuse myself in all cases involving permanent replacement of economic strikers. My wife commented that a prisoner would be spoken to with more respect than I was in this derisive and insulting letter from the House's Republican labor-law troika.

In responding to it two weeks later, I took issue with all their characterizations of my position and their advocacy of "the idea that I should recuse myself in striker replacement cases." Of course, I said, it was important for me to act as an adjudicator in connection with the statutory issues that came before the agency. But, I pointed out, the expression of views by the chairman of an agency is "in the greatest tradition of administrative agencies, including the National Labor Relations Board." I cited instance after instance in which the chairs of other administrative agencies had spoken and, in some cases, been called upon to testify about legislative proposals that affected the statutes they interpreted and administered. These agencies—for example, the Federal Trade Commission and the Federal Communications Commission—were, like the NLRB, quasi-judicial agencies, a fact of which they and others who thought like them seemed completely unaware.

Proceeding on the assumption that ethical standards applicable to federal judges were appropriate to agency heads as well, I noted that judges were permitted to speak about issues of law as long as their statements do not compromise their impartiality.

There is a significant difference between the statement, "I will grant all divorce actions that come before me—whatever the strength of the evidence to support the statutory ground for divorce—because I believe that persons who no longer live in harmony should be divorced" and the statement "I believe that limited statutory grounds for divorce are not in the public interest. The law should be changed to allow persons who no longer live in harmony to obtain a divorce."

After quoting numerous judges—Chief Justice Rehnquist, Chief Justice Burger, and Chief Judge Abner Mikva, among others—who had expressed their views on legislation and argued for statutory change, I pointed out that I was not the first NLRB chairman to speak publicly on matters related to the NLRA. Moreover, I noted, senators Hatch, Durenberger, and Kennedy had all expressed interest in hearing my views on legislation.

Although I extended an invitation to discuss this question with the congressmen in person, I received no response. And on more than one occasion subsequent to this 1995 exchange, Chief Justice Rehnquist spoke publicly about legislation relating to the federal courts.[17]

In reference to the replacement of economic strikers, it became clear to me that the different rules applied to such strikers and those striking over unfair labor practices—the former group are not entitled to reinstatement whereas the latter are—produced wasteful and artificial litigation to determine which category employees belonged to. The union had to prove an unlawful firing or an illegal refusal to bargain in order to obtain the right to reinstatement, engendering sometimes-unnecessary litigation that is burdensome to the Board. If we argue (as some writers have) that the legislative proposals offered by Rehnquist and Burger were related only to their caseloads, then my ideas about the delay inherent in determining the rights of economic strikers versus unfair labor practice strikers should also be seen as related to our caseload.

A second series of statements I made (which are also set forth in *Agenda for Reform*) dramatizes how difficult it is for a chairman with previous expertise and scholarship about the subject in question to remain silent. My comments concerned the relationship between schemes to enhance employee participation or partnership with management and the NLRA. A number of considerations drove the movement for greater employee participation that began in the 1970s and 1980s. Employers concerned with competition saw it as a way to enhance productivity, while for employees and union interests the pursuit of social and economic justice were foremost. The objective on both sides was to substitute a greater degree of cooperation for what was perceived as an excessively adversarial "them and us" system that divided and harmed both labor and management.

However, such partnerships were limited by Section 8(a)(2) of the Act, which was designed to prohibit so-called company unions in which workers had no autonomy. In *Agenda* I propose amending the act to facilitate employee participation—participation with autonomy for workers. I also thought, however, that the Board could do more to facilitate such cooperation even within the framework of the law as written.

In several cases in which a quality circle group was used only in one or two very minor instances, I was successful in getting Cohen and Truesdale to switch their votes to allow employee participation to be viewed as consistent with the act.[18] In a concurring opinion in *Keeler Brass* I said the following:

This movement [employee participation] is a major advance in labor relations because, in its best form, it attempts nothing less than to transform the relationship between employer and employees from one of adversaries locked in unalterable opposition to one of partners with different but mutual interests who can cooperate with one another. Such a transformation is necessary for the achievement of true democracy in the workplace. However, it does pose a potential conflict with the National Labor Relations Act, enacted in 1935 at a time when the adversarial struggle between management and labor was at its height.[19]

The statute prohibits support or assistance for labor organizations that include employee committees, quality work circles, and teams of employees. But my view was—and is—that even where such committees can be viewed as a labor organization within the meaning of the statute, there is a difference between support or assistance and legitimate cooperation. As I said in my concurring opinion:

The court [the Seventh Circuit Court of Appeals] defined support as the presence of "at least some degree of control or influence," no matter how innocent. Cooperation, on the other hand, was defined as assisting the employees or their bargaining representatives in carrying out their "independent intentions." The court went on to find that assistance or cooperation may be a means of domination, but that the Board must prove that the assistance actually produces employer control over the organization before a violation of Section 8(a)(2) can be established. Mere potential for control is not sufficient; there must be actual control or domination. . . . I do not think that these [cooperative] efforts are unlawful simply because the employer initiated them. The focus should, instead, be on whether the organization allows for independent employee action and choice. If, for example, the employer did nothing more than tell employees that it wanted their participation in decisions concerning working conditions and suggested that they set up a committee for such participation, I would find no domination provided employees controlled the structure and function of the committee and their participation was voluntary.[20]

In the 1995 and 1996 debates about the so-called TEAM Act, which the Republicans promoted to both further employee participation and eliminate the anti–company union features of the National Labor Relations Act, the sponsors purported to rely on my ideas. Representative Steve Gunderson of Wisconsin and, ironically, Senator Kassebaum were the first to do so. This round of discussion demonstrated what seemed to be the prevailing attitude toward me of the Republicans, and of some other establishment people in Washington: "Don't speak unless spoken to!" For the Republicans who objected to my speeches about striker replacement were all too happy to invoke my writings about employee participation when they thought it suited their purposes in devising legislation to undermine collective bargaining.

Gunderson began it all on September 27, 1995, with a "Dear Colleagues" letter to Republican members of the House—itself a response to a letter from representatives Bill Clay, George Miller, and Matthew Martinez opposing the TEAM Act. The latter asserted that "current labor law places no barrier whatever to establishment of legitimate employee involvement programs." Gunderson's reply referred to my "salient observations" in *Agenda,* in which I had advocated reform of the NLRA to promote employee participation. Gunderson's letter, entitled "Current Law IS a Barrier to Workplace Cooperation—Just Ask the Current Chairman of the NLRB," attempted to confuse my views on employee participation with those contained in the proposed TEAM Act. If enacted, this bill would have allowed the imposition of top-down company unions in the form of employee committees like those of the 1920s and 1930s. In none of the series of proposals put forward by the Republicans in 1995 and 1996 was there any guarantee of employee autonomy or free choice in the selection of representatives to teams or in other participation mechanisms.

Also on September 27, 1995, the same Representative Talent who would hold rule-making hearings in early 1996 said on the floor of the House that the National Labor Relations Act needed to be revised to promote employee participation.

Here is what Chairman Gould, the Chairman of the National Labor Relations Board, appointed by President Clinton two years ago said. Let me read this real slowly, specifically addressing this issue. He said, "The difficulty here is that Federal labor law, because it is still rooted in the Great Depression reaction to company unions through which employers controlled labor organization that might affect employment conditions and additionally" here is what he said the additional problem was—"the term 'labor organization' has been provided with a definition so broad as to include, potentially, employee quality work circles, other employee groups, 'teams,' and the like. Amendments to the NLRA that allow for coopera-tive relationships between employees and the employer are desirable."

That is his quote, and he meant including any kind of employee involvement. He sug-gested amendments to the NLRA that allowed for cooperative relationships.[21]

A few minutes later, congratulating Gunderson on his sponsorship of the amend-ments, Talent said: "People say there is not any problem, take it up with the Chairman of the National Labor Relations Board. He says there is a problem and so do the employees and the employers and the consultants who came and testified at these hearings."

Representative Goodling, who a few months earlier had attacked me for speak-ing out on legislation related to strikebreakers and permanent replacements, then quoted the same portion of my book alluded to by Talent. My writings were debated yet again when Talent and Representative Tom Sawyer (D-Ohio) joined issue:

Mr. Talent: So the gentleman agrees with Chairman Gould who says amendments to the NLRA that allow for cooperative relationships between employees and employers are desirable. There is a need to do something. I hope in the interest of not polarizing this that we can establish consensus that there is a need to do something.

Mr. Sawyer: Mr. Chairman, indeed, and I agree with the Dunlop Commission that we ought to facilitate that growth of employee involvement. But I also agree with Chairman Gould when he argues that he does not support the TEAM Act because it does not contain the basic safeguards against company unions that he feels are absolutely necessary.[22]

While the Republican House ultimately passed the TEAM Act in 1995, it did not go through the Senate, and in 1996 the matter was brought forward again. At that time, in light of the way they had been characterized in 1995, I thought I needed to get my views on the record in a more detailed fashion. I did so in a series of speeches in Indiana and Nebraska and, ultimately, in op-ed pieces in the *San Francisco Chronicle* and *St. Louis Post-Dispatch*. I emphasized my accord with President Clinton's 1996 State of the Union statement that "When companies and workers work as a team, they do better. And so does America."

This time, Senator Kassebaum, my leading critic during the confirmation hear-ings, offered a clarification the Republicans had not provided in 1995.

William Gould, who was appointed Chairman of the National Labor Relations Board in 1994 by President Clinton made the following statement on employee involvement to a sem-inar at the Indiana University School of Law on February 29, 1996. I want to state that Chairman Gould is opposed to the TEAM Act, but he did say that although he opposed it, he does feel that an amendment to Section 8(a)(2) is necessary to promote employee involve-ment. He said: "Nonetheless, as I wrote three years ago in *Agenda for Reform*, a revision of 8(a)(2) is desirable. The difficulties involved in determining what constitutes a labor organi-zation under the act as written subjects employees and employers to unnecessary and wasteful litigation and mandates lay people to employ counsel when they are only attempting to promote dialogue and enhance the participation and cooperation."

Mr. President, I can think of no more effective statement than that of the Chairman of the National Labor Relations Board.[23]

As a result of Kassebaum's commentary, Senator Dianne Feinstein of California queried me about my views on the law. I reiterated to her my opposition to the TEAM Act as antidemocratic in its refusal to guarantee employee autonomy. The legislation passed both the Republican-controlled House and the Senate in 1996 but ran into the president's veto on July 30. In his veto message President Clinton stated that the act would "undermine crucial employee protections"; he set forth his support for the kind of "cooperative labor-management relations" necessary to make the country globally competitive. Taking note of the widespread acceptance of cooperative workplace efforts, he recommended that cooperation proceed within the parameters of the law and that the Board "provide guidance to clarify the broad legal boundaries of labor-management teamwork." In concluding, President Clinton noted that cooperative efforts must be based on "true partnerships" and that ambiguities in the legislation—ambiguities I had pointed to in my writings and speeches since becoming chairman—should be resolved without weakening or eliminating the "fundamental rights of employees to collective bargaining."

Later that fall during oversight hearings, Senator Kassebaum again referred to my writings on the TEAM Act. This time, however, she said that they brought into question my impartiality, alluding to some of the same considerations noted the preceding year by Hoekstra, Goodling, and Fawell. Senator Kennedy, however, responded wryly that "I was interested to hear Senator Kassebaum talking about Chairman Gould and the TEAM Act, because on May 8th of this year, my good friend and colleague, the Chairman of the committee quoted Bill Gould on the TEAM Act [and said that] 'I could think of no more effective statement than that of the Chairman of the NLRB.' So it looks like you are being courted by our good Chair ... as well as others, so I think that is interesting."

Now, however, there was an added twist to the story. Not only was I attacked for my statements on the TEAM Act by the very same people—as Kennedy had noted—who praised them when they thought that their views on the legislation could be confused with mine—but also by the AFL-CIO. As my diary records, the federation, which had previously been silent on the issue, became concerned about my views on labor-law reform.

May 23, 1996   A phone call this morning from Jonathan Hiatt, the new general counsel of the AFL-CIO. Hiatt said that he was calling me about something about which I would probably be hearing from Sweeney and Trumka this afternoon (although I have not as of yet—it is now 5:04 P.M. as I write this). [Neither Sweeney or Trumka ever did call.] Hiatt said that he and Sweeney and Trumka were extremely concerned about the statements that I had made on the TEAM Act and proceeded to discuss this from the assumption, as he said, "We have always been against the idea of your speaking out on legislation." I pointed out that this in fact was not the case—although I recognized from comments that he had made about my speeches and his view that it would have an impact on the budget that this would be a logical corollary to these views that he had expressed. Hiatt expressed the view that organized labor was having a difficult time from people like Senator Feinstein because of the fact that I had expressed the idea that some amendment to Section 8(a)(2) is appropriate. I told him that my view was that I would be remiss in my responsibility of the NLRB not to speak out on an important issue involving the interpretation and administration of the Act. I pointed out to him that this was in the tradition of previous chairmen like Madden and Millis. Hiatt's response to this was that they operated in a different and less political environment. I said that I wasn't so sure of that given the fact that Millis was chairman at a time when Congress was considering ideas that were, in some sense, the precursor to the Taft-Hartley amendments and that this was a highly-charged subject.

I said that I welcomed any conversation with Sweeney or Trumka, although I pointed out to Hiatt in two instances that the whole question of pressure by organized labor on me—as Hiatt said he was not doing—to "muzzle me" would raise a separate issue.

Washington insiders like Sarah Fox and Fred Feinstein and the Republicans maintained that my speeches prompted budget retaliation. A related line of attack was that even speeches chronicling our work—like rule making and oral argument—brought undue attention to the Board and triggered budget slashing.

But the fact of the matter was that the Republican attacks on our budget were motivated by their hostility to the NLRA and the Board itself. Our use of Section 10(j) antagonized them, and our rule making and scheduling of frequent oral argument—all of which I take responsibility for—caught their attention and prompted them to move against us on particular issues before we could institute needed reforms. Moreover, the AFL-CIO's active involvement in the 1996 campaign enraged the House Republicans and made them all the more determined to move against any labor legislation thought to be favorable to organized labor. Only repeal of the National Labor Relations Act and, perhaps, its replacement with repressive legislation would have satisfied them.

I also disagreed strongly with the argument that my speeches describing the Board's achievements harmed us. I thought that it was important for the Board to re-establish its credibility, which had declined for so long during the crippling years of the 1980s and early 1990s. Moreover, as early as the fall of 1994 some of my critics, like Feinstein, were themselves giving speeches advertising the fact that the Board's use of Section 10(j) applications was increasing four- and five-fold![24]

It might be argued that I should have refrained from speaking out if, in so doing, I could have speeded up our lagging case production—a problem that intensified in 1997 and 1998. But I think that the same considerations that made it so difficult for me to get other Board members to finish their work, produce decisions, and issue even one isolated case position on an issue like *Marquez* would have remained no matter what I said. The best proof of this assertion lies in what happened in 1998, 1999, and 2000 subsequent to my departure. Two years after my departure none of the major policy cases then pending had been issued, although two important ones were finally released at the end of July 1999.[25] One of these was issued because it had been argued at the American Bar Association convention three years earlier. The Board was embarrassed by the fact that—with yet another oral argument scheduled for the ABA convention in August of 1999—its work on the earlier case was still incomplete. All the others, including some that went back to the early- and mid-nineties, were still at the Board.

The contingent-worker cases on which a vote was taken in January of 1998, and for which drafts were circulated, were still there, notwithstanding the fact that they had been with the Board since the middle of 1995 and were argued in late 1996.[26] Indeed, in an unprecedented move, the Court of Appeals for the District of Columbia seriously entertained issuing writs of mandamus (requested by the National Right to Work Committee and Legal Foundation) on cases that had been pending with the Board for almost a decade. Only such writs made the Board move at all. It seems highly unlikely that I could have gained any points in the case-production arena if I had been silent on law reform.

In fact, several of the speeches I was criticized for making (e.g., on employee participation and Proposition 226 in California) came about as a result of legislative invitations or references to my writings. Indeed, as I pointed out to Goodling in early 1995, at my confirmation hearing senators Kennedy, Durenberger, and Hatch had all asked me to comment on legislation in the future. Hatch had questioned me about legislation to prohibit union violence; Durenberger on striker-replacement case priorities; and Kennedy on more efficient administrative procedures for the Board.

For all these reasons—and particularly where a matter was before the Congress or a legislature and I had been invited to respond—I thought it appropriate to do so. The lesson of my four and a half years in Washington was that individuals only objected to my speaking out when they objected to the substance of my commentary. In the final analysis, little else seemed to be involved.

10

"The Clamor of Legislators"

Meanwhile, much more than my public utterances were at stake. The heart of our struggles with Congress in both 1995 and 1996 involved the budget. In September of 1995, the Senate reversed the House's action, restoring the funds cut but not providing for any increase.

Tom Harkin of Iowa, the ranking Democrat, played a key role for us on the budget committee. The Republican chair, Senator Arlen Specter, enjoyed a good relationship with organized labor generally, particularly in his home state of Pennsylvania. Because he aspired to the Republican presidential nomination in 1996, and because the Iowa caucuses would be important at the beginning of the primary campaign, he was eager to connect with the state's union leadership. Harkin arranged a meeting for him with the president of the Iowa AFL-CIO.

As the budget struggle continued, Washington lawyer Bill Coleman was also invaluable. His help in arranging contacts with the auto companies, as I noted in my diary, paid big dividends for us.

September 22, 1995 A few days ago General Motors, Ford, and Chrysler announced their support for our position or, more precisely, "adequate" funding in the budget. This came about because of telephone conversations that I had with Steve Yokich [president of the UAW] a few weeks ago in which I asked him to make an approach to the Big Three to see if they would support us. When I was in Detroit two weeks ago to speak at a tribute to Walter Reuther, Yokich, who had been scheduled to speak, cancelled his appearance and cancelled his meeting that he had scheduled with me that afternoon. I assumed that nothing had come of this particular initiative. But this week I was pleasantly surprised to get a copy of the September 14 letter sent to Senator Hatfield by the American Automobile Manufacturers' Association on behalf of the Big Three.

September 25, 1995 I spoke with Senator Hatfield at about 1:00 P.M. today in what was a very friendly and cordial conversation, but nonetheless, alarming. It was his view that because President Clinton will veto the labor, health, and human services budget, it will be dealt with by a continuing resolution and that the lower amount, that is, the House cut of

30 percent, would apply. I pointed out to him how alarming this was, and he stated that he understood this. I asked him how we might be able to avoid what would be clearly the disastrous consequences of this and he said a phone call to Panetta or [Alice] Rivlin would be the best way to go about it. He also stated—and I had heard this earlier—that the White House was insisting upon an across-the-board cut, that is, 1 or 2 or 3 percent—although he did not mention these precise figures. He said that what he had been stating, that is, the lower amount, was Congress's view. He pointed out that negotiations were now proceeding with regard to those agencies that were excised altogether. For instance, he stated that he personally favored the National Service Program of President Clinton and other "social" programs like it. In the case of such agencies, the negotiations were about so-called "minimum funding." He opined that we would be in a better position if we had been excised altogether in the budgetary process. The conversation ended on a good note. He said that he has had the flu bug for some time and was going to read a new book about Lincoln, and we said that "when things calmed down" (my words) we would get together and talk about the United States around 1860–1865.

Leon Panetta called at about 6:20 P.M. and presented a very different scenario. He said that the White House was going for "across-the-board cuts" not to exceed 10 percent. The agencies that were being eliminated altogether would continue to function with some kind of—this is Hatfield's language—"minimum" funding. I pointed out to Panetta how concerned I was with Hatfield's scenario, that is, 30 percent, that it would decimate us. He agreed and expressed the view that this would not happen. Again he used the words "across-the-board cuts.' He said that he thought that the entire matter would be coming to a head between Thursday and Friday.

October 1, 1995   This weekend President Clinton signed into law a so-called continuing resolution, which will allow us to continue to function without layoffs. Precisely what our budget level is [under the resolution] is not yet known to me at this point. We will have a briefing on this on Tuesday from Harding Darden [Board budget analyst]....

October 2, 1995   In response to my call last week, Senator Harkin called today. I thanked him profusely for his help on the budget. In response to my inquiry, he stated that the problem now would be to get the White House to explicitly refer to us in the budget message. He said that he would draft a letter with Ted Kennedy urging the White House to take us into account in the veto message. He also suggested that I call the leadership of the House and both Reich and Panetta in this regard.

Last week another minicrisis emerged here in connection with this issue. Senator Specter's office called to say that Senator Gorton of Washington was going to the floor with an amendment to restore the House language on the salting cases. I immediately sent a letter to Senator Specter saying that I had instructed the [Board's]executive secretary, through an oral statement on September 13, not to issue any more salting cases. Subsequently, this was sent to Senator Gorton as well and nothing happened.

But Browning, Truesdale, and Cohen found out about the letter and complained that I had not consulted with them—although they were careful to state that they agreed with my position substantively. At a meeting last week Cohen moved that my letter be rescinded and a new letter be sent on behalf of the entire Board. I got up and said that I could not call this to a vote and Cohen called it himself as I walked out the door. I did nothing to change my letter in any way and subsequently the others wrote to Specter stating that they supported my position. All of this left me with a dreary, exhausted, and tired feeling last Wednesday night. I took off part of Thursday morning to jog and work at home before I came into the office.

October 26, 1995 I had lunch with Ab Mikva today. He is leaving his position as counsel to the president next Thursday, the last day of October. Mikva said to me what he said to the newspapers, that is, that he was simply tired and found the job too exhausting in terms of the amount of hours and energy that had to go into it. He had told the president, as he said in public and to me earlier, that he [had] wanted to serve with him until the end of his term in January 1997 but that exhaustion rather than any kind of discord had taken over and dictated his decision....

Two subjects were the focus of our discussion today. The first was related to a meeting that I had had a couple of days ago with Congressman Steve Gunderson of Wisconsin when he said the following: "Your agency is in difficulty because the parties are polarized. —You won't be able to get your agency out of these difficulties until you are able diminish polarization between labor and management."

He had then gone on to suggest that I convene a group of labor and management representatives who would look at the question of ways in which they could reduce their differences. When I told this to Mikva, he expressed deep concern—not because of the potential political trap, that is, Gunderson's attempt to circumvent Reich or the White House, but rather the incompatibility of this kind of role with my adjudicative responsibilities. That is to say, Mikva was concerned that I would be compromised in adjudicating cases that might come before me from the very parties with whom I would be discussing reform or policy changes [a concern similar to the one I had expressed to Senator Hatch in September 1993].

We also discussed the budget generally and my concern that I needed to not only reach out to moderate Republicans like Gunderson but also make sure that my support was solid within the White House and OMB. Mikva said that he would explore the question of who I might link up with in the White House to shore up my position and get a good veto message so that the Senate–House conferees would not fashion a compromise that would work against the Board's interest.

November 1, 1995 I met with Congressman Tom Sawyer of Ohio [D] yesterday ... we discussed the oversight hearings, which had been held by Hoekstra on October 30. Actually the committee never even advised us, but [Executive Secretary] Jack Toner came in and informed us about it. Sawyer said that the hearings were very rough and that there was a good deal of combat in them. He believes that Hoekstra is really trying to run with this as an issue—particularly on the "salting" cases. Clearly a tremendous amount of opposition is building up against this line of cases—regardless of what the Supreme Court does in the *Town & Country* case that is now pending before them.[1]

We also talked about the budget, and he expressed dismay at what Steve Gunderson had suggested—though he emphasized the fact that he did not believe that Gunderson was acting in bad faith.

November 19, 1995   This past week was both eventful and uneventful with the big federal government shutdown for the past five days. I am the only person in this office and there are only about ten people in the entire building. We have kept one person in about a half dozen regional offices. Essentially, the agency is shut down, as many conservatives wished it were permanently....

I pointed out to [Browning] ... both orally and in a memorandum that I circulated the next day that we have an obligation to be at our workstations at all times. That is why I had to return from Chicago on Monday, rather than proceeding to speak in Los Angeles to Morgan, Lewis and Bockius, as I had planned.

Now it appears as though there is a possibility that this shutdown could go through Thanksgiving. Indeed some believe that it could go through Christmas itself, although I find that a bit of a stretch. But, this is truly a debacle with the government paying people for doing nothing and creating, in our case, an even greater backlog.

December 5, 1995   Last week a remarkable situation developed on Friday. I put a foot-note in *California Saw & Knife*, dealing with the Supreme Court's 1963 ruling in *NLRB* v. *General Motors* stating that because employees did not know what membership meant as defined by the Supreme Court, that is, the payment of initiation fees and dues, [rather than full membership], they had to be put on notice—not only as nonunion members are pursuing their *Beck* rights, but also unionists who do not know that they have the right to refrain from full membership and thus be in a position to enforce *Beck*. This caused a great deal of consternation inside the Board, and Bill Stewart told me on Friday that several of the Board members are saying that the opinion could not issue if I insisted on placing this footnote in it. I went to see Browning, who said that I should understand that Chuck [Cohen] had a "political problem" and that I was making it more difficult for him. Apparently, the idea was that the position asserted was more conservative than Cohen's, who has now joined in several or at least one of my opinions about employee participation (probably for the same reasons)—and did not want to seem to be outflanked with his conservative constituency.

I said to Browning that it was important for us to be a judicial agency and to enforce the law and not be concerned about political support or lack of support for political Board members and their reappointment. She opined that perhaps we should be more judicial but seemed to indicate that this is what the facts were.

Congressman Porter called this afternoon to bring me up to date on the current status of budget negotiations. He indicated—as had Nancy Pelosi last week when I met with her—that staffs had begun to meet on a conference basis on our budget. He stated that it was his view that we must find "common ground" with the Senate and the budget cuts by the House had been much too "severe."

December 7, 1995   ... One [meeting] was with Craig Higgins and Meg Snyder of Senator Specter's staff. Basically they had no news for us, except to say that our appropriations bill was the last in line and that no one knows what the outcome will be at this particular point. Higgins alluded to the fact that it is possible our bill could take the form of a continuing resolution for a year with a formulaic approach, that is to say, an across-the-board mechanistic approach to an increase or decrease. The difficulty is that it would   provide the administration with an opportunity to revive programs that Congress would otherwise eliminate, like the National Service Program. This would mean that more entities would be pursuing the same amount of funds. Moreover, it is possible, given the fact that we are the last in line, some of the funds for HHS [Health and Human Services] would be reallocated from our bill to some other bill. Thus, although it is in the interest of the administration to obtain such a continuing resolution, it may work against our interest. There Specter seemed to be shoring up his Republican base and showing his muscle against us.

December 19, 1995   I had lunch with Harold Ickes at the White House today, and I thought that it was a good session. Essentially, as I stated to him frankly, I was making a "pitch" on behalf of the Board, particularly in connection with our budget. Ickes professed not to know the details of the budget or of the negotiations between the president and Gingrich and Dole. He stated that he was deeply involved in Whitewater, which we did not pursue in our discussion.

I told Ickes about a number of our innovations, including Section 10(j) injunctions, postal ballots, rule making, and our approach to simplifying procedures generally as exemplified by our *Management Training* decision [asserting jurisdiction over government contractors without litigation about the extent to which they could make labor relations decisions] last summer.[2] He said that he would make sure the president mentions the NLRB in any veto message. This would have the effect of making the NLRB nonnegotiable, relatively speaking....

Our session lasted about an hour and it was a friendly one. Ickes had been described to me as blunt and difficult, but he did not come across that way in this session. The week before last we (the general counsel and I) met here with Larry Matlack and Janet Himler of OMB. This was a very forthright and frank discussion. Matlack said: "Why not bite the bullet now? Things are not going to get any better in 1997 with the budget. Why delay the pain?"

Here he was referring to the potential for layoffs to which we had alluded. Matlack said that we would never get back to 1995 funding and that most agencies would be cut in 1996 at about 10 percent below their previous funding. He thought that the best agencies could do in 1997 was a freeze. He said that in all probability 1997 would not look better than 1996.[3]

The budget battles between the White House and Congress made the Board's prospects for fiscal year 1996 appear very ominous indeed. Two shutdowns crippled the government that winter: the first, in November 1995, lasted for six days and the second commenced on December 15 and lasted through the second week of January. For weeks before, right-wing Republicans had been touting the need to shut down government and arguing that many social welfare services the government funded were not needed anyway. As I drove across the frozen plains of Illinois and Iowa just before returning to Washington on the eve of the first shutdown, I listened incredulously to talk-show host Rush Limbaugh continuously spouting on nationwide radio his view that it was intrinsically desirable to shut down the government.

When I returned to Washington after the shutdown, I often trudged to and from the Board offices in what seemed like an interminably cold Washington December; in between I watched on C-SPAN the puerile antics of Gingrich and Congressman John Kasich of Ohio, who thought they had "one upped" Clinton in the negotiations. The fate of the Board was, of course, on the periphery of these discussions; as Tom Harkin had noted, the sums in our budget were relatively small potatoes—to them!

Our own regulations decreed, incredibly, that Bill Stewart (my chief counsel) and Mary Ann Sawyer (my confidential secretary) were not essential personnel. In fact, I was being deprived of the presence of the two *most* essential people at the agency.

Political writer Elizabeth Drew captured the mood of the shutdown when she described the "eerie feeling in Washington" and the "giddiness over the question of whether one was 'essential,' and was to keep working or 'nonessential.'"[4] When it finally ended, I was in balmy northern California, my return from Christmas holidays delayed by the inclement weather in the East.

January 17, 1996   Yesterday the Board met and we discussed, amongst other things, the question of what we should do with the cases that have accumulated since the shutdown began. This was really the second day of work after a month-long absence beginning with the shutdown of December 15. The Board had opened last Thursday, January 11, but quickly shut down in the midst of the second of two major snowstorms, now called the Blizzard of 1996.

We had worked a good deal during the shutdown although only nine of us were here in Washington under the plan—the same number that had been here during the November shutdown.

January 23, 1996   [General Counsel] Feinstein indicated ... that he had word that we would be facing serious financial problems as the result of the continuing resolution that the Congress is now fashioning, attempting to avoid yet another shutdown by the January 26 deadline. Late yesterday afternoon I was advised that the result could be that, as was the case previously under the last two continuing resolutions, we could be cut 25 percent because the fund was the lower of the two House figures, but no lower than 25 percent in earlier resolutions. . . . Under the earlier continuing resolutions, we operated under 94–96 percent. As of yesterday, however, it appeared that there was no antifurlough language [carving out an exception to cuts if layoffs were necessitated by them].

Last week I telephoned Nancy Pelosi in San Francisco, and she stated that she did not think that any action would be taken until after Clinton's State of the Union message of January 23, which will take place in less than two hours from the moment that I am dictating this.

Today's newspapers indicated that Senator Dole wanted to move more quickly and that he would not wait until Thursday or Friday as Nancy Pelosi had thought would be the case.

This morning I met with Senator Harry Reid of Nevada [D] and told him that I was fearful that we would have to furlough people for as many as ten days because of the formula. He said to me: "That's the best of the scenarios."

He said, "The Republicans in the House have singled out programs that they don't like and yours is one of them." I had been through a sleepless night last night, and I think that my exhaustion and shock showed in my face quite clearly as Reid delivered this message.

I spent the rest of the day on the telephone with a variety of people including Bob Reich, George Kourpias [president of the International Association of Machinists], Steve Yokich [president of the United Auto Workers] and Bill Coleman. As usual, Coleman was ... most helpful, stressing both the importance of my talking to Tom Campbell—who appears to enjoy a close relationship with Gingrich [a year later it proved to be a short-term relationship when Campbell voted against Gingrich for the speakership] and the need to get some major auto companies behind us. Coleman said: "I'm going to try to deliver one of the auto companies to you." ... Kourpias was very quick to realize what was at stake and said that he would scramble to the telephones to talk to Senate Republicans and the White House and others with whom he has a good relationship and that he would urge others to do the same.

... The Bob Reich conversation began with him stating that he was "fine—because we have a CR [continuing resolution or temporary appropriations bill]." But I then said to him that this continuing resolution was "devastating" to us because of the large number of furlough days that we would incur, and he was surprised by this information. He said that he would call people in the Senate. ...

This day—a day in which I did not complete work on any single case on my desk—was one which left me exhausted and demoralized. But this is the challenge and responsibility of this position. As Mikva said to me some time ago, "If the job was an easy one, they would ask anyone to do it." So I must listen to President Clinton's State of the Union speech this evening, hope that it goes well, get a good night's sleep, and attempt to struggle with the problems that we confront tomorrow morning.

February and March brought a series of congressional hearings—three in the House and one in the Senate. The first one, on February 6, was in the Senate and was presided over by Specter, who was aggressive and gruff in questioning both me and Feinstein. I don't think I've ever endured an interrogation in which I felt more defensive.

Before the hearing began, however, Specter pulled me aside and asked me a number of friendly questions: Where was I from to begin with? How long had I resided in California? Did I think of myself as a Californian? etc. But in the hearing itself he took a very different tone.

John Sweeney advised me later that much of what took place that day was Specter posturing for the antilabor Republicans who hated our agency. After my opening statement, Specter began a very intimidating series of questions.

Senator Specter: Let me start with the basic question: Are you able to make at least some cuts?

Mr. Gould: Well, there are cuts that we are attempting to make. We have a streamlining committee which has been put into existence and that is looking at all aspects of our operation and wherever we find that there is scope for cuts we are prepared to make those.

Senator Specter: Well, that does not really answer the question. Wherever we find a scope for cuts we intend to make them. You have been on notice for a long time. Let me ask you the question again. Is the NLRB prepared to make some cuts?

Mr. Gould: We are prepared—I believe that we can make cuts in some instances through the consolidation of various operations that we have.

Senator Specter: Can you give me a figure as to what cuts the NLRB can make?

Mr. Gould: I cannot give you a figure.

Senator Specter: Well, why not?

Mr. Gould: Well, because we have not completed the investigatory work which is a necessary prerequisite.

Senator Specter: ... Given the current budget and the downsizing of government generally, I would ask your Board to give us a definitive statement. Are you saying that you cannot make any cuts?

Mr. Gould: No, I am not saying that we cannot make any cuts.[5]

And so it went throughout February 6. Trumka, with whom I had clashed over the UMW contempt matter and was seemingly reconciled with at Jack Sheinkman's retirement party, seemed to smirk at my discomfort as I looked back to aides in search of props and rescue. The next day I made the following entry in my diary:

February 7, 1996   The one voice of calm and reason that day seemed to be Senator Harkin, who was supportive of us and who noted that any cuts in our budget would make virtually no contribution whatsoever to reduction in the deficit because we constitute 1/10 of 1 percent of the total budget!

February 22, 1996   The biggest event of these past few weeks has been the hearing held by Senator Specter on our appropriations.... Specter has us very much on the defensive and is [himself] responding to the House Republicans, stating to them that he will lean on us in exchange for what appears to be a reprieve that he gave us on February 1, when the most recent continuing resolution expired. We are going to have to go back up at the new [continuing resolution] expiration date, March 15. Feinstein's inclination is simply to recite the savings that have been made thus far in the field [regional offices], but I have tried to impress upon him the fact that this clearly will not be enough. Whether he will move or not will become clearer next week when we get to the stage of finalizing everything.

That afternoon [after the February 6 hearing] I swore in Sarah Fox. Both Ted Kennedy and Bob Reich were here, and it was a very nice occasion. Before the ceremony, Reich told me that he had had a similar encounter with Specter and that Specter had asked him during his appropriations hearing whether, when he made a speech attacking Republicans, he meant all Republicans. Reich made light of it and Specter responded: "I don't think you understand, Secretary Reich. I am the chairman of your appropriations committee, and I determine how much money you get. Now, I want to know whether you meant all Republicans in your speech." When Reich said he did not, Specter showed him a copy of the speech and said that this contradicted his assertion and wanted to have any other document that would indicate anything to the contrary.

On March 14, another round of hearings relating to labor, health and human services, and education commenced before the House subcommittee on appropriations. It was a barrage on a number of fronts. Both Representative Bonilla of Texas and Chairman Porter went after me on my rule-making proposal. The former led off the hearing:

Mr. Bonilla: I did want to close on this round by making an observation. Recently, a union scored this subcommittee's voting record for the past year and for our entire public career. I would just say that seven of us have zeroes for the past year and this side of the dais has a lifetime average of 8 percent while my friends and colleagues on the other side have four members with 100 percent score last year. Mr. Hoyer got 92 percent and 93 percent for a legislative lifetime. So I guess my advice to you and members of the NLRB with all due respect, take care of the senior Senator from Pennsylvania [Specter] because he seems to be the guardian angel of the NLRB. Make sure he's happy, healthy and elected because our 30 percent cut proposal has the votes in this subcommittee and it will continue to have the support this year as well. We will continue to be persistent on that.[6]

Chairman Porter then urged me and the Board to withdraw from our jurisdiction over small business. I pointed out to him that the jurisdictional yardsticks were frozen at the time of the Landrum-Griffin Act of 1959, something I had learned as a law student almost forty years earlier. I advised Porter that the relevant statutory provisions had emerged from a compromise as a result of detailed litigation about the preemption doctrine expounded by the Supreme Court. Porter said that the members of the subcommittee would "disagree with your interpretation of that section and believe that it was never written with that understanding because in 1958 there was no inflation in the economy; that you could interpret that more broadly."[7]

This proposal became a favorite of the Republicans. It allowed them to promote the idea that small business should not be regulated by labor law and, simultaneously, gave them a knife with which to cut our budget, on the theory that our caseload would decline. I sparred with Porter on this issue, suggesting that if Congress thought it desirable to have the Board relinquish jurisdiction over small employers they could always do so by statutory amendment; they could also hold hearings to see whether this would, in fact, produce a smaller caseload. I knew, of course, that the House Republicans had precious little interest in obtaining facts and enacting legislation in light of them. They had once again chosen the road of "legislation by stealth," as the *New York Times* later called it, knowing that any proper legislation along the lines they favored would produce a Clinton veto.

In my testimony I also noted that my colleague at Stanford, Bob Flanagan of the Business School, had written about this subject, and I commended his work to the subcommittee. Yet, although Congress did not seem to be interested in holding hearings and obtaining facts, the small business issue would not go away. It was taken up by Representative Istook, who began sending out memos entitled "Free the NLRB," meaning that we could be freed from the work of handling so many cases if the Board was deprived of jurisdiction over certain cases. When our advisory panels examined this proposal, both union and employer representatives disagreed with it on the grounds that the states might not adequately regulate violations of the act by employers or unions.

Next, the subject of the March 14 hearing shifted to more general rhetoric and there followed this long colloquy with our most persistent critic on the subcommittee, Representative Dickey of Arkansas:

Mr. Dickey: I want to ask a question, Mr. Gould, to which I really want to hear the answer. It's not that I know what the answer is. It's two questions that are general, and you may think that they are not sincere but they are. So many people tell me that either the AFL-CIO is a branch of the NLRB or the NLRB is a branch of the AFL-CIO. Can you tell me why that's not true?

Mr. Gould: Yes sir. It's not true and it's false because of the fact that I and my colleagues act as an impartial arbiter—a neutral ...

Mr. Dickey: The Department of Labor is said to be a branch of the AFL-CIO, and you all are too. I'm being facetious there.

Mr. Gould: I would hope so.[8]

This long, dreary hearing went on until about 6:00 P.M. or so. Dickey and Frank Riggs, a Republican from the Mendocino area in California, took over questioning toward the end. Riggs's thinking seemed to be dominated by the idea that unions opposed to him politically in his own district were not adopting the kind of non-adversarial, cooperative approach to management that I was espousing.

Naturally, in the weeks after this hearing, the matter of our appropriations was constantly on my mind, and in the air, as my diary illustrates.

April 6, 1996—Easter Eve   These have been a very busy past two weeks since I returned from California. On March 29, I had lunch with John Sweeney, the newly elected president of the AFL-CIO and his general counsel, John Hiatt. We talked about a number of things. I told Sweeney how the Republicans who have attacked me roundly for the proposed rule on single-unit facilities really think that we, Sweeney and I are working hand in glove. Sweeney replied, "Of course we are, Bill. We will just have to convince them that that is the real case."

Sweeney was very upbeat about his new initiatives in the AFL-CIO vis-à-vis both politics and organizing of the unorganized. I had been to a reception at the White House on March 25 where both Sweeney and Trumka were present, and the AFL-CIO had endorsed the Clinton–Gore ticket that morning. A new, very close relationship has emerged, which has prompted the Republicans to attack labor more viciously and the NLRB as well. Jay Dickey, at the most recent set of March 14 hearings in the House, said to me, "Isn't the NLRB a department of the AFL-CIO?" He and Congressman Riggs that day seemed to be obsessed with the AFL-CIO and their attempt to go after Republicans in marginal districts. Sweeney said that he was pleased with both efforts and the summer campaign is well underway.... Another development over these past few weeks related to the attempt by the Republicans to get riders on our appropriations bill. Another temporary spending bill went through on March 29, which will expire on April 24. Dickey has apparently obtained a vote in the House that has produced another 5 percent cut and has put forth new riders on our single-unit location rule and Section 10(j).

Feinstein was in touch with both OMB and the AFL-CIO about 10(j) but ... did not advise me until I confronted him with it a couple of days later. The single-location rule has succeeded in stirring up a letter from thirty-eight Republicans and sixty-eight members of Congress [as recounted in chapter 9]. Specter wrote me and, indeed, through his aide telephoned me while we were in the midst of discussing the aftermath of Brown [*Brown* v. *Pro Football*] on March 27. He wanted me to promise him that I would not move forward with the rule until there was a "consensus" between labor and management. I indicated that this was impossible. On March 28, I testified on Congressman Gekas's legislation on administrative law judges. [Representative Zoe Lofgren of San Jose was particularly helpful in asking good questions about this legislation, which would harm our ALJ corps]. When I came out of the hearing, I was told that there was a call from Specter for me. I eventually spoke with Craig Higgins since Specter was in the midst of a House-Senate conference, and Higgins stated that he wanted some kind of promise of not moving ahead on the proposed rule. I told him that, as a practical matter, it was unlikely that we would move forward with it until the fall. But I said that I couldn't promise him anything and that I was the chairman of an independent regulatory agency. Higgins said: "Perhaps you would prefer a rider on the single-unit location." I said that, "I would be less uncomfortable with that" than making some kind of promise to Specter....

On March 30, I went to the Gridiron Club Dinner at the invitation of Jim Risser [Chairman of the Stanford Communications Department].... Earlier in the day, I attended a pre-Gridiron luncheon at the Gannett facilities in Arlington and met the president of the Detroit Newspapers, Frank Vega. Both he and the vice president [of Gannett], at whose table I sat, made reference to the fact that they hoped that differences could be resolved with the unions and the strike in Detroit. But it does not appear as though that is going to happen. They seem to be in a fight to the finish.

April 11, 1996 I had lunch with Bob Nash, the director of presidential personnel at the White House today. Bob said that things look so good for the president's reelection that it is "scary." ... I noted that Chief Justice Rehnquist with his speech, reported in yesterday's newspapers, attacking those who would attempt to undermine the independence of the judiciary, would help us more than it would help the Republicans—a point with which Bob enthusiastically concurred. . . .

I told Nash how I had refused to respond to inquiries about my "extracurricular" or social activities—the Republicans had put a series of interrogatories to all Board members asking all of us what we did with our spare time [after work, when we were on travel in another city] and he expressed amazement that the Republicans would go this far.

Later in the month, on April 26—seven months into fiscal year 1996 and after a series of continuing resolutions and two government shutdowns—President Clinton signed the 1996 budget into law. The Board wound up with a 3-percent cut for fiscal year 1996. The riders relating to Section 10(j) and "salting" were dropped from the bill, but it included (as related in chapter 9) the first in a series of riders preventing us from continuing our single-facility rule making.

Unquiet Interim

Rule making also figured in the new round of debates and worries about the fiscal 1997 budget that began almost as soon as the 1996 budget was signed. Meanwhile I continued my attempts to make friends on both sides of the aisle, insofar as it was practical to do so.

May 2, 1996   On Monday of this week, I met with Senator Chafee and his assistant David Sloane. It was a very cordial and friendly meeting in which Senator Chafee said that he had never regretted his support of me. I brought him up to date on what we were doing and he, Senator Chafee, was particularly interested in the settlement judge process. He then asked me about the *Brown & Sharpe Manufacturing Company* case [which involved a very bitter, protracted strike in Rhode Island], which really blindsided me—although it shouldn't have. I should have been briefed on it before I went over there. I told Senator Chafee that I believed that the *Brown & Sharpe* case had issued prior to my arrival at the Board. I thought that it was gone. He expressed some doubt about this. In fact, it turns out the Board decisions were rendered in 1990 and 1993—prior to my taking office here—but the case has been remanded by the Court of Appeals for the District of Columbia. I should have remembered that we considered the question of whether certiorari should be granted last summer. I had Al Wolff call David Sloane to fill him in, and I wrote Senator Chafee a letter about this yesterday. Now I am sitting here in my office trying to get this case to move forward.

Yesterday another development when we inadvertently discovered that Congressman Hoekstra is looking into possible contact between Rick Sawyer [a good friend of mine from California], who was dismissed from the Department of Labor as the result of his involvement in a labor dispute [in which he was alleged to have displayed bias or partisanship towards SEIU{Service Employees International Union}] and our Region 20 [in San Francisco]. The contention made by employers and Congressman Hoekstra and

Congressman Doolittle [R-Calif.] apparently is that Sawyer had access to our Region 20 offices and that, as a result, we are showing bias toward SEIU in a dispute that they have with the same company that got Sawyer into difficulty with the Department of Labor. Feinstein and Al Benson and another official in operations actually met with the Republican Congressman to discuss this but did not advise me.…

I expressed considerable concern to Feinstein when I reached him by telephone in New Orleans this morning and said that I should have been notified. [I actually had a meeting scheduled with Senator Boxer, which was cancelled—and the subject could have been brought up]. Feinstein and I went back and forth at it a bit—Feinstein stating that there are plenty of things that I did without advising him. I said that I always advised him where his jurisdiction was implicated in any subject matter discussed. Feinstein said that it really "grates with me" that I want to be involved with everything and don't tell him about everything. In any event, I did have a discussion with Mary Joyce Carlson [the deputy general counsel serving under Feinstein], Al Benson, and one other fellow from operations and learned something about the nature of the charges being leveled against us.…

This is another example of both politics affecting the agency and also Feinstein arrogating to himself any and all decisions about matters that are of extreme sensitivity and that could embarrass or cause concern for both me and the Agency. Feinstein said that he would have apprised me when he had taken action, but I told him that I should have known from the "get go." Feinstein said that I really was getting that information, but it is clear that I would not have even known about this if the faxes from Congressman Hoekstra had not been inadvertently sent to my office.

May 7, 1996   We had one of our better Board agendas this morning. We discussed a number of cases dealing with the contingent-employee question and attempted to come to grips with a number of difficult issues. I am not sure that we solved anything in particular, but I think that the discussion was a good one and served to get a lot of problems out in the open about the *Greenhoot* doctrine, which has denied contingent employees effective collective bargaining rights for a long period of time. I regard these cases as perhaps the most important of my term, and I so stated today. I would like to see us bring such employees into the mainstream of the collective-bargaining process and remove what I perceive to be existing impediments to their effective participation. I also stated that I would like to see some of the independent-contractor cases argued orally as well as the contingent-employee cases. All of these issues really relate to the new employment relationship and somehow we must find a way to bring employees together, notwithstanding the relationship that employers enter into with temporary agencies.… Everyone seemed to be very pleased with the way in which the agenda worked this morning.…

Yesterday, a new report by the New York City management labor law firm [Nixon, Hargraves, etc.] that studies Board members' voting came out. It says that Cohen is the most proemployer Board member since Donald Dotson.… [H]e has to tow the party line and dissent from everything we do—and he is certainly doing that! On the other hand, I am sure that he will not like the comparison to Dotson.…

I went to a White House press correspondents' dinner on Saturday night and spent a good deal of time talking with Tom Campbell—although when Steve Horn from southern California came along (a so-called moderate Republican), I lost my cool a bit when he began to try to justify the current antiaffirmative action initiative that will be on the ballot in California this fall. President Clinton's remarks [at the dinner were very funny—even better than I recall them two years ago]. Al Franken went on a bit, although he was very funny—again as he was two years ago.... He said that certain things would be beyond discussion: "President Clinton's personal life, Senator Dole's first wife, Senator Gramm's first wife, Congressman Gingrich's first wife, Rush Limbaugh's first wife, Rush Limbaugh's second wife, Rush Limbaugh's third wife!" He is one of those guys who makes you laugh just the way he says things, let alone the content of what he says.

May 19, 1996   I have just returned from a few days in San Francisco and Stanford. On Friday, May 17, after a speech to the Pipe Trades Council at the Park 55 Hotel—which I think went rather well given the fact that my speech was interrupted on about a half a dozen occasions with applause—I went to the Board regional office in San Francisco. [A senior Board official] ... told me that the office was very much concerned about the intervention of Washington on a couple of matters. He said that Mary Joyce Carlson had telephoned to advise him that a complaint should issue on a new theory ... for checked-off dues—a theory that has not been used [to date] by the Board. He said that the general counsel [of a major union] ... had telephoned him and indicated that he [the senior Board official] really didn't know what his current Board was thinking, and soon thereafter he got a call from Carlson. He was very concerned about this matter because he thought that the Republicans could use it as an instance of (1) intervention by Washington in an undue and inappropriate matter; (2) a situation where Washington was working with one of the unions and the union knew about the policy before the region did.

... On Friday evening [while in San Francisco] we went to the Getty home in Pacific Heights. The whole thing was organized by Nancy Pelosi, who was just elegant and her beautiful self. She introduced me to those in attendance at the dinner. I was the only individual who was not a member of Congress who was introduced.... Leon Panetta was the guest of honor and gave a very nice and short talk after being introduced by [Representative] George Miller. The evening had just the right touch to it. I was seated next to Jack Henning [the head of the California Federation of Labor] and Anna Eshoo [my representative at Stanford] was a few seats over from me.

May 30, 1996   Yesterday, we prepared a memorandum ... asking questions of Fred Feinstein about the amount of staff and resources in the various regions so that we could have this information prior to our June 3 meeting about regional director vacancies. This afternoon ... Feinstein came here to discuss it with me. As we anticipated, his initial point was that nothing that we can do will change the minds of the Republican leadership so why do anything at all? I responded by stating that this was a problem that would not go away, regardless of whether the Democrats or Republicans prevailed [and there was the problem of Senator Specter's attitude], and I said that it would be very much with us in the future. He seemed to accept this, although from time to time he returned to this theme of our inability to affect the Republicans....

He raised another argument against review [of staff resources] ... as well. He said that it would affect office "morale." but I said that morale could be affected much more severely if we are faced with more severe attacks upon our budget in the future. He said that he didn't think this would happen because the White House and the Senate would fend off anything that the House does. I said that this would probably be the case but that from a public relations perspective, we wanted to be ahead of the curve. One of Feinstein's initial concerns was that we would "give away our cards" if we talked about making sacrifices now. [I found it both curious and ironic that Feinstein had "given away our cards" so quickly in the 1994–1995 Mine Workers contempt dispute—but now argued against it.] I said that we were simply trying to get information on which we could base an objective judgment.... Confronted with this argument, Feinstein relented.

Another point that Feinstein raised was related to political opposition. He said that Milwaukee was one of the least active offices—a fact that all of us know—and that we would face opposition from Congressman [David] Obey, with whom he is particularly close, the ranking Democratic member of the appropriations committee. I said that the same point could be made with regard to New Orleans and that we would face difficulties with Senator [John] Breaux, and Feinstein noted that Congressman [Robert] Livingston [R-La.] would be even more important in this regard. However, I said that it would be important to deal with this in the same manner in which we deal with rule making under the Administrative Procedures Act. We could run the flag up the pole and then wait for public commentary and public reaction. We could deal with the political onslaught and point to those that opposed it on the basis of harm to their own constituencies and ask the congressmen and senators what they want to do in light of the opposition of their own colleagues. Again, Feinstein seemed to relent. I pointed out to him that it was important to have this conversation now because: (1) we have a brief respite and are now faced with an ongoing attack, and (2) we need to address these matters before filling the many regional director positions that Fred wants us to fill now.

July 8, 1996   A month ago Congressman Jay Dickey came to see us here in my offices. I was able to kill the first twenty minutes or so by simply showing him the baseball photos and the material on the wall in which he expressed a great deal of interest. It was a very puzzling and perplexing meeting because Dickey said—as he had said so often in the past—that he really doesn't know very much about the agency or the National Labor Relations Act and that he needs our help in this connection. He said that he had been surprised by the fact that there was so much support for us and that people on his side did not feel as intensely about the issue as our supporters did.

... Dickey said that "I'm not afraid." A rather bizarre comment that apparently [was, it] seemed to me, in response to the June 2 *New York Times* piece about me and the agency in which I had emphasized my unwillingness to back down. Dickey seemed to be saying that he wouldn't back down either, although he had noted that Congressman [Tom] Lantos [D-Calif.] ... had called him, and he said that perhaps Lantos would play a good role in mediating the dispute.

Whatever conciliatory message was sent to us in the June 5 meeting, the fact is that it was soon dissipated by an article that Dickey authored in the June 24 issue of *Roll Call* entitled, "It's Time Washington Bureaucrats Join the Team," which was critical of the Board in a number of respects.

As I write this, although the subcommittee on appropriations has voted a 15-percent cut initiated by Congressman Porter, coupled with the single-facility rider ... as well as a rider by Congressman Istook purporting to limit Board jurisdiction, the [1997] appropriations bill has not come before the House for a vote. I spoke with Marsha Simon of Senator Harkins's office today and she indicated that the matter would probably not be addressed by the Senate until September. She thought that the final compromise would be embodied in an omnibus temporary resolution that would carry us through until after the elections. There are a number of newspaper reports to this effect as well.

Right after the January shutdown, at Bob Reich's suggestion, I had made sure that our decision on undocumented workers was issued quietly so as to avoid intrusion into the budget process (see chapter 7). But I always knew that it was only a matter of time before lawyers and the corporations brought their concerns to Congress. That happened in the summer of 1996.

July 17, 1996, Stanford, California   Last Thursday, July 11, the House debated our appropriations bill and passed legislation that provided for a 15-percent cut and three riders. Senator Hatfield advised me last week that he would obtain level funding in the legislation passed by the Senate. But on the riders he was less certain, he said, because the position of Arlen Specter was less certain. He said that Specter was for the single-facility rider. He also said the Specter had not made up his mind on the Istook rider dealing with jurisdictional disputes. At the time of our discussion, which I think was on July 10 or 11, he was not aware of a new problem for us, the origins of which I am not completely sure of at this point, the so-called Campbell amendment, introduced by my Stanford Law School colleague, Tom Campbell.

Campbell called me on July 10 and advised me that he had been made aware (precisely how I am not sure) of one of our decisions providing for an interpretation of the 1984 Supreme Court *Sure-Tan* decision providing for back pay for undocumented workers who are unlawfully dismissed. He read a sentence from Justice O'Connor's 1984 opinion, which does indeed support the view that such an award is barred. However, I pointed out to him in the first and in subsequent telephone conversations that there are four or five references in the opinion—and the Court of Appeals for the Ninth Circuit as well as Judge Cudahy in dissent has made this clear—that discussed the fact that these particular individuals were unavailable for work because they left the country, presumably because they were threatened with potential deportation proceedings. Justice O'Connor went on to say at great length that these employees could not be said to be in the relevant labor market and, thus entitled to back pay, because they were out of the country. There is an inherent tension between this theme—which promotes the view that some undocumented workers will be eligible for back pay because they may be available for work and the view that all are barred as one particular sentence of Justice O'Connor seems to say. My point in my conversations with Campbell was that, given this tension, we have resolved the matter by looking to the basic philosophy that underlines the Court's rationale; that is, that the lack of protection for undocumented workers creates a new subgroup of employees whom the employer will then have an incentive to employ because of their status, thus depriving workers who are lawfully entitled to be here of solidarity and the ability to act collectively. I think that *Sure-Tan* was properly decided, and I think that our decision was correct. Campbell vehemently disagreed, and he kept returning to the one sentence of Justice O'Connor.

Eventually Campbell said that he was looking for—and wanted my reaction to it—a compromise that would allow the Board to obtain civil fines against employers who engaged in unfair labor practices and which would be remitted to the federal Treasury, rather than back pay to those who are not lawfully here in the first instance. I said that this was not a perfect resolution of the matter but that it was certainly something that "intrigued me" and that I wanted to explore it. Campbell said that he had not discussed it with any other person in the Clinton administration.... One of the first things that I said to Campbell when we discussed it last week was "your party has profited from this issue considerably." He immediately jumped in and said that he was not doing it for this reason and that he had opposed Proposition 187 [which denied benefits to undocumented people] here in California when [Governor] Wilson had supported it.

On Monday, July 15, I noted in the *Daily Labor Report* that Campbell had said that our decision was "absurd." This upset and angered me, and I called him and told him that there was an "escalation of the rhetoric" and I was concerned about this and personally offended by this. Campbell responded by saying, "Is this why you are calling me?"

I said, "Yes." Then there was a bit of a pause. He said that he could not remember using that word, and I went on to argue about our opinion in his legislative plans. Finally after denying that he made the statement—he pointed out to me that he had only spoken about it on the floor of the House; and while I had not heard the remark on television, I tuned in that night in the midst of his remarks. (I told him this.). He said that, "If you are offended by this comment, I apologize." [In fact, Campbell had used the word *absurd* on the floor of the House.] I said that I accepted his apology and looked forward to working with him on his legislative proposals....

One peculiar outgrowth of all this is that I very much favor the idea of civil penalties and the explicit notion that the Board's role is to punish and regulate future conduct as well as to compensate individual employees—a matter that has often gotten confused in the debate of our remedies under the statute. Although I did not say this to Campbell, my hope is that this can be a building block for reconsideration of the remedy issue on a more general basis and more explicit recognition of the policies involved. [But the Campbell legislation got nowhere because Democrats opposed his proposal to eliminate back pay for undocumented workers but supported the idea of fines and Republicans did not want to give the Board any new powers. Thus, the legislation was "doomed," in Campbell's words.]

About this time, there appeared a new indication of the lengths to which people ideologically opposed to the NLRA would go to discredit the Board.

July 30, 1996, Los Angeles, California   Over the past day, the Republicans have begun a new attack based upon what the Labor Policy Association started a month ago. They have induced the staff of Congressman [Christopher] Shays [R] of Connecticut to write a draft letter—it is dated July 25 and as of this afternoon of July 30, the office in Washington has yet to receive it—alleging that I am neglecting my duties by attending baseball games on government-financed trips. No matter how many times they keep hitting me, I never fail to feel some sense of emotional jar and upheaval after they do so. Certainly that has been the case here. The letter drafted for Shays has come to our attention because it was leaked to the *Washington Times*, which sent it to us. I am rather surprised that Shays—who has the reputation of being a moderate—would be involved in this. Perhaps the delay in receiving the letter indicates that he will not lend his name to this rather shabby effort.

Gene Orza, [general counsel of the Major League Baseball Players' Association] telephoned and was concerned enough to suggest that the Dodgers-Marlins tickets that he had arranged for me—of course, I paid for them myself—for tonight's game here in Los Angeles should be reserved under another name. I have done that....

The reception that I received here at the California Federation of Labor Convention was a very good and warm one. A standing ovation ... and sustained applause at the end of my speech. Probably some of the things that I said about undocumented workers and the like will create a new round of crisis for us back in Washington. This is one of the reasons that I am not particularly anxious to return from California too soon. But I must get back there this week.

Senator Hatfield to the Rescue, Again

September 11, 1996   Last night I attended a very fine party that Stanford University threw to honor Senator Mark Hatfield [at the Capitol]. When Senator Hatfield arrived, I was the first person that he spotted and he came over to me and said, in his usual gracious and courtly way: "Now we have another bond with one another—Stanford University!" He thanked me profusely for coming to the party, given all the work that we have in front of us. At the end of the evening, he said that he thought that I had done a great job as a "Commissioner".... Ironically, in light of our previous meetings and conversations, he was given a book on President Lincoln that has just been published by the Stanford University Press.

When ... we were about to part, Senator Hatfield said, "Now there is one thing that I want to change in our relationship. From now, if you are agreeable, I would like it to be Mark and Bill." I mumbled something in a very inarticulate way, I'm sure, concurring with him. And so when he left he said, "Now, good night Bill." And I said, "Good night Mark"—though I felt awkward in doing so because he ... [and] Bill Coleman are the two people that I am really in awe of in this city.

September 23, 1996   Senator Mark Hatfield telephoned me this morning with some rather somber news. He said that he had run into Senator Specter and that he had asked Specter what the budget would be for the NLRB. Specter said to him that they would have to "bring the Board into line." Hatfield inquired about this and stated that he wondered what the Board had done wrong. All the reports that he had heard were very good. Specter said that the Board was engaging in forum shopping—not his words—mine, but that we were usually looking around for good judges in pursuit of antibusiness positions. Hatfield said that he would make another attempt to convince Specter that he was wrong, but he urged me to go in and see Specter and try to use whatever methods I thought would be appropriate. I said to him that I would try to reach people that Specter would listen to and, although I did not say it to Hatfield, I was clearly thinking of people like Ron Carey of the Teamsters, Bob Georgine of the Building and Constructions Trades Department [AFL-CIO], and other union leaders who I thought would be important to him. Late today I put in a call to John Sweeney of the AFL-CIO, but he was on the road....

Early in the week I was deeply involved with preparations for Senate oversight hearings to be chaired by Senator Kassebaum. I met on late Monday afternoon with Senator Ted

Kennedy, and he was very helpful indeed—as he proved to be in the hearing itself. Kennedy was very impressive and seemed to understand all the ideas that I and others presented. And, interestingly, when I became a bit obtuse he looked at me in a way that indicated I ought to speak more clearly—this was in reference to the single-facility rule, which is quite abstract but which, ironically, has now drawn an op-ed piece in yesterday's *Washington Times* by Senator [Christopher] Bond of Missouri [R]. Earlier I met with Paul Simon [Ill.], who gave me lots of his time, but was equally attentive. He was particularly interested in the travel matters, on which I anticipated questions—although I never got them. [On the Labor Policy Association's accusations that I was traveling in connection with baseball games.] ... I will always remember Simon sitting there with his prominent ears and his good-natured and intelligent facial expression. At the end of the meeting with Simon, I said to him that this would probably be our last meeting together [he was not running for reelection in 1996] and that I wished him the best. But he said to me that he was being placed in charge of a public policy program at Southern Illinois University in East Carbondale, Illinois, and that he was sure that we would be in touch with one another.

September 30, 1996 Last Saturday, September 28, I awoke in my apartment to hear the NPR broadcast that a deal had been cut on the budget between 4:00 A.M. and 6:00 A.M. that morning. After a number of phone calls in which I was unsuccessful in finding out how the agency had done, I suddenly remembered that the House was still in session debating the bill that afternoon, and I called Steve Morin in Nancy Pelosi's office. He responded by saying, "Congratulations!" He advised me that we had received $175 million-plus and that apparently this constituted about a 3-percent increase. He said that we had done "very well" and that we were the "most contentious part of the labor budget."

After Senator Hatfield's call of last Monday, alerting me to the fact that Senator Specter was concerned and upset with us ... he urged me to meet with Senator Specter to bring any pressure that could be brought to bear, [and] we arranged a September 24 meeting with him. And, along with Fred Feinstein, I met with him in the Senate Cloakroom. Specter asked, "Why do people complain about the Board so much?" I said that one of the problems was that there had never been a consensus reached about the statute and that the agency had been attacked for years. I stated that the Supreme Court was affirming our positions and deferring to our expertise and that the circuit courts of appeals were acting in a similar fashion. Later on in the conversation, I noted the small number of dissents and reversals of precedent—the very point that I had made in the Senate oversight committee the previous week.

Senator Specter then raised the question of shopping for judges. He said, "I hear that you are shopping for friendly judges." I told Specter that I had heard that he was concerned about this and that I questioned many inside the agency about this, including Fred Feinstein, and that I was unable to find out what had triggered this remark. He [Specter] had no further information on it. (Subsequently, I ran into [former Board member] Dennis Devaney and the general counsel for Caterpillar in the hallway, and they told me that they had just been to a meeting with Feinstein. It turned out that Caterpillar is making this complaint about us ... [in reference to] the regional director's requests for assignment of administrative law judges [this was the forum shopping], but Feinstein never advised me of the meeting with Caterpillar either before or after.)

Specter asked us both, Feinstein and myself, whether we had met with the Republicans on the House Appropriations Committee. I told him that I had and I mentioned meetings with Congressman Porter and Congressman Riggs. Specter said, "Have you met with Congressman Dickey?" Feinstein began to laugh and Specter said, "What's so funny?" Feinstein was unable to provide a response, and Specter immediately went after him, saying that he didn't think that this was a funny matter. Feinstein assured him that he didn't think it was funny either. This was a low moment in the entire discussion.

Specter said that he had received a call from Leon Panetta about our budget and that Panetta had been very insistent upon the administration's request.

Perhaps the high point of the meeting was when, during one of the moments in which Specter was raising criticisms and concerns with me, along came Senator Hatfield, who leaned over Specter's shoulder and said, "Good afternoon Mr. Chairman, it's so good to see you!" After shaking my hand in the friendliest way, he then turned to Senator Specter and greeted him and said to me, "He is one of my best subcommittee chairmen." He [Hatfield] then went on his way. The timing couldn't have been better. Both Feinstein and I commented afterwards how this had really been helpful to us with Specter.

One bad piece of news was that the rider to the legislation will stay in on single facility. Since it is an omnibus appropriations bill, apparently this will keep the rider in place and preclude us from engaging in rule making for another year.

John Sweeney telephoned us late this afternoon—in response to my call from earlier in the week subsequent to Senator Hatfield's communication—to congratulate us and to say that he thought that Specter had simply been posturing during this process to help himself with his own party. I am not sure that this is the case, but I didn't express much skepticism to Sweeney directly. Whether it was posturing or not, his position caused us considerable difficulty. In the evening at Primi Piatti [a Washington restaurant near Washington Circle], I ran into Bob Georgine [president of the Building and Construction Trades Workers, AFL-CIO]. I expressed my thanks to him as I had to Sweeney without even referring to the problems with Specter because I know that Georgine has a very close relationship with Specter.

1996 Case Production

Miraculously, throughout the political turmoil of 1996, we had somehow continued to issue cases and decisions. Yet in retrospect, as the diary extracts make clear, productivity was declining. The political attacks on the agency took their toll internally and were translated into inaction. The high water mark was fiscal 1995. That year the Board produced 935 cases, and we were just beginning to catch our stride. But in fiscal 1996 case production was to show the first of a number of marked declines. The first skid took us down to 709 cases.

The presidentially appointed personnel, of course, were changing. The first to go was the former chairman, James Stephens, who, like Sarah Fox and Fred Feinstein, had been a congressional staffer. When President Clinton's fortunes were lagging before the government shutdown in 1995, I said to Stephens, "If a Republican is elected, you will be chairman again." Stephens replied, "Perhaps. But first I have to get reappointed." But although he was a Washington survivor, Stephens was not able to survive in the Clinton administration. He departed in August 1995 when his term expired.

Charles Cohen's term expired in 1996, and the president replaced him with a recess appointment, Republican John Higgins. Higgins had been appointed (to a recess appointment) during the 1980s, but his confirmation was blocked by the National Right to Work Committee, which considered him to be less than simon-pure on union security issues. Initially, I thought Higgins's objective was simply to keep the Republican seat warm until his party could find their candidate—much as John Truesdale had done for me between January and March of 1994. I was later disabused of that idea. At the American Bar Association Convention in San Francisco in August 1997 he announced straightforwardly: "Bill Gould has said that the Republicans may have thrown some names across the transom for the vacancy. I hope that mine is one of them." According to the rankings of the New York City management labor law firm of Nixon, Hargrave, Devans, and Doyle, "During his first Board term in 1988–89, Higgins voted for the union's position 82.1 percent of the time. Approximately a decade later, John Higgins voted for the employers position 91.4 percent of the time."[9]

Like Stephens and Cohen, Higgins was tied to the rightward drift of his party and its insistence that their nominees possess all of the indicia of this trend. He had no hope of Senate confirmation without an unmistakable manifestation of ideological purity. It was a pity, I always thought, that an insufficient number of Republicans were aware of the delight with which he had greeted the 1994 election results. I shall never forget the broad smile on his face when I walked into the Board agenda meeting the next morning.

During 1996 the other Democrat serving with me and Margaret Browning was Sarah Fox, a former aide to Ted Kennedy. She was very smart and possessed a fiery temperament, but she also could be a very nice, warm person. For some reason—initially I thought that it was the political environment but many on the staff believed that it was simply her inability to do the job—she could not produce decisions and sign off on them. She was the greatest cross I had to bear while in Washington.

While Browning was still in office, we were able to issue some important decisions that shaped the law. For instance, in *Caterpillar, Inc.* a majority of the Board affirmed the administrative law judge's finding that the employer had violated Section 8(a)(1), which prohibits employer interference and coercion.[10] The firm had contravened the antidiscrimination features of the NLRA by making and enforcing a rule prohibiting employees from displaying various union slogans, including one reading "Permanently Replace Fites" (the company president). The Board found that the slogan was a response to the employer's stated policy of using permanent strike replacements rather than a serious attempt to cause Fites's removal as chief executive officer. Even if that had been their intention, the Board held, such conduct was protected activity that immunized employees from retaliatory discharges or discipline.

In a separate opinion, I concurred but expressed my dissatisfaction with Board and judicial precedent with respect to employee activity that seeks to influence management policy and its protected status.

[T]he level of managerial policy or hierarchy protested by the Union or employees should have little of anything to do with whether such employee activity is protected. Quite obviously, the level at which managerial representatives are involved in employment conditions will vary from company to company. While I am of the view that concerted activity for the purpose of influencing management policy, which is unrelated to employment conditions, is not protected under the Act, the fact of the matter is that the presence or absence of a particular corporate hierarchical structure or internal organization does not provide the appropriate answer to the question of whether employee activity is protected under Section 7 of the Act.

In *Novotel New York,* a very important case involving union organizational tactics, a union had commenced an organizational drive among hotel workers in the midst of complaints about alleged irregularities involving the payment of overtime.[11] The union filed a suit in federal district court alleging violations of the Fair Labor Standards Act of 1938 (the minimum-wage and maximum-hours statute) and was represented by outside counsel. Consent forms were signed and filed. The issue presented was whether the union's legal services [on the FLSA suit] constituted a "benefit" that interfered with the conduct of the election. (Unions, like employers, are prohibited from providing benefits to employees during campaigns leading to NLRB elections; the most extreme illustration of such a "benefit," of course, is an outright bribe or payment by either side.)

In *Novotel,* the Board noted that, historically, unions have undertaken a wide variety of actions and tactics to protect and advance the rights of workers. The decision observed that unions have used, for example, training programs, litigation, and the advocacy and monitoring of legislation to advance their goals. I took particular interest in this case and the shaping of this opinion, though I did not write a separate concurring opinion. I thought that there was a confluence between concerted activity on the part of unions and employees and the availability of litigation services and the freedom-of-association cases that had arisen in the civil rights arena, beginning with *NAACP v. Alabama*.[12] Moreover, I was concerned about the "T-shirt" litigation, in which union victories and representation campaigns had been voided because possible recruits had been given something of "value, " such as a T-shirt or a cap. The standard of what was unlawful was inherently vague and, to my mind, sometimes created a terrible and silly waste of Board resources.

The Board's *Novotel* decision took note of the freedom-of-association cases in which the Court held that First Amendment protection applies to advocacy that takes place in the context of litigation. We held that constitutional and statutory precedents provide protection for employees in an organizational campaign and that that protection was not removed "the moment the union took the next logical step and sought financially or otherwise to assist nonmembers in gaining access to the courts for vindication of their lawful rights."

The major employer argument in *Novotel*, which Cohen accepted in his dissent, was that, notwithstanding the protection afforded employees, the result of litigation by the union was an objectionable grant of benefits that would warrant setting the election aside.[13] But, said the Board,

[W]e would be standing the statute on its head if we were to set the election aside on the ground that the legal services [provided by the union to] ... employees were a "financial benefit to which they would otherwise not be entitled." ... Because the Act protects the Petitioner's conduct, we conclude that the legal services it provided Novotel employees were a benefit to which they were entitled under national labor policy.[14]

The Board also noted the employees' lack of familiarity with the legal process and remedies and their lack of financial resources. It observed that resort to the judicial process might well have been "fruitless" without union assistance. Said the Board: "The Petitioner here did precisely what the Act intended labor organizations to do: it aided employees engaged in concerted activity."

In other cases involving benefits in the form of money paid to employees prior to an NLRB election for coming to the election (whether paid by unions or employers), the Board held that such benefits (if they exceed reimbursement for transportation expenses) could "reasonably tend to influence the election outcome."[15] Initially, I was reluctant to buy into this idea, because of my view that the parties ought to have a more wide-open unregulated environment in which to campaign prior to an election, particularly when a benefit is involved. But eventually I was dissuaded from this viewpoint, in part because of the persuasive arguments of my chief counsel, Bill Stewart, who made the point that this lack of regulation would promote outright bribery, something generally prohibited in the political process itself.

In yet another important case involving a high-visibility employer, *McClatchy Newspapers, Inc.*, the majority held that an employer could not unilaterally implement merit-pay proposals, even when bargaining had taken place to the point of impasse or deadlock (the stage at which management can generally put its position into effect). We held that if the employer were given carte blanche authority over wage increases fashioned without regard to time-and-standards criteria, it would be "so inherently destructive of the fundamental principle of collective bargaining that it could not be sanctioned as part of a doctrine created to break impasse and restore active collective bargaining." The majority went on to say: "[W]e are preserving an employer's right to bargain to impasse over proposals to retain management discretion over merit pay while, at the same time, maintaining the guild's opportunity to negotiate terms and conditions of employment."[16]

As the Board moved on with its cases in 1996, the White House sought to fill the existing vacancies. The administration became increasingly concerned that congressional Republicans might contend that the absence of a full membership complement should prevent the Board from acting on cases or might even try to shut it down for lack of a quorum. (This had actually happened between November 1993 and January 1994, when the Senate's failure to confirm me left the Board without a quorum of three.) Yet Senator Kassebaum, notwithstanding numerous invitations from the White House, refused throughout the year to provide a list of acceptable Republican candidates.

Calm before Yet Another Storm

November 7, 1996   The 1996 elections have come and gone last Tuesday and, while there is considerable rejoicing here and amongst my friends throughout the country about President Clinton's convincing election, the results in Congress are truly depressing and ominous. The Senate, notwithstanding the reelection of Paul Wellstone [who had been particularly helpful in the September 1996 Senate Oversight hearing] and Tom Harkin, and the fine victory of Robert Toricelli in New Jersey and Jack Reed in Rhode Island, will be more conservative and, without Mark Hatfield [who did not run for reelection], will be less of a moderating influence—particularly on matters affecting us. There are some who believe that the narrowed margin in the House, where the Democrats appeared to have picked up a dozen seats, will have a moderating influence on the Republican leadership. But in our area, the tension should grow since the Republicans are extremely angry with union efforts to defeat incumbent Republicans through their use of thirty-five million dollars. (They appear to have been outspent . . . but that doesn't really matter to the Republicans!)

Probably the focus will be upon our rulings interpreting the Supreme Court's *Beck* decision . . . particularly our lead cases. . . . Earlier in the year, the Republicans began to focus upon us with more intensity, and organized labor committed itself to the political campaign. I am fearful that the Republicans will try to seek revenge against organized labor and, derivatively, against us as well. I think that the Board would have been well advised to have taken my suggestions about reorganization and the consolidation of regional offices but . . . they didn't! I think that we will have considerable problems as a result of this.

This morning I gave a speech to the Associated Building Contractors' lawyers' conference [a major nonunion group], and the questioning was quite hostile indeed. Much of it seemed to buy into the ideas put forward by the Labor Policy Association, for instance, that the Board should be eliminated by statute [the idea has been put forward for years by anyone dissatisfied with the Board] and that somehow the administration has failed to appoint management labor lawyers. I am afraid that I got into an exercise of diversion when I responded to a question put to me along the lines of "Given the tradition of appointing management and union lawyers . . ." by disputing this tradition. I pointed out to the questioner that, except for Gerry Reilly (I should have mentioned Guy Farmer as well), there was no tradition of appointing management labor lawyers until the Nixon administration in the early seventies. I also noted that Browning was the first union lawyer in the history of the Board. Meanwhile, internal developments grow ominous here at the Board. Both Fox and Higgins appear to be joining Browning on a variety of [administrative] issues. . . .

Things may get so bad that I still do not rule out the possibility of leaving next summer, shortly after Bill Stewart retires in March. It will be difficult to fight the other Board members as well as the Republicans simultaneously. I. . . . have tried to do it for more than two and a half years now, but I am not sure I can continue to carry this on. . . .

But that is exactly what I did during the slightly less than two years that followed. My problems emerged on two fronts. The most exhausting one was the task of simply getting decisions issued and out the door. Meanwhile a whole raft of congressional interventions, investigations, and criticisms from the Hundred and Fifth Congress created a formidable second front and made this last period of my tenure the most challenging one.

The intensity of the Republicans' opposition increased. The AFL-CIO's financial commitment to the Clinton-Gore ticket had extended to many House Democrats as well in a campaign lost by a narrow margin. Now that the dices' roll had come up short in some districts, the Republican sword was to be used against the unions. The most persistent and wide-sweeping part of this attack was the so-called paycheck protection bill (put forward in a variety of forms at both federal and state levels). It required unions to obtain explicit permission from any worker whose union dues they planned to spend on political issues or candidates. Though rhetorically framed as a protection of workers' liberty against union coercion, the initiatives were really designed to bar unions and workers from the political process in which they had participated so effectively in 1996. And, as I explain at length in chapter 12, this was also what California Proposition 226 was all about in 1998—putting unions out of business politically and thus eroding their strength in the workplace.

In this context, any government agency related to labor, particularly one whose adjudications in both the representation and unfair labor practice arenas could actually provide power and autonomy for workers, was automatically in the Republican crosshairs. The departure of Senator Hatfield from Congress and from the chairmanship of the appropriations committee was particularly distressing for the Board. There was no one on the Republican side of the aisle who could replace him.

As 1996 wound down and 1997 began, therefore, we faced a barrage of interrogatories and investigations. All too frequently, I would hear Mary Ann Sawyer exclaim as if she had been personally assaulted as she opened the most recent document sent to us from some committee chair (perhaps Hoekstra of Michigan or Shays of Connecticut). It was a stressful and trying time for all of us. I always tried to recall the advice given me by Representative Miller of California: Never show weakness and always fight back!

The travel subject (which Shays would raise again in 1997 in connection with my attendance at baseball games) had originated with Congressman John Boehner of Ohio in an attack on me and Secretary Reich in early 1996. Boehner, who headed up the Republican congressional campaign, distributed widely a document entitled "Union Bosses: A Look Behind the Rhetoric." It began with the statement that the AFL-CIO had announced its intention to "steer a considerable amount of union money and resources toward the goal of reestablishing liberal Democrat [*sic*] control of the U.S. House of Representatives." The document went on to describe in some detail the intent of the federation to place a hundred union activists in every congressional district in contention; it asserted that the "AFL-CIO has steadily increased the number of Republican House members who are targets for its political activities."

Moreover, an election-eve letter embossed with the American flag—it purported to come from the House Labor Committee but carried no committee members' names or any indication that it was an official House document—excoriated me for my travel, not only renewing Shays's baseball charges but also alleging that in May 1994 I had gone "uninvited" to President Nelson Mandela's inauguration in South Africa. In fact, my old friend, Cyril Ramaphosa, who represented the African National Congress in the constitutional negotiations that led the 1994 elections, had invited me in 1993, and I also went as an official U.S. government representative. When a formal invitation did not arrive, my staff inquired about it, and the Republicans seized on these communications as a basis for asserting that I engaged in wasteful travel.

This document, which was distributed a week before the election, caused great concern to Congressman Sawyer of Ohio, the ranking Democrat on the House Labor Oversight Committee and someone with whom I had a good deal of contact. We both saw it as a sign of what was to come after the election.

Meanwhile, inside the Board I pushed on with a variety of policy issues, some of which would inevitably have attracted Republican attention had I left them unattended.

November 13, 1996   Yesterday we had a very extensive meeting involving *Beck*. Sarah Fox raised numerous objections, stating that we had expanded our class far beyond that contemplated by the general counsel, that is, individuals who had been hired prior to the Section 10(b) period. [This provision provides that unfair labor practice charges must be filed within six months of their occurrence.] Harold Datz, in a memo to the other chiefs, has now advocated that we basically buy into the Fox–Browning line. (Browning was with me on most of the *Beck* issues when others were on the Board. But now that Fox has jumped in trying to limit *Beck*, she sees an opportunity to do the same and feels emboldened by Fox's efforts.) The crisis for me—and this is a point that I emphasized to the Board yesterday—is that the Republicans, angered by organized labor's support of their opponents in the 1996 elections, will raise *Beck* as soon as they return in January and will come after us at that time. If we don't have these *Beck* cases decided—and I said in a speech to the Associated Builders and Contractors that I would get the *Beck* cases out by the end of the year—we will be the convenient whipping boy for the Republicans. (That may happen to us in any event, but why give them an extra opportunity?)

December 4, 1996   ... On December 2 and 3 ... we had oral arguments on the status of temporary workers and independent contractors under our Act.... The oral arguments went very well. Tuesday's presentation dealing with independent contractors was particularly skillful and helpful in dealing with a wide variety of factual problems. Monday was fairly predictable and straightforward. Most of the unions were saying change the rule—and clearly the rule does need changing—it requires both the referring agency and the user to consent to an election amongst temporary and permanent employees working alongside one another. The rule makes no sense and the employers almost uniformly said, "Leave it just like it is. It suits us just fine." Naturally, it suits them fine because they cannot be subjected to an NLRB election in which employees can exercise their free choice about their desire to be affiliated with the union and the collective-bargaining process. So many of the smug, self-satisfied, and affluent members of the Bar who got rich in the eighties and 1990s came forward and told us just to leave things alone. . . .

This evening John Hiatt of the AFL-CIO called to say how dismayed he was by the recent Tallmer report [Matthew Tallmer, a kind of "yellow journalist" who wrote for a publication called *Labor Notes*] that the AFL-CIO was disillusioned with me. Tallmer quoted people in Trumka's office saying that he had never been enthused about me because of my position on the Mine Workers' contempt citation and also, secondarily, my views on union access to company property. The headline for Tallmer was "AFL-CIO Seen Backing Away from NLRB Chairman Gould." Hiatt said that he was concerned about this, that he had checked this with numerous people in the AFL-CIO, and no one had said any of the things that Tallmer had reported. Hiatt said that he wanted me to know this because of any concern that I might have. But I assured him that I knew that Tallmer's work was always fabrication—nothing more; nothing less—and that I was very much aware of the fact that his article would have no basis in reality. . . .

December 5, 1996   I spent a good deal of time today drafting a dissent in *Sheridan University City Hotel*. [This secondary-boycott case was never issued during my tenure.] This case deals with the attempt of the Board and the Ninth Circuit in an opinion by Judge Wallace to distinguish between successorship clauses that are concededly lawful, notwithstanding the obvious secondary impact upon nonunion employers who would like to purchase the facility, on the one hand, and prohibitions against leasing the same facilities to an employer who is nonunion or who would not assume the collective-bargaining agreement. The attempt is to draw a demarcation line between these two situations [one—the purchase and the other the lease arrangement] is entirely synthetic, and I think [that my draft] will make that point fairly clear. As I discussed this matter with Bill Stewart today, he said, "This is the reason you came here." Indeed, this is true—certainly not to go through all of the altercations and attacks from fellow Board members.

On the point of fellow Board members, I had a good discussion with Sarah Fox this afternoon in which I beseeched her to do whatever she wants to do with the *Beck* cases, but that to do it so that we can either vote it up or down. Personally, I will vote it down, but I don't care whether she is in the majority or the dissent. As I told her, I am only concerned that the cases actually issue, because when the Republican Congress returns here shortly after the New Year, they are going to train their attention upon unions and politics, union campaign expenditures, the role that the *Beck* decision as interpreted by the Board plays in furthering union political interests and—most important of all—our own ability to actually issue decisions. This failure to issue decisions is completely inexcusable, and it is attributable to the fact that new people, particularly Sarah Fox, have come in with their own ideas and have created absolute turmoil for us on issues that we thought we had resolved at the time of *California Saw & Knife*.

Jack Toner [the Board's executive secretary] told me that Browning had not been able to come into the office over the past couple of days. In his words, apparently she was able to "suck it up" and to participate in our oral argument on Monday and Tuesday. When I asked her whether she was able to continue for two hours back to back, she responded without any hesitation that she was able to do so. But apparently she has [only] been able to come into the office for a couple of hours or so each day for the last couple of days. She is functioning, but not at full speed.

I had an interesting discussion with Congressman John Porter today, in which he expressed enthusiasm about our idea to bring his staff and other staff of the Republicans and Democrats on the appropriations committee in both the Senate and the House over here to look at our facilities, to get an understanding of what we do, and to attend our Advisory Panel meetings in late January.

Subsequently, I spoke to Senator Specter's chief of staff and he expressed similar enthusiasm. I have not yet been able to reach Senator Tom Harkin, Congressman David Obey, and Congresswoman Nancy Pelosi on the Democratic side, but I hope to do so soon. We will need every technique and tactic possible to keep the Republicans at bay during 1997.

That prediction was to prove all too accurate. In the wake of the 1996 elections, the Board entered its most volatile and explosive period. By the second week of the new year it was obvious, as I said in my diary, that "a real crisis is building up here." The principal internal problem continued to be Fox's refusal to sign off on the large number of cases—first and foremost the *Beck* cases—that should have been decided a long time ago. I was also pretty sure that there would be some big changes on the Board in 1997. Browning was very ill and frail, and it seemed unlikely that Fox would be confirmed (she was) or that Higgins would be re-nominated (he wasn't). Although the moderate Senator Jim Jeffords of Vermont succeeded Kassebaum as chairman of the Senate Labor and Human Resources Committee after the 1996 elections (she had not sought reelection), authority over the critical arena of Republican nominees was transferred to Majority Leader Trent Lott. And, like Kassebaum, Lott would refuse throughout most of 1997 to send a list of nominees to the White House—despite numerous entreaties to do so!

11

"The Lights Will Not Go Off"

The year 1997 brought with it a confluence of problems, many of which we had been dealing with since 1995. There was the ongoing battle with the House appropriations subcommittee and the promise of new hearings of Shays's Government Oversight Subcommittee. Notwithstanding later protestations that it did not regard the matter of my attendance at baseball games as a serious matter, Shays's committee continued to harp on the games I went to while out of town—generally to give a speech about labor law or visit a Board regional office—and even in Oakland and San Francisco when I was in the Bay Area during summer vacations. The subcommittee was evidently also computing the number of evening baseball games I had attended in Baltimore and Bowie, Maryland, after working hours.

In early February Margaret Browning went into the hospital with fluid on her lungs. This appeared to be an ominous development and something akin to pneumonia. However, she was able to come home, and for the next couple of weeks she continued to work on her cases as much as she could. Sarah Fox still would not or could not move forward with the cases in front of her, first and foremost the *Beck* decisions.

January 9, 1997 ... I promised—reasonably it seems to me—in a speech to the Associated Building Contractors' Lawyers Conference on November 7, that all the pending *Beck* cases would be out by the end of the year, that is, 1996. Very few have issued since, and this is primarily because of the fact that Fox has a wide variety of new ideas—she did not participate in *California Saw & Knife*—and simply cannot either express her opinions or get off the cases in question....

I would imagine that there would be some big changes in the Board this year. Browning is very ill and frail, and I simply don't know what will happen on that front. It seems somewhat unlikely that Fox will be confirmed. Higgins was not renominated [Fox was], and I hope that the White House looks for Republicans like Leland Cross (a management labor lawyer from Indianapolis and member of our advisory panel) or Ken Hipp, member of the National Mediation Board, or Saul Kramer [management labor lawyer from New York City]. It is quite possible that there will be Democratic seats to be filled as well.

February 5, 1997   I met with Congressman John Porter today.... I brought him up to date on the kinds of initiatives that we had undertaken to make the Board more efficient, and he seemed impressed with them.... But what was interesting, of course, was what Porter was interested in. He asked my views about the NLRB jurisdictional indexing proposal, and I repeated my point: (1) no one knew what the real impact would be; (2) that employers as well as unions were opposed to it because of the fact that states had no mechanisms in place that would regulate unfair labor practices. I mentioned to Porter that the advisory panels—management and labor—had unanimously rejected the position of the committee. I went into a fair amount of detail—probably too much detail—about the delicate compromise that was negotiated between President Eisenhower and the Democratic Congress. I seemed to get through to Porter when I reminded him that I was in law school when all of this was happening, and he said, "Oh, I was in law school also." And we then went on to talk about his labor-law class with Russell Smith [at the University of Michigan Law School] and the fact that he had done very well on the examination.

February 7, 1997   I met yesterday with Senator [Jeff] Bingaman [D-N.M.], Senator [Patricia] Murray [D-Wash.], Senator [Jack] Reed [D-R. I.], Senator Jeffords [R-Vt.] and Senator Susan Collins [R-Maine] to report to them about the agency and recent legal developments. Bingaman, with whom I had met when we spoke together at Stanford last October, was particularly interested in the TEAM Act and Section 8(a)(2). He asked me whether it would be illegal for an employer to bring in a group of employees and to ask them to communicate with him about conditions of employment, and to ask anyone else who wanted to come in, to come as well. I said that it would not be illegal and pointed his attention to my *Keeler Brass* opinion. He seems to be interested in doing something, and yet, of course, does not want to act in an antiunion manner. We promised to keep in touch in the coming days about this, given the hearings that are coming up in the Senate on February 12.

Senator Patty Murray of Washington was particularly interested in this subject and agreed with my point that this was an issue that was in search of a problem. I had a greater opportunity to talk with her about the precise nature of the law than I did with Bingaman. Jack Reed was similarly interested and stated that Kennedy had convened a breakfast meeting for next Tuesday with AFL-CIO President Sweeney. Both Murray and Reed expressed interest in the data relating to the number of cases that actually come before us, and I provided this to them today with copies to Bingaman, so that they will have this in advance of the hearings.

Senator Collins was particularly interested in the *Beck* cases and I told her of our *California Saw & Knife* and *Weyerhaeuser Paper Company* decisions.... She was very attentive and listened carefully to what I had to say generally—and about *Beck* as well as the TEAM Act in particular.[1]

The Jeffords meeting was a very different one. He greeted me warmly and effusively, but was very much at arm's length in our discussions. When he mentioned the TEAM Act, and I told him that I had given him a copy of my *Keeler Brass* opinion he said, "so there's no need to legislate in this area, is there?" His voice was dripping with sarcasm and he looked away with a half-smile on his face. When we spoke about the vacancies on the Board, he expressed awareness of Browning's illness and said that he would try to get people that were impartial and acceptable to all. I said that I thought that I had acted in this manner, but he made a remark to the effect that "you can see that not all members of the Senate are in agreement on this."

It was a cordial meeting, but not a particularly friendly one. Yet, when all is said and done, he is about the best Republican that we can ever get in that position. . . .

This morning . . . we had a real battle about postal ballots. The regional director in Indianapolis, Chavarry, ordered a postal ballot where he would have to send an agent two hundred and twenty (220) miles round trip, and where two elections were to be conducted in two units, the employer stating that they should be conducted on two separate days. Fox sided with Higgins, who began to pontificate about how manual ballots are the crown jewel of the act and the heart of the act. Of course, the act nowhere mentions manual ballots or the particular method for conducting a ballot. Both Bill and I made it clear that we thought that he, Higgins, was talking a great deal of nonsense and Higgins became testy, asking us to allow him to complete his sentence. But Fox played the truly pernicious role, weighing in with Higgins. She has been destructive in the postal-ballot cases generally and now has done a draft in the *Spectacor* case, which has been here forever—more than a year—which would not allow us to hold postal ballots on the basis of resources alone. Higgins said that we need to spend money on ballots, and I pointed out to him that Congress was asking us to conserve monies, although I have no doubt that they will side with him on this particular matter because . . . one of his motivations for holding the manual ballot is to allow the employer to effectively use the captive audience. . . .

Wayne Gold [Head of the Office of Representation Appeals] told us afterwards that Chavarry was really angry about the fact that the Board had undercut him and said that he would never hold another postal ballot again. Regrettably, in *Willamette Industries* the Board is sending that message and discouraging the regional directors from doing what I have tried to get them to do in 1994 and 1995.[2] . . . .

February 26, 1997   We continue to be in a period of limbo and quasi-crisis here at the Board. For some reason Sarah Fox holds on to cases forever under the guise of reworking them and then inserts only slight modifications after a substantial period of time. This happened most recently in connection with the *PECO Energy* decision which she held for about three months and which we finally issued on February 14.[3] This has prompted Elliott Bredhoff [a Washington union lawyer] and Donald Wightman (president of the Utility Workers Union) to contact me about changing our procedures through statute and to give the chairman the authority to discharge cases. I am going to have lunch with Elliott next week to discuss this. And the most troublesome aspect of what Fox is doing relates to the *Beck* cases, which she continues to sit on. We finally received yesterday her revisions in [one case], which presumably could spring loose a whole bunch of these cases. She has been sitting on *Connecticut Limousine* forever, which simply involves a remand to the administrative law judge amongst other issues, the question of whether union expenditures for co-organizing are germane to collective bargaining.[4] Of course, I believe that they are, as I have said in law review pieces a decade ago. But the problem is [that] the Supreme Court, albeit within the context of the Railway Labor Act, says otherwise in the *Ellis* decision.[5] Accordingly I have dissented in *Connecticut Limousine* on the Board's remand on this particular issue, taking the view that we are foreclosed from considering evidence, given the Supreme Court's decision. This must be the matter that Fox is taking months to respond on because it is the only issue of any significance. [No response was ever provided on this issue in the decision when it was issued a half year later!]

Higgins is proving to be both difficult and politically mischievous. I had asked him to let the *Burlington* case go—*Burlington* involving a common-site secondary picketing issue in which I was dissenting against Browning and Fox, and he had said that he would seriously consider not participating.[6] [The law prohibits secondary boycotts and other forms of pressure designed to involve a so-called neutral in a dispute with another employer, the primary.] But when he saw my draft [at that point, a dissent in support of the management position], he came in to tell me that he would have to participate, thus deadlocking the case and keeping it here until the foreseeable future. He said that he would be "impeached" ... if he let this go forward. I reminded him of his promise to me that he would seriously consider not participating and that he has deadlocked other cases, which exacerbates our probable backlog, but that is not as important to him. Similarly, he holds up the *Detroit News and Free Press* secondary-boycott settlement, where he and Browning have voted together to approve the general counsel's settlement, [thus bringing to end Board litigation against secondary-boycott activity engaged in by the Detroit newspaper unions], and I have stated that it [the settlement] is deficient.[7] Again, I feel that he views himself as being outflanked politically and simply sat on the case without comment for two or three weeks. Now, this week he takes the position that he wants to examine the general counsel's handling of new secondary-boycott charges that have been filed by the employers against the union. I objected to this, but I am sure that Browning will side with him, and she is saying that she may change her vote if, in fact, the new charges demonstrate—as they may well—the deficiencies of the settlement that I have already identified ... .

Meanwhile, Browning has become gravely ill. She was in the hospital last week for more than a week to drain fluid from her lungs. For the past week she has been home confined to bed. I called her on Sunday and her husband, Joe, answered and expressed the view that she was "fine" and said that while she could not speak to me then, she would call me back if I wished her to do so. I said that would be fine—but she has never called. I'm told that she is not communicating with most of the people that call her and that much of the time now she is unable to handle cases.

I have kept Bob Nash and Patsy Thomasson [deputy director of presidential personnel] alerted on this.

In Limbo and Quasi-Crisis

March 3, 1997   On Friday morning at 2:00 A.M. [February 28th] Margaret Browning died. While we had been expecting this for some time, it still comes as a shock. It is hard to believe that she is gone ... She put up a valiant struggle, continuing to work on her cases until the very end. I wonder whether I could do the same with the sense of dedication and courage that she exhibited. Now we were down to three, and today ... we spent a good deal of time at agenda talking about what we'll be doing. I believe that we should press on with all the cases in the same way. Higgins took the position, which seems to be supported by most people here, that we should not reverse precedent. But I asked whether this was written down someplace in the way of policy guidance or even in Board decisions. No one seemed to come up with any kind of examples, although Howard Datz seemed to recall that some Board members had assumed, in their opinions, that this would be done. I said that we should press on with the contingent-worker cases which were argued here in December. But Higgins was very much against this and the discussion was inconclusive. We will be having another agenda in a few weeks to focus upon where we are now in some of the cases that have been here for a long time.

Still the *Beck* cases do not emerge. Finally, Fox has signed off on a draft of [one case] ... which is on my desk now. That, apparently, will spring a whole bunch of them loose. At today's agenda, Fox still talked of her draft in *Connecticut Limousine* as though it was something that would be emerging at some point in the future. I pointed out that it was simply a remand, but she said there are a lot of issues that she could recall—although no one seemed to mention what the issues were. When I mentioned *Legal Aid,* [the supervisory status of professional employees] which is perhaps our oldest case which has been here far before I got here, she seemed unaware that anything was to be done with that case coming out of her shop, until Lafe Solomon pointed out that he was preparing something for her.[8] ...

This past weekend I was in North Carolina, where I walked the path walked by the first William Benjamin Gould in the previous century....

March 5, 1997   Inspector General Bob Allen was here yesterday and complained about the fact that his investigation of alleged improper procurement practices in Feinstein's office—the principal focus being upon Gloria Joseph—is moving slowly because, amongst other matters, Joe Frankel [special assistant to Feinstein] and others in Feinstein's office are insisting upon the presence of counsel while being interrogated. [The Inspector General's Office, created by Congress, is charged with eliminating fraud, waste, and mismanagement and promoting efficiency and economy.] Allen opined a great deal about the investigation and asked whether I would mind having my name used as someone who was willing to proceed with the investigation, which he completed a few weeks ago, about my travel and reimbursement of baseball people [without the presence of counsel]. I assured him that I would be perfectly willing to have him use my name. Today, Bill Stewart said that Bob has telephoned back because he had inquired with other inspector generals, and they were absolutely amazed that any senior official would insist upon the right to counsel. I would imagine that Bob is going to forge ahead with this and that Frankel and others will relent. But this could be a scandal waiting to happen, given the kinds of allegations and counter-allegations that are moving back and forth.

Earlier this week the *Wall Street Journal* ran a piece criticizing Feinstein—of course, they did not distinguish between Feinstein and myself—on refusing to issue a complaint against a union involved in a right-to-work controversy with the National Right to Work Committee that is, Feinstein taking the position that the complaint should not issue in a *de minimus* situation. My own view is that Feinstein should have issued the complaint and left us to interpret the matter.... Frankly, it may be that I would have come to a different conclusion than Feinstein. But the important point is that we, the Board, should have made the decision and not the general counsel.

Baseball, Bedrooms, and Representative Shays

The Republicans simply could not let loose the of the baseball matter. I think that this is what had initially prompted representatives Shays and Hoekstra to send written interrogatories to all Board members asking what they did with their spare time when they were out of town on speaking engagements for the Board. This first step in their process seemed to imply that I was in another city simply to attend a baseball game rather than to fulfill my Board functions.

My first inclination was to respond that it was none of Congress's business what I did with my free time after my workday ended. But OMB dissuaded me from taking this position, and I simply avoided answering the question altogether.

Their next step was more interesting. Both Shays and Hoekstra were fascinated with my connection with Gene Orza and wanted to know all about who had attended a Cleveland–New York game we had gone to in the spring of 1996 (after a lecture I gave at St. John's Law School). Their inquiry then moved in a different direction.

March 5 (continued)   Today I received a rather insulting and argumentative letter from Shays and Hoekstra requesting yet more information—and I got off a letter to Shays, with whom I had the most discussion about this entire baseball ticket and travel controversy, that will surely get his attention. It looks as though we are in for another battle. Shays and Hoekstra have said that since I have requested a hearing they want to give it to me. I pointed out in my letter of March 5 that they failed to state the basis for my request, their leaking of their communications to me to the *Washington Times* and another publication, which had telephoned me about the communications before I had even received them.

In their March 4 letter, after surveying my correspondence with baseball people relating to baseball tickets, they had spent the taxpayers' money by asking the following question: "Please identify 'Dusty' by gender, position, and relationship to the San Francisco Giants, if any." The answer I provided was as follows "Dusty Baker is a male. He is the manager of the San Francisco Giants and, in that connection, his relationship to the Giants is a prominent and important one." When I related this interrogatory to Dusty at a later point, he said "Bill, they simply wanted to see if you had a girlfriend with the Giants!"

Case Production

March 6, 1997   Early in the day I had lunch with Elliott Bredhoff, where the ... subject [of filling Board vacancies] came up, and I told Elliott that I would press both Bob Nash and John Hiatt to see if the White House would move affirmatively next month if the

Republicans do not respond with some names for the Republican seat. Elliott and I also spoke about how we can be more effective with case handling, and he advised me that Jack Toner had told him that rule 76-1 permitted the Board to get cases out if two Board members would vote to do so. But I pointed out to Elliott that when I first came here in 1994, I had asked to have rule 76-1 reinstated—it is not in effect now as Elliott and I guess Jack Toner seemed to believe—and that I was voted down four to one on this as well as on the question of having individual Board members author particular cases. I told him that I was reluctant to bring this rule up again with the Board because Fox would be particularly sensitive on this score. This morning I reviewed and slightly revised [a] the draft ... [in] ... one of the lead *Beck* cases. Fox had sat on this one for about three months just to make a few small revisions, mostly substituting language like "the employee may elect non-membership," as opposed to the employee "may resign." All this could have been done in about two hours. Instead it took more than three months. Rule 76-1 would, in fact, be an important provision. But we will not get it—and another way of looking at it is that it would be difficult to get a majority of the Board to discharge a case because of the concern of offending colleagues.

March 13, 1997 I was in Philadelphia today for a retirement luncheon for Peter Hirsch [Philadelphia's regional director]. ... There was a very good feeling throughout the audience about Peter and about the way in which things were conducted. I was warmly received and felt that I made some good friends. ...

When I returned here at about 5:30 P.M. I found both Bill Stewart and Sarah Fox. Fox made one of her most revealing remarks when I pressed her to sign off on *Connecticut Limousine* and move it. She asked me why it was so important and she said "Do you want to have the case revealed before the House Appropriations Subcommittee hearing so that you can show that you are against the remand?" I immediately said to her "Is that why you were holding this case up?" Of course, clearly she denied this.

But the more I thought about it the more I realized that she is sitting on these cases because she believes these cannot help but be harmful for her with the Senate. My interests are to see the *Beck* cases promptly decided, and I am also proud of my [substantive] positions that I have taken throughout. I'm sure that she is proud of her positions. But she sees the revelation of them to be politically disadvantageous to her. I don't think that she truly believes that she can keep these cases under wraps during the entire 105th Congress. But clearly she hopes to keep these cases hidden while the Congress focuses upon us. The Congress, of course, will focus upon us next week when the House holds the appropriation subcommittee hearings ...

... Then at the conclusion of my conversation with Fox, she had the audacity to say that if we came around to her point of view on a case involving the Mine Workers and the Department of Interior—where it is the view of Bill Stewart and myself that we need to get a formal submission from the Department of Labor in order to be adequately advised— that she would then issue *Connecticut Limousine*. This, from someone who had said to me a few months back that I was acting in a manner inconsistent with my oath of office because of my willingness to join her or not join her depending upon what she was ... doing ... in [a] personnel dispute involving the New Orleans Region!

... I don't think that Fox is motivated ... to stop me from looking good with the Republicans in the *Beck* cases. I think that she just doesn't want to look bad. Therefore, I would imagine that she will not be concerned with any attention that the *Detroit News–Free Press* secondary boycott cases may get because here she is taking a position—the one that I stood by these past two months—which is against the interest of the unions. [I was correct—the case finally issued on March 14!]

A New Round of Appropriations Hearings

March 26, 1997   Last week was far more tumultuous than expected. We had a hearing before the House Appropriations Subcommittee, and it is clear that they are going to be much more aggressive than they have been in 1995 and 1996. More people are participating. For instance, Congressman Wicker of Mississippi, who has never been at the hearings before, asked me numerous questions about contacts with Vice-President Gore's office on his proposals relating to procurement and labor law violations. Congresswoman Northrop, whom I had met with and tried to promote a good relationship with, was quite irate and antagonistic in a series of questions about single-location facilities and salting cases. Indeed, the *Wall Street Journal*, the day before ran a piece entitled "The NLRB's Secret War against Small Business," suggesting that readers should get my telephone number and call me about the proposed rule on single-facility location.[9] Istook came after me and suggested that I had been lying about testimony on the number of cars that the Board had. Bonilla called Feinstein the most biased general counsel in the history of the Board, and Feinstein did not respond immediately [though I urged him to do so].

When I got down to Florida to speak at the Stetson Law School, the office faxed me the written questions [propounded by the subcommittee]. And they were numerous and aggressive. We are in for a very long struggle, particularly triggered by the desire of the Republicans to retaliate against organized labor—they see us as a tool of organized labor—for the AFL-CIO's involvement in the 1996 elections.

The sad thing was that no Democrats were present at the hearings. Nancy Pelosi was there for a minute or so and Congresswoman [Nita] Lowey from New York came in for a minute or so. But no one was there to jump in and work with us—a very sharp contrast to the oversight hearings in 1995, when I went to each of the Democrats and had urged them to attend. This time I didn't have time to do that, although I probably should have talked to some of the union leaders to see if they would make contact with the Democrats.

"Our Productivity's Gone South"

With Browning gone, the Board was down to three members and faced the Republican argument that we should do nothing on any case of policy import or take any action that involved the reversal of precedent. Yet a fully constituted Board was impossible to achieve because the Republicans would not put forward their own nominees. Higgins posed the worst problem in this regard, and his inaction was increasingly aided and abetted by Fox.

To my extraordinary friend, Bill Gould, who will make history for our Country! With all my best, Anna G. Eshoo, M.C. 4.94

At the Senate Labor Committee Confirmation Hearing, October 1, 1993. I was accompanied by Howard Jenkins Jr., my former boss and the first black member of the NLRB (left) and Representative Anna G. Eshoo (D-Calif., right). Not pictured, but also at my side, were Senator Dianne Feinstein (D-Calif.), Senator Barbara Boxer (D-Calif.), and Representative William Clay (D-Mo.).

February 1994. San Francisco Giants manager Dusty Baker visited Stanford University Law School to lecture. In 1993 he was the winningest rookie manager in the history of baseball—in 2000 he was to become the winningest San Francisco Giants manager ever—and he was extremely helpful in providing support and arranging California contacts during the long confirmation process.

*My first Board, March 1994.
The 1994–1995 period when
these members served with
me was the most productive
in NLRB's recorded history.
From left to right, James M.
Stephens, Margaret
Browning, myself, Charles J.
Cohen, and Dennis M.
Devaney.*

*Part of the chairman's staff. Deputy
Chief Counsel Kate Dowling
(1997–1998) is in the back row third
from the left. Below her to the right
between the middle and back row is
my chief counsel for 1997–1998, Al
Wolff. Also pictured are two of the
Four Horsemen, Ella Chatterjee (first
row, center) and David Schwartz
(middle row, fourth from left).*

*Other members of the chairman's
staff. The heart and soul of the
NLRB in Washington consisted of
my confidential assistant, Mary Ann
Sawyer (standing, third from left),
and Chief Counsel Bill Stewart
(standing, fifth from left).*

With President Clinton at the White House, April 1994. To the right of board member Charles Cohen (center) is Lane Kirkland, who was then president of the AFL-CIO.

With Paul Wellstone (D-Minn.). Senator Wellstone was my principal defender at the October 1993 confirmation hearing and a close and valued friend throughout my Washington tenure.

With Edward Kennedy (D-Mass.), April 1994. Senator Kennedy steered my nomination through the shoals of the Senate and brought it safe to harbor with no defecting Democrats.

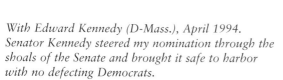

DRABBLE/KEVIN FAGAN

The NLRB and baseball. The name of the Board was emblazoned on the minds of the fans when the Board's petition for an injunction induced the players to return to the field to begin the 1995 baseball season. From Prince George's Journal, *April 26, 1995; reproduced with the permission of Kevin Drabble and United Features Syndicate, Inc.*

April 1995, Hofstra University, commemorating the 100th anniversary of the birth of Babe Ruth. I am pictured here with Phil Rizzuto, who played shortstop for the New York Yankees when I was a child. At dinner, the conference organizer, Dean Eric Schmertz, paid tribute the Board's role in ending the 1994–1995 baseball dispute.

With the Reverend Jesse Jackson, Atlanta, May 1995. Reverend Jackson, who was the first person to congratulate me on my nomination by President Clinton, is shown presenting me an award on behalf of the Rainbow Coalition. His inscription on the photo reads: "Keep hope alive!"

August 1995, Camden Yards, throwing out the first ball in the Red Sox–Orioles Game. Orioles owner Peter Angelos assigned me this honor because of the Board's help in settling the baseball strike.

White House reception for Presidential Medal of Honor winners, September 1995. The honorees on this occasion were my friends (not shown) attorney William Coleman of Washington, D.C., and the eminent historian John Hope Franklin, professor emeritus of history at Duke University.

With Senator Mark Hatfield (R-Ore.), summer 1996. This giant of the Senate—along with Senators Tom Harkin (D-Iowa) and Paul Wellstone (D-Minn.)—frequently came to the NLRB's rescue during its struggles with the 104th and 105th congresses. My best friend and the Board's best supporter in the Senate, the Lincolnesque Senator Hatfield was greatly missed after he left Washington in January of 1997.

With Representative Nancy Pelosi (D-Calif.), San Francisco, May 1996. Rep. Pelosi, a member of the House Appropriations Subcommittee, was one of the staunchest supporters of the NLRB.

Four Bills at the White House, October 1997. On this occasion, President Clinton congratulated retiring NLRB Chief Counsel Bill Stewart (second from right), winner of the President's Award for Distinguished Federal Civilian Service. On the far right is Bill Stewart's companion, the late William Dresser.

Dealing with the growing backlog, 1997. We were never sure whether the two other characters at the table represented Board members Sarah Fox and John Higgins or my Deputy Chief Counsel Kate Dowling and Chief Counsel Al Wolff. From the Washington Post, *October 31, 1997.*

My last Board, 1997–1998. From left to right: Sarah Fox, Peter Hurtgen, myself, J. Robert Brame, and Wilma Liebman. For two principal reasons, this was the most inactive and least productive of all my Boards.

With Senator Tom Harkin (D-Iowa), July 1998. A supportive friend from the time I first met him in the fall of 1993, Senator Harkin was an invaluable ally and advocate for the Board. At this private luncheon in his office, while discussing the number of Senate Republicans who had voted against my confirmation, Harkin declared, "Bill, that was your badge of honor."

March 26 (continued)   On Monday I had lunch with Steve Yokich, George Kourpias, George Becker and the new Machinist leader, R. Tom Buffenbarger.... When I met with them I related the budget hearings to them and the frontal attack that we are under. They expressed concern and said that they would round up the Democrats in our future hearings. They were rather confused and wondering about what should be done on the Board appointments. I pointed out to them that it was important to get a recess appointee because of the so-called tradition that it takes more than two votes to overrule prior Board precedent. Higgins, as it turns out, is resisting my proposal that we vote case-by-case on the question of whether a particular case should emerge with a reversal of precedents. I told them that it is important to get somebody there now—preferably someone who did not want to be nominated so that they could do the right thing on their votes in case handling.... At one point during the conversation I suggested—in response to the point that the president seemed to have forgotten his allies in organized labor now that he was reelected—that a good point of contact would be Vice-President Gore and his office, especially given his many appearances before AFL-CIO Executive Council. But Yokich poured cold water on this idea....

Yesterday I spoke with Sarah Fox about pushing union-organizing initiatives on a number of fronts: (1) formulating some kind of right of unions to rebut captive-audience speeches in lieu of *Peerless Plywood*[10] [which precludes all captive audience speeches twenty-four hours prior to the election]; (2) formulating the rule on single-location presumptions through adjudication rather than rule making; (3) undertaking more initiatives on dealing with hearings in a prompt and expeditious way so that we can get votes. But Fox, probably because of her own confirmation problems, was lukewarm to all of this. ... [She] felt that any attempt to deal with the single-facility issue through adjudication would be too confrontational with the Congress....

March 28, 1997   ... No offer or names [of Republican appointees to the Board] have been received from Senator Lott as of yesterday—and it seems unlikely that they will be. As I said to Peg [Clark of the President's Personnel Office], the Republicans believe that time is on their side, and if they can bring the agency to a screeching halt later in the year it will require the president to make more recess appointments. The only counter of that strategy is to make a recess appointment that scares the Republicans and would drive them to the bargaining table....

April 3, 1997   Yesterday we had a very important meeting involving *stare decisis* in Board decisions. Higgins has argued that we cannot depart from stare decisis when the Board is down to three members because we are required to have more support for such a proposition. He even stated that even a 3 to 0 decision by a three-member Board would be wrong, but he seemed to back away from this. The problem for his argument is that it is not supported in statute, decisions by either the Board or the courts of appeals, or any policy document anywhere! [However, it was supported by most of the Republican members of Congress who took an interest in the Board!] The best argument that can be made for his point is that, as Harold Datz said at the Board meeting on the subject yesterday, it [reversal of precedent with a 2 to 1 vote with two Board members in majority] hasn't been done before—at least when the Board was down to three members. It was done 3 to 0 when there were four members, and also the Dotson Board did it on numerous occasions [3 to 0] when there were three Board members. However, everyone agrees—Higgins claims to be amongst this number—that the Dotson Board's decisions brought the Board into disrepute. I argued that that was a peculiarity because of the fact that the Dotson Board was waiting until the appointees of the Carter administration departed and then immediately lined up all their people to provide a series of 3 to 0 votes.

... I referred to the fact that the so-called practice or custom that required a 3 to 0 or, in Higgins' view, a 3 to1 vote has no basis in practice or custom or case law or anything.... Higgins said it was part of "Board lore." He said that Board people "knew" this. I put the question to him "Am I a Board person?" He didn't respond. I should have said, as I thought afterwards, "Is Bill Stewart a Board person?" Bill having been here some thirty-three years prior to his retirement.

I said that we had taken an oath of law to perform our job and to decide cases and this is what the United States Government had hired us to do. To Higgins's and Datz's point that we somehow needed credibility, I pointed out that our credibility had never been better with the judiciary and with the public. They had no response to any of this.

Sarah Fox joined in by telephone hook-up from Buffalo, New York, and said that the language of the statute clearly required Board members to discharge their obligation on all matters, including the reversal of precedent. And I think that she is right. I pointed out that Jeff Weddekind [the acting solicitor of the Board] had been able to find out that the Federal Communications Commission and the Securities and Exchange Commission had no such tradition. No one had any information on any other administrative agency.

In short, I argued, and I think effectively, that all the evidence was in support of our position. The GAO [General Accounting Office] had criticized the Board in the 1980s for having refused to move forward with cases on the ground that vacancies existed. Here, as I emphasized, there was no prospect for any break in the [Congress–White House] stalemate. Indeed, as I said, all the objective evidence and indicia support the proposition that the stalemate will continue for some period of time, perhaps well into 1998 or 1999, and that we will not have new Board members. (Although I did not say this, it seems to me clear that the Republicans believe that they can stiff Clinton and bring the Board to a complete halt with one member in November, unless Clinton either capitulates or makes new recess appointments....) Higgins really irritated me by saying "If you were back in Stanford as a commentator would you be saying the same thing?" As I told Harold Datz today, no one at Stanford or any other university has ever even heard of this idea that is being put forward by Higgins, let alone adhered to it or supported it. Higgins was way off the mark and insulting in his suggestion that I would act in an unprincipled fashion.

Higgins, almost as a desperation gasp, toward the end of the meeting began to pursue the idea that our involvement in this issue would somehow impede our ability to deal with the backlog. He opined about how he was concerned about how the backlog had grown "on his watch" and said "why can't we get on with the cases that will cure the backlog rather than focusing upon this issue?" I said that this was a "red herring" and "distraction" and that it had nothing to do with the issue at hand. The problem was that there was no concern with taking on the backlog as well as taking on cases that involved a reversal of precedent.

April 10, 1997 Fox and Higgins are becoming very aggressive about having some input into the answers as to the House appropriations subcommittee. On April 7, they set up a conference call with me, and I said that I welcomed their input. However, Al [Wolff, my new chief counsel] sent them a memo on my behalf indicating that I would have the final say on any answers, and I heard very little out of them thereafter. Then on this past Friday, Fox began to press again. We went back and forth with a series of memos ... and it turned out to be a kind of cat-and-mouse game with them—Sarah claimed to be speaking always for Higgins, who had gone off to attend a memorial service for Browning in Philadelphia. ... On Friday afternoon Fox and I had a long talk in which amongst other things, she claimed that I was "inviting" the hostile questions from the committee. I responded by saying that I didn't think it was my speeches, as she claimed, that provoked them, but rather the actions that we took. She harkened back to my March 1994 speech when I said that I would view the Senate vote [on my confirmation] as a badge of honor. This really shows where she is coming from.

Fox went on a great length about how her role was a valuable one because she had had Senate committee experience. She said she had called Larry Matlack of OMB, who had assured her that the answers [to the subcommittee] were to be provided on a consensus basis. I responded by saying that I would never agree to a majority-rule system and she agreed that that was not what was in order. I also said that I thought that she knew a lot about the committee system. Once I said that, the tension began to ease a bit and she stated that we had a lot of friends in common, that she has never attacked me "publicly." However, she said an amazing thing, that is, that while I went to great pains to be impartial between labor and management I was extremely partisan, thereby indicating that that had apparently antagonized the Republicans. I didn't have the presence of mind ... to tell her that, aside from White House staunch and steadfast support, the thing that had really saved the agency budget was my friendship with a Republican, Senator Hatfield....

On Thursday morning I met with Senator Bingaman and some of his staff aides, at his request, for a breakfast meeting to discuss the TEAM Act. He clearly wants to support some version of it and is skeptical of Kennedy's rigid opposition. I told him that I thought if an employer selected employees randomly or selected someone and allowed employees to select others, that could be acceptable. He thought that Senator Jeffords might be opposed to the language to the effect that "whenever practicable" democracy would rule might be enough. I said that I thought that some kind of affirmative obligation had to be placed upon the employer to pursue democracy rather than a hierarchical relationship in establishing the committee or team....

It seemed to me that Bingaman was looking for a way to break with the Democrats. I'm not sure when and where the next step is that will be taken by him....

Friday, April 18 was an extremely exhausting day. Everything moved so quickly that I didn't even think about picking up clothes that I needed from the cleaner and money that I needed for the weekend—until everything had closed late in the day. I spoke with Peg Clark [from the White House], who advised me that Senator Lott had still not proposed Republican candidates for the Board. She said that she wanted Bob Nash's office to go ahead with "another strategy," which I took to mean that they will put together a couple of names for recess appointments later in the year if the Republicans don't move. Apparently, Bob Nash is sending Lott a letter this week, which states that the president regards the Board as a very important institution and wants the Republicans to cooperate on providing names. But I would imagine that they continue to believe that time is on their side and that they can either shut us down or create havoc by bringing in two more recess appointees and therefore won't be moved by any letter—any more than Kassebaum was in all of 1996. . . .

April 21, 1997 I have been trying to think about the worst aspect of my job at Stanford Law School and at the National Labor Relations Board. I think that the worst part of the job at Stanford is grading the papers of students. The worst part of my job at the Board is dealing with fellow Board members. It was made very clear to me this afternoon that the worst part of the job at the Board is worse than the worst part of the job at Stanford Law School.

Sarah Fox was a character to behold today! She came into a meeting that I had called at her request to get her input on answers to Congress arising out of the appropriations hearing, without any kind of written proposal. When I suggested to her that she should provide us with proposals she was very angry and looked at me with one of those glaring stares. She came back ten minutes later and said that she couldn't get it out of her computer and that she was calling people to do it. She then proceeded to challenge a whole series of matters that I had put forward. I agreed to take both Feinstein's and my name out of the first five pages and simply to substitute "answer" to an answer rather than Gould or Feinstein. It really didn't matter to me because I take no pride of authorship in this part of it. Then she began to insist that I remove my name from anything that didn't involve me as an individual, e.g., travel and the like. I said that I wouldn't do this. She said that I should really take this up with OMB because they were saying that I should. I said that I didn't believe that OMB was saying that I should, and I would keep my name in the answers. Then she said that she felt my statement that members of the Advisory Panel had said that there would be more litigation in the event that the jurisdictional yardsticks were raised was in error . . . and she asked me what the possible rationale could be. I said I couldn't recall the rationale but I was pretty sure that it had been said at the meeting and I would have someone check it. I will be surprised if there isn't a statement in there to that effect. [In fact, I was correct. The Advisory Panel was in complete opposition to the jurisdictional-yardsticks proposal of the Republicans. This whole discussion was a complete waste of time.]

Last week on a postal ballot matter where Fox was telling me that I had to join in her opinion, Datz laughingly said, "You guys work it out. That's something for the two of you to work out." I am sure that Higgins must have been laughing to himself this afternoon to watch Fox's performance. One other thing that Fox kept pounding away on and which I resisted [in response to the subcommittee questions was] her assertion that the agency does not comment on cases. I acceded to her view that I should speak in my individual capacity when talking about cases. But she kept saying that it was not the agency's tradition to speak on cases. This, of course, is the view that all the "old wise" establishment types that the Board have accepted—people like Higgins himself, as well as Truesdale, and others and Browning, Feinstein, and all the rest. But we left matters as they are with me simply saying that I would speak in my individual capacity and leaving open the question of what the agency tradition is. When one looks at what she said last Friday, today and in March when Bill Stewart and I asked her about *Connecticut Limousine*, one has to assume that she at a minimum is a very hostile Board member.

... When Fox finally left she said she had to leave because she had been there two hours, I said that I had been there two hours also—after all I had been there, and I stayed there, at her request! I told her that I had been able to work on two cases all day because she and Higgins wanted to have this meeting. But she was very angry and said that I always left meetings when I had appointments to keep and she had an appointment to keep....

A day like this leaves me with a feeling—a feeling that may be more pronounced tomorrow morning—that it will be much more enjoyable to be a former chairman back at Stanford Law School than to be chairman.

May 3, 1997   This was an interesting week internally in the Board. At the Board Agenda on Tuesday, Higgins threatened to stop all cases from going out. He got into what seems to be a perennial dispute with me over the *Farm Fresh* case [involving a nonemployee organizer's access [to snack bars in retail establishments].[11] Again, insisting that he was not reversing precedent on nonemployee union organizer access to public lunchroom areas by reversing *Montgomery Ward*, Higgins had to insist that the Supreme Court *Lechmere* decision had already accomplished this because, otherwise, he would be reversing his own position—in a situation where it is politically convenient to do so—and stating that [Board] precedent could indeed be reversed.[12] He kept saying to me "Help me." And when I didn't, he then said that he would stop the case from going out. I stated that it would be intolerable for any Board member to act in this manner, and Fox joined in and said that Higgins was "blackmailing" us. Higgins quickly retreated and said that that wasn't what he had been saying and then came into my office on Wednesday afternoon to reiterate the same view. "Of course," that isn't what he had been saying, said Higgins.... Fox is, of course, undermined in pressing Higgins on this because she, herself, is holding up so many cases. In her case because of perhaps a combination of writers' block—which always winds up with very little in the way of changes of substance—and, perhaps even more important, political maneuvering.

... When Higgins raised the argument that I should help him in connection with *Farm Fresh*, I said that I would insist upon intellectual honesty and that I was troubled by the fact that he, in our previous discussion on *stare decisis* had indicated that he thought that I might have a different position if I was at Stanford Law School as opposed to voting on the Board. I said that my position would be the same at Stanford Law School or at the Board. Higgins said that he "apologized" for making such a statement, although he couched it in terms of being misunderstood and I said that I "accepted" his apology.

... We then began to talk about regional directors, and I pointed out to him that he was obliged to follow our affirmative action provisions. He said that he had put an affirmative action plan into effect involving SES [senior executive] positions when, in fact, as I advised him, we put the first such plan into existence when we got here in 1994 after a considerable amount of controversy and debate—and that he should abide by these procedures....

May 18, 1997   The backlog continues to escalate. Cases are just not going out. Until the early part of mid-1996 I was able to make great progress in moving us forward. Since then, we have been moving backward and now it seems as though it is coming at a gallop. Although I had an "Old Dog" agenda [on cases that had been with us for more than two years] a couple of weeks ago and set deadlines, all the deadlines—except those that I set by myself and a few by Higgins—have come and gone without being met. None of the cases, except for *Anchor,* have gone out.[13] . . . And most of them are not difficult ones. But Fox, apparently because she does not want to be identified with any case in which there could be political problems for her confirmation in the Senate, or perhaps, for some other reason which is not known to me, simply won't sign off on anything! I really need to step back and go to work on other cases that are before me and think about my upcoming series of talks in Europe. Otherwise, the work here is too demoralizing and depressing. . . .

At our Tuesday meeting, Fox resumed the shouting technique and said "Do you think that I am not working on these cases, that I'm simply goofing off." She refused to accept any deadlines on any further cases and . . . didn't adhere to the deadlines that have already been established and that she had agreed to be bound by. . . .

There is still no movement from the Republicans on the appointment process. No word from Senator Lott about Republicans who would be acceptable to him. They know very well what they are doing. They have the recess appointees scared to death as they run for office and are unwilling and unable to do much of anything . . . The underlying dynamic is their antipathy for the Board, which has been exacerbated with the AFL-CIO involvement in the 1996 elections.

This past week on Wednesday, May 14, I had a very interesting meeting with Senator John McCain of Arizona [and I spoke] . . . about our settlement initiatives. McCain expressed great interest in this and talked about a Udall environmental mediation program in Arizona.

I . . . mentioned that our regional directors' conference was going to take place in Phoenix in late June, and he said that that was not a good time to be there in terms of weather. But this gave me an opportunity to introduce our appropriations and budget problems, and I said that that was precisely the reason that we were there—because our budget wouldn't permit much else. . . .

I told Senator McCain about our *Beck* decisions and that we had obliged the unions to tell workers not only about their *Beck* rights but also what degree of union membership they were obliged to accept under union security agreements. He expressed a great deal of interest in this because of his work in campaign finance legislation. Senator McCain said that he wanted campaign finance to be bipartisan, and the problem was that the Democrats didn't want to apply restrictions to the unions but were only interested in business, and that the Republicans only wanted to apply restrictions to the unions and were not concerned about corporations. He felt that both had to come within the strictures of law and expressed an interest in having me comment on the constitutionality and lawfulness of his ideas in the future. I said that I would be glad to be of any help to him and that, although there were people who undoubtedly "knew more than me," I would be of any help possible. McCain said that he was sure that I could give him valuable help with my kind of background and qualifications.

At this point McCain asked me if there was anything else that I wanted to discuss with him in this meeting and I said that there really wasn't, although there was what I characterized as the "perils of Pauline" problems involving appropriations. I then mentioned our experience over the past couple of years, the growing antagonism to us in the House—and I said that "members of your party in the House do not like us very much"—and that Senator Hatfield had been such a good friend to me personally and to the agency. . . . McCain then said "Well, I will play that role now that he is not here." [But he did not do so.] As I left the office he said "I don't envy your job." I said that I enjoyed it very much but that it was a "challenge," and he nodded enthusiastically. It may well be that I have a good Republican friend as the result of this.

May 22, 1997 Yesterday I had a very interesting discussion with Darla Letourneau [Secretary of Labor Alexis Herman's budget person]. She told me that she had been with Alexis Herman for recent meetings with the House appropriations subcommittee and that the name of the Board came up quite frequently. In particular she mentioned Congresswoman Northrop, who was featured in today's *Washington Post* and about whom I had considerable hope at one point.... Darla said that Congresswoman Northrop said that the Board was "tyrannical and always on the side of the union" saying "don't confuse me with the facts." She said that the Board made the same basic decision even after it was overturned by the judiciary, apparently not recognizing our role as an expert agency.... When either Herman or Darla said that the NLRB was not part of the Department of Labor budget, she said "then you won't mind if I cut the NLRB budget."

... Tomorrow the first of the many cases that Fox committed to work on—and thus far hasn't worked on (at least to the extent of completion)—*Q-1 Motor Express* [involving the duty to bargain in corporate relocation cases] will issue.[14] ... Kate Dowling played such an important role [in writing the concurring opinion]. [Recently] I offered [the deputy chief counsel position] to Kate.... She is a delight to work with and very bright and dedicated to me and to our operation. I know that this is one of my truly good choices. Undoubtedly she is one of the youngest to ever assume this position, she is only [my oldest son] Billy's age, 34. And she is one of the first women to ever be in the position. I am hopeful that the agency will give her appointment a good deal of publicity in June.

Appropriations

May 23, 1997 I met with John Sweeney of the AFL-CIO and John Hiatt this morning. It was a very pleasant and cordial meeting and lasted about an hour. I thanked Sweeney for his help in the past and said that I was really counting on it in the future.... I said that I thought the Republicans were really seeking revenge against the AFL-CIO through their attack on us and he agreed.

Sweeney said that as soon as he had heard about the appropriations hearing and the fact that no Democrats were there to defend us, he met with Gephardt and Bonior and a group of fifty Democrats who are well placed on various committees in the House, and he obtained from them a pledge to focus on the Board and labor matters as the appropriations process moves forward.

... I told Sweeney that our "productivity had gone south" and that we were in big trouble. I was able to get into this because Hiatt asked me about one of the *Beverly* cases, which he said had been sitting with us for a long time. I told him that I would put this front and center, and I've checked with Al [Wolff] and Kate this afternoon and they brought me up to date on the status of them....

Sweeney was very informal and relaxed. A number of times we talked about the way in which the appropriations committee hearing had gone. I told him about the previous year's hearing when I [had] told Dickey that I would not be swayed by any kind of political pressure from them, that is, that I would not vote for less 10(j) because of the squeeze that they were putting on us in the appropriations arena. I looked Sweeney right in the eye when I said that no pressure from any source would ever make me change my vote on anything. Although our meeting was a friendly one and he is an ally and a good ally, I know from earlier discussions with Hiatt about the TEAM Act that he would like to put pressure on me, albeit in a very different arena.

... Hiatt expressed a concern about the decline of Section 10(j)s. I told them that while I publicly proclaimed that the decline in Section 10(j) cases was attributable to the fact that more employers are getting the message about obeying the law, I didn't believe that that was really the case. Sweeney quickly said, "I don't believe it either."

... One of the funny parts of our discussion today was Sweeney's question to me, "Do you keep a diary?" I hesitated in responding and, before I could get an answer out, Sweeney began to joke about Reich's book and asked me whether I was reading it. He said he thought that it was really improper for Reich to have spoken about [Lane] Kirkland in the manner he did ... after being invited into his home. Both of us thought that Reich was a little funny in the way in which he kept speaking about his height and was a little too showbiz.

June 10, 1997   Much of yesterday and today, I spent most of my time on one of the things that really makes this job interesting. I dealt with a wide variety of issues in a case involving the *New York Post* and Newspaper Guild, which could have easily been—perhaps it will become at some point—a nice law school question. Even the names of the parties that is, Acquisition, one of Murdoch's alter-ego creations, are perfect for this. The *New York Post* case is a law professor's dream, like a number of the issues that come before me.

I had a fine time—more than an hour of conversation, something in the order of an hour and a half—talking through the issues with Dave Schwartz [of my staff], Kate Dowling, Al Wolff, and Kirk Franklin from Sarah Fox's staff. Murdoch had come in to save the *New York Post*, it being in bankruptcy and losing about $300,000 a month. His company, specially devised for the management of the firm during an interim period, did not make an absolute commitment to buy but did create arrangements that made it unlikely that another buyer could come in with much ease. The administrative law judge had found Murdoch's operation not to be a successor on the basis of a narrow reading of a 1988 ruling, and both Fox and I will reverse in that regard. There has to be an employer at some point. Who is it? The *New York Post*, which is now in bankruptcy? Clearly the arrangement provided for Murdoch to run the paper and that is where the labor-law liability lies.

But that is simply the first of a whole host of questions that I engaged in discussions with Kirk Franklin in particular.... The next question related to the bankruptcy code and its presumption that the collective-bargaining agreement remains in force in bankruptcies where the property and assets are being managed by the trustee, as well as a debtor. The practical significance of this conclusion is that a strike, which the Guild engaged in, is unprotected, and their members are subject to dismissal by virtue of an implied no-strike obligation in the agreement. Here, Fox will probably part company with me, although I would find that Murdoch's subsequent refusal to recognize the Guild is unlawful, thus joining issue with her conclusion on this score, and finding that the strikers are unprotected and subject to dismissal, thus joining with Higgins, who would affirm the administrative law judge, in this regard. It was a fine morning's work—but here I am this afternoon with seemingly hundreds of cases to deal with, some of them small and some of them complex. [This case was never issued.]

Yesterday, a *New York Times* article appeared that gave a very different cut to the kind of work I do here.[15] It was a detailed description of a dispute that came to us for adjudication—*Domesey Trading Corporation*, 310 NLRB 777 (1993) ([decided by] Stephens, Devaney, and Oviatt); [subsequently enforced by the court of appeals] ... [it] involved the dismissal of Haitian workers in Brooklyn who had been the object of racial epithets by the owners and had prevailed before both us and the courts, but achieved what the writer, Deborah Sontag, characterized as a "Pyrrhic victory." According to her piece, the conditions remained "oppressive"; workers were not addressed by their names, but rather by numbers that they are required to wear on their chest, and the union, apparently UNITE [United Needletrades Industrial & Textile Employees], had lost the election. The strikers, said the writer, had not yet received a "dime," although the matter had been pursued vigorously. Apparently, she was critical of us because of the long delay in obtaining compliance. Her article concluded by noting that the first organizer to be dismissed died before he could receive the $44,000 that was owed him by the company and that his widow had borrowed money to bury him. The piece notes that all that we can do is obtain compensation and that the "legal system is incapable of effectively punishing" law breakers and that an order of back pay "if contested ... can take years to bear fruit." This was a good piece, and it told something that needs to be told in the country more often. Rather than focus upon this, the Senate Labor Committee is today holding hearings today on union organizers in salting campaigns. This Congress doesn't seem to care very much about people who need the benefits of our statute. What they want to do is build limits on the already-limited powers that we have. Small-minded legislators, uninterested in doing an effective job for our people who really need help through laws such as ours.

...

Last Friday night I had dinner with Sarah Fox in an attempt to restore our friendship and to see if she would be willing to push some cases out of here. We went over to Tuscana West, and it was a very nice evening. She told me about a lot of personal troubles that she has caring for her mother in Buffalo, and she said that her rather angry reaction at my attempt to get her to move forward with cases in the last Board agenda was really attributable to the fact that she felt that everyone was trying to get after her these days for matters both professional and personal. I think that we soothed a lot of the troubled waters in this evening, and she assured me that she would move forward on all of the cases—although many of them have still not appeared as of this Tuesday afternoon ... Before she had said that she couldn't sign off on *Connecticut Limousine*, which doesn't involve what she perceived to be the relatively complex issues contained in the *Chevron* case [involving the mathematical formula for allocation of "chargeable" and "non-chargeable" dues under *Beck*]. [The case finally issued on August 24, 1998, with a very skimpy opinion, which could have been written about seven years earlier in *Chevron Chemical Company* 326 NLRB No.34] ... another one that she is sitting on—but on Friday night she said that she agreed with my assertion that this was not the case and that *Connecticut Limousine* could issue right away, and she said she would sign off on it very quickly. We haven't seen it yet, but perhaps we will see it soon. Now I've scheduled a Thursday night dinner with her, and my hope is that we will really work effectively to turn around what is the growing problem at the agency—a problem that I felt was under control in 1996 ...

I'm very upbeat at this moment about Sarah, and I really hope that we can work well together. This evening had the effect of not only making her feel more favorably toward me, but also, quite frankly, dissipating some of my anger over those cases that have been kept in her office for so long. Some of them, of course, contain brilliant dissenting and concurring opinions by a well-known law professor and therefore I want to really try to move these cases forward for personal reasons.

The *Detroit Newspapers* Case

During my tenure the Board had used injunctions under Section 10(j) in an unprecedented number of instances. And, as we saw in chapter 9, doing so was the surest route to getting the attention of the Republican Congress. In the *Detroit Newspapers* dispute, which began with a strike in 1995, the employers had installed permanent replacements. The issue before the Board was whether the strike had been caused by the employers' unfair labor practices. If so, the strikers were entitled to reinstatement. If the Board held that the strike had not been prompted by such conduct, the strikers could be permanently replaced. In this case, as in many disputes involving dismissal of workers involved in organizing activity, it was contended that the passage of time might erode the effectiveness of a meaningful remedy (i.e., reinstatement).

When I returned from Europe. I began to dig into the case, in which the general counsel was asking us to request an injunction against the newspapers. Earlier in the year (as chapter 9 records), several Republican members of the Senate Labor Committee had written to me to object to authorizing an injunction. I met with Fox and Higgins on June 5, one day after my return. Although I was leaning toward voting for the injunction, I was unsure about critical elements in the general counsel's theory, particularly his attempt to compare the approach we use in dismissal cases—in which workers typically "scatter to the winds" and are difficult to locate (let alone compensate) to situations (like that in Detroit) in which the union has a well-established organization and bargaining relationship and striking workers are refused reemployment at the end of the strike. It was clear that the case was going to take some analysis.

June 10, 1997 ... At the meeting with Fox and Higgins, Higgins was the first one to take note of the fact that the unfair labor practice cases are before Administrative Law Judge Wilkes. As a result of his suggestions, I reexamined the papers and found that briefs were submitted to [the ALJ] ... in January. I then inquired with Bob Giannasi to see about the status of the case, and Bob advised me that he expected a decision between June 20–25. It made no sense, and I can't understand why the general counsel's office was constantly calling us on this—to go ahead with this matter while it is still pending. Fox has decided to authorize the issuance, and Higgins has stated that he is against it although the reasons provided—I can't recall what they were right now—quickly evaporated under cross-examination by Fox. Still Higgins's mind was made up, even though his rationale had disappeared into thin air. I am undecided. But, particularly in light of the Republican party's great interest in this case, it will be a big one which will affect us, quite conceivably very much as *Overnite Transportation* and *Caterpillar* did.

June 26, 1997, Phoenix, Arizona   Here for the regional directors' meeting, which has proved to be informative. It is always good to talk to people in the field who, in this arena know so much more than those sitting in Washington simply dealing with paper.

We met today on *Detroit News* and *Free Press*....

Higgins came up with the most extraordinary idea today, which both Fox and I rejected. I did so a little more out of hand than Fox did. Higgins's idea was that we shouldn't authorize Section 10(j) relief against the *Detroit News* and *Detroit Free Press* and that we should take up Andrew Kramer's suggestion—Kramer is counsel to the Detroit newspapers—that we devote all our resources toward expediting the administrative hearing rather than seek Section 10(j) relief. Higgins's idea was that we could get the case out by August 15. I said that that was absolutely beyond imagination, given the fact that we are not able to even get the little cases out within six weeks, let alone a big one like this one with a 3,000-page transcript, issues of law, and indeed at least one case with novel issues of law, that is, the duty to bargain with regard to replacement workers.... Fox said that we could go ahead with an expedited procedure for August 15 and seek Section 10(j) relief. But I said that I thought that any kind of expedited procedure for August 15 was totally unrealistic both for ourselves and for our staffs. Meanwhile I noted that we have a whole host of cases that are undecided on our docket that we need to devote time to, let alone new cases that are coming in the door everyday. There is no way that we could devote a substantial percentage of our time to this matter [and there would be an appeal in any event]. That would take, in all probability, at least an additional two years, during which relief would be denied.

Higgins, who had earlier in the week said to me that he would vote to authorize Section 10(j) relief, now said that he wasn't sure how he would vote and when he would vote. However, at times he indicated that he would vote by Friday which means that he will vote perhaps on Monday June 30.

The Detroit newspapers, anticipating our action, said earlier in the week that they understood the fact that the administrative law judge, Wilkes, would rule against them—as he did on June 19 in a 113-page opinion—because he was appointed by the Board. They have written us off completely and their strategy is to attack us.

Last week, on June 19, Fox came into my office late in the day after the ALJ's ruling and talked about Judge Wilkes's decision, claiming that she had read it already, even though it was 113 pages and took me most of the weekend to get through it—even skipping over large paragraphs where he dealt in detail with credibility. She wanted to move on Thursday afternoon. The following day I began to learn why this was so. John Hiatt, general counsel of the AFL-CIO telephoned to say that he was simply calling about *Detroit Newspapers* to find out the status of the case. I said that we are working on it and I hope to get it out "early next week." Hiatt asked if there was any possibility that it could be done that day,

Friday June 20. When I said that this would be impossible, Hiatt sighed in a very exasperated way and said that there was a big rally in Detroit that Sweeney was speaking to and he hoped that Sweeney could announce the Board's action. I pointed out to him that this couldn't happen, and he was quite upset....

July 3, 1997   Two days ago we initiated injunction proceedings in the *Detroit Newspapers* case—a case that has caused quite a stir. In the end, part of the delay was caused by my insistence that the Board publish my opinions on Section 10(j). Higgins sought to prevaricate as much as possible but finally relented on July 1.

One of the tragic aspects of this case is that it could have been resolved, and should have been resolved, on the ground that it is simply an unfair labor practice to permanently replace strikers. But this would require the reversal of the Supreme Court's 1938 ruling in *Mackay*. And that, of course, neither the Board nor the federal judiciary can undertake— particularly because both the Congress and the Court have assumed the viability of *Mackay* in a variety of contexts since then. This case, unlike baseball, where only temporary replacements were threatened by the owners, involved the workers' deprivation of their jobs through the permanent replacement technique in a strike that has gone on for two years now and one in which the unconditional offer to return to work was only made in February of this year. Of course, for the baseball players in 1995 when we were successful in obtaining injunctive relief, the temporary replacements would have been the equivalent of permanent in light of their short playing lives and in light of the insecurity they would have felt had others taken the field. I hope that we get the same grand result that we obtained in baseball. But very much will depend upon the selection of the federal judge next Monday, when our regional director goes into federal district court. Once we know the answer to that question, we will have a good sense of how successful we are going to be.

Ultimately Judge John O'Meara of Detroit denied our petition for injunctive relief in *Detroit Newspapers*, and the Court of Appeals for the Sixth Circuit in Cincinnati affirmed his denial. Discussion of the Board's own decision on the issues involved in this case continued at intervals over the next year as I struggled to get Fox and Higgins, and later the new appointees, to issue the case (see chapter 12).

A Farewell to Bill Stewart

One of the major events of the first part of 1997 was the retirement of my friend and chief counsel, Bill Stewart, a thirty-three year veteran of the NLRB wars. We held a great party for him in March—the night before the appropriations subcommittee hearing—at a place called "The Mansion," a very nice 1890s-style restaurant. Bill seemed very pleased with everything about the party, including really funny and witty speeches by Bernie Reis and John Ferguson (career NLRB lawyers) that were kind of a roast. My speech was much more straightforward and not as funny, although people seemed to receive it fairly well. There was a great deal of warmth and conviviality throughout the evening.

But there is no doubt that Bill's retirement was a tremendous loss for me. When he came in earlier that week, we began going through the whole bonus business for staff, and I remembered how he had really scurried around the agency and found the extra money for it. This is just one of the numerous things that he did besides case handling and responding to congressional inquiries and to attacks on me from other Board members.

In early June I was delighted to inform Bill that he had received the President's Award for Distinguished Federal Civilian Service—the first employee in the NLRB's history to do so. It is the highest-ranking and most prestigious award a career federal employee can receive, and he was absolutely overjoyed. We put out a press release about it, and the news just swept through the building. Bill got a beautiful medallion to wear as well as $5,000 and a terrific party.

Few knew the difficulties I encountered with Fox and Higgins over this matter. I had wanted to give Bill $25,000, but in order to do that I had to get the permission of Fox and Higgins. They vetoed it. Higgins was very angry about the award and said that "my nose is out of joint" over this, claiming that the other Board members' concurrence was necessary, though this simply isn't true. I researched this fairly carefully. But he was quite unhappy and said "I would like to see the justification for this."

July 3, 1997 (continued) ... Yesterday, we had a wonderful party for Bill Stewart celebrating his award.... Everything seemed just right. My speech went reasonably well, and Bill gave really funny and lovely extemporaneous remarks. So many of the good people at the Board were there and many of his old pals from around Washington, including his brother and sister-in-law and niece and her husband. It really gave me a special pleasure to note again and again that Bill is the very first person in the sixty-two-year history of the agency ever to receive the award.... Bill really kept this office [and the Board] going in the most difficult days of 1994–1996.

Subsequently, in October, Bill, his friend Bill Dresser, and I went to the White House to meet with President Clinton. When I introduced them, I said, "Mr. President, I would like you to meet Bill Stewart and Bill Dresser. And so we really have four Bills here." Without missing a beat, President Clinton said, "Well, if we were in a lineup, then we could all say 'Bill did it.'" We all roared!

Congress and Case Production

July 12, 1997, Stanford, California   This is the twenty-fifth anniversary of my arrival at Stanford. Here I sit on a lovely beautiful cloudless Saturday afternoon working on Board decisions and thinking about what my legacy at the Board will be in thirteen months time when my work comes to an end there.

This past week I've tried yet another avenue to which to get at the problem of producing our cases, and more particularly, inducing Sarah Fox to release cases that she is simply sitting on. I spoke with Congressman Tom Lantos about this, and he is enthusiastic about bringing this up in the July 24 [oversight hearing].... Meanwhile Bill Stewart approached Fox to say that I had been contacted by Congress about this. When Bill first came in to see her, she said "Oh, have you come as an emissary of the chairman?!" When Bill told her about the communication with Congress she became very angry and said that "the chairman can tell the Congress that I am holding up a number of cases!" She said to Bill that she resented the idea of memos being sent around about cases that she had not finished working on and she wondered aloud how "the chairman would feel if he received memos from me about cases that he has not worked on." Bill replied "Why don't you send such memos to him?" No answer to this rhetorical question was received.

The only thing left is Congress, and I think that, as desperate as it is, this was the only route that I could responsibly take.

July 19, 1997   Incredibly busy past week and an even busier one coming up. On Friday, the day after House oversight subcommittee hearings chaired by Shays of Connecticut, we will have a Board agenda on contingent employees, which was postponed once before because of Fox's intransigence. [A week before the hearings we received notice, that—notwithstanding all of the committee's leaking to the *Washington Times* about my attendance at baseball games, questions about whether I had obtained the tickets gratis from the clubs, and such weighty matters as the sexual identity of Dusty Baker—no questions would be asked about the baseball games at all because now the committee did not regard it as a serious matter.] Al Wolff has heard that she [Fox] will not participate in the upcoming Friday meeting—or at least prepare very much—because she hopes to delay any kind of decision, hoping that she will be confirmed before an opinion issues.

I met with all the Democrats on the Government Reform and Oversight Subcommittee on Human Resources this past week, and they seem like a very good bunch.... I ... met with Tom Lantos [Calif.] ... [Edolphus] Towns of New York, [Bernard] Sanders of Vermont, [Henry] Waxman, who is the leading Democrat on the full committee, of Los Angeles, California, [Tom] Allen of Maine, and [Thomas] Barrett of Wisconsin. My most memorable meeting was with [Dennis] Kucinich of Ohio, with whom I had breakfast on the morning of July 17 at Sherrill's near the capital itself. It is a little, almost cafeteria-style diner run by a few old ladies and populated by senior citizens entirely, except for Kucinich and, arguably, myself. Kucinich went on at great lengths about the importance of collective bargaining and workers rights to him and how he felt that the right of workers organized was a "moral" and indeed "spiritual" right. I pointed out to him how important the issue of inequities was to me both because of race, and the desperate circumstances of the Great Depression, and religion through the Episcopal Church in my case and the Roman

Catholic Church in his. . . . Kucinich . . . urged me to go back to basics and explain what the act was all about in terms of its origins.

All the Democrats expressed admiration and respect for Shays and said that he was really the best of the Republicans. Allen of Maine said that he was concerned about . . . our regional director in Boston and had been receiving complaints about our salting cases. Quite clearly, we are going to have to be ready on salting and *Beck*. We spent a good deal of time talking about politics in Maine. I had been interrogated by his predecessor whom he defeated in 1996, James Longley, in the House Small Business meetings chaired by Talent in 1996. This is a subject that I was able to continue that very evening when I sat next to Senator George Mitchell in Peter Angelos's box at the Red Sox–Orioles game. He was quite high on Allen and delighted to see him defeat Longley.

In the Shays Committee hearing itself, the Democrats, most of whom I had spoken with in the days leading up to this proceeding, were fulsome in their praise for the Board and my chairmanship:

Mr. Towns [of New York]:   . . . In an effort to eliminate the backlog of cases, Chairman Gould has appointed an advisory panel of prolabor and promanagement lawyers to recommend ways to improve the processing of cases and improve the agency's service to the public, and I applaud him for that. Additionally, the chairman has instituted speed teams that reduce the time and paperwork involved in hearing a case. These procedures have enabled the Board to reduce its backlog. As the Committee on Government Reform and Oversight, we should also say thank you.

Mr. Barrett [of Wisconsin]:   I think you have responded very well and have given a glimmer of hope to what has been otherwise a very sad situation in my district.:

Mr. Lantos [of California]:   . . . I have been enormously impressed by the Gould chairmanship of the NLRB. . . . I think you have been subjected to unfair criticism from many quarters. I have very carefully looked at and analyzed those bits of criticism and I have found them to be wanting. I think you are performing in a remarkable fashion in an almost untenable situation with only three members of a five-member Board, with two of the three members not having been confirmed. . . . So let me commend you and congratulate you, Mr. Chairman

Mr. Sanders [of Vermont]:   I just want to applaud Mr. Gould for the work that he has been doing, and I hope that this Congress can give him the staff and the associates so that he can do his job adequately.

Mr. Kucinich [of Ohio]:   I have to say that Mr. Gould, among all the NLRB chairs that I have been familiar with or have read about, stands out as someone who has fearlessly defended workers' rights.[16] . . .

Later that week, however, as I recorded in my diary, we received bad news. Specter had turned on us again and was recommending level funding—the very approach taken by the House Appropriations Subcommittee, which we regarded as a victory in that case. I was on the phone with a good number of people including

Ron Carey (president of the Teamsters) whose own situation had become somewhat tenuous.

July 19 (continued) Carey was upbeat and promised to help. He said that he would have someone who has influence in his union in Pennsylvania—I am sure that is was Morris of Philadelphia—call Specter. When I suggested that it might be good to call Senator Stevens of Alaska because of the fact that the Teamsters have many members there, Cary said, "Bill, I've become quite skillful at saying the things I am supposed to say and not saying the things that I am not supposed to say in this situation, and I know what you want and I will do it." I tried to reach Trumka and Georgine, but they have not returned my calls. My old pal Paul Wellstone called me back immediately and said that he would join in and reach Harkin and help with statements on the floor during the floor debate. The Senate Subcommittee voted Tuesday, and I will have to deal with the phone calls from Los Angeles where I will be to speak at the Orange County Labor Law Luncheon.

Keeping the Board Lights Burning

September 7, 1997 I returned from California on the Sunday before Labor Day, and Labor Day itself was typical Washington, sweltering hot and humid. It made me want to get on the first plane to go back to California. [A few weeks earlier the *Washington Post* had run a piece on our appointment problem which began "William B. Gould, IV, Chairman of the National Labor Relations Board, may soon find it very lonely at the top; by the end of the year he could well be the only member left on the five-seat Board which resolves disputes between organized labor and management."[17] The *Post* was referring to the fact the recess appointments would expire when Congress left in the fall.]

In discussions with Feinstein about an investigation involving a contractor doing computer work for us and the [retaliation against] one of our employees, who had complained of the work [done by the contractor], [Bob] Allen [the Board's inspector general] said that Feinstein had approached him—... and said to him that he hoped that he, Allen, would act as Higgins had and keep the agency's interests "at heart." But Allen said that that remark and Feinstein's conversation with me [in which he had characterized Allen's findings that the firing of our employee for complaining of the contractor's deficiencies were "soft"] convinced him that Feinstein hadn't learned the lessons of Nixon and Watergate. If Nixon had acted like Kennedy in the wake of the Bay of Pigs fiasco and taken the blame for himself, he would have continued to be president, said Allen.... Allen said that Feinstein wasn't interested in what was good for the agency but rather what was good for him.]

September 10, 1997 I had two meetings at the White House today, first in the Executive Office Building in the morning with Bob Nash and Tom Shea ... Both Shea and Nash reiterated that they had not received any word from the Republicans about the so-called Republican list....

I walked back to my office through Lafayette Park and ran into Jack Golodner [of the AFL-CIO] on the other side of 16th Street in the same block of the AFL-CIO (in front of the Hay Adams). I told him what had transpired and he said that I should really go by and see Sweeney. And so I did.... I told Sweeney of my concerns, and the fact that we might be faced with a shutdown prospect, and he agreed with my view.... Sweeney said that he thought that Podesta had a better hold of things, and I said that I would be meeting Podesta in the afternoon. Sweeney said that this was a good idea and that if I had any concerns after meeting with Podesta that I should get back to him or John Hiatt.

In the afternoon I met with Podesta and, as Sweeney anticipated, it was a much better and more informative meeting. Podesta began by saying that he would not allow "the lights to go off" at the Board. Podesta said that the recess appointees were lined up and that they could go through.... Podesta, like Nash, thought that Fox's chances of confirmation were zero and said that he would have to talk to Fox to see what she wanted to do and to see if they could find her another position. However, he did opine that perhaps Fox could still get through as part of a deal with the Republicans on a total package.

Podesta said that he had been promised by a senior staff guy that the list by the Republicans would get to him by the end of this week. He thought that this promise was a little stronger than the ones that had been previously given ...

... [A]fter my meetings and my return to the office, the House of Representatives beat back an attempt to cut our budget by 10 percent and to transfer the funds to impact schools. Nancy Pelosi was brilliant in her presentation, and Patsy Mink was quite sharp and emotional and eloquent in her ringing refusal to stand second to none on money for so-called impact schools. Both she and Pelosi said that this was simply a ruse to hurt workers. Pelosi said that it was impossible to talk about education for children when the job and income security of the workers that have the families was being undermined.

... The past couple of days have been absolutely frantic as we have struggled to get answers ready to both Lantos and Hoekstra as well as a variety of other things, including a speech in Baltimore last night, which I gave for Earl Shaw. This morning I had some difficulty in getting out of bed.

September 16, 1997 ... Bob Allen came down in the afternoon to tell me about a meeting with Fred Feinstein. Even at this point, Feinstein appears not to have read his [Allen's] report, a fact that concerned both Bob and me. Bob attempted to draw them out by providing criticisms of his report, but they refused to respond. They clearly have adopted a "circled wagons" defensive mode in dealing with this.

September 17, 1997 Today, we received word that Senator Lott has proposed two Republicans for the Board and would allow Sarah Fox and [Wilma] Liebman to be appointed as the Democrats. The Republicans are Peter Hurtgen of Morgan, Lewis in Miami and J. Robert Brame III of [a] law firm in Richmond. Brame would appear to be the more right-wing of the two and apparently has been counsel for the Republican party in Virginia, which is hardly a good sign. Sarah Fox told Bill Stewart that these fellows are not regarded as extremists, and certainly that comports with my telephone-call conversations with both Dick Hotvedt and Bill Emanuel [both of Morgan Lewis] today. More important, if Senator Kennedy is placing his imprimatur on these guys as a way to get Fox through, it should go through—although when it will go through is anybody's guess.... Although I am slightly encouraged by the idea that Hurtgen may be someone good to work with, I am depressed about the prospect of having to work with Fox until the summer of 1998 and also the possibility that my opinions, which she has blocked, might not emerge by the time that I leave in 1998....

September 18, 1997   I spoke with Tom Shea on the telephone this morning and he said that he and representatives of Nickles and Lott as well as two individuals from Senator Kennedy's staff ... had met to discuss the "package." Shea is somewhat cautious and skeptical and says that he is not sure that Nickles and Lott will go along with Fox and Liebman. Apparently, one of them said to Shea during the meeting, "We are disappointed. We thought that you would come up with a career NLRB person for one of the seats." Shea said to either of them or me that he thought that they should come up with an NLRB person as well. So the deal is not completely cut at this point.

One of the great ironies here is that the Republicans are really deciding not only the Republican Board members but also holding a veto over the Democratic Board members as well. During the Reagan and Bush years the Republicans named phony Democrats of their own choosing for the Democratic seats and, of course, did not allow the Democrats to influence directly or indirectly the Republican seats....

September 23, 1997   Yesterday was the day of deadline for my response to Congressman Lantos's questions [about the reasons for delay and our increasing backlog]; when it got to be the afternoon, I began to assume that no one would contact me and that we would send ... off [our responses] ... indeed, I spent a good part of the day revising the final draft.

Then toward the middle of the afternoon Higgins came in and wanted me to revise it because he maintained that I was "confusing" his opinion on reversal of precedent and policy. His conversation was broad and rambling, ranging over a number of subjects. At some point he talked about his criteria for blocking or not blocking decisions where he felt the Board was improperly reversing precedent—although in the past he had been at great pains to tell me that he would not block decisions but would simply dissent on this basis. Then he raised an entirely new issue: that is, that he had taken his positions because of the short period of time before the recess. He had never mentioned this before. Indeed, during our discussion of *Detroit Newspapers* in Arizona, he was talking about timetables that would require us to issue the decision in the fall and had to be reminded by Fox ... that neither of them might be around at that point for which he was establishing a deadline. He was clearly out of sorts, because he then began to speak about the fact that he had not even been nominated and that he would be "going on to his glory" at some point in the very near future.

... I then proceeded around ten of five to meet with Secretary of Labor Alexis Herman at the Department of Labor. When I arrived, the secretary advised me that my staff needed to speak to me immediately, and Mary Ann said that a message marked "confidential and personal" had arrived from Fox, and she had asked that the letter not be sent to Lantos....

Before I returned and read the letter—... Al read it in part to me on the phone ... [I decided then] to hold up sending the Lantos letter—I met with Herman. I began by telling her that our charge and petition activity was increasing a bit.... I pointed out to Secretary Herman that Section 10(j) was what had really attracted Congress's attention to us and explained to her what Section 10(j) meant in terms of union organizing drives and refusals to bargain.

I then went on to talk about our productivity and the fact that, while we had brought the backlog to its lowest level in 1995 and had established numerous procedural reforms that facilitate the handling of cases more quickly, as well as new principles of law consistent with the purposes of the act, our backlog was rising now to approximately 550, in contrast to 330 or so that we had in November of 1995. I said that this was attributable to the fact that we have fewer Board members and that we are also operating within an environment of intimidation and retaliation. I said that this was impeding our case processing as a general manner, and I alluded to the fact that we had a large number of high-profile, old cases that disproportionately involved the *Beck* issue....

I returned here to my office to a much more difficult meeting. I ... read the ... letter from Fox when I returned and it was rather rambling and incoherent. I went in to see her and suggested that we talk, and she was on the phone with Susan Greene from Senator Kennedy's office. She came back here ... and I told Sarah that, contrary to her note, I bore no hostility toward her, that I had great respect for her intellect and was, indeed, attracted to her as a person. This seemed to calm her, and we began to have a discussion. I pointed out to Fox that ... my interest was in not releasing the response to Lantos as written. We agreed to meet on Wednesday at 2:00 P.M. to discuss all the cases that I raised in my memo to her. In her memo to me and in our conversation she acknowledged that she was responsible for the backlog problems and the failure to issue the old cases and that these needed to be given priority. I told her that I had been shouted at by many people, and I expected that this would happen to me in the future—but I did not appreciate being shouted at by her in Board meetings, and she said that she was sorry and attempted to ascribe this manner of behavior to some of the frustrations and difficulties that she is confronted with [on a personal level] in her family....

In the late afternoon I spoke with Congressman Donald Payne of New Jersey, a prominent member of the Black Caucus, who was at the hearing [he was at a recent oversight hearing investigating our handling of *Detroit Newspapers* and other matters] ... and criticized the Republicans for failing to invite me to testify ... [particularly given the fact that] Fawell attacked me personally ... Payne said to me that the conduct of the Republican majority was "scary" in that they are trying to attack any labor legislation or entity that is designed to enforce it out of their desire to tear down working conditions and seek revenge against the labor movement. [A month later Payne issued a very thoughtful statement, which criticized the "intentional interference with" the adjudicatory activities of an "independent agency" as an "improper abuse" of the subcommittee's oversight responsibilities—noting that management lawyer G. Roger King, who criticized my handling of the *Detroit Newspapers* case, had not properly identified himself as affiliated with the firm that represented [the] Detroit newspapers!]

September 24, 1997   I had a conversation with Tom Shea this morning ... [and] asked him what the status of the nominations is now. Shea said that he is still waiting to hear from Lott and Nickles on the package. Really, Shea stated, they are waiting to see whether Lott and Nickles will approve the president's own nominees! This is an absolutely ridiculous and extraordinary state of affairs where the president is now in the position of not only seeking Republican consent on Republican nominees and not even selecting them himself from a list [as he did during my confirmation process] but simply receiving one list on a take-it-or-leave-it basis ... and the list submitted by the White House is being subjected to consent of the Republicans. Quite frankly, I wonder whether anyone has ever done this in the history of the Republic! ...

October 29, 1997   The conference between the House and the Senate will meet this afternoon on our budget. So these past few days I have been talking to union leaders because of the fact that Specter's office through Craig Higgins had advised me that on Monday that we were not getting enthusiastic support from the White House for an increase, but only pro-forma support. When I repeated this in a telephone conversation with John Sweeney this morning, he said "Whoever is telling you that is lying. And they are full of shit." Sweeney expressed the view that they have had some difficulty with Specter's office in the past and that Specter's office was misrepresenting this. He, Sweeney, said that he had talked directly to Vice-President Gore, Erskine Bowles, John Podesta.... He said that he would make some more calls over to the White House—although he doubted whether he could get through right now because of the Chinese president's state visit today....

Since Monday, I have spoken to Steve Yokich of the UAW, Tom Buffenbarger of the machinists, Mort Barr of the Communications Workers, and Bruce Raynor of UNITE. All of them said that they would swing in to support us....

Meanwhile yesterday, the White House advised us that the nominations for the three people—Wilma B. Liebman, Peter J. Hurtgen, and Joseph Robert Brame—had gone to Capital Hill ... I spoke with Patsy Thomasson [of personnel] on the phone, and she said that she was not particularly confident that the nominations would be confirmed prior to the recess. "Why?", I asked. Patsy replied, "I don't trust them," referring to the Republicans and their leadership, I just hope that she is right, because the confirmation of this package means great difficulties for me. On the one hand, although Fox will not be quite as timid as she has been once she is confirmed and will perhaps issue some cases—she will not be dissenting alone representing unions, Liebman will be with her—but she will be obstreperous and difficult. Brame may start writing decisions challenging the constitutionality of the act, given his far right-wing views and his deep involvement in the Virginia Republican party political affairs. It is not an inviting prospect, and by the time that this whole story begins to unfold it will be time to return to Stanford next summer.

October 31, 1997   Yesterday I received a most disturbing telephone call from Congressman David Obey of Wisconsin. He was quite angry with the appeals that I and apparently Fred Feinstein had made to trade union leaders to pressure both the Congress and the White House on our budget.... His comments were consistent with what I subsequently read in the *Daily Labor Report*. He said that "I [Obey] have busted my ass for the National Labor Relations Board" and "no one got more done for the Board than me" and that he had "voted for the agency every time." He said that obtaining level funding for us had caused him great problems, and he said that you are the "number one enemy of the Republicans."

I told him that I was extremely grateful to him for all of his help and that I appreciated what he had done. I said that if I had offended him by telephoning union leaders as I had,

I apologized, I explained that Specter's people ... had told us that the White House didn't have us on the short list and thus I was alarmed and had called the union leaders. Obey said that he was upset about having to explain to each of the union presidents the facts of life on Capitol Hill and that we were lucky to obtain level funding. He said: "If you are not satisfied with level funding, perhaps you would like a 5 percent cut!" At some point I'm sure that I assured him that we would not like that.

This stormy phone call from Obey, who impressed me as both boorish and arrogant, was the very first contact I had had with him. In the three preceding years, he had never deigned to attend any of the subcommittee hearings, even when we were savagely attacked by the Republicans and when many of his colleagues on the Democratic side of the aisle were in attendance. But this was not the last that we would hear from him. Just as my contacts with Senator Hatfield—as well as Senator Chafee, Susan Collins, and McCain—were proof of the proposition that there were moderate Republicans of good sense and sound principle, so my discussions with Obey quickly disabused me of the idea that Democrats, whatever the merits of their public policy pronouncements, possessed any kind of monopoly on a civilized sense of balance about intergovernmental relations. The biggest fights were yet to come—and they were to be with Obey as well as the GOP.

As 1997 wound down, confirmation of the new Board members brought us back to full strength. This was not, however, the end of our backlog problem. The list of undecided cases continued to soar, because of (1) the natural start-up time involved with new Board members; (2) a series of unrelenting dissents by Brame, some of which were produced and written in great length and detail; (3) Fox's unchanging conduct; and (4) my inability to revive Rule 76-1—though I tried again in 1998—or to get the Board to adopt any policy providing timetables for reaching decisions and preparing opinions.

The wild scramble involved in attempting to deal simultaneously with external political problems and internal Board matters was more frantic than ever. A *Business Week* column about the appointment process by Aaron Bernstein carried the ominous headline, "How Business is Winning Its War with the NLRB."[18] The piece observed that, as the result of the deal struck between Senator Kennedy and Senator Lott, business was getting a more "employer-friendly Board." Noting that Feinstein had allowed the number of injunction requests to the Board to decline, it claimed that he had "blinked and bowed to the political pressure" of the Republicans.

Of my tenure, Bernstein said "the former baseball arbitrator had moved the agency toward a more impartial stance after years of pro-business ruling under Presidents Reagan and Bush. That angered business, which urged Congress in 1995 to slash the NLRB's $174 million budget by a third. Clinton balked, but the 1998 budget is still $2 million less than in 1995." After describing that fall's oversight hearings and the bias displayed by management labor lawyer King—who had failed to disclose his involvement in the case the hearings was purportedly examining— the piece concluded by noting that my calls for law reform now went "largely ... unheeded. After years of grousing about that tiny agency with the huge influence, Corporate America finally seems to have the NLRB in check."

In 1998, my last eight last months as chairman were spent much as they had been throughout 1997 attempting to induce Board members—particularly one Board member—to do their work, just as I had years earlier urged my sons to do their homework. In 1998, 1999, and 2000 the pattern continued as the dog continued to eat the homework of some Board members a full two years after I left Washington.

Meanwhile the Republicans' unrelenting questions about my attendance at baseball games, both professional and college, and what I did with my personal time drew this comment from Major League Players Association General Counsel Gene Orza to Dusty Baker: "Dusty, it would be great to go to a baseball game with Bill Gould. But I'm afraid that if we did it, Congress would subpoena us."

12

The House Republicans' "Number 1 Enemy"

Obey had advised me well. I had indeed become the House Republicans' number one enemy. This status was hardly surprising, given the Republican view of the National Labor Relations Act, my confirmation difficulties, the policies I pursued, and the balanced relationship between labor and management I promoted during my tenure. The home stretch of my journey was, therefore, the most perilous and difficult part. The writer of an interview article in the *Asbury Park Press* (the closest thing to a hometown paper for Long Branch, New Jersey, where I grew up) summed it up this way:

In times of adversity, William Benjamin Gould IV takes cues from his late father, a man who didn't believe in giving up.

"My father, like myself, was not fast moving. He once had a track meet, and he was one of the last persons in the race; some said he wouldn't finish, but his pals said 'Bill Gould will finish,' and he did finish," said Gould, who grew up in Long Branch. "And I want to finish."

... Don't count on Gould leaving office before his term expires.

"I would never give my opponents or critics that satisfaction," Gould said during a recent interview in his Washington office, which boasts photographs of those he holds dear, such as the Boston Red Sox team, South African President Nelson Mandela and members of the Kennedy family.

"These past two months have left me bone weary, but as tired and discouraged as I get, I will never leave before the race is finished."[1]

I didn't give up, but in 1998, on a Board with three entirely new Board members and Fox—who was widely mentioned as my successor—I assumed lame duck status. When Robert Reich offered me the job on May 25, 1993, I made it clear that I wanted to stay for only one term, ideally until 1996, After my confirmation was delayed until March of 1994, I stated that I would return to California in the summer of 1998. In fact, I had advocated amending the statute to prohibit second terms for Board members because I believed—and continue to believe—that their conduct in office is too often influenced by concerns about reappointment.

The continuing problem of case production was well illustrated in a conversation I had with Howard Jenkins Jr. as I drove him to "Doc" Penello's funeral in early 1998. When I complained about my inability to get Board members to sign off on cases, Jenkins said: "Whenever I had a problem with Fanning [former Chairman John Fanning], when I thought that he was sitting on a case, I simply told him that I would release one of his if he would move on mine." "But," I said, "the problem is different now—there is no case that they have that they want me to release!" Jenkins smiled and allowed that that sort of situation had simply not arisen in his experience.

A second complicating factor in the last months of my term was the sharp ideological divide between members of the new Board. Hurtgen and Brame, on the one hand, had probusiness credentials, although from the very beginning Hurtgen seemed genuinely anxious to see the Board produce cases promptly. Liebman and Fox sat firmly on the other end of the political spectrum. This split caused me to vote with the Republicans on a variety of issues. More frequently, I voted with the Democrats but found it necessary to write separate concurring opinions because my views of a case did not fit with those of either side. And, in much the same vein, when a consensus emerged between the Democrats and Republicans, I sometimes felt called upon to write a separate dissenting opinion. In all cases, my overriding concern was to actually issue a decision—no easy feat in the late 1990s.

The problem was twofold. The full Board's clear ideological divide meant that I had to write more separate opinions while continuing to focus on the overriding issue of case production. The crisis of 1997 had emerged with a three-member Board, and five members simply increased the number of separate opinions and added time for the new people to become acquainted with the issues Fox and I had been dealing with for some time. And Fox, for almost the entire remainder of my term in office, refused to finish her work on the outstanding cases.

In a speech I gave in San Francisco to the California Federation of Labor in July of 1998. I also noted that

... the backlog of cases before the Board is rooted in political intimidation ... Correspondence [from the Congress] ... coupled with the resistance, until November 1997, to the confirmation of any Board members, may have produced a reticence on the part of some members to issue decisions as cases languished for years in Washington. This cause is difficult to prove, since it is always denied, but there is a high likelihood that it plays a significant role in the process.

This problem carried over to the two years following my retirement from the Board, even though none of the incumbents faced confirmation problems until late 1999.

In the same San Francisco speech I also pointed to the increased complexity of unfair labor practice cases (during 1996 the average length of transcripts had increased from 473 to 602 pages) and the rise in such complex unfair labor practice cases as a percentage of our caseload (from 78.8 percent of new cases in 1990 to 82.6 percent in 1997). In addition, there was the problem of declining staff size. In 1998, in inflation-adjusted dollars, our budget was 8.7 percent below that of fiscal 1995, and the number of Board employees had fallen by 15 percent.

Nonetheless, the fundamental problem was at the top, with the presidential appointees. Moreover, the political environment again heating up in Washington— especially in the House, where Republicans were eager to cut our appropriations further and control our activities through appropriations riders—presaged a tumultuous 1998.

January 1, 1998   In early November, the package [of NLRB appointments] put together by Senator Kennedy and Senator Lott went through the Senate without debate or any hitch [late Saturday night on November 8, 1997]. The major problem as I saw it then, and as I continue to see it now, is the difficulty of getting cases out of Sarah Fox. The new Board members, particularly the Republicans, and Peter Hurtgen most of all, have brought a real enthusiasm and commitment to handling these cases. . . .

I set a series of Board agendas dealing with the important cases that I hoped to be a part of my work prior to my departure. Hurtgen was very enthusiastic about it. Brame expressed some tentativeness, stating at one point, "You are such a slave driver. If you were an employer, a union would come in to organize your employees!"—although he quickly said that he was just joking. [Months later he came into Al Wolff's office and spoke of me with obvious reference to my great-grandfather: "Isn't it ironic. Gould is the biggest slave driver of all!"] Liebman came in and complained that she didn't know if she could meet this schedule, and Dennis Walsh, whom she has chosen as chief counsel [he was Browning's chief counsel previously] . . . wrote a memo stating that my previous practice had been one agenda a month in 1994. This was completely untrue, and in our first agenda I pointed out that I had held thirty-five Board agendas in 1994, beginning in April. . . .

The December 17 [1997] session was our first one and was quite interesting. The votes were rather predictable. I lined up with the Republicans on the secondary-boycott case (*Burlington Northern*) and also on the bargaining-tactic case (*Telescope Casual Furniture*) as well as the newest *Lechmere* case (*Farm Fresh*). [It was very old, however, having been lodged with us in 1993.] In the case where I voted for the union position [where I was all alone] (*Hale Nani Rehabilitation*), Liebman stated that her staff had told her that this was not a good case to assert employee rights—where no-solicitation rule had been disparately enforced by management [and] management itself had disobeyed the rule. I wanted to say to her that she, Liebman, should make the decision, not her staff. But she is very meek and mild and quite under the influence of both Fox and Feinstein.

This became very clear in a major budget discussion that we had on December 17 with Feinstein [attending] as well. Feinstein had us hire a large number of employees between July and October, when it became apparent that it was very likely that we would have only a minimum level of funding, and then came to us recommending that all employees be furloughed because of a shortfall—a shortfall that he himself had created by hiring the fifty-one additional people. Fox and Liebman fell in completely behind Feinstein, but through aggressive questioning of his technology people, we were eventually able to get reduction in that area and make either furlough or layoffs unnecessary because of the other cuts. My position was that rather than furlough people—assuming we couldn't get cuts elsewhere—we should lay off those who had been recently hired over the past few months, as Draconian and regrettable as that would have been. But we were able to escape, and my belief is that it is generally known that I led the charge in moving us away from the furlough idea that Feinstein had proposed.

I also suggested again that we had to consider consolidation of field operations in order to deal with the Republicans and the appropriations process in 1998. On this I seem to have struck a sympathetic note with the Republicans, particularly Brame. Feinstein simply glowered when I put this idea forward. But I think that we are going to have to do something like this—I suggested the consolidation of Milwaukee with Chicago—because of Republican insistence. Senator Specter keeps pounding away on this theme, and the Republicans in the House are sure to keep after us. We did, however, institute a hiring freeze.

A number of interesting exchanges took place at the Board agenda. I said that I viewed the employer's position in *dba/Hale Nani Rehabilitation and Nursing Center* as similar to the idea that the "king could do no wrong." I said that that had been rejected in both the Nixon Watergate situation as well as the *Paula Jones* litigation before the Supreme Court. When I mentioned the *Paula Jones* litigation, Brame just beamed all over. Of course, I wasn't supporting the *Jones* litigation at all, but rather the proposition accepted by the Supreme Court in *Jones* v. *Clinton*, as well as *Nixon* v. *United States*.

Also, Brame said about my position: "If that position is accepted, the Labor Policy Association will simply go wild." . . . I responded in mock despair saying: "Heavens, we can't have that!" . . .

Hurtgen got off a couple of good quick comments. When Fox, in her usual overbearing fashion, said that she wanted to make another point, Hurtgen said: "Haven't we heard enough from you already?" This stopped Fox in her tracks, speechless. Not another word was said. I steered the conversation to another subject. . . .

Yesterday, I had lunch with Bob Brame. The most interesting thing to come out of that was his belief that any attempt to [re]name Feinstein as general counsel without confirmation by the Senate would burden the appropriations process and really cut us adrift in the Senate. He said that his belief was that if the White House renamed Feinstein in this manner it would be an insult to the Senate and it would constitute "holy war." When he used that expression, I was so surprised, I asked him to repeat it and he said, "holy war." Brame [being] a right-wing fundamentalist [that] may influence his terminology [in fact, Feinstein *was* named as acting G.C. and the Congress did nothing].

. . . I . . . didn't venture out into the cold evening air on New Year's Eve [still being on California time].

January 25, 1998 On Friday, I had a meeting with Fred Feinstein, who advised me that the White House will appoint him as acting general counsel, notwithstanding ... [what appears to be] a prohibition in the statute on this action. He said that he thought he would be here throughout 1998 and that he would stay on "as long as he could stand it" or as long as he could....

Immediately after my meeting with Feinstein, I met with both Brame and Hurtgen. Brame expressed great displeasure about the news that Feinstein would be appointed and said that the Senate would react negatively "particularly in light of Bill Lan Lee" [the Asian-American attorney general for civil rights, who was appointed on an acting basis in the absence of confirmation], a comment ... that ranked alongside an earlier one he had made about Hitler's armies at a [January 15] Board agenda.

... On January 15 at the Board Agenda, Brame had said that when we were discussing what cases we were going to deal with and when we were going to deal with them, "I feel like Hitler's army. I don't know where to put my troops first when I am fighting on so many fronts." One of the lawyers on Fox's staff, who is Jewish, looked at me and rolled his eyes.

Another amazing comment came out of this [session]. We were ready for our decision to both accelerate and provide briefing in the *Kroger* case, where we are considering—hopefully before the Supreme Court does under the Railway Labor Act in late March—the question of whether a union may mandate impartial arbitration of *Beck* union dues disputes. [We didn't succeed because the case was settled out.] Said Fox to the other Board members with a very stern face: "We have to move quickly on this. We can't dawdle." Fox, who has tied this Board up with her delays and inability or unwillingness to write opinions for the past couple of years was truly amazing at making such a comment. Kate Dowling and I just looked at each other and ... smiled.

This past week was frantic and exhausting in a number of respects. I returned from a speech in Sacramento, after spending a few days in Stanford, on Wednesday night and immediately threw myself into a number of matters. Somehow Al and I were able to grind out my concurring opinion in the *Bloom* decision, which we are supposed to produce by February 2, involving the question of whether a union security agreement, which does not explicitly express union membership obligations is facially invalid....

The week was also made crazy—though it didn't affect my work at all—by revelations about President Clinton in connection with the sex scandal involving an intern at the White House. The most serious aspect of this is possible perjury or subornation ... by Clinton.... I am puzzled about how Paula Jones's lawyers were able to get into Clinton's sexual history in a sexual harassment case. When I last taught the subject, admittedly about five years ago, this could not be done with regard to a woman who complained. It is hard for me to see how it would be fair to do it to the person who is accused, given the other prohibition.

This week we consider cases involving both the status of contingent employees and the *Detroit Newspapers* case as well as other issues. It promises to be an active and difficult week for us here.

At about this time, we ran into the complicating problem of the American Bar Association's two winter meetings. In my view, we simply had no time for these meetings—at least not both of them. But they were being held in Hawaii and Puerto

Rico in the middle of the cold Washington winter. This was a very difficult decision to make. It was important to the ABA to have the Board members and the general counsel there, apparently so that they could show their clients that they had a special relationship with the Board. When I was successful in convincing the Board to attend only one of these functions, some ABA people became irate. Former Board member Charles Cohen, who had been a thorn in our side throughout his tenure, stated at an ABA-Board meeting that "Bill Gould is trying to embarrass us in front of our clients." (Cohen was precluded by law from appearing in cases before the Board for five years after his term expired in 1996, but that didn't stop him from unofficially representing his clients in the meetings the Board held with the ABA Labor and Employment Law section from time to time.)

When I heard about this remark, I did something that, in retrospect, seems foolish. I backed out of the one meeting I had planned to go to. I regarded these sessions as a complete waste of time in which I would undoubtedly be confronted with nothing but hostility. But I should have remembered that back at the beginning of my term one of the leading officials of the section had planted a story with the *Washington Post* to the effect that I had "stood them up" by leaving one of their Washington meetings early in order to attend the staff Christmas party. I had simply thought that the party with my staff was more important. But I could also see that if they would resort to the *Washington Post*—and I was surprised that a reputable paper like the *Post* would print something so trivial—I would face real problems at their meetings.

Leonard Page of the UAW legal staff tried to convince me to go, but I refused. Leonard was right and I was wrong. I should not have backed out of the meeting— that is exactly what Cohen wanted me to do.

The *Caterpillar* Dispute

Early in 1998 one of the older pending cases, *Caterpillar*, seemed to be coming to a head. The dispute centered around the company's failure to address a large number of unfair labor practice charges filed by the United Auto Workers in an early-1990s strike. When in 1994 the Board sought (ultimately unsuccessfully) a Section 10(j) injunction to have the workers reinstated in their jobs, the company complained bitterly to the House Republicans (see chapter 9) and charged the Board with "forum shopping"(looking for a friendly judge).

February 24, 1998 Two weeks ago we had a very major discussion on what we thought would be an important settlement in *Caterpillar*. In essence, all of the NLRB litigation would be withdrawn. All of the strikers, except fifty, would be reinstated without back pay, and the company could object to these fifty, with those matters being submitted to arbitration and such workers entitled to back pay with a two-year cap. The collective-bargaining agreement was to be negotiated alongside of [the] settlement ... [and] taken to the union for ratification. What was unusual about this was the fact that the parties wanted the Board's endorsement of the settlement prior to ratification—although the settlement was conditioned upon ratification.

All of us were supportive except Fox. I spoke out emphatically in favor of it, notwithstanding the fact that the union didn't seem to be getting a lot out of it for the strikers because the collective process was being reestablished and the parties were negotiating a [new] collective-bargaining agreement. Fox agonized a great deal about the acceptability of the package for the individual employees, but after a recess she agreed to accept the package without further meetings and discussion.

On early Friday morning, February 13 [subsequent to our meeting], Dick Shoemaker, the Director of the UAW Agricultural Implement Section, whom I have known for a number of years, called me to say that a deal had been cut and that a collective-bargaining agreement had been negotiated and would be submitted to the membership, although probably not during the long Presidents' Day weekend.

This past weekend the package went to the membership, and they rejected it by 58–42 percent. They apparently were deeply concerned about the two-tier provisions in the collective agreement—they weren't before us—as well as the amnesty provision for strike-breakers or scabs—that wasn't before us either.

Right now, all is in a state of confusion. I don't know whether the parties will attempt to negotiate a new settlement and send it back to us. Caterpillar, which still seems to be sitting in the driver's seat, has said to us that it doesn't feel that further negotiations will be fruitful. The settlement, albeit for a weakened union, made a good deal of sense because of the well-established position of the UAW and its reputation as a bona fide representative. It fits right in with my opinion in *Flint Iceland Arenas,* where I dissented, stressing the importance of settlements even where the union is the losing party and the outcome reflects an imbalance in bargaining resources.[2] It seems to me that we ought to put our imprimatur upon a settlement in such circumstances. [A second agreement was negotiated, ratified, and approved by the Board shortly thereafter.]

Cases and Congress

February 25, 1998   This was one of those mad, crazy days when an awful lot happened administratively and very little happened in terms of case decisions. More arguments and discussions about oral argument on cases and more fears expressed by my staff that Fox will never act on important decisions in which employer rights are being upheld where I am voting with the Republicans, for example, *Farm Fresh* and *Telescope Casual.*

Three major initiatives went out the door today. The first was my proposal that the Board be briefed by the [our] inspector general on March 5 on the cases arising in our regions where staffers have given union-busting management consultants information about the cases that are coming before us so that such firms can represent the companies involved. In some instances, the Board officials who gave the information were actually supervising the election itself. If the labor movement knew about this it would be fit to be tied. On January 14 both Fred [Feinstein] and I were advised of this, and on January 22 I wrote Fred stating that we should dismiss the employees involved. No response. No inquiry of any kind. I advised the Board of all of this today.

I also sent a memo advocating finality [some mechanism through which cases could be produced within a given period of time] in our procedures. I am not optimistic about this because Brame will probably not join me, and Fox and Liebman will undoubtedly be opposed because of their concern about protecting Fox. Brame has already told me that [John] Penello had warned him against getting involved in such matters because they would harm him, Brame, as a dissenter.[3] But, in any event, I must make the attempt.

Finally, although this is to be distributed tomorrow morning, I put together a detailed memo prepared by Dave Parker and Al Wolff on the restructuring of the agency, outlining my many attempts to move the Board forward on this during the past couple of years. Here it is *possible* that something might happen because the Republicans have us under such pressure.

In that connection, the Republicans on the House Appropriations Subcommittee wrote me today, undoubtedly at the behest of the Labor Policy Association (because the letter tracks the association's language), stating that we are carrying out our proposed rule making through adjudication and citing two recent cases. Of course, that is exactly what we are doing. As I attempt to point out to these Republicans, our rule making is a mirror image of what the Board has been doing for three-and-one-half decades through adjudication. The rule-making initiative was simply relevant to codification and to eliminating wasteful litigation. They didn't listen, and therefore they didn't learn.

More troublesome, however, is the invasion of our adjudicative responsibilities.... There is another theme to all of this and that is that the Board, by taking rule making off the table, as it did a few weeks ago, simply invited more aggression by the bully. If the Board is afraid enough to remove proposed rule making from the table in order to placate Congress, surely it will accede to more demands. Thus, the House Republicans wind up stating that I should "provide assurances that the long-standing policy regarding approval of single-facility units are [*sic*] still in effect, including evidence, if any, of Board approvals of multiple facility units against the wishes of the petitioning unions." Moreover, they "request" that I should communicate to all regional directors that determinations on this issue will be made in accordance with the rules in effect as of September 28, 1995, when we first put the proposed rule into effect. Of course, there has been no change in the handling of such cases.

We began to review the lengthy, rambling, and somewhat repetitive dissent of Board member Brame in *Hale Nani Rehabilitation*. It is an extremely ambitious job, which covers the waterfront and engages in a discussion about a wide variety of issues that he perceives to be directly presented by the issue in this case: that is, does an employer violate the statute when its supervisors distribute antiunion literature during working time and employees are prohibited from distributing literature during working time. I will work on this a bit more tonight and have already spent about a half an hour discussing this with Steve Rappaport after reviewing most of this dissent—I still haven't read all of it.

Today I had lunch with Howard Jenkins, who was in good form mentally, notwithstanding his inability to walk very far because of emphysema and his macular degenerative disease in his eyes. I think he was genuinely pleased at my invitation to visit with us. Mary Ann took a photo of us that will appear in *All Aboard*, the NLRB newspaper.

March 5, 1998   [Feinstein] ... sent me a copy of the letter that he sent to President Clinton in which he frankly acknowledged that his reason for withdrawal [for renomination] was that he didn't have the votes. Though I told Feinstein that he had shown "courage" for withdrawing rather than allowing this debate to damage the Board's appropriations struggle, in fact I think that he hasn't shown much courage as general counsel in either the issuance of complaints—no minority bargaining orders or an attempt to take on the question of union constitutional limitations of the right to resign—and as an administrator he has been a disaster because of his failure to reorganize, a failure that is going to get us in a great deal of difficulty with the Republicans in the House, in particular, this spring. I have sent the Board a memo on this, advocating regional office reorganization and, of course, the inspector general's reports have revealed a wide variety of other deficiencies. But it does no good to speak ill of the dead, and I, when asked by Glenn Burkins of the *Wall Street Journal* for a comment on Feinstein, did not provide one.

A new controversy emerged about this time in relation to my attempt to appoint a new inspector general for the Board. Bob Allen had indicated to me that he would like to retire prior to my departure. I was concerned that Feinstein, Fox, and Liebman would not support the appointment of an individual at the SES level because of Allen's investigations into the general counsel's office and the fact that only someone at an SES level would have had stature and independence enough to stand up to a presidential appointee as he did. In a March 11 memo to me, Bob Allen stated the following:

I write to convey my concern about what I view as the continuing interference and obstruction by the Office of the General Counsel with the Office of the Inspector General.

It would by naiveté of the greatest degree on my part not to recognize that the increasing level of obstruction has coincided with our [two most recent major] investigations ... regarding issues ... which flow directly back to the Office of the General Counsel.

This is an Agency charged by law with the prevention of interference with the exercise of legally protected activity, and which deals daily with retaliation, pretextual actions, and nexus with animus. Indeed, the General Counsel was recently quoted in the *NY Times* as stating: "Prosecutors are, generally speaking not very popular ... and an agency that prosecutes and enforces laws having to do with protecting workers' rights can run into particular problems in terms of popularity." Yet this very reaction is one that has become increasingly more practiced by the Office of the General Counsel with regard to the investigations and reports of the Office of the Inspector General: our statutory duty, just like that of the General Counsel, is to investigate workplace complaints and to issue reports without regard to rank or identity of the subject. This we have done, but surprisingly with interference by the Office of the General Counsel, particularly in high profile cases involving high ranking officials. We have also been surprised by the hostility displayed towards the OIG as a result of reports which are not completely to the liking of the Office of the General Counsel.

... OGC [Office of the General Counsel] [conduct] triggers a serious question of obstruction of justice, witness tampering and criminal conflicts of interest.

... a strong, independent Inspector General is critical to this Agency. I regret that the actions of the Office of the General Counsel have reached the point where I find the need to cite it to you as the head of the Agency, as a serious management problem, consistent with the requirements of the Inspector General Act ...

Thus, when I met resistance from Feinstein and Fox with regard to my attempt to continue the inspector general position at the SES level, I swung into action and sought the assistance of Congress.

March 12, 1998 ... I have made arrangements to go see both Congressman Shays and Congressman Towns, the ranking Democrat on the Human Resources Subcommittee of the House Committee on Government Reform and Oversight, which last year expressed a great deal of interest in our inspector general program with Bob Allen. Today, we did that and Towns expressed general interest and sympathy. Shays was not there, but we laid it out to his subcommittee counsel, Halloran, and Shays called me later in the afternoon. Shays said that he would support me in any dispute about whether the inspector general's job should remain at SES level. He brought Halloran in on our conference call and said that he was supportive and said: "Should we do anything further?" Halloran said that perhaps a call to Feinstein was in order [because of] the refusal of Feinstein to submit himself or his representatives in the Tampa investigation—which Hoekstra, Shays, and Towns also have copies of—to be interviewed for the purpose of affidavits without the presence of the general counsel's special counsel. Shays was quite friendly and personable and seemed to be supportive.

I am sure that I will face another attack by Feinstein, Fox, and Liebman on the SES issue—or at least would have until they become aware that Congress has been alerted to what they are doing. I am quite sure that they will know that Mo [the NLRB driver] took both Bob Allen and myself up to Capitol Hill at the conclusion of the union advisory panel meeting today.

These last couple of days have left me exhausted and drained. I was on the phone Tuesday night for about three hours with not only Feinstein, Bill Stewart, Bob Allen, Peter Hurtgen about this matter, but also back-to-back meetings and discussions yesterday when I came here before preparing for the union advisory panel meeting—my last as chairman—today.

I have often thought that the internal struggles, first with Feinstein and Browning, in particular, and now with Feinstein, Fox, and Liebman, were even more draining than those with the Republicans, and this proves to be no exception to the rule.

March 18, 1998 Yesterday was a watershed in a number of respects. It marked the beginning of the transition for my departure from Washington. I had my last meeting with the management attorneys on our advisory panels, and it went very well indeed, notwithstanding a number of criticisms that were aimed at us in connection with Section 10(j). Incidentally, I think that most of the management people knew that, had I not insisted upon it, there would have been no discussion on this subject.

As in the past, Feinstein fiercely resisted it and Liebman rushed around to do his bidding with the other Board members, particularly with Hurtgen. But, eventually, I pushed a reluctant Hurtgen to side with me, and the discussion went forward. Of course, I thought some of the management criticisms were justified: that is, the failure to provide for unimpeded access to the Board rather than filtering matters through the general counsel, the failure to provide for oral argument in selected cases, the failure to articulate a rationale for a decision arrived at. The other Board members and Feinstein remained silent as I set forth my views.

The meeting involved a lot of good give-and-take, and I think that I surprised the management attorneys by pointing out that as a percentage of cases received, the 10(j) requests that came to Washington had actually declined during fiscal year 1996 compared to the early 1990s, when Jerry Hunter had sought Section 10(j) relief so infrequently. One of the great ironies of the meeting was that there was much more warmth toward me—particularly by those who were the management leadership types—than was demonstrated by the union people last week, at least their leadership in the form of Hiatt. All that Hiatt could do was to bemoan Feinstein's inability to get confirmed in angry language. Nary a word was spoken about me. But yesterday the vibes were not only better as a general matter, but Betty Murphy [a Washington management lawyer and former chairman under President Ford] chimed in at the end to the effect that I would be "much missed in Washington."

Thus, in the morning, it was my farewell to my first innovation.... In the afternoon, it was really my farewell to the Board, as I got into one of my intractable fights, this time over the inspector general issue. The backdrop, of course, is that Fox and Liebman want to denigrate the office so that the vigorous investigation of the general counsel will not be continued. And, of course, the complementary goal of Fox (and probably Liebman as well) is that she would like to select the inspector general herself....

At a Boilermakers legislative function in the evening—the fourth or fifth that I have been to since arriving here (I think that I went to my first in the first few days after I got here on March 14, 1994)—it turned out that Brame had never read the report on Feinstein's political selections of lawyers ... [the subject of one of the inspector general's investigations of the general counsel]. I strongly suggested to him that he do so. Liebman chimed in with this remark: "You always come across as so morally superior." This set me back a bit, but [it] clearly reflected her outright hostility.

I told Hurtgen [because of his lack of support on the inspector general issue] that I felt that he had led me into the Iadrang Valley, one of the early and bloody battles of the Vietnam War, around 1965 or 1966, in which American troops were slaughtered. The day ended on a very angry note, indeed.

All of this made me start thinking about the point that Betty Murphy had made to me when I had lunch with her yesterday; that is, that I should stop participating in new cases pretty soon. I have talked to Al Wolff about this this morning and will probably relinquish new cases when I send my letter of resignation to President Clinton in the first week of May. I think that I will stick with the July 14 Bastille Day resignation date and have this week asked Frank Brucato at Stanford Law School to put me back on the ... payroll on July 15. We are now moving into the final stretch.

In March 1998, while I struggled to produce cases and get the inspector general's status on a firm footing, the House of Representatives was at work amending the

National Labor Relations Act, this time through legislation rather than appropriations riders. While a number of House Democrats were in Africa with President Clinton, the House Republicans attempted to amend the statute through passage of the Fairness for Small Business and Employees Act of 1998. It passed in the House by a narrow vote of 202 to 200.

The bill sought to substantially reverse the Supreme Court's decision on "salting" in *NLRB* v. *Town & Country Electric, Inc.* (often referred to as *Town & Country*). In a provision sure to generate considerable litigation, the House articulated a test to determine the "primary purpose" of an individual seeking employment; that is, to determine whether he or she is a bona fide applicant. The bill was a project of Speaker Gingrich, who had long taken great interest in pressuring the Equal Employment Opportunity Commission, with apparent success, to rule against the use of "testers" in unfair employment practice cases.)

A second provision of the bill sought to reverse the single-facility presumption that had been addressed in our (now withdrawn) rule-making proposal. The Republican majority wanted to eliminate that presumption from Board adjudication in representation cases as well. According to the House report on the legislation, "the reason unions prefer smaller units is because they are easier to organize, as it is easier to get members of the unit to agree on a mutually advantageous course of collective bargaining—which is why the proposed rule was so attractive to them."

The third provision, a particularly cynical move even by the standards of the Republican House, sought to require the Board to resolve individual discrimination cases within a year of the time they are filed. The difficulty (and irony) with this idea is that most such cases could not even be heard by an administrative law judge before a year had elapsed—and that the same Congress that purported to be so interested in prompt resolution of disputes had cut Board funding!

Finally, the amendment required the Board to pay the attorneys' fees and other related costs of employers who prevailed against the Board if they had fewer than a hundred employees and a net worth of less than $1.4 million. The present rule requires as a prerequisite to such a recovery a substantial justification or a very special set of circumstances.

At the Las Vegas AFL-CIO executive council meeting later that month, President Clinton pledged to veto the bill. In the fall, an attempt by Senate Republicans to obtain the sixty votes necessary for a vote on a bill outlawing the "salting" of nonunion companies was beaten back by 52 to 42. Senators Kennedy and Harkin led the Senate fight against this legislation.

Internally, my greatest struggle continued to be issuing cases. On April 6 I went to a luncheon with Chief Justice Rehnquist and asked him publicly how he managed each year's cases so as to get them all out by July 1 or 2.

April 8, 1998 ... [On the podium] he went through an explanation in which he said that he categorized cases and tried to focus the justices' minds on cases that were analytically related, and so on. But then when the formal presentation was over (there was a Stanford Law Society meeting), he shook my hand as he left the room and I said to him that nothing had frustrated me more than dealing with the problem of case processing and getting Board members to act. Rehnquist said: "Let me ask you one thing. Do you have the authority to assign cases?" When I answered in the negative, he said: "Oh, that would make a big difference. Because what I do with the nonproducers is not to assign them the cases." That would, indeed, make a big difference with us here, but, regrettably I don't have this kind of authority.

My one major accomplishment over the past few days lies in the creation of a committee that will oversee Board reorganization, configuration, and closing of [some] regional offices. Feinstein had always resisted this bitterly, but for some reason Fox and Liebman relented and, with Hurtgen's support, I was able to push it through. Questions remain about the composition of the committee and precisely what it will do. But I want to make much of this when I testify before the House on April 29.

Proposition 226

By late April it seemed that, despite my best efforts, the forces of political confrontation and the logjam at the Board were hurling us toward disaster. Early in the month, Dave Sickler of the California AFL-CIO telephoned to say that the proponents of California Proposition 226 (which requires unions to get prior permission from members to spend their dues for political purposes) were arguing that it was needed because the Clinton Board was not enforcing *Beck*. I pointed out to him that our predecessors had decided no *Beck* cases at all while we have issued seventeen rulings, including the comprehensive *California Saw & Knife* decision of December 1995.

In mid-April I was invited by California State Senator Hilda Soulis to speak to the California legislature about Proposition 226, which was on the ballot for the June 2 election. This proposition provided what the Republicans called "paycheck protection," but it was actually designed to cripple the financial relationship between the trade union movement and the Democratic party. As a practical matter, requiring unions to obtain explicit authorization from represented workers before spending dues for political purposes would put the unions out of business politically and would eliminate one of the major funding sources of the Democratic party. My own principal concern, however, was about the relationship between Proposition 226 and the National Labor Relations Act.

A hearing of the House Appropriations Subcommittee prevented me from testifying at the joint hearing in Sacramento. Instead, on April 28 I submitted a written statement in which I noted that I planned to vote "no." Proposition 226, I stated, was flawed from a policy perspective; one of the core elements of trade union activity, I pointed out, is involvement in the political process. Indeed, political activity in the form of lobbying legislatures is protected by the very National Labor Relations Act that the Board administers. I stated that as in American labor law there is no presumption that workers should be represented by unions, the political involvement of a given union might well be an issue touched on during a union organizing campaign. If workers subsequently become dissatisfied with their union's political activities, they can obtain new leadership in the periodic elections guaranteed by the Landrum-Griffin Act. In any event, they can object to the expenditure of political dues under the *Beck* decision itself. Thus workers have always been free to decline having their dues spent for political purposes.

Second, I stated that Proposition 226 was a misguided attempt to convince California voters that the Board had not enforced *Beck*. I pointed out that when I first arrived in Washington, six years had elapsed since the Court had handed down that decision—yet not one single decision had been issued by the Board, whereas my Board had made issuing *Beck* cases one of its priorities and had done so in rulings affirmed by the circuit courts of appeals.

Third, I contended that Proposition 226 was flawed constitutionally because it was preempted by the National Labor Relations Act's exclusive jurisdiction over the labor-management subject matter covered by that statute.

Thus, I concluded, Proposition 226 was both bad policy and bad law. "As a California voter and a citizen and chairman of the National Labor Relations Board, which interprets *Beck*, as well as a California law professor, I have an obligation to speak out and address the issues in light of your invitation to me."

In an e-mail responding to my arguments David M. Sander of Congressman Porter's staff accused me of partisanship:

Today—of all days—Chairman Gould submitted testimony to the California State Legislature attacking Proposition 226, a state paycheck protection measure. The press release and testimony appear on the NLRB web page.... one particular quote of interest:[prop 226] would "cripple a major source of funding for the Democratic Party." That sounds a little partisan to me, and is especially interesting considering his recent response to our letter.

As you no doubt recall, we were verbally slapped by Gould for trying to interfere politically in an adjudicatory process. He suggested that the mission of the Board was above politics, and such political influence might "erode the system of independent adjudication and democracy in the workplace...."

Now, however, he is clearing [*sic*] making partisan statements as the Board Chairman, and posting them on his web page.

A few days later, on May 4, President Clinton expressed his opposition to Proposition 226 at a breakfast meeting in Los Angeles. He argued that the initiative would "basically muffle the ability of the collective voices of working people to be heard by putting on them a far, far greater administrative burden than corporations face when they spend their own money...." Rhetorically, President Clinton asked why labor unions should be treated differently from corporations.

The Sander e-mail set off the biggest conflict of all—or so it seemed at the time.

May 7, 1998   A veritable firestorm emerged during these past couple of days on my statement on Proposition 226. On Monday I held off doing anything about the ... web site ... [which had been set up by Dave Parker, a staff member, with my approval]. I had heard nothing from any of the members of the Board, but Porter's office called again and expressed their displeasure at the press release still being on the web site.

Tuesday, May 5 was the truly eventful day. After consulting with Bill Stewart (Bill had agreed to come in to work on this particular crisis) and Al Wolff, I decided to tell Dave Parker to take the press release off the web site because so many investigations were pending: that is, the inspector general, GAO at the request of the House Republicans, and possibly the Office of Legal Counsel. Dave was relieved at this because it took him out of the crossfire....

When I returned to my office things began to go very badly with a phone call from David Obey, who is the ranking Democrat of the appropriations subcommittee and had been particularly abusive to me last fall when he claimed that I didn't know how things operated in Washington ... [because I had contacted both the executive and legislative branch on behalf of our budget]. This time Obey began the conversation in a more venomous, derisory tone than the previous one, if that is possible: "What in the world did you think you were doing going to California to make a statement like the one that you made?!" Then he said: "How could you possibly refer to the Democratic party as losing funds and make such a partisan statement! Don't you realize that you have opened yourself up and the agency up to an attack by the conservative Republicans—you have laid yourself open, and you are not in a position to lead the agency." Obey also said: "Why did you make this statement *before* the hearing?" I pointed out to him that the timing of it all was dictated by the California legislature and the June 2 vote in California, and I said, "It really doesn't matter when I made the statement. The Republicans would attack me at any time for saying this and would threaten to retaliate against the budget for any speech that I may make at any time." At this point ... I said: "Perhaps someone else can do it better and

I should simply step aside." ... He said to me: "I think that you should resign as chairman." I was absolutely stunned and devastated. A few more comments went back and forth, but I simply stopped responding to him. There was a long pause on the telephone. Earlier he had said—when I began to respond in some detail—that he had to leave quickly because he had to vote. But now there was simply a silence on the phone. When we concluded the conversation, I sprang into action quickly to call a number of friends.

I telephoned Nancy Pelosi, but she did not turn out to be very helpful. In fact, when I mentioned the Obey statement, she said: "Well Bill, if the Republicans are going to ask for your resignation wouldn't it be better to resign before they ask for it?" At this point I was beginning to toughen up a bit, and I said that no, it would not, and that I did not intend to resign under any circumstance. She said that there was some sentiment—when I asked her where this was coming from beyond identifying it as in the legislative branch she refused to do so—that I should resign and when I said that I was going to be leaving in August she said that there was some belief that August was not soon enough. She said poignantly: "This place [the House] is a very rough place." I said to her: "I find it hard to believe that after more than four years of making the kind of contribution that I have to the Board that it would make sense for me or the president to resign on the basis of one line in a statement to the California legislature to which Congressman Obey objects." In a second telephone conversation in the evening from her home, Pelosi began to take a more conciliatory [tone] ... and began to speak of "we" as one of my supporters and expressed the view that the women on the committee, that is, Lowey and DeLauro, would be supportive of me. However, it became apparent to me that [Steny] Hoyer [D-Md.] had bought into some of Obey's thinking [and] that undoubtedly Pelosi was referring to Hoyer. But the underlying assumption in all of her remarks was that the Republicans would be climbing out of the woodwork after my scalp, and they would seek my resignation.

I called Lou Stokes and reached him in Cleveland and described everything that had happened with Obey to him. He said to me: "Obey is a wild man and has behaved this way before." Indeed, this squared with what Pelosi said, although Pelosi, in her words, said, "David cares so much about the issues and does it so well." Stokes said that he wanted a copy of the statement and that he would talk to Obey and try to calm him down. I also telephoned John Conyers, and Conyers put in a call immediately to Gephardt and then in a second telephone conversation with him on Wednesday morning reported to me that he had reached Gephardt and that Gephardt "had the fire hoses out." Conyers said at that point—this was late Wednesday morning—going into a House Judiciary Committee meeting that he planned to come to my hearing at 2:00 P.M. (In fact, he did not get there.) I also called Steve Yokich of the UAW, and Mary Ann was successful in getting me out of a meeting by stating that it was "urgent." When I got Yokich on the phone, he said: "Bill, I have all kinds of urgent things that are going on this morning. Daimler-Benz is merging with Chrysler, and everyone is telling me that that is urgent. What is your urgent situation about?" I then told him what had taken place, and he expressed absolute amazement. He said he would call Obey and try to calm him down. Yokich said he thought that I had been a fine chairman and that, although a number of the UAW people complained about the fact that I didn't vote with them in many cases where they wanted me to do so, he said that he had always said to them: "Where are we going to find someone who will be a better chairman?"

The common thread that seemed to run through the discussions with Stokes, Conyers, and then Maxine Waters, whom I reached late Tuesday afternoon . . . was that Obey was "wild."

But at the hearing on Wednesday it proved to be different.

It was a tough hearing, but most [people] seemed to think I did pretty well in dealing with what was said. Porter began with a statement that I felt mischaracterized the facts, and I made brief note of what I felt was accurate. Istook called me a liar as he had done last year. Dickey was as aggressive as ever and zeroed in on this particular theme. Dickey asked me how I could tell Californians what to say and do, and I said that I was a Californian, a fact of which he seemed to be unaware. Obey was not his caustic and abusive self but stated that I should have exercised more caution. I opined that I had spoken in the first-person singular and that my reference to Democratic party funding should have spoken of the Republican party interchangeably. My point was—and I expressed it to the committee—that the position of both the National Labor Relations Act and the National Labor Relations Board had been mischaracterized in the California debate. Thus, the need to set the record straight.

At one point, Dickey said that I was partisan and only interested in meeting with Democrats and not Republicans and alluded to Obey's criticism of me last fall (Obey had aimed his criticism at Feinstein as well) for rounding up Democrats to support me. But I pointed out to him that I had tried to reach him and schedule all kinds of meetings with him, including a recent meeting with Brame and Hurtgen, only to be rebuffed. He denied this, but I said it was true, I was sure that it had been done and that we had tried to do it but were denied the opportunity. He pointed out that he had met with Brame, and I was tempted to say that that was only because he wanted to meet with Republicans, but I bit my tongue and said nothing. I said that I would meet with Dickey any time and any place; and I said to him that I was going to Blues Alley that evening and that he could join me there. Steny Hoyer said: "You don't really mean that. You don't really mean that." Of course, Hoyer was correct.

It was an exhausting and grueling day and set of events leading up to it. May 5 was the lowest [day] of my four-year-plus tenure. May 6 brought me back a bit, although I found that the articles that were written about this—even in the *Los Angeles Times*—and, of course, the *Washington Times* (which regards me as a criminal who only takes actions in response to its urgings) focused too much on the criticisms of me and not my explanations. But I suppose that that is the way it is.

One bright note today: Tom Rankin of the California AFL-CIO called to thank me for my support on Proposition 226. Earlier in the day, David Sickler of the Los Angeles County Federation had called to say how enthused people were about the position I have taken. But I have yet to hear from the AFL-CIO here in Washington.

May 7, 1998 (addendum, 10:48 P.M.)   As I reflect on the events of Wednesday and Thursday, I think that the major mistake in my Proposition 226 press release is in its reference to trade union support for the Democratic party, for the Democrats don't want to focus upon the fact that they get so much money from the unions. And this point, in their view, makes them vulnerable to attack from the Republicans. I made this point to Pelosi, and she said that this wasn't the reason for Obey's reaction. But I think that it is—a point buttressed by the fact that the Zubrenskys [friends of mine from the early 1960s] in Milwaukee this evening pointed out to me how much money Obey gets from the unions, even though he is in a relatively conservative and rural district where the unions are not strong. This might be my error. Karen Tramontano [of the White House] seemed to say as much when she said that this is something that we don't want to talk about, that is, union support for the Democratic party.

Of course, my predecessors had gone much further in involving themselves in the political process. As I noted in an earlier chapter, both Chairman Millis (FDR's chairman) and Chairman Herzog (Truman's) had communicated with the White House and filed memoranda. Chairman Herzog, along with General Counsel Van Arkel, had even worked on legislation with a number of senators. And, as James Gross relates, the special assistant of Chairman McCulloch (Kennedy's chairman) actually drafted a congressional report, the so-called Pucinski Report.[4]

Thus, by the standards of the NLRB of the 1940s, 1950s, and 1960s, my statement on Prop 226 was a cautious and mild venture into the political arena. Had I done anything remotely comparable to what my predecessors did, I would have been burned alive! I thought (and still think) that my testimony to the California legislature, delivered at its request, was appropriate. In my mind the legislature's invitation was similar to the inquiries I had received about the TEAM Act from senators Feinstein, Bingaman, and others and the requests for information senators Durenberger, Hatch, and Kennedy made at my 1993 confirmation hearings.

But in addressing this sensitive issue publicly—even though my communication was delivered much more at arm's length from the legislative branch than those of prior Board chairmen—I had pressed the hot button of labor law and politics in the 1990s. The Republicans were pressing their so-called paycheck protection—the heart of their campaign financial reform initiative—on both the federal and state levels. And Proposition 226, which was to go down in flames the following month, was at the heart of their efforts. All the Democratic and moderate Republican attempts to sponsor campaign-reform legislation ran aground on the shoals of this issue. The so-called poison pill amendment to the campaign reform bill introduced by Senate Majority Leader Trent Lott would have reversed *Beck*, just as Proposition 226 would have done—though its supporters contended that they were only putting it forward to *enforce* the Court's decision.

California Governor Pete Wilson seemed to believe that the issue could take him to the White House in 2000. Echoing the House Republican sentiments, he attacked my views, insisting that the opponents of Proposition 226 in the Clinton administration really were not enforcing *Beck*.

National Labor Relations Board Chairman William Gould boldly claims that the administration does enforce *Beck*. But this is misleading at best. First, *Beck* doesn't apply to the 6.7 million union members in the U.S. who are public employees.

And what Gould calls "enforcement" is really a burden that workers must assume in order to obtain refunds for political spending taken unlawfully from their paychecks.

The grievance process they must follow is complex and frustrating. It can take as long as 800 days before the NLRB resolves a worker's claim.[5]

There are major flaws in Wilson's argument and in much of the Republican commentary. First, to the extent that it does take time for charges to be pursued by the Board, that problem was being exacerbated by Wilson's own party in the House of Representatives, which was then attempting to cut our budget (again). Only a couple of months earlier, the House had pursued the same cynical theme by passing the Fairness for Small Business and Employees Act of 1998, even though it knew that inadequate funding made the time limits established by the bill impossible to meet.

Second, *Beck* provided that employees must object and file objections with the union. Wilson seemed to assume that the status quo under the law operated in favor of the dissident workers rather than of the union. Thus, the promotion of Proposition 226 was actually an attempt to overrule *Beck*, not enforce it.

Third, Wilson's statement embodies another basic misunderstanding that the Republicans had about *Beck*. Like Wilson, they kept speaking and writing about the rights of "union members," whereas the Court had made it clear that the rights contained in *Beck* related only to nonmembers or limited members. These were the people the Court sought to protect against union coercion. Representative Fawell of Illinois, a staunch critic of the Board, also seemed to misunderstand this aspect of *Beck* when he spoke—during the August 1998 debate about campaign reform—of workers who would be unable to get their *Beck* "rights" under the proposed legislation because it applied only to nonmembers.[6] Of course, the legislation applied to nonmembers—just as *Beck* did. Representative Goodling's remarks, made on the House floor the same day, illustrate a similar lack of understanding.[7] But perhaps they did not understand because—as so often happens in Washington—they simply did not want to understand, or to listen to something that departed from their ideological preconceptions. Earlier, I had seen that tendency at work in its most exaggerated form in the debate about rule making.

Meanwhile, much to the consternation of the House Republicans, Inspector General Bob Allen conducted a thorough investigation of whether my statement to the California legislature and having it typed at the Board constituted an unlawful expenditure of agency funds under the Appropriations Act, as the Republicans contended. That legislation supposedly prohibited statements by presidential appointees involving "legislation pending before any State Legislature." The IG, however, found that because the statement involved an initiative that would be decided by the voters of California, not a bill being debated and voted upon in the California legislature, it was not legislation within the meaning of the law. Thus, there was no violation. That finding infuriated Chairman Porter and the rest of the Republicans, who nonetheless continued to claim that I had violated the law!

"We Must Do Both"

That May, I felt completely under siege. In one speech I said I was "reminded of British Prime Minister Harold Wilson's comment when faced with a great deal of criticism and challenge from within and without: 'I know what's going on. I'm going on.'"

And so I continued to move forward, but the old problem of case processing was not easily solved. During the summer and fall of 1997, in addition to urging Fox to move on cases in person, I had sent numerous memos to her and the rest of the Board. Now, in the spring of 1998, I moved back to that approach. I had no choice. As I noted in a memo to the Board, we were not doing "... either the routine or the major cases. We must do both."

I devised a "hit parade" of priority cases and implored Board members to "roll up our sleeves and ... turn this around." Subsequently, I conducted a number of meetings with individual members—particularly Fox—to talk about the status of cases. At the conclusion of one Board meeting in which we had reviewed all the outstanding cases and simply reported on what stage we were each at in our work, Fox smiled and said, "Don't you think that that meeting went very well?" Even her faithful ally Liebman smiled, as if to say, "It's one thing to review the work. It's another thing to actually do it."

In my memo, I noted that *Farm Fresh* had been with us for five years and that in the more than three years that we had had *Telescope Casual* there were "many inquiries from Capitol Hill." Pointing to the doubled backlog, I said: "We are paid handsome salaries by the people of the United States to do this work. I do not understand why we cannot do it and implore and urge you to do it and, more importantly, I am sure that neither the judiciary or the Congress will understand if we do not."

Meanwhile, an avalanche of letters came in about the *Detroit Newspapers* case, for which we had unsuccessfully requested an injunction in 1997. I received a letter from the president of the Detroit Mailers Union and another from Morty Bahr, president of the Communications Workers of America, in which he said he hoped that the Board would act on *Detroit Newspapers* "before your term ends and you leave. A lot of families want to put their lives together again."

I circulated these inquiries to the Board with the comment that "despite my many memos, meetings, exhortations, etc., nothing issues—with the exception of *Burlington* [the secondary-boycott case], we have not issued anything from the December 17 Board Agenda, held now almost one half year ago." I went on:

I share the anger and cynicism of Messrs. Young and Bahr—but I share it because of the failure to act on a whole host of cases.

I think that most individuals asked to accept this Chairmanship would have despaired at this failing performance long ago. Again, nonetheless, I ask you to do the work that we are paid handsome salaries to do and issue our cases. No one from the public, Congress or the judiciary could possibly understand this rock-bottom performance.

The next day Peter Hurtgen, who had stated that Fox's inaction was "maddening," joined in, although no member acceded to my repeated attempts to revive Rule 76.1. As Hurtgen pointed out:

In two days, it will be May Day, which at the Board means the Chairman will be with us for only two more months.... It seems to me that we must issue all the cases presently pending before the full Board and upon which the Chairman is one of a three-member majority. Regardless of who the two dissenters are in all such cases, if they do not issue while the Chairman is here, they will become tied cases which will further exacerbate our backlog problem.... It will be my urging of my colleagues that we commit ourselves to issue in these cases while the Chairman is here, for it seems to me there is no legitimate reason not to do so, regardless of who the two dissenters are.

But still no cases moved. In retrospect, notwithstanding Hurtgen's statement of interest in our productivity and his comments about Fox, he too wanted very much to be reappointed. As he told me, he had, therefore, to "get along with Fox" so that his term in Washington would be a smooth one. Thus I did not have in reality the help that the Hurtgen memo seemed to give me on paper. My reliance on the Republicans for case productivity was pathetic in a Democratic administration when it should have been in the interest of the Democrats to work with me.

Inspector General Fracas

In the early summer the dispute over the inspector general position erupted. When Bob Allen retired, I decided to appoint to the position a very qualified lawyer, Aileen Armstrong of the general counsel's office. My thinking was that if I allowed the position to be posted it would certainly be delayed and the opponents of keeping the job at an SES level that provided complete independence might ultimately prevail. I needed someone with Armstrong's capabilities and qualities and knowledge of the Board. Representative Shays, however, now supported the Board members who favored Feinstein's position on this matter.

June 25, 1998   Today was one of those furious quick days on Capitol Hill. In a sense it was a good one, not only because of apparent success but also because it could take my mind away from the fact that the same old story prevails here at 1099 14th Street: that is, absolutely no cases of any consequence continue to issue. This has been true throughout my absence of two weeks in Europe—between June 7 and 21—and it remains true now.

One reason that the Board apparently doesn't produce cases is that they continue to spend so much time on administrative matters. They are attempting to rebuff the inspector general on her investigation of case processing.... Now with an impending new financial crisis, which will be discussed on Monday, I am quite confident that they seek to deny the inspector general the monies [that she had requested for computers].

I met with Halloran and Chase of Congressman Shays's office this morning. It brought to mind some of the old discussions about baseball tickets that Shays started with me in 1996 in which Halloran figured so prominently. He didn't disguise his hostility and smirked and smiled a good deal of our discussion. I said that I was there to talk about: (1) the appointment of the IG and my response to Congressman Shays's concern that I did not follow the appropriate procedure; (2) the budget request that is being resisted by the Board; and (3) the resistance to the inspector general's investigation. I quickly learned that I was in hostile territory when Chase began to say that it would have been better for me to have selected the inspector general from outside the agency because that individual would have been more independent. I pointed out that we had had a history of investigations and ... negative responses to ... [previous] IG investigations. It was almost as though they hadn't heard what I had said. Halloran then stated that he couldn't understand why I had made the appointment so late in my chairmanship. I said that it didn't matter when in my term of office I made it and that, if anything, the fact that I was leaving soon all the more highlighted the fact that the IG would be independent. But they didn't appear to be very interested in that.

Halloran then stated that it seemed as though the IG was commencing her investigation to retaliate against the people who opposed her appointment. I said that this was in error. If anything, I asked, why weren't they focusing upon the resistance to the investigation. It seemed as though the resistance indicated retaliation for her appointment.

I then decided to get in touch with the Democrats and met with Towns right after noon, and Towns was sympathetic and said that he would talk to Shays; and when I asked what else I should do, he suggested that I talk to Congressman Kucinich of Ohio and Barrett of Wisconsin. Kucinich had been extremely friendly toward me in last summer's hearings, and the meeting that I had with him in the afternoon proved to be no exception to the pattern. Kucinich invited me in and said that I was always welcome in his office anytime and that I should feel free to use it as a base to make telephone calls, etc. He said: "You have been a friend of working people in the country and you have changed the direction of your agency. Wherever I go labor recognizes this." When I would thank him, as I did on a number of occasions, he would say that thanks were not appropriate because of the fact that he was committed to the National Labor Relations Act and working people in the country and he appreciated what I had done in this connection. He then asked for me to put a letter together to prepare for Shays, and Al and Aileen Armstrong did this very quickly. He called Barrett, Sanders, Towns (and I think that there might have been someone else) and they agreed to sign immediately. Barrett called me later in the evening and said that he had signed and that he had seen Allen of Maine's signature on it. The only person Kucinich may not have been able to contact, although he tried to reach him as well, was Lantos ... In any event, right now it looks as though a letter will be delivered to Shays tomorrow, which will state the concern of all the Democrats with the way in which the IG matter is being handled. Shays's office let it drop that Feinstein is coming in tomorrow to speak with them....

I don't know what will happen, but I suppose that this gave me a badly needed lift. I have had a number of good meetings over the past few days—the first one with my old pal Paul Wellstone, who congratulated me on my work and with whom I discussed the budget and case-processing problems. I told him that I had seen him on C-SPAN in New Hampshire in his run-up to the primary in that state, and he said that he was quite serious about pursuing the presidency in 2000 and probably would do it. He said to me: "As a lawyer, you can understand Oliver Wendell Holmes's interest in 'memorable opinions' and I hope that that is what my campaign in 2000 will be." He said that he would help with Harkin. [Ultimately, Wellstone withdrew from the presidential stakes. He and I both supported Senator Bill Bradley's unsuccessful candidacy in 2000.]

Although I didn't have a meeting with Tom Harkin, he called me and, on learning that my term would expire soon, said to me: "I feel like the Shoeless Joe Jackson story: 'Say it isn't so.'" But I explained to him that I had really made up my mind. He said that he talked to so many labor people throughout the country who spoke highly of me and the work of the agency these past four-plus years, and he said "Your predecessors didn't believe in the Act or collective bargaining—they were just going through the motions." [Later, during the following month, Senator Harkin hosted me at a lunch in his office for just the two of us. It was a memorable and touching gesture that I very much appreciated.]

I also met with Jack Reed of Rhode Island and that, too, was a pleasant one. He also asked whether there was some way I could stay on, at least beyond my expiration date. After the pounding that I have been taking on the Proposition 226 and inspector general matters, all of these meetings these past few days were a welcome respite. But, regarding the inspector general matter, one can never celebrate early. I am sure that Fox and Feinstein, as soon as they get wind of what has developed, will begin their own counterattack among the Democrats. Then the fur will begin to fly, and we will have to see how this plays out. Tomorrow we will have to sit down and devise a strategy for the Monday meeting on the IG budget and the budget generally.

July 3, 1998 The big event of this week was a budget meeting, which took place yesterday and which appeared to be engineered by Toner and Fox so as to deny the inspector general her request for funds without making it look like it was retaliation. Kucinich had called me the night before, and we spent about a half an hour on the phone. He told me that Fox had called him a couple of times and had called many others and was name-dropping, presumably Senator Kennedy's name. A letter had been sent that day by

Congressman Shays to Towns indicating that he would not back off on his position on the inspector general. Kucinich said that Shays had been calling the Democrats "furiously" to try to turn things around.

Although I used these words first, Kucinich indicated, by his tone of voice and content that we didn't really hold the cards. Kucinich said that his only leverage was to call for hearings and that he was inclined to do this, but that Shays was saying, and some of the Democrats were saying, that this would not be in the interest of the Board or the Democrats because it would provide another vehicle for the House Republicans to beat us up in the appropriations process. I said to Kucinich that I agreed with this . . . essentially Kucinich was telling me to know when to fold them.

Surprisingly, the Board members and Feinstein did not seem to realize the full strength of their hand, although Fox had come running over to our office on Wednesday afternoon with the Shays letter so as to make sure that I would know that she had orchestrated a political counterattack on me. (This happened when I was in Philadelphia for Frank Hoeber's retirement party and Mary Ann, Al, and Kate were holding down the fort.)

The program [of the budget meeting] began with a very detailed description of all the adversities confronting the Board, particularly in the regions, in light of the austerity program, including lights going out and some air-conditioning going out because of con-tractual requirements. The hostility and coolness to me by all of the Board members was so thick that you could have cut it. The only banter or informality took place when Hurtgen, while getting a cup of coffee and coming over to where I was sitting, was asking about whether mail ballots were costing a great deal of money and started laughing with me about that. Fox and Liebman did not even look at me or acknowledge my presence when I came into the room. . . .

I continue to believe that *I am going to get some cases out.* Now my inclination is to stay in office beyond July 14, although I still plan to depart for California on July 15. I remain hopeful that we can get the package of eight that Toner put together that were due on June 11 and then forge ahead with *Detroit Newspapers, Telescope,* and *Roadway Express* and *Dial-a-Mattress.* I was somewhat encouraged by a meeting this afternoon at the office with Bolles [Brame's chief counsel], who seemed to indicate that he thought that all of these cases were in shape to go and he thought that they could go. I think the most formidable problem will remain one Sarah Fox on *Telescope.* She will simply refuse to produce as long as she thinks she can wait me out and flip the majority on that case. But I will try to stay beyond my planned departure date in July and take it "day-to-day," as the expression is used in baseball.

Right now, 1099 14th Street is a very, very depressing place and it will be good to get out of there, hopefully with a few cases produced.

Dennis Kucinich urged me stay until my very last day, August 27, to make sure that all the cases, including *Detroit Newspapers,* were issued. He pointed out that if I left early Fox and the Republicans would immediately say that I was responsi-ble for the failure to issue the cases. I got the same advice from several others, par-ticularly when I tarried in Detroit to watch two Red Sox–Tigers games. (The Sox cracked four home runs in one inning in the second game!) As my wife and I drove back across the country in mid-July, I decided to stay until the very end and to return to Washington after moving back to California. A delay of a month or so in returning to Stanford was a small price to pay if there was even the slightest chance I could induce the Board to issue decisions.

In the meantime, I submitted my letter of resignation to President Clinton, stating that it was my hope to leave office "at some point prior to August 27" and summarizing what I perceived to be our major accomplishments during my chairmanship. On July 29, shortly before my last return to Washington, the president wrote to me, accepting my resignation and saying that we had "helped to restore the American public's confidence in the NLRB."

When I returned to Stanford, Dean Paul Brest welcomed me back and then told me to call the Stanford general counsel's office. It turned out that that office had been in touch with Dean Brest to determine whether the Law School was paying me a salary beginning in July. Earlier, Brame and his chief counsel, Kenneth Bolles, had repeatedly questioned me and my staff about my precise date of departure. They said they needed to know in order to establish deadlines for their work. We had told them that I hoped to resign and go back on the Stanford payroll on Bastille Day, July 14. The Stanford legal department had received word that the House Republicans, who seemed to know when I was supposed to leave and that I had not yet resigned, wanted to know if I was collecting salaries from both Stanford and the NLRB. This, of course, would have been illegal if I had done it, which I had not. This inquiry was the my enemies' last-gasp attempt to accomplish what they had failed to do in the Proposition 226, travel, and baseball investigations. Said one Stanford lawyer at the beginning of our conversation, "Someone in Washington doesn't like you very much."

As the month of July unfolded back at Stanford, I still could not push many cases out, though some fissures in the wall of resistance began to open. The National Right to Work Legal Defense Foundation filed a mandamus against us for delay in issuing one of the *Beck* cases: "It's obvious that organized labor has the NLRB on a short leash," it said. But that was not true. As I had said on numerous occasions, this process was remarkably similar to one I had encountered earlier in my life: the struggle to get my sons to do their homework and do it in a timely fashion. But at the Board I was dealing with presidential appointees, who reminded me, as Fox did on numerous occasions, that they were not only adults but also the possessors of the presidential seal. The implied message was that they were immune to timetables or deadlines. No chairman could tell *them* what to do! (Indeed, Fox had earlier argued against deadlines, stating that she was a presidential appointee and that, as such, no one could tell her what to do!)

I had written to Congressman Lantos in the fall of 1997—after negotiations with Fox over moving cases out of her office had collapsed—that we had been unable to move a great many cases because of "one member only." By July, ten months later, the number of five- and six-year-old cases still unissued had doubled. Those four years old had increased from 19 to 22, a 15.8 percent rise; and those at least three years old had increased by 78.6 percent, from 28 to 50. Cases at least two years old—which should be the worst-case scenario in the Board's handling of cases—had increased from 65 to 119, an increase of 83 percent. The same pattern prevailed for the *Beck* cases. While the National Right to Work Foundation sought to discredit me, the agency, and the statute, action that might have averted—or at least belied— their criticism was not taken.

Cracks in the Wall

The very first crack in the wall actually appeared in the spring—shortly after Hurtgen's April 28 memo—when we were able to issue *Arizona Public Service Company*.[8] In three separate opinions (the majority consisted of Hurtgen and myself), the Board held that an employer did not engage in objectionable conduct by conducting a raffle for employees on the same day as a Board-conducted election. Fox, who had sat on the case for 191 days without taking any action (and had been the only member holding it up for at least 50 days), finally removed herself from the panel, thus making it possible to issue the case. So perhaps, I thought, there was hope for action on more cases. In July I voted with the Democrats in *San Diego Gas & Electric* to approve a mail ballot, a significant policy issue that Hurtgen wanted to move on as much as I did.[9]

Yet the overwhelming number of unresolved cases remained, and it was not clear that they ever would be issued. During a few weeks in Stanford, I continued to push and prod and write and review drafts sent to me by Mary Ann. On August 17, with eleven days remaining in my term, I flew back to Washington for the last time as chairman.

Slowly at first, some of the resistance weakened. One of the old cases we issued in those waning days, *Chevron Chemical Company*, was a classic example of the Board's inexplicable prevarication.[10] It had been with the agency since 1992, and Fox had stated over and over that the draft prepared by my staff was unacceptable.

Finally, in a majority opinion in which Hurtgen joined, Fox, rather than withdrawing from the case altogether, simply refused to address the basic issue that had held it up so long: how to calculate the amount of dues *Beck* objectors had to be pay and how much they should be reimbursed. In my concurring opinion, I took the same position I had been taking for years in the drafts I circulated: that is, that in *Machinists* v. *Street* the Court had stated that the purpose behind an accurate calculation formula is to ensure that a union does not use the dues of objecting nonunion employees solely for representational activities, thereby impermissibly freeing up more of the members' dues for nonrepresentational activities. To preclude such unlawful subsidization, I noted, the Court in *Street* had suggested that an appropriate formula would refund to the objector the "portion of his money . . . in the same proportion that the expenditures for [nonrepresentational] purposes bore to the total union budget."[11] I stated, therefore, that the converse of the *Street* formula would apply in this case: that is, "an objector is required to pay that portion of the dues that is equal to the ratio of dues spent for chargeable representational purposes to total dues collected."

While I was glad to see the opinion issued, I was irritated that no amendments or ideas were put forward in the other members' opinion that could possibly account for the many years of delay. The majority opinion was short, skimpy, and could have been issued in a matter of weeks, not years! And still outstanding were several major cases I was determined to push out.

When I arrived back in Washington on the seventeenth of August, I received two telephone calls—from representatives David Bonior of Michigan and Bernie Sanders of Vermont. (I had had a good deal of contact with Sanders during the Shays Government Reform Committee hearings the previous summer.) Both calls were very important. In retrospect, I realize that Bonior, who was worried that *Detroit Newspapers* would not issue prior to my departure, had the greatest impact on the Board's actions in those last few days. Both Bonior and Sanders reiterated their dissatisfaction with the Board's inaction. Sanders had long been concerned about *Telescope Casual*, a lengthy strike involving the IUE (International Union of Electrical, Radio and Machine Workers) in or near his congressional district.

So, as time grew shorter, I did something I should have done much earlier. I revealed to Bonior and Sanders that Fox alone was impeding the issuance of *Detroit Newspaper* and *Telescope Casual*. Both asked whether they could telephone her directly to ask whether she could possibly take action; under the circumstances, I said, I thought such inquiries were completely appropriate. Immediately after their calls, Fox finally began to move and circulated the draft in *Detroit Newspapers* we had been waiting for. It affirmed the employer's duty to bargain about strike replacements. But at this point, with no more than forty-eight to seventy-two hours left in my term, the Republicans balked. They said, with some justification, that they could not respond to her views in such a short period of time. Nonetheless, we reached a consensus allowing the other portions of the case to issue. The other three other continuing Board members took no position on the issue in her draft and severed it for subsequent adjudication.

Therefore, on August 27 *Detroit Newspapers* was finally issued. The Board held, unanimously—both Democrats and Republicans—that the employer had committed unfair labor practices and that, inasmuch as such conduct had caused a prolonged strike, the strikers were unfair labor practice strikers entitled to reinstatement.[12] The majority of the Board also (1) held that the employer's attempt to modify or withdraw from multiunion joint bargaining on one or more particular bargaining subjects was not an unfair labor practice; (2) affirmed the administrative law judge's dismissal of another aspect of the complaint; and (3) unanimously affirmed the administrative law judge's ruling that the employer had refused to bargain in good faith by unilaterally implementing its proposals regarding merit pay and television assignments and by its refusal to furnish the Newspaper Guild with requested information regarding both merit pay and overtime-exemption proposals. Finally, the Board, over my dissent, refused to address the employer's duty to bargain with regard to the conditions of employment for strike replacements. It is ironic that when it did so the following spring, the vote was 3 to 2 to uphold the employer's position on this issue.[13] Had the work been done—as it should have been—the preceding summer, the vote would have been 3 to 2 in favor of my position, inasmuch as both Fox and Liebman dissented from the March 1999 decision.

The burst of activity in that final week made it possible for us to issue forty-seven cases on my last day in office, August 27, and for a good number to go out in the days immediately before. Quite a number of them were "Old Dogs" that had been pending with us for many years; some were cases involving important policy issues; and some were both old and important.

One of them was the case Representative Sanders was interested in, *Telescope Casual Furniture, Inc.*[14] In it I joined Hurtgen to dismiss a complaint involving the lawfulness of an employer's bargaining tactic. The employer had made a final offer accompanied by a threat to implement an alternative position containing more onerous terms if the final offer was rejected. Almost two years earlier I had written a concurring opinion in which I noted that although this employer had utilized the exact same tactic on numerous previous occasions, the parties had then resolved their differences without a strike. I nonetheless viewed the tactic as distasteful:

I do not like the employer's tactics in this case and, like Member Liebman [dissenting], I do not find them to be conducive to good industrial relations. Indeed, my personal view is that impasse—a concept inherently vague and thus conducive to perilous litigation for both sides—and unilateral implementation weight the scales against the labor movement improperly in a democratic pluralistic society such as ours. But, we are obliged to subordinate our personal views to the rule of law.

I am quite confident that Bernie Sanders's union constituents did not like my opinion upholding the employer's position. But, as Sanders had said to me, "I don't care how the decision comes out. I just believe that I'm entitled for it to issue." That was my view too. Moreover, Sanders's intervention, like that of Bonior, was nothing like the incessant attempts of the congressional Republicans to influence the substance of our decisions. In this respect, they distinguished themselves fundamentally from the House Republicans, who not only advised the Board about *what* to decide but also about *when* not to decide it.

In another significant case, *Farm Fresh, Inc.,* I tipped the majority 3 to 2 toward the Republicans to deny a nonemployee organizer's access to the snack bar of a retail establishment.[15] I concurred, noting, however, that we were required to reverse Board precedent in light of the Supreme Court's 1992 decision in *Lechmere.* This was the case John Higgins had refused to move on unless I specifically stated that *Lechmere* had overruled Board precedent. This view was part of his argument that the Board could take no decisions that reversed Board precedent while there were only three members. But there had been another impediment as well: Fox took no action on it throughout 1997 (for 340 days), and, after her confirmation on January 22, 1998, neither did Liebman. (Frequently when Fox would not take action, Liebman, notwithstanding her ostensible commitment to productivity, would not either.)

On some cases, I stood completely alone, as in *Pike's Peak Pain Program.* In this case, the Board, by a 4 to 1 vote refused to find that a single worker protesting an employer's action was engaging in concerted activity (which is protected by the act), even though the subject matter of his or her protest affects the whole group of employees.[16] Another example was *Hale Nani Rehabilitation*; again, mine was the only vote for invalidating a decertification election because the employer had violated its own no-solicitation rule.[17] But I did not mind dissenting alone—not in the least! In 1997 I had done so in the related area of union access to cyberspace on company property.[18] What was important to me was to issue cases serving the public interest and demonstrating to the parties in dispute the Board's commitment to working at and resolving their problems according to law.

In *Lafayette Park Hotel* I joined with the two Republican members to find that the employer's rules of conduct were facially lawful and did not implicate the prohibitions contained in the National Labor Relations Act.[19] These rules required employees to be "cooperative," to support the company's "goals and objectives," not to divulge information about the company to unauthorized people, and not to engage during nonworking hours in "improper conduct" that affected their relationship with other employees and the "hotel's reputation or goodwill in the community." I wrote a separate concurring opinion because I was concerned that the dissent of members Fox and Liebman failed "to appreciate the importance of civility and good manners for all people, including employees."

I also joined with Hurtgen, in *Central Illinois Public Service Company*, to hold that an employer could lock out union-represented employees in response to their "inside-game" strategies. The latter involved refusals to work voluntary overtime, strict adherence to safety rules, and other work-to-rule tactics.[20] The Supreme Court had already held in *American Ship Building* that an employer could institute a lockout if it feared that a lawful strike was a real possibility.[21] Whatever the protected status of the "inside-game" tactics of the union in *Central Illinois*, it was difficult for me to see how we could give a different answer to the question in this case than the Court had provided in *American Ship Building*.

In that last week we also issued extensive remedial orders involving recidivist behavior.[22] I was particularly pleased with a case in which numerous unfair labor practices were remedied by the Board affirmatively, leading ultimately to the election of the union at a complex employing 5,200 workers.[23] "Suddenly we've got a beacon to show other textile workers that they can do it. And it sent a message to other owners that they're going to have to take into account the needs of workers as they modernize," was the enthusiastic response to our decision of Bruce Raynor, UNITE's organizing director.[24] A collective-bargaining agreement between the parties was negotiated.

In the final analysis—given the inaction that had plagued me during most of 1997 and 1998, the advent of three new Board members who had relatively little time to acquaint themselves with the cases, and the deep ideological divisions on basic issues—the achievement was remarkable.

Unresolved Issues

Despite our last-minute progress, a number of important issues were left pending. Foremost for me was one of several cases involving the status of contingent employees; the question was whether temporary workers referred to the employer by an agency could vote in the same election as the employer's regular workers without the consent of both employers (see chapter 9). The case, which had drawn so much attention from the Republicans, had been argued in December 1996 and was still pending when I left the Board. It remained unresolved well into 2000. Similarly, the question of whether employers challenging an incumbent union's continued majority status could be required to petition the Board for an election had disappeared, as one commentator noted, into the "black hole" of the Board's offices in 14th Street.[25] This issue also remained pending in Washington—at least for the first half of 2000. The inability of the Board to move on both these cases left me deeply dissatisfied.

And there were other cases I very much wanted to push out. They involved the employee status of graduate students working as teaching assistants at universities and residents, interns, and fellows on the house staffs of hospitals. I also particularly regretted not having a chance to participate in a case involving the question of whether the right of employees at a union facility to be accompanied by a union representative in a disciplinary proceeding could be applied to employees at nonunion plants.

Another important question left unanswered was whether a negotiated check-off clause for union dues could be enforced beyond the expiration date of a collective-bargaining agreement. It is ironic that in this case, as in most of the cases left pending, I would have joined the Democrats to form a majority, whereas in most of the important policy cases we ultimately issued, I joined the Republicans to form a majority. Under the rules of the Board, all members had to consent to issuing a case. Notwithstanding the recalcitrance of Brame on most of these cases, I shall never understand why Fox and Liebman could not or would not push forward for resolution cases in which a majority supported what were presumably their own positions. Aside from my lone exhortations, no pressure whatever was brought to bear on the Republican members to induce them to decide these leading policy cases. All of them, save one, lay dormant in Washington well into 2000.

Much of the eleventh-hour flurry of activity was attributable to cooperative efforts by Hurtgen and, to a lesser extent, by Liebman, who clearly found it difficult to move without Fox's consent. At the same time, Hurtgen's initiatives were relatively mild. His effort to work both sides of the street and establish a modus vivendi with Fox for future work considerably circumscribed his ability to make substantial progress.

Yet the overriding factor in our last-minute productivity was without a doubt the intervention of Bonior and Sanders. The prominence of Bonior, the House minority leader, galvanized Fox and Liebman and produced the *Detroit Newspapers* ruling. Representative Sanders, who undoubtedly did not like the result in *Telescope Casual,* pried that case loose. Neither man, nor any of the other interested Democrats who had expressed their concerns earlier, pressed us for a particular result—that, they said, was the Board's job. They simply urged the Board to issue decisions that were important to their constituents.

It seemed to me that Senator John McCain's similar insistence that the Federal Communications Commission decide a case that had been pending for some time was also entirely appropriate and desirable. (He was criticized for this intervention in the 2000 presidential primary campaign.) I only wish I had had more Senator McCains and more House members like Bonior and Sanders nipping at my heels to produce decisions.

The day before my last day in office, I flew back to California. On August 27, my very last day, I spent a beautiful afternoon at Candlestick Park, talking with Dusty Baker and watching the Giants trounce the Phillies. Around the fourth inning or so I telephoned back to the office, and Al Wolff confirmed that everything we thought could issue had issued. Relieved and emotionally drained, I then drove up to the San Francisco regional office to say goodbye to the staff there.

13

"The Dilatory Virus"

The job was completed. Yet beyond my success at moving out some of the most important policy cases lay the inescapable fact that the Board's backlog had risen since early 1996. Although I disagreed with the Court's 1998 *Marquez* ruling, which declined to obligate unions to notify dissidents of their rights in the collective-bargaining agreement, I admired its ability to decide the case within a month of hearing oral argument![1]

The Board has continued to move in the opposite direction. By early 1999, half a year after my departure, the backlog had escalated to 714 cases! Indeed, as a March 2000 report of the NLRB inspector general chronicles, all relevant indicia point to *more* delay.[2] This increase in cases pending occurred between 1997 and 2000 during a period in which there was no Board turnover (other than Truesdale's replacement of me as chairman) and in which, therefore, the Board should have gained from members' improved efficiency derived from experience.

As the inspector general's report makes clear, during the first two years of my chairmanship the Board expedited cases at a rate unprecedented since records were first kept. We achieved this productivity notwithstanding high turnover, a number of recess appointments, illness, and the fact that we often operated at less than full strength—that is, with four- and even three-member Boards. As my diary indicated, and the report confirms, between late-1996 and early-1997 these gains were beginning to be eroded.

Specifically, in the early days, the median days for processing cases were down to 162, 155, and 137 in 1995, 1996, and 1997, respectively (see figure 1). In 1998, however, operating with three new Board members (and a fourth one confirmed after a recess appointment), the number of days rose to 239 (a 75-percent increase). And in 1999, after my departure, a five-member Board took two and a half times longer to issue cases than my Board did during the first two years.

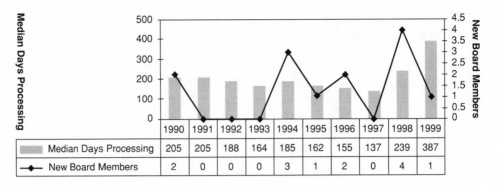

Figure 1
Median days processing v. new board members

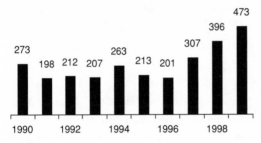

Figure 2
Cases pending at end of fiscal year

Similarly, in 1999 the number of cases pending with the agency in Washington (473) had more than doubled from our low of 201 in 1996 (figure 2). The same was true of cases that had been pending for more than two years (figure 3). This distressing pattern of wastefulness occurred against a backdrop of appropriations plenty and increased staffing.

Ironically, while this inspector general's report was begun by my appointee, Aileen Armstrong, it was completed by Chairman Truesdale's own appointee. While Board members echoed Brame's "slavedriver" characterization of me and purportedly stated that I had delayed case processing through my testimony about Proposition 226, the IG report makes it clear that the Board's new self-touted collegiality had translated into indecision and indolence. Moreover, this record was achieved while the Washington case intake was actually declining! In my view, this is exactly the result sought by the House Republicans and many of those in the

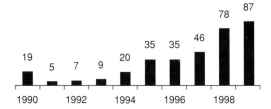

Figure 3
Cases pending over two years at end of fiscal year

Senate. As G. Calvin Mackenzie has described the situation in relation to use of the "batching" process, ideology and inaction reigned supreme.

And the same was true of the more important policy cases. Until late July 1999, except for some *Beck* cases affected by the *Marquez* ruling or by the mandamus action filed by the National Right to Work Committee, no major policy decisions were issued. (The NRTW mandamus required the NLRB to advise the courts when a decision would be rendered.) Indeed, except for a November 1999 ruling holding that hospital interns and residents were employees under the act, no major policy decision was issued for two full years after my departure from Washington.[3] Moreover, the pattern of inaction in 1999 and 2000 featured a sharp decline in Section 10(j) injunctions initiated by the Board. In fiscal 1999 the number of petitions filed was approximately one-third of those filed by my Board during our first year in office. The trend noted by *Business Week* (cited in chapter 11) and confirmed by the IG's March 2000 report took the Board back perilously close to the low point of the Bush Board.

The decline in productivity was sustained in spite of the presumed gains in the experience of Board members (figure 4) who had joined the agency in 1997 (the so-called learning curve) and in spite of the Board's enhanced budget. There were several reasons for the appropriations increase: (1) the anticipated surplus; (2) the Republicans' weariness of confronting Clinton in this arena; and (3) their recognition that policy initiatives, case production, and Section 10(j) injunctions in 1999 and 2000 had fallen off so far as to become virtually unimportant. The white flag of surrender had already been raised! It appeared that a Faustian bargain was made for both appropriations and appointments. Regrettably, the larger budget and the experience learning curve only serve to dramatize more vividly that the problems of 1996–1998 had originated at the top of the agency.

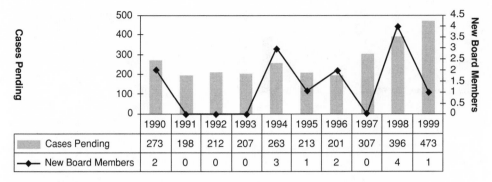

	1990	1991	1992	1993	1994	1995	1996	1997	1998	1999
Cases Pending	273	198	212	207	263	213	201	307	396	473
New Board Members	2	0	0	0	3	1	2	0	4	1

Figure 4
Cases pending v. new board members

This slow progress has not escaped the attention of the courts. In confirming the decision in *Anchor Concepts,* Judge John Noonan, speaking for the Court of Appeals for the Second Circuit, warned the Board about the effect of delays:

No decisionmaking body is totally immune from the dilatory virus and delay is sometimes the too human way of grappling with a thorny issue of policy. Nonetheless, the Board stands out as a federal administrative agency which had been rebuked before and for what must strike anyone as a cavalier disdain for the hardships it is causing. We have on other occasions indicated that extraordinary delay of this kind will itself be reason to refuse to enforce an order of the Board ... although we have no occasion in this case to apply this doctrine, we call it to the Board's attention as a reminder that, whatever its internal problems, the Board has a duty to act promptly in the discharge of its important functions.[4]

In the 1980s I had testified before a House subcommittee on the theme "Has Federal Labor Law Failed?" The committee's report stated that the long delays forcing workers to wait years for Board decisions could be so frustrating that they would "prefer to have the case decided immediately by the flip of a coin."[5] That was the way I felt so frequently during 1997 and 1998.

In a few cases, the courts had actually refused to enforce the Board's decisions because of delays in issuing decisions. In 1990 Judge George Pratt did so in *Emhart Industries, Hartford Division* v. *NLRB*; and in a 1992 Seventh Circuit opinion, Judge Richard Posner called the Board's eight-year delay in another case "inexplicable" and refused to enforce its order providing back pay for this lengthy period of time.[6] During oral argument on an Eighth Circuit opinion also issued prior to my arrival in Washington, the Board could offer no explanation for its slothlike pace in issuing the order. Addressing counsel for the NLRB, Judge Richard Arnold asked:

[O]ne thing about this really concerns me ... the ALJ's opinion [was] filed in 1982, [but] the Board d[id]n't decide the case until 1989. Can you tell us why?

Counsel for the NLRB: I must confess, Your Honor, that I'm embarrassed by that myself. ... [A] deputy counsel of the Board ... had a mental block in deciding [this] case.... I have no explanation for it and, frankly, I must confess it's inexcusable and unfortunate....

Judge Arnold: We agree with you.[7]

Of a similar case issued in 1991 after a ten years' delay, the Court of Appeals for the Ninth Circuit noted that the employees were the "victims" no matter how it was decided. Yet, "because we conclude that fewer policies are frustrated by enforcement than by nonenforcement, we choose the former."[8] Regrettably, these delays inevitably undercut some of the remedies the Supreme Court had made available to the Board![9]

Most of these decisions were rendered prior to my chairmanship. But *Anchor Concepts*, about which Judge Noonan wrote in the above opinion, was a case before my Board. As chapter 12, in particular, makes clear, the internal Board dynamics were at the heart of the productivity problem. Even more than our battles with Congress over budgets and appointments, delays were caused by the presidential appointees. Most of the career staff people in Washington, D.C., and in the regions were committed to the charge of the statute.

Part of the built-in delay, of course, was a result of ideological divisions. This factor was reflected not so much in arguments about the decisions themselves as in the time required for so many opinions to be written and circulated. In the long-pending contingent worker cases voted upon by the Board in January of 1998, Brame never finished his dissent. (The majority draft and my concurring draft had circulated in April of 1998.) He also took a considerable amount of time to write a very lengthy opinion in *Hale Nani*, though—to his credit—he actually did the hard work involved and produced something. All too often, other members simply did not do so.

Peter Hurtgen, a relatively strong supporter of case production, in the actual votes taken, hardly ever found an employer he did not like. As of the beginning of 1999, according to the New York law firm Nixon, Hargreave, Bevins & Doyle, Hurtgen had voted for the employer's position in 98.9 percent of the cases in which dissenting votes were cast. This surpassed even the record of President Reagan's chairman, Donald Dotson, who voted with employers in comparable circumstances in 97.2 percent of the cases.

No one illustrates the difference between ideological perspective and commitment to case production more dramatically than Sarah Fox. None of the remaining gang of four voted with me more often than she did. Again according to the Nixon firm's compilation, we were in agreement in 29 out of 49 cases. Yet, for her, and so often for others, the combined effects of being a Washington insider and the batching process insisted upon by the Republicans meant deadlock, inaction, or both. In contrast to earlier Boards, which were criticized for sudden oscillations from their predecessors' positions, our Board panel was more frequently taken to task—by objective and constructive critics rather than partisan ideologues—for its paralysis. The primary victims, of course, were those who supported the statute and the idea of the rule of law.

Areas of Reform

For me especially, the events of the last year and a half on the Board pointed emphatically to the need for reform legislation designed to expedite internal procedures. Far too much was being decided through inaction—through, for example, the failure of one member to act because of political intimidation or her own Hamlet-like indecision.

During my term, the only thing President Clinton could do to prevent the effectiveness of the Board and the NLRA from being undermined was to veto or threaten to veto damaging legislation. A whole host of reforms, both procedural and substantive, need to be instituted at different levels to address the issues reflected so dramatically in my experience in Washington, D.C. The ability of the Board and the courts to implement the goals of the act also needs to be enhanced through amendment.

In the first place, it seems to me that the Senate's constitutional role in the confirmation process is distorted by requiring sixty votes to break a filibuster over the president's candidate. The Senate could, if it were willing, change its rules to make the filibuster inapplicable to nominations. It should do so.

Nominees should also get an up or down vote. I was never sure whether any particular senator had placed a "hold" on my nomination, although I was told informally that that was the case. So far as I am aware, this is a matter for the Senate's inner sanctum, as no records are kept and voters are not advised of such actions. Senate rules should not allow one member to obstruct debate and the vote on a nominee, just as the objections of 41 out of 100 senators should not be permitted to thwart the president's selection.[10]

Even when votes are taken, some of my experience in 1993 and 1994 plays itself out anew. Though more moderate than the right wing House, the Senate voted down a qualified black nominee for the Court of Appeals for the Eighth Circuit in the fall of 1999. President Clinton properly denounced this rejection as "disgraceful" and an example of the unequal treatment of minority and women judicial nominees.[11]

Nominees to the Board should reflect America geographically, as well as with regard to race, sex, disability, and other considerations. President Clinton was more supportive of diversity than any of his predecessors in the White House, but his focus did not extend to geographical considerations and the need to reach outside the Washington inner circle.

In the passage by Mackenzie quoted in chapter 2, he notes that past nominees to federal agencies were much more likely to come from many areas of the country.[12] They worked in Washington for a limited period of time, bringing with them expertise and experience accumulated outside the capital. And when their terms were over, they returned home. Insiders who reside in the district and have followed a career-path inside the Beltway should not, of course, be excluded. But the process is presently too top-heavy with such appointees. All the Board members with whom I served, except for Browning and Hurtgen, were Washington insiders in the sense that they had resided there or in the immediate vicinity prior to their appointment. Even Browning, who never once voted against a general counsel's recommendation for a Section 10(j) injunction, was closely associated with that group. (The insider view in the 1990s was that a Democrat should never break with the general counsel.) Hurtgen (like Browning) very much hoped for a second term, and Brame, though initially a resident of geographically proximate Richmond, was a former member of a prominent Washington management labor law firm.

When the term of such nominees expire, they generally choose to stay in Washington. Thus, they are almost inevitably affected by the political environment and the necessity to survive in it. In my last two years in office, heightened Republican hostility to the Board made internal paralysis on case processing a very serious problem—particularly with regard to policy cases and the *Beck* cases that had languished at the Board for so long. It was no coincidence, I believe, that cliquish insularity reigned at the same time.

It is also true, of course, that my own tenure coincided with what may have been a political aberration—the first period in which Republicans had controlled both houses of Congress since 1953–1955 and the first time that this had happened with a Democratic president since the Eightieth Congress passed the Taft-Hartley amendments over President Truman's veto in 1947. Yet we cannot, I think, assume that the hateful emotions that fashioned the Clinton impeachment trial are behind us. The similar treatment meted out to the Board in numerous hearings took place far away from the television cameras—whereas the impeachment was on television for all the world to see. For congressional Republicans, as Mark Shields of the *Boston Globe* has noted, the "red scare" of the 1950s became the "fed scare" of the 1990s.[13] Regardless of who occupies the White House in this new century, the animosity toward the National Labor Relations Act and the Board demonstrated during my confirmation process and tenure as chairman seems certain to be a significant part of the political scene.

In view of this likelihood, how can we get the very best people to serve in the U.S. government? First and foremost, I would argue, we must create procedures that encourage such people to come forward and do the best they can to implement the public interest. An amendment to the NLRA, and to other regulatory statutes, should provide for one term, albeit an extended one of perhaps seven or eight years. Such a reform would give the public the benefit of the experience members obtain while in office; it would also diminish the political considerations and calculations appointees use to protect themselves from the political flak emanating from a recorded vote or opinion that is unpopular with some special interest. (It would also make it more likely that votes would be public and not secret, as they have been all too frequently.) Members not distracted by considerations involving their reappointment could press ahead with their public duty to make decisions—including those sensitive policy issues that inevitably attract criticism!

I would point out that this proposal is based on concerns that are very different from those informing the debate on term limits for elected officials. There the concern is that long-serving incumbents who gain too much power may become unresponsive to the needs and wishes of the electorate. My own view has always been that the people should decide for themselves, through the electoral process, who their elected representatives will be and how many terms they should serve. I have also argued (successfully) for this point of view in the context of local residency requirements that formerly limited candidates for public office.[14]

The problem with regard to regulatory and judicial appointees is very different. In both administrative agencies and the judiciary, the principal concern is that the incumbent might become too dependent on elected officials whose support is necessary for reappointment. Public policy should emphasize anew its commitment to sealing off such commissioners or members of quasi-judicial agencies from the immediate political passions surrounding a given case or issue.

The fact that I came to Washington in 1994 with an understanding that I would only serve one term divided me fundamentally from the rest of the Board and from the general counsel. I first publicly advocated one term for NLRB members in 1995, shortly before the term of the former chairman, James Stephens, expired. I was told that he took my position as a personal slight; but my view was in no way aimed at Stephens or at any particular Board member. It was then, and is now, simply my view that the best people would be attracted to these positions for the best reasons if they knew that at the end of their service they were required to return from whence they came.

In regard to another, related issue, prompt case resolution, it seems to me that if agencies like the NLRB are unwilling to undertake their own internal reforms, then a procedural scheme should be imposed by statute. The Federal Trade Commission, for instance, has specific time limits built into its adjudication procedures, and they are binding on the commissioners themselves. The NLRB, which has time limits and timetables for everyone in the agency except the presidential appointees, refuses to accept the obligation to function properly and expeditiously—a matter of critical importance in labor law. There is no reason why the presidential appointees cannot subject themselves, or be subjected to, the same discipline that they impose on administrative law judges and regional directors.

A major step in this direction would be to give the chairman authority to assign cases—and to move old cases and policy cases to Board members able and willing to deal with them expeditiously. Along with lack of deadlines, the existing system of leaving this task to the Board's executive secretary allows malingerers to frustrate prompt case production. Mandated procedures for disgorgement and assignment of cases by the chairman are both necessary. An additional procedural change, the writing and signing of opinions by individual Board members, would improve the quality of the Board's work without interfering with prompt delivery of the service. Indeed, concurring or dissenting opinions could issue, if necessary, subsequent to the Board's decision—a rejected proposal I put forward in 1994.

The fact that I did not have the authority to assign cases or institute a procedure requiring the issuance of decisions under a specific timetable or within certain time limits contributed substantially to the problems I confronted internally. Of course, my life in Washington would have been considerably less turbulent, and in many respects more enjoyable, if I had simply turned a blind eye to the problem of case production. But I could not. That approach was totally inconsistent with my reason for coming three thousand miles across the continent.

Admittedly, some of the internal dissension on the Board was attributable to inaction or lack of sensitivity on my part. I should have reached out to Stephens beforehand and let him know that my proposals about reappointment were in no way aimed at him. And because I knew that confronting Fox directly in the beginning could be politically harmful to me—given her association with Ted Kennedy—I attempted, mostly in vain, to cajole her over to my side. On a number of occasions I had dinner with her; and I took her as my guest to see the Baltimore Orioles play at Camden Yards and introduced her to club owner Peter Angelos. But none of this personal outreach seemed to make any difference to the problem of case production. In the final analysis, the only thing that energized Fox were those last-minute phone calls from Bonior and Sanders.

Like senators Harkin and Chafee, who had asked about earlier cases, both of these House members were expressing appropriate concern about the status of particular cases, something members of Congress have done from time immemorial. Given all the pressure that was being imposed on us by congressional Republicans *not* to produce decisions or to decide them in a particular way, it seemed to me that responding to Bonior and Sanders as I did was in no way inconsistent with the Board's independence. I saw it as just as appropriate as working with congressional Democrats in preparation for oversight and appropriations hearings.

Another institutional factor that created instability and uncertainty during my term was the division of responsibility between the chairman and the general counsel. Fred Feinstein never brought Board complaints involving the two important policy issues I most wanted to adjudicate during my term: (1) minority bargaining orders, which are designed to remedy employer unfair labor practices that deprive the union of its majority; and (2) the extent of union disciplinary authority during strikes when strikebreakers cross the picket line and solidarity is eroded.[15] These two important issues of law, which I touched on in my 1993 confirmation colloquy with Senator Hatch, were among those that could not come before the Board for adjudication without the cooperation of the general counsel.

Even more disturbing were the administrative conflicts and tensions between the two entities. The general counsel (the prosecutorial side) was one person and we, at the Board (the judicial side), were five. He could, and often did, try to play one Board member off against another (as he did, unsuccessfully, during the baseball strike). A genuinely constructive Congress would amend the statute to make explicit what has for too long been implicit (and frequently ignored): that is, the subordination of the general counsel to the chairman of the NLRB. In 1949 and 1950 the Board itself—as well as President Truman and Senator Taft—advocated this position. As former NLRB solicitor Ida Klaus pointed out a few years later,

... there are vital engineering defects in the statutory plan for this system of separation and ... its practical workability is at all times dependent upon the spirit of cooperation between the Board and the General Counsel. Thus, the potentials for conflict are there, and the threat to realization of the basic congressional policy remains, so long as the formula of internal management and the lines of authority continue as they are. When and where conflict may erupt will depend upon the personnel and policies of the future. A swing of the pendulum in any direction may upset the balance.

In other words, whatever may be said about the theory of this genre of internal separation of functions, the blueprint for bringing it into effect is seriously imperfect. One wonders whether true and pristine separation can ever be achieved under this blueprint and, if so, whether the price to be paid in struggle and conflict is not far too high for the dubious and vague value received."[16]

Successful Reforms

In all of these areas, my role as chairman would have been facilitated if the procedural and statutory reforms I allude to above had been promulgated. But a number of the reforms I advocated were instituted, and they did work.

The advisory panels, for example, were a helpful venue for advancing and reacting to ideas in labor relations. While the panels could help very little with issues that sharply divided labor and management, such as postal ballots, they did speak with one voice about several ideas the House Republicans tried to promote—for example, abolishing the NLRB's jurisdiction over small employers. I am sure that Chairman Porter and representatives Istook and Dickey received a rather rude surprise when management labor lawyers joined with union lawyers in opposing this idea.

On certain of our innovations, such as bench decisions and settlement judges, both advisory panels were initially skeptical but came to support them when they saw them in action. The Board, too, learned from the positions the parties advanced in their questions on issues like Section 10(j) injunctions. I had to overcome considerable internal opposition even to get that issue on the agenda for discussion, but I think it proved worthwhile.

Oral arguments and rule making, if they had not been held up by appropriations riders, would also have been extremely useful to the agency's ability to accomplish its objectives. However, in the political environment of the time it was futile to pursue rule making—although in 1998 it became clear that our retreat in the face of Congressional hostility only made the bully more impudent.

In any event, it was impossible to carry on a deliberative process with leaders of Congress who do not believe in the rule of law. Until March of 1998 the House insisted on legislating through appropriations riders imposed without hearings or findings or reliance on expert testimony. The rule upheld by the House Republicans seems to have been "Don't confuse us with the facts"!

So, while we achieved many changes, such procedural reforms, in an arena as politically charged and volatile as labor law, have limited utility without more fundamental and sweeping reforms. The National Labor Relations Act itself needs to be amended to incorporate the kinds of proposals I made in *Agenda for Reform* (1993). In recent years some union leaders, discouraged by the antiunion climate in Washington have stated that they are abandoning the Board and looking elsewhere for more effective solutions. My term in office saw no increase in the number of union petitions filed for representation elections—even though this period coincided with the AFL-CIO's increased attention to union organizing and larger expenditure for these efforts—prompted in part by the changing of the guard at the federation's offices in Washington. Nonetheless, the unions still need the law and the provisions of the National Labor Relations Act, even though its weaknesses, as well as other considerations, made it impossible for the Clinton Board to arrest the decline in collective bargaining and the dwindling number of workers who feel confident enough to express support for unionization.

Although representation petitions are down nationally, in regional offices like Las Vegas, where unions have been effective in obtaining voluntary recognition from employers through persuasion and pressure, the amount of unfair labor practice litigation has escalated. This increase is principally due to employer retaliation against these organizational efforts in the form of discharges, discipline, intimidation, and the like. My point here is that the filing representation petitions is not the sole test of whether unions are using the NLRA. The rise in unfair labor practice litigation reflects the increase in self-help organizing activity and employers' responses to it that would otherwise take the form of representation petitions. In Las Vegas and elsewhere, unions have turned to such other methods of organizing as "salting"—using paid union organizers in industries, such as construction, where workers have generally not petitioned for elections.

In addition, there are several situations in which unions can obtain recognition without Board assistance: when, for example, the employer is a government contractor and can be influenced by political considerations; or when the company is part of a joint venture in which one of the other employers has already been organized by the union. This is what occurred in Fremont, California, at the NUMMI car assembly plant (a General Motors–Toyota joint venture); and in places like Las Vegas, where unionization could take place fairly easily because the dominant ethos is prounion in industries like casinos, hotels, and construction and employers are more willing to accede to union demands for recognition agreements without an election.

Legal scholar Professor Catherine Fisk and her colleagues have also demonstrated how in common-situs situations a group called Justice for Janitors has been able to use self-help—in the form of picketing and demonstrations—without resort to law and without running afoul of the strictures of the secondary-boycott prohibitions.[17] (*Common situs* refers to a situation in which a building contractor shares a work site with a party with whom they have a commercial contract.) Neutrality agreements that oblige employers to refrain from antiunion campaigns or to allow nonemployee organizers access to company property—which they could not obtain through the National Labor Relations Act—are other lawful paths to unionization that do not require Board elections.[18] And, although Board precedent casts some doubt on the proposition, it may also be possible to negotiate terms and conditions of employment *before* the union has obtained majority status but to condition their implementation upon the union's actual achievement of such status.[19] In several cases the Board has facilitated the recognition of this type of bargaining agreement.[20] Finally, in 1999 the United Automobile Workers presented yet another legal issue involved in obtaining recognition without the NLRB by seeking an agreement with the Big Three to facilitate organization of their suppliers' factories.[21]

Unions' efforts to organize temporary workers and new kinds of employees (e.g., home care workers, physicians, and teaching assistants)—cases that are pending before the Board—suggest a potential for revitalization.[22] This new round of emphasis on organization by the AFL-CIO began in 1995. Nothing better illustrates the innovativeness of this trend than the unions' attempt to reach out to physicians.[23] Organizing such new workforces is not only a vital part of labor's mission but one that will inevitably require methods other than Board-supervised representation elections.

Yet in many, if not most circumstances, unions will continue to need the recognition procedures of the National Labor Relations Act. As I said to the *Washington Post* in 1997: "If a union can obtain recognition without going to us [the Board], they will always be better off.... there's more delay going through us."[24] But I also said: "Most unions can't obtain representation without our help.... they need us because many employers won't recognize unions without the compulsion of law." As Bruce Raynor, executive vice president of UNITE said in the same piece, "Anyone who thinks we're going to revitalize the labor movement with card checks is kidding themselves."

As I said, the act itself needs to be reformed in both the substantive law area as well as remedially; that is, by expanding the relief available to unions and employers when things go wrong. During my term the Board was able to use Section 10(j) injunctions, bench opinions for administrative law judges, postal ballots, and a wide variety of internal reforms that, during our first couple of years, expedited case handling. But the absence of effective remedies for labor troubles—for example, the kind of first-contract arbitration now available in Canada—frustrates successful implementation of the act.[25]

Statutory reform should not only sponsor a more balanced or level playing field between labor and management, it should also make war against the "them and us" mentality rooted in divisiveness and distrust. This is the road I advocated in my *Keeler Brass* concurring opinion and in other Board rulings dealing with employee participation. Whatever their form, participation schemes must be genuine and respectful of the dignity of labor, not phony ploys like the Republican-sponsored TEAM Act, which was aimed at undermining employee autonomy and free trade unions.

The Clinton administration's labor and race relation policies were designed to bring us together as a people, to help us reach one another across racial, class, and economic lines. Our adjudication initiatives at the Board and the kind of balanced amendments to the NLRA sought, for example, by such Democrats as Tom Sawyer of Ohio, were efforts to promote both employee rights and a common ground where labor and management can each gain through their interdependence while producing a better, more competitive product.

Whatever the specific situation, the law must stand ready to intervene when cooperative procedures break down and employees are harmed—for instance, by being permanently replaced in strikes. It is wasteful and harmful for society to engage in the kind of lengthy litigation involved in the *Detroit Newspapers* case. An infinitely better approach to the problem from the perspective of equity would be a clearly defined set of rules that everyone—the public, the employees, and the employers—can understand in advance.

The need for statutory reform was one of the reasons why it was so important for me to speak out on the striker-replacement issue at Yosemite in early 1995. The law relating to the status of economic strikers is, first of all, inconsistent with democracy in the workplace; but it also fosters wasteful litigation, forcing unions and workers to search out the unfair labor practices that enable employees to be reinstated at the end of the strike. Regrettably, on other occasions when I spoke out on labor law reform, and was asked to do so by members of Congress and others (e.g., on employee participation and the TEAM Act and Proposition 226 in California), the effort was defensive. I felt that I was taking part in a kind of holding operation to ward off bad legislation that would only make labor relations worse.

Political Realities

I recognize, of course, that none of the reforms I advocated in *Agenda for Reform* or during my term of office can happen in the political environment of the turn of the new century. The Republicans in the hundred and sixth (and perhaps also the hundred and seventh) Congress are simply interested in reversing progress. The approval of the Board's diminished use of Section 10(j) expressed by Representative Jay Dickey in March of 2000 is indicative of their attitude.[26] They want to reinterpret (or abolish) *Beck* to make it easier for dissidents to cripple the unions' political muscle (and the muscle of the Democratic party). They seek to tie up union "salting" campaigns with a de facto reversal of the Supreme Court's *Town & Country* decision and to eliminate the Board's jurisdiction over small employers through nostrums not subject to hearing and debate. The Fairness for Small Business and Employees Act proposed in 1998 was illustrative of that kind of approach.

Short of such Draconian legislation, congressional Republicans, particularly the House Republicans, will do what they can to make it difficult for a vigorous Board to function. Further interference in the adjudication and rule-making process is ever present on the horizon. The financial backers of many Republican legislators make it unlikely that rule making and other significant reforms will see the light of day as long as the Republicans control Congress.

Unfortunately, the position articulated by Congressman Obey makes it clear that some Democrats are also not particularly enthusiastic about campaign finance reform. Any such legislation would necessarily focus on their donors, and any restraints enacted would affect them as well as the Republicans. The failure to even consider labor law reform seriously prior to the advent of the Republican majority in the hundred and fourth Congress makes it clear that the political, and perhaps the economic, circumstances of society will have to change substantially before the matter is revisited. Even election of a Democratic president and a Democratic Congress in 2000 would by no means assure serious consideration for labor law reform, although in 1999 the dialogue between them was promising.[27]

No logical trade-off between employee-participation reforms and deregulation of employer free speech in union organizational campaigns, on the one hand, and enhanced organizational access and tough remedies for statutory violations such as I advocated in *Agenda*, on the other, will produce labor law reform. My proposals were fashioned to create a sensible and balanced scheme of labor law reform that would be fair to all parties. But they were not political prognostication. They were, in essence, what *should be*, not necessarily what *would be*. The latter, in my estimate, is the kind of grand compromise advocated by Paul Weiler of Harvard Law School.[28] His view seems to be predicated upon the idea of a "consensus" that would promote support for labor law reform by both labor and management. The failure of both Democratic and Republican congresses to consider such reforms seriously heretofore, as well as the unremitting attacks on the Board and myself between 1994 and 1998, make it clear that his conception, though rooted in logic, bears no relation to reality. There is simply no interest in such ideas by substantial elements of the business community; indeed there is considerable hostility toward them. This was evident in the warfare waged against the Board's attempts to enforce the statute as it is now written by using Section 10(j), rule making, postal ballots, and the like.

Yet another discouraging loss from the recent political scene was the retirement of John Chafee of Rhode Island not long before his death. His absence, like that of Senator Hatfield after 1998, further reduced the already-weakened moderate wing of the Republican party. (Of the five moderate Republican senators who voted for my confirmation in 1994, only two—Arlen Specter of Pennsylvania and

James Jeffords of Vermont—were still serving in 2000.) Whether Congress is subsequently controlled by the Democrats or the Republicans, any attempt to amend the National Labor Relations Act to more readily achieve its objectives will require the support of some moderate Republicans.

Whether dominated by Democrats or Republicans, Congress will inquire, as it should, about the views on labor law reform of the nominated chairman of the NLRB. The chair of any quasi-judicial administrative agency should have the background and qualifications necessary to express such views in appropriate circumstances. I thought that my own public commentaries fit this standard because in two of these three circumstances—the TEAM Act and Proposition 226—I was invited to address outstanding issues of interest to Congress and the California legislature. If the chairman of the National Labor Relations Board, an academic who had written on labor law for many years, was not the appropriate person to speak, who in the world would be! My third public comment, on the important striker-replacement issue, was not only appropriate but directly involved Board case management.

Several of my critics stated that it was as inappropriate for the chairman to speak about law reform as it would be for the chief justice of the U. S. Supreme Court to do so. Yet, both Chief Justice Rehnquist and Chief Justice Burger repeatedly spoke before the courts and Congress on such important issues as habeas corpus. As Ab Mikva said bluntly when he was chief judge for the Court of Appeals for the District of Columbia, "Civil RICO [Racketeer Influenced Corruption Organization Act] was bad legislation: it has turned out to be bad law. We ought to get rid of it."

By the standards of these eminent jurists, my speeches met the standards of judicial propriety. Yet, some said, although it was ethical for a chairman to speak out, it was still not wise—because it invited more of the budget slashing we were already confronting. That argument became the mantra of many of my Washington-insider critics. Yet it was clear that the response of the Republican Congress was attributable to several other causes: (1) hostility to the National Labor Relations Act itself; (2) the Board's vigorous enforcement of the statute during my tenure; (3) the desire to seek revenge against the AFL-CIO for its involvement in the 1996 elections and to punish it by visiting retribution upon all labor-related agencies; and (4) the fact that in rule making and oral argument we tipped our hand about what we intended to do before we did it. My occasional speeches on law reform had very little, if anything, to do with the actualities of the appropriations process. When I told the chairs of other quasi-judicial administrative agencies in Washington of the controversy and debate about my statements on labor law reform, they were completely flabbergasted.

In the month following my departure from the Board in August 1998, the House of Representatives leadership put on a full public display—in the Clinton impeachment trial—of the belligerent partisanship the Board had already seen far too frequently. Congress had become obsessed with its attempt to defy the political will of the people duly expressed in the 1992 and 1996 elections.

From the beginning of my involvement in this vituperative environment in 1993, I had stated that a democratic society was one in which the rights and obligations of both labor and management were recognized. The 1980s and early 1990s had already seen a strong shift in the power balance away from organized labor. Yet, in spite of the decline of unions in the United States and other industrialized countries, the Republicans and the right-wing organizations that supported them continued to see democratic institutions in the workplace as a central threat. The intensity of their attack on the NLRB was the mirror image of their fear that a renaissance of unions was beginning in both the economic and political sphere.

In this sense, the Republicans were correct. There is no more important public policy issue than democracy in the workplace at the beginning of the twenty-first century. The challenge for elected representatives and policy makers is to address this issue in a balanced manner that takes into account the competing interests of unions, employers, and individual employees. The framework of a statute like the National Labor Relations Act remains the best means of dealing with the issue— particularly if it is amended along the lines I have advocated. Without the NLRA, the alternatives are a labor law of the jungle or a transfer of jurisdiction (which some conservative groups have advocated) to general courts that have never shown themselves equipped to perform this function. As our management and labor advisory panels properly noted, given the labor law vacuum that exists at the state level, the Republicans' proposal to withdraw Board jurisdiction from certain arenas would deprive both employers and unions of their rights and obligations under federal law.

None of the goals I pursued while in Washington or the reforms I have outlined above can be realized without a commitment to public service. My objectives as chairman were not only to institute numerous procedural and substantive reforms but also to demystify the law and make it more understandable and equitable for the average layperson—whether a worker or a business person. That was one of the reasons why I fought to reveal publicly the votes the Board took on Section 10(j) cases and why I advocated issuing written opinions in these cases, a practice I also followed in *Detroit Newspapers*. And that is why I spoke out about the way in which our agency functioned and the internal and statutory reforms it needed to be more effective.

One hundred and thirty-three years prior to my departure from Washington in August of 1998, my great-grandfather, William B. Gould, received his honorable discharge papers from the United States Navy after serving his country for more than three years in the War of the Rebellion. It was my privilege to serve the same U. S. government—"Uncle Samuel," as he frequently referred to it in his diary—in this century past, albeit under less perilous circumstances. I sought to achieve some of the same aims for which he fought so bravely against the same forces of repression.

Notes

Introduction

1. Ironically, Obey, the ranking Democrat on the House Appropriations Committee, was the ugliest and most prideful personality we encountered during those difficult hearings. It did not surprise me to see him quoted, during President Clinton's impeachment, as stating that President Andrew Johnson "was impeached because he showed some restraint toward the South" (David Rogers and Jeffrey Taylor, "Chamber Maid: A President Impeached and a Congress Torn—the Show Must Go On," *Wall Street Journal,* December 21, 1998, p. 1). This comment comparing President Clinton's imbroglio with the refusal of Johnson to enforce civil rights legislation in the South—which, in the view of the radical Republicans of the time was an attempt to reverse the results of Appomattox—revealed, I think, Obey's sympathies and lack of knowledge.

2. *Bailey* v. *Alabama, 219* U.S. 219 (1911), quote at 241. See also James Pope, "Labor's Constitution of Freedom," *Yale Law Journal* 106: 941, 943–48 (1997).

3. For the effect of these new players, see, e.g., Glenn Burkins, "SEIU [Service Employees International Union] Union Wins Right to Represent California Home Health-Care Workers," *Wall Street Journal,* February 26, 1999, p. A4; Steven Greenhouse, "In Biggest Drive since 1937, Union Gains a Victory," *New York Times,* February 26, 1999, p. A1.

4. *NLRB v. Jones & Laughlin Steel Corp.*, 301 U.S. 1 (1937).

5. James A. Gross, *Broken Promise: The Subversion of U.S. Labor Relations Policy, 1947–1994* (Philadelphia: Temple University Press, 1995), pp. 232–33. See also idem, *The Making of the National Labor Relations Board: A Study in Economics, Politics, and the Law, vol. 1, 1933–1937* (Albany: State University of New York Press, 1974); idem, *The Reshaping of the National Labor Relations Board: National Labor Policy in Transition, 1937–1947* (Albany: State University of New York Press, 1981); and Harry A. Millis and Emily Clark Brown, *From the Wagner Act to Taft-Hartley: A Study of National Labor Policy and Labor Relations* (Chicago: University of Chicago Press, 1950).

Chapter One

1. The strategy was also a direct descendant of the Dixiecrat walkout over civil rights at the 1948 Democratic convention, which was led by Strom Thurmond of South Carolina. Later,

Thurmond switched parties over a 1960s civil rights bill and became, like many conservative southern Democrats, a Republican.

2. Recent developments in the much-touted cooperative union experiment at General Motors' Saturn plant leave the future of such relationships uncertain. See Keith Bradsher, "Saturn Plant's Leaders Are Voted Out," *New York Times*, February 26, 1999, C1.

3. See *Compania Gen. De Tabacos De Filipinas* v. *Collector of Internal Revenue*, 275 U.S. 87, 100 (1927).

4. "Those black veterans of other wars were the backbone of this nation" (W. Gould, Letter to the Editor, "Equal Opportunity for Black Civilians," *New York Times*, March 7, 1991, A18).

5. *Brown* v. *Board of Education*, 347 U.S. 483, 74 S. Ct. 686 (1954).

6. Archibald Cox, "The Uses and Abuses of Union Power," *Notre Dame Lawyer* 35 (1960): 624.

7. Curiously enough, although in the 1970s the AFL-CIO had roundly attacked my views on seniority and, in particular, on discrimination, twenty-plus years later both labor and management officials conveniently forgot our disagreements and supported me during the prolonged confirmation debate over my nomination.

8. Cf. Roger Undy, Annual Review Article: "New Labour's 'Industrial Relations Settlement': The Third Way?" *British Journal of Industrial Relations* 37 (1999): 315.

9. "According to the Bureau of Labor Statistics, union membership in 1998 inched up by 101,000 to 16.2 million people.... Overall, labor's percentage of the work force dropped to 13.9 percent last year from 14.1 percent a year earlier. Its share of the work force was as high as 20.1 percent in 1983, the first year for which comparable data are available" (Glenn Burkins, "Number of Labor Unions Grew Last Year," *Wall Street Journal*, January 26, 1999, B3). See also Thomas Geoghegan, *Which Side Are You On?: Trying to Be for Labor When It's Flat on Its Back* (New York: Farrar, Straus & Giroux, 1991): "Organized labor comprises just 16 percent of the labor movement now, down from 20–25 percent ten years ago."

10. *Sure-Tan* v. *NLRB*, 467 U.S. 883, 104 S. Ct. 2803 (1984).

11. *NLRB* v. *Mackay Radio and Telegraph Co.*, 304 U.S. 333, 58 S. Ct. 904 (1938).

12. Joe Klein, "The Town That Ate Itself," *New Yorker*, November 23, 1998, 79, 80–81.

13. Southern states are: Alabama, Georgia, Mississippi, South Carolina, North Carolina, Virginia, Florida, Louisiana, Texas, Tennessee, Arkansas, and Oklahoma. Border states are: Kentucky, Missouri and West Virginia.

14. Andrew Hacker, *Two Nations: Black and White, Separate, Hostile and Unequal* (New York: Scribners, 1992), p. 201.

15. See Paul M. Barrett, "Conservatives Tear A Page From Liberals' Book, 'Borking' Clinton's Nominees for Legal Positions," *Wall St. Journal*, November 29, 1993, A14.

16. John Kifner, "Lott, and the Shadow of a Pro-White Group," *New York Times*, January 14, 1999, A9.

17. Quoted in Peter Applebome, "Impeachment Republicans, 130 Years Later; Dueling with the Heirs Of Jeff Davis," *New York Times*, December 27, 1998, 4: 1.

18. Sarah A. Binder and Steven S. Smith, *Politics or Principle: Filibustering in the United States Senate* (Washington, D.C.: Brookings Institution, 1997), p. 136.

19. G. Calvin Mackenzie and Robert Shogun, *Obstacle Course: The Report of the Twentieth-Century Fund Task Force on the Presidential Appointment Process* (Washington, D.C.: 1996).

Chapter Two

1. William B. Gould IV, "Bush: More Tolerance with Labor? *Sacramento Bee,* January 17, 1989, B13.

2. The Amalgamated Clothing Workers Union subsequently merged into UNITE, the Union of Needletrades, Industrial and Textile Employees, AFL-CIO, CLC.

3. The now-deceased Interstate Commerce Commission, born in 1887, was the first agency established to regulate aspects of economic activity.

4. Herb Caen, "The Morning Line," *San Francisco Chronicle*, May 4, 1993. Stanford University is often referred to as "The Farm."

5. Reich, "Labor Law, Reform, and the Japanese Model," *Harvard Law Review* 98 (1985): 697.

6. G. Calvin Mackenzie, *Starting Over: The Presidential Appointment Process in 1997* (Washington D.C.: Twentieth Century Fund/Century Foundation White Paper, 1997), pp. 39–40.

7. See, e.g., Kevin G. Salwen "Gould Expected to Be Named Head of NLRB," *Wall Street Journal*, June 17, 1993, A2.

8. No major reform of American labor law had been fashioned since 1959 when new unfair practices by labor unions were defined by a heavily Democratic Congress, largely as a result of the McClellan Committee hearings in which John and Robert Kennedy played an influential role. The result was a bill of rights for workers against unfair union practices.

9. Terry M. Moe, "Interests, Institutions and Positive Theory: The Politics of the NLRB," *Studies in American Political Development: An Annual* 2 (1987): 273.

10. See Robert D. Hershey, "Washington Watch, The Magnet for Lobbyists," *New York Times*, August 18, 1980; Martin Tolchin, "Republicans Fight Carter Nominees," *New York Times*, September 14, 1980, A31.

11. Moe, "Interests, Institutions and Positive Theory," p. 272.

12. Quoted in Mike Weiss, "Bill Gould's Ordeal: The Anatomy of a Character Assassination," *Sacramento Bee,* July 10, 1994, F1.

12a. See also Paul C. Light and Virginia L. Thomas, *The Merit and Reputation of an Administration's Presidential Appointees on the Appointments Process* (April 28, 2000).

13. Paul Craig Roberts, "Clinton May Be Term-Limited by Nominees," *Los Angeles Times*, October 31, 1993, 5.

14. James A. Gross, *Broken Promise: The Subversion of U.S. Labor Relations Policy, 1947–1994* (Philadelphia: Temple University Press, 1995), pp. 16–17.

Chapter Three

1. *Pattern Makers* v. *NLRB,* 473 U.S. 95, 105 S. Ct. 3064 (1985).

2. *NLRB* v. *Granite State Joint Bd., Textile Workers Union of America, Local 1029, AFL-CIO,* 409 U.S. 213, 218, 93 S. Ct. 385, 388 (1973) (Burger, C.J., concurring).

3. Unfortunately, the opportunity never came during my term as chairman, because the general counsel did not issue a complaint the Board could use to adjudicate the theory.

4. Jeremy Campbell, "Getting Away with Murder," (London) *Evening Standard,* November 3, 1993, 27.

5. Paul Craig Roberts, "Clinton May Be Term-Limited by Nominees," *Los Angeles Times,* October 31, 1993, 5. See also "Questions for Professor Gould," *Detroit News,* December 5, 1993, B2 (which offers substantially the same viewpoint as the Roberts article); "Blocking the NLRB Nominee" *Sacramento Bee,* December 14, 1993, B6; and "Labor Board: Senate Roadblock Holds up an Outstanding Nominee," *Detroit Free Press,* January 23, 1994.

6. Mike Weiss, "Democracy Inaction," *San Jose Mercury News,* June 26, 1994, 10; idem, "The Prey," *Mother Jones,* July 1, 1994, 50.

7. Neil Lewis, "While Senator Deliberated a Top Aide Politicked," *New York Times,* November 5, 1993, A9.

8. *Communications Workers of America* v. *Beck,* 487 U.S. 735 (1988).

9. Mathew M. Bodah, "Congressional Influence on Labor Policy: How Congress Has Influenced Outcomes Without Changing the Law." Paper delivered at the 51st Annual Meeting of the Industrial Relations Research Association, New York, January 5, 1999.

10. G. Calvin Mackenzie, *Starting Over: The Presidential Appointment Process in 1997.* A Twentieth Century Fund/Century Foundation White Paper (Washington, D.C., 1998).

11. *NLRB v. Wooster Division of Borg-Warner Corp.* 356 U.S. 342 (1958). The Court held that wages, hours, and conditions of employment are mandatory subjects for bargaining and that both sides must engage in bargaining about them until impasse occurs.

12. Anthony Lewis, "... Running the Gauntlet," *New York Times,* January 31, 1994, A11.

Chapter Four

1. The chief ALJ, who is appointed to the post by the Board at the recommendation of the chairman, assigns cases, oversee schedules and travel, and otherwise allocates resources. Like other ALJs, he or she is independent of the Board insofar as decision making is considered. The chief ALJ's office is in Washington, where the majority of ALJs also sit; the remainder are in Atlanta, New York City, and San Francisco.

2. The Federal Trade Commission's procedures manual establishes deadlines for commissioners' opinions and final orders; the Federal Communications Commission deals with the problem by simply designating the chairman its chief executive officer. Both agencies have procedures for issuing decisions regardless of the tardiness of individual commissioners.

3. *National Labor Relations Board: Action Needed to Improve Case-Processing Time at Headquarters* (Washington, D.C.: U.S. General Accounting Office, 1991).

4. James M. Landis, Letter to the editor, *New Republic*, June 9, 1958; reprinted in Leon I. Salomon, ed., *The Independent Federal Regulatory Agencies* (New York: Wilson, 1959), pp. 174–75.

5. *Lone Star Northwest*, Case 36-RD–1434, rev. granted April 17, 1994 (unpublished).

6. *Shepard Convention Services, Inc.*, 314 NLRB 689 (August 3, 1994), enf. denied 85 F.3d 671 (D.C. Cir. 1996).

7. NLRB Case No. 21-RC–19234, rev. denied April 14, 1994.

8. NLRB Case No. 5-RC–14033.

9. NLRB Case No. 5-RC–14351.

10. William B. Gould IV, "Four-and-One-Half Year Report," *Daily Labor Report*, August 28, 1998 (Washington D.C.: National Labor Relations Board).

11. *Management Training Corp.*, 317 NLRB 1355 (July 28, 1995).

12. *Teledyne Economic Development* v. *NLRB*, 108 F.3d 56 (4th Cir. 1997); *Pikeville United Methodist Hospital* v. *USW*, 109 F.3d 1146 (6th Cir. 1997); *NLRB* v. *YWCA*, 192 F.3d 1111 (8th Cir. 1999); *Aramark Corp.* v *NLRB*, 179 F.3d 872 (10th Cir. 1999).

13. *Angelica Healthcare Services Group, Inc.*, 315 NLRB 1320 (January 18, 1995).

14. Merton C. Bernstein, The NLRB's Adjudication-Rule Making Dilemma under the Administrative Procedures Act," *Yale Law Journal* 79 (1970): 571; Cornelius J. Peck, "The Atrophied Rule-Making of the National Labor Relations Board," *Yale Law Journal* 70 (1961): 729; idem, "A Critique of the National Labor Relations Board's Performance in Policy Formulation: Adjudication and Rule-Making," *University of Pennsylvania Law Review* 117 (1968): 254; David L. Shapiro, "The Choice of Rulemaking or Adjudication in the Development of Administrative Policy," *Harvard Law Review* 78 (1965): 921. Cf. *NLRB* v. *Wyman-Gordon Co.* 394 U.S. 759 (1968); see also Judge Henry Friendly's dissent in *NLRB* v. *Lorben Corp.* 345 F.2d 346 (2d Cir. 1965). He suggests that the Board consider using either rule making or adjudication for disputes about employer interrogations of employees.

14a. See Robert Greenberger, "Microsoft's Fate May Depend on the Computer, Which Picks Panel from Diverse Appeals Court," *Wall Street Journal*, May 24, 2000, A28, describing a meeting between the court and the owner of the Washington Redskins—a potential litigant before the court.

15. See, for example, *Black & Decker Mfg. Co.*, 147 NLRB 825 (1962); *Sav-On Drugs*, 138 NLRB 1032 (1962).

16. *American Hospital Association* v. *NLRB*, 499 U.S. 606 (1991).

17. 487 U.S. 735 (1988).

Chapter Five

1. The full work of the Board during my tenure (1994–1998), except for decisions issued on the last day or so, is described in William B. Gould IV, "Four-and-One-Half Year Report," *Daily Labor Report*, August 28, 1998 (Washington D.C.: National Labor Relations Board).

2. *North Macon Health Care Facility*, 315 NLRB 359 (October 26, 1994).

3. *Speedrack Products Group Ltd.,* 320 NLRB 627 (1995).

4. *Speedrack Products Group Ltd. v. NLRB,* 114 F.3d 1276, 1282 (D.C. Cir. 1997).

5. *James Luterbach Co. Inc.,* 315 NLRB 976 (December 16, 1994).

6. *Lexington Fire Protection Group, Inc.,* 318 NLRB 347 (August 15, 1995).

7. *Canteen Co.,* 317 NLRB 1052 (June 30, 1995), enf'd. *Canteen Co. v. NLRB,* 103 F.3d 1355 (7th Cir. 1997).

8. *NLRB* v. *Burns International Security Services,* 406 U.S. 272 (1972).

9. *Providence Hospital,* 320 NLRB 717 (January 3, 1996), enf'd. 121 F.3d 548, (9th Cir. 1997); *Ten Broeck Commons,* 320 NLRB 806 (February 2, 1996). In *Providence,* the Board held that as the record did not establish the use of independent judgment by charge nurses, they were not statutory supervisors. In *Ten Broeck* we held that licensed practical nurses serving as charge nurses were not supervisors because they did not exercise independent judgment.

10a. Professors John Delaney of the University of Iowa and Lamont Stallworth of Loyola University in Chicago, wrote approvingly of these reforms. See Michael Bologna, *NLRB: Study Shows Unions, Employers, Judges Support NLRB's New Settlement Programs.* 84 D.L.R. A-4 (May 1, 2000).

10. *Providence Alaska Medical Center* v. *NLRB,* 121 F.3d 548 (9th Cir. 1997); *Grancare, Inc.* v. *NLRB,* 137 F.3d 372 (6th Cir. 1998).

11. *NLRB* v. *Beverly Enterprises-Massachusetts Inc.* 174 F.3d 13 (1st Cir. 1999).

12. Ibid. at 34.

13. Ibid. at 36.

14. *San Diego Gas & Electric,* 325 NLRB 218 (July 21, 1998) (W. Gould concurring).

15. NLRB Case Nos. 7-CA-24872 and 7-CB-6582. That 1980s dispute arose out of a new cooperative relationship between the United Auto Workers and General Motors' newly created Saturn subsidiary. The question was whether the preferential hiring of UAW-represented workers prior to its selection as majority union representative was compatible with labor law. Rather than submit this important issue to the Board for adjudication, the general counsel had decided the issue herself and dismissed the complaint.

16. Gould, "Taft-Hartley Comes to Great Britain," *Yale Law Journal* 81 (1972): 1421; see also idem, "On Labor Injunctions, Unions, and the Judges: The Boys Market Case," *Supreme Court Review* 70 (19): 215.

17. *U.S.* v. *United Mine Workers of America,* 330 U.S. 258 (1947).

18. *Buffalo Forge Co.* v. *Steelworkers,* 428 U.S. 397 (1976); Gould, "On Labor Injunctions Pending Arbitration: Recasting *Buffalo Forge,*" *Stanford Law Review* 30 (1978): 533.

19. "NLRB Seeks Contempt Citation against UMW for Strike Misconduct,"*Daily Labor Report,* May 6, 1994.

20. Harry Bernstein, "Coal Miners Get the Shaft from the NLRB: The Board's New Chairman, a Liberal, Takes a Tough Stance against Workers," *Los Angeles Times,* July 5, 1994, B5.

21. 512 U.S. 821 (1994).

22. Ibid., at 831.

23. *NLRB* v. *Ironworkers Local 433*, 169 F.3d 1217 (9th Cir. 1999).

24. 800 F.2d 1136 (3rd Cir., 1986).

25. *Lechmere* v. *NLRB*, 502 U.S. 527 (1992).

26. *Makro Inc.,* and *Renaissance Properties Co., d/b/a Loehmann's Plaza*, 316 NLRB 109 (January 25, 1995), rev. denied sub. nom. *UFCW Local No. 880* v. *NLRB*, 74 F.3d 2992, 151 LRRM 2889 (D.C. Cir. 1996), cert. denied 117 S. Ct. 52 (1996); *Leslie Homes Inc.*, 316 NLRB 123 (January 25, 1995), rev. denied sub. nom. *Metropolitan District Council United Brotherhood of Carpenters and Joiners* v. *NLRB, 68* F.3d 71, 150 LRRM 2641 (3d Cir. 1995).

27. *Farm Fresh, Inc.,* 326 NLRB 81 (August 27, 1998). When not limited by Supreme Court precedent, however, I expressed views similar to those contained in my earlier law review articles. See my dissent in *Beverly Enterprises-Hawaii, Inc.* dba/*Hale Nani Rehabilitation,* 326 NLRB No. 37 (August 26, 1998). On the general issue, see Derek Bok, "Reflections on the Distinctive Character of American Labor Laws," *Harvard Law Review* 84 (1971): 1394; W. B. Gould, "The Question of Union Activity on Company Property," *Vanderbilt Law Review* 18 (1964): 73; and idem, "The Union Organizational Rights and the Concept of Quasi-Public Property," *Minnesota Law Review* 49 (1965): 505.

Chapter Six

1. *National Basketball Association*, NLRB Case No. 2-RD-1454, July 26, 1995. These were not the only sports industry case by any means. See, e.g., *Delaware Racing Association*, 325 NLRB 156 (1997) (Chairman Gould concurring), where I voted to take jurisdiction over horse racing. Regrettably, no other member of the Board addressed this issue. For a wide-ranging discussion of the Board and sports cases, see Daniel Silverman, "Hard-ball Labor Relations in Sports Lead to Government Involvement: An NLRB Regional Director's Life in Sports," *New York State Bar Journal* 71 (September/October 1999): 80.

2. Professional Baseball Clubs and Baseball Players Assn., *Labor Arbitration* 66 (1975): 101 (Seitz, Arb.).

3. 259 U.S. 200 (1922).

4. *NLRB* v. *Jones & Laughlin Steel Corp.*, 301 U.S. 1 (1937).

5. The three others were Max Lanier; an excellent St. Louis Cardinals left-hander and father of former Houston manager Hal Lanier; the Brooklyn Dodgers' Mickey Owen (who had dropped the infamous third strike in the 1941 World Series and was later sold to the Chicago Cubs); and Sal "the Barber" Maglie.

6. 346 U.S. 356 (1953).

7. *Milwaukee American Assn.* v. *Landis*, 49 F.2d 298 (N.D. Ill. 1931). Of course, by the time of *Toolson,* Commissioner Landis was dead and the commissioner's powers were considerably diminished.

8. 407 U.S. 258, 282 (1972). Flood's brilliant defensive plays in the 1967 and 1968 World Series and his unique underhanded throws from the outfield are unforgettable in the annals of baseball.

9. Ibid.

10. See, e.g., *Robertson Class Plaintiffs* v. *NBA*, 479 F.Supp. 657 (S.D. N.Y., 1979), aff'd in part, reversed in part, 625 F.2d 407 (2d Cir. 1980); *Mackey* v. *NFL*, 543 F.2d 606 (8th Cir. 1976).

11. *Silverman* v. *Major League Player Relations Committee*, 516 F.Supp. 588 (S.D. N.Y. 1981).

12. Murray Chass, "Owners Pull So Hard on Cap, They Can't See Strike in Their Path," *New York Times*, June 7, 1994, B11.

13. Chass, "Labor Secretary's Plea Is Hardly a Solution," ibid., August 9, 1994, B15.

14. Chass, "Next Two Weeks Critical for Salvaging Season," ibid., August 29, 1994, C9.

15. Chass, "Baseball Talks Are Collapsing as Impasse Nears," ibid., December 22, 1994, B13.

16. "Selig, Angelos Unite in Praising Clinton," *Washington Post,* January 27, 1995, D3; Claire Smith, "Orioles Say They Won't Play without Regulars, *New York Times,* January 20, 1995, B9; "A Sane Baseball Owner," ibid., January 25, 1995, A20.

17. Chass, "President Pressuring Baseball's Negotiators," *New York Times*, February 3, 1995, B13.

18. Chass, "Salary Cap Vanishes; Problems Don't," *New York Times*, February 5, 1995, A13; idem, "It's Clinton at the Bat in Labor Negotiations," ibid., February 6, 1995, C1; Douglas Jehl, "All Is Quiet on the White House Front," ibid., February 7, 1995, B14; Robert B. Reich, *Locked in the Cabinet* (New York: Knopf, 1997), pp. 237–40. See also Mark Maske, "Clinton Seeks Intervention on Strike," *Washington Post*, February 8, 1995, A1.

19. Michelle Levander, "Chairman of NLRB Could Play Key Role in Baseball Conflict," *San Jose Mercury News*, February 8, 1995; Chass, "Bill to Curb Antitrust Exemption on Way," *New York Times*, February 11, 1995, 25.

20. Chass, "Baseball Outlook Appears Gloomy," and "Baseball's Unreal World," *New York Times*, February 9, 1995, B11, 22; John Helyar and David Rogers, "Congress Resists Taking a Swing in Baseball Strike," *Wall Street Journal*, February 9, 1995, A3.

21. Mark Maske, "Usery Plans to Stay Involved; Despite Criticism, Baseball Negotiator Wants to Continue," *Washington Post*, February 9, 1995, D1; Bill McAllister, "Reluctantly Congress Takes a Swing at Strike: No Quick Legislation Likely, Say Senators," ibid., February 16, 1995, B2.

22. Chass, "Labor Board Slows Action in Bid to Get Owners and Players Back to Table," *New York Times*, March 24, 1995, B14.

23. Wolf died in 1999 at the age of 94; his work with the original NLRB is chronicled in his obituary, ibid., July 28, 1999, C25.

24. *Silverman* v. *Major League Baseball*, 67 F.3d 1054, 1062 (2d Cir. 1995).

25. Nick Cafardo, "Sox Drop Orioles; Clemens on Target; Vaughn Hits No. 18," *Boston Globe,* June 23, 1995, 37.

Chapter Seven

1. Robert E. Cushman, *The Independent Regulatory Commissions* (New York: Oxford University Press, 1941), p. 362.

2. 295 U.S. 602 (1935).

3. Marver H. Bernstein, *Regulating Business by Independent Commission* (Princeton: Princeton University Press, 1955), p. 140. The work Bernstein refers to is James M. Landis, *The Administrative Process* (New Haven: Yale University Press, 1938).

4. William Cary, "The Federal Regulatory Commissions," Lecture delivered at Princeton University, April 4, 1952, mimeo., p. 3.

5. Peter L. Strauss, "The Place of Agencies in Government: Separation of Powers and the Fourth Branch," *Columbia Law Review* 84 (1984): 573, 590.

6. William L. Cary, *Politics and the Regulatory Agencies* (New York: McGraw-Hill, 1967), p. 7.

7. Terry M. Moe, "Interests, Institutions and Positive Theory: The Politics of the NLRB," in *Studies in American Political Development: An Annual* (New Haven: Yale University Press, 1990), p. 237.

8. See, e.g., William B. Gould, "The Question of Union Activity on Company Property," *Vanderbilt Law Review* 18 (1964): 73; Gould, "Union Organizational Rights and the Concept of 'Quasi-Public' Property," *Minnesota Law Review* 49 (1965): 505; Robert A. Gorman, "Union Access to Private Property," *Hofstra Labor Law Journal* 9 (1991): 1; Derek C. Bok, "Reflections on the Distinctive Character of American Labor Law," *Harvard Law Review* 84 (1971): 1394.

9. See, e.g., *Holly Farms Corp.* v. *NLRB*, 517 U.S. 392 (1996); *Auciello Iron Works, Inc.* v. *NLRB*, 517 U.S. 781 (1996); *NLRB* v. *Erie Resistor Corp.*, 373 U.S. 221 (1963); *NLRB* v. *Town & Country Elec. Inc.*, 516 U.S. 85 (1995).

10. Cary, "Federal Regulatory Commissions," p. 11.

11. The Republicans continued this practice into the 106th Congress subsequent to my departure: "Soon after the Republicans swept to power on Capitol Hill in 1994, they adopted a strategy of attaching last-minute legislative proposals, or riders, to essential appropriations bills. The point is to ensure passage of controversial changes in policy that might not survive if subjected to full hearings and debate as freestanding bills. The Democrats have used this profoundly undemocratic device, but the Republicans have perfected it" ("Legislation By Stealth," *New York Times*, August 2, 1999, A18).

12. *Super grade* is an advanced-level salary designation reserved for a limited number of agency personnel. The super grades constitute the most prestigious and well-paid portion of the senior federal workforce.

13. Steven G. Breyer and Richard B. Stewart, *Administrative Law and Regulatory Policy: Problems, Text, and Cases,* 3d ed. (Boston: Little, Brown, 1992), p. 684. For a general discussion of the relationship beween politics and administrative law, see Matthew Holden Jr., *Continuity and Disruption,* (Pittsburgh: University of Pittsburgh Press, 1996), pp. 107–67.

14. 487 U.S. 735 (1988).

15. This account is based on a conversation with former Chairman Stephens in my office, October 7, 1994.

16. No final rule was issued. When the Clinton Board came into existence, it issued several decisions in 1995. It is ironic that the Clinton Board, which was heavily castigated by the right-wing press for failing to produce *Beck* decisions, moved forward on a ruling providing for union regulation, while the Bush people had avoided it.

17. This is particularly ironic given the fidelity to the rule of law so often proclaimed by the House Managers in the 1998–1999 impeachment proceedings.

18. Cary, "Federal Regulatory Commissions," pp. 19–20.

19. Editorial, "Herman on Hold," *Wall Street Journal*, April 17, 1997, A22.

20. William B. Gould IV, Letter to the Editor, "NLRB Independent from Birth in 1935," *Wall Street Journal*, May 12, 1997, A15.

21. 320 NLRB 224 (December 20, 1995); *Paperworkers Local 1033 (Weyerhaeuser Paper Co.)*, 320 NLRB 349 (1995), enf. denied in part sub nom. *Buzenius* v. *NLRB*, 124 F.3d 788 (6th Cir. 1997), vacated 119 S. Ct. 442 (1998).

22. *A.P.R.A. Fuel Oil Buyers Group*, 320 NLRB 408 (1995), aff'd. 134 F.3d 50 (2d Cir. 1997).

23. U.S. Congress, House, Committee on Appropriations, *Hearings before the Subcommittee on Appropriations: Education and Related Agencies for 1998*, 105th Cong., 1st sess., 1997, p. 711.

24. 326 NLRB Nos. 64 and 65 (August 27, 1998).

25. 119 S. Ct. 292 (1998).

26. G. Calvin Mackenzie, *Starting Over: The Presidential Appointment Process in 1997*, Twentieth Century Fund/Century Foundation White Paper (New York: Twentieth Century Fund Press, 1997).

27. 513 U.S. 88 (1994).

28. Seth P. Waxman, "Presenting the Case of the United States As It Should Be: The Solicitor General in Historical Context," web site (visited April 13, 1999), http://www.usdoj.gov/osg/sgarticle.html.

29. 518 U.S. 231 (1996).

30. William B. Gould IV, "Players and Owners Mix It Up," *California Lawyer* (1988): 56.

31. James Mauro, "The Case of the Missing NLRB," *Legal Times of Washington*, April 8, 1996.

32. 119 S. Ct. 250 (1998).

33. Frankfurter's view was expressed in a dissenting opinion in *Machinists* v. *Street*, 367 U.S. 800 (1961). My own views were set forth in some detail in a speech given in Amana, Iowa, on October 8, 1997: "Campaign Finance Reform and the Union" (see Appendix I).

34. 119 S. Ct. 292 (1998).

35. *Monson Trucking, Inc.*, 324 NLRB No. 149 (October 31, 1997); *Group Health, Inc.*, enf. denied sub. nom. *Bloom* v. *NLRB*, 153 F.3d 844 (8th Cir. 1998), cert. granted, *Office and Professional Employees International Union, Local 12* v. *Bloom* 119 S. Ct. 1023 (1999).

36. Cary, "Federal Regulatory Commissions," pp. 19–20.

37. *Jefferson Smurfit Corp.*, 326 NLRB No. 74 (August 27, 1998).

38. Cary, "Federal Regulatory Commissions," p. 10.

39. 320 NLRB 224 (December 20, 1995); *Paperworkers Local 1033 (Weyerhaeuser Paper Co.)*, 320 NLRB 349 (1995), enf. denied in part sub nom. *Buzenius* v. *NLRB*, 124 F.3d 788 (6th Cir. 1997), vacated 119 S. Ct. 442 (1998).

40. *IUE & IUE Local 444* (Paramax Systems Corp.), 311 NLRB 1031 (1993), enf. denied, 41 F.3d 1532 (D.C. Cir. 1994).

Chapter Eight

1. Such disputes were frequent in the distrustful days prior to the 1955 merger of the two labor organizations.

2. James A. Gross, *The Reshaping of the National Labor Relations Board: National Labor Policy in Transition, 1937–1947* (Albany: State University of New York Press, 1981), p. 25.

3. U.S. Congress, Senate, Committee on Labor and Public Welfare, *Hearings on Nominations to National Labor Relations Board*, 80th Cong., 1st sess., 1947, p. 2; cited as Denham Confirmation Hearings, 1947 in Seymour Sher, "The National Labor Relations Board and Congress: A Study of Legislative Control of Regulatory Activity" (Ph.D. diss., University of Chicago, 1956).

4. Ibid., pp. 14–15.

5. *International Brotherhood of Teamsters* v. *United States* 431 U.S. 324 (1977).

6. *Painters and Allied Trades District Council No. 51 (Manganaro Corporation)*, 321 NLRB 158 (May 10, 1996).

7. U.S. Congress, Senate, Committee On Labor and Human Resources, *Hearing Examining the Activities and Progress of the National Labor Relations Board*, 104th Cong., 2d sess., 17 September 1996, pp. 12–13.

8. U.S. Congress, Senate, Committee on Labor and Public Welfare, *Hearings on S. 249, a Bill to Diminish the Causes of Labor Disputes Burdening or Obstructing Interstate and Foreign Commerce and for Other Purposes*, 81st Cong, 1st sess., 1949, pp. 201–202.

9. U.S. Congress, House, *Congressional Record*, 105th Cong., 1st sess., 1997, 143, no. 119: 7169.

10. U.S. Congress, House, *Hearings before a Subcommittee of the Committee on Appropriations*, 105th Cong., 1st Sess., March 19, 1997, part 6, p. 715.

11. *Federal Express Corp.*, 317 NLRB 1155, 1156–1158 (July 17, 1995) (Chairman Gould dissenting).

12. Aaron Bernstein, "The Long Knives Are Out for Bill Gould's NLRB, but the labor board chief isn't cowed by house budget threats," *Business Week*, September 25, 1995.

Chapter Nine

1. *Painters and Allied Trades District Council No. 51 (Manganaro Corporation),* 321 NLRB 158 (May 10, 1996).

2. *Brown & Sharp Manufacturing Company,* 321 NLRB 924, 925 (1996) (Chair Gould dissenting).

3. Quoted in Barbara Yuill, "NLRB: House Small Business Subcommittee Grills NLRB's Gould on Proposed Rule," *Daily Labor Report,* March 8, 1996.

4. "Way Out of Step," *Wall Street Journal,* November 29, 1996.

5. See "Legislation By Stealth," *New York Times,* August 2, 1999, A18.

6. A third variation on this theme, which did not come before the Board, is when a temporary agency sends employees to one employer for a relatively brief period of time and subsequently sends them to another.

7. The initial decision was *Greenhoot Inc.,* 205 NLRB 250 (1973). But it was not until the early-1990s that the Bush Board explicitly applied this doctrine to temporary-agency referrals: *Lee Hospital,* 300 NLRB 947 (1990); *International Transfer of Florida,* 305 NLRB 150 (1991); *Hexacomb Corporation,* 313 NLRB 983 (1994).

8. 326 NLRB, No. 72 (August 27, 1998); 326 NLRB, No. 75 (August 27, 1998).

9. *Roadway Package System Inc.,* 326 NLRB No. 72 (August 27, 1998*); Dial-A-Mattress Operating Corporation,* 326 NLRB No. 75 (August 27, 1998); *AmeriHealth Inc.,* 326 NLRB No. 55 (August 27, 1998).

10. *NLRB v. Town & Country,* 513 U.S. 1125 (1995).

11. Lewis, "A Lobby Effort that Delivers the Big Votes: Federal Express Knows Its Way Around Capitol," *New York Times,* October 12, 1996.

12. *Federal Express Corp.,* 323 NLRB No. 157 (May 30, 1997).

13. Laurence Zuckerman, "FedEx Pilots Decide to End Strike Threat," *New York Times,* November 21, 1998, B-1.

13a. Steven Pearlstein, FTC Proposal Accepts Savings As a Justification for Mergers; FTC Proposes New Merger Guidelines, *Washington Post,* June 4, 1996, at C1.

14. See, for example, NLRB proposals on amending Taft Act 22 LRRM 54 (1948).

15. *NLRB v. Mackay Radio & Telegraph Co.,* 304 U.S. 333 (1938).

16. 373 U.S. 221 (1963). I set forth the incompatibility of *Erie Resistor* and *Mackay* in detail in *Agenda for Reform* (Cambridge: MIT Press, 1993*),* p. 191.

17. "Too Many Offenses Are Made U.S. Crimes, Rehnquist Says," *New York Times,* January 1, 1999, A-13.

18. For example, *Vons Grocery Co.,* 320 NLRB No. 5 (December 18, 1995).

19. 317 NLRB 1110, 1117 (1995).

20. Ibid., p. 1119.

21. U.S. Congress, House, *Congressional Record,* 104th Cong., 2d sess., 1995, vol. 141, no. 152: 9523.

22. Ibid.

23. U.S. Congress, Senate, *Congressional Record*, 104th Cong., 2d sess., 1996, 142, no. 63: 4822.

24. Feinstein's remarks are discussed and cited in Michael Gottesman and Michael Seidl, "A Tale of Two Discourses: William Gould's Journey from the Academy to the World of Politics," *Stanford Law Review* 47 (1995): 749.

25. *Randell Warehouse of Arizona, Inc.*, 328 NLRB No. 153 (July 27, 1999); *Mississippi Power & Light Co.*, 328 NLRB No. 146 (July 26, 1999).

26. W. B. Gould, "The Labor Board's Ever Deepening Somnolence," *Creighton Law Review* 32 (June 1999): 1505.

Chapter Ten

1. *NLRB v. Town & Country Electric*, 516 U.S. 85 (1995).

2. *Management Training*, 317 NLRB 1355 (1995).

3. Clearly, Matlack could not anticipate Monica Lewinsky and the beneficial impact that scandal would have on the Board's fiscal 1999 budget (see chapter 9).

4. Elizabeth Drew, *Showdown: The Struggle between the Gingrich Congress and the Clinton White House* (New York: Simon & Schuster, 1996), p. 330.

5. U.S. Congress, Senate, Hearings Before Committee on Appropriations, 104th Cong., 2d sess. (February 6, 1996) (unpublished).

6. U.S. Congress, House, *Hearings before a Subcommittee of the Committee on Appropriations*, 104th Cong., 2d sess. (March 14, 1996), pt. 6, p. 1289.

7. Ibid., p. 1290.

8. Ibid., p. 1309.

9. *Employment & Law Alert*, no. 44 (April 1998): 8.

10. 321 NLRB 1178 (August 27, 1996).

11. *Novotel New York,* 321 NLRB 624 (July 8, 1996).

12. *NAACP v. Alabama ex rel. Patterson*, 357 U.S. 449 (1958). The Court held that an order to produce a list of the names and addresses of an organization's members unconstitutionally limited their freedom of association.

13. Cohen's position was also adopted by Judge Douglas Ginsberg in *Freund Baking Co. v. NLRB*, 165 F.3d 928, 160 LRRM 2299 (D.C. Cir. 1999).

14. 321 NLRB 636.

15. See *Sunrise Rehabilitation Hospital*, 320 NLRB 212 (December 19, 1995); *Good Shepherd Home*, 321 NLRB 426 (May 31, 1996).

16. 321 NLRB 1386 (August 27, 1996) enf'd. 131 F.3d 1026 (D.C. Cir. 1997) cert. denied 524 U.S. 937 (1998).

Chapter Eleven

1. *Paperworkers Local 1033 (Weyerhaeuser Paper Co.)*, 320 NLRB 349 (1995), rev'd. On other grounds sub nom. *Buzenius* v. *NLRB*, 124 F.3d 788 (6th Cir. 1997), vacated 119 S. Ct. 442 (1998). The Court held both that a union must inform all employees in the bargaining unit of the rights of nonmembers under *Beck*, and that members have a right under the Supreme Court's ruling in *NLRB* v. *General Motors* to become nonmembers of the union in order to be eligible to exercise *Beck* rights.

2. 322 NLRB 856 (January 10, 1997). We held that a distance of 80 miles from the Board's office to the employer's facility was not reason enough to hold a postal-ballot election instead of a manual election. In a concurring opinion I stated that resources alone were a basis for a postal ballot. Id at 856.

3. 322 NLRB 1074 (1997). The Board approved a multifacility unit over the wishes of the union).

4. 324 NLRB No. 105 (October 2, 1997). This decision limited the information required by *Beck* to major categories and found that organizational expenses were chargeable to *Beck* objectors. Chairman Gould's dissent found that the Supreme Court's ruling in *Ellis* required that these expenses not be charged to nonmembers. The Board subsequently held that such expenses are chargeable under certain circumstances (*UFCW Local 951* [*Meijor Inc.*], 328 NLRB No. 69 [1999]).

5. *Ellis* v. *Brotherhood of Railway Clerks*, 466 U.S. 435 (1984). The Court held that organizing expenses are nonrepresentational under the Railway Labor Act.

6. *Oil Workers Local 1–591 (Burlington Northern Railroad)*, 325 NLRB No. 45 (January 27, 1998).

7. *Teamsters Local No. 372, International Brotherhood of Teamsters, AFL-CIO*, 323 NLRB 278, 280 (1997) (Chairman Gould, concurring).

8. *Legal Aid Society*, 324 NLRB No. 135 (October 21, 1997).

9. Arleen Goodman, "The NLRB's Secret War on Small Business," *Wall Street Journal*, March 19, 1997.

10. *Peerless Plywood Co.*, 107 NLRB 427 (1953).

11. 326 NLRB No. 81 (1998).

12. *Montgomery Ward*, 288 NLRB 126 (1988).

13. *Anchor Mining Co.*, 324 NLRB No. 52 (1997).

14. 323 NLRB No. 142 (1997). The Board found that the union had a right to receive notice of and an opportunity to bargain over the employer's entire plan when that plan consisted of an employer's decision to relocate the bargaining unit and to change from a single-driver system to a team-driver system.

15. Deborah Sontag, "U.S. Victory Is Empty to Workers' Insults, Dismissals, and a Four-Year Wait for Pay They Won," *New York Times*, June 9, 1997, B1.

16. U.S. Congress, House, Hearings of the Government Reform and Oversight Subcommittee on Human Resources, 105th Cong., 1st sess., August 1997 (unpublished).

17. Cindy Skrzyck, "Top Regulatory Posts Remain Unfilled: Dozens of Federal Jobs Are Vacant as Politics Bogs Down Appointment Process," *Washington Post*, August 2, 1997, A1.

18. Aaron Bernstein, "How Business Is Winning Its War with the NLRB," *Business Week*, October 27, 1997, 59.

Chapter Twelve

1. Jacqueline Sergeant, "Standing His Ground," *Asbury Park Press*, November 16, 1997, B16.

2. *Flint Iceland Arenas* 325 NLRB 318, 321–23 (1998) (Chairman Gould, dissenting).

3. Former Board member John Penello, who was appointed by President Nixon and with whom I had much contact when he was a management labor lawyer in Washington. He died in 1998.

4. James A. Gross, *Broken Promises: The Subversion of U.S. Labor Policy, 1947–1994*, (Philadelphia: Temple University Press, 1995), p. 160.

5. Pete Wilson, *Investor's Business Daily*, May 21, 1998, p. A30.

6. U.S. Congress, House *Congressional Record*, 105th Cong., 2d sess, 1998, vol. 133, no. 107: 6940.

7. Ibid. p. 6942.

8. 325 NLRB No. 137 (May 4, 1998).

9. 325 NLRB No. 218 (July 21, 1998).

10. 326 NLRB No. 34 (August 24, 1998).

11. *Machinists v. Street* 367 U.S. 740 (1961). One of the seminal cases for the *Beck* doctrine, this case applied to the Railway Labor Act and established portions of the dues-objection principles.

12. 326 NLRB No. 64 (August 27, 1998).

13. *Detroit Newspapers* 327 NLRB No. 146 (March 4, 1999).

14. 326 NLRB No. 60 (August 27, 1998). See also my concurring opinion in *White Cap Inc.*, 325 NLRB 1166 (1998), pet. for review denied, No. 99-1118, 2000 U.S. App. LEXIS 4686 (D.C. Cir. March 24, 2000), which stressed freedom-of-contract principles.

15. 326 NLRB No. 81 (August 27, 1998).

16. 326 NLRB No. 28 (August 20, 1998).

17. 326 NLRB No. 37 (August 26, 1998).

18. *Technology Service Solutions*, 324 NLRB 298, 302 (1997).

19. 326 NLRB No. 69 (August 27, 1998).

20. 326 NLRB No. 80 (August 27, 1998).

21. 380 U.S. 300 (1965).

22. *Beverly California Corporation*, 326 NLRB No. 29 (August 21, 1998); *Beverly California Corporation*, 326 NLRB No. 30 (August 21, 1998). Earlier in my term the Board had

devised special notice and access remedies to dissipate the coercive effects of violations of the statute where they were numerous, pervasive, and outrageous. On my last day, the Board majority imposed negotiation and unfair labor practice strike costs as a remedy to be obtained by a union under certain circumstances (*Alwin Manufacturing Co. Inc.*, 326 NLRB No. 63 [August 27, 1998], enf'd 192 F.3d 133 [D.C. Cir. 1999]).

23. See *Fieldcrest Cannon, Inc.* 318 NLRB 470 (1995), enf'd. in part 97 F.3d 65 (4th Cir. 1996). See also "Textile Union Wins Fight at Six North Carolina Mills," *New York Times*, November 10, 1999, A23.

24. Quoted in "Victory for Union at Plant in South Is Labor Milestone," *New York Times*, June 25, 1999, A1, A16.

25. See Joan Flynn, *Allentown Mack: A Happy Exemplar of the Law of Unintended Consequences?* 49 Labor Law Journal 983, 991 (1998).

Chapter Thirteen

1. *Marquez v. Screen Actors Guild*, 525 U.S. 33 (1998).

2. Inspector General's Office, *Review of Board Casehandling Timeliness* (National Labor Relations Board, Report No. OIG-AMR-26-00-02, March 2000).

3. *Boston Medical Center*, 330 NLRB No. 30 (November 26, 1999).

4. *NLRB v. Anchor Concepts,* 160 LORM 2304, 2308 (2d Cir. 1999).

5. "Report of a House Government Operations Subcommittee on Manpower and Housing Decisional Delay and Case Backlog at the NLRB," *Daily Labor Report*, October 5, 1984, D1.

6. 907 F.2d 372, 378 (2d Cir. 1990); *NLRB v. Thill, Inc.,* 980 F.2d 1137, 1141 (7th Cir. 1992).

7. *NLRB v. Mountain Country Food Store*, 931 F.2d 21 (8th Cir. 1991).

8. *NLRB v. Hanna Boys Center*, 940 F.2d 1295, 1299 (9th Cir. 1991).

9. See, e.g., James Brudney, "A Famous Victory: Collective Bargaining Protections and the Statutory Aging Process," *North Carolina Law Review* 74 (1996): 939.

10. In 1999 senators Trent Lott and Mitch McConnell (R-Ky.) placed an "anonymous hold" on the Senate's confirmation of Richard C. Holbrooke as ambassador to the United Nations in the hope that President Clinton would nominate their choice for a seat on the Federal Election Commission (FEC). See "Pincus, Lott and McConnell Also Have 'Hold' on Holbrooke," *Washington Post*, July 7, 1999, A4.

11. Editorial, "A Sad Judicial Mugging," *New York Times*, October 8, 1999, A26; Charles Babington and Joan Biskupic, "Senate Rejects Judicial Nominee," *Washington Post*, October 6, 199, A1.

12. G. Calvin Mackenzie, *Starting Over: The Presidential Appointment Process in 1997* (Washington D.C.: Twentieth Century Fund/Century Foundation White Paper, 1997).

13. Mark Shields, "So Senator, Tell Us What You Think," *Washington Post*, May 6, 1995, A15.

14. *Mogk* v. *City of Detroit*, 365 F. Supp. 698 (E.D. Michigan 1971).

15. *Nabors Alaska Drilling*, 325 NLRB No. 104 (April 8, 1998) (Chairman Gould dissenting as to bargaining-order remedy).

16. Ida Klaus, "The Taft-Hartley Experiment in Separation of NLRB Functions," *Industrial and Labor Relations Review 2* (1957): 389.

17. Catherine L. Fisk, Daniel Mitchell, and Christopher Erickson, *Union Representation of Immigrant Janitors in Southern California: Economic and Legal Challenges* (Ithaca, N.Y.: Cornell University Press, forthcoming).

18. *Hotel Employees Local 2* v. *Marriott Corp.*, 961 F.2d 1464 (9th Cir. 1992); *UAW* v. *Dana Corp.*, 679 F.2d 634 (6th Cir. 1982); *Kroger Co.*, 275 NLRB 1478 (1985); *Coamo Knitting Mills, Inc.*, 150 NLRB 579 (1964). But the employer's practice can run afoul of the law. See, for instance, *Anaheim Town and Country Inn*, 282 NLRB 224 (1986); *Department Store Food Corp. of Pa.*, 172 NLRB 1203 (1968), enf'd 415 F.2d 74 (3d Cir. 1969).

19. *Majestic Weaving Co.*, 147 NLRB 859, enf. denied 355 F.2d 854 (2d Cir. 1966). The decision of the Supreme Court the Board relied upon to cast doubt on such arrangements is *International Ladies Garment Workers Union* v. *NLRB (Bernhard-Altmann Texas Corp.)*, 366 U.S. 731 (1961).

20. *Lexington Health Care Group*, 328 NLRB No. 124 (June 30 1999), holding that a union may waive its right to organize and petition the Board in a side agreement.

21. Again, the issue, as in the *Justice for Janitors* case, is whether the union's action is secondary or not. See the "UAW's Next Battleground," *Business Week*, July 26, 1999, p. 26; Jeffrey Ball and Fara Warner, "UAW to Seek Car Firms' Tacit Accord in Bid to Organize Supplier Factories," *Wall Street Journal*, May 13, 1999, A3.

22. In *Yale University*, 330 NLRB, No. 28 (November 29, 1999) the Board, after holding onto the case for more than two years, remanded to the administrative law judge the question on the employee status of university teaching assistants. Meanwhile, New York Regional Director Daniel Silverman has held that graduate teaching assistants at New York University are employees (New York University, Case No. 2-RC-220982 [April 3, 2000]). However, this decision is appealable to the full Board in Washington, and NYU has announced its intention to appeal it (*Chronicle of Higher Education*, May 21, 2000, p. A20. If the past is any case, it will be resolved in 2003 or 2004, at best.

23. See "Should Physicians Unionize?" *Wall Street Journal*, July 7, 1999, A22; Michael A. Weinstein, "Economic Scene: If Doctors Win the Right to Organize Patients Could Lose," *New York Times*, July 8, 1999, C2.

24. Frank Swoboda, "To the AFL-CIO, There's No Place Like Home: Unions Increasingly Turn to Door-to-Door Organizing, Bypassing Employer Opposition," *Washington Post*, March 16, 1997, H1.

25. Glenn Burkins, "For Unions, First Contracts Are Tough Fights," *Wall Street Journal*, November 23, 1998, A6.

26. Referring to the reduced number of requests for injunctive relief under Section 10(j), "Dickey said 'Constituent complaints have died down.'" (*Daily Labor Report*, March 29, 2000).

27. Steven Greenhouse, "U.S. Is Issuing New Rules for Contractors," *New York Times*, July 9, 1999, A12.

28. See Alan Hyde, Book Review, *Columbia Law Review* 91 (1991): 456. A different point of view seems to be held by Professor Paul Weiler; see his, "A Principled Reshaping of American Labor Law for the 21st Century," NYU Conference on Labor Law, June 1999.

Appendixes

A

Statement of William B. Gould IV at His Confirmation

Released March 2, 1994

I am pleased that a clear majority of the United States Senate has this day confirmed President Bill Clinton's nearly nine-month-old nomination of me to be Chairman of the National Labor Relations Board. Today, I reiterate my gratitude to the President for his support of me and express thanks to Senate Democrats, particularly Senator Edward Kennedy, who managed the floor debate, and those moderate Republicans who voted to confirm me. I am especially grateful to so many friends and supporters throughout the United States and, indeed, on every continent of this earth who have communicated so many expressions of support to me during this recent period of adversity.

Today's vote is a victory over a determined campaign of cynical character assassination waged against me for the past nine months by right wing ideologues in the Republican Party and in some elements of the business community. My hope is that careful examination of my nomination's extraordinary and unwarranted delay will galvanize the public and our political leaders to fight back against the antidemocratic politics of gridlock so assiduously practiced by those who have promoted partisan politics over good government.

I look forward to taking up my responsibilities as Chairman of the Board in a matter of days. As I told the Senate Labor Committee during my October 1, 1993 hearings, I intend to make expedited processes and effective dispute resolution machinery genuine priorities during my tenure. My goal is to reduce polarization both at the Board and also between labor and management. Within a few weeks, I shall announce the appointment of panels of labor lawyers representing both sides—panels which will provide the Board with valuable input about the strengths and deficiencies about the Board's processes.

The National Labor Relations Board—traditionally one of the most well-respected governmental agencies—lost considerable credibility during the 1980s. Its one-sidedness served poorly the ever-necessary objective of respect for law in industrial relations, which is so vital to a democratic society like ours. This approach also impeded the goal of our globally competitive economy, which is forever dependent upon harmonious and cooperative relationships between labor and management.

My three decades' work as a labor lawyer who represented management, labor and individual employees, as a law professor and labor law scholar and an impartial labor arbitrator has made me a vigorous proponent of rights and obligations for both labor and management. During the coming four and one-half years of my term, I shall endeavor to return the Board to the center, to promote a balance between the parties—a policy that is inherent in both the National Labor Relations Act and in good sense—and, most important, to let workers, union officials and business people know that they will be treated with respect, civility and fairness.

Before God, my family and friends, and the American people, this is what I pledge to do. I shall do the best job that I can to vindicate President Clinton's expression of confidence in me.

B

The National Labor Relations Board Today

An Address by
William B. Gould IV, Chairman
National Labor Relations Board

Fifteenth Constitutional Convention
Metropolitan Detroit AFL-CIO
May 6, 1994, Westin Hotel
Detroit, Michigan

It is indeed a pleasure and privilege to speak to you here today and to return to Detroit—a city of which I think fondly in connection with my youth and early professional development. As you know, Detroit not only has always been one of the genuine centers of the trade union movement—it is also the birthplace of modern industrial unionism in our country.

Out of the Great Depression of the 1930s, you forged the new unions of this country—the United Auto Workers, by whom I was employed in the early 1960s; the United Rubber Workers, who organized so many of the major tire companies here throughout the Midwest; and the United Steelworkers providing a few of the major examples.

Trade unions are a basic part of our democratic and pluralistic system. As a society, our ability to resolve our differences peaceably, notwithstanding basic differences in race, religion, national origin, language, and culture, is in substantial part attributable to the advent of the unions and the collective-bargaining process in the 1930s, 1940s, and 1950s.

I salute you as agents of this change and for being an integral part of the democratic system which has made our country so well-respected in the eyes of the world. It is often forgotten that your affiliates shaped a very real alternative to violence, riots, and indeed revolution.

I am particularly pleased to be here today for two reasons. The first is a sense of personal nostalgia for which I hope you will indulge me. My first professional work occurred in this city and it all began when I arrived here on June 19, 1960, on a flight from Newark, New Jersey, to Detroit. My first job was at Solidarity House, where I worked as a law clerk between my second and third years at Cornell Law

School in Ithaca, New York—a job to which I walked every day down East Jefferson Avenue from the Hannan YMCA.

Later, again as the result of the recommendation of my professor, the late Kurt Hanslowe, I was to return to the legal staff of the United Auto Workers as an assistant general counsel in 1961 and 1962. In the late 1960s and early 1970s, I returned yet again as a law professor at Wayne State Law School and as an impartial arbitrator. This period of my life contains some of my fondest memories, and to this day, a disproportionate number of my friends are found in this city in the labor movement, the civil rights movement, and the business community. I have a great sense of warmth and emotional involvement with my friends and colleagues in this wonderful city.

The second is more philosophical. As a young boy, I was raised a Democrat in the tradition of President Franklin D. Roosevelt—indeed some might say that I was born into the Democratic party! Because, in the previous century, the Republican Party was the supporter of Reconstruction and rights for blacks in the South, my grandfather and great uncles were Republicans. However, the racial politics of each party was turned on its head in this century. My father told me as a young boy that the last time that he had ever crossed over the line to support those Republicans was 1928, when he voted for Hoover over Al Smith. "Never again" he said to me—and I have followed his commitment to the Democratic party all of my voting life.

Thus, it is a pleasure to come here as a representative of the Clinton administration, albeit as the chief executive officer of an independent regulatory agency. I am grateful to President Bill Clinton for his support of me and to Senator Edward Kennedy for managing my confirmation in the Senate. I thank you in the AFL-CIO as well for your support.

As you know, I received the largest number of "No" votes of any Clinton nominee. I have said earlier—and I say again today—that I intend to let bygones be bygones. But I want you to know that I wear that 58–38 confirmation vote in which every single Democratic Senator voted for me—along with the opposition to me—as a badge of honor.

Now we must look forward. The National Labor Relations Board and the statute that it is charged to interpret are at the vortex of American political debate today—most recently in connection with my own confirmation hearings.

It should never be forgotten that the National Labor Relations Act in its preamble states the following:

It is hereby declared to be the policy of the United States to eliminate the causes of certain substantial obstructions to the free flow of commerce and to mitigate and eliminate these obstructions when they have occurred by encouraging the practice and procedure of collective bargaining and by protecting the exercise by workers of full freedom of association, self-organization, and designation of representatives of their own choosing, for the purpose of negotiating the terms and conditions of their employment or other mutual aid or protection.

These words were first set forth by Senator Wagner as part of the Act as it was written in 1935. They have remained unaltered, notwithstanding the attempts of many to change the law, right through 1994.

The Act is and will remain committed to the collective-bargaining process, and I am here to say to you that, as chairman of the National Labor Relations Board, so am I!

But I am also here to tell you that there are both labor rights and labor wrongs. Last month, at my urging, the Board initiated contempt proceedings against the United Mine Workers in the Court of Appeals for the Sixth Circuit—which covers the State of Michigan—and in the Fourth Circuit as well. These contempt proceedings grew out of extensive violent conduct in which the Mine Workers were involved during last year's bituminous coal strike.

I am against employer lawlessness in attempts to frustrate unions organizing and collective bargaining—but I am also against union lawlessness which undermines the peaceable resolution of disputes. And I say to you today that during my four-years-plus as chairman of the Labor Board, the agency and the statute will be at war with attempts by any side to undermine the process. I shall be even-handed in my approach to statutory violations and contempt. We must be vigilant against lawbreaking, no matter what its source!

As many of you know, I am the first Chairman of the NLRB nominated by a President with a background as an impartial and neutral arbitrator since President Franklin Roosevelt selected University of Chicago Professor Harry Millis in 1940. In the 1990s, I intend to see to it that the Board discharges its obligation to be fair and impartial to both sides and to protect both the collective-bargaining process and peaceable procedures!

In the coming months you will be hearing about a number of initiatives that we are undertaking at the Board. I have long advocated, both prior and subsequent to my appointment as Chairman, the greater use of rulemaking authority which will simplify and expedite our procedures. Justice delayed is justice denied and all too often our procedures are cumbersome and slow-moving.

In the summer months I believe that we will announce a number of changes designed to expedite representation procedures, both through rulemaking, changes in our rules and regulations, and through other means which will make all too often cumbersome procedures move more quickly. These measures can diminish wasteful litigation which undermines employee free choice through delay. When extensive delays occur, employees and employers lose faith in the law.

We have made progress with the backlog of unfair labor practice cases in recent years. But that, in part anyway, is because of our declining credibility during the Reagan 80s. Fewer workers were willing to file charges and petitions with us.

I want to turn both problems around, i.e., encourage parties to use our processes and, at the same time, to respond expeditiously. That is no mean trick in our current period of deficit reduction and budgetary austerity. But we must change some of our behavior so as to serve the public, our customers, more effectively. We will need to work with you, enlightened business representatives, and all of those who have the public interest at heart in achieving these objectives.

In a related area, we are in the process of examining the issue of postal or mail ballots in NLRB-conducted elections. All too often, workers who are laid off, ill, retired or on strike are not able to participate in the franchise because they are scattered and absent from the workplace. Some of these categories are excluded from the ballot altogether. I hope that we will expand the franchise and allow more people to participate in our processes.

On another front, we have already been active in obtaining injunctions against unfair labor practices. In the almost eight weeks that I have been in my job, I and my colleagues have signed 10 requests for temporary injuctions against Employer fair labor practices which were designed to frustrate the collective-bargaining process—one of them aimed at the Caterpillar Company and methods that it used in its ongoing dispute with United Auto Workers.

As I have written in a book of which the Republicans made much during the confirmation process, the use of temporary injunctions by the Board has declined in recent years. This is a trend that has been already reversed since we have come to Washington—and it is a trend that I believe will continue in the future months and years to come.

Finally, on April 11, I appointed panels of union and management lawyers composed of 50 of the country's most distinguished labor law practitioners. These panels are designed to advise us about procedural problems and our need to be more efficient. Ted Sachs, your General Counsel, is a member of our panel—and I think the participation of Ted and other like-minded, public-spirited lawyers will help us foster more genuine cooperation and dialogue.

For, in the final analysis, I hope that this will be the legacy of my chairmanship that in this period of the 90s the Board assisted the parties coming together and gaining a greater sense of mutuality. The parties, labor and management, are inevitably interdependent. You, here in Detroit, have played an important role in recognizing and promoting this truth.

It is a pleasure to come back to Detroit again and to see so many good and old friends. Detroit, like California where I reside and New Jersey where I was raised, is a real home to me. I look forward to working with you and other interested parties during my term as Chairman in Washington. I pledge to you that I will do the very best job I can during my tenure in the Capitol. Thank you for giving me this chance to speak to you and to return yet, again to a city, that I love.

C

This Generation's Reconciliation

Address by
William B. Gould IV, Chairman
National Labor Relations Board

Distinguished Speaker Luncheon
National Academy of Arbitrators
Forty-Seventh Annual Meeting
Minneapolis Hilton and Towers
Minneapolis, Minnesota
May 28, 1994

It is a special pleasure to have the opportunity to speak to you here today. This occasion is proof positive for the proposition that you can, indeed, come home again; for, as you may know, I became a member of this organization almost a quarter of a century ago in 1970, a period so long ago that it now seems lost in the distant haze of another era.

At that time, I was in Detroit as a law professor at Wayne State University Law School and a neighbor of such Academy worthies as Dick Mittenthal, the late Harry Platt, Ron Haughton, and Mark Kahn, with whom I taught a seminar available to law, economics, and industrial relations students at the university. Thus the academy holds old and fond memories for me, and it is good to see so many old friends and to have the opportunity to make new ones as well.

Once in each generation or so, a broad theme emerges which characterizes that particular era. In the Eisenhower 1950s, the first period which influenced me, it was McCarthyism and anti-Communist hysteria which went with it, and the contentment and middle-class prosperity that was attracted to "I like Ike."

In the 1960s it was intense conflict and upheaval vaguely reminiscent of the Great Depression, New Deal, and Wagner Act—first over civil rights and related domestic inequities and then, with regard to the Vietnam conflict and the various forms of civil disobedience which arose out of that engagement. For the next decade, it was Watergate, which accelerated a sense of cynicism already rampant by virtue of the Vietnam War.

Disraeli said, "We, all of us, live too much in circles"—and yet, the1980s brought with them another round of moral torpor and greed reminiscent of both the 1950s and 1920s. Now President Clinton's focus on a comprehensive national medical insurance program—an idea first put forth by President Truman almost a half a century ago—suggests a renewed sense of morality which brings to mind the domestic initiatives undertaken in both the Kennedy and Johnson administrations and the New Deal and Fair Deal which went before them. The end of the Cold War in the 1990s not only allows for more attention to domestic issues but also reminds us of St. Matthew's aphorism that the peacemakers are blessed.

We have been in the business of peacemaking for some years—though I know that most of us would have difficulty recognizing ourselves in the laudatory and effusive passages of the *Steelworkers Trilogy* written by Justice Douglas thirty-four years ago. Yet it seems obvious that the need to substitute peaceable procedures for conflict and to promote cooperation in human relationships in a period of change is a subject with which we have considerable familiarity.

The bulk of the arbitration which blankets unionized industry and much of the public sector in this country has emerged since the emergency conditions of World War II and the promotion of arbitration under the auspices of the War Labor Board. It is often said that the developments of the 1940s, of which the War Labor Board and arbitration procedures were a major part, outrank the importance of the 1930s and the rise of the new unions at that time. The institutional developments, of which you have been such a major part, principally voluntary and private, are associated with events which are now half a century old.

The emergence of our voluntary system of private arbitration in the United States is one of the best illustrations of new methods to deal with a changing social circumstance, in this case, in the workplace. As the United States Supreme Court has noted on countless occasions, this system has served to function as a substitute for industrial strife for labor and management. If it has had difficulty completely adjusting to the new world of employment discrimination and individual employee rights, nonetheless, it seems clear the new field of alternative dispute resolution owes its existence to the success of arbitration in employment.

This May 1994, reminds us of other profound changes even more considerable than the arbitration process of which you have been a part—changes which contain graphic parallels to your work. Last week, we celebrated the fortieth anniversary of *Brown* v. *Board of Education*, the Supreme Court's decision in which separate but equal in public education was declared to be unconstitutional under both the Fourteenth and the Fifteenth amendments to the Constitution. Tony Lewis of the *New York Times*, in his important book, *A Portrait of Our Times,* highlighted the significance of *Brown* and its role in substituting reconciliation in the place of conflict.

For *Brown*, whatever its limitations and the frustrations associated with desegregation of public education, produced a nonviolent revolution in our country which led to agitation for civil rights legislation in the late-1950s and the 1960s, beginning with the Civil Rights Act of 1957 and carrying forward to the important and consequential legislation enacted in 1964 (employment and public accommodations), 1965 (voting rights), and 1966 (private housing). As Lewis noted last week: "What happened was that protests, and brutal suppression of those protests by white officials, aroused the conscience of Americans who had not known or cared much about segregation. President Kennedy made the first speech ever from the White House calling racism a moral issue. President Johnson pressed for action."

Inequities, along racial and social lines, are ever with us—and in some respects more deep and divisive than those which existed thirty years ago. The big cities are overwhelmed with the problem of drugs, crime, and the tawdriness associated with both. But the fact is that *Brown* presaged a nonviolent revolution where blacks moved into positions of responsibility in both the private and public sector, and where black political representation increased enormously.

Two weeks ago, I participated in events reminiscent of *Brown* and its progeny at a ceremony which in some respects was even more startling. I stood outside the Union Buildings in Pretoria, South Africa, and witnessed the inauguration of Nelson Mandela as the first black president of the Republic of South Africa. The May 10 inauguration was, in some respects, the logical culmination of efforts that have taken place throughout the West during the past three hundred years, beginning with England's bloodless revolution of 1688, the Declaration of Rights in France and its revolution, as well as our own Declaration of Independence, the Constitution, its Bill of Rights and, ultimately and most important, the post–Civil War amendments.

In the United States, of course, even when the country attempted to correct the previous century's *Dred Scott* decision, which declared that blacks were property, the promise of the Constitution was not realized through actual deeds of government or private parties. The result of the Civil War was the abandonment of human rights through both the 1877 Compromise, which brought Rutherford Hayes to the

White House, and Supreme Court decisions which narrowly limited the post–Civil War amendments. The emergence of Jim Crow and the Supreme Court's proclamation of the constitutional acceptability of "separate but equal" in public transportation in the 1896 ruling of *Plessy* v. *Ferguson*, as well as congressional abdication of its role in the post–World War II era, made it necessary for the Supreme Court to speak out against apartheid in this country in the 1954 *Brown* ruling.

But in South Africa, the situation was quite different. No written constitution or independent judiciary with the capability to render legislation invalid through judicial review existed. Until the 1990s, blacks had no right to move freely throughout the Republic. And again, until that decade, interracial marriage or sexual relations were prohibited by statute—and blacks were excluded from jobs by statute on the basis of race. Indeed, until this decade, all rights of citizenship and political participation were nonexistent.

My first published writing was a review of Alan Paton's book, *Hope for South Africa* in *The New Republic*, in September 1959. But at that point there appeared to be precious little hope indeed. The only prospect was that of recurrent violence between the political and economic leadership, which possessed modern weaponry and an efficient military fighting force, and the black masses who attempted to resist the laws of oppression. The prospect was Armageddon.

President Mandela's appointment of so many of his major opponents to key positions in his cabinet vividly demonstrates his commitment to the politics of reconciliation between the races and contending points of view in that country. In the broadest sense, the new government's commitment of the politics of inclusiveness dramatizes its belief in innovative methods of conflict resolution. As President Mandela put it on May 10: "We must ... act together as a united people, for national reconciliation, for nation building, for the birth of a new world.... Never, never and never again shall it be that this beautiful land will again experience the oppression of one by another."

Thus, the challenge in South Africa is to devise a new institutional mechanism to respond to the need to both tackle racial and social inequity and to simultaneously preserve the infrastructure which the country possesses.

I would like to explore with you today four areas in this country where efforts to achieve a similar goal are ongoing, two of which affect my agency, the National Labor Relations Board directly, and one indirectly. All of them, in my view, involve attempts to cut through the barriers of wasteful litigation or confrontation responsible for unnecessary acrimony.

The first relates to our attempts to process litigation at the Board without excessive delay. One of the most vexatious areas under our Act relates to the finding of what constitutes an appropriate unit for the purpose of collective bargaining and, more immediately, for a vote amongst employees to determine whether a union will represent them. All too frequently, disputes about what constitutes the unit for such purposes have provided the basis for substantial delays, conflict, and maneuvering under numerous criteria, some of which play no actual role in the Board's decision. This problem was a principal factor in the Board's decision a few years ago to devise a mechanical rule which would diminish, if not eliminate, the potential for such disputes in the acute healthcare industry.

Where the employer possesses more than one facility, frequently there have been disputes about whether the single facility is the appropriate unit or whether it shall consist of multiple facilities. Over the past almost sixty years of the Act there has been extensive litigation involving such factors as geographical separation, autonomy of the location manager, extensive employee interchange, contact between facilities, functional integration, and various other matters—and in 1994 the litigation still continues!

If the Board devised a relatively mechanical rule which focused upon one or two factors and allowed for dispute only in the most extraordinary of circumstances— an approach already used in acute health care cases—the potential for delay in representation proceedings and the consequent impact that would have upon employee loss of faith in the law might be diminished considerably.

The agency committed itself to rulemaking in the acute health industry area prior to my arrival on March 14, and the results, if measured by the frequency of resort litigation in the courts, are dramatic and positive. As many of you know, this venture has successfully concluded with affirmance of our authority by the United States Supreme Court.

A process begun by my predecessors, and one in which I am involved now, relates to the Supreme Court's 1988 ruling in the *Communications Workers of America* v. *Beck* case, where the Court held that the National Labor Relations Act prohibits a union, over the objections of dues-paying nonmember employees, from expending funds collected from those employees (pursuant to a union-security clause) for purposes not germane to collective bargaining. A whole host of issues has emerged under *Beck* for the agency. Again, prior to my appointment, the rule-making process was invoked.

It may be that a variety of other issues lend themselves to rulemaking. Some issues relating to the jurisdiction of the Board might be good examples. Moreover, the whole area of campaign tactics (i.e., captive audience speeches and other matters) may appropriately fall in this arena—just as the Board has utilized its authority to oblige employers to provide unions with the names and addresses of employees when an election is ordered.

The second area in which litigation could be diminished again relates to the Labor Board itself. A number of years ago I wrote a book, *Japan's Reshaping of American Labor Law*, which suggested that the American NLRB has much to learn from its Japanese counterpart, established, as it was, at the end of World War II by virtue of the MacArthur occupation. As a general, proposition, the Japanese Board is much more active in promoting settlements than its American counterpart.

Of course, two cautionary notes are very much in order in this regard. The first is that the American Board does promote a substantial number of settlements, generally in excess of 96 percent of the charges filed. However, the difficulty is that most of this settlement activity occurs prior to the issuance of a complaint, that is, before the battle lines are drawn and hardened. The second is that the ability to transplant practices from another country are difficult indeed because of the obvious cultural differences—particularly between Japan and the United States—which are part of the industrial relations systems and the law, contrasts which impose limits upon the ability to compare practices and law.

Nonetheless, it is possible to learn something from the experience of another country. It appears that our administrative law judges, who have a direct involvement at the time that a complaint is issued, vary substantially in terms of their degree of intervention with a view toward promoting settlement and discouraging litigation. I shall be meeting a group of senior administrative law judges early next week with a view toward promoting a greater potential for the dispute resolution process—and, indeed, have sought the views of others both inside and outside of the agency on this matter.

It is ironic that the American system has devoted such considerable energy to sophisticated dispute resolution techniques in both the private and public sector on grievance and interest disputes, matters frequently discussed and analyzed at your Academy meetings—but yet comparatively little attention has been given to procedures which might operate in the area of public law so as to diminish the amount of litigation which would otherwise take place. One of my major initiatives, with a view toward diminishing administrative litigation before our agency, is to institute more effective mediatory initiatives by our administrative law judges to resolve unfair labor practices prior to hearing.

A third area is one which Academy members are familiar with and which I spoke to you about in Chicago a decade ago. This is the subject of wrongful or unfair dismissals and the extent to which new procedures, arbitration constituting the best example, could be put in place in lieu of the existing system of litigation in courts of general jurisdiction. Causes of action in the employment relationship over the past ten to twenty years have increased considerably in number. The Civil Rights Act of 1991, which amended in significant respects the 1964 legislation, and the Americans With Disabilities Act of 1990 will cause an even greater increase in such litigation.

The prospect of expensive and substantial litigation which is vexatious to both sides has led to a consideration of alternatives to such law suits. In the wrongful discharge area, the expense of litigation is undoubtedly harmful to most employees and the disproportionate number of managerial and white collar employees who have used the wrongful discharge theories demonstrates the importance of income to litigation and the necessary involvement of an attorney whose financial stake is frequently predicated upon a contingency-fee arrangement.

The system is also harmful to employers because of the erratic and unpredictable nature of juries, which sometimes have been known to award multimillion dollar punitive and compensatory damage judgments predicated upon the depth of the defendants' pockets.

Another problem here is the inherent vagueness of many of the concepts used in wrongful-discharge litigation. For instance, it has been held that longevity of employment is an important prerequisite to maintaining an action under the covenant of good faith and fair dealing concept. But how long must the employee be employed? Since these are common law actions, the matter cannot be addressed with precision as would be the case under a statute. Moreover, the idea that an employee may not be dismissed for reasons inconsistent with the public policy of the state is not only inherently vague but also of benefit primarily to higher-echelon employees who are likely to be in a position to blow the whistle on the misdeeds of the employer.

Moreover, the problem of liability is considerable. As I have already indicated, many of these judgments are of the multimillion variety. This is because of the availability of punitive as well as compensatory damages, and it encourages, perhaps excessively, employees to roll the dice in the hopes that their number may emerge in the lottery before a sympathetic jury.

A decade ago a special California State Bar Committee which I co-chaired recommended comprehensive legislation providing for arbitration and limited liability. Two years ago the National Conference of Commissioners of Uniform State Laws recommended a similar model. But, no state, except Montana, has enacted legislation which regulates this matter.

In the meantime, subsequent to the California report, an increasing number of employers have introduced so-called at-will clauses, under which employees agree to be subject to dismissal at will or without cause. The Supreme Court in the *Gilmer* decision has facilitated the binding nature of wrongful-dismissal agreements which provide for arbitration—a process which may be controlled and/or financed by the employer unencumbered with the presence of any other party.

Both developments are one-sided and unfair and thus argue even more persuasively for legislation along the lines of that proposed in California ten years ago.

On the other hand, it is said that the California proposals would be the full-employment act for arbitrators and thus swell the Academy's ranks to untold numbers! I leave for your consideration and discussion the implications of such prosperity. I cannot resist noting that it would provide you with a wonderful opportunity to increase the numbers of minorities and women in your ranks—an area where you could use lots of improvement!

But your numbers may be diminished by the last area that I want to discuss. This is the attempt to develop, in both nonunion and unionized circumstances, non-adversarial procedures through which cooperation between employees, employers, and the unions, is promoted. The emergence of employee committees and other cooperative mechanisms in the organized sector in some circumstances heralds a more infrequent invocation of grievance-arbitration machinery. But the verdict is still out on whether the same results apply in nonunion firms where arbitration is used to ward off the dreadful prospect of punitive and compensatory damage awards.

Numerous issues relating to the introduction of procedures facilitating cooperation will be coming before the Board shortly. So also will the cases relating to employee committees in the nonunion context.

Two of the most prominent relationships where the interdependence of labor and management and the need for cooperation have been recognized are at the Saturn Corporation, a wholly owned subsidiary of General Motors, and NUMMI, New

United Motors Manufacturers, Incorporated, the General Motors/Toyota Joint Venture in Freemont, California—both relationships being with the United Automobile Workers. The attempt in both situations has been to eliminate archaic work rules and rigid job classifications, to compress job categories into a very small number so as to promote managerial flexibility. Part and parcel of this is the development of a team system where workers assume the challenge of designing their job and, in some instances, possess disciplinary functions as well. Indeed, at Saturn, both the lines between the employees and their supervisors have been blurred if not obliterated by virtue of supervisory responsibility in the discipline area undertaken by union *and* employer representatives who work together as "unit module advisors."

The payoff, if you will, for employees, is twofold. First, both NUMMI and Saturn provide strong pledges against potential for dismissals. In NUMMI the employer obligated itself to utilize alternative methods including "the reduction of salaries of its officers and management" before economic dismissals or layoffs are instituted. At Saturn the union is involved in virtually all aspects of decision-making in the management-prerogative arena—the investment planning and the like.

Our statute does not mandate such procedures and relationships. But the fact that the parties have undertaken such efforts independently demonstrates maturity and means, in my judgment, that a greater measure of economic democracy is reaching the workplace, notwithstanding the limits of law. The new economic democracy is a mirror image of the political democracy produced by the *Brown* decision and President Mandela.

But just as the wrongful-discharge arena giveth more business to your members, so also the parties' reliance upon their own mechanisms may taketh it away. Notwithstanding my good wishes to old Academy colleagues, primary reliance upon new mechanisms are the bedrock of autonomy, the virtue so frequently associated with your work.

All these developments that I have discussed with you today—beginning with *Brown*, on through Nelson Mandela's inauguration, as well as our four labor issues—present opportunities to promote dialogue, understanding, and reconciliation between old adversaries.

Justice William Brennan—your distinguished speaker at this luncheon a few years ago—stressed the role of antagonistic viewpoints and self-interest in collective bargaining in a 1960 opinion issued a few months before *Steelworkers Trilogy*. To suggest some modifications to that well-accepted philosophy does not necessarily mean that the lion will lie down with the lamb or that old foes will love their enemies. But you peacemakers of this world are best positioned to promote and practice reconciliation through word and deed—to bring the political changes in the United States and South Africa into the workplace of this decade and the next.

I wish you good luck on this and on your deliberations here in Minneapolis generally!

D

The Last Chairman of the National Labor Relations Board?: The Law and Politics of Labor Policy in the First Hundred Days

Address by
William B. Gould IV, Chairman
National Labor Relations Board

The Commonwealth Club of America
Luncheon Meeting
Sheraton Palace Hotel
San Francisco, California
Friday, June 10, 1994

It is a pleasure to be back with you in the Bay Area today. This is my first opportunity to return to my home after what has been approximately a hundred days in office since the United States Senate confirmed me on March 2, 1994, by a vote of 58–38. I am particularly grateful to both President Clinton for his nomination of me a year ago and his support in what was a difficult confirmation process—I received the most "No" votes of any Clinton nominate thus far nominated—and to Senator Edward Kennedy of Massachusetts for handling the confirmation process in the Senate and managing the floor debate on my behalf.

Similarly, I am most appreciative for the unstinting support provided me by Congresswoman Anna Eshoo, of my congressional district, and Congresswoman Nancy Pelosi of San Francisco, along with Senators Dianne Feinstein and Barbara Boxer. I have enjoyed immensely the opportunity to work with Congresswoman Pelosi on appropriations for the Board, and I look forward to a good and constructive relationship with her in the future.

The National Labor Relations Board, of which I am Chairman, is a relatively small agency which has 2,100 employees and 33 regions throughout the United States, 2 of them here in the Bay area in San Francisco and Oakland. As the collective-bargaining process has declined throughout the nation—and the number of workers represented by unions in the private sector which our statute covers has gone down to 11.2 percent, according to the Bureau of Labor Statistics, and some think that it will decline further, a phenomenon attributable to many factors which I and others have written about in books and articles—some have speculated about the decline of our own agency.

Some say that the decline in union-represented employees is attributable to the law and the interpretation of it provided by the Board and the judiciary. Although the factors involved in this phenomenon are numerous and complicated, I have expressed the view in testimony given to a House Labor Subcommittee a decade ago that federal labor law has failed in implementing the statutory objectives and that the Board, during the Reagan and Bush years, was excessively one-sided. Its credibility with labor, some elements of management, and the public and thus the respect for law suffered as well, a factor which a democratic society can ill afford.

Whatever the reasons, the decline is there for all to see. And there are some who believe that the unions' share of the workplace can decline to as little as 5 percent of the private sector before the turn of the century.

This much is clear. Both the labor movement and the collective-bargaining process are in difficulty—and the labor law, which my agency administers—is in considerable difficulty as well.

The problem is best described, though in somewhat exaggerated form, by an acquaintance, the wife of a prominent federal judge in Washington, who introduced me at a cocktail party in that city shortly after my arrival in Washington. She said to the person to whom I was introduced: "This is Bill Gould. He is the last chairman of the National Labor Relations Board."

Now I don't believe that I will be the last chairman of the National Labor Relations Board—and I certainly don't want to obtain such a dubious distinction. But the comment does highlight the crises that confronts both this agency and the statute.

In 1994, the Board and the Act are confronted with hostility and suspicion from both labor and management. Segments of management have not believed in the mission of the Act, which is to promote the practice and procedure of collective bargaining as well as freedom of association for workers. Unions have grown increasingly skeptical of our willingness and our ability to deliver on the statutory promise.

As I have expressed in earlier writings, the collective-bargaining process, which the statute properly supports, is still one of the best ways to resolve employee-employer problems—and this policy is contained in the preamble which states:

It is hereby declared to be the policy of the United States to eliminate the causes of certain substantial obstructions to the free flow of commerce and to mitigate and eliminate these obstructions when they have occurred by encouraging the practice and procedure of collective bargaining and by protecting the exercise by workers of full freedom of association, self-organization, and designation of representatives of their own choosing, for the purpose of negotiating the terms and conditions of their employment or other mutual aid or protection.

It is important to note that this policy—first expressed in the original Wagner Act—was not amended or changed by the 1947 or 1959 amendments to the Act in spite of efforts to do so.

In order for there to be an environment in which this statutorily-mandated policy flourishes, at least three things must happen. First, the unions themselves must be reborn perhaps along the lines of what happened in the Great Depression in the 1930s, both here on the west-coast docks as well in industry throughout basic manufacturing across the country. Secondly, as I have written during the past decade, the Act itself must be strengthened through amendment.

But today I am here to speak with you about the statute as it is written and as I and my colleagues at the Board are charged to administer it. For this is the third and most immediate avenue through which the preamble objectives can be implemented.

It is difficult to achieve major changes in an independent regulatory agency such as the National Labor Relations Board, let alone in the first 100 days of a chairmanship. But I am encouraged at the progress we have made to date at moving in some constructive new directions.

The first steps about which I shall speak to you relate to the way in which we conduct our own business. I have re-instituted the weekly Board agenda at which all Board members meet in a collegial fashion to discuss and vote on the most important impending issues. Such meetings have been scheduled through Thanksgiving of this year—and we have been at work on a considerable backlog of significant cases, with decisions anticipated as Washington's languid summer becomes more intense.

One of the reasons that some would believe or would like to believe that I would be the last chairman of the Board is that our procedures have become cumbersome, creaky and open to exploitation aimed at obtaining delay. One of my first initiatives at the Board has been to focus attention upon procedures which can streamline if not cure some of the immediate problems. These initiatives are important for a number of reasons.

The first is that we are operating within a period of austerity. We need to find ways in which, to use the parlance of Vice President Gore, we can more effectively satisfy our customers, i.e., labor, management and the public interest.

One of the basic problems that we confront is the proliferation of wasteful litigation under our Act—particularly as it relates to disputes about representation and whether a union will represent employees in some kind of collective bargaining process. I have said elsewhere that notwithstanding whatever good the act accomplishes, one of its unintended consequences has been to become a full employment Act for labor lawyers on both sides of the fence who creatively re-invent the litigation wheel in NLRB proceedings.

On June 3 a unanimous Board held in *Bennett Industries, Inc.* (313 NLRB [1994]) that a party's refusal to take a position at a representation hearing precludes further litigation on the issue in dispute because: (1) the refusal to take a position when introducing evidence "... may in some circumstances signify a lack of good faith"; (2) to permit further litigation would be unwise because it condones "... duplicative procedures, unjustified delays, and unnecessary expenses for all parties, including the Board."

The Board needs to speak more simply and clearly so that both sides will know what their rights and obligations are in advance of initiating procedures before us. Thus, in a third initiative, on June 2 of this year, the Board filed an advance notice of proposed rulemaking in the *Federal Register* and invited the comments of all interested parties on the way in which the Board can best fulfill its statutory obligation to determine an appropriate unit when a single location unit is sought by one side and where there is a dispute about whether this constitutes an appropriate unit for the purpose of collective bargaining in the trucking, retail, or manufacturing industries.

Let me just give you an illustration of what this is all about. Frequently, a union files a petition to represent an employee in a particular facility, be it a fast food outlet or a trucking facility. The employer responds by stating that the union is seeking the wrong appropriate unit or grouping of employees for the purposes of collective bargaining. The matter must go to a hearing and be litigated on the basis of how close the facilities are and how much the employees are interchanged between the facilities and a whole host of other considerations—many of which are rarely viewed by the Board as critical or dispositive. Adversarial litigation is encouraged by the hearing process in which counsel are invited to joust about the numerous criteria announced by our decisions of these past 59 years.

Would it not be simpler to advise the parties through a stated rule in advance with substantial precision? A limited number of factors could make the appropriate unit determination more understandable—and this would provide parties with precise guidance, i.e., the facilities cannot be merged together as a unit where two facilities are more than one mile apart from one another.

If we speak with precision on these issues it seems to me that it diminishes the potential for litigation and consequent delay. This is particularly important in the 1990s where we are in the period of budget austerity and where it is quite possible that changes in our rules will invite more parties to use our processes because of our enhanced credibility.

The same cost savings consideration is one of the reasons that I have tentatively accepted the arguments of some unions in favor of a wider use of the postal or mail ballots in NLRB-conducted elections and voted for their use in the *Lone Star* case in last month Seattle, Washington. I have established a task force which will report back to me about the feasibility of introducing postal ballots under more circumstances than used in the past.

A basic rationale for the postal ballot is that we need to expand the franchise and to reach more employees so that the question of whether the union is to represent employees or not will be more truly democratic. But equally important, it seems apparent that in many portions of the country—particularly in many of our large western regions where Board agents have to travel for substantial miles when they are conducting an NLRB election held at the workplace—it may be less expensive to do it this way.

Traditionally, as you may know, these votes are conducted at the work site on plant premises. But one difficulty is that workers who are scattered by virtue of being ill or retired or laid off or are on strike are not able to have access to the ballot under these circumstances. Postal ballots, on the other hand, would reach a broader group of workers, some of whom are now excluded by the Board's own rules no matter what the form of the ballot.

In spacious states like Nevada and Arizona where vast expanses of land are served by one Board agent in a given electoral process, it may be more practical and efficient and inexpensive to use the postal ballot rather than the traditional manual one.

If we gain the credibility of the public in establishing the democratic procedures for which workers can express their right to freely associate and designate their representatives, more parties would use our process and, of course, our budget problems will grow. But simultaneously, whatever the future caseload is, we must save public monies and one way that we can do this is through the postal ballot that we have used in *Lone Star*.

Of course, postal ballots may present a range of problems not present in manual elections. These will be studied by my task force before the Board makes a final decision. But as California and others provide more absentee ballots—I sent mine through the Postal Service two weeks ago—the idea that more mail ballots are incompatible with democratic civilizations appears even more implausible.

One other area is of vital importance. Since my first day on the job on March 14, I have signed 24 requests for temporary injunctive relief. If the National Labor Relations Act redeems its statutory promise of freedom of association and the promotion of collective bargaining, prompt relief must be available under appropriate circumstances.

The General Counsel, in May, made requests of the Board for authorization to institute discretionary injunctive proceedings under Section 10(j) of the act in 14 cases—this is the highest number of requests in a single month made by the General Counsel to the Board since 10(j) was enacted in 1947.

In concluding, let me mention two other noteworthy developments. As a labor law professor and arbitrator I have always taken the view that in a modern system of industrial relations, not only does democracy mean that the collective-bargaining process is to be promoted, but that also there must be rights and obligations for both sides. I shall adhere to the same evenhanded approach at the Board.

Accordingly, I have voted with a Board majority to initiate contempt proceedings against the United Mine Workers where violent and unlawful behavior was engaged in in violation of a consent decree entered into with our agency. The UMW has a proud and honorable tradition in the annals of labor-management relations in the United States. It played a central role in the birth of the industrial unions during the Great Depression. But no party, union or employer, is above the law.

I agree with Justice Brandeis's view when he said:

The unions should take the position squarely that they are amenable to law, prepared to take the consequences if they transgress, and thus show that they are in full sympathy with the spirit of our people whose political system rests upon the proposition that this is a government of law, and not of man.

As I stated, in my October 1, 1993, confirmation hearings, my professional life has been dedicated to an even and balanced approach to labor-management relations. I intend to enforce the law in a balanced fashion and to use our remedies and contempt proceedings against all who break the law, whether they be labor or management representatives.

Finally, in order to discharge my responsibilities more effectively, in April of this year I appointed a panel of fifty of America's most distinguished labor law practitioners. Half of them represent unions and the other half employers. Serving on these panels are some of San Francisco's most distinguished labor lawyers from both sides of the table—like Duane Beeson, William Coday, Maureen McClain, and Morton Orenstein.

I expect these individuals to provide us with valuable recommendations as we fashion solutions to procedural problems that have plagued the Board over the years.

The first meeting of these labor and management lawyers will be later this month. My hope is that the panels not only will provide us with input but also promote dialogue between the parties. For, in the final analysis, as the first impartial neutral selected by a President to chair, let alone be a member of, the National Labor Relations Board since President Franklin Roosevelt appointed Professor Harry A. Millis of the University of Chicago in 1940, my hope is to promote a dialogue and a more cooperative environment between the parties.

As you can see, the problems confronting the Board and indeed the National Labor Relations Act today are formidable. Thus, my hope is that the Board can be a principal agent in fostering a genuine dialogue and more cooperation between labor and management where both sides have an understanding for each of the others' rights and obligations and where an inevitable interdependence and a sense of mutuality is recognized. In turn, this will encourage the collective bargaining process as promised by the statute.

I will do the best that I can to accomplish this objective. For what is the alternative? To allow further erosion of the process? Surely that is not the answer of democratic pluralism.

I take the view, as has former Secretary of Labor George Schultz, that our democracy needs unions as "a system of checks and balances" against arbitrary conduct, both potential and actual. You can rest certain that I do not intend to be the last chairman of the National Labor Relations Board.

E

Tribute to Jack Sheinkman

An Address by
William B. Gould IV, Chairman
National Labor Relations Board

The Jack Sheinkman Endowment Fund Dinner
National Labor Relations Board
Sheraton New York Hotel & Towers
New York, N.Y.
November 2, 1994

Sixty years ago the Great Depression brought forth new unions and leadership—the likes of Hillman, Reuther, Lewis, Murray, Randolph, and Bridges—who took giant steps across the pages of history. In the midst of profound upheaval, Congress and President Franklin Roosevelt gave birth to a new bill of rights for workers in the form of the National Labor Relations Act of 1935, an important part of which was and is an independent administrative agency, the National Labor Relations Board, which I now chair.

The eighties and nineties have brought new challenges to both the labor movement and the policies of the NLRA—and to the idea expressed by President Lincoln in his first Annual Message to Congress: "Capital is only the fruit of labor and could never have existed if labor had not first existed."

This period of history, in which the Reagan-Bush assumption that one side of the bargaining table should possess unfettered discretion, was uncritically accepted by too many and has sorely tested the resolve and talents of a new union leadership, of which Jack Sheinkman stands second to none.

I first came to know Jack Sheinkman in 1959 when he was general counsel to the Amalgamated Clothing Workers and I was a first-year student at Cornell Law School aspiring to be a labor lawyer. Though the passage of time over these thirty-five years of friendship makes us more like contemporaries, he was and is a genuine role model for me at every step of my career—and for countless others as well!

The beginnings of our friendship were sparked, in part, by the reality that we both had lived at 109 Williams Street in Ithaca as young law students. And it was Jack Sheinkman, ever full of generous counsel and support, who brought me to the attention of President Kennedy's Chairman of the NLRB so that I was able to join his staff in 1963.

The President Jack Sheinkman that I know today is principled, tough and no-nonsense, ever the worthy adversary at the bargaining table and in politics—and yet compassionate and—Cornell graduate and drum major that he is—always open to new ideas and new friends. His leadership and tenure have promoted innovative, cooperative partnerships between labor and management, the type of which President Clinton extolled in his 1994 Labor Day message.

On November 3, 1932, at the end of an earlier campaign which promoted the human condition as well as the hopes and aspirations of all men and women in this country—like this one in 1994 can now do again—President Roosevelt said: "There is no indispensable man."

So it is today and will ever be. But our friend Jack Sheinkman, with his un-questioned vision and humanity comes closest to the unattainable. Like all of you, I salute and applaud him as both a friend and leader—and not only wish him the best for himself and his good family, but also I count upon the benefit of his wise counsel for us in the years to come.

F

Baseball and the Sultan of Swat: The Curse of the Bambino

An Address by
Willliam B. Gould IV, Chairman
National Labor Relations Board

Charles A. Beardsley Professor of Law
Stanford Law School
A Conference Commemorating the 100th Birthday of Babe Ruth
Hofstra University
Hempstead, New York
April 27, 1995

Issuing the injunction before opening day is important to insure that the symbolic value of that day is not tainted by an unfair labor practice and the NLRB's inability to take effective steps against its perpetuation.—Opinion of Judge Sonya Sotomayor, Southern District of New York in *Silverman* v. *Major League Baseball Players Relations Committee, Inc.*, April 3, 1995.

Like the Constitution, the Flag, and "straight ahead" jazz, baseball, to paraphrase President Clinton, is the "glue" which holds the nation together. Combining the analytical and cerebral with the country's passion for that which is romantic, it is one of life's eternal verities in which the clock stands still forever, transcending all periods of one's life—a game in which there is no buzzer or horn in the form of an arbitrary or predestined time limitation. Like life itself, it gives one the sense and hope that it could go on forever, but in reality, meanders through streams and corners which defy all earthly predictions.

The "Babe" made the dramatic home run central to this game, and the expressions associated with the "roundtripper" as well as the game's other aspects have permeated the entire English language, at least on this side of the Atlantic. And it is certainly appropriate in a paper which addresses the "curse of the Bambino" to note that this tradition of grand majestic long drives has lived on in Red Sox lore over the years, first with Jimmy Foxx—and then, in my memory, in the 1940s, 1970s, and early 1980s in the form of Williams, Stephens, York, Doerr, Yaz, Tony

C., Rice, Lynn, Scott, Evans, and so many others. Canseco, Vaughn, and Whiten carry on this great tradition in the new shining season of 1995, which burst forth this week, like spring itself, full of promise, hope and fantasy.

On March 31, the day of Judge Sotomayor's oral bench opinion in the baseball case in which the National Labor Relations Board successfully sought an injunction against alleged owner unfair labor practices, she said:

The often leisurely game of baseball is filled with many small moments which catch a fan's breath. There is, for example, that wonderful second when you see an outfielder back-pedaling and jumping up to the wall, and time stops for an instant as he jumps up and you finally figure out whether it is a home run, a double or a single off the wall, or an out.

More than a quarter of a century before the 1995 baseball case, on a typically warm, humid night in D.C. (later RFK) Stadium, Dick Ellsworth was on the hill for the Red Sox against the hometown Washington Senators and was tiring in the late innings. But, Dick Williams, the Bosox manager from 1967 through 1969, had no one in the bullpen to relieve Ellsworth and, thus stayed with him as Hank Allen stepped in at the plate with the Senators trailing by two with two-on and two-out in the bottom of the ninth. Allen hit a long shot to deep left center which Reggie Smith, the then Sox center fielder, tracked down and raced to the wall for—and leaped high against the fence.

As he descended to the center field grass, there was that precious moment of which Judge Sotomayor spoke. But in this case, if the ball was over the fence the Senators had won by one run on what the Japanese call a sayonara home run—and if it was caught , the game was over with the Red Sox the victors.

Only when the Sox bullpen erupted racing down the left field line and onto the field to greet Smith, as he held the ball high, was the result apparent. This was that breathless inescapable moment. . . .

And on a brisk Oakland, California, evening twenty years later a ground ball is hit into the hole between short and third, for which Alfredo Griffin ranges far to his right. Griffin turns, as if to throw to first base and the runner from second base advances off the bag, anticipating an effortless capture of the third sack on the throw to first—and in mid-air, with the skill of a ballet dancer, Griffin gracefully twirls and throws to second, eliminating the lead runner from the base paths.

No game is more basic to America's essence than that of baseball. Its elegance and dignity, the big sweep of Burt Blyleven's breaking curve, the heavens opening to the soaring deep fly ball into the distant horizon, as well as the major league pop-up which disappears into the stream of brilliant sunshine and the virtuosity of the double play or "twin killing." And no player is more associated with it than Babe Ruth, the Bambino.

As a young boy, listening to the radio during the 1946 season, I heard Ted Williams strike out with the bases loaded—and my father was able to console me with this comment: "It has happened to the Babe also." And Ruth himself said: "I swing big, with everything I've got. I hit big or I miss big. I like to live as big as I can."

The Babe's early years were in Baltimore, where Cal Ripken and Peter Angelos now hold forth. But his major league professional baseball career began with the Red Sox—as a pitcher who eventually hit twenty-nine homers when switched to the outfield in 1919. And a very fine pitcher he was—particularly in the 1916 and 1918 World Series, which culminated in the Red Sox last World Championships ever. His ERA's in those two post-seasons of play were 0.64 and 1.06 respectively. In those two series he pitched 29-2/3 consecutive scoreless innings, a record that was not broken for forty-three years!

The sale of Babe Ruth to the Yankees from the Red Sox in 1919 to finance owner H. Harrison Frazee's Broadway ventures, does seem to have placed the "Curse of the Bambino" upon the Red Sox.[1] No world championship has been won by the Townies since then, the ultimate goal having been tantalizingly just missed in the seventh games of the 1946, 1967, 1975 and 1986 World Series and in countless other playoffs and tense pennant drives decided on the last day—or, as in 1972, the penultimate day of the season.

I followed every last step of those tense come-from-behind pennant races in 1948 and 1949 when the Sox, having come back from an enormous deficit, in both seasons, lost the pennant on the last day—in 1948 on a play-off date itself, only to be repeated in 1978 when, this time around, a double-digit lead had been squandered against the Yankees.

Like Ruth's $125,000 sale itself, those just-missed championships remind us not only of Luis Aparicio falling to the ground as he rounded third base in 1972, but also the 1946 and 1949 groundouts of Tom McBride and Tom Wright—and even more important, the deficiencies of the Supreme Court's ruling in 1922 in *Federal Baseball* when Justice Holmes, on one of those bad days that all great baseball players have, concluded that baseball was not a business in interstate commerce within the meaning of the Sherman Antitrust Act.[2] But, of course baseball has always been a business—as the National Labor Relations Board recognized when it took jurisdiction over this sport in 1969.[3]

Accordingly, Denny Galehouse would not have been on the mound for the Red Sox in the 1948 play-off game if the St. Louis Browns, like the infinitely more successful 1995 Montreal Expos, had not decided to send their players to big market teams for cash and minor leaguers. Mike Torrez would not have been on the hill in that fateful 1978 play-off game in which Bucky Dent homered, had not Andy Messersmith and Dave McNally prevailed in the arbitration case which made them free agents and produced the first of a series of collective-bargaining agreements allowing major league players to exercise a measure of free agency.

And had not Carlton Fisk, the hero of the sixth World Series game in 1975 by virtue of the extra inning home run that he figuratively willed fair, been able to become a free agent as the result of the Red Sox failure to tender an offer under the 1976 collective agreement, he, rather than Rich Gedman, might have been behind the plate in that nightmarish after-midnight (by daylight saving time) final inning of the 1986 sixth game and would have then gloved Bob Stanley's inside wild pitch which produced the tying run—and thus would have made Bill Buckner's infamous error anticlimactic.

Nothing has more directly affected baseball's on-the-field developments than the legal developments off-the-field. The 1975 *Messersmith* arbitration decision of Peter Seitz, alongside the salary-arbitration provisions first negotiated in 1973, provided the Players Association with a surrogate for antitrust law which *Federal Baseball* and its progeny had earlier denied them.[4] This is the first of a number of ironies affecting baseball and modern employment and labor law.

The second lies in the fact that *Federal Baseball* was never followed by the courts in other major league professional sports such as football, basketball, and hockey. These decisions were influential in establishing unions in these sports because the owners could not avail themselves of the nonstatutory labor exemption to antitrust law without a collective-bargaining agreement and the players could leverage this liability against them. Accordingly, the antitrust decisions initially gave great impetus to unions and an obligation to recognize and bargain collective-bargaining agreements because, in the absence of such agreements, which could provide them with a nonstatutory labor exemption, the owners would be liable for antitrust violations for unreasonable restrictions upon player mobility in the form of reserve clauses, draft procedures and the like. By virtue of *Federal Baseball*, and the Supreme Court's affirmance of it in both the *Toolson* and *Curt Flood* decisions, baseball players did not have the same advantage.[5]

But the second phase of the antitrust decisions dealing with the nonstatutory labor exemption has produced a more profound irony. For in at least two circuit courts of appeals—the District of Columbia and the Second Circuit—the courts have said that owners may avail themselves of the labor exemption after having negotiated an agreement, even when unsuccessful in negotiating a subsequent agreement—unless the employment relationship becomes nonunion altogether. The result of this is that, as Judge Wald properly noted while dissenting in the recent *Brown* v. *Pro Football, Inc.*[6] case, the nonstatutory labor exemption becomes available only under "bizarre" circumstances—that is, where the union pretends to eliminate itself altogether, as the National Football League Players Association did in the wake of the 1987 strike—and as the National Basketball Players Association threatened to do—and then uses the antitrust laws as a vehicle to revive itself for the purpose of negotiating a new agreement and the consequent labor exemption.

The other major result of both *Brown* and *National Basketball Association* v. *Williams*, decided here in the Second Circuit, is that any kind of balance between the properly competing policies of labor and antitrust laws is eliminated altogether.[7] Thus in football, basketball, and presumably hockey, antitrust law and its treble-damages remedy is relegated exclusively to the nonunion sector, thereby creating an incentive for the players in the major professional sports to be nonunion and for employers to foster unionized relationships regardless of their bona fide origin or status—a result which is hardly compatible with the promotion of freedom of association, collective bargaining, and autonomous labor-management relationships—goals all enshrined in the National Labor Relations Act.

In my judgment the new approach to the nonstatutory labor exemption is flawed in another major respect as well. It misconceives the role of National Labor Relations Act. National labor law does not provide for balance, parity, or equality of power, as the D.C. Circuit said.[8] Illustrative of this point is the rule which establishes the lawfulness of permanent economic replacements of strikers engaged in protected activity of the Act.[9] Notwithstanding the Court's comment in *American Ship Building* to the effect that the strike and lockout are "correlative," the economic weaponry provided the parties is not equal and, most important, the statute, as interpreted, does not contemplate such equality.

This, then, is the current backdrop to any discussion about the appropriate relevance of antitrust and labor law to the business of baseball. The Supreme Court, of course, can change both *Brown* and *Williams* and limit the labor exemption to either the point of impasse in the bargaining relationship or, as I have advocated in a book and a couple of articles published during the past fifteen years, at some point subsequent to impasse—perhaps a reasonable period of time transpiring in its wake.[10]

The difficulty with either approach, as Justice Harlan remarked in his separate opinion in the *Borg Warner* decision about some of the rules relating to impasse, is that it is inherently vague—a point noted by the Court of Appeals in *Brown*.[11] But this limitation is infinitely preferable to the untoward policy consequences involved in eliminating antitrust law from basketball and football as the Courts of Appeals in the District of Columbia and New York have done.

Congress, should it apply antitrust law to baseball—and there is no earthly reason why the same standards should not apply to baseball as other major professional sports—would have to address the labor exemption issue and establish some kind of demarcation line for availability of the exemption and a balance between it and the good faith bargaining objectives contained in the National Labor Relations Act.

Whatever the outcome of the antitrust debate, it is clear that labor law has been extremely relevant to the 1994–1995 strike. The difficulty with the National Labor Relations Act—and this has made the unions in professional sports all the more interested in using antitrust law—is its ineffective remedies and poor procedures.[12] My agency, the National Labor Relations Board, can do little about the ineffectiveness of our remedies because of limitations which have been established by the Supreme Court or the language of the act itself. It is difficult for the Board to level the playing field of any relationship within the parameters of existing law.

But there is much that the Board can do within its procedures—particularly with regard to the use of its authority under Section 10(j) to seek temporary injunctive relief against employer and union unfair labor practices. Since I and President Clinton's other NLRB appointees arrived in Washington, D.C. almost 14 months ago, we have used this provision of the law against both employer and union unfair labor practices with unprecedented frequency—a total of 132 times. The purpose is to bypass an unduly time consuming and burdensome administrative process where, by virtue of delay, the relief fashioned would be too late to effectively implement the statute's objectives.

In *Silverman* v. *Major League Players Association*, the Board voted to authorize the use of temporary injunctive relief to restore the status quo ante in the employment relationship which had been altered by virtue of the owners discontinuance of the free agency and salary arbitration system.[13] On March 26, the Board voted to seek injunctive relief against such conduct and, in my view, therefore concluded that there was reasonable cause to believe that this conduct constituted an unfair labor practice and that relief was just and proper—principally because the passage of time would make the remedy, when provided, relatively meaningless.

The Board has no authority to oblige the parties to resume or continue the season—or to fashion an agreement for them. Under our system of voluntary collective bargaining that process is for the parties themselves. The Board's only role is to insure adherence to proper procedures to rid the process of unlawful impediments, and to provide for an appropriate framework for future collective bargaining.

If the administrative process was the only avenue available, restored employment conditions might have been realized in the 1997 season. Meanwhile, the 1995 and 1996 seasons might not have taken place—or under circumstances in which quickly eroding baseball skills could not be compensated under processes established voluntarily by labor and management.

Thus, the use of Section 10(j) so as to preserve the status quo ante can be particularly significant in established bargaining relationships—as well as in the unorganized sector. It was, as Judge Sotomayor said in her opinion, critical to the 1995 baseball season and, a back-to-work agreement. The Board's remedy provided the proper legal framework for future bargaining.

My own judgment is that my agency's use of labor law in the 1995 baseball strike may be yet another instance of baseball constituting a mirror image of other societal developments. The most dramatic example of that proposition in my lifetime is the advent of Jackie Robinson at first base for the Brooklyn Dodgers in 1947—and the hiring of Larry Doby and Dan Bankhead soon thereafter. Robinson, who hit .296, playing at an entirely new position in his rookie year, broke baseball's color barrier before President Truman desegregated the Armed Forces and seven years before the Supreme Court's historic ruling in *Brown* v. *Board of Education* declaring segregation in education to be unconstitutional. The example and contribution of these brave men against odds truly incalculable can never be forgotten.

The Board's reliance upon Section 10(j) injunctions reflects a renewed conviction about our National Labor Relations Act and its purposes and, to the rule of law, in the workplace itself. Our weekend work on March 26, and the importance of baseball to our country, made our law and its procedures known to millions who may not have heard of the Board or the Act previously. It was the mirror image of injunctions sought throughout industry in this country and, like Robinson's contribution, it could conceivably influence other relationships. My hope is that this will trigger more awareness of the law and promote voluntary compliance with its provisions.

In particular, I want to pay tribute here in New York to Regional Director Dan Silverman and his staff who not only played an extremely competent role in investigating the matters brought before us, but also presented the case to Judge Sotomayor. The Board's prompt intervention is properly seen as the vehicle through which the parties put aside their differences and resumed baseball and began the 1995 season this week. Meanwhile, of course, the Board is adjudicating the baseball case on its full merits in its administrative process.

Of course, the owners and players themselves have not yet negotiated a new collective-bargaining agreement. It was their failure to do so which triggered the 1994 strike, the longest dispute in the history of professional sports in this country and anywhere in the world! Under our system, these negotiations are for the parties themselves under their own voluntary autonomous system of collective bargaining.

But, what the Board and, ultimately the judiciary, have done through the use of Section 10(j) is to create a framework in which the collective bargaining process is fostered. This is the kind of objective that our law was designed to accomplish when first enacted by Congress in 1935 in the form of the Wagner Act. Over the years we have sometimes lost our way because of the failure to use the provisions which give our statute strength.

My belief is that our March 26 determination to seek injunctive relief in the 1995 baseball dispute was consistent with the law, has been good for the game of baseball and its 1995 season in particular, and, most important of all, important to the effective administration of our statute.

As is true of all of American society, we need to have the game of baseball be one in which the interests of all parties—players, owners, and fans—are taken into account. This is consistent with the policies of the National Labor Relations Act which my agency administers. A balanced relationship in which genuine voluntary collective bargaining is encouraged and warfare is diminished is consistent with our national labor policy and with the honor that we appropriately bestow upon Babe Ruth.

This spring of 1995 represents a new season in which a long deep drive was hit for baseball, for effective labor law enforcement, and for so much of what is truly great about our country on this 100th anniversary of the Babe's birth.

Notes

1. This theme has been eloquently chronicled in Dan Shaughnessy, *The Curse of the Bambino* (1990). I have found this work to be an informative one, although some of the connections between Ruth and the Red Sox performances in recent years are a bit overdrawn.

2. *Federal Baseball Club of Baltimore, Inc.* v. *National League of Professional Baseball Clubs*, 259 U.S. 200 (1922).

3. *The American League of Professional Baseball Clubs*, 180 NLRB 190, 191 (1969).

4. *Professional Baseball Clubs* v. *Major League Baseball Players Association* 66 Labor Arbitration Reports BNA 101 (1975).

5. *Toolson* v. *New York Yankees, Inc.*, 346 U.S. 356 (1953); *Flood* v. *Kuhn*, 407 U.S. 258 (1971).

6. *Brown* v. *Pro Football, Inc.*, 50 F.3d 1041, 148 LRRM (BNA) 2769 (D.C. Cir., March 21, 1995).

7. *National Basketball Association* v. *Williams*, 45 F.3d 684 (2d Cir. 1995).

8. In *Brown*, the court stated that under federal labor policy, there prevails "a delicate balance of countervailing power," which "favors neither party to the collective bargaining process, but instead stocks the arsenals of both unions and employers with economic weapons of roughly equal power" (*Brown*, 148 LRRM [BNA] 2769, 2776; *First National Maintenance Corp.* v. *NLRB*, 452 U.S. 666 [1981]); *American Ship Building* v. *NLRB*, 380 U.S. 300 (1965).

9. *NLRB* v. *Mackay Radio & Telegraph Co.*, 304 U.S. 333 (1938). President Clinton recognized that the balance of economic power is tipped heavily in favor or employers under this rule, leading him to issue an executive order banning the federal government from contracting with companies that hire permanent replacements during strikes (Executive Order 12954, 60 *Fed. Reg.* 13023 [March 8, 1995]). I have often addressed this troublesome issue myself, most recently in a speech I gave before the Bar Association of San Francisco on February 25, 1995. See 38 *DLR* (BNA) A8, February 27, 1995. Of course, in the recently concluded 1994–1995 baseball strike, the owners hired temporary replacements for the striking ballplayers during the spring training exhibition season and have now hired temporary replacements for the umpires during the regular season.

10. See R. Berry & W. B. Gould IV, "A Long Deep Drive to Collective Bargaining: Of Players, Owners, Brawls, and Strikes," 31 *Case Western Reserve Law Journal* 685, 774 (1981); Gould, "Players and Owners Mix It Up," *California Lawyer* 8 (August 1988): 56. See generally, Robert C. Berry, William B. Gould IV, and Paul D. Staudohar, *Labor Relations in Professional Sports* (Dover, Mass.: Auburn House, 1986).

11. *NLRB* v. *Borg Warner*, 356 U.S. 342, 351 (1958).

12. Gould, *Agenda for Reform: the Future of Employment Relationships and the Law*, (Cambridge, Mass., MIT Press, 1993).

13. *Silverman* v. *Major League Baseball Player Relations Committee*, 880 F. Supp. 246, 148 LRRM (BNA) 2922 (D. N.Y., April 3, 1995).

A Tale of Two Centrist Countries: Taft-Hartley, the Thatcher Reforms 1997, and All That

An Address by
William B. Gould IV, Chairman
National Labor Relations Board

The Royal Institute of International Affairs
Chatham House, London
June 2, 1997

This is my very first visit to the Royal Institute of International Affairs since becoming chairman of our United States National Labor Relations Board in March 1994. But, this is the fifth time that I have had the chance to speak to the Institute and, as always, it is a pleasure to be here. I think that it is Boswell's maxim that a man who is tired of London is tired of life, and there is no city outside of the United States with which I have had more contact over the years than this one.

This all goes back to 1962–1963 when I was a graduate student at the London School of Economics rushing over to the House of Commons to hear live what Norman Shrapnel of the *Guardian* was reporting about when Harold Wilson squared off, first with Harold Macmillan and later with Alec Douglas Home; to see Hugh Gaitskell in the bracing October wind of Brighton at the Labor Party Conference there; and to meet with members of Parliament in all of the major political parties of that time—and, yes, to watch the fabulous *That Was the Week That Was* political satire every Saturday night on British television. My principal reason for being in London then was to get my baptism in comparative labor law with Professor Otto Kahn Freund of the LSE, and when I compare the scene then with what it is in 1997, I can't help but note the profound change in the industrial relations and labor law landscapes on both sides of the Atlantic.

In the United Kingdom, the unions, of course, had a much greater influence than that ever possessed by their trade union counterparts in the United States. George Woodcock, the General Secretary of the Trades Union Congress, with whom I met shortly after my arrival in the Chalk Farm section of London in the fall of 1962, was, along with his organization, a formidable force in not only the Labor party, which the unions had shaped, but in Conservative governments as well. I don't believe that Mr. Woodcock was entirely uncomfortable with the unflappable Prime Minister Macmillan, though he stressed to me that he could never say anything of the sort in public.

In the collective-bargaining arena, although there was a union presence and strength, the story was more complicated. Here, by virtue of multiunion fragmentation and a crazy-quilt trade union structure which had grown like Topsy, along with a low dues structure, which was a result of union competition for the same workers, power drifted in key industries, like automobiles, into the hands of shop stewards. Through their autonomous negotiating committees, these stewards undertook action, including stoppages and the threat of them, without any reference to the national unions with which they were affiliated and sometimes without adherence to union constitutions and procedures. Conflict resolution was frequently undertaken as the result of guerrilla warfare, stoppages, slowdowns, or "working to rule," which frequently emerged as a form of intermittent economic pressure.

The trade union view was that the law should stay out of all of this—both from the perspective of protecting unions as well as regulating them—in part, because of the unfortunate experience with the judiciary which they shared with their American cousins. But, more important, the view was that the status quo suited the unions just fine—notwithstanding the Cassandralike warning provided by many foreigners about the need to be competitive. Britain had not found her new role in the world, said Dean Acheson. But that was then the world of *I'm All Right Jack*.

Similarly, young American labor lawyers like myself thought that we had a system which worked just fine in the United States. I touted my experience and the experience of workers and employers with the National Labor Relations Act and the agency that I would come to head thirty years later, the National Labor Relations Board. I thought that it was a system which resolved disputes relating to union representation and unfair labor practices applicable to both unions and employers in a rational and sensible way. I proclaimed to all of my British friends who would listen—and listen politely they did, although they didn't think that my points had much applicability to Britain—that NLRB secret ballot box elections would provide for a more sensible form of union representation involving exclusive bargaining agents and appropriate units and that this, even more than our Taft-Hartley jurisdictional dispute prohibitions, would diminish the jurisdictional warfare which was so prevalent in Britain.

And, in fact, the American system, albeit with enormous deficiencies, endured. What is particularly remarkable about this lengthy legacy is that the labor relations framework of law in the United States has outlasted that of all the modern industrialized countries including Great Britain, Germany and France, as well as Australia and New Zealand. Only the Scandinavian countries have established a procedure and substantive system with a longer history than ours.

The assumption in Britain, though, was that law in industrial relations which compelled an employer to recognize a union which possessed majority support simply was not then suited to British soil. Even our arbitration system, which I discussed with so many here, was deemed to have little relevance. I shall always remember my good friend John Cole, at that time the labor correspondent for the *Manchester Guardian*, duly noting that the word *arbitration* is derived from the word *arbitrary* and surely that did not provide for more effective dispute resolution procedure than the existing system in Britain.

The 1970s brought change to these patterns in both countries. When Edward Heath was elected prime minister in an upset victory in 1970, true to the promise of the Conservative party, comprehensive labor law reform imposing restraints upon unions was enacted in the form of the Industrial Relations Act of 1971. There followed three years of confrontation in which the Heath government ultimately was toppled by virtue of a miners' dispute unrelated to the Industrial Relations Act itself. But this precedent set the stage, along with what was viewed as increasingly irresponsible behavior on the part of the unions during the "winter of discontent" of 1979, for a series of Thatcher labor law reforms which fashioned limits on union power far more wide-sweeping than those legislated in the United States through Taft-Hartley, Landrum-Griffin, or antitrust law. Even prior to the 1980s and the early 1990s, in which the Thatcher reforms were realized—this time without the governmental trappings that the Industrial Relations Act provided in the form of an Industrial Relations Court—the unions had conceded the logic of the Conservative position in the second Wilson government by accepting legislation in 1975 that was designed to assist them but not restrain union action.

Meanwhile, in the United States, the National Labor Relations Act, which I had thought of as a model in my London student days, began to unravel. In the 1970s, employers resisting trade union organization, found loopholes in the act which permitted them to delay administrative procedures and defeat union organizational efforts with greater ease unrelated to the merits of a union case. The cost of unlawful conduct was suddenly found to be cheap. The absence of an expeditious process made the unavailability of wide-sweeping remedies—the traditional NLRB orders simply provide for reinstatement, back pay, or an order to bargain in good faith—appear all the more ineffective.

Labor law reform to cure these obvious deficiencies failed because of the Senate's filibuster, which made it impossible to get a vote in that chamber.[1] In the 1980s, while the Thatcher reforms were being instituted in Britain, during the Reagan-Bush era a decision was made not to repeal the legislation—though those administrations viewed the National Labor Relations Act itself with little enthusiasm—but rather to emasculate the statute with appointments to the Board by some members who were unsympathetic to its basic goals. This produced the best of all worlds for conservatives, who opposed legal intervention in the employment relationship and those employers (it should always be remembered that many employers then and today are law-abiding in their conduct) which sought to resist union representation at whatever the cost. The issue could be fought out on terrain during those twelve years which was inhospitable to the Act's objectives. While other factors surely were at work in the decline of trade unions in the United States, the Act, as interpreted and administered in the 1980s and early 1990s, most certainly was a factor.

In both countries, trade union representation declined precipitously, as did industrial stoppages. Here, in particular, the role of law in the United States was an important consideration because employers could permanently replace economic strikers under a 1938 Supreme Court ruling,[2] which had not been used by employers in well-established and mature relationships until the 1980s. Arbitration in the United States ran into difficulty in connection with its application to new areas of dispute like employment discrimination and to the employment relationship in 90 percent of the workforce where unions were not present.[3]

Now, in 1997, we are at one of those rare moments where similar changes in the political landscape allow each country, the United States and Great Britain, to step back and reexamine not only what has happened in their own countries but across the Atlantic. The reelection of President Clinton in 1996—providing four more years of the first Democratic administration in twelve years—and the election last month of Prime Minister Tony Blair with the first Labor government in eighteen years—have changed the political landscape as it relates to industrial relations and other issues in both countries.

Both the Democratic party in the United States and the Labor party in Great Britain, under the leadership of Clinton and Blair, have moved to the center. The American transformation began in 1952 when Governor Adlai Stevenson became the first Democratic party nominee to refuse to pledge the repeal of the 1947 Taft-Hartley amendments, which imposed restrictions upon organized labor. Today, Taft-Hartley's golden anniversary exists alongside of progressive administrations in the United States and United Kingdom, which are committed to a form of managed capitalism and a balanced approach to the competing interests of freedom of association and solidarity for workers, on the one hand, and, on the other hand, the need for American and British employers to be competitive in the global marketplace. In an interdependent democratic society these goals are not incompatible—a truth long accepted in a good number of mature collective-bargaining relationships.

In my country, the appointments made to our National Labor Relations Board during these past three years have been, for the most part, individuals who are committed to the objectives of our legislation—that is, with the promotion of the practice and procedure of collective bargaining and freedom of association amongst workers. In Britain, Prime Minister Blair has pledged to leave intact the labor law reforms of the past twenty years under both Labor and Conservative governments and to provide a framework through which unions which represent the majority of the employees may obtain compulsory recognition—a framework which exists in imperfect form in the United States.

Suddenly, in the 1990s, there is commitment to the idea of rights and obligations for both labor and management on both sides of the Atlantic. My sense is that this stems from a belief in both the United States and Great Britain that democracy in the workplace means that government must focus upon the interests of workers as well as employers and a commitment to the resolution of differences through the parties' own autonomous structures.

There are, of course, issues aplenty for our National Labor Relations Board in the United States and for whatever mechanism is established here in Britain in the Blair administration in the future. How does one establish expeditious administrative procedures which, within the parameters of Supreme Court authority, fashion opportunities for employees to hear both the merits and demerits of the case for unionization? After three decades of Board decisions which established the right of unions to have the names of addresses of employees so that they can communicate with them and send them literature and recruit them, the Board still is trying to apply the principles established so that both sides have an equal opportunity to communicate.

In your country, the Labor governments in the 1960s were of the view that postal ballots for unions were particularly important, given the potential for coercion in the union hall itself, particularly, with a "show of hands" procedure. This policy was enacted into law as part of the Thatcher reforms of the 1980s. Now, in the United States, our Board has used postal ballots in representation disputes where workers have the opportunity to vote for or against a union to represent them, in a greater number of instances than was the case prior to the time that we came to office. (Our friends over at the National Mediation Board who administer the Railway Labor Act, which applies to railways and airlines, use postal ballots in practically every instance—and haven't used a manual ballot at an employer's facility since 1987!)

The challenge which prompts more focus upon postal ballots is that workers are not always likely to have ready access to the ballot box at the workplace—particularly when they are part-time or in a "call in" or staggered shift status. How do we insure both fairness and the opportunity for all who wish to possess the franchise to vote? Both countries must attempt to address these problems.

Both the United States and the United Kingdom are confronted with a global marketplace which has increased competitive pressures for employers. The British Government's commitment to sign the European Union Social Chapter will establish a mechanism which parallels in some limited respects the duty to bargain which exists under our statute. The practical problems that arise in both countries will emerge from the need for corporations to reorganize themselves and for unions and representatives of workers to protect the job security of those whom they represent and enhance their employment prospects generally.

In both countries, the attempt is and will be made to promote procedures through which employees and trade unions can be involved and, at the same time, employers can function competitively. Both countries must attempt to address the problems of contingent or atypical workers, as they are called here and across Europe, insofar as the ability to participate in the shaping of their employment relationship is concerned. The need for employees to participate in the enterprise, through both collective bargaining procedures as well as other mechanisms will be part of the discussion. In my country this debate has taken place in the context of a discussion of whether the so-called TEAM Act should be passed by Congress.

Through both administrative initiatives as well as statutory interpretation, my agency, which undertakes such responsibilities independent of immediate supervision by the executive branch, (or any other governmental entity except the Supreme Court's mandates interpreting the National Labor Relations Act) will attempt to continue the sometimes daunting task of providing for workplace democracy. I look forward to a dialogue as your government, committed as is mine, to finding the center or impartial ground between labor and management, undertakes a task which in some broad respects is similar.

This is the role that I have assumed as an impartial arbiter between labor and management in the three decades since I left the LSE. This is my role as chairman of the National Labor Relations Board.

Now that our two countries find themselves on a centrist course, where will it lead next? My belief is that we are at a turning point in industrial relations where a fundamental shift is taking place—a shift from the presumption underlying the traditional labor relations framework of a natural conflict between labor and management, to more cooperation. While traditionally, cooperation was viewed as inconsistent with genuine robust representation by autonomous unions or employee groups, the fact of the matter is that a better understanding of employer sales and product problems can enhance both the system of representation and the viability of the enterprise.

This shift arises from a recognition of two important factors, among others, by labor and management. First, is a realization that to successfully compete in the new global marketplace, American companies, unions, and employees have it in their self interest to cooperate with each other. The same principle holds true on British soil, and in non-union settings. The parties are beginning to wake up to a recognition that the survival of their industries is at stake.

A second growing recognition—and this is more on the part of management—is that a company's employees are its greatest asset. Instead of asking workers to check their brain in at the factory or establishment gate, enlightened management views them as a wellspring of ideas on improving operations and production.

Evidence of these two factors in the United States is seen in the proliferation of quality of worklife (QWL), employee participation, and team programs. Notwithstanding the economic success in my country, regarded as the great jobs machine, smart managers recognized the deficiencies in our old industrial relations model and borrowed heavily from successful practices in Japan, Germany, and other countries, that promote labor-management cooperation.

In my own work at the Board, and previously in my scholarly writings, I have attempted to advance more constructive, cooperative, harmonious labor-management relations to reach the middle ground—or "vital center," as President Clinton has described it. Two recent Board decisions in which I wrote concurring opinions illustrate this point. In *Keeler Brass Automotive Group*,[4] the Board found the employer had violated the Act by dominating an employee participation committee and interfering with its administration. In that case, I spoke approvingly of decisions which are

consistent with the movement toward cooperation and democracy in the workplace which I have long supported. This movement is a major advance in labor relations because, in its best form, it attempts nothing less than to transform the relationship between employer and employees from one of adversaries locked in unalterable opposition to one of partners with different but mutual interests who can cooperate with one another. Such a transformation is necessary for the achievement of true democracy in the workplace. However, it does pose a potential conflict with the National Labor Relations Act, enacted in 1935 at a time when the adversarial struggle between management and labor was at its height.

In the other case, *Q-1 Motor Express, Inc.*,[5] the Board found the company's failure to bargain over its decision to relocate a terminal was unlawful. I said in my concurring opinion:

In my view, the act requires decision bargaining where the reasons underlying the relocation of unit work are amenable to bargaining and not solely to those decisions which implicate labor costs. And the issue is particularly vital and central to the new global marketplace of competitive pressure which affects both employers and unions as well as the public interest.

As I have stated on previous occasions, the genius of the Act is that it provides a legal framework for industrial relations designed to keep government out of the workplace, leaving most problems to resolution by the parties who are best equipped to solve them using the kinds of creative means preferred by those most directly affected. This has been the overriding theme of my opinions in both *Keeler Brass* and *Q-1 Motor Express, Inc.* In both situations accepting the ideas advanced would diminish wasteful litigation as well as foster communication and greater understanding for employers and employers. And since March 1994, our decisions have attempted to reflect a balance and consideration for the competing interests of labor, management, and individuals, as well as a commitment to the practice and procedure of collective bargaining and the promotion of voluntarily negotiated procedures by the parties.

This is then the sensible, centrist course upon which I see our countries embarking in the years ahead as the industrial relations field braces for the twenty-first century.

Notes

1. Cf. William B. Gould IV, "Prospects for Labor Law Reform," *Nation*, April 16, 1977.

2. *N.L.R.B. v. Mackay Radio & Telegraph* Co., 304 U.S. 333 (1938).

3. This is an issue that is often referred to these days as alternative dispute resolution.

4. 317 NLRB 1110, 1117 (1995).

5. 323 NLRB 767, 770 (1997).

President's Award for Distinguished Federal Civilian Service Presented to William R. Stewart

An Address Delivered by
William B. Gould IV, Chairman
National Labor Relations Board
Charles A. Beardsley Professor of Law
Stanford Law School (on leave)

On the occasion of the bestowal of the President's Award
NLRB Headquarters
Wednesday, July 2, 1997

This is a great day for the National Labor Relations Board—the greatest one, with the possible exception of some of our landmark Supreme Court rulings, that the agency has ever had.

Bill Stewart is the finest public servant I have ever known, and I've known plenty. Since he retired in March not a day goes by that I don't think: "I wish Bill were here to help me deal with this." From the distance of his comfortable retirement, I find I appreciate and miss him all the more.

During these past three years plus, the assault on our National Labor Relations Board and National Labor Relations Act has been extraordinary. A host of internal challenges has afflicted us and me, in particular, as head of the agency.

The buck stops right here in the Chairman's Office—as it should! And that meant that my ever-resourceful and loyal chief counsel, Bill Stewart, was in on every minute of it!

There are so many good memories that I have of our time together. And I shall never forget Bill's statement two years ago in response to one of the internal attacks:

[T]he Chairman made it explicitly clear ... that he would not allow the Board members to muzzle him. Bill Gould was not appointed to be Chairman by President Clinton to speak only when and to say only the things that a majority of the Board deigns that it will permit him.

And, Bill, when I think of the struggles, I can't help but take special pride in President Bill Clinton's reference to your contribution to "preserving the ability of workers to vote by mail in union elections." Because of your work and that of so many professionals and clericals throughout the agency, we are expanding the franchise in NLRB elections, and it is good to know that this has not escaped White House notice.

Last March when Bill retired, I noted President Clinton's March 18 letter to Bill and its reference to his work at the Board as "unparalleled"—and I said that we should all "stay tuned" for future Bill Stewart developments at the White House.

It is meet and right that President Clinton has bestowed the highest honor in the federal government, the President's Distinguished Federal Civilian Service Award, upon my good friend and counselor, Bill Stewart. It is meet and right that he should be the first NLRB employee in the sixty-two-year history of the agency to receive it—the award generally going to the State and Defense Departments or to individuals involved with national security.

On this special occasion honoring Bill, I'd like to reflect briefly on the type of person he is and those personal attributes which he had brought to bear on his forty-year career in the government. In doing so, I want to touch upon two points for you all to consider as friends and former colleagues of Bill laboring in the vineyard of public service.

The first theme is that you can advance very far professionally in the government through dedication and hard work. Exhibit number one is Bill Stewart. Bill is a role model, an inspiration to federal government employees everywhere. He has done it all!

The second and related theme is that this work we do as government employees—whether as a political appointee like myself, or as a career employee at any grade level—is important and counts greatly toward the public good.

Let me start first by telling you something about Bill's background. Most of you are aware that he is a son of Terre Haute, Indiana, the middle of America, and that he did his undergraduate work, majoring in government, at Indiana University. It is commendable that he graduated with high honors and was to elected Phi Beta Kappa. It is remarkable that he did so working virtually full time as a student on scholarship.

Out of college, Bill moved on to law school at the same university in the fall of 1954, again on full scholarship. No sooner than he arrived, he was called to active duty. By May 1956, Bill was an officer with the Third Armored Division stationed in Germany. He was selected to be the courts and boards officer and assistant adjutant of a combat command of over five thousand men. After eighteen months of active duty, he was promoted to first lieutenant.

In the fall of 1957, Bill returned to Indiana University Law School and was awarded a J.D. with distinction in 1959. During law school, he was invited to join the staff of the *Law Journal* and was elected to be a Note Editor. He also was elected to The Order of the Coif.

My association with Bill began in 1963 when he and I joined the staff of President John F. Kennedy's appointee as NLRB Chairman, the late Frank McCulloch. Bill had come from the Atomic Energy Commission, where he had been employed four years as an attorney. I had just returned from the London School of Economics after a tour of duty with the United Auto Workers in Detroit.

While I left the agency in 1965 to pursue my career goals elsewhere, Bill stayed, as they say, for the duration. Isn't it wonderful and interesting that our paths would find their way back together at this agency: I as the Chairman and Bill as my Chief Counsel, although I'm convinced that Bill from time to time thought it was the other way around.

The intervening years for Bill brought a series of promotions and awards, which of course came as no surprise to any of us who knew of his considerable talents. He was a gifted attorney and leader in the Appellate Court Branch. His leadership was evidenced by, among other things, his election—twice—as president of the NLRB Professional Association.

Against that backdrop of professional success is another side of Bill that those of us close to him know and respect. It is his remarkable ability to relate to people of all economic and social backgrounds, all races and creeds on the enlightened basis that we share a common humanity. He sincerely believes—and I do too—that progress is dependent on hard work and making the most of individual talents, and on the ability to perceive and develop the talents of others. And that, as much as anything, is the lesson that Bill leaves with this fine agency.

Throughout his career Bill has assisted the agency in recruiting lawyers committed to his high standard of excellence and performance. Once hired, he has made sure that all have been given the opportunity to succeed. Bill has been an outstanding teacher, not only to young attorneys but to individuals in all grade levels.

Bill's special ability to get along with all types of individuals enabled him to know what really was going on at the agency. Let's face it, with his intelligence network, he knew just about everything about everybody. And, of course, his special insights were enormously helpful to me as I came into this job unaware of where the land mines were buried.

My relationship with Bill, and working with so many talented people here at the Board, has convinced me that the dedication and idealistic verve of the 1930s still is very much part of the agency's work today.

And it was Bill who steered me toward the best of them all, my Confidential Assistant, Mary Ann Sawyer, who is unsurpassed in every great capability that exists! I have seen the torch passed from Bill to the extremely capable hands of Al Wolff with the very able and talented Kate Dowling as his deputy. To my mind, Kate—and other bright lights like her at the NLRB—represent the new generation who are advancing to positions of leadership as Bill Stewart did in his time. They can and will follow in his footsteps.

The second and related point is that public service is a high and noble calling— a point that seems sometimes forgotten in the drumbeat of attacks on government over the past two years. Along those lines, Paul Volcker, former Federal Reserve Board chairman, said recently: "This is not the happiest of times to be in the civil service. There are those ominous polls that indicate that confidence and trust in government are at a low point." Mr. Volcker went on to say:

We can be sure of one thing. Whatever the angst today, whatever the challenges of tomorrow, government is here to stay. We can argue about the proper boundary lines of the public sector. But we will not be able to do without people—first rate people, people imbued with a sense of mission, willing and able to devote a good share of their life to public service.

All of us, inside or outside of government, need to recognize that fact. Public employees make a valuable contribution to our daily lives. They are essential to the success of our government and our individual lives.

As I pointed out in two recent commencement addresses to law school graduates, we need to hold public service as an important calling—because it truly is—and to respect the public employees who contribute to the quality of American life. As a nation, we need to value a professional civil service whose highest principle is one of patriotism, whose foremost commitment is to excellence, and whose experience and expertise are a national resource to be used and respected. As President Kennedy said:

Let the public service be a proud and lively career. And let every man or woman who works in any area of our national government, in any branch, at any level, be able to say with pride and with honor in future years: "I served the United States Government in that hour of our nation's need."

In a similar vein, President Lyndon Johnson said:

So very much of what we are as a nation—and what we are to achieve as a people—depends upon the caliber and character of the federal career people. In no other endeavor can we more directly serve our country's cause—or the values on which we stand—than in the public service.

Now there are awards, and there are awards. This one is the highest honor the federal government can grant to a career civilian employee. The award, which was established by executive order in 1957, is presented "for the best achievements having current impact on improving government operations or serving the government interests." Bill is the first NLRB employee to receive it.

Between 1957 and 1979, no more than five to six career federal civil servants received this prestigious award each year. Since 1984 only about eighteen individuals throughout the entire United States government were singled out for such a high recognition.

So you see, this is a rare honor indeed. Let me conclude by reading President Clinton's statement in bestowing this award:

With Profound Appreciation, Highest Esteem and Great Satisfaction.

William R. Stewart is cited for his exemplary service to the Nation throughout a distinguished 37-year Federal career. For over 30 years, Mr. Stewart served with the National Labor Relations Board as an attorney working on a wide variety of significant cases. As Chief Counsel to the chairman, he became a recognized legal scholar and litigation expert and was instrumental in winning national labor law cases that have had a major impact on American workers, such as protecting the rights of blind workers and preserving the ability of workers to vote by mail in union elections. Additionally, Mr. Stewart has been an outstanding teacher and role model for innumerable young attorneys. Mr. Stewart's dedication, scholarship, and leadership have served as an example for all in public service. His distinctive accomplishments culminate a long and distinguished career in public service and reflect the highest credit upon himself and his country.

And so Bill, if you would please step forward, it is my privilege and high honor to present you with the President's Award for Distinguished Federal Civilian Service, medal, rosette, and certificate. Congratulations.

I

Campaign Finance Reform and the Union Dues Dispute under *Beck*

An Address by
William B. Gould IV, Chairman
National Labor Relations Board
Charles A. Beardsley Professor of Law
Stanford Law School (on leave)

Iowa Chapter of the Industrial Relations Research Association
Co-Sponsored by the Federal Mediation and Conciliation Service
Amana, Iowa
October 8, 1997

It is good be to back here in Iowa. This is my first professional visit to this state since becoming chairman, although I had the opportunity to give a series of lectures at the University of Iowa Law School and Institute of Industrial Relations in 1969 and 1970 and then again, in this decade, in 1992 and 1994.

On my return to this state, I want to pay homage and tribute to my good friend, Senator Tom Harkin, the ranking Democrat on the Senate Appropriations Committee, Labor, Health and Human Services, Education and Related Agencies Subcommittee. From the first time that I met him four years ago in the fall of 1993 during my confirmation process, Senator Harkin has been a good and loyal friend both to me and to the National Labor Relations Board. He has stood with me and the agency during the difficult struggles that have affected our appropriations process as the Hundred and Fourth and Hundred and Fifth congresses, particularly in the House of Representatives, have expressed so much hostility to our policies and decisions and, indeed, to the National Labor Relations Act itself. Iowa is indeed fortunate to have such an excellent representative in the United States Senate and I count myself fortunate to have a friendship with Senator Harkin.

Here in Iowa—and I will be in Iowa City tomorrow—I want to say what a pleasure it is to see the great accomplishments of my former students at Stanford Law School who are now on the faculty of the University of Iowa Law School, Peter Blanck and Adrien Wing, I was their teacher at Stanford in the 1980s and I am so proud of the great work that they have done on such a distinguished faculty.

Being here in Amana reminds me of Bill Zuber's Dugout Restaurant, where I have dined in neighboring Homestead, and his part on the pitching corps of the 1946 Red Sox, who won the pennant the year that I first fell in love with baseball. Along with Jim Bagby, Bob Klinger, Earl Johnson. Mike Ryba and others, he made the long walk from the Sox bullpen in that fantasy-rifled year.[1]

I speak to you today about a subject which occupies the President, the Congress, and policymakers and the press everywhere throughout the United States; that is, campaign expenditure reform legislation, particularly as it relates to trade unions. The issue of union dues and their use for political expenditures by trade unions has come to the forefront anew, a controversy fueled by the intense and deep involvement of the AFL-CIO in the 1996 elections.[2] Labor, as I shall develop, has always been deeply involved in the political process because of the direct relationship between the conditions of trade union members, working people generally, and public policy fashioned in the political arena.

Samuel Gompers, the first president of the American Federation of Labor, spoke of rewarding labor's friends and punishing its enemies. And since 1952, with the exception of George McGovern's candidacy in 1972, the trade union movement, on a national level, has endorsed every Democratic party candidate for president.

Now the issue returns in the form of the current debate about campaign finance reform legislation. Members of Congress, on the Republican side of the aisle, are angry about the support given by the AFL-CIO to the Democratic party candidates in 1996 and the attacks made upon Republican members of the Hundred and Fourth Congress through television issue advertisements. Some have maintained that the Clinton Board is in some way responsible for alleged wrongs and abuses, relating to dissidents who disagree with the politics and political preference of their unions, that the Republicans perceive to exist.

The area of union dues and political expenditures is a confused one with a long and meandering past. Its origins lie in two separate lines of authority developed by the United States Supreme Court. One doctrine is rooted in Supreme Court dicta in 1954 and the ultimate holding in *NLRB* v. *General Motors* in 1963, that where unions can negotiate union security agreements compelling membership as a condition of employment—and they can do so in twenty-nine of the states of the Union where there are no right-to-work laws prohibiting such—unions only may compel the payment of "periodic dues and initiation fees" as opposed to full membership.[3] In other words, as the Supreme Court said in *General Motors*, under a union security agreement, membership as a condition of employment for workers within the meaning of the law is the payment of such monies and nothing more.

This means that there are two categories of employees under a union security agreement—"limited" or "financial core" members: really nonmembers, who are obliged only to pay dues and initiation fees and full members who assume all the rights and obligations of union membership. As full members, their rights traditionally have included the right to participate in strike votes, ratification votes, and other related internal procedures of the union. And as the Supreme Court explained in its 1967 landmark *NLRB* v. *Allis-Chalmers Mfg. Co.* decision, union members also have certain obligations and are subject to disciplinary authority in the form of fines and other sanctions when, for instance, they engage in strikebreaking.[4] To complicate matters further, the Supreme Court in 1985—in a decision that I believe to be completely erroneous under the National Labor Relations Act—said that union members could resign at any time that they wish to do so and thus escape union discipline when, for instance, they engage in strikebreaking activity and cross a valid picket line.[5]

Meanwhile, a second line of authority began to emerge in the 1950s and the 1960s. This doctrinal development proceeded upon the assumption that the First Amendment's rights of free speech and association are implicated where the dues of nonunion members who were obligated to pay such under a union security agreement were expended for political purposes with which they disagreed. But, of course, as I alluded at the outset, the trade union movement was born out of political protest that is directly related to working conditions. Justice Frankfurter, dissenting in *Machinists* v. *Street* saw this clearly when he wrote the following:

To write the history of the Brotherhoods, the United Mine Workers, the Steel Workers, the Amalgamated Clothing Workers, the International Ladies Garment Workers, the United Auto Workers, and leave out their so-called political activities and expenditures for them, would be sheer mutilation. Suffice it to recall a few illustrative manifestations. The AFL, surely the conservative labor group, sponsored as early as 1893 an extensive program of political demands calling for compulsory education, an eight-hour day, employer tort liability, and other social reforms. The fiercely contested Adamson Act of 1916, see *Wilson* v. *New*, 243 U.S. 332, was a direct result of railway union pressures exerted upon both the Congress and the President.[6]

As Justice Frankfurter observed in *Street*—and this is the pattern that has evolved in the overwhelming number of cases where the dispute has arisen—no claim is made that "freedom of speech in any form or in any forum" is interposed by the unions.[7]

Nonetheless, in a series of decisions involving the public sector and the Railway Labor Act, ultimately the Court upheld the right of dissidents to object to expenditures that are not germane to collective bargaining and contract administration.[8] That principle was applied to the National Labor Relations Act in *Beck* v. *Communication Workers of America*.[9] As I indicated in a September 29, 1997, letter to the Democratic Senate Minority Leader from South Dakota, Senator Thomas Daschle, responding to an inquiry about the status of *Beck* cases, our Board decisions in this area of the law these past two years are based upon the Court's holding in that case. I said to Senator Daschle:

> The Court held that a union was not permitted "over the objections of dues-paying non-member employees" to expend funds on activities not related to collective bargaining, contract administration or grievance adjustment. The Court fashioned an accommodation between the right to "object"—not the right to withhold permission prior to riling an objection—and the "union's ability to require every employee to contribute to the cost of collective bargaining activities."

My predecessors had never dealt with the many *Beck* issues that have been presented in the six years from *Beck* until we took office in 1994. Thus, in a series of decisions beginning in 1995, we held that a union must inform every nonunion employee who is obliged to pay dues and fees under a union security agreement that he or she has the legal right not to do anything more than pay dues and fees relating to representational purposes. We also said that a union could notify such employees through an annual publication and that newly hired employees must be given notice before they are asked to join the union and pay dues under a union security clause.[10]

In many instances, however, I do not believe that this kind of notice is sufficient. This is because many or most collective-bargaining agreements define "membership," which is a condition of employment in a union security agreement, as simply membership—and not the payment of periodic dues and initiation fees. As Judge Posner has recently stated, "the only realistic explanation for retention of the statutory language in collective bargaining agreements ... is to mislead employees about their right not to join the union." Although our *Beck* decisions oblige unions to notify both full members as well as nonmembers or "financial core" members of the fact that they only have the obligation to pay periodic dues and initiation fees, the fact is that this is inadequate where the collective-bargaining agreement simply speaks of "membership" in the union security provision without defining it in accord with the statute as interpreted by the Supreme Court![11]

Generally speaking, neither workers nor employers understand that "membership" is what the Supreme Court has defined it to be in its 1963 *General Motors* holding. Each year, prior to my assumption of my current duties in Washington, when I had completed my lectures on this subject to my Labor Law I students at Stanford Law School, I would then pause and tell them that they were amongst the select few in the country—including both lawyers and nonlawyers—who had an exposure to the law of union security and its implications. In substantial part, this is why I have stated in my October 2 dissenting opinion in *Connecticut Limousine* "that I would oblige unions and employers to revise their collective bargaining agreement to define membership as only the obligation to pay periodic dues and initiation fees."[12]

From a policy perspective, this paradigm, rooted in all of the Supreme Court authority to which I have referred, is a disaster. Under federal labor law—as it has evolved through Supreme Court teachings—a union must notify full members that they first must resign from the union before they can exercise their *Beck* rights. This requirement induces the union to act against its self-interest (and who amongst us does that?!) and promotes antiunionism in the workplace—a result which is completely at cross-purposes with our act which, properly in my view, promotes the collective-bargaining process and the right of the freedom of association itself in the preamble of the Act.

Second, as some of the Republicans are beginning to point out—and it is a valid point—the only way that a worker can object to political expenditures is through exercising the right of resignation. But, by resigning, these workers relinquish, in most circumstances, participation in the strike and ratification votes which affect the employment relationship. This has led some Republicans to say that *Beck* rights should apply to members as well as nonmembers."[13] I subscribe to this Republican idea but for very different reasons than those which they would put forward.

I think that the statute ought to compel one class of membership, not limited membership or different degrees of membership, which invites litigation because of their inherent ambiguity. This would mean, for instance, where employees are covered by a valid union security agreement they have the right to participate in the strike and ratification procedures and the obligation to submit to appropriate union disciplinary sanctions for strikebreaking, for instance, as outlined in *Allis-Chalmers*.

Contrary to the United States Supreme Court in *Pattern Makers* v. *NLRB*, my view is that strikebreakers who are members do not have the right to resign at any time they want or for any reason[14]—and I believe that the Board has the authority to uphold responsible restrictions on resignation—and thus consider the issue anew without statutory amendment.[15] In my judgment, *Pattern Makers* is inconsistent with the statute's objectives in that unions may impose sanctions under some circumstances in the interest of solidarity.

As I said in my *Detroit Newspapers* opinion on the propriety of Section 10(j) relief, my view of national labor policy contemplates rights and obligations for all parties. Here, I believe that the statute should be amended so that unions may function actively and employees be informed with genuine and responsible participation.

Second, my dissent in *Connecticut Limousine*, in which I concluded that *Beck* objectors may not be charged for organizational activities, and that the Supreme Court decision in *Ellis,* which is the precedent upon which my opinion is based, should be reversed by Congress and the president on policy grounds. Monies expended for organizing activity—and the AFL-CIO has attempted to restore some vitality to the trade union movement by putting more resources in this area—are the lifeblood of a strong and independent trade union movement which is a prerequisite for a pluralist democratic society. Contrary to *Ellis*, dues monies spent for organizational activities are germane to collective bargaining and, thus, Congress should reverse the opinions—including mine—to which I have alluded. As I said a decade ago, the Supreme Court's decision in *Ellis*:

totally ignores what all observers of labor-management relations have known since the beginning of organized relationships between the two: Unions must organize and recruit new members to protect the gains and standards of those in the bargaining unit. This is especially so when the organizational activities are taking place amongst employers which are direct competitors of the enterprise in which the dues are collected.[16]

But in this area the job is for Congress or the Court—not the Board!

Third, Congress should reject out of hand, either in a campaign reform context or not, legislation such as the Worker Paycheck Fairness Act, which would require workers to opt in, that is to provide permission for trade union expenditures for political purposes (the British in their debate about this matter between 1913 and 1945, and about the new restrictions during Prime Minister Thatcher's reign, characterize it as "contracting in"). It is inappropriate for a number of reasons. In the first place, workers already have presumptively given permission for unions to make such expenditures by voting in the union in NLRB-conducted elections or through some other method demonstrating majority support. Workers may be very much influenced by whether a trade union is aligned with the Democratic party, the Republican party, or some other party in determining whether they want the union to represent them. Under our system, employees are not required to be represented by a union in every corporation, nor should they be. NLRB-conducted elections or some expression of majority support is a prerequisite. Consent is given at this stage.

Moreover, the *Beck* problem only arises where union security agreements have been voluntarily negotiated between labor and management as a part of a collective agreement. No dispute generally arises until the parties have devised such an arrangement. And, under *Beck*, dissident employees represented by the union have the right to object and, under our decisions, are informed about the choice. As we said in *California Saw*: "The union … must apprise the objector of the percentage of the reduction [of dues], the basis for the calculation, and that there is a right to challenge the calculation."[17] Penultimately, the Lott Amendment, which is attached to the Worker Paycheck Fairness Act, for the first time establishes comparable rights for stockholders in corporations. Yet corporations, which are reputed to have outspent trade unions in soft money by 26-1, do not have the same raison d'être as do unions. I rather doubt that Congress would have enacted much-needed minimum wage legislation in 1996 without trade union prompting. Again, one must recall Justice Frankfurter's instructive commentary about the origins of trade unions and the inevitable overlap between political activity and collective bargaining.

Finally, it is interesting to note that the Worker Paycheck Fairness Act provides for damages for any violations equal to double fees and interest, a private right of action to recover damages, attorneys fees, and posting requirement in all facilities. It would be interesting to determine whether the proponents of such legislation would apply the same provisions to all rights protected by the National Labor Relations Act, such as, for instance, the firing of workers involved in union organizational campaigns who can only obtain back pay minus interim earnings or those that would have been obtained with reasonable diligence under existing law. What accounts for this difference in approach? Perhaps the debate in the Congress will provide us with some answers to this question.

And, of course, if our society is to promote fairness and stability in labor-management relations, it would seem that a democratic society would put real substance in the right to strike and to reverse existing precedent which allows employers to permanently replace strikers. What good is the right to strike if an employee loses his or her job? My sense is that many of the disputes about union discipline of full members, and who is a full member and a limited member, mask the real issue which underlies the debate—and that is that there is no effective right to strike in this country today where the employer is willing to use the permanent-replacement tactic.

To sum up: the idea that workers have not provided presumptive consent for political expenditures under our law is simply false. They have selected, through their own initiative, the union as their exclusive bargaining representative. Their union and an employer voluntarily negotiate the union security clauses in question—and even then workers may object to such expenditures under *Beck*.

Under our decisions, employees have notice of their rights—although I believe that they should have more effective notice through revisions of collective-bargaining agreements which require "membership" as a condition of employment.

And under our decisions of these past few years, workers have full knowledge of trade union expenditures—so that they may file an objection. In this respect, the law as defined by our Board is working well.

Under the current system, unions are obliged to tell members that they have a right to resign in order to object under *Beck*. This should be changed by Congress to provide all workers the right to object under *Beck* and to participate in strike and ratification procedures; to provide unions the right to limit resignation (those who resign should not be able to use internal procedures); and to provide that all workers who are lawfully members be subject to union disciplinary sanctions.

It is difficult to know whether these issues will be definitively addressed, let alone resolved this week in the Senate and in the foreseeable future in the Congress. I suspect that the issues will be with us for sometime—as they have been for most of the post–World War II era. In the meantime, as I have stated many times, I will adjudicate the cases that come before me involving *Beck*—or for that matter, any other issue—fairly, impartially, in accordance with the principles of the law and in accordance with the rule of law.

It is a pleasure to be back here in Iowa with you. I hope that my remarks will generate some discussion and thoughts on these important aspects of federal labor policy which now have the attention of the Congress and the President.

Notes

1. As Ryba strolled in—and in those days relievers would walk deliberately—the late New York Yankee announcer, Mel Allen, would sing from the hit ballad of that time: "Hey, Baba Reeba. Yes, your baby knows."

2. Elizabeth Drew, *Whatever It Takes: The Real Struggle for Political Power in America* (New York: Viking Press, 1997) is a particularly thorough and informative discussion of the tactics of many organizations during the 1996 campaign.

3. *Radio Officers' Union of Commercial Telegraphers Union, A.F.L.* 347 U.S. 17 (1954).

4. *NLRB* v. *Allis-Chalmers Mfg. Co.*, 388 US 175 (1967).

5. *Pattern Makers' League of North America, AFL-C10*, 473 US 95 (1985).

6. See *Machinists* v. *Street*, 367 US 740 (1961).

7. Ibid., at 800.

8. *Abood* v. *Detroit Board of Education*, 431 US 209 (1977) and Chicago Teachers v. Hudson, 475 U.S. 292 (1986); *Railway Employees Dept.* v. *Hanson*, 351 U.S. 225 (1956); *Railway Labor Clerks* v. *Allen*, 373 U.S. 113 (1963); *Ellis* v. *Railway Clerks*, 466 U.S. 435 (1984).

9. 487 U.S. 735 (1988).

10. *Wegshied* v. *Local Union 291, International Union, UAW, Aerospace and Agr. Implement Workers of America*, 117 3F.3d 986, 990 (7th Cir. 1997).

11. *Weyerhaeuser Paper Co.*, 320 NLRB 349 (1995); enf. denied in part *Buzenius* v. *NLRB*, No. 96-5139 (6th Cir. 1997).

12. 324 NLRB 633 No. 105 (1997), relying upon the Sixth Circuit's decision in *Buzenius* that the union security clause in *Connecticut Limo*usine was unlawful on its face.

13. See "Trent Lott's Poison Pill," *New York Times*, October 1, 1997, A30.

14. William B. Gould IV, "Solidarity Forever—or Hardly Ever. Union Discipline, Taft Hartley and the Right of Union Members to Resign," *Cornell Law Rev.* 74 (1980).

15. In *Pattern Makers* (473 U.S. 105 (1985)) the Court affirmed the Board's view expressed in *Neufeld Porsche-Audi* (270 NLRB 1330 [1984]), that the right to resign is absolute. But the deciding vote cast by Justice White in that 5-4 decision was predicated on deference to the Board's exercise of its expertise (116–17). Indeed, a substantial part of Justice Powell's majority opinion in *Pattern Makers* is similarly rooted in this policy (473 U.S. 114–15).

Therefore, the Board can change its position when it exercises its expertise: "The responsibility to adapt the Act to the changing patterns of industrial life is entrusted to the Board ... and its special competence in this field is justification for the deference accorded its determinations" (*NLRB* v. *J Weingarten, Inc.*, 420 U.S. 251, 266 (1975) and cases cited therein). To be sure, *Weingarten* involved a shift in the Board's construction of the Act prior to a ruling by the Supreme Court. The reasoning, however, is equally applicable where the Board's construction of the Act shifts after the Court has deferred to the Board's expertise. Interestingly, in the context of Section 8(f) of the Act, the Board shifted its views, the Court deferred to the Board's then-current view, and, after the Court's decision, the Board announced a different interpretation intended to better serve the statutory policies of industrial stability and employee free choice in the construction industry. Thus, *in NLRB* v. *Iron Workers Local 103 (Higden Contracting Co.)*, 434 U.S. 335 (1978), the Court rejected the union's assertion that the Board's construction of Section 8(f) was not entitled to deference because the Board had shifted its position: "An administrative agency is not disqualified from changing its mind; and when it does, the courts still sit in review of the administrative decision and should not approach the statutory construction de novo and without regard to the administrative understanding of the statute" (*Higden*, 434 U.S. 351). After the Court deferred to the Board's construction of Section 8(f) in *Higden*, the Board again shifted its position in *John Dekleva & Sons*, 282 NLRB 1375 (1987), enf'd. 843 F.2d 770 (3d Cir. 1988). The Board acknowledged "certain tensions" between the new interpretation of Section 8(f) announced in *Dekleva* and the language in *Higden*.

The Board noted, however, that *Higden* had "to be read in the context of the Board's then-current efforts to balance the multiple legitimate conflicting interests present in Section 8(f)." And, since the *Higden* decision, the Board had experienced the application of its 8(f) rules in a multitude of circumstances and been able to evaluate the extent to which those rules served their objectives (282 NLRB 1388 (1987)): "'Cumulative experience begets understanding and insights by which judgments ... are validated or qualified or invalidated. The constant process of trial and error, on a wider and fuller scale than a single adversary litigation permits, differentiates perhaps more than anything else the administrative from the judicial process" (*NLRB* v. *Seven-Up Bottling Co.,* 344 U.S. 344, 349 (1943)). Based on its experience, the Board concluded that its old 8(f) rules had failed to achieve the objectives for which they had been created and that the new rules would correct the problems that had become evident and better achieve the objectives of the act (282 NLRB 1389).

16. William B. Gould IV, "The Burger Court and Labor Law: The Beat Goes On— *Marcato*," 24 *San Diego Law Review*, 51, 61 (1987).

17. *California Saw & Knife Works, Inc.,* 320 NLRB 224, 233 (1995).

J

Proposition 226: Political Contributions by Employees, Union Members and Foreign Entities

Statement of William B. Gould IV, Chairman
National Labor Relations Board
Charles A. Beardsley Professor of Law
Stanford Law School (on leave)

To the Joint Hearing
Senate Committees on Industrial Relations,
Elections and Reapportionment and Assembly Committee on Labor and Employment
April 28, 1998

On June 2, 1998, California will vote on a ballot initiative, Proposition 226, which would provide for sweeping changes in the relationship between unions and employees that they represent as it relates to the political expenditure of union dues. As one who has been involved in the field of labor-management relations for 37 years as a practitioner representing both unions and employers, an impartial arbitrator in a wide-variety of disputes between labor and management, an academic for most of my career as Charles A. Beardsley Professor of Law at Stanford Law School teaching labor law and other subjects, as well as Chairman of the National Labor Relations Board for more than four years, I am of the view that Proposition 226 is deeply flawed from both a policy and constitutional perspective. I plan to vote "no" by mail absentee ballot on June 2 and I would urge all voters in California to do the same.

I plan to vote "no" for a number of reasons set forth below.

Proposition 226 Is Flawed from a Policy Perspective

One of the core elements of trade union activity is involvement in the political process. Indeed, union involvement in politics and legislation antedates union participation in the collective bargaining process in many industries. As Justice Frankfurter noted in *Machinists v. Street*, 367 U.S. 740 (1961), the trade union movement was born out of political protest related to working conditions. As Justice Frankfurter wrote:

To write the history of the Brotherhoods, the United Mine Workers, the Steel Workers, the Amalgamated Clothing Workers, the International Ladies Garment Workers, the United Auto Workers, and leave out their so-called political activities and expenditures for them, would be sheer mutilation. Suffice it to recall a few illustrative manifestations. The AFL, surely the conservative labor group, sponsored as early as 1893 an extensive program of political demands calling for compulsory education, an eight-hour day, employer tort liability, and other social reforms. The fiercely contested Adamson Act of 1916, see *Wilson v. New*, 243 U.S. 332, was a direct result of railway union pressures exerted upon both the Congress and the President. 367 U.S. at 800.

This, then, is the historical backdrop for the Supreme Court's conclusion that union political activity constitutes "mutual aid or protection" protected under Section 7 of the National Labor Relations Act which my Agency, the National Labor Relations Board, is charged to interpret and administer. An essential part of union activity is an appeal to legislators to affect employment conditions.

In concluding that union political activity is protected by federal labor law the Supreme Court in *Eastex, Inc.* v. *NLRB*, 437 U.S. 556 (1978), said:

The 74th Congress [which enacted the National Labor Relations Act] knew well enough that labor's cause often advanced on fronts other than collective bargaining and grievance settlements within the immediate employment context. It recognized this fact by choosing, as the language of §7 makes clear, to protect concerted activities for the somewhat broader purpose of "mutual aid or protection" as well as for the narrower purposes of "self-organization" and "collective bargaining." Id at 565.

If enacted, Proposition 226 would exclude trade unions from participation in a democratic pluralist society and, at the same time, cripple a major source of funding for the Democratic Party, given the fact that most donations by unions go to Democrats rather than Republicans.

As Justice Frankfurter noted in *Street*, no denial of free speech is involved through union political expenditures in the sense that no worker is being denied an opportunity to express his or her view in any form within or without union circles. Moreover, although the proponents of Proposition 226 appear to support its enactment on the ground that it would promote worker liberty, the fact that existing law adequately protects such liberty gives the lie to this claim. Employee liberty and free choice are protected in a number of ways.

In the first place, under American labor law there is no presumption that workers will be represented by unions. The burden is upon employees who seek such representation to obtain an adequate "showing of interest" to convince the National Labor Relations Board to hold a secret ballot box election or, on the basis of some other evidence of majority support in an appropriate unit, to convince the employer to voluntarily recognize it. In the ensuing campaign for the workers' allegiance, employer free speech 2 and campaign efforts, as well as union recruiting tactics, are protected by the Act. During the election campaign, the employer, as well as dissident employees, can bring the political preferences of the trade union or trade union leadership in question to the attention of all employees and these preferences can be a basis for the workers' votes or expression of choice in the election or some other forum. If workers do not like the fact that the union in question gives its money to the Democratic Party, they can vote against the union and not even be represented, let alone be subject to a union security agreement which compels "membership" as a condition of employment.

Secondly, the Labor Management Reporting and Disclosure Act of 1959, more commonly known as the Landrum-Griffin Act 3 states that all union members have the right to elect their leaders on a periodic basis, i.e., at least once every three years. If the workers have selected the union as exclusive bargaining representative and if there is a belief that the union leaders are out of touch, not only may the workers challenge union leadership and both the leadership's preferences for union security clauses as well as political expenditures, and decertify the union before the Board, they also may vote out the union leadership in a statutorily guaranteed election procedure. Again, free choice and liberty are paramount considerations built into existing law.

It is interesting to note that Proposition 226 does not cover expenditures by corporations notwithstanding the fact that stockholders do not have the same rights to object as workers represented by unions do and that the stockholder may suffer injury by virtue of withdrawal of his or her investment, and finally corporations, unlike unions, were not born out of political protest relating to their concerns. All of this illustrates the double standard that Proposition 226 applies to corporations and trade unions.

Third, even if employees are unsuccessful in ridding themselves of a union or union leadership which has political views with which they disagree, they may object to the expenditure of any dues for political purposes under the Court's ruling in *Communications Workers* v. *Beck*, 487 U.S. 735 (1988). Thus, as the United States Supreme Court has noted in *Austin* v. *Michigan Chamber of Commerce*, 494 U.S. 652, 665–666 (1990):

An employee who objects to a union's political activity thus can decline to contribute to those activities, while continuing to enjoy the benefits derived from the union's performance of its duties as the exclusive representative of the bargaining unit on labor-management issues. *As a result, the funds available for a union's political activities more accurately reflect members' support for the organization's political views than does a corporation's general treasury.* Id. (emphasis supplied).

Under the precedent upon which *Beck* relied in establishing the right to object, it is clear that the burden is upon the dissident who wishes to object. Thus, although it is frequently said that Proposition 226 is designed to *enforce Beck*, in fact, it is designed to *reverse* the Court's decision in *Beck*.

As the Court of Appeals for the District of Columbia has said: "Dissent is not to be presumed—it must affirmatively be made known to the union by the dissenting employees." *Abrams* v. *Communication Workers*, 59 F3d 1373–1382 (DC Cir. 1995). In this connection *Abrams* directly relied upon the early Supreme Court authority which led to *Beck*.

And, most important, the Court of Appeals for the Ninth Circuit which covers California is in accord with this view. Said the court in *Mitchell* v. *Los Angeles Unified School District*, 963 F2d 258, 261 (9th Cir. 1992):

The Supreme Court has repeatedly held that nonunion members' rights are adequately protected when they are given the opportunity to object to such (political) deductions and to pay a fair share fee to support the union's representation costs.... The Supreme Court has clearly held that the nonunion employee has the. burden of raising an objection. The non-members' "burden" is simply the obligation to make this objection known.

Further, relying on the precedent of the U.S. Supreme Court, the California Supreme Court, in *Cumero* v. *Public Employment Relations Board*, 49 Cal. 3d 575, 581 (1989), reached the same conclusion—that the employee's right to object must be affirmatively raised or else it is waived—in a case arising under the California Educational Employment Relations Act.

Thus, in my view, Proposition 226 is bad policy because it reverses the carefully balanced ruling of the Supreme Court in *Beck* pursuant to federal labor law. Moreover, under *Beck* only nonmembers under union security agreements have the right to protest against expenditure of dues for political purposes. But Proposition 226 extends this right to "members" as well. The assumption of the *Beck* line of authority has been that nonmembers who do not wish to join the union are the only ones who are coerced and possess "standing" to protest. Again, Proposition 226 contradicts *Beck* rather than enforces it.

Proposition 226 Is a Misguided Attempt to Convince California Voters That the National Labor Relations Board Has Not Enforced *Beck*

Preliminarily, it is important to note that while the Board is referred to as the Clinton Board, given the fact that the President has made the appointments to the Agency, there is no contact between the Agency and the Executive Branch, White House or Department of Labor, about any matter of policy relating to adjudication or rulemaking. This approach has been scrupulously followed by the Clinton Board and all of my votes are in accord with my views of the policies of the Act and have nothing whatsoever to do with the political relationships between the Clinton Administration and the AFL-CIO or anyone else.

As we can see from the above, the proponents of Proposition 226 have spread a great deal of confusion and misunderstanding about *Beck* itself. The same holds true with regard to the role of the National Labor Relations Board.

When I arrived in Washington in March 1994, subsequent to my appointment by President Clinton and my confirmation by the Senate in the 103rd Congress, six years had elapsed since *Beck* had been handed down. Not one single decision on *Beck* had emerged from the Board although numerous unfair labor practices charges had been filed here.

The Board made *Beck* one of its priorities and in 1995 issued a landmark ruling in *California Saw & Knife Works*, 320 NLRB 224 (1995). The Board in this case addressed a wide variety of issues that had been pending for a number of years. Amongst other matters, the Board held that notice of *Beck* rights could be provided by a union in a monthly publication which was provided to both members and non-members—though the question of whether a union is obliged to provide such information through the union security provision of the collective bargaining agreement itself through an obligation to notify through the collective agreement remained unresolved. But, subsequently, I have expressed the view that the agreement must articulate the fact that the workers' only obligation is to pay periodic dues and initiation fees as a condition of employment and that no worker is obliged to have his or her dues used for non-representation purposes. 4 A majority of the Board has now taken the position that union security provisions which do not define membership are not adequate under federal labor law and this view will be expressed to the United States Supreme Court in *Marquez* v. *Screen Actors Guild*, 124 F3d 1034, cert. granted Mar. 23, 1998. The *Beck* dissidents' rights have been strengthened increasingly by my Board.

In *California Saw & Knife*, the Board also held that information would permit an objector to challenge the union's calculation about what should be deducted must be provided to the objector and it is also concluded that appropriate time periods for challenges by objectors may be established.

The Court of Appeals for the Seventh Circuit, in an opinion authored by the conservative jurist Judge Richard Posner, has upheld the Board's *California Saw & Knife* conclusions. Said Judge Posner:

> It is hard to think of a task more suitable for an administrative agency that specializes in labor relations.' and less suitable for a court of general jurisdiction, than crafting the rules for translating the generalities of the *Beck* decision (more precisely of the statute as authoritatively construed in *Beck*) into a workable system for determining and collecting agency fees. *International Association of Machinists & Aerospace Workers, et al. v. NLRB*, 96-1246, 96-2928 & 96-3467, slip op at 4 (7th Cir. 1998).

In sixteen decisions since *California Saw & Knife* the Board has issued rulings enforcing *Beck*. The National Labor Relations Board is enforcing *Beck*. Proposition 226 would, for the reasons stated above, reverse it.

Proposition 226 Is Flawed Constitutionally

Proposition 226 is quite clearly preempted by the National Labor Relations Act. In fashioning the doctrine of preemption for the Act, the Court had prohibited state activity where Congress has occupied the field through the Act. See *San Diego Building Trades Council* v. *Garmon*, 359 U.S. 236 (1959). As the Court has said:

> The Garmon rule is intended to preclude state interference with the NLRB's interpretation'and active enforcement of the integrated scheme of regulation established by the NLRA. *Golden State Transit Corp.* v. *City of Los Angeles*, 475 U.S. 608, 613 (1989).

As Judge Posner noted, the task of formulating rules and guidelines and the making of details is peculiarly "suitable" for an administrative agency like the Board. But Proposition 226 does not simply invade an area occupied by the Act—it contradicts the Act and the Court's rulings pursuant to it itself! By contradicting the Act and the Supreme Court's precedent on both the burden to object and the member-nonmember dichotomy, Proposition 226 is outright subversion of the principles of federal labor law.

In a line of cases beginning with *Machinists* v. *Street*, 367 US 740, 774 (1961), the Court has held that "dissent is not presumed—it must affirmatively be made known to the union by the dissenting employee. The union receiving money exacted from an employee under a union shop agreement should not in fairness be subjected to sanctions in favor of an employee who makes no complaint about the use of his money for such activities." In *Abood* v. *Detroit Board of Educ.*, 431 US 209, 235–236 (1977), the Court held that the "Constitution requires only that such expenditures be financed from charges, dues, or assessments paid by employees who do not object to advancing those ideas and who were not coerced into doing so against their will by the threat of loss of governmental employment." In *Chicago Teachers Union, Local No. 1* v. *Hudson*, 475 US 292, 309 (1986), the Court stated that "the nonunion employee has the burden of objection." Citing the Court's decisions in *Street*, *Abood*, and *Hudson*, the United States Court of Appeals for the Ninth Circuit, in *Mitchell* v. *Los Angeles Unified School District*, 963 F.2d 258 (9th Cir. 1992), rejected the contention that affirmative consent to deduction of full dues is required in order to protect nonmembers' First Amendment rights. The court stated:

The Supreme Court has repeatedly held that nonunion members' rights are adequately protected when they are given the opportunity to object to such [political] deductions and to pay a fair share fee to support the union' s representation costs.... The Supreme Court has clearly held that the nonunion employee has the burden of raising, an objection. The nonmembers' "burden" is simply the obligation to make his objection known. 963 F.2d at 261 (citing *Greenwald* v. *San Bernadino City Unified Sch. Dist.*, 917 F.2d 1223 (9th Cir. 1990) and quoting *Hudson* 475 U.S. at 306 n. 16)).

The United States Court of Appeals for the 6th Circuit also relied on the Supreme Court's rulings in rejecting the contention that nonmembers should only be required to pay those costs related to collective bargaining unless they affirmatively consent to pay for the union's political expenditures. In *Weaver* v. *University of Cincinnati*, 970 F.2d 1523 (6th Cir. 1992), cert. denied, 507 US 917 (1992), the court stated that

[this] argument must fall because it seeks to shift the balance of interests underlying all of the Supreme Court's pronouncements on the subject of agency shop fees. An "opt in" procedure would greatly burden unions while offering only a modicum of control to nonunion employees whose procedural rights have already been safeguarded by [the Supreme Court's decision in] *Hudson*. 970 F.2d at 1533.

In finding that a union could satisfy its obligations under the Court's decision in *Communication Workers v. Beck*, 487 U.S. 735 (1988), by requiring employees to object within a "window period" each year and to renew their objections annually, the United States Court of Appeals for the Seventh Circuit, in *Nielsen* v. *Machinists Lodge 2569*, 94 F.3d 1107 (7th Cir. 1996), cert. denied, 117 S.Ct. 1426 (1996), stated that

[i]t is not unreasonable for a union to require existing members or full fee nonmembers to voice their objections in a timely fashion, and to be aware that the price of not doing so will be to wait at most ten or eleven months before implementing their new status. Life is full of deadlines, and we see nothing particularly onerous about this one. 94 F.3 d at 1116.

In *Cumero* v. *Public Employment Relations Board*, 49 Cal. 3d 575 (1989), the California Supreme Court upheld a labor organization's right under the California Educational Employment Relations Act (EERA), to collect fees through involuntary payroll deductions pursuant to its organizational security arrangement with an employer. The California Supreme Court stated that the procedures prescribed by the Supreme Court in its decision in *Chicago Teachers Union, Local No. 1* v. *Hudson*, 475 U.S. 292 (1986), for protecting nonmembers' constitutional rights against a union's improper uses of their agency fees are sufficient and appropriate for the protection of nonmember employees' statutory rights to prevent improper use of their service fees collected under an EERA organizational security arrangement. The Cumero court stated

[t]he only limit expressly imposed by the EERA on the amount of the nonmember fee the union may collect is that the fee may not exceed the union's standard initiation fee, periodic dues, and general assessments. That limitation implies a general prohibition against putting the service fees to any use to which the union could not property put the funds voluntarily paid by its members.

In addition to rights stemming from that general constraint, each nonmember has a right to prevent the use of his or her service fee for purposes beyond the uniores representational obligations. Since ... that additional right is an aspect of the right of an employee to refuse to participate in a union's activities, it must be affirmatively asserted or else it is waived. Accordingly, that right is satisfied if the nonmember is given sufficient information about union expenditures, an opportunity to challenge the amount of his or her financial obligation to the union before an impartial decisionmaker, and protection in the form of an escrow of amounts reasonably in dispute while such challenges are pending, all in accordance with *Hudson*. (citations omitted) 49 Cal. 3d at 590.

And, as noted above, *Beck* is contradicted in the sense that members as well as nonmembers are given the right to withhold permission. Only nonmembers have the right to protest under federal labor law. *Kidwell* v. *Transportation Communication Union*, 946 F.2d 283 (4th Cir. 1991), and *Farrell* v. *Fire Fighters Local 55*, 781 F. Supp 647 (N.D. Cal. 1992).

Of course, it is important to note that Proposition 226 extends beyond union security agreements to the regulation of dues themselves. In *Motor Coach Employees* v. *Lockridge*, 403 U.S. 274 (1971), the Court invalidated a state law action complaining that the union had wrongfully obtained an employee's discharge for nonpayment of dues on the ground that it was preempted by federal labor law.

Accordingly, the states have no jurisdiction. See also, *SeaPak* v. *Industrial, Technical & Professional Employees*, 400 U.S. 985, 91 S. Ct. 452 (1971); *Operative Potters* v. *Tell City Chair Co.*, 295 F. Supp. 961, 965 (S.D. Ind. 1968); *Electrical Contractors* v. *Hamilton County*, 101 Ohio App.3d 580, 656 N.E.2d 18, 20–21 (1995). The Board itself has expressed a similar position, *Shen-Mar FoodProducts, Inc.*, 221 NLRB 1329 (enf'd as modified), 557 F.2d 396, 399 (4th Cir. 1977); *Syscon International Inc.*, 322 NLRB 539 (1996).

I would imagine that the defenders of Proposition 226, confronted with the argument that their ballot initiative is unconstitutional under the doctrine of preemption, would attempt to sweep their provision within Section 14(b) of the National Labor Relations Act. But it is difficult to see how this approach can succeed, particularly with regard to the Proposition's regulation of the payment of wages by employers inasmuch as that obligation exists independent of any union security provision. But even the attempt to regulate fees paid by members or nonmembers or agency shop fees, the argument must fail as well.

In *Algoma Plywood & Veneer Co.* v. *Wisconsin Employment Relations Board*, 336 U.S. 301 (1948), the Court, speaking through Justice Frankfurter, concluded that Section 14(b) extended to the application of union security agreements as well as their prohibition. See also *Intern Union of the United Assoc. of Journeymen and Apprentices of the Plumbing and Pipefitting Industry* v. *NLRB*, 675 F.2d 1257 (DC Cir. 1982).

Subsequently, the Court in a seeming endorsement of the view that Section 14(b) extends to state laws that regulate as well as prohibit union security agreements appeared to reaffirm this approach in *Retail Clerk Int. Assn, Loc. 1625* v. *Schermerhorn*, 375 U.S. 102 (1963) (*Schermerhorn II*). Accord, *Sheet Metal Workers* v. *Nichols, 89 Ariz. 187*, 360 P.2d 204, 47 L.R.R.M. 2856 (Ariz. 1961); *CWA* v. *Western Electric Co., Inc.*, 191 Colo. 128, 551 P.2d 1065, 93 LRRM 2176 (1976), appeal dismissed, 429 U.S. 1067 (1977) and *Ruff* v. *Kezzer,* 199 Colo. 182, 606 P.2d 441, 104 L.R-R-M. 2295 (Colo. 1980). But the fact of the matter is that Proposition 226 does not provide for regulation of union security agreements in any sense comparable to that which is used in the above-referenced cases approving state law jurisdiction under Section 14(b). Here, where California is attempting to regulate dues relationships both in and outside the union security context, the Proposition is not directed at the compulsory aspect of union security or agency shop clauses and thus is not within the ambit of Section 14(b).

Conclusion

For all of the reasons stated above, Proposition 226 is both bad policy and, in all probability, unconstitutional. Voters of California should reject it out of hand. It is based upon erroneous understandings and omissions about the nation's labor law.

Though I cannot be in Sacramento to testify before the Informational Joint Hearing of the Senate and Assembly on "Proposition 226: Political Contributions by Employees, Union Members and Foreign Entities," my hope is that this statement is of some assistance to the California Senate. As a California voter and a citizen and Chairman of the National Labor Relations Board, which interprets *Beck*, as well as a California law professor, I have an obligation to speak out and address the issues in light of your invitation to me. I stand ready to respond to any questions that you may have in the future and wish to be of help to you in any way possible.

Respectfully submitted,

William B. Gould IV
Chairman, National Labor Relations Board
Charles A. Beardsley Professor of Law
Stanford Law School (On Leave)

Notes

1. Chapter 4 of the proposition provides for the following changes to the California Government Code:

Code Section 5990:
(a) No employer or other person responsible for the disbursement of funds in payment of wages shall deduct any funds from an employee's wages that the employer knows or his reason to know will be used in whole or in part as a contribution or expenditure except upon the written request of the employee received within the previous 12 months on a form as described by subdivision (b).

Code Section 5991:
(a) No labor organization shall use any portion of dues, agency shop fees, or any other fees paid by members of the labor organization, or individuals who are not members, to make contributions or expenditures except upon the written authorization of the member, or individual who is not a member, received within the previous 12 months on a form described by subdivision (b).

Subdivision (b) of both sections specifies the authorization form's details including the size of the font to be used. Section 5991(c) requires labor organizations to maintain records including copies of the authorization, amounts withheld, and specific contributions. Section 599 1 (f) requires a reduction of dues, agency fees or other fees for individuals who do not sign authorizations. Chapter 8 provides that the measure's provisions in the case of legal invalidity are severable and that any provision found to be in conflict with federal law will remain in force to the maximum extent permitted by federal law.

2. *Eldorado Tool*, 325 NLRB No. 16 (W. Gould, concurring and dissenting in part at slip op. pgs. 4–7) (Nov. 9, 1997).

3. This statute is not administered by my Agency, the NLRB, but rather the Department of Labor with certain controversies within the jurisdiction of the federal courts.

4. *Monson Trucking Inc. and Calvin Anderson*, 324 NLRB No. 149 (W. Gould, concurring at slip op. pgs. 6–8) (Oct. 31, 1997), and *Group Health, Inc.*, 325 NLRB No. 49 (W. Gould, concurring at slip op. pgs. 4–7) (Feb. 2, 1998)

K

Labor, Civil Rights and the Rule of Law: Reflections of the NLRB Chairman

Delivered by William B. Gould IV, Chairman
National Labor Relations Board
Charles A. Beardsley Professor of Law
Stanford Law School (on leave)

NAACP Convention
Labor Luncheon
Atlanta, Georgia
Tuesday, July 14, 1998

The views expressed are those of Chairman Gould, and do not necessarily reflect those of the Board or other Members.

It is a pleasure to be with you today. I want to thank you for inviting me to speak here and particularly my old and dear friend, Bill Lucy, Secretary-Treasurer of American Federation of State, County and Municipal Employees Union who seems to have set this process in motion. This is one of my last opportunities as Chairman of the National Labor Relations Board to pay homage to Bill Lucy. His work is so valuable and tireless on behalf of not only his union and workers throughout the world—including South Africa which he and I have visited on numerous occasions—but also, as you know, for the NAACP to whom he has made such a substantial contribution over the years.

Nothing could be more timely and appropriate to the National Association for the Advancement of Colored People convention, in my view, than this celebration of Bastille Day 1998 and the historic recognition of inalienable rights of men and women, and the rights, as well as obligations, of labor. This day is critical to the advancement of human rights here and abroad over the past two centuries. It is one of a few sparks for the idea of a movement which speaks for large numbers of people who cannot effectively speak for themselves as individuals and which is at the heart of the birth of this organization, the NAACP, near the beginning of the century. This idea also was the premise of the New Deal legislation, which brought forward our own National Labor Relations Act, protecting the rights of workers to engage in concerted activities, which my Agency, the National Labor Relations Board, administers.

This legislation, the National Labor Relations Act, has endured for more than 63 years now and it is sometimes fashionable to say that it is no longer relevant to the modern high-tech information age in which knowledge and proficiency in math is so frequently substituted for jobs that were previously composed of brawn and muscle. But I think that this latest idea fad has just about as much validity as the view, so often propounded in this century, that the great post–Civil War amendments have no relevance to our times.

President Lincoln and his Administration, whatever its stance on slavery and the right to equality prior to the Emancipation Proclamation, and the War of the Rebellion, brought with them commitment to the idea of free labor. And it is that same philosophy which is enshrined in our National Labor Relations Act of 1935— a policy which has just as much validity in 1998 as it ever did. Whatever the Act's imperfections—and there are many of them—its framework is designed to promote and instill democracy in the workplace. And it has outlasted labor law systems in every major industrialized country of the world—Germany, France, Great Britain and Japan. The legacy of 1935 endures for me and the Agency which I head and, I dare say, most of the American people.

My professional life has been intimately connected with this philosophy. Now in large part, I came to the law because of the relationship between attempts to eradicate arbitrary barriers which exclude or limit people on the basis of race, sex, religion, national origin, disability or sexual orientation and the rights of employees to band together so as to improve their living standards and conditions of employment. Specifically, I was drawn to the law during my senior year in high school because of the Court's landmark May 17, 1954, ruling in *Brown* v. *Board of Education*[1] and my belief that lawyers could make a contribution both, through the interpretation of existing legal instruments and, as the debate on civil rights moved into Congress and the state legislatures, through the political process as well.

My heroes in the 1950s were two gentlemen who played leading roles in this organization. The first was Thurgood Marshall who, prior to his ascent to the High Court, argued *Brown* and participated in so many other cases along with such legal worthies as Charles Houston and James Nabritt. Nothing made the law more vivid for me as a high school youngster than *Brown* and a role model like Thurgood Marshall. They did, in the words of Charles Houston's biographer, the real "spadework." They were and are an inspiration for my generation—and it is my belief that they will be for those who are to follow.

The second individual was Roy Wilkins. His principled, unyielding, calm and deliberative manner put me in mind of my own father—and I never missed an opportunity to read to his comments in the *New York Times* and to hear him speak on programs that were gaining popularity at that time like "Meet the Press."

But my path was directed once I entered Cornell Law School in the fall 1958 and began my study of law. The first epiphany was that I quickly became aware of the fact that there were very few civil rights or constitutional lawyers around— Thurgood Marshall had three or four people working with him in New York and a few practitioners, principally around the south, who worked with him on cases on the NAACP docket. Remember, Title VII of the Civil Rights Act of 1964, which I followed with considerable interest while with the Board in Washington as a junior attorney, was not yet even on the books!

The second moved me toward my career and ultimately the Chairmanship of the National Labor Relations Board—the first black American ever to be Chairman of the Board in this Agency's history. My law school professor, Kurt Hanslowe devised a problem in first year legal writing dealing with the duty of fair representation under the Railway Labor Act and the attempt by the railway unions to remove black workers from the fireman's job as it was transformed from the dirtiest, least desirable classification to a cushy feather-bedded position with the advent of the diesel engine. The problem that Professor Hanslowe devised for us during that first year focused on the Supreme Court's ruling in *Steele* v. *Louisville & Nashville Railroad*[2] and it concentrated my attention on ways in which labor and civil rights were unalterably infused with elements of each.

For the central theme contained in the *Steele* decision, in attempting to retard the exclusion of black workers in the railways, was overriding the importance of the dignity of labor, and the need to protect the workers against arbitrary treatment of all kinds, including racial discrimination as it seemed to me, by implicating other forms of discrimination. For in the '50s I could see that the work of Walter Reuther, for whom I always had considerable admiration,[3] and the United Auto Workers for whom I went to work in the early '60s, was aimed at protecting those who could not protect themselves individually, on employment discrimination, education and social welfare issues.

And thus it was clear to me at this point that unions, notwithstanding the sins of those involved in the railway industry and in *Steele,* were quite necessary. Any society which is both democratic and pluralist in the industrialized world must have free and autonomous trade unions as part of its system. It is clear that the decline of the labor movement has been unhealthy for our democracy and a contributing factor in the growing inequality between rich and poor in our country and the gap between the haves and the have-nots—white, black, brown or yellow—that threatens the stability of any society predicated upon free institutions.

But *Steele* itself made me aware of another problem in the workplace, i.e., that there are labor rights and labor wrongs, labor uses and labor abuses. Both labor and management are capable of overreaching and misdeeds. I bore personal testimony to this proposition as I served as lead counsel in the case involving Judge Keith's landmark 1973 ruling in *Stamps* v. *Detroit Edison Co.*[4] that at the time provided the greatest per individual affected judgment in employment discrimination litigation in history. It was an action instituted against a company and the two unions with which they bargained.

Thus, these early experiences have helped shape my view that it is vital for the state to intervene in the labor market to redress inequality between employees and employers, as the National Labor Relations Act obliges us to do—and that both parties—labor and management—should have rights and obligations and that both should be answerable to the rule of law. The philosophy of the Act mandates intervention to ensure workers freedom and autonomy—so that labor, if it wishes, may sit down with management and negotiate so as to resolve their own peculiar problems. While my position in Washington makes it impossible to comment on the merits of either side's position or tactics in the ongoing UAW-General Motors dispute in Flint, Michigan, disagreements (and they cannot be avoided in a democratic society) about job protection, work rules, methods to reduce labor costs and future investment planning are inevitably part of or related to the bargaining process promoted by our statute.

Now we are engaged in a difficult struggle in Washington over the continued viability of the Act and the National Labor Relations Board. In a sense, this chapter of our story began in the winter of 1995–1996 when we endured government shutdowns because of the unwillingness of the House Republicans to accept statutes like our Act as part of the social fabric of America. But during this era of divided government the votes have never been there to repeal our Act—or at least to override a potential White House veto of such a repeal.

Meanwhile, numerous Members of Congress wrote to me about decisions or policies with which they had disagreement. The House in 1995 voted for a 30 percent cut in Committee for our budget and then, on the floor, ultimately a 15 percent cut. Ultimately, we wound up with a 2 percent cut, then the following year a slight 3 percent increase and, at present, we are operating under a freeze—a cut in real terms which has required us to not only engage in a hiring freeze throughout '98 but to stop all hearings for the entire month of September.

That represents a real cut of 5 percent and I can tell you that our resources are stretched to the limit. The House of Representatives Appropriations Subcommittee on Labor, Health and Human Services has voted a "hard freeze" for Fiscal Year 1999 which is in effect a decrease of 4.4 percent. If this level of funding is provided it would mean:

- Case backlogs would increase by one-third
- Case processing times and delays would continue to increase
- Loss of an additional 125 FTE or 6.6% staff reduction over current year
- Staff loss of 15% since 1993
- Staff reductions would require furloughs and possibly RIFs
- Agency ability to be Year 2000 compliant seriously hampered

Under my Chairmanship the backlog in Washington was reduced to the lowest level ever achieved since statistics were kept by late '95. But since early '96 we have been moving backward and our productivity at the highest level in Washington is going south. The gains obtained in '94 and '95 are imperiled.

As my late father used to say to me when we would have our telephone conversations about the *Detroit Edison* case which was pending lo those many years: "Bill, do those fellows have their money and jobs yet?" That is the key—for in the absence of expeditious resolution of issues, we build criticism and disrespect for the law into our labor law system and, of course, the concept that justice delayed is justice denied has applicability to employers as well as unions. Workers who lose their jobs because of discrimination prohibited by our Act have to wait far too long to receive the reinstatement and backpay remedy. Employers are victimized by the accumulation of backpay liability that could be diminished if we moved more promptly. An employer, which can file unfair labor practice charges under our statute, also loses benefits through the passage of time.

As you may know, I instituted numerous reforms to get at our delay problem. For the first time we authorized our Administrative Law Judges to issue bench decisions and to use new methods to settle and conciliate cases that would be a drain to the taxpayers and private parties. My judgment is that our use of Section 10(j) to obtain injunctions in more than 300 occasions since March 1994 represents a major step forward for law enforcement. Never before in its 63-year history has the Board acted with such frequent conviction and commitment—and I am particularly proud of this accomplishment.

I have been after the backlog problem since the beginning of my Chairmanship and I tell you today that, both before and after my departure from Washington, as long as there is the breath of life in me, I will not retreat. I will press again and again and speak out again and again against both the indolence and the cynical calculated delays which injure the parties and erode the respect for law which a democratic society must possess. And I shall continue to urge the Congress to provide us with the appropriations to do our job, reminding them that our staff support in Washington has declined by 15 percent during the four-and-one-half years of my watch.

In the years immediately following *Brown*, we lost one of the best opportunities for law and order down here when this part of the country was encouraged to believe that it could say "never." Recently, one of our court of appeals, while reviewing an important case now pending before us on the merits, presumed, it said, that the Board would act with all "deliberate speed." The irony was not lost on me. We cannot countenance another round of "deliberate speed" in labor law. We owe it to the people to devote our energies toward the production of decisions! The alternative is cynicism and disrespect for the rule of law which we cherish.

What a pleasure it is to speak to you at this NAACP Convention. It is an honor to recall the great men associated with this organization like Marshall and Wilkins and so many others.

It has been an honor for me to serve as President Clinton's nominee as Chairman of the National Labor Relations Board during these past four-and-one-half years. I appreciate your support—particularly during the sometimes lonely and difficult period of the confirmation process.

I recall Wade Henderson's attendance at the Senate hearing on October 1, 1993 and when the Senate cast the greatest number of "No" votes against my nomination on March 2, 1994, I rolled up my sleeves to do the job at hand. As one of our Agency's great friends, Senator Tom Harkin of Iowa, said to me at lunch last week about that vote: "Bill, that was your badge of honor," and I shall always wear it proudly.

I think that we have confounded those "No" votes in the Senate and have made great strides towards upholding the rule of law impartially and to promote some measure of balance between labor and management.

Thank you for the invitation to be here. I wish you and your leaders Godspeed in the hard work that is to be done in eliminating and diminishing the barriers of inequity that exist in our society and I look forward to working with you in the future on these as a former Chairman.

Notes

1. 347 U.S. 483 (1954).
2. 323 U.S. 192 (1944).
3. See "In Memory of Walter Philip Reuther," BNA Daily Labor Report No. 174 at D-12, E-1 (September 8, 1995).
4. 365 F. Supp. 87 (E.D. Michigan 1973).

L

Resignation Letter

United States Government
National Labor Relations Board
Washington, D. C. 20570
Hand Deliver via Messenger

July 7, 1998

Honorable William Jefferson Clinton
The President of the United States
The White House
Washington, D.C. 20500

Dear President Clinton:

This is to advise you that at some point prior to August 27, 1998, the date on which my term of office expires, I shall resign as Chairman and Member of the National Labor Relations Board. When first approached about this position in May 1993, I stressed my intent to serve only one term and now the time has come for me to depart and to return to my duties as a law professor at Stanford Law School.

It has been an honor to serve in your Administration as head of our independent quasi-judicial Agency in which so many career employees serve with distinction. You will recall that last year you bestowed the President's Award for Distinguished Federal Civilian Service upon my former Chief Counsel, William R. Stewart, the first individual with the National Labor Relations Board ever to receive the President's Award. This award symbolizes the standards of excellence adhered to by the career employees with whom I have served.

I am of the view that during the past four and one half years of my tenure as Chairman we have made considerable strides toward the substitution of cooperation for conflict and the goal of bringing our people together as one Nation which promotes and respects the rights and obligations of both labor and management. Thus, we have diminished the polarization and contentiousness that prevailed at the Board's beginnings, and that of the National Labor Relations Act, 63 years ago, notwithstanding its continued existence in some labor-management relationships in the private sector within our jurisdiction.

During this period the Board has promoted new settlement procedures so as to lessen the amount of otherwise wasteful litigation, reduced (at least during our first two years) the case backlog, stressed the National Labor Relations Act's principal focus upon both the promotion of collective bargaining and freedom of association for workers, and restored the Board's credibility as an impartial arbiter of labor-management disputes. Our success in enforcing our orders in the courts has never been better. Based upon all of these indicia, the state of the National Labor Relations Board in 1998 has improved considerably during my Chairmanship.

Nearly 133 years ago, my great grandfather, having had the chance to serve the United States Government as an escaped slave under the most perilous and arduous circumstances of the War of the Rebellion, received his discharge papers in Charlestown, Massachusetts after three years of service in the United States Navy. I have been privileged to carry on this tradition of public service and I thank you for the opportunity to have done so.

I wish you Godspeed during the remainder of your term of office.

Sincerely yours,

William Benjamin Gould IV
Chairman

M

Letter from President William J. Clinton

The White House
Washington

July 29, 1998

Mr. William B. Gould IV, Chairman
National Labor Relations Board
1099 14th Street, N.W.
Washington, D.C. 20570

Dear Bill:

I have received your letter of July 7, and it is with regret that I accept your resignation as Chairman of the National Labor Relations Board, effective not later than August 27, 1998.

Your vision and expertise over the past four years have helped to restore the American public's confidence in the NLRB. With a strong commitment to promoting stable labor-management relations, you have skillfully guided the NLRB through the challenges posed by today's rapidly changing work environment. I am especially grateful for your commitment to my Administration's reinvention initiative. At the NLRB, this commitment has translated into more efficient administrative processes, expedited legal procedures, and a reduction in the need for lengthy and costly litigation.

The NLRB's forward thinking, innovative agenda is more important than ever, as our country strives to meet the social and economic challenges of the 21st century workplace. I know that your wise counsel and judgment will be missed, as will the dedication and energy that you have brought to the NLRB. I know, too, that these extraordinary qualities will serve you well as you return to private life.

Best wishes for every future success.

Sincerely,

Bill Clinton

N

Glossary of Cases

I   Some Supreme Court Decisions prior to Clinton Board

Communication Workers v. Beck, 487 U.S. 735 (1988) held that a union was not permitted "over the objections of dues paying nonmember employees," to expend funds on activities not related to collective bargaining, contract administration or grievance adjustment. The Court concluded that such expenditures violated the union's duty of fair representation.

Lechmere, Inc. v. *National Labor Relations Board*, 502 U.S. 5327, 112 841 (1992). This case requires the Board not to make an employer's exclusion of nonemployee organizers where the union is trying to reach the public an unfair labor practice. Chairman Gould has noted on this issue that the Board must protect a union's ability to present its views by those means of communication that remain available to it within the confines of the Court's decision in *Lechmere*, where the Court established the broad presumption that nonemployee union organizers do not have access to private property.

NLRB v. *General Motors Corp.*, 373 U.S. 734 (1963) in which the Court held that "membership" means financial payments of dues and assessments under a union security clause.

NLRB v. *Mackay Radio & Telegraph Co.*, 304 U.S. 333 (1938) in which the Court said that an employer may permanently replace economic strikers.

NLRB v. *Wooster Division of Borg-Warner Corp.*, 356 U.S. 342, 351 (1958) in which the Court held that mandatory subjects of bargaining about wages, hours and conditions of employment must be engaged in by both sides until impasse.

NLRB v. *ILA*, 473 U.S. 61 (1985). The Longshoreman's union had successfully bargained for a requirement that some cargo containers owned or leased by marine shipping companies must be unloaded by longshoremen, as opposed to anywhere within the local port area. This rule was bargained for as a result of the reduction in work following the increased use of local port workers instead of longshoremen in this type of work. The Board held that such a provision constituted secondary activity pursuant to Section 8(e) of the NLRA. The Supreme Court reversed, finding that the provision constituted a lawful work preservation agreement, and was not directed at affecting the business relations of neutral employers.

In *American Hospital Association* v. *NLRB*, 499 U.S. 606, 610 (1991), the Court described the Board's authority to make broadly applicable rules as follows: Section 6 [of the NLRA] granted the Board the "authority from time to time to make, amend, and rescind . . . such rules and regulations as may be necessary to carry out the provisions' of the Act. Section 156." The Petitioner *in American Hospital* claimed that the Board had a statutory responsibility to make decisions on a case-by-case basis instead of rulemaking. The Court disagreed, saying, "the meaning of Section 9(b)'s mandate that the Board decide the appropriate bargaining unit 'in each case' is clear and contrary to the meaning advanced by petitioner. . . . In resolving such a dispute, the Board's decision is presumably to be guided not simply by the basic policy of the Act but also by the rules that the Board develops to circumscribe and to guide its discretion either in the process of case-by-case adjudication or by the exercise of its rulemaking authority. . . . [Furthermore, our own precedent establishes that] even if a statutory scheme requires individualized determinations, the decision maker has the authority to rely on rulemaking to resolve certain issues of general applicability unless Congress clearly expresses an intent to withhold that authority."

II Supreme Court Decisions Rendered during Clinton Board

Brown et al. v. *Pro Football Inc.,* 116 2116 (1996). Here, while concluding that the federal labor law shields football from antitrust liability when the owners act unilaterally subsequent to bargaining to impasse, the Court noted that it could not resolve the ultimate issue of accommodation between the competing statutes until it hears "the detailed views of the Board, to whose 'specialized judgment' Congress 'intended to leave' many of the 'inevitable questions' concerning multi-employer bargaining bound to arise in the future. . . . " 116 S. Ct. at 2127. Again, the Court stressed the central role of the Board and the Court's policy of deference to this agency.

Marquez v. *Screen Actors Guild, Inc.,* 119 S. Ct. 292 (1998). The plaintiff raised the issue of whether the union had a responsibility to advise her of her rights under

Beck pursuant to the union security clause in the collective bargaining agreement. The Supreme Court, in an opinion written by Justice O'Connor, held that: (1) union's mere negotiation of union security clause tracking NLRA language does not breach duty of fair representation; (2) organization's negotiation of union security clause with language derived from NLRA section authorizing such a clause was not arbitrary; (3) organization did not act in bad faith by negotiating union security clause that tracked NLRA language; and (4) challenge to grace period provision of union security clause fell squarely within primary jurisdiction of National Labor Relations Board.

Textron Lycoming Reciprocating v. *United Automobile, Aerospace and Agricultural Implement Workers*, 523 U.S. 653 (1998). The Supreme Court held that the section of the National Labor Relations Act conferring subject-matter jurisdiction over disputes about refusals to bargain in good faith does not confer exclusive jurisdiction over a union's complaint that an employer had fraudulently induced the union to sign a collective-bargaining agreement. Such actions may be entertained as suits involving the alleged breach of a collective-bargaining agreement in federal district court as well.

NLRB v. *Town & Country*, 116 S. Ct. 450 (1995). "Salting" case in which the Supreme Court upheld unanimously the Board's decision that paid union organizers are "employees" within the meaning of the Act, and therefore are protected against employer retaliation in the form of discharge or discipline for protected activity.

Allentown Mack Sales and Service, Inc. v. *NLRB*, 118 818 (1998) held, by a 5-4 vote, that the Board's "good-faith reasonable doubt" standard for determining whether an employer lawfully may poll its employees to determine if the union retains majority support was "facially rational and consistent with the Act." However, the Court concluded, again by a 5-4 vote, that the Board erred in its factual finding that Allentown lacked a good-faith reasonable doubt. The Court held that certain employee statements, such as expressions of dissatisfaction with the quality of union representation by employees who hope to be hired by a successor employer interviewing them for employment discounted by the Board, could "unquestionably be probative to some degree of the employer's good-faith reasonable doubt." However as Justice Breyer said in dissent: The Board in effect has said that an employee statement made during a job interview with an employer who has expressed an interest in a nonunionized work force will often tell us precisely nothing about that employee's true feelings. That Board conclusion represents an exercise of the kind of discretionary authority that Congress placed squarely within the Board's administrative and fact-finding powers and responsibilities.

Auciello Iron Works Inc. v. *NLRB*, 116 1754 (1996), the Court again unanimously upheld the Board's position and held that an employer may not refuse to bargain with an incumbent union on the ground that it has lost majority status where it has previously entered into a contract with such a union. The Court stated that "the Board's judgment is entitled to prevail. To affirm its rule of decision in this case, indeed, there is no need to invoke the full measure of the 'considerable deference' that the Board is due" (116 at 1759).

III   Some Leading Clinton Board Decisions

Angelica Healthcare Services Group, Inc., 315 NLRB 1320 (January 18, 1995), a unanimous Board held that a hearing in some form is required prior to the time that the election takes place. From a policy perspective, the Chairman's view is that employees should have ballots in most instances before a hearing so that representation matters may be resolved expeditiously and so that the electorate does not lose faith in the prompt delivery of the protections provided by the Act. Under the statute, a "hearing" is required—although it was not addressed in *Angelica* precisely how one would define a hearing.

A.P.R.A. Fuel Oil Buyers Group, Inc., 320 NLRB 308 (December 21, 1995) enfd. 134 F.3d 50, 157 LRRM 2001 (2d Cir. 1997), Chairman Gould joined a Board majority which interpreted the Supreme Court's *Sure-Tan* decision, which had concluded in 1984 that undocumented workers are employees within the meaning of the National Labor Relations Act. The question in *A.P.R.A Fuel* was whether such workers are entitled to backpay and the Board answered this question in the affirmative. The Chairman, along with member Truesdale, rejected the view of Member Browning that the employer could be ordered to hire applicants referred by the union in the event that dismissed workers were not eligible for reinstatement. The Chairman explicitly stated that the Board does not have the authority to grant such a remedy.

Arizona Public Service Company, 325 NLRB No. 137 (May 4, 1998) A Board majority, Chairman Gould and Member Hurtgen, held in separate opinions that an employer did not engage in objectionable conduct by conducting an election-day raffle for employees voting in the election. Chairman Gould disagreed with the Board's prior approach to determining if an election-day raffle is objectionable, i.e., consideration of whether the raffle prizes are of a substantial nature, and stated his view that "the Board should modify its analysis … to place primary consideration on whether the employer has, in the past, held raffles of a similar nature for employees." Because the record failed to show that the employer's raffle was inconsistent with past practice, Chairman Gould found the raffle not objectionable.

Alwin Mfg., 326 NLRB No. 63 (1998), enf'd. 192 F.3d 133 (D.C. Cir. 1999) A Board majority held that a union's negotiating and unfair labor practice strike costs might be imposed as a remedy for certain employer violations of the duty to bargain.

Bennett Industries Inc. 313 NLRB 1363 (1994), a unanimous Board held that in a representation hearing where an employer did not take a position about an issue in dispute, the hearing officer properly refused to allow the employer to introduce evidence as to that issue and that it would be inappropriate to permit relitigation of the same issue to the challenged ballot process.

Beverly Enterprises-Hawaii, Inc. d/b/a Hale Nani Rehabilitation and Nursing Center, 326 NLRB No. 37 (August 26, 1998). A Board majority, Members Fox, Liebman, Hurtgen, and Brame, in separate opinions, held that an employer did not engage in objectionable conduct by having its supervisors distribute anti-union literature to employees in areas where employees were prohibited from distributing literature. Chairman Gould dissented, finding that the employer's conduct constituted disparate enforcement of its no-distribution rule.

California Saw & Knife, 320 NLRB 224 (December 20, 1995), enfd. sub nom. *Assn. of International Machinists* v. *NLRB*, 133 F.3d 1012, 157 LRRM 2287 (7th Cir. 1998). The Board held that a union must inform every nonmember employee that s/he has a legal right to remain a nonmember, and that this information must be communicated to the nonmember before the union seeks to obligate the employee to pay dues and fees under a union-security clause. Also, the Board held that the information communicated should include those responsibilities articulated by the Supreme Court in *Beck*; i.e., information relating to non-bargaining union activities. In a companion case—*Paperworkers Local 1033 (Weyerhaeuser Paper Co.)*, 320 NLRB 349 (December 10, 1995)—the Board held that a union must inform all employees in the bargaining unit, not just nonmembers, of the rights of nonmembers under *Beck* if they were not informed of those rights prior to assuming obligations under a union-security clause. In addition, the Board held that a union must inform all such employees that they have a right under the Supreme Court's ruling in *NLRB* v. *General Motors*, to become nonmembers of the union in order to be eligible to exercise *Beck* rights.

Caterpillar, Inc., 321 NLRB 1178 (August 27, 1996), a majority of the Board held, in affirming the Administrative Law Judge, that the employer violated Section 8(a)(1) by prohibiting its employees from displaying various union slogans including a statement, "Permanently Replace Fites," and violated Section 8(a)(3) by enforcing the rule. The Board stated that it agreed with the Administrative Law Judge that the slogan was a response to the employer's stated policy of using permanent replacements rather than an attempt to cause the removal of Fites as the chief executive officer. But, even if they were attempting to remove the chief executive officer, the Board's view was that the conduct was protected.

Chairman Gould concurred in a separate opinion expressing his dissatisfaction with Board and court precedent with respect to employee activity which seeks to influence management policy and its protected status. He said:

[T]he level of managerial policy or hierarchy protested by the union or employees should have little if anything to do with whether such employee activity is protected. Quite obviously, the level at which managerial representatives are involved in employment conditions will vary from company to company. While I am of the view that concerted activity for the purpose of influencing management policy, which is unrelated to employment conditions, is not protected under the Act, the fact of the matter is that the presence or absence of a particular corporate hierarchical structure or internal organization does not provide the appropriate answer to the question of whether employee activity is protected under Section 7 of the Act.

Detroit Newspapers I & II, 326 NLRB No. 64, 65 (August 27, 1998). The first issue was whether the employer's withdrawal from multiunion joint bargaining constituted a violation of Section 8(a)(5) of the National Labor Relations Act. A majority of the Board (Member Liebman dissenting) concluded that it did not. The second issue was the employer's proposal to permit the assignment to non-unit employees of work traditionally performed by unit employees in Local 18. Again, a majority of the Board determined that this proposal was not an unfair labor practice. The third issue raised involved proposals by the employer on merit pay, television assignments, and a refusal by the employer to furnish relevant information. On this issue, the Board (with Hurtgen and Brame dissenting about certain "aspects of information") did find that an unfair labor practice had been committed, and that the strike was an unfair labor practice strike. Over Chairman Gould's dissent, the majority of the Board did not address the issue of whether the employer had violated section 8(a)(5) by unilaterally determining wages and conditions of striker replacements. Chairman Gould did find a violation of 8(a)(5) in this action.

Dial-A-Mattress Operating Corp., 326 NLRB No. 75 (August 27, 1998), and *Roadway Package System, Inc.*, 326 NLRB No. 72 (August 27, 1998). These cases concerned determinations of whether particular employment relationships designated workers as employees or independent contractors. Chairman Gould maintained that one has to look at aspects of the employer-independent contractor relationship that are attributable to government regulation. The Board focused particularly on the following four issues in determining that the workers in *Dial-A-Mattress* were independent contractors, while the workers in *Roadway* were employees: (1) the Board's authority to change or modify the common law right-of-control test to determine if an individual is an employee under Section 2(3) of the Act; (2) the relative importance of factors indicative of employee or independent contractor status; (3) the applicability of three specific cases; and (4) evidence of financial gains or losses by the drivers in the *Roadway* cases.

Douglas-Randall, Inc., 320 NLRB 431 (December 22, 1995), a majority of the Board sustained the dismissal of a decertification petition when a subsequently-entered settlement agreement provided a bargaining provision with the incumbent union. This decision facilitated both settlement and the collective bargaining process.

Fieldcrest Cannon, Inc., 318 NLRB 470 (1995), enfd. In part 97 F.3d 65, 153 LRRM 2617 (4th Cir. 1996), petition for rehearing denied February 10, 1997, the Board (Chairman Gould and Member Browning; Members Stephens concurring and dissenting in part) found that the respondent employer's unfair labor practices were so numerous, pervasive, and outrageous that special notice and access remedies were necessary to dissipate fully the coercive effect of the violations.

Kalin Construction Company, Inc., 321 NLRB 649 (July 8, 1996), the Board adopted a new rule, similar to the anti-captive audience approach endorsed four decades ago prohibiting eleventh-hour captive audience speeches in *Peerless Plywood*, by prohibiting other forms of last minute campaign tactics. In this case, employees could only gain access to the voting area by entering through an area where, contrary to past practice, the company handed them their pay envelopes. Here, each employee received two checks for the pay period whereas in the past one paycheck per pay period had been issued. One was for the amount the employer claimed the employees would receive under union representation. The other was for the amount the employer claimed would be sent to the union. The Board concluded that, because last minute campaign speeches and electioneering and changes in the paycheck process have an unsettling impact on employees and disturb the laboratory conditions which are a prerequisite for a fair election, a change in the paycheck, paycheck distribution, the location or method of the paycheck distribution would be a basis for setting the election aside. It noted that, if a change in the paycheck process was motivated by a "legitimate business reason unrelated to the election," the new rule would not be violated. The Board sounded a theme that is similar to much that they have done elsewhere, i.e., an additional virtue of this approach was that it was both understandable and predictable and, therefore, would be less likely to give rise to "... extensive litigation, delay, and rulings that are difficult to reconcile."

Legal Aid Society, 324 NLRB 135 (October 21, 1997). The Board addressed the issue of whether professional employees possess supervisory authority over nonunit support personnel. The Board was confronted with the issue of whether four of the Society's attorneys should be excluded from the petitioned—for unit of attorneys on the ground that they exercise statutory supervisory authority over nonunit law clerks, paralegals and/or clericals or otherwise exercise statutory supervisory authority. Members Fox and Higgins in the majority opinion, adhered to *Detroit College of Business*, 296 NLRB 318 (1989), in which the Board held that a number of factors should be appropriately taken into account in determining whether professionals possess supervisory status which would exclude them from statutory coverage. The majority found that attorneys should be excluded who supervise paralegals on the ground that the individuals' work is comparable to part-time faculty members in Detroit College. In *Legal Aid*, the Board majority said that the functions of one attorney were not "ancillary to her professional duties as an attorney" and because of the independence of such nonunit individuals they could not be regarded as support personnel which might provide the basis for an exception to supervisory status.

In a concurring and dissenting opinion, Chairman Gould stated that, because of the confusing and wide variety of separate factors set forth *in Detroit College*, that decision should be overruled. But he endorsed the principle that the professionals who only supervise non-unit support employees could be included in the professional bargaining unit. Chairman Gould stated that there is not divided loyalty problem—the basis for supervisory exclusion—because the professional supervisory authority is set apart from their "primary interest as employees in professional matters and concerns." He expressed the concern that *Detroit College* would deprive employees of their rights and protections under the Act and was contrary to the purpose of the Act.

Management Training Corp., 317 NLRB 1355 (July 28, 1995). The Board found that private employers, whether government contractors or not, are within its jurisdiction. (The National Labor Relations Act excludes public employers.)

McClatchy Newspapers, Inc., 321 NLRB 1386 (August 27, 1996) enfd. 131 F.3d 1026, 157 LRRM 2023 (DC Cir. 1997) cert. denied (1998), a Board majority held that an employer could not unilaterally implement merit pay proposals even when bargaining had taken place to the point of impasse. The Board said that if the employer was given carte blanche authority over wage increases without regard to time, standards, criteria it would be " ... so inherently destructive of the fundamental principles of collective bargaining that it could not be sanctioned as part of a doctrine created to break impasse and restore active collective bargaining." The majority went on to say: "[W]e are preserving an employer's right to bargain to impasse over proposals to retain management discretion over merit pay while, at the same time, maintaining the Guild's opportunity to negotiate terms and conditions of employment."

Monson Trucking, Inc., 324 NLRB 933 (October 31, 1997), the Board found that the union violated the National Labor Relations Act by failing to withdraw its request to have an employee discharged after he complied with demands to satisfy delinquent dues obligations, and by failing to inform him of his *Beck* rights in connection with the notice of his dues delinquency. In a concurring opinion, Chairman Gould expanded his view that "membership in good standing" language in a union security clause is unlawful.

North County Humane, Columbia, Baltimore Gas & Electric: Where placement or status questions are raised to the Board in pre-election proceedings, the Board traditionally has followed a policy of permitting up to approximately fifteen percent of the voting group to vote under challenge. The Board and most parties deem this to be preferable to having extensive pre-election litigation that would delay the ballot and/or the court. In early 1994, shortly after its confirmation by the Senate, the Board proceeded to a ballot where 33 percent of the voters in one unit, and 22 percent of the voters in a second unit, were in dispute. See *North County Humane Society*, 21-RC-19324, review denied April 14, 1994. The theory behind this approach is that where the numbers of employees in dispute is manageable, it may be unnecessary to resolve such disputes even after the ballot is taken because the numbers ma not affect the outcome of the election. This also proved the case in *Columbia Hospital for Women Medical Center, Inc.,* Case 5-RC-14033, at a time when the anticipated ratio of challenged ballots were in dispute. Since the challenged number was 700, the election would have been delayed some period of time—and again the numbers in dispute were not determinative.

Novotel New York, 321 NLRB 624 (July 8, 1996). The Board held that a union's litigation on behalf of organizing employees was not a "benefit" which interfered with the conduct of the election.

Oil Workers Local 1-591 (Burlington Northern Railroad), 325 NLRB No. 45 (January 27, 1998), the Board held that he union, which was engaged in a labor dispute with a subcontractor working on the premises of a neutral refinery, violated Section 8(b)(4)(B) by picketing at the refinery gate reserved for the neutral railroad that transported the product of the neutral refinery.

Texaco, the neutral refinery owner, operated a facility on refinery grounds that produced "coke," a byproduct of oil. Texaco subcontracted part of its coke-making operation to WPS, the primary employee with which the union had a labor dispute. Texaco set up a reserve gate system. One gate was for Texaco employees and suppliers, another gate was for WPS employees and suppliers, and a third gate was for Burlington Northern-the neutral railroad that came into the refinery to pick up the coke for delivery to Texaco customers. In furtherance of its dispute with WPS, the union picketed not only the gate reserved for WPS employees and suppliers, but also the gate reserved for Burlington.

The Board majority, consisting of Chairman Gould and Members Hurtgen and Brame, found that the picketing was common-situs picketing because it took place at the refinery, which was owned by neutral Texaco and was the location where multiple neutral contractors worked.

Painters and Allied Trades District Council No. 51 (Manganaro Corporation), 321 NLRB 158 (May 10, 1996), Chairman Gould and Member Browning, with Member Cohen dissenting, held that the anti-dual-shop clause sought by the union had a primary objective and thus did not violate Section 8(b)(4)(B) of the Act. The majority agreed with the judge's finding that the clause was a primary work-preservation clause and that the clause was not unlawful on its face.

Providence Hospital, 320 NLRB 717 (January 3, 1996), enf'd.121 F.3d 548, 156 LRRM 2001 (9th Cir. 1997). The Board stated that the record evidence did not establish that charge nurses' assignments of registered nurses was anything more than a routine clerical task and that their direction of employees did not require the use of independent judgment within the meaning of Section 2(11). The Board noted that while the charge nurses exercised considerable judgment in assessing patients' conditions and treatment, this was part of their professional judgment shared by all staff registered nurses.

San Diego Gas and Electric, 325 NLRB No. 218 (July 21, 1998). This case addressed the policy of using mail ballots to maximize the opportunity of workers to exercise their statutory right to vote in representation elections. In this case, the majority abandoned the Board's *Casehandling Manual* "infeasibility" standard, which stated that "the use of mail balloting, at least in situations where any party is not agreeable to the use of mail ballots, should be limited to those circumstances that clearly indicate the infeasibility of a manual election." Noting that the Manual has not been revised since 1989 and does not reflect current Board precedent regarding mail ballots, the majority stated that the direction of a mail ballot election is appropriate: (1) where eligible voters are "scattered" because of their job duties over a wide geographic area; (2) where eligible voters are "scattered" because of their work schedules; and (3) where there is a strike, a lockout, or picketing in progress.

Chairman Gould concurred in a separate opinion, stating that he would find the use of mail ballots appropriate in all situations where the prevailing conditions are such that they are necessary to conserve Agency resources and/or enfranchise employees and joined in the decision to abandon the "infeasibility" standard. Chairman Gould also stated that he would find that budgetary concerns standing alone could justify the direction of a mail ballot election.

Shepherd Tissue, Inc., 326 NLRB No. 38 (August 26, 1998): In his concurring opinion, Chairman Gould stated the following: "In my view, the *Sewell* prohibition [against racially inflammatory campaign appeals] is inapplicable in the instant case where the Petition, in a campaign handbill, included a statement by a discharged unit employee concerning a sexual harassment investigation that "black folk have been wrongly touched by whites for over 300 years." Racial remarks and campaigning which takes race into account involving the employer-employee relationship are part of the reality of the workplace and therefore a legitimate campaign issue. Such appeals are germane to the solidarity and the working conditions of a racial group during an organizing campaign and accordingly are not objectionable regardless of their truth or falsity."

Speedrack Products Group Limited, 325 NLRB No. 109 (April 9, 1998), a case on remand from the United States Court of Appeal for the District of Columbia Circuit, where the Board reconsidered its earlier decision, re-ported at 320 NLRB 627 (1995), in which a majority had held that work-release inmates did not share a community interest with the regular "free-world" unit employees, and were ineligible to vote. Chairman Gould dissented from that earlier decision, stating that he would find the work release employees eligible under the Board's decisions in *Winsett-Simmonds Engineers, Inc.*, 164 NLRB 611 (1967), and *Georgia Pacific Corp.*, 201 NLRB 760 (1973), which represent the Board's determination that whether work-release employees share a community of interest with their fellow employees depends on their status while in the employment relationship and not on the ultimate control they may be subjected to at other times. In remanding the case to the Board, the D.C. Circuit agreed with Chairman Gould's dissenting opinion, finding that "work-release employees were 'completely integrated' into Speedrack's workforce," and "[t]hus under *Winsett-Simmonds* and the Board's other cases, *Speedrack*'s employees appear to share a community of interest and to be eligible to vote in the representation election." *Speedrack Products Group, Ltd.* v. *NLRB,* 114 F.3d 1276, 1282. In accepting the remand, the Board stated that it had reconsidered its original determination regarding the work-release employees and, in agreement with Chairman Gould's dissent in the underlying representation case, decided to apply *Winsett-Simmonds* to ding that the work-release employees share a sufficient community of interest with the unit employees.

Sunrise Rehabilitation Hospital, 320 NLRB 212 (December 19, 1995) The Board held that monetary payments, that are offered to employees by unions or employers, as a reward for coming to a Board election, and that exceed reimbursement for actual transportation expenses, amount to a benefit "that reasonably tends to influence the election outcome." Accordingly, the Board overruled established precedent. It noted that the standard for whether the offer of pay or monetary benefits is objective and not subjective, i.e., "... whether the challenged conduct has a reasonable tendency to influence the election outcome." The Board further stated that it takes into account, "... such factors as the size of the benefit in relation to its stated legitimate purpose, the number of employees receiving it, how the employees would reasonably construe the purpose given the context of the offer, and its timing."

Teamsters Local 618 (Chevron Chemical Co.), 326 NLRB No. 34 (August 24, 1998). The principal issue raised in *Chevron* centered on the methodology that the union used in calculating reduced dues for *Beck* objectors. The union offset interest and dividend income that it received against nonchargeable expenditures prior to determining the respective percentages of chargeable/nonchargeable expenditures. In a very brief opinion, the Board found this method unlawful because there was no evidence that the interest and dividend income was generated solely from non-dues income and, hence, it was impossible to determine whether "objectors were required to pay their 'fair share' of the union's representation expenses." Chairman Gould concurred separately.

Telescope Casual, 326 NLRB No. 60 (August 27, 1998). Chairman Gould and Member Hurtgen found, over Member Liebman's dissent, that regressive bargaining was not bargaining in bad faith. In regressive bargaining, the party (in this case, the employer) claims that if the offered deal is not accepted, then when negotiations come to an impasse, the same party will only offer a worse deal. The opinion noted that regressive bargaining is not per se unlawful. See, e.g., *McAllister Brothers, Inc.,* 312 NLRB 1121 (1993). In the Board's view, regressive bargaining is unlawful if it is for the purpose of frustrating the possibility of agreement. In *Telescope Casual,* however, the Respondent was determined to have used its alternative proposal to press the Union to come to an agreement. In this connection, we note that, as the judge pointed out, there is no allegation of bad-faith bargaining on the part of the Respondent.

Contrary to Member Liebman's dissent, the majority did not conclude that the Respondent's alternative proposal was merely an ultimatum or club to force the Union to accept the final offer. Rather, they found that the alternative was a bona fide proposal in its own right, as evidenced by the fact that not only did the Respondent offer to bargain over it but, further, the Respondent offered to modify its terms in several respects in order to make it more acceptable to the Union.

Ten Broeck Commons, 320 NLRB 806 (February 2, 1996), the Board held that licensed practical nurses serving as charge nurses in a nursing home were not statutory supervisors. As in *Providence Hospital*, in connection with assignment and direction, the question was whether the direction required the use of independent judgment or involved directions which were merely routine.

United Food and Commercial Workers International Union, Local 400, AFL-CIO (Farm Fresh), 326 NLRB No. 81 (August 27, 1998). This case presented two main issues: (1) whether the Respondent established a sufficient property interest to exclude nonemployee organizers from certain portions of the sidewalks in front of its grocery stores and (2) whether it unlawfully ejected nonemployee organizers from the snack bar at on of its grocery stores. Chairman Gould and Members Brame and Hurtgen joined in dismissing the complaint allegation that the Respondent unlawfully ejected nonemployee organizers from its grocery store snack bar. On the second issue, all Board Members joined in finding that the Respondent possessed a sufficient property interest in sidewalks outside some, but not all of its stores and that the Respondent violated Section 8(a)(1) only at the stores where it removed nonemployee organizers from the sidewalks in which it retained an insufficient property interest.

IV Rulemaking on Single-location Bargaining Units

A rule like that proposed by the Board during Chairman Gould's tenure would have facilitated the election process by setting forth rules about how units are to be determined. Because of the propagation of misinformation about the rule, the Board met with considerable opposition to the proposed rule. The rule would not have changed with substance of the law, but would have codified it in such a way that both the parties and the agency would have saved considerable amounts of money and time which instead continues to be squandered on unit-determination investigations and negotiations.

V TEAM Act

A Republican proposal designed to eliminate anticompany union prohibitions of the National Labor Relations Act so as to foster employee committees or teams.

O

Board Members and General Counsels of the National Labor Relations Board, 1981–1999

I Board Members

John C. Truesdale[1] (D)
October 23, 1980–January 26, 1981
January 24, 1994–March 3, 1994
December 23, 1994–January 3, 1996
December 4, 1998–

John R. Van de Water (R)
August 18, 1981–December 16, 1982

John C. Miller (R)
December 23, 1982–March 7, 1983

Donald L. Dotson (R)
March 7, 1983–December 16, 1987

Patricia Diaz Dennis (D)
May 5, 1983–June 24, 1986

Wilford W. Johansen[2] (R)
May 28, 1985–June 15, 1989

Marshall B. Babson (D)
July 1, 1985–July 31, 1988

James M. Stephens (R)
October 16, 1985–August 27, 1995
December 17, 1987–March 6, 1994

Mary M. Cracraft (D)
November 7, 1986–August 27, 1991

John E. Higgins Jr.[3] (R)
August 29, 1988–November 22, 1989
September 3, 1996–November 13, 1997

Dennis M. Devaney[4] (D)
November 22, 1988–December 16, 1994

Clifford R. Oviatt[5] (R)
December 14, 1989–May 28, 1993

John N. Raudabaugh[6] (R)
August 2, 1990–November 26, 1993

William B. Gould IV (D)
March 7, 1994–August 27, 1998

Margaret A. Browning[7] (D)
March 9, 1994–February 28, 1997

Charles I. Cohen (R)
March 18, 1994–August 27, 1996

Sarah M. Fox[8] (D)
February 6, 1996–

J. Robert Brame III[9] (R)
November 17, 1997–

Peter J. Hurtgen[10] (R)
November 14, 1997–

Wilma B. Liebman[11] (D)
November 14, 1997–

II General Counsels

William A. Lubbers[12] (D)
December 24, 1979–April 24, 1984

Wilford W. Johansen[13] (R)
April 27, 1984–October 12, 1984

Rosemary M. Collyer[14] (R)	October 16, 1984–April 3, 1989
Joseph E. DeSio[15] (R)	April 4, 1989–November 22, 1989
Jerry M. Hunter (R)	November 28, 1989–November 27, 1993
Daniel Silverman[16] (D)	November 28, 1993–March 2, 1994
Frederick L. Feinstein[17] (D)	March 3, 1994–November 19, 1999
Leonard R. Page[18] (D)	November 29, 1999–

Source: National Labor Relations Board, Division of Information.

Notes

1. Mr. Truesdale served as a member under several recess appointments: October 23, 1980–January 26, 1981 (by President Carter); January 24, 1994–March 3, 1994, December 23, 1994–January 3, 1996, and December 4, 1998–November 19, 1999 (by President Clinton). He was confirmed by the Senate on November 19,1999, for a term that officially expires on August 27, 2003.

2. Term expired August 27, 1988; recess appointed by President Reagan effective August 29, 1988.

3. Recess appointment by President Read from August 19, 1988–November 22, 1989; subsequently received a recess appointment from President Clinton from September 3, 1996–November 13, 1997.

4. Served under recess appointments by President Reagan from August 29, 1988–November 22, 1989, when he was confirmed by the Senate for a term expiring December 16, 1989. Received second recess appointment from President Bush from December 17, 1989 until August 3, 1990, when he was confirmed by the Senate for a term ending December 16, 1994.

5. Recess appointed by President Bush from December 14, 1989–August 3, 1990, when he was confirmed by the Senate.

6. Mr. Raudabaugh's term expired on December 16, 1992. He subsequently received a recess appointment from President Bush on December 19, 1992.

7. Ms. Browning died in office. Her term was to expire on December 16, 1997.

8. Served under recess appointment by President Clinton from 2/6/96 to 11/8/97, when she was confirmed by Senate for term expiring 12/16/99. Currently serving under second recess appointment by President Clinton on 12/17/99.

9. Confirmed by Senate on 11/8/97. Term expires 8/27/2000.

10. Confirmed by Senate on 11/8/97. Term expires 8/27/2001.

11. Confirmed by Senate on 11/8/97. Term expires 12/16/2002.

12. Served under a recess appointment from December 24, 1979–April 22, 1980.

13. Acting General Counsel.

14. Served under a recess appointment from October 16, 1984–April 3, 1985.

15. Acting General Counsel.

16. Acting General Counsel.

17. Upon expiration of term on 3/2/98, President Clinton appointed Mr. Feinstein Acting General Counsel. On 10/22/98, he received a recess appointment to serve as General Counsel.

18. Serving under a recess appointment by President Clinton.

Index